Brecon

Blaenllyfni

Abregavenny

Castell Nos (UW 4)

Twyn Castell (MO 9)

Glamorgan

Gwynllŵg

Ynyscrug (MO 11)

Rhymni

nwyd (MR 2)

Gwern-y-domen (CR 9)

Tomen-y-clawdd (MO 7)

Taff

Ruperra (MO 4)

Ogwr

Twmpath (MO 8)

Coity (MR 1)

Morganstown (MO 3)

Ely

Treoda (MM 2)

Newcastle (EM 3)

Llanilid (CR 12)

Felin Isaf (MO 2)

Pen-y-pil (CR 19)

Gelli-Garn (CR 8)

Rumney (MR 7)

E 4)

Ty Du (MO 10)

Cardiff (MM 1)

Ogmore (MR 5)

Ystradowen (MO 12)

Peterston (EM 5)

Caerau (CR 4)

Penllyn (EM 4)

Cottrell (MO 1)

St. Nicholas (CR 20)

Brynwell (CR 3)

Llanquian (MR 3)

Llantrithyd (CR 13)

Coed-y-cwm (CR 6)

Dinas Powys Ring (CR 7)

ow (CR 11)

Bonvilston (CR 2)

Dinas Powys Castle (EM 1)

Howe Mill (CR 10)

Walterston (CR 21)

Thaw

Pancross (CR 17)

Sully (EM 6)

Castles Treated in Part 1a:

The Royal Commission on Ancient and Historical Monuments in Wales

An Inventory
of the Ancient Monuments in
Glamorgan

Volume III ~ Part 1a

Medieval Secular Monuments

The Early Castles

From the Norman Conquest to 1217

London: HMSO

Fig. 1. *(Opposite)* Ogmore Castle (MR 5) viewed from the west across the Ewenni.

© Crown copyright 1991
First published 1991

ISBN 0 11 300035 9

A CIP catalogue record for this book
is available from the British Library

Printed in the United Kingdom for HMSO
Dd 291117 C8 8/91 63215

Contents

Chairman's Preface

This Inventory forms Part 1 of Volume III of the series planned for the county of Glamorgan. The volume will deal with the medieval secular monuments of the county. All known medieval non-defensive secular sites have been treated in Part 2. Part 1 was originally envisaged as a single work dealing with the castles, town walls, and other fortified sites. The subsequent decision to divide the material between Part 1a and Part 1b is explained in the first section of the Introductory Survey, along with an outline of the chronological division chosen. Part 1a, *The Early Castles (to 1217)*, deals with fifty-seven sites comprising thirty-seven earthwork castles, sixteen masonry castles, and four vanished sites of uncertain character. Part 1b, *Later Castles (after 1217)*, will treat twenty later masonry castles and a varied range of strong houses, town defences, and post-medieval fortifications, concluding with an annotated list of over fifty alleged castles rejected after examination.

Each Inventory section opens with a distribution map and a preamble discussing the particular type of castle under consideration. These sectional maps and preambles also notice typologically related sites treated in other sections of Part 1a or Part 1b, explaining the reasons for their separate treatment where this is not self-evident.

The *Introductory Survey* consider more general matters in four sections. Following the explanation of the division of the material between Parts 1a and 1b (I), successive sections (II–IV) considers the geographical background, the historical background, and general aspects of the early castle. Section III outlines the wealth of relevant historical studies and printed sources available for Glamorgan, and draws upon them to furnish a detailed context for the castles in the period 1072–1217. The lordships of Glamorgan and Gower are treated separately, and a brief account is given of Gwynllŵg, providing an historical context for the two castles which lie in the small area of that Gwent lordship falling within the county of Glamorgan. An important reinterpretation of the formative years of Norman settlement between 1072 and 1083 is offered, accepting Cardiff as a foundation of the Conqueror in 1081. Section IV considers the

distribution and siting of early castles, and discusses those which were provided with partial or complete stone defences before 1217. In addition, the eccentric and mutually exclusive distribution patterns of mottes and castle-ringworks are examined, and a geological determinant is proposed, while a further sub-section notices the many excavations undertaken at Glamorgan castles and summarizes the evidence they provide. The *Introductory Survey* concludes with an annotated list of nineteen early castles which remained in use after 1217, and were strengthened with additional masonry after that date. All such later fabric, extant or vanished, is fully described in the relevant Part 1a accounts, and briefly noted in this list as a convenient means of reference for those concerned with later castles. Further to assist reference between the Parts, an alphabetical list is given at the end of the Inventory following the General Index (pp. 391), and maps on the end-papers provide more rapid reference to both parts: that to the front plots all sites described in Part 1a, that at the back the fifty-one sites to be treated in Part 1b. Fieldwork for the latter part is well advanced and the addition of further sites is not expected.

Illustrations in Part 1a follow the arrangement devised for the recent Brecknock Inventory (Volume I, Part ii, 1984). No distinction is made between photographs and drawings; all are numbered consecutively as 'figures', and placed as close as possible to the most relevant textual matter. The illustrations are considered in detail in the introductory section explaining *The Presentation of Material*. Monuments described in Part 1a were investigated between 1980 and December 1988. Before the latter date much work had been undertaken on the later castles which will complete Volume III. To complete the planned series of volumes for the county of Glamorgan further work will be undertaken on the Ecclesiastical Monuments (Volume II). Industrial Monuments will be treated in a separate series of publications.

The list of monuments 'most worthy of preservation' follows the practice of indicating those of quite exceptional importance, recognizing that there are many other monuments of considerable interest which should be preserved if at all possible. To enhance the value of the present list an indication is given of those monuments which are known to preserve very significant buried fabric, and those which are neglected and seriously threatened by unrelenting erosion.

Corrections or criticisms of the contents of this volume will be welcomed with the view to their possible inclusion in some future edition. They should be sent to the Secretary. Properly accredited persons may consult the records of the Commission in Aberystwyth.

The contents of the volume are Crown Copyright, including most of the illustrations. Copies of these can be purchased through the Secretary of the Commission.

November 1989   Glanmor Williams

Report

To The Queen's Most Excellent Majesty

May It Please Your Majesty

We, the undersigned Commissioners, appointed to make an *Inventory of the Ancient and Historical Monuments and constructions connected with or illustrative of the contemporary culture, civilisation and conditions of life of the people in Wales from the earliest times, and to specify those which seem most worthy of preservation*, humbly submit to Your Majesty the following Report, being the nineteenth on the work of the Commission since its first appointment. This Report will accompany Part 1a of the third volume of the Inventory of Monuments in the County of Glamorgan.

2. It is with deep regret that we record the death of our former Chairman, Professor William Francis Grimes, and of our former Secretary, Dr Alexander Hubert Arthur Hogg.

3. We have to thank Your Majesty for the re-appointment as Commissioners under Your Majesty's Sign Manual dated 8 June 1988 of Dr Michael Ross Apted from 1 May 1988 to 31 May 1990, and of Dr Ronald William Brunskill for a period of seven years from 1 May 1988.

4. We have pleasure in reporting the completion of our enquiries into those early defensive secular monuments of the Middle Ages dating before 1217 in the historic County of Glamorgan, which we have retained as the framework of our report in preference to the administrative units which came into being in 1974. We have made detailed records of 57 monuments. A total of 170 sites were visited, of which 59 were rejected and 51 were assigned to the following Inventory of later castles.

5. We have prepared a full Inventory of these Monuments which will be issued as a non-Parliamentary publication.

6. We desire to record our special thanks for valuable assistance from the owners and occupants of land where monuments exist. We would also like to acknowledge the help received from Dr David Crouch of the Institute of Historical Research; Professor Rees Davies of the University College of Wales, Aberystwyth; Mr Gareth Dowdell of the Glamorgan–Gwent Archaeological Trust; our former investigating officer, Mr C. N. Johns; Mr Richard Kay; the late Mr D. J. Cathcart King; Mr John Kenyon of the National Museum of Wales; Mr John Lewis, lately of the National Museum of Wales; Mr Kenneth Lightfoot of Neath Museum; Mr Donald Moore, formerly of the National Library of Wales; Mr Bernard Morris; Mr Derek Renn; our former Commissioner, Dr A. J. Taylor; Dr Ronald Walker of the University College of Wales, Aberystwyth; and Dr R. A. Waters of the British Geological Survey. In addition we would like to acknowledge the valuable assistance rendered by officers of South Glamorgan County Council during the survey of Cardiff Castle, and particularly by Mr J. R. C. Bethell, Mr P. Eriksen, Mrs P. Eyles, Mr G. Gray, Mr D. St. J. Griffiths, Mrs P. Sargent, and Mrs M. Stone; and by Mr R. J. Avent and Mr J. K. Knight of Cadw in regard to those monuments which are in the care of the Welsh Office.

7. We desire to express our acknowledgement of the good work of our executive staff; their names, and indications of their particular contributions, are included in the Inventory volume.

8. We humbly recommend to Your Majesty's notice the following Monuments as most worthy of preservation, indicating with an asterisk those which undoubtedly possess significant buried fabric, and with a dagger those which are threatened by serious erosion:

Mottes without Masonry:
MO 6   Talybont Castle†

Castle-Ringworks without Masonry:
CR 4   Caerau, Ely
CR 12   Llanilid
CR 14   Mountyborough
CR 20   St Nicholas Gaer

Unclassified, probably Welsh:
UW 5   Plas Baglan*

Masonry Castles built over Mottes:
MM 1   Cardiff Castle

Masonry Castles built over Castle-Ringworks:
MR 1   Coity Castle
MR 2   Llangynwyd Castle*†
MR 4   Loughor Castle
MR 5   Ogmore Castle
MR 6   Pennard Castle

Early Masonry Castles:
EM 1   Dinas Powys Castle*†

EM 2   Kenfig Castle*†
EM 3   Newcastle, Bridgend
EM 5   Peterston Castle*

The monuments in this list have been selected solely with regard to their manifest archaeological potential or their architectural and historical importance. They are considered to be of quite exceptional importance. There are many other monuments of considerable interest and less conspicuous archaeological potential which also deserve protection.

All of which we submit with our humble duty to Your Majesty.

(*signed*)
Glanmor Williams (Chairman)
L. Alcock
M. R. Apted
G. C. Boon
R. W. Brunskill
D. Ellis Evans
R. M. Haslam
J. G. Jenkins
J. B. Smith
J. G. Williams
G. J. Wainwright
P. Smith (Secretary)

List of Commissioners and Staff

During the preparation of this volume (1980–1989) the following members, appointed by Royal Warrant, have served on the Commission:

Hubert Newman Savory, M.A., D.Phil., F.S.A., formerly Keeper of Archaeology in the National Museum of Wales. (Appointed Chairman 1979, retired 1983.)

Richard John Copland Atkinson, C.B.E., M.A., F.S.A., Emeritus Professor of Archaeology in the University College, Cardiff. (Appointed Chairman 1984, retired 1986.)

Glanmor Williams, C.B.E., M.A., D.Litt., F.B.A., F.S.A., F.R.Hist.S., Emeritus Professor of History in the University College of Swansea. (Appointed Chairman 1986 for four years.)

Michael Ross Apted, M.A., Ph.D., F.S.A., formerly Assistant Chief Inspector of Ancient Monuments in the Department of the Environment. (Reappointed 1988 for two years.)

Leslie Alcock, M.A., F.S.A., F.R.Hist.S., Professor of Archaeology in the University of Glasgow. (Appointed 1986 for seven years.)

George Counsell Boon, B.A., F.S.A., F.R.Hist.S., F.R.N.S., formerly Keeper of the Department of Archaeology and Numismatics in the National Museum of Wales. (Re-appointed 1984 for ten years).

Ronald William Brunskill, O.B.E., M.A., Ph.D., F.S.A., Hon. Fellow and formerly Reader in Architecture in the University of Manchester. (Re-appointed 1988 for seven years.)

David Ellis Evans, M.A., D.Phil., F.B.A., Jesus Professor of Celtic in the University of Oxford. (Appointed 1984 for ten years.)

Sir Idris Llewelyn Foster, M.A., F.S.A., formerly Jesus Professor of Celtic in the University of Oxford. (Re-appointed 1981, retired 1983; died 1984.)

Richard Michael Haslam, M.A., F.S.A., Architectural Historian. (Appointed 1986 for seven years.)

John Geraint Jenkins, M.A., D.Sc., F.S.A., F.M.A., Curator of the Welsh Folk Museum. (Appointed 1984, retired 1989.)

Edward Martyn Jope, M.A., B.Sc., F.B.A., F.S.A., Emeritus Professor of Archaeology in the Queen's University, Belfast. (Re-appointed 1984, retired 1986.)

Jenkyn Beverley Smith, M.A., F.S.A., F.R.Hist.S., Professor of Welsh History in the University College of Wales, Aberystwyth. (Appointed 1984 for ten years.)

Arnold Joseph Taylor, C.B.E., M.A., D.Litt., F.B.A., P.P.S.A., F.R.Hist.S., formerly Chief Inspector of Ancient Monuments and Historic Buildings. (Re-appointed 1980, retired 1983.)

Dewi-Prys Thomas, B.Arch., F.R.I.B.A., M.R.T.P.I., Emeritus Professor and formerly Head of the Welsh School of Architecture, Cardiff. (Re-appointed 1984; died 1985.)

David Gordon Tucker, Ph.D., D.Sc., C.Eng., Emeritus Professor and Hon. Senior Research Fellow in the University of Birmingham. (Re-appointed 1983, retired 1984; died 1990.)

Geoffrey John Wainwright, B.A., Ph.D., Dir. S.A., M.I.F.A., Principal Inspector of Ancient Monuments and Historic Buildings, English Heritage. (Appointed 1987 for seven years.)

John Gwynn Williams, M.A., Emeritus Professor of Welsh History in the University College of North Wales, Bangor. (Re-appointed 1987 for five years.)

Raymond Bernard Wood-Jones, M.A., B.Arch., Ph.D., F.S.A., A.R.I.B.A., formerly Reader in Architecture in the School of Architecture of the University of Manchester. (Re-appointed 1973 for ten years; died 1982.)

Staff

During the preparation of this volume (1980–1989) the following have served as Staff of the Commission:

Secretary
Mr. P. Smith, B.A., F.S.A.

Principal Investigators
Mr C. H. Houlder, M.A., F.S.A.
Mr W. G. Thomas, M.A., F.S.A. (to 1988)

Investigators
Mr C. S. Briggs, B.A., Ph.D., F.G.S., F.S.A., M.I.F.A.
Mr H. Brooksby, F.S.A.
Mr D. M. Browne, M.A., M.I.F.A., F.R.G.S.
Mr M. Griffiths, M.A., D.Phil. (1982 to 1988)
Mr W. E. Griffiths, M.A., F.S.A. (to 1980)
Mr D. B. Hague, A.R.I.B.A., F.S.A. (to 1981)
Mr S. R. Hughes, B.A., M.Phil., F.S.A.
Mr D. K. Leighton, B.Sc., M.I.F.A.
Mr C. R. Musson, B.Arch., M.I.F.A. (from 1986)
Mr A. J. Parkinson, M.A., F.S.A.
Mr D. J. Roberts, N.D.D. (from 1981)
Mr C. J. Spurgeon, B.A., F.S.A.
Mr H. J. Thomas, M.A., F.S.A.

National Monuments Record Staff
Mrs S. L. Evans
Ms N. P. Figgis, M.A. (from 1988)
Mr N. J. Glanville
Miss R. A. Jones, M.A. (from 1985)
Mrs H. A. Malaws, B.Lib., M.I.F.A.
Mrs. S. Spink, B.A., A.L.A. (from 1987)

Field Recording Staff
Mr B. A. Malaws, M.I.F.A., (from 1984)
Mr D. J. Percival
Mr R. F. Suggett, B.A., B.Litt.

Illustrating Staff
Mrs J. B. Durrant
Mr C. W. Green (from 1987)
Mr J. D. Goodband (to 1983)
Mr J. W. Johnston (from 1987)
Miss D. C. Long, B.Sc. (1984 to 1987)
Mr B. A. Malaws, M.I.F.A. (to 1984)
Mr M. Parry (from 1984)
Mr D. J. Roberts, N.D.D. (to 1981)

Mr I. Scott-Taylor S.I.A.D. (1984 to 1988)
Mr G. A. Ward

Photographic Staff
Mrs F. L. James (from 1983)
Mr R. G. Nicol
Mr C. J. Parrott (to 1983)
Mr I. N. Wright, F.B.I.I.P.

Administrative and Clerical Staff
Miss C. A. Griffiths
Mr D. M. Hughes
Mrs L. M. Jones
Miss D. M. Ward (to 1985)

Authorship and Compilation

The following officers were allocated leading roles in the preparation of this Inventory:

Editing, General Arrangement, Introductory Survey, and Sectional Preambles	Mr C. J. Spurgeon
Inventory Accounts and Field Survey	Mr D. J. Roberts Mr C. J. Spurgeon Mr H. J. Thomas
Illustration	Mrs J. B. Durrant Mr C. W. Green Mr M. Parry
Layout	Mr J. W. Johnston
Photography	Mr I. N. Wright
Typing	Mrs L. M. Jones

Mention must also be made of other specific contributions to the work by certain members of Staff: Mr D. K. Leighton and Mr D. J. Percival provided the basic framework for the plotting of the ground plan of Coity Castle; Mr C. W. Green made a significant contribution during the later stages of work on the maps and line-drawings, and Mr I. Scott-Taylor prepared the plans of several earthworks at an earlier stage; Mr C. R. Musson directed and advised in regard to Aerial Photography, working with Mr I. N. Wright; Mr R. G. Nicol, director of the photographic staff, made valuable contributions to the work; finally, as a temporary member of staff, Mrs A. Collis assisted in the work of typing.

Presentation of Material

General Arrangement

At the outset it was decided that the Inventory of the historic pre-1974 county of Glamorgan should comprise five volumes, each considering particular categories of monuments pertaining to a specific period. In practice, the preparation of three of these volumes has called for the further sub-division of the subject matter between two or three separate parts. It has also been decided that Volume V, which was to have considered industrial and later monuments, will be replaced by a separate series of publications treating different categories of such monuments and beginning with the canals and tramroads. All parts constituting Volumes I and IV are already in print; with the present part, two of the three parts constituting Volume III will have been published. With the dates of publication of those parts in print, the Inventory now envisaged comprises the following volumes and parts:

I *Pre-Norman*
   Part 1 The Stone and Bronze Ages (1976)
   Part 2 The Iron Age
           and the Roman Occupation (1976)
   Part 3 Early Christian (1976)

II *Ecclesiastical Monuments*

III *Medieval Secular Monuments*
   Part 1a Defensive: The Early Castles, to 1217
   Part 1b Defensive: The Later Castles, after 1217
   Part 2   Non-defensive (1982)

IV *Domestic Architecture, from the Reformation*
    to the Industrial Revolution
    Part 1 Greater Houses (1981)
    Part 2 Farmhouses and Cottages (1988)

Part 1b will complete Volume III, which will be followed by the preparation of Volume II on the Ecclesiastical Monuments.

Monuments included

This publication, Part 1a of Volume III, considers fifty-seven castles which were established by 1217 and are here styled 'early castles', although in some cases their history or surviving remains indicate continued occupation beyond that date. Part 1b will deal with over fifty 'later castles' and other fortifications, most of them founded after 1217. These defensive monuments were originally intended to form a single Part 1 of Volume III. Section I of the Introductory Survey to this part (pp. 1 and 2) explains the need for a further sub-division of the material and justifies the choice of 1217 as an appropriate date for a chronological division: in that year the lordship of Glamorgan passed to Gilbert de Clare, the first of four eminent lords and notable builders of castles. No other division could assure an approximate parity between the parts. That section of the Introductory Survey also explains the relatively obvious allocation of some three-quarters of the monuments considered to Part 1a or Part 1b. There remained a minority less easily deemed

'early' or 'later' castles; their structural histories began before 1217, but continued well after that date. Such castles were allocated to the parts according to the perceived greater significance of their 'early' or 'later' remains in terms of military architecture. Cardiff Castle (MM 1), for example, is assigned to Part 1a on account of its great motte and Norman shell keep and despite its more substantial later masonry; Castell Coch (LM 4), in contrast, is placed in Part 1b on account of its substantial restored 13th-century masonry and despite its underlying motte. Once allocated to a part, all such sites are then the subject of comprehensive inventory accounts treating their full structural histories. In consequence, the full descriptions of the lesser aspects of their structural histories are unavoidably divorced from the appropriate sections of the other part. To minimize this inconvenience all such divorced descriptions are taken into account in the relevant sectional preambles dealing with each category of monument. For immediate reference these preambles begin with a distribution map and list of all relevant sites, including those described in other sections.

The fifty-seven castles assigned to Part 1a are arranged in seven sections, each considering a recognisable category of monument. Each section has been assigned two capital letters derived from the type of monument being considered (e.g. CR = Castle-Ringwork without Masonry). The entries in each section are numbered separately and prefixed by the appropriate capital letters. The seven sections in Part 1a are placed in the following order:
Mottes without Masonry (MO 1–12)
Castle-Ringworks without Masonry (CR 1–21)
Unclassified, Probably Welsh (UW 1–5)
Vanished Early Castles (VE 1–4)
Masonry Castles Built over Mottes (MM 1–2)
Masonry Castles Built over Castle-Ringworks (MR 1–7)
Early Masonry Castles (EM 1–6)
Sectional preambles introduce and discuss each of these categories of monument.

All known sites to be considered in Part 1b have been inspected and many of them have been surveyed. Only new discoveries might modestly alter the following proposed arrangement of that part:
Later Masonry Castles (LM 1–20)
Tower-Houses (TH 1–5)
Strong-Houses (SH 1–3)
Town Defences (TD 1–5)
Possible Castles or Strong-Houses (PC 1–12)
Forts and other Post-Medieval Fortifications (FO 1–6)

In addition, Part 1b will conclude with an annotated list of *Rejected Sites* (RS 1–59).

Form of Entries

The detailed inventory accounts which make up each section are arranged in alphabetical order and numbered separately, with two-letter prefixes, as described above. Alphabetical ordering necessitated the choice of a preferred name in those cases where there were recognized alternatives. In such cases alternative names not given priority are cited in parentheses after the preferred names heading the entries, and to ensure direct reference to the relevant account all such alternatives are also listed in the index. On the question of names, it should also be noted that D. J. C. King in his *Castellarium Anglicanum* (Vol. I) listed many of the Glamorgan castles under the name of the parish in which they fell, although they are known by more historic or adopted names. As an example, King's 'St Nicholas No. 1', 'St Nicholas No. 2' and 'St Nicholas No. 3' are here respectively designated St Nicholas Gaer, Cottrell Castle Mound, and Coed-y-cwm. The importance of King's gazeteer and bibliography, despite its eccentric choice of names in certain instances, merits a reference at the termination of each entry, and citing his name for each site where this is at variance with that used here.

All entries in Part 1a are illustrated. These illustrations range from simple location maps which plot the known or suspected locations of vanished sites, to the many plans, profiles, sections, elevations, details and other drawings which are required to record fully the most substantial monuments. The exceptional range of detailed historical and documentary studies available for medieval Glamorgan also ensures that for many sites it is possible to present a reasonably informed account of their manorial descent. The single-line reference to D. J. C. King's Glamorgan list at the end of each entry is followed by: (i) the parish, designated E for Ecclesiastical and C for Civil if there is a divergence between them, otherwise undesignated when there is no divergence; and (ii) the quarter-sheet number of the new, National Grid based, O.S. 6-in. map; the eight-figure National Grid reference (in brackets); the date of the last visit to record or check the site; and the old O.S. quarter-sheet number.

Illustrations (General)

All illustrations, whether photographs, maps, prints or drawings, are here designated as Figures and combined in the same serial numbering. As far as possible they are placed within or conveniently close to relevant textual matter.

Distribution Maps

A map introducing each section shows the distribution of the relevant monuments in relation to the relief and the boundaries of the lordships of Gower and Glamorgan. Related sites necessarily described in Part 1b (see above) are also plotted. The symbols devised for these simple distribution maps are specifically designed visually to proclaim the type of site in question. These symbols are used consistently in more detailed maps illustrating the Introductory Survey and plotting different types of castle to illustrate various topics discussed. The front end-paper provides an overall distribution map of the fifty-seven monuments considered in Part 1a, while the rear end-paper similarly plots those to be treated in Part 1b.

Line Drawings

All but a few vanished sites are illustrated at the very least by a ground plan and one or two overall surface profiles. With one exception the general overall plans are reproduced at a scale of 1:500. Cardiff Castle (MM 1) is the exception; on account of its large area this is reproduced at 1:1000. With certain castles retaining substantial masonry, overall plans at upper levels are also provided. For such castles there are also more detailed plans and sections of their most significant structures (e.g. the keeps at Coity, MR 1, and Ogmore MR 5; the Black Tower at Cardiff Castle, MM 1; and the Gatehouse at Pennard, MR 6). These more detailed drawings are reproduced at 1:200. Finally, certain significant individual features such as doors, windows, or fireplaces, are reproduced at 1:40. All scale drawings have imperial and metric scales.

With the obvious exception of vanished sites, all monuments were the subject of fresh surveys, even where the remains were severely eroded, as at Ynys-crug (MO 11) and Llandow (CR 11), where such plans may prove to be the final records of sites soon to disappear. In the section dealing with four well-documented vanished sites (VE 1–4) individual area maps indicate their known or suspected locations. These and other area maps presented are variously reproduced at 1:2500, 1:5000, or 1:10,000, according to the size of the area to be shown.

Castles key

On the site plans and inset maps, the following conventions are used:-

Ancient features

Medieval scarp

Iron Age scarp

Stones or breaks on scarp

Conjectured scarp

Conjectured feature

Stone revetment

Post holes rock cut

Post holes conjectured

Post holes earth cut

Church

Churchyard boundary

Medieval Track

Natural features

Natural scarp

Merging of scarp types

Conjectured natural scarp

Contours

Water

River or stream

Marsh or bog

Sand dunes

Cliff

Flat rock

Woodland

Undergrowth

Modern features

Modern scarp

Merging of scarp types

Hedge or fence

Hedge bank

Building

Wall

Track

Modern road

Trig. point

Quarry

Railway line

Canal

To distinguish clearly between the ancient, natural, and modern features necessarily portrayed on the general site plans, certain conventions have been applied throughout Part 1a. By reproducing these plans against a tonal background it is possible to use solid black to emphasize all ancient features, grey to represent natural scarps, rivers or other features, and white to clearly distinguish any modern features.

Pencil drawings provide perspective views of several earthwork castles where effective photography was not possible, and the same medium is used to portray a few significant features or especially significant artifacts associated with certain sites.

Excavations

Where possible, significant structural evidence derived from important excavations is transposed from the excavators' plans and indicated in simplified form on site plans. This evidence greatly enhances the plans of Dinas Powys Ringwork (CR 7), Llantrithyd Ringwork (CR 13), Penmaen Castle Tower (CR 18) and Cardiff Castle (MM 1). In the case of Rumney Castle (MR 7), however, it was clearly impossible to indicate the six phases of development on the main site plan; instead, with the excavator's collaboration, a series of simplified phase plans was assembled to help explain the structural development of the site.

Parish Lists and Index of National Grid References

Readers who are concerned with the monuments in a particular locality may refer to the lists of the ecclesiastical and civil parishes (pp. 350–358). These are arranged alphabetically and a map is provided for each list to show the location of the parishes. In these lists the numbers of all monuments which fall within a given parish are cited.

An index of national grid references follows the parish lists (pp. 358–359). This list furnishes direct reference to an entry which corresponds to a site located according to the National Grid, but for which the proper name is not known.

Town Defences

The defences of five medieval boroughs are to be considered in Section TD of Part 1b. The five boroughs are Cardiff, Cowbridge, Kenfig, Neath, and Swansea. Although all these boroughs except Cowbridge were in existence before 1217, it was only in the 13th century that they approached their medieval peaks. Furthermore, these sites retain little of their former defences. Surviving remains of town defences are limited to sections of the rampart at Kenfig, one simple gate and sections of the wall at Cowbridge, and one restored gate and a small fragment of wall at Cardiff. In all cases, including Neath and Swansea where nothing survives above ground, these sites will be described and illustrated with reference to past records, old maps and reported sighting of the defences.

Rejected sites

The list of rejected sites (Section RS) which will complete Part 1b includes certain sites which were claimed to have been mottes, castle-ringworks or other early castle types. Such sites, albeit rejected, might have been listed in Part 1a. On consideration, however, it was considered preferable to delay the final listing of these rejected sites until the last moment, since there are already fifty-nine of them and others may well be added. Section RS will consist of an annotated alphabetical list of all these sites, briefly stating the reasons for their rejection as castles.

Introductory Survey

Preliminary Note

This introduction is in four sections: I – The Division of the Material; Parts 1a and 1b Explained; II – The Geographical Background; III – The Historical Background (1072–1217); and IV – The Early Castles Discussed. Volume I, Part 1 of this work provides a detailed account of the physical background and soil structure. For a detailed study of the historical background, *Glamorgan County History*, Volume III, *The Middle Ages* should be consulted. The *Inventory of the Medieval Non-defensive Secular Monuments*, Volume III, Part 2, provides a brief summary of the medieval history of the area; a detailed discussion of agrarian history and patterns of settlement is given in Volume IV, Part 2.

Section II emphasizes those geographical factors relevant to the study of the early castles. Section III considers the extent, nature and development of Norman lordship in Glamorgan and Gower to 1217, stressing the importance of castles in the territorial reorganisation initiated in this formative period. General aspects of the early castles are considered in Section IV. All references to inventory accounts or figures in this or other volumes are made in brackets.

I The Division of the Material; Parts 1a and 1b Explained

Volume III, Part 1, as originally envisaged, would have formed an inventory of 108 castles and related structures. No county in Wales, and only four in England, can boast a greater number of castles. Adequately to describe and illustrate these monuments, and to draw upon the quite exceptional and extensive range of printed sources and works of history available for the county, it has been necessary to divide the material to produce two parts of approximately equal size. Any semblance of parity in text and illustrative content could not be achieved with any division on the basis of castle-types (*e.g.* earthwork castles and masonry castles), geographical zones (*e.g.* highland and lowlands) or medieval administrative areas (*e.g.* Gower/Kilvey and Glamorgan/Gwynllŵg). All such divisions would produce greatly unequal parts. A chronological division was chosen which achieves the necessary balance and respects a logical divide in the medieval history of Glamorgan: Part 1a, *The Early Castles (to 1217)*, treating 57 sites; and Part 1b, *Later Castles (after 1217), including Strong-Houses, Town Defences and Post-Medieval Fortifications*, treating 51 sites. With little offence to historical terminology, Part 1a might be regarded as a study of castles of the Norman period. Strictly, this period ended with the loss of Normandy in 1204, but for Glamorgan and its castles 1217 is historically an altogether more important date to use in defining *early* and *later* castles. In that year Glamorgan passed to its first de Clare lord, whose successors later in the century would raise impressive new castles at Caerphilly, Morlais, and Castell Coch, and refortify many others, which all figure so largely in any consideration of the *later castles*. This date is also close to the death of King John (19 October 1216), who had been lord of Glamorgan from 1189 to 1214. The brief tenure of his former wife, Countess Isabel (1214–17), furnishes a convenient and inconsequential hiatus in the tenurial history of the lordship of Glamorgan which constituted by far the greater part of the historical county.

Most categories of monument under consideration were clearly appropriate to one or other part of Volume III. Despite occasional evidence for continued occupation after 1217, all *Mottes* and *Castle-ringworks* with no imposed masonry defences were clearly early foundations to be assigned to Part 1a (MO 1–12; CR 1–21). To these were added five unclassified sites, four earthworks and one with masonry, which are taken to be 12th-century *Welsh Castles* (UW 1–5), and four *Vanished Early Sites* (VE 1–4). Part 1b was similarly the obvious place for any consideration of the *Tower Houses* (TH 1–5), *Strong Houses* (SH 1–3), *Town Defences* (TD 1–5), *Possible Castles or Strong Houses* (PC 1–12), and *Forts and Other Post-Medieval Fortifications* (FO 1–6). Part 1b will conclude with an annotated list of rejected sites (Section RS). This relatively obvious allocation of four categories of monument to Part 1a and five categories to Part 1b gave a reasonably balanced division, with forty-two *early sites* almost entirely made

Fig. 2. *(Opposite)* Coity Castle (MR 1): the grand staircase.

1

up of simple earthworks, and thirty-one *later sites* with only a limited degree of surviving or former masonry for consideration. There remained a large group of masonry castles far less easily divided between the parts to achieve the required overall balance.

The thirty-five masonry castles are mostly substantial works worthy of lengthy descriptive text and much detailed illustration. Only eight of these are known to have been founded after 1217 or lack any evidence indicating an earlier date. The eight furnished a large proportion of the twenty monuments classed here as *Later Masonry Castles* to form the first inventory section of Part 1b (LM 2, Bishops Castle; 3, Caerphilly; 9, Morgraig; 10, Morlais; 13, Penlle'r Castell; 15, Penrice; 17, St Fagans; and 20, Weobley).

The remaining twenty-seven masonry castles were all certainly or probably founded well before 1217, but were occupied and developed long after that date. Most of them retain or formerly displayed fabric or features of both *early* and *later* date. For these, a strictly chronological separation was impossible and a subjective allocation to the parts was necessary. After consideration of the surviving remains of each of them, twelve were chosen to complete the section designated *Later Masonry Castles* in Part 1b (LM 1–20, including the eight *later* sites listed above). In these cases substantial masonry of the *later* period was far more significant in terms of military architecture than the lesser or vanished traces of *early* work. They are more suitably discussed along with the purely later castles. Two of them had mottes (LM 4, 18), four retain lesser vestiges of early masonry (LM 5, 6, 7, 12), and the other six were possibly raised upon castle-ringworks of the 12th century (LM 1, 8, 11, 14, 16, 19); these lesser aspects of their structure or development will be discussed in the detailed inventory accounts in Section LM, but they are also mapped, listed and taken into consideration in the preamble to relevant sections treating early earthwork and masonry castles in Part 1a.

Fifteen sites were selected for inclusion in Part 1a and arranged in three sections: *Masonry Castles Built Over Mottes* (MM 1–2); *Masonry Castles Built Over Castle-Ringworks* (MR 1–7); and *Early Masonry Castles* (EM 1–6). With three exceptions, the sites thus classified and treated here as *early castles* are those at which surviving or adequately recorded early remains are altogether more significant than those of the later period, though these are also fully described and illustrated in the inventory accounts. The exceptions are Llangynwyd, Loughor and Pennard (MR 2, 4, 6), where only later masonry survives but the former existence of primary castle-ringworks is not in doubt. Excavations have proved this sequence of development at Loughor and Pennard; at Llangynwyd the remains proclaim a similar development, despite the imposed great gatehouse and other works of the 13th century. The inclusion of these three sites in Section MR thus assembles all certain masonry castles raised over castle-ringworks, leaving suspected cases with far more substantial later masonry in Section LM of Part 1b. As mentioned above, preambles to Sections MM, MR and EM take into consideration, list and map all known or suspected cases to be described in Section LM on account of the greater importance of their later fabric. Similarly, the preamble to Section LM in Part 1b will notice later fabric fully described in accounts included in Part 1a and included there because of the significance of associated earlier remains. In this way it is hoped that each preamble will give a comprehensive general account of each category of monument defined, overcoming the difficult but necessary division of the multi-period masonry castles between the two parts.

II   The Geographical Background

The historic county of Glamorgan (Fig. 3) is a most convenient region for medieval studies, its bounds having been established in the 'Acts of Union' (1536–1543) by the simple merger of the lordship of Glamorgan and the lesser lordship of Gower to its W., together with the latter lordship's dependent manor of Kilvey between them. The united bounds of these medieval lordships were preserved intact until the present century, when contiguous encroachments into Monmouthshire incorporated the parish of Rumney (1937) and a portion of the parish of St Mellons (1950) within the city of Cardiff, adding two castles pertaining to the adjacent Monmouthshire lordship of Newport or Gwynllŵg (CR 19; MR 7).

The historic county is bounded by the Bristol Channel to the S., and to the W. and E. respectively by the south-flowing Llwchwr and Rhymni rivers.[1] Its N. limit broadly corresponds with the northern border

---

[1] G. M. Howe and H. Carter provide a detailed geographical study of Glamorgan in E. G. Bowen (ed.), *Wales: a Physical, Historical and Regional Geography* (1957), chapters XV and XVI, pp. 353–430; see also *Glam. Co. Hist.*, I (1936) and H. J. Randall, *The Vale of Glamorgan* (Newport, Mon., 1961), pp. 1–53. *Glamorgan Inventory*, Vol. I, Part 1, pp. 3–8 offers a detailed discussion of the physical background and soil structure.

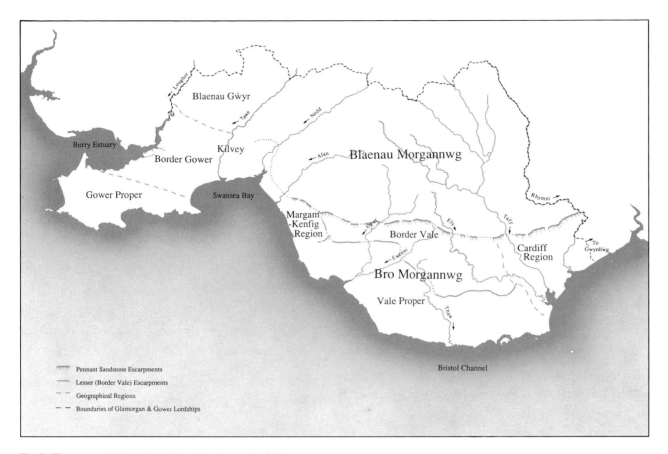

Fig. 3. The geographical regions of the historic county of Glamorgan.

of the South Wales Coalfield along a series of north-facing escarpments. Within these limits the area presents a clear division into a fertile lowland area fringing the coast and comprising the Vale of Glamorgan (*Bro Morgannwg*) and the peninsula of Gower, and a comparatively inhospitable interior upland, *Blaenau Morgannwg*. A further sub-division of relevance to the geographer and medievalist is imposed by the post-glacial rise of the sea level and the consequent flooding of the Burry Estuary and Swansea Bay. These marine transgressions created the peninsula of Gower, which along with its adjacent lowlands was almost isolated from the more fertile Vale of Glamorgan. For 12km between the estuaries of the Nedd and Cynffig the coastal plain was reduced to a narrow corridor 2km wide between the sea and the steep border escarpment of the *Blaenau*. For the geographer this constricted plain is the natural divide between Gower and *Bro Morgannwg*; for the medievalist the Afon Tawe, and the E. boundary of Kilvey on the E. side of its lower reaches, divide the lordship of Glamorgan from the lordship of Gower and its

dependent manor of Kilvey. Thus delimited, the medieval lordships of Gower and Glamorgan correspond closely with areas defined by geographers as *pays* on the basis of their distinctiveness and individuality.[2]

The northern uplands of Gower and Glamorgan, the *Blaenau*, share certain characteristics. To the E. of the valley of the Nedd they are generally in excess of 1,000ft (305m), but rarely as high to the W., within Gower. Physiographically they are a southern extension of the high plateau of Central Wales, from which they are separated by their north-facing border-escarpments. They constitute a tract of high and level moorland trenched by many steep sided and deeply incised river valleys trending southwards to the sea. The valleys of the Llwchwr and Tawe define the flanks of Gower to the W. Between the valley of the Tawe and that of the Rhymni to the E., *Blaenau Morgannwg* is cut by the valleys of the Nedd, Afan, Ogwr, and Taff and their many tributaries. A series of steep

---

[2] H. Carter, in E. G. Bowen (ed.), *ibid*, p. 401.

south-facing Pennant Sandstone escarpments sharply define the southern edge of the *Blaenau*. This eroded sea cliff runs E. from Margam and is particularly prominent at Llanharan, Llantrisant, and between Tongwynlais and Ruperra to the N. of Cardiff. The uplands of Gower are generally less elevated than those of *Blaenau Morgannwg* and less abruptly divided from their coastal lowlands. The *Blaenau* in general, however, shares the same infertile soils deficient in lime and supporting a moorland vegetation of coarse grasses, bracken, rushes, gorse and heather. Its unfavourable climate and the dense woodland of its sheltered slopes and deep valleys were further impediments to successful agriculture. Communications were poor and virtually limited to the ancient tracks trending N.–S. along the moorland ridges between the deep valleys which impeded all lateral movement. Before the exploitation of their mineral resources since the 18th century, these bleak uplands supported only a sparse and scattered population of largely Welsh farmers subsisting mainly on the grazing of cattle and sheep, with negligible arable farming on the few areas suitable for improvement by liming.

In its broadest sense the Vale of Glamorgan, *Bro Morgannwg*, is traditionally taken to embrace all that area of the lowlands between the coast and the prominent Pennant Sandstone scarp marking the S. limit of the *Blaenau*. The Vale of Glamorgan is in no sense the physical feature suggested by its name, nor the uniform tract of agriculturally rich country portrayed by Rice Merrick in the 1580s. He characterized it as an area '*renowned as well for the fertility of the soil, and abundance of all things serving to the necessity or pleasure of man*', praising its climate and its '*pleasant meadows and fruitful pastures, the plains fertile and apt for tillage, bearing abundance of all kinds of grain.*'[3] In reality only a broad dissected coastal plateau at a general level of 200ft befits Merrick's description. Now termed the Vale Proper, this supremely fertile tract of undulating land extends between the Ogmore river and the Barry area. Its fertility is owed to its shallow but freely-drained soils upon limestone which provide excellent land for tillage or pasture. To the E. and W. of the Vale Proper rather less productive regions may be added to define a continuous coastal tract from Margam to Rumney where medieval manorial exploitation was most concentrated. These peripheral regions may be termed the Margam-Kenfig region to the W., and the Cardiff region to the E. This recognition of the Vale Proper and its extensions permits a basic twofold division of *Bro Morgannwg*

which is demonstrably valid to both the geographer and the medievalist.[4]

The Border Vale to the N. constitutes a well-defined secondary region of the Glamorgan lowlands. Its N. limit abuts the well-marked Pennant Sandstone escarpment of the *Blaenau*. South of this, a crudely lunate former interior surface at 400ft is defined by a broken line of lesser south-facing escarpments falling to the 200ft surface of the Vale Proper. These escarpments define a line running eastwards from Cefn Cribwr, near Kenfig Hill, to the high down E. of St. Nicholas and incorporating the escarpments at Cefn Hirgoed, St. Mary Hill, and St. Hilary Down, near Cowbridge. To the N. of Cardiff this inner boundary is merged with the *Blaenau* escarpment from Tongwynlais to Ruperrra. The former interior plateau thus defined is greatly dissected and eroded, with few eminences attaining its original 400ft level and an irregular surface offering a variety of soil conditions generally unfavourable for agricultural exploitation, if more productive than the high moorlands of the *Blaenau*. The Border Vale broadly coincides with the southernmost fields of glacial drift; between Taironnen and Coedarhydyglyn this coincidence is almost exact for 5km along the A48, the medieval Port Way. This drift is absent on the surface of the Vale Proper, though it extends further S. to blanket the area of the Cardiff Region around the Taff-Ely estuary. The drift produced largely impermeable soils deficient in lime and inferior to those of the coastal lowlands. The mediocre nature of its soils matched the moderate nature of its internal communications; lateral movement, hindered by deeply incised valleys in the *Blaenau*, was here easier over its irregular terrain and heavy soils. The Romans pioneered the main E.–W. road across South Wales along a route skirting the southern limit of the drift and the Border Vale, a route followed in turn by the medieval Port Way and the A48, and only recently superseded by the M4.

Gower presents a similar threefold division into an interior upland or *Blaenau*, an intermediate Border Gower and a southern and agriculturally richer Gower Proper.[5] In Gower these three regions are less well defined. The Gower *Blaenau* matches *Blaenau Morgannwg* in its bleakness and infertile moorlands, but it is less elevated and lacks the abrupt southern bounding escarpments so well marked in Glamorgan. The

[3] Merrick, *Morg. Arch.*, p. 14.
[4] H. Carter, in E. G. Bowen (ed.), *op. cit.* (n. 1), pp. 401–20.
[5] H. Carter, in E. G. Bowen (ed.), *op. cit.* (n. 1), pp. 420–30.

inundations of the Burry Estuary and Swansea Bay isolated the peninsula of Gower. Border Gower may be defined as the tract of land extending across the neck of that peninsular from Swansea and its immediate area to Loughor and Talybont, but also comprising land lying N.E. of a line drawn between Landimôr and Oystermouth. Unlike the boundary between the Border Vale and the Vale Proper, this line is not coincident with any relief features and areas of drift, but marks a divide between the good permeable soils with a high lime status which are characteristic of Gower Proper, and the thin less fertile soils of Border Gower.

Having defined the basic threefold division of both Gower and Glamorgan into their upland *Blaenau*, their intermediate Border regions and their coastal regions of agriculturally superior land, it remains only to indicate those aspects of this basic geography which influenced their conquest, settlement and manorial exploitation in the Middle Ages. In the concluding section of this introduction certain aspects noted here will be considered more fully in relation to the castles.

Communications are an obvious factor involved in the conquest, settlement and subsequent domination of any region (Fig. 9, p. 33). The major E.–W. route through Glamorgan, the Port Way, with its extension through Gower between Neath and Loughor, was clearly of importance in the initial settlement and exploitation of both lordships. Little can be said of the network of lesser roads which existed south of this main highway. These lesser lines of communication, to some extent mapped by Rees,[6] are discussed in Volume III, Part 2, along with the tracks running N. through the Border Vale and the *Blaenau*. Excellent maritime communications were a further significant factor in the settlement and successful economic exploitation of this coastal region. Gower was served by good harbours at Loughor and Swansea, with others at Porteynon and Oystermouth. No fewer than eleven harbours served the coast of Glamorgan, the most significant being those beside the chief lord's castle-boroughs of Neath, Cardiff, and Kenfig. Despite much debate, it is uncertain whether the Norman invaders arrived by sea or by land; there is no doubt, however, that the estuarine castles at Loughor, Oystermouth, Swansea, Neath, Kenfig, Ogmore, Cardiff, and Rumney were all early foundations, and that all but Loughor and Ogmore were founded by the respective chief lords. The rôle of these maritime centres in the consolidation of lordships may not be doubted, particularly as all of them except

Oystermouth and Ogmore were sited upon or close to the Port Way.

Geographical factors are the most obvious of all in any consideration of the phases by which feudal domination was extended with full authority to the very limits of Gower and Glamorgan. It is not surprising that the primary settlement under William I was first extended by Fitzhamon (*ca.* 1093–1107) to embrace the especially productive agricultural lands of the Vale Proper, but little beyond its limits in his time. The remainder of the coastal lowland beyond the Ogwr was similarly absorbed by his successor, Earl Robert (*ob.* 1147), and limited encroachments were made into the Border Vale. There, it may be noticed, such lords as the Turbervilles were granted particularly extensive lands on most favourable terms, a reflection, perhaps, of their exposed nature on the edge of the unsubdued *Blaenau* and a recognition of the limited agricultural quality of their lordships. The even more inhospitable *Blaenau* remained in the effective control of the native rulers, subject only to the nominal and virtually meaningless overlordship of the lord of Cardiff. These rulers retained their independence until the eventual appropriation of the hill commotes in the mid-13th century, and even then this final expansion of unqualified feudal overlordship was to ensure the continued and unmolested manorial exploitation of the south, and not in any serious expectation of a profitable return on such barren moorlands. In these uplands very few castles were founded or improved in the later period after the annexations, and these were works of an essentially military nature: on the southern fringe of the uplands such works at Llangynwyd, Llantrisant, Castell Coch, and Morgraig primarily served to stiffen the outer perimeter of the lowlands, while Caerphilly, Penlle'r Castell, and Morlais were advanced garrison-castles. The dependent borough at Caerphilly never prospered, while that at Morlais was abortive and the prime purpose of its castle was to define the northern frontier of Glamorgan and deter the encroachments of the English lords of Brecon, just as Penlle'r Castell was raised to define and protect the northern frontier of Gower.

The distribution of the castles which may be associated with the successive phases in the extension of alien lordship demonstrates underlying geographical determinants. The prime purpose of most castles was to secure their dependent lands for profitable exploit-

6 *Glamorgan Inventory*, Vol. III, Part 2, Section RO, pp. 347–58; Rees, *Map*, S.W. and S.E. sheets.

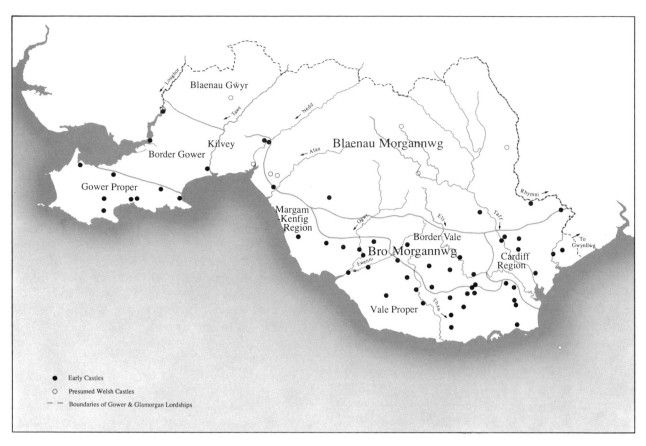

Fig. 4. The geographical regions and all early castles.

ation. Not surprisingly, the great majority of early castles identified are located on the most profitable coastal regions (see above). Excluding the seven presumed to be Welsh (UW 1–5; MO 9, 11), some thirty-five appear to lie in these most favoured areas. About twelve lie in the intermediate lands of Border Gower and the Border Vale. This leaves only four early sites within the *Blaenau*, or three if we exclude the lord of Glamorgan's Llangynwyd (MR 2), for this was located on a low elevation within the exceptionally broad and fertile re-entrant valley of the Llynfi, which thrusts into the northern hills and was sufficiently productive to support the only medieval nucleated village within the uplands.[7] The other three (MO 4, 7; CR 9) are all unrecorded earthworks with no known manorial context and situated just within the Blaenau to the N. of Cardiff. It is suspected that they represent a short-lived demarcation of a primary enclave established at that estuarine centre by the Conqueror in 1081.

Rice Merrick was quite as advanced for his time in his appreciation of local geography, as he was in

assembling the historical matter available to him. He was well aware of the broad divisions of variable agricultural quality which we have defined, and his appreciation of the differing attributes of the Border Vale and the Vale Proper was further apparent in his listing of the castles of Glamorgan.[8] He identified fifty-seven castles, including many which we have designated as later castles and fourteen which may be discounted. He classified them into four groups on the basis of their location. Two of his groups respectively fall within the *Blaenau* and the Border Vale; the other two groups assemble those sites which lie within the Vale Proper and its eastern and western extensions. By sheer coincidence we have designated fifty-seven sites as *early* castles, but there is little correspondence between these and the same number comprised in Merrick's lists, with only seventeen common to both. In terms of a common appreciation of topography, as demonstrated by the variable density of sites in the

---

[7] H. J. Randall, *op. cit.* (n. 1), pp. 26–7.
[8] Merrick, *Morg. Arch.*, pp. 75–6, 125.

three divisions of Glamorgan-Gower, however, the respective totals are strikingly similar. Merging Glamorgan and Gower, and including the presumed Welsh sites, the respective totals of *early* castles in the *Blaenau*, the Border regions and the Vale and Gower Proper, are 7, 14 and 36, as compared with Merrick's totals of 7, 15 and 35.

The foregoing discussion might seem to imply that the Norman settlers were infallible in their choice of productive lands for settlement and castle-building, but in fact it is possible to discern instances of foundations which were not found to be viable. We have noticed three *early* castles to the N. of Cardiff, just within the mountain zone and lacking any records or manorial contexts, where early abandonment is assumed. Such retraction is clearly recorded in five other cases in which castles and the whole of their dependent lands were conveyed to monastic houses by gift, lease or exchange. The earliest and most striking case is Granville's Castle (VE 2), granted by Richard de Granville on his foundation of Neath Abbey in 1130. By 1183 Roger Sturmi had conveyed his fee of Stormy (MO 5) to Margam Abbey for 6s. 8d. a year, and Samson de Hawey had exchanged his sub fee (of St Fagans) at Gelli-garn (CR 8) with Neath Abbey for a vill in Devon. The knight's fee of Llangewydd (VE 3) was leased to Margam in 1202 by David Scurlage for the wardsilver payment of 6s. 8d. he owed annually at Cardiff. Finally, as late as *ca.* 1250, Robert de Bonville conveyed the whole of his fee of Bonvilston (CR 2) to Margam for three marks a year. Excepting Bonvilston, which lay within the fertile Vale Proper, the other four sites were on far less productive land. It has been suggested that Granville's Castle and Gelli-garn were given up because of their proven vulnerability to Welsh attacks. The four were certainly exposed, Granville's Castle on the western fringe of Glamorgan and the other three N. of the Port Way and very close to the Border Vale. Gelli-garn certainly proved a profitable grange for Neath (Vol. III, Part 2, MG 16), with ten carucates of arable, but Stormy, Llangewydd, and Granville's Castle appear to occupy less fruitful land, and this, as well as their exposed locations, may help to explain their early desertion as lay manors.

The glacial drift present in Glamorgan, or more precisely its presence or absence, played a hitherto unsuspected rôle in the early Norman settlement of Glamorgan and Gower. It will be demonstrated in the final section of this introduction that mottes are located only to the N. of the Port Way, which largely coincides with the southern limits of the drift, for they could not be raised on the shallow soils over rock which largely covered the more fertile lands to the S., where we find castle-ringworks. In Glamorgan and Gower only two of the sixteen mottes identified do not appear to be sited on glacial drift, suggesting that a tractable subsoil was usually requisite for the construction of this type of castle.

A further aspect of the historical geography of Glamorgan to be pursued below is the clear survival of the broad patterns of settlement and communication pioneered by the Romans. While both Romans and Normans were equally constrained by topographical considerations, it is clear that the latter benefited from the routes and settlements bequeathed by their predecessors. The Port Way, the main highway through the territory, followed the line of the Roman road across south Wales, and many of the most important early castles lay on its line and within or adjacent to Roman forts.

III The Historical Background (1072–1217)

The historian or archaeologist concerned with medieval Glamorgan is fortunate in the most exceptional and extensive range of relevant printed sources and historical studies that are available. Complemented by the equally exceptional number of excavations that have been undertaken, as detailed in the succeeding section, this wealth of historical information permits an unusually informed discussion of its castles which would not be possible in most other areas. We have noticed Rice Merrick as an observant late-16th-century topographer of Glamorgan; above all, however, his *Morganiae Archaiographia* constitutes a precocious and indispensable study of local history and antiquities which will be frequently cited, and is particularly valued for its demonstrably reliable citations from the lost cartulary of Neath Abbey. Of later works, none is cited in succeeding pages as regularly as those of G. T. Clark (1809–98). This engineer, historian, and father of castle-studies was born in London. After working under Brunel on the Great Western Railway, and a period in India, he settled in Glamorgan. From 1852 until 1897 he was the controller of the Guest ironworks at Dowlais, near Merthyr Tudful, but it was the consuming interest in medieval fortification which occupied his leisure hours that has ensured the enduring gratitude of succeeding generations far beyond the bounds of his adopted county. Besides many papers in learned journals, his works included the splendid six-volume collection of Glamorgan charters, the *Cartae*, a substantial volume of Glamorgan pedigrees, the *Limbus Patrum Morganiae et Glamorganiae*, and a general history of the medieval lordship of Glamorgan, *The Land of Morgan*. His detailed studies of individual castles have seldom been equalled; nine of these describing Glamorgan sites were included in over a hundred such studies which were brought together in his two-volume *Mediaeval Military Architecture*. A large but unindexed and inadequately sorted collection of his manuscripts in the National Library of Wales includes notes, plans and sketches made on visits to castles and churches between the 1820s and the 1890s, some never published, including his records of the vanished keeps at Newcastle and Sully (EM 3, 6) and of the vanished rectangular entrenchment which formerly enclosed the motte at Treoda (MM 2). His writing is difficult to decipher, and often in faint pencil, but a thorough search has yielded information incorporated in certain Inventory accounts, besides the frequent references to his published works.

Since the death of Clark in 1898 an unbroken succession of scholars has built upon his pioneering works on medieval Glamorgan and bequeathed a particularly detailed historical background against which we have been able to set the present study of the castles. A particularly heavy debt is owed to J. H. Matthews, J. S. Corbett, L. D. Nicholl, William Rees, J. Conway Davies, J. Beverley Smith, and R. B. Patterson, and to Michael Altschul, whose study of the de Clare earls is equally prominent in the annotations in Part 1b. The six volumes of *Cardiff Records* (1898–1911), edited by J. H. Matthews, incorporate much information on the lordship as a whole. Corbett (*Glamorgan Lordship*, 1925) and Nicholl (*Normans*, 1936) provide detailed analyses of the manorial development of Glamorgan lordship, the latter extending his study to include the lordship of Gower. In addition to detailed monographs on the Glamorgan possessions of Tewkesbury Abbey and Cardiff lordship, William Rees furnishes the authoritative history of Cardiff (1969) and incorporates much Glamorgan material in his general history of the *Order of St John in Wales* (1947); his *Map* (1932) is quite indispensable. The *Episcopal Acts* of the Dioceses of St Davids and Llandaff (1946, 1948), edited and discussed by Conway Davies, assembles very many translations of Gower and Glamorgan manorial deeds; the infor-

mation they contain and their witness lists are frequently relevant to castles, even if these are rarely mentioned. (A revised and extended collection of the *Llandaff Episcopal Acta, 1140–1287*, edited by David Crouch and published in 1988 by the South Wales Record Society, was not available in time for consideration in Part 1a.) The many contributions of J. Beverley Smith to *Glamorgan County History* (Vol. III, 1971), together with Rees Davies' discussion of the lordship of Ogmore, provide the essential historical background for the early castles. Finally, R. B. Patterson's *Earldom of Gloucester Charters* (1973) furnishes corrected and annotated transcripts of many charters which appear in Clark's *Cartae*, adding a further ten not previously published.

The lordships of Glamorgan and Gower are now considered in turn from the arrival of the Normans until 1217. An attempt is made to relate the early castles to the historical development of each lordship in this period. In order to place the two castles formerly in Monmouthshire in their historical context a brief note on the lordship of Newport (or Gwynllŵg) is appended to the discussion of Glamorgan.

A The Lordship of Glamorgan to 1217

It is convenient to consider the lordship of Glamorgan during this period in five successive phases coincident with the tenures of four chief lords of the formally constituted lordship and a preceding phase of initial Norman activity in the area which is now seen to have culminated in the first permanent settlement at Cardiff under William I from 1081. This pioneering phase spans the years 1072–93. The successive chief lords were Robert Fitzhamon (*ca.* 1093–1107), Robert, earl of Gloucester (*ca.* 1113–47), Earl William (1147–83), and John of Mortain, King John from 1199 (1189–1214). The two gaps which punctuate the otherwise consecutive tenures of these four lords were periods of direct royal control during the wardships of heiresses, whose marriages took the lordship to Earl Robert and John of Mortain. The brief and inconsequential rule of John's divorced wife, Countess Isabel (1214–17), provides a convenient hiatus before the accession of the de Clare earls and the start of our later period.

The recent recognition of *the primary settlement at Cardiff under the Conqueror (1081–93)*, and a general appreciation of its character and historical context, stem from a timely and fruitful collaboration combining the mutually consistent independent conclusions of a numismatist (George Boon), a historian (David Crouch), and the Commission's staff engaged on the archaeological survey of the early castles. Such is the general interest of the revised sequence of events now perceived in Glamorgan in the period 1072–83, and the central role played by William I, that the evidence has already been published from each of these standpoints and is readily available in detailed support of the following summary account.[9]

In 1072 unidentified Normans are first recorded on the eastern fringe of Glamorgan when they assisted Caradog ap Gruffudd, the Welsh prince of neighbouring Gwynllŵg, in his defeat of the army of Maredudd ab Owain of Deheubarth on the banks of the Rhymni.[10] Previously regarded as a brief inconsequential episode, it is now possible to understand this appearance on the scene as one with lasting implications which directly involved Glamorgan in events of national significance in 1075 and 1081, long before the traditional, but no longer tenable, foundation of Cardiff by Fitzhamon ca. 1093. The defeat and death of Maredudd at the battle on the Rhymni earned Caradog ap Gruffudd the kingship of Morgannwg, the territory that was to constitute the lordship of Glamorgan. It is now possible to discern limitations to that kingship, imposed in return for Norman help in defeating the Deheubarth prince, and to identify the Norman mercenaries as the knights of Roger Fitzosbern of Breteuil, who was conveniently and firmly established in Gwent to the E. of the River Usk bordering Caradog's Gwynllŵg. There is clear evidence that Caradog was established in 1072 as a client king of William I, as appears in the Book of Llandaff and a previously un-noticed and quite credible episode in the account of a posthumous miracle incorporated in the early-12th-century Life of St Gwynllyw of Newport. The miracle describes the flight of three knights to Caradog's court, where he received them '*though he should lose everything he held from the king*', for they had been in rebellion against William I. That they were the men of Roger of Breteuil, whose abortive conspiracy led to his downfall in 1075 and provoked their flight, may hardly be doubted; their generous reception by Caradog, despite his acknowledged obligations to the English Crown, most strongly suggests that they were among his allies in the battle three years earlier, and the King's dispatch of William Rufus to Glamorgan on an otherwise unrecorded punitive campaign appears to confirm Caradog's status as a vassal.[11] Despite this episode, he was restored to royal favour, to appear as the sole

Welsh dignitary at the consecration of St Mary of Monmouth between 1075 and his death in 1081.[12]

Caradog was slain at the battle of Mynydd Carn in 1081 contesting for supremacy in south Wales with Rhys ap Tewdwr, the prince of Deheubarth. As now perceived, this event deprived William I of the ruler of a client kingdom vital in maintaining stability on the fringes of his dominions. Thus viewed, the King's immediate expedition to St Davids to treat with the victorious Rhys ap Tewdwr is far more comprehensible, and the implications of his long-recognised pact with that prince may be seen as extending to the kingdom of Morgannwg. That vital border territory would surely have been foremost in his mind in his deliberations with Rhys, and essential to the treaty between them in which the Welsh prince agreed to render £40 annually to the King, as recorded in Domesday Book. Far more credible, also, is the King's foundation of Cardiff on his return journey; as an obvious attempt to ensure the continued stability of this border territory, it must surely have been agreed with Rhys. The three Welsh chronicle references which record William's founding of Cardiff in 1081 were unfortunately dismissed by Sir John Lloyd early in this century.[13] These chronicles are credible in the revised context outlined, and confirmed by numismatic evidence.

A mint of the Conqueror at Cardiff has now been recognized by George Boon. He lists five of its coins, including one from the castle of a type just going out of fashion, probably in 1081 and from local dies, and renews the claim for a contemporary mint at St Davids.[14] The Domesday evidence for Rhys ap

---

[9] George Boon, *Welsh Hoards 1979–1981*, National Museum of Wales (1986), pp. 40, 46–8 and notes 35–37 (pp. 66–7); David Crouch, *Morgannwg*, XXIX (1985), pp. 20–41; C. J. Spurgeon, in John R. Kenyon and Richard Avent (eds.), *Castles in Wales and the Marches; Essays in Honour of D. J. Cathcart King*, University of Wales Press (1987), pp. 38–42 and Château Gaillard, XIII, 1986 (1987), pp. 204–5.

[10] *Bruts (B.S., Pen. 20, R.B.H.)*.

[11] *Liber Land.*, pp. 277–79; *Vitae Sanctorum Britanniae et Genealogiae*, ed. A. W. Wade-Evans (Cardiff, 1944), pp. 188–91. These and other sources of evidence illustrating Caradog's relationship with William I and the Normans of Gwent are fully discussed by Crouch, *op. cit.* (n. 9), pp. 23–7.

[12] *Liber Land.*, p. 277.

[13] *Ann. Margam*, p. 4; *Breviate Ann.*, f. 29 (= *Arch. Camb.*, 1862, pp. 272–3); *Brut., B.S.*, p. 83 (s.a. 1080); J. E. Lloyd, *Trans. Soc. of Cymmrodorion* (1899–1900), pp. 160–4 and *Hist. Wales*, II (1912), pp. 393–6, 402.

[14] Boon, *op. cit.* (n. 9).

Tewdwr's annual tributes of £40 to the King is good reason for the presumption that these mints were established to furnish a means of exchange to pay the military garrisons which must have protected them, and also to enable the Prince to render his tribute, for the Welsh had hitherto minted no coins.

At Cardiff it is now possible to envisage the great motte (MM 1) raised within the partially rehabilitated Roman fort functioning as the strongly garrisoned centre administering a Norman enclave in the area. The mint was no doubt within the ancient walls. The motte itself is the largest in Wales; its size and location within a Roman fort are typical of the mottes raised by the Conqueror at such places as York, Lincoln, and Cambridge. There is no record of this formative settlement during its presumed existence between 1081 and 1093. Its omission from Domesday Book may suggest that it enjoyed a special status under the terms of the King's treaty with Rhys ap Tewdwr and was thus subsumed in his annual tribute there recorded. A strong Norman presence doubtless continued until 1093, when it is believed that Robert Fitzhamon gained control of Glamorgan. Fitzhamon's conquest, the 'Winning of Glamorgan' as it is termed in Merrick's most detailed traditional account, is in fact an episode lacking the slightest shred of contemporary supporting evidence, despite the records of other Norman advances into Wales in that year after the death of Rhys ap Tewdwr. The silence of the records may indicate that Merrick's dramatic 'Winning' was cobbled together to explain subsequent infeudation, and that with the strong pre-existing Norman presence at Cardiff Fitzhamon was simply allowed to assume control in 1093.

The castles of the Cardiff area appear to shed some light on the extent and nature of the Conqueror's initial settlement. On the reasonable assumption that the mint-workers, garrison, and servants based at Cardiff would need to be self-supporting, it follows that a sufficient area of the adjacent countryside would have been annexed and administered from the new castle. The present historical and archaeological study of the surrounding castles has identified a number of mottes which might indicate the approximate extent of such annexed lands. To the N. of Cardiff an arc of 13km drawn between the Ely and Rhymni rivers embraces seven mottes and a curious hybrid ring-motte (Fig. 5). Only two of these sites may be identified with recorded medieval manors (Treoda, MM 2; Castell Coch, Vol. III, Part 1b, LM 4). The other mottes are Felin Isaf, Morganstown, Ruperra,

Tomen-y-clawdd, and Twmpath (Rhiwbina) and the ring-motte is Gwern-y-domen (respectively MO 2, 3, 4, 7, 8; CR 9). Even Treoda and Castell Coch are certainly known in a manorial context only from the 13th century, and the other six are either situated in areas where there is no known medieval manor of any date, or, in the case of Morganstown, where the motte lies distant from the later manorial centre at Radur. As castles, only Treoda and Castell Coch figure in the records, but not until they were given stone defences in the 13th century. Considering the almost universal and obvious identification of the close-set and minor earthwork castles to the S. and W. of the Ely with recorded manors, it is significant that this arc of earthwork castles N. of Cardiff is so lacking in documented contexts. It is tempting to consider them as early sites buttressing the primary settlement at Cardiff; a presumed military purpose might explain the location of four of them within the southern fringes of the infertile *Blaenau*, those at Castell Coch and Ruperra being on particularly strong elevated sites. With the formal establishment of the lordship of Glamorgan after 1093 by Fitzhamon, and the acquisition of the fertile lands further W., these pioneering castles were perhaps abandoned.

Robert Fitzhamon (1093–1107), first lord of the formally constituted lordship of Glamorgan, is believed to have established his rule there in 1093 during the widespread advances into Wales immediately after the death of Rhys ap Tewdwr in an engagement with the men of Bernard de Neufmarché near Brecon. We have noted the singular lack of any contemporary record of his acquisition of Glamorgan, and the strong probability that this is to be explained by his simple assumption of authority in the pre-existing Norman settlement around Cardiff, which furnished a base for further encroachment. At the same time, it is also clear that he acquired Wentloog, the coastal plain of neighbouring Gwynllŵg between the Rhymni and Usk rivers, and maintained it as a separate lordship with its *caput* at Newport. Fitzhamon, lord of Creully in Normandy, was loyal to William Rufus during the rebellion of that King's elder brother, Duke Robert. For this service he was granted extensive lands in Gloucestershire *ca.* 1089, where he was conveniently placed to participate in the general Norman advances into Wales in 1093. His tenure of Glamorgan and Gwynllŵg, if not his coming, is well attested in the records.

The Welsh kingdom of Morgannwg, until the fall of Caradog ap Gruffudd in 1081, extended from the

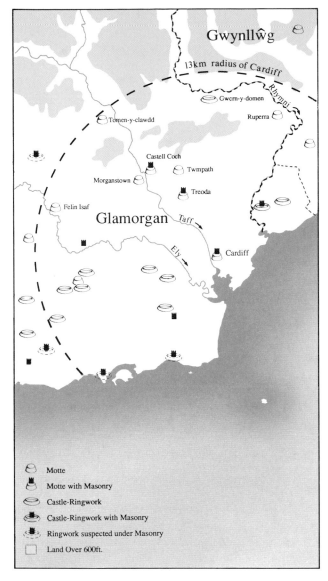

Fig. 5. Mottes in the Cardiff area.

Motte

Motte with Masonry

Castle-Ringwork

Castle-Ringwork with Masonry

Ringwork suspected under Masonry

Land Over 600ft.

reached the E. bank at Caerleon by the time of the Domesday Survey.[16] The upland commotes of Senghennydd, the cantref between the Taff and the Rhymni, fell to an obscure family represented in the mid 12th century by Ifor ap Meurig (Ifor Bach); Cardiff occupied its lowland commote of Cibwr. Finally, in the remainder of Morgannwg between the Taff and the Tawe, there emerged Iestyn ap Gwrgant. This prince asserted his authority over the ancient cantrefs of Gorfynydd and Penychen, which were divided in the lowlands by the River Thaw, and he figures prominently and alone as the leader of Welsh resistance to Fitzhamon's legendary 'Winning' of Glamorgan. Setting aside the legend, it was Iestyn's power which most seriously confronted Fitzhamon in 1093, and it was by right of conquest that Norman governance was established under Fitzhamon over the whole territory of ancient Morgannwg.

Robert Fitzhamon's assertion of his authority provided him with a basis for regal jurisdiction as heir to the kings of Morgannwg. The full rigour of unfettered feudal authority, however, would not be extended over the entire territory until long after Fitzhamon's time. For the whole of the 12th century, and well into the next, the heirs of the three Welsh princes we have noticed retained effective control of the upland commotes, acknowledging the nominal overlordship of the lord of Cardiff. To the S., the fertile Vale Proper and large tracts of the intermediate Border Vale fell to the rule of the Normans. This appropriation of the more productive areas of Glamorgan was completed only in the time of Earl Robert (ca. 1113–47), to produce an overall division of Morgannwg into areas subject to three distinct forms of secular rule. Firstly, to the N., there were the virtually independent Welsh commotal lordships in the *Blaenau*. Further S., extending over much of the intermediate Border Vale, there were certain Norman member lordships held on generous terms, their lords holding 'with royal liberty', to use a late 13th-century gloss. Finally, there were the fertile coastal plains, and a few adjoining areas of the Border Vale, which were appropriated and organized on feudal lines and subjected to the complete and effective rule of the lord of Glamorgan at Cardiff.

[15] David Crouch, *Morgannwg*, XXIX (1985), pp. 30–1.

[16] This possibility favours the view that Fitzhamon advanced to Glamorgan by land in 1093. The Roman road from Caerleon to Carmarthen traverses Wentloog before entering Glamorgan at Rumney.

Tawe to the Usk and comprised the lands that were to constitute the separate medieval lordships of Glamorgan and Gwynllŵg. The Conqueror's settlement in the Cardiff area destroyed this unity. In the period 1081–93 it would appear that authority over the remainder of the kingdom was divided between three surviving representatives of Welsh princely houses.[15] The son of Caradog ap Gruffudd, Owain Wan, retained only the barren uplands of Gwynllŵg, suggesting that the Conqueror's appropriations may well have extended to its fertile coastal plain, Wentloog, and as far as the Usk, establishing links with Norman settlements beyond that river which had

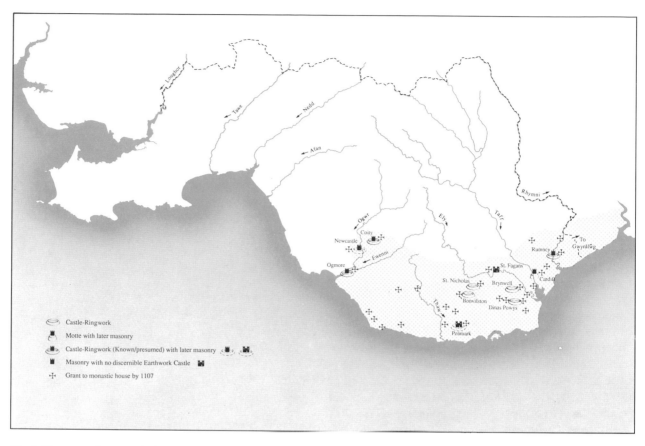

Fig. 6. Norman settlement under Robert Fitzhamon (1093 - 1107).

Fitzhamon's appropriations extended only as far as the Ogwr River, and marginally beyond it at Newcastle, where he had established a castle (EM 3) by 1106. This limited extension of his lordship beyond Cardiff was a logical annexation of the entire area of the Vale Proper, the most fertile area of the Welsh kingdom of Morgannwg. The extent of these appropriated lands may be deduced from the grants which Fitzhamon and his *barones* made to the abbeys of St Peter's, Gloucester, and Tewkesbury, his own foundation. The grants to Tewkesbury were confirmed by Henry I on Fitzhamon's death in 1107, and were to be augmented by further grants made in the Margam-Kenfig region beyond the Ogwr, largely under Earl Robert of Gloucester, which were added to the later confirmation of Bishop Nicholas (1148–83).[17] The map (Fig. 6) plots those churches, chapels and lands which may be identified among the grants to Tewkesbury by Fitzhamon and his named followers, together with the tithes of the manorial rents of 'all his barons' (un-named, but identified by reference to the detailed list of their particular lordships

in Bishop Nicholas' later confirmation). The map also indicates Fitzhamon's castles at Cardiff and Newcastle, the only ones recorded in his time, together with nine others which must have been founded before 1107 by his knights. These nine castles are the ringworks at Bonvilston, Brynwell, Dinas Powys and St Nicholas (CR 2, 3, 7 and 20); the castle-ringworks later to receive masonry at Coity, Ogmore, Rumney and Penmark (MR 1, 5, 7; LM 14); and the primary castle of the le Sores presumably underlying the later stone castle at St Fagans (LM 17). Only Rumney lies outside the lordship of Glamorgan, and in neighbouring Gwynllŵg; its particular historical context is outlined below. With Fitzhamon's castles at Newcastle and Cardiff, ten castles are thus identified as foundations of his period within Glamorgan lordship. Brynwell is unrecorded, but might constitute a third demesne castle, given its location within the lord's manor of

[17] Clark, *Cartae*, I (xxxvi, xxxvii, cxxxvi), pp. 39–40, 133–35. See Beverley Smith in *Morgannwg*, II (1958), pp. 20–3 and in *Glam. Co. Hist.*, III, pp. 14–18.

12

Leckwith. Only Coity was the castle of a Norman member lordship, to which we will return. The remaining six castles at Bonvilston, Dinas Powys, St Nicholas, Ogmore, Penmark and St Fagans, along with their appurtenant lands, were all held by military tenure. The knights that held them were obliged to perform castle-guard at Cardiff commensurate with the value placed on their fees. They were also called upon to attend the chief lord's court or *comitatus*, a word also applied to the territory occupied by the manors of those attending the court, but hereafter referred to as the 'shire-fee' to avoid confusion.

The *shire-fee* is seen to have occupied the Vale Proper, with a northern extension into the Border Vale to embrace the le Sore fee at St Fagans. It is quite probable that other castles were established within this area under Fitzhamon in addition to the six we have listed, especially in the wide area between Bonvilston and Ogmore. These might be sought among the castles which are believed to have existed under Earl Robert before 1135. The large lordship of the Nerbers at St Athan, in particular, must surely have had a castle before 1107. St Athan was one of the four most valuable and extensive holdings within the shire-fee which were all situated upon the coastline. From the W., these lordships were Ogmore, St Athan, Penmark and Dinas Powys, respectively held by de Londres, Nerber, Umfraville and de Somery. Dinas Powys was held by the service of three and a half knights, the others by the service of four knights. Only the chief lord's large demesne manor at Llantwit, situated between Ogmore and St Athan, intruded into this otherwise unbroken line of especially valuable lordships. St Athan, it will be noticed, is the only one for which we have not listed a castle of Fitzhamon's time, though one must surely have existed, probably at Castleton, where only late medieval masonry vestiges survive within the buildings of a defensibly-sited farmhouse of that name (Vol. III, Part 2, MH 29 and Vol. III, Part 1b, PC 2). Further E., the four fees held by de Sully at Sully and Wenvoe formed a comparably rich holding, but that family appears in Glamorgan only at the end of the 12th century. The St Quintins, who came to hold Llanblethian, were certainly companions of Fitzhamon in Glamorgan in 1102,[18] but it is not possible to identify Walter of Llanblethian as their forebear. Walter granted land at Llanblethian to Tewkesbury in Fitzhamon's time, and it may be noted that the 14th-century castle there encloses the stump of a large square keep (LM 7).

The knights of the shire-fee were provided with houses within the outer bailey of Cardiff Castle to facilitate their service of castle-guard and attendance at the *comitatus*. The repair of these houses was the responsibility of the knights, as appears in King John's writ to them in 1208 during his tenure of Glamorgan.[19] By 1262, when a detailed survey was made, the service of castle-guard had been commuted to the payment of 6s. 8d. as ward silver for each knight's fee. In that year a total of £12 5s. 0d. was rendered in respect of 36¾ fees.[20] Twenty-five of these fees, shared between twelve families, have been identified with fees that appear in *Liber Niger* (1165) and *Liber Rubeus* (1166), where they are listed as fees of the 'Old Enfeoffment', *i.e.* established before the death of Henry I in 1135. The twelve families holding these fees in 1262 were also the holders in 1165–66, and seemingly in 1135. Many of them were certainly enfeoffed by Fitzhamon (le Sore at St Fagans, de Umfraville at Penmark, de Somery at Dinas Powys, and de Londres at Ogmore), and the others were enfeoffed by Earl Robert, if not earlier (Nerber at St Athan, de Winton at Llandow, de Cardiff at Llantrithyd, Butler at St Donats, de Constantin at Cosmeston, and Walsh at Llandough). The remaining eleven and three-quarter knight's fees of 1262 were either newly enfeoffed after 1135 or, in two cases where early enfeoffment might be suspected, they may have been omitted in 1165 and 1166 during wardship (de Sully at Sully and Wenvoe, Corbet at St Nicholas) The extent of 1262 and the 1165 and 1166 lists of fees are cited in the very many cases where they furnish vital evidence for the tenurial history of individual castles.

Within the shire-fee Fitzhamon retained for himself the demesne manors of Llantwit, Leckwith, and Roath. The largest of these, at Llantwit, included the vill of Llysworney, a name suggesting that this was the site of the pre-Norman *llys* or administrative centre of the cantref of Gwrinydd (or Gorfynydd), and that here Fitzhamon gave the abstract regality won by conquest a clear and concrete expression by retaining part of the demesne of the Welsh kings of Morgannwg. Despite the agricultural richness of Llantwit manor there is no evidence that a castle was ever raised there, but merely a moated manor-house at Llysworney (Vol. III, Part 2, MS 2). The far smaller

---

[18] R. A. Griffiths, *Glamorgan Historian*, III (1966), p. 166.
[19] Clark, *Cartae*, II (cccxxi), p. 320.
[20] Clark, *Cartae*, II (dcxv), pp. 649–5 and n., pp. 621–7; Corbett, *Glamorgan Lordship*, pp. 34–9, 116–20.

demesne manor of Leckwith had a small and quite unrecorded castle-ringwork within its bounds at Brynwell (CR 3). Roath demesne manor lay to the E. of Cardiff within Cibwr, the southernmost commote of Senghennydd, and was a constituent of the shire-fee where there was another moated manor-house (Vol. III, Part 2, MS 13), but no castle.

The Norman Member Lordships to the N. of the shire-fee, and largely occupying lands within the intermediate Border Vale, were Coity, Rhuthin and Talyfan. The latter was entirely within the Border Vale except for a small southern protrusion into the shire-fee which constituted its dependent manor of Llanblethian. The whole of Rhuthin fell within the Border Vale, as did the greater part of Coity, where another southward protrusion of its bounds embraced a lesser but agriculturally richer area of the Vale Proper in which Coity Castle (MR 1) served as its *caput*. These three member lordships are thought to have been independent conquests which were no doubt encouraged by the chief lord who permitted them to be held on generous terms, with royal liberty reserving to the lord of Cardiff only the rights of wardship and marriage of minor heirs. From their great size, and the especially regal status of their lords, it is likely that these lordships were created within the bounds of pre-existing commotes. These virtually autonomous lordships constituted what amounted to a march within the lordship of Glamorgan, buttressing the northern flank of the shire-fee. Coity is a special case, being held with royal liberty by serjeanty of hunting.

The Turberville lordship of Coity and its castle must have been established before 1106, when Fitzhamon's castle at Newcastle on the W. bank of the Ogmore is first recorded, for Newcastle could scarcely have been founded before the W. bank of that river had been secured, a function so clearly served by Coity, and virtually proved by the early grant of the tithe of its rents to Tewkesbury. Talyfan was appropriated by the St Quintins, who may also have been established there under Fitzhamon. They are recorded in the company of Fitzhamon as early as 1102, and we have noted the enigmatic Walter of Llanblethian who granted lands to Tewkesbury before 1107, and may perhaps have been their forebear in that dependent manor of Talyfan. The much smaller Norman member lordship of Rhuthin lying between Coity and Talyfan was largely retained in Welsh hands well into the 12th century, deprived only of the small sub-fee of Gelli-garn (CR 8) established at its southern end by the de Haweys under the le Sores of St Fagans.

Rhys, as son of Iestyn ap Gwrgant, still held the greater part of Rhuthin in 1130, but not long after that it fell to the St Quintins of Talyfan.

The Welsh Commotal Lordships, like the Norman member lordships, were virtually independent. These lordships represented the least fertile upland commotes or cantrefs, which originally extended southwards to embrace the good agricultural lands of the coastal plain, though there the bounds of lowland commotes are lost in the proliferation of imposed manorial boundaries. Following the annexation of the southern commotes, Iestyn ap Gwrgant maintained his dominion over the hill commotes between the Taff and the Nedd until his death by 1127, after which they were divided among his sons, of whom Caradog ab Iestyn came to assert an overall dominion. At this time the forbears of the dynasty of Ifor ap Meurig were similarly established in the two upland commotes of Senghennydd between the Taff and the Rhymni.

To return to the shire-fee established in the time of Fitzhamon, it is clear that it was only there that the chief lord's authority was absolute. There, he had his sheriff, his seal, his courts, and probably his chancery. Fitzhamon was wounded in the head at the siege of Falaise in 1105, surviving deranged until his death in March 1107. He was buried at Tewkesbury Abbey, leaving an heiress, Mabel, in ward to Henry I. The king's confirmations to Tewkesbury have been noticed, though little else may be discerned during his tenure which lasted about six years. Eventually, *ca.* 1113, Henry I's natural son, Robert Fitzroy, was granted seisin of Glamorgan after his marriage with Mabel Fitzhamon.[21]

Robert, Earl of Gloucester (as he became in 1121/22) was lord of Glamorgan from about 1113 until 1147. As well as his lands in south Wales and Gloucester, he possessed extensive lands in Normandy including the Honours of Évrecy and St. Scholasse-sur-Sarthe. Loyal and active in support of his father's cause in Normandy in 1119 and 1123, he was given custody of his uncle, Robert, duke of Normandy, who was confined at his castles at Devizes and Bristol, and finally at Cardiff from 1126 until his death there in 1134. In 1126 Earl Robert concluded an important agreement with Bishop Urban of Llandaff in the presence of his royal father at Woodstock. Later, already one of England's most extensive landholders, his leadership of Empress Maud's cause from 1138 would bring him to the forefront of national events.

---

[21] Patterson, *Glouc. Charters,* p. 3 and n., p. 152.

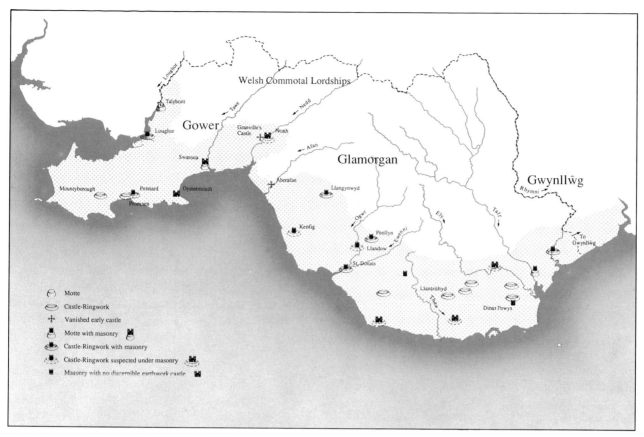

Fig. 7. Norman settlement under Earl Robert of Gloucester (*ca.* 1113 - 1147). For names of pre-existing castles shown, see Fig. 6.

In Glamorgan the tenure of Earl Robert was a period which saw the consolidation and extension of the lordship which had been imposed by Fitzhamon only as far as the Ogwr. Robert was joined in Glamorgan by Richard de Granville, his constable (*i.e.* commander of the knights of his household). Before 1130 they advanced far beyond the Ogwr to appropriate the Margam-Kenfig region, and beyond that the lowlands flanking the Nedd estuary, and the narrow Aberafan coastal corridor which linked those two areas (Fig. 7). There are no records of this campaign, but four early castles were clearly central to its accomplishment. Moving W., Kenfig Castle (EM 2), at an important river-crossing and upon or adjacent to the main Roman road, would have been the primary base for further advances, well placed to oversee the Margam-Kenfig region. By 1140, we first hear of the fortified vill which was established beside this demesne castle. Beyond lay the constricted coastal strip, and there a castle was built at Aberafan (VE 1), again at a river-crossing. There is evidence to indicate that this castle was a Norman foundation, and before it

was destroyed by the Welsh in 1153 it appears to have been held by William Fitzhenry. Its strategic siting at a river-crossing in the coastal corridor would suggest it as the next castle established in the advance to Neath. At Neath two castles were built, one on each side of the river. That to the E. was retained by Earl Robert and would form the nucleus of the borough of Neath (Vol. III, Part 1b, LM 11). The castle and appurtenant lordship on the more vulnerable W. bank of the river was established by Richard de Granville (VE 2), probably within or near the Roman fort; yet again, the Roman road had led to the most suitable river-crossing and sites for the castles which flanked it. Granville's castle was short-lived. In 1130 he granted his lordship and castle to the abbey he founded at Neath in that year. In a similarly generous gesture Earl Robert gave a large tract of land for the foundation of Margam Abbey in 1147, shortly before his death.

The westward advance by Earl Robert effectively brought to a close the period of Norman expansion in Glamorgan. The Welsh commotal lordships in the

15

Blaenau and the Norman member lordships would continue to enjoy virtual autonomy for the remainder of the 12th century, and, if anything, the tenures of the next two lords of Glamorgan witnessed marginal contraction, rather than expansion, of effective rule.

Neath and Kenfig, together with their appurtenant lands, were not incorporated in an enlarged shire-fee. With the exception of Richard de Granville's short-lived fief beyond the Nedd, these newly annexed western lands were administered from the lord's new castles at Neath and Kenfig, and that previously founded on the W. bank of the Ogwr at Newcastle, and described as the 'territories' of Newcastle, Kenfig, etc. Within these demesnes freeholders were endowed with parcels of land, but there is no evidence that any of these were held by military service under Earl Robert. A small number of knight's fees were to be established in these territories by Earl William, only two of which appear to have had castles. The contrast between these demesne castleries with their freeholders and the proliferation of the knight's fees and minor castles to the E. of the Ogwr is accentuated by another notable feature of the settlements established in the western territories. The freeholders who colonized those lands were not only Normans (Sturmy, Luvel, de Hereford etc.) but also Welsh (Einion ap Rhirid, Rhys Goch, John Ddu etc.); the survival of Welsh freemen is not unknown within the shire-fee, but there it was far less characteristic of a social structure dominated by military tenants of Norman origin.[22]

It is possible that Earl Robert established the primary castle at Llangynwyd (MR 2). This lay in the fertile re-entrant of the Llynfi Valley which protrudes into the Blaenau to the N. of Kenfig. A third castlery of the chief lords, known as Tir Iarll (The Earl's Land), must have been based on that castle before the 13th century but early documentation is lacking, though the chapel of Llangynwyd (*capellam sencti Cunioth' de Leveni*) was confirmed to Tewkesbury by Bishop Nicholas (1148–83).

The map (Fig. 7) adds, named, those early castles known to have existed by the end of Earl Robert's tenure. As well as the castles within the western territories, it is now possible to add further castles within the shire-fee. These may be discerned from the lists of knight's fees in *Liber Niger* and *Liber Rubeus*. Considered with the extent of 1262, as explained earlier, these lists enable us to identify those fees which had been established by 1135. On this evidence it is possible to add castles of this phase at St Donats (Vol. III, Part 1b, LM 16), Llandow (CR 11), Penllyn (EM 4), Llantrithyd (CR 13), and Dinas Powys Castle (EM 1, replacing CR 7, the nearby ringwork, abandoned before 1135).

Castles, thus, were demonstrably central to Robert's consolidation of lordship within the shire-fee and its extension to embrace the western lowlands. Before his time the walled inner ward of Cardiff, partly formed by rehabilitating two sections of the Roman walls, would appear to have been the only masonry castle within the Honour of Glamorgan. Earl Robert was noted as the builder of a great keep at Bristol regarded by a 13th-century chronicler as the 'flower' of all keeps in England.[23] In Glamorgan the square keep at Kenfig (EM 2) and the shell-keep at Cardiff (MM 1) may be attributed to him; it is also probable that the keeps at Ogmore (MR 5) and Penllyn (EM 4) were built in his time by de Londres and Norris respectively, and that others may have also been raised by his tenants at Coity (MR 1), Dinas Powys, Peterston, and Sully (EM 1, 5, 6).

Although Earl Robert had annexed the remaining coastal lowlands to the W. before 1130, he wisely chose to come to terms with the Welsh lords of the commotes in the *Blaenau*. Only this might explain the fact that Glamorgan was spared the savage assaults of the general Welsh rising that followed the accession of Stephen in 1135. The Normans were overwhelmed in neighbouring Gower, and the Welsh of his eastern lordship of Gwynllŵg devastated large areas of the Wentloog lowlands and seized Caerleon, the neighbouring lordship to the E. In Gwynllŵg Robert restored order by granting rich areas of his demesne at Rumney to Morgan and Iorwerth, the sons of Owain Wan. In Glamorgan an isolated attack on Neath was made by Rhys and Rhiwallon ab Iestyn, but the situation was again stabilized by a settlement conceding large areas of demesne to the insurgents. Even in the shire-fee the quiescence of the Welsh lords of Senghennydd appears to have been assured by granting them the demesne lordship of Leckwith.[24] Such actions recall his acceptance of so many Welsh freeholders within his new demesnes to the W.

---

[22] Matthew Griffiths provides a detailed discussion of native social structure and landholding in Glamorgan in the 12th and 13th centuries in *Welsh History Review*, XIV (Dec. 1988), No. 2, pp. 179–216.

[23] *Hist. Kings Works*, II, p. 578.

[24] This thesis is well argued by David Crouch in *Journal of Medieval History*, XI (1985), pp. 227–43 and especially pp. 229–30 and n. 5–7.

The exceptionally pacific diplomacy of Earl Robert in regard to the Glamorgan Welsh was no doubt inspired by his wider involvement, as a leading magnate of the realm, in the constitutional disputes which followed Stephen's seizure of the Crown. Reluctantly, from 1135 until 1138, Robert remained loyal to Stephen. Thereafter, he was the leading supporter of Empress Maud, and her most valued commander in the field with the support of Welsh troops, minting coins for her at Cardiff. It is an interesting and not improbable speculation that the celebrated contemporary hoard of coins from Coed-y-wenallt, a little N. of Cardiff, and mainly minted at Cardiff, was connected with the payment of his Welsh mercenaries or with the purchase of military supplies.[25]

In the last months of his life, more concerned with his spiritual than his worldly needs, he turned his attentions to the founding of Margam Abbey. His surrender of the large tract of land W. of Kenfig for that foundation in 1147 emphasizes the confidence he could place in the success of his policy of pacification. His son and successor, Earl William, would neither deserve nor enjoy the freedom to make such a bold gesture without fear of provoking a violent response from the commotal lords. Earl Robert was undoubtedly the greatest of the early lords of Glamorgan; of those that followed him, only the second Earl Gilbert de Clare achieved such great advances in the development of the lordship.

Earl William (1148–83) inherited an honour in which his father had achieved a considerable measure of stability. It remained, however, an honour which was only in part effectively conquered. He inherited mastery only over the productive coastal lowlands between the Nedd and the Rhymni, and in marginal areas of the Border Vale further N. The commotal lordships of the *Blaenau* were still virtually autonomous, as were those Norman member lordships of the intermediate Border Vale. During the latter half of the 12th century and well into the next, this tripartite division of the honour survived with little if any change. Only from the 1240s, under Earls Richard and his successor Gilbert (II) de Clare, was there a concerted and ultimately successful attempt to bring the entire honour under the effective lordship of the lords of Cardiff. Meanwhile, under Earl William and his successor John (1189–1214), there was a period of stagnation and retraction, during which the Welsh lords of the commotes in the *Blaenau* were no longer content to accept as final their loss of the more productive southern lowlands. For most of this time the leading Welsh prince was Morgan ap Caradog (*ca.* 1147–*ca.* 1207), grandson of Iestyn ap Gwrgant. Morgan, who became lord of the commote of Afan around the same time that Earl William succeeded, was able to assert his authority over all the upland commotes between the Nedd and the Taff. Beyond the Taff, in Senghennydd, N. of Cardiff, lordship was exercised by Ifor ap Meurig, the celebrated Ifor Bach of Gerald of Wales. The resistance of Morgan and Ifor to the feudal domination of the lords of Cardiff is more easily comprehensible in the light of their close family ties with the princes of Deheubarth. Morgan ap Caradog's mother, Gwladus, was the sister of Rhys ap Gruffudd; Ifor ap Meurig was himself married to that great prince's sister, Nest.

The first outward demonstration of a resurgence of Welsh resistance in Glamorgan appears to have come as early as 1153. In that year the Norman castle at Aberafan (VE 1) was burnt by Morgan ap Caradog's uncle, Rhys ap Gruffudd, an action which could only have been contemplated with Morgan's approval. Margam Abbey's granary was next attacked, in 1161, and in 1167 Morgan ap Caradog was bold enough to mount an assault upon Kenfig Castle (EM 2) in which the borough was destroyed by fire. Meanwhile, Earl William had been even more dramatically confronted by the discontent of the Welsh lord of Senghennydd. Gerald of Wales and the Margam chronicler record that in 1158 Ifor ap Meurig led a most spectacular raid on Cardiff Castle at dead of night. Earl William, his countess, and their son were abducted and carried off to the hills, where they were held until Ifor secured the restoration of lands taken from him, together with further lands as compensation. The lands in question are not named, though there is reason to suspect that Leckwith was involved in this celebrated affair and perhaps Whitchurch.

There is no evidence that Earl William made any further effort to appease his disgruntled Welsh tenants, as his father would surely have done. Instead, by 1175, they were able to present their complaints to the king himself. In that year Morgan ap Caradog and Ifor ap Meurig's son, Gruffudd, represented the Morgannwg commotes as members of a delegation of Welsh princes conducted to a royal council at Gloucester by Rhys ap Gruffudd, who by then was acknowledged by the Crown as leader of the south Welsh. Still, no discernible efforts were made to calm

---

[25] Boon, *Welsh Hoards*, pp. 37–82.

the discontent building up in Glamorgan. We may suspect that Roger Sturmy and Samson de Hawey had correctly sensed impending disaster when, before 1183, they disposed of their respective fees of Stormy and Gelli-garn (MO 5; CR 8) to Margam and Neath Abbeys; indeed, Merrick claims that Samson's fee had already been ruined by the Welsh, according to the Neath Cartulary available to him but now lost. Disaster certainly came, but not before the death of Earl William in 1183.

The revolt of 1183–84, following Earl William's death, was so destructive and threatening that Henry II delayed the intended marriage of his son, John of Mortain, with William's heiress Isabel. The king did not deem it advisable to permit this marriage and give seisin to John during his lifetime. The recorded facts of the revolt and Henry II's tenure of Glamorgan are noticed in the accounts of the castles that were central to events; contemporary references may be found in the inventory accounts of those castles, and particularly in those concerning Kenfig and Newcastle (EM 2, 3).

The leading figure in the revolt was clearly Morgan ap Caradog of Afan, the acknowledged Welsh overlord of the commotes between the Nedd and the Taff. The Welsh of the uplands of Senghennydd and Gwynllŵg were also involved, but the western demesne lordships were the main area of conflict where a powerful and concerted military campaign was mounted and the castles at Neath, Kenfig, and Newcastle were all attacked. To the E., Cardiff and the Gwynllŵg *caput* at Newport were also attacked. The Pipe Rolls record shipments of materials to repair and strengthen the threatened castles and the efforts made to victual and garrison them under the leadership of tenants of the shire-fee and demesne lordships. These included William de Cogan (at Neath), Reginald Fitzsimon (at Kenfig) and Walter Luvel (at Newcastle); Payn de Turberville and William le Sore were also active. Two adherents of the Norman resistance are of particular interest: Peter de Meulan, not known in Glamorgan, refused to go to aid the besieged castle at Neath and forfeited his lands for this dereliction of duty; Hywel ab Iorwerth, the Welsh lord of Caerleon, chose to support the Crown, rather than his kinsmen of the Gwynllŵg uplands, in order to retain the lands in Wentloog restored to him by Earl Robert.

The revolt was over before July 1184 when the king met Rhys ap Gruffudd of Deheubarth at Worcester. To stabilize the situation royal garrisons were maintained at the Glamorgan castles and works to repair and strengthen them are recorded, even as late as 1187–88 when houses in Cardiff Castle were repaired on the king's behalf. The Pipe Rolls do not indicate massive expenditure at Newcastle (EM 3); the most significant possibility, that it had been entirely rebuilt in stone for Henry II, is discussed in the account of that particularly interesting castle. The rebel leader, Morgan ap Caradog, survived despite his ruthless and unsuccessful onslaught on the western demesnes which he had clearly hoped to repossess. A significant reference to him in 1188 suggests that he was restored at least to a small but strategically significant area of the lowlands, and must therefore have made his peace with the Crown. In that year it was Morgan who conducted Archbishop Baldwin and Gerald of Wales through the hazardous quicksands of the Nedd estuary as 'the prince of those parts'.[26] The lost Register of Neath Abbey, as cited by Merrick, claimed that Caradog built a castle on a steep hill to control this dangerous crossing, and this must surely be identified with the vestiges noticed at Briton Ferry (UW 1).

John of Mortain (1189–1214), the last Norman lord of Glamorgan, was King of England from 1199. The fourth son of Henry II, he had been betrothed in 1176 to Isabel, the youngest of the three daughters of Earl William and the one declared to be sole heir to the earldom of Gloucester and the lordship of Glamorgan. The marriage was finally celebrated on August 29 1189, seven weeks after the death of Henry II, and John assumed lordship in right of his wife. He was to remain lord until 1214, despite the annulment of his marriage to Isabel in 1199.

We have noticed that Morgan ap Caradog had recovered a small area of the western lowlands around the estuary of the Nedd by 1188. A far more significant area of the lowlands was restored to him by John, namely the demesne castle and lordship of Newcastle (EM 3). The date and details of this grant are not known from any contemporary document, but there is no reason to doubt the claim made in the course of 16th-century litigation that John granted Newcastle to Morgan by the service of a fourth part of a knight's fee.[27] There is a considerable body of contemporary documentary evidence which bears witness to Morgan's exercise of lordship at Newcastle, not least

---

[26] Giraldus, *Itin. Kamb.*, p. 72.

[27] J. Beverley Smith, *Glam. Co. Hist.*, III, pp. 38–9 and in *Morgannwg*, II (1958), pp. 25–7.

the grants of land he made within this territory and those made by his followers with his stated approval. Discontent with a Welsh overlord may have contributed to David Scurlage's grant of his castle and knight's fee of Llangewydd (VE 3) to Margam Abbey in 1202. Morgan ap Caradog held Newcastle until his death *ca.* 1208, and was succeeded by his son, Leison, who was still its lord in 1213 shortly before his death. His brother Morgan Gam succeeded him as lord of Afan, but did not inherit Newcastle which reverted to the lords of Cardiff. Morgan Gam was deeply affronted at this reversion; his efforts to re-possess the fee were to be directed against the first de Clare lord, after 1217.

The surrender of Newcastle to Morgan ap Caradog was an act of considerable generosity, especially as the castle had only recently been rebuilt in stone in a very advanced fashion and with a lavish use of free-stone embellishment. It is very probable that the grant to Morgan was made at the time John became lord, in the summer of 1189. This gesture to the troublesome prince was surely motivated by a clear appreciation of the limitations of the lordship that could be exercised in the upland commotes, and was an attempt to ensure the loyalty of the most powerful Welsh lord, who might be expected to maintain stability in those parts. By implication, the withdrawal from Newcastle signalled the abandonment of any intentions of further territorial encroachment into the *Blaenau*. The high summer of advance under Earl Robert was over. The lethargy, and the neglect of Welsh sensibilities displayed by Earl William had provoked the savage uprising of 1183–84. John now acknowledged an uneasy *status quo* which would endure, with periodic outbreaks of violence, until Earl Richard de Clare turned again to the *Blaenau*, in the 1240s, and set in train the final conquest of the upland commotes, which would be completed by his son.

Meanwhile, during John's long tenure, there were no significant developments in Glamorgan. The policy of pacification paid off, in so far as we hear of Morgan ap Caradog's son, Leison, and Ifor ap Meurig's sons, Gruffudd and Cadwallon, leading large contingents of Welsh troops to serve King John in Normandy in 1202–04. The same Cadwallon, however, was moved to mount an attack from Senghennydd on the Glamorgan lowlands in 1211, for which six of his men were beheaded. The growing power of Llywelyn ab Iorwerth of Gwynedd preoccupied John at this time, and his successive custodians of Glamorgan were William de Braose (1202–07) and the dreaded mer-

cenary leader, Falkes de Bréauté (1207–14), men of stature whose presence suggests a growing concern for the continued stability of the lordship. By 1212 Llywelyn ab Iorwerth had won the allegiance of most Welsh princes. In Glamorgan Cadwallon ab Ifor Bach of Senghennydd was active in his cause, and Gilbert de Clare (1217–30), the first Glamorgan lord of that name, would soon face a resurgent Welsh power under the vigorous leadership of Morgan Gam of the line of Iestyn ap Gwrgant. The problems of the de Clares and their ultimate solution, however, are matters for consideration in Part 1b. The brief and inconsequential tenure of King John's former wife, Countess Isabel, concludes our 'early' period.

Countess Isabel (1214–17) was divorced in 1199. John took Isabel of Angoulême as his second wife, but held Isabel of Gloucester in custody until January 1214, when he was in desperate need of funds to finance an expedition with Otto of Brunswick to recover Normandy, and to enable him to placate the church by reimbursing the losses suffered by the clergy during the Great Interdict. To these ends he sold the marriage of Isabel, with title to her earldom, to Geoffrey de Mandeville, earl of Essex, for 20,000 marks, the largest sum known to have been given for an heiress in medieval England.[28] Earl Geoffrey predeceased her in 1216, but she married yet again, on this occasion taking her lands to Hubert de Burgh, Justiciar of the new young king, Henry III. Hubert de Burgh lost seisin, claimed *iure uxoris*, on Isabel's death on 14 October 1217; and so Glamorgan and the earldom of Gloucester passed to Gilbert de Clare, the son of Isabel's sister, Amicia, who was herself recognised as countess until her death in 1233.

Countess Isabel's short tenure of Glamorgan is most notable for the remarkable series of detailed confirmations she granted to Margam Abbey, which have been published by Clark and Patterson. It appears probable that it was during her time that Morgan Gam lost the possession of Newcastle as heir to his brother, Leison; to this extent she might be blamed for the renewed Welsh unrest which soon afflicted her de Clare successors.

The Castles of Glamorgan 1147–1217 (Fig. 8)

The advances made under Fitzhamon and Earl Robert have been given visual clarity by plotting those castles

---

[28] Patterson, *Glouc. Charters*, Introduction, pp. 7–8; Clark, *Land of Morgan*, pp. 71–73.

which may be regarded as foundations of their respective tenures (Figs. 6 and 7). No such patterns emerge by plotting the very few new castles which are known to have been founded between 1147 and 1217. The records permit us to add only five as probable foundations of this long period and, paradoxically, even these illustrate the reduced power of the chief lords in this long period of comparative stagnation. Two of these late foundations were Welsh: Morgan ap Caradog's castle at Briton Ferry (UW 1), seemingly in being before 1188, and Cadwallon ab Ifor's little motte at Gelli-gaer (MO 9) in Senghennydd (if correctly identified as *castrum cadwallon* of the 1197–98 Pipe Roll). The others were the Norman castles at Stormy and Llangewydd (MO 5; VE 3), respectively within the territories of Kenfig and Newcastle, and that at Gelligarn (CR 8) at the southern extremity of the commote of Rhuthin. All three are known to have been enfeoffed by 1154. Their contribution to the stability of the lordship was short-lived. We have noticed that before 1183 Roger Sturmy and Samson de Hawey had disposed of their respective fees of Stormy and Gelligarn to the abbeys of Margam and Neath. Similarly, in 1202, David Scurlage made over the whole of his knight's fee of Llangewydd to Margam and the monks dismantled his castle there.

All other castles recorded between 1147 and 1217 are known or believed to have been founded earlier, and in one case a solitary record of this period may indicate a further retraction at Aberafan (VE 1). In 1153 that castle, presumably founded during Earl Robert's advance to Neath, was destroyed by Rhys ap Gruffudd; there is no evidence that this strategic position was refortified before a Welsh borough was founded at the outset of the 14th century. The stone castle at Dinas Powys is first mentioned in a record of 1193–1203, but is attributed on archaeological and historical grounds to the early 12th century. The castles most frequently recorded are those previously founded by the chief lords at Neath, Kenfig, Newcastle, and Cardiff, though it remains a mystery that the castle at Llangynwyd (MR2) is not on record before 1246; it was presumably founded by Earl Robert (*ob.* 1147), and a chapel certainly existed there in the time of Bishop Nicholas (1148–1183).

There remain many early castles for which there is no historical or archaeological evidence sufficient for their attribution to the periods of the respective chief lords up to 1217. Their form or architecture, however, indicates that they were established at some time during this period. A further more detailed map (Fig. 8) is therefore needed. Drawn to a larger scale, and differentiating the various categories of castles, this map plots all early castles in the county, adding those of Gower to those of Glamorgan and Gwynllŵg. Manorial boundaries are shown in so far as they are known and within the limitations of scale. Later castles assigned to Part 1b, but with some fabric of the early period, are also plotted.

Clark has identified thirty tenants of the chief lords of Glamorgan who also held estates within the Honour of Gloucester in the counties of Gloucester, Somerset, Devon, Dorset, and Wiltshire, all but ten of them being listed in *Liber Niger* (1165).[29] The Glamorgan castles of many of these tenants survive, and it would be worthwhile to compare them with any castles surviving in their estates in the Honour of Gloucester, whether they are classified here as 'early' or 'later' castles. Unfortunately such an investigation was beyond the scope of this work. To facilitate such an inquiry, however, those families whose castles are described in this Inventory are listed, followed by the names of their Glamorgan castles, and, where known, the location of their English lands.

It will have been noticed that many of these families gave their names to parishes or villages, both in Glamorgan and the Honour of Gloucester. Many of them also assisted in the 12th-century settlement of Ireland, along with others whose Glamorgan castles have not survived (*e.g.* Barry, Basset, Bonville, Cogan, Constantine, Fleming, Norris, Scurlage and Walsh). Historical and archaeological investigation in Ireland might identify castles built there by these followers of Strongbow and offer further opportunities for comparative study.

B The Lordship of Gwynllŵg

A brief account of this lordship is required to place Rumney and Pen-y-pil (MR 7; CR 19) in their historical context. These castles were brought within the boundaries of the historic county of Glamorgan when the parish of Rumney (1937) and a part of the parish of St Mellons (1950) were incorporated into the city of Cardiff. Before then they were within Monmouthshire. They occupy the south-western corner of the medieval lordship of Gwynllŵg, in the angle between the coast and the Rhymni River which divided the lordship from Glamorgan. The lordship extended as far as the lower reaches of the Usk to the E., and

---

[29] Clark, *Land of Morgan*, pp. 3, 29; Clark, *Limbus Patrum.*

Family	Castles at:	English Estates, if known
Barry	Barry (1b, LM 1)	Silverton Park (Dev.); Bychenstoke, nr. Chewstoke, Lufton, Hornblotton (Som.)
Bonville	Bonvilston (CR 2)	Minehead, Chewton (Som.); Bonvileston (Devon); Craumer St Peter (Glos.)
Cardiff	Llantrithyd (CR 13)	'Toppesfield, Grancendon, Hameldon' (?Devon); Walton Cardiff (Glos.)
Cantelupe	Candleston (1b, TH 1)	Calne (Wilts.)
Constantin	Cosmeston (1b, PC 4)	—
Granville	Granville's Castle (VE 2) (vanished)	Bideford, Littleham, Kilkhampton (Devon)
Hawey	St Donats (1b, LM 16) Gelli garn (CR 8)	Compton-Hawey (Dorset); Combe-Hawey, Halwey (Som.)
Londres	Ogmore (MR 5)	'Hanedon' (?Hindon, Wilts.)
Norris	Penllyn (EM 4)	—
St Quintin	Llanblethian (1b, LM 7) Llanquian (MR 3)	Frome-St-Quintin (Dorset)
Sore	St Fagans (1b, LM 17) Peterston (EM 5)	Backwell-le-Sore (Som.)
Somery	Dinas Powys (EM 1)	Dudley (Staffs.)
Sully	Sully (EM 6)	Winchcomb (Glos.)
Turberville	Coity (MR 1)	Pidley-Turberville, Bere-Turberville (Dorset); Acton-Turberville, East-Leach-Turberville (Glos.)
Umfraville	Penmark (1b, LM 14)	Down-Umfraville, Lappeford, Torriton (Devon)
Walsh	Llandough (1b, TH 2)	—
Winton	Llandow (CR 11)	—

deep into the mountains to the N. Its geography matched that of Glamorgan – a fertile lowland to the S., Wentloog, and a barren northern upland, the commote of Machen. These lands constituted a cantref of the ancient kingdom of Morgannwg, but in medieval times they formed a separate lordship held by the lords of Glamorgan, but with its own *caput* established at Newport. Gwynllŵg was held by Caradog ap Gruffudd in 1072, when he won the kingship of Morgannwg, with Norman help, at the battle on the Rhymni. We have suggested that Wentloog might have been annexed along with some land around Cardiff when the Conqueror founded that town in 1081. If this was the case, it could explain the separate administration established in Gwynllŵg by Fitzhamon from 1093, and would favour his arrival by land along the Roman road running W. from Caerleon, where the Normans had long been established. It is interesting, in this regard, that the arc of castles

to the N. of Cardiff, tentatively related to the Conqueror's settlement, is matched by two similarly sited mottes which, like them, are unrecorded; these lie on elevated sites just within the Machen uplands at Twmbarlwm and Twyn Tudur.

Gwynllŵg shared the same lords with Glamorgan until the division of the de Clare inheritance in the early 14th century. Until then, the general course of its history also followed the same pattern as that of Glamorgan. Under Fitzhamon and Earl Robert only the lowlands of Wentloog were appropriated and, as in Glamorgan, Earl Robert pacified Welsh unrest after his father's death in 1135 by granting the prince of Machen some of his demesne at Rumney. The upland commote would also remain in Welsh hands until the 13th century, like those in Glamorgan.

Fig. 8. *(Overleaf)* Distributions of all the Early Castles founded by 1217 and the main manorial boundaries.

Kidwelly

Is Cennen

Cantref Bychan

Carnwyllion

Welsh Gower (Supra Boscus)

Talybont

Nedd

Llangyfelach

Loughor

Kilvey

LM 1

Sub Boscus
(to Welsh Gower)

Neath

Llanmadog

Swansea

Landimor

Llanrhidian

LM 18

Bishopston

Penmaen

Oystermouth

Penrice

Pennard

Rhosili

LM 12

Oxwich

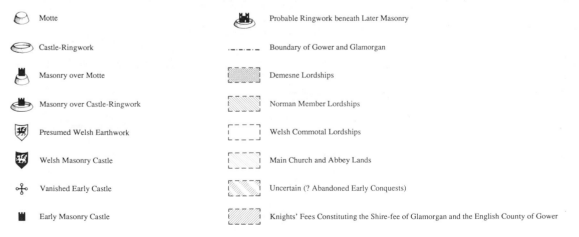

Motte		Probable Ringwork beneath Later Masonry
Castle-Ringwork		Boundary of Gower and Glamorgan
Masonry over Motte		Demesne Lordships
Masonry over Castle-Ringwork		Norman Member Lordships
Presumed Welsh Earthwork		Welsh Commotal Lordships
Welsh Masonry Castle		Main Church and Abbey Lands
Vanished Early Castle		Uncertain (? Abandoned Early Conquests)
Early Masonry Castle		Knights' Fees Constituting the Shire-fee of Glamorgan and the English County of Gower

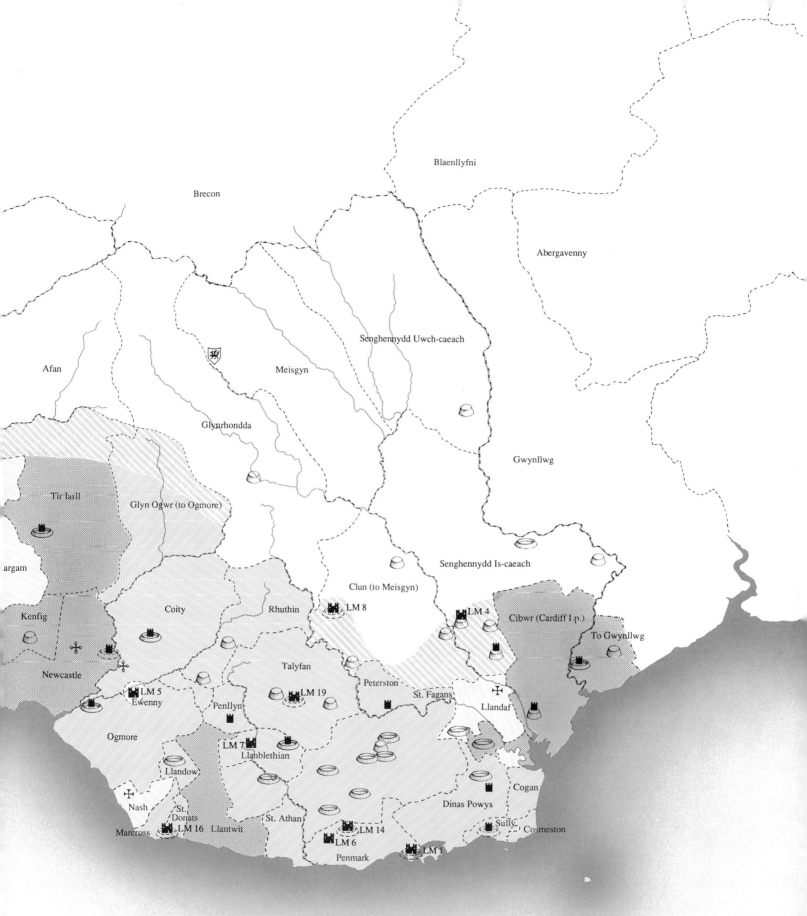

Blaenllyfni

Brecon

Abergavenny

Afan

Senghennydd Uwch-caeach

Meisgyn

Glynrhondda

Gwynllwg

Tir Iarll

Glyn Ogwr (to Ogmore)

Senghennydd Is-caeach

argam

Clun (to Meisgyn)

Kenfig

Coity

Rhuthin

LM 8

LM 4

Cibwr (Cardiff l.p.)

To Gwynllwg

Newcastle

Talyfan

Peterston

St. Fagans

LM 5
Ewenny

Penllyn

LM 19

Llandaf

Ogmore

LM 7
Llanblethian

Llandow

Cogan

Nash

St. Athan

Dinas Powys

St. Donats

LM 14

Sully

Marcross

LM 16

Llantwit

LM 6

LM 1

Cosmeston

Penmark

23

The *caput* at Newport was at first centred on a motte (buried in upcast during construction of the railway tunnel beneath it in the 19th century) close to St Woolo's (St Gwynllyw's) church. Later a new castle and borough were developed on lower ground beside the Usk. A second motte was raised at Castleton in the central part of Wentloog between Newport and Rumney. Except for a former castle of undetermined type or date thought to have existed at Maesglas, to the S. of Newport, the two sites now incorporated in Glamorgan are the only other early castles in Wentloog.

Pen-y-pil (CR 19) is not recorded, but Norman fabric formerly existed at nearby St Mellon's church. Rumney Castle (MR 7) lies beside the main A48 road which follows the course of the Roman road. Its position, at the point where that road crossed the Rhymni, is sufficient evidence to assume that the castle was very early, and was possibly founded along with Cardiff in 1081. It would appear that at first Fitzhamon enfeoffed Robert de Haia in Wentloog.[30] That lord is found very early at Newport and at Basaleg. His important grant of the church at Basaleg to Glastonbury in 1102 furnishes the earliest list of the followers of Fitzhamon, who served as witnesses. Robert de Haia soon relinquished his lordship, however, and Earl Robert was in control by the 1120s, with his *caput* at Newport and a productive demesne manor centred at Rumney. The subsequent tenurial history of Rumney, and therefore of Gwynllŵg, is outlined in the account of that castle. It need not be repeated here, except to notice the manner in which the territory became separated from Glamorgan. This separation occurred in 1317 when the Clare lands were partitioned three years after the death of Gilbert de Clare at Bannockburn; while Glamorgan passed to Hugh Despenser as husband of Gilbert's daughter Eleanor, Gwynllŵg went to Hugh Audley who was married to her sister Margaret. Thereafter the lordship remained quite separate and was one of those merged in Monmouthshire in 1536.

C   The Lordship of Gower to 1217

The range of printed sources and historical studies that are available for those concerned with the medieval lordship of Glamorgan is quite exceptional. No such wealth of information serves the historian or archaeologist when he turns to the lordship of Gower. There is marginal notice of Gower in some of the general works we have noticed in introducing this section of the Introductory Survey. Merrick's *Morganiae Archaiographia*, in its latest edition, provides useful information and further reliable evidence from the now lost cartulary of Neath Abbey. Clark's *Cartae* also incorporates some important charters vital to the manorial development of the lordship, and we have noticed that Nicholl (*Normans*, 1936) furnishes a study of its manorial development. More information on medieval Gower may be found in Conway Davies' *Episcopal Acts* (Vol. I, 1946); the works of Corbett, Matthews, and Patterson cited in relation to Glamorgan do not extend to Gower. Rees provides information regarding the Templar and Hospitaller lands in Gower (*Order of St John in Wales*, 1947), but his *Map* (1932) is less informative in its portrayal of medieval Gower than it is for Glamorgan, reflecting the disproportionate quantity and value of surviving records for these lordships. Of specific historical studies of Gower, mention should be made of the works of J. D. Davies, W. Ll. Morgan, and W. H. Jones.[31] There are also valuable papers concerning the lordship by G. T. Clark, C. A. Seyler and F. R. Lewis.[32] All these contributions by earlier generations of scholars incorporate much information and interpretation well worthy of consideration. Their combined efforts have been drawn together and developed in the most recent general studies of medieval Gower contributed by J. Beverley Smith and T. B. Pugh, and by David Crouch.[33] The first of these provides the most comprehensive general account available for the medieval lordship; Crouch confines his most informed and widely researched paper to an elucidation of the vexed question of the descent of the early Norman lords of Gower. Their work provides the broad out-

---

[30] David Crouch, *Morgannwg*, XXIX (1985), p. 29 and n. 37, pp. 38–39. Patterson, *Glouc. Charters*, No. 156, n., p. 146.

[31] J. D. Davies, *A History of West Gower* (4 Vols., Swansea 1877–94); W. Ll. Morgan, *An Antiquarian Survey of East Gower, Glamorganshire* (London, 1899); W. H. Jones, *History of Swansea and the Lordship of Gower from the earliest Times to the fourteenth Century*, Vol. 1 (Carmarthen, 1920) and *History of the Port of Swansea* (Carmarthen, 1922).

[32] G. T. Clark, 'The signory of Gower', *Arch. Camb.*, 1893, pp. 1–16, 292–308 and 1894, pp. 122–30; C. A. Seyler, 'The Early Charters of Swansea and Gower', *Arch. Camb.* (1924), pp. 59–79, 299–325; F. R. Lewis, 'A History of the Lordship of Gower from the Missing Cartulary of Neath Abbey', *B.B.C.S.*, IX (1938), pp. 149–54.

[33] J. Beverley Smith and T. B. Pugh, 'The Lordship of Gower and Kilvey in the Middle Ages', *Glam. Co. Hist.*, III, pp. 205–65; David Crouch, 'Oddities in the Early History of the Marcher Lordship of Gower, 1107–1166', *B.B.C.S.*, XXXI (1984), pp. 133–41.

lines of a most troubled period in the history of Gower, from 1106 until 1217, as the context of the eleven early castles identified within the lordship.

We have noticed the well-defined natural bounds of the territory of Gower: its sea-girt southern peninsula, and its extensive inland region running far to the N. into the high moorlands between the Llwchwr and Tawe rivers. Known to the Welsh as Gŵyr in the period preceding the arrival of the Normans, Gower is believed to have constituted the easternmost commote of a cantref, named Eginog in some texts, which incorporated the commotes of Carnwyllion and Cydweli (later to form Kidwelly lordship). By the 11th century the political associations of these commotes were with the kingdom of Deheubarth to the W. Had Maredudd ab Owain defeated Caradog ap Gruffydd at Rumney in 1072 he would have incorporated Glamorgan and Gwynllŵg within its dominions. With Norman help Caradog defeated Meredudd and won the kingship of Glamorgan, but Gower remained beyond his lordship. Even when Rhys ap Tewdwr vanquished Caradog in 1081, and won an ascendancy in south Wales which endured until 1093, it is not clear how far he was able to control Iestyn ap Gwrgant who emerged as the native ruler of the lands between the Nedd and the Taff, while a Norman presence was firmly established beyond the latter river around Cardiff. The quite independent Norman advances which subsequently won Iestyn ap Gwrgant's fertile coastal lands from the E. beginning in 1093, and those into Gower after 1107 from a Norman centre to the W., do suggest that Iestyn may well have established a measure of independent kingship, albeit less extensive than that presumed in the traditional accounts.

In 1093, as Fitzhamon advanced into Glamorgan, William Fitzbaldwin, the sheriff of Devon, was dispatched by William Rufus to establish Rhydygors Castle, at or near Carmarthen, and named *RYDCO* on a surviving coin soon minted there.[34] From there Gower was ravaged by the Normans in 1095, but not occupied before Rhydygors was abandoned on the death of William Fitzbaldwin in the following year. Gower is next heard of following the rebellion of Robert and Arnulf de Montgomery in 1102. At that time Richard Fitzbaldwin, brother of William, restored the castle and settlement at Rhydygors and Henry I granted Gower, Ystrad Tywi and Cydweli to Hywel ap Goronwy, who may also have been granted the lordship over the Welsh of Glamorgan. Conflict between Richard Fitzbaldwin and Hywel led to the latter's death in 1106 and the Norman appropriation of Gower, probably in the following year, though not by Fitzbaldwin, who leaves the story.

Henry de Beaumont, earl of Warwick, secured Gower soon after the death of Hywel ap Goronwy. Henry was the son of Roger de Beaumont, a close associate of the Conqueror. Like Fitzhamon, he was rewarded for his loyalty to William Rufus during the uprising of 1088, being created the first earl of Warwick. His continued loyalty to the new king, Henry I, in the Montgomery uprising of 1100–1102 no doubt prompted his nomination as the successor to Hywel ap Goronwy in 1106. There are no records of his conquest of Gower, which probably began in 1107, but in 1116 he is recorded under attack by the Welsh of Deheubarth at his main castle at Swansea (Vol. III, Part 1b, LM 18). Before his death in 1119 he had granted the ancient church at Llangennydd to the Norman abbey of St Taurin of Evreux, and granted the fees of Loughor and Talybont to Henry de Villers, who no doubt founded their castles (MR 4; MO 6).

Henry de Beaumont left five sons and the subsequent descent is complicated, not merely by this fact and by the paucity of adequate records, but also by the added confusion caused by the three names which have been applied to the family. The name 'Beaumont', first applied to this family by a French genealogist in the 18th century and now generally adopted, derives from the ancestral lands of Earl Henry's father at Beaumont-le-Roger (*Bellomonte*), near Eure in Normandy. The *Bruts* (excepting the *B.S.* version), in describing the attack on Swansea in 1116, name the earl as Henry Beaumont, but the Warwick branch used the surname 'du Neubourg' or 'de Novo Burgo', which is preferred by many scholars and anglicized as 'de Newburgh'. This name derives from the small lordship of Le Neubourg in central Normandy which Earl Henry received from his father. The third surname also encountered in the 12th century is 'de Warwick' (and one of Henry's sons, also Henry, adopted the name 'de Gower').

The succession of the de Beaumont lords of Gower has been established by David Crouch.[35] Following Earl Henry (lord *ca.* 1107–19) these were: Earl Roger of Warwick (1119–*ca.* 1138, *ob.* 1153, presumed eldest son of Earl Henry); Henry du Neubourg (*ca.* 1138–*post* 1166, youngest son of Earl Henry); and Earl Wil-

[34] *Bruts*: *B.S.*, *R.B.H.*, *Pen 20* (entries now correctly ascribed to 1093–96); Boon, *Welsh Hoards*, n. 11, p. 56.

[35] Crouch, *op. cit.* (n. 33), which also discusses the complex issue of the family surnames.

liam of Warwick (*post* 1166–84, son of Earl Roger of Warwick). Crouch explores in detail the strong possibility that Earl Henry's widow, Countess Margaret, held Gower by right of dower from 1119 until at least 1156 when she is last on record. This circumstance would explain how her youngest son, Henry du Neubourg, was able to hold Gower well before the death of his brother, Earl Roger, in 1153, and for at least thirteen years after the succession of his nephew, Earl William.

Earl Roger of Warwick (1119–ca. 1138) granted lands at Pwllcynan and Pennard to Neath Abbey on its foundation in 1130, the first indication of the existence of the demesne manor at Pennard. On 1 January 1136, a month after the death of Henry I, a Welsh force under Hywel ap Maredudd advanced into Gower and '*when knights and footmen to the number of 516 massed in one body against them they surrounded them on every side and laid them all low with the edge of the sword*'.[36] After this signal victory, somewhere between Loughor and Swansea and possibly upon Mynydd Carn Goch, Gower was ravaged, according to a 16th-century transcription by Sir John Stradling from the missing cartulary of Neath Abbey: *terra illa vastata fuit et depopulata*.[37] The same text adds that Gower was reconquered by Henry du Neubourg, and this is confirmed by the same assertion in the inserted memoranda of *ca.* 1300 on the fly leaves of the *Breviate of Domesday*.[38] The disaster of 1136 certainly terminated Earl Roger's tenure of Gower and there is no doubt that Henry du Neubourg was soon in control there.

Henry du Neubourg (ca. 1138–post 1166) probably recovered Gower before 1139; his family supported King Stephen, and since south Wales and the west country was dominated from 1139 by a strong rebel army under his neighbour, Earl Robert of Gloucester, this successful expedition must have been mounted earlier. His reconquest is now indisputably attested by coins from the recently discovered Coed-y-wenallt hoard. Minted from *ca.* 1140 at Swansea (rendered SWENSI, SVENSHI etc.) the earliest issue was in the name of Stephen, while from 1141 Henry's name was substituted (HENRICI DE NOVOB = Novo burgo or Neubourg). A grant of 1156 provides the strongest indication that Gower was indeed in dower to Countess Margaret, and that Henry du Neubourg and his brother before him were her custodians. In that year the countess granted the manor of Llanmadog in Gower to the Templars with the agreement of Henry du Neubourg, 'my son who is heir of this land'.[39]

Another brother, Robert du Neubourg, died in 1159. Avoiding confusion with Robert's successor in the Norman *caput*, another Henry du Neubourg, Henry deservedly adopted the name Henry of Gower ('Henricus de Goher'), and appears as such in 1166 in Earl William of Warwick's list of fees in *Liber Rubeus*. This record is the last mention of Henry. No details are known of the campaign by which Henry du Neubourg reconquered Gower. During his long tenure there is only one record to illuminate the study of at least one of its castles. In 1151 the Welsh chronicles record that Rhys ap Gruffydd attacked and burned the castle at Loughor.

Earl William of Warwick, who succeeded his uncle in Gower at an unknown date after 1166, was its last Beaumont lord. He died in 1184 without a son. His brother Waleran succeeded to the earldom, but never possessed Gower. Two suspect sources claim that Earl William sold Gower to Henry II to meet debts to the Jews. At his death the earl certainly owed £44 to a rich Jew, Bruno of London, for which he had pledged Gower as security, as appears in the Pipe Roll of 1184. Henry II settled this debt, which presumably explains subsequent Crown tenure of the lordship.[40] It is not difficult to see the motive for the king's action. Only the previous year Glamorgan had escheated to him on the death of Earl William of Gloucester and was still unsettled after the savage revolt that had then erupted and continued into 1184. His concern at affairs in south Wales would persuade him to retain Glamorgan until his death in 1189; the late lord of Gower's pledge to Bruno offered a simple and opportune means of acquiring Gower which would greatly assist his efforts at stabilizing the area.

The period from 1184 until 1217 which closes this outline of the early history of the lordship of Gower was most troubled; beginning with a long term in strongly disputed royal custody, Gower finally succumbed to persistent Welsh pressure and fell in 1217 to Rhys Gryg, a prince of Deheubarth. Before then the lordship was subjected to savage Welsh invasions in 1189, 1192, 1212 and 1215. There were five distinct periods of tenure: royal custody (1184–1203); William

---

[36] *Gesta Stephani*, ed. and transl. by K. R. Potter, Oxford (1976), pp. 16–17.

[37] F. R. Lewis, *op. cit.* (n. 32), p. 150; Stradling's contemporary, Rice Merrick, similarly attributes this information to the Neath cartulary: *Morg. Arch.*, p. 146.

[38] PRO., E. 164/1, f. 481.

[39] Boon, *Welsh Hoards*, pp. 49–50, 53–5.

[40] J. Beverley Smith, *Glam. Co. Hist.*, III, pp. 218–9.

de Braose the elder (1203–08); royal custody (1208–15); Reginald de Braose (1215–17); and Rhys Gryg (1217–20).

The royal custody from 1184 to 1203 was first put to the test in 1189. The death of Henry II was immediately followed by a savage campaign waged by that king's trusted ally Rhys ap Gruffydd and aimed at the centres of Anglo-Norman power in the S.W., including Gower which was ravaged.[41] At this time William de Londres was the custodian of Swansea, where in 1192 he was himself besieged in the castle for ten weeks by Rhys ap Gruffydd during a further incursion. Only the dispatch of the feudal host of England saved the castle.[42] John of Mortain, lord of Glamorgan, probably assisted in the relief of Swansea Castle, and in 1199 Gower came to him on his accession to the throne. In 1202 John granted custody of Gower, Glamorgan and Gwynllŵg to William de Braose, the lord of Brecon and Builth and other lands in the Middle March. In the following year William was granted the lordship of Gower by the service of one knight's fee.

William de Braose (1203–1208) did not enjoy his lordship of Gower for long. In 1208 he fell from royal favour and escaped to France where he died in 1211, avoiding the fate of his wife and eldest son who starved to death at Windsor. He left two sons, Giles and Reginald, but the Braose claim to Gower now devolved upon John, the son of William, who had been put to death at Windsor.

Royal Custody (1208–1215). When John resumed custody of Gower he placed it in the charge of Falkes de Bréauté, who was also his custodian of neighbouring Glamorgan where he had succeeded William de Braose in 1207. John visited Swansea in 1210 on his way to Ireland and a successful campaign there. Soon, however, he faced a mounting and powerful Welsh resurgence headed by Llywelyn ab Iorwerth of Gwynedd whose primacy was recognized by other Welsh rulers. In 1212 Rhys Gryg and Maelgwn, the sons of Rhys ap Gruffydd, led a force from Deheubarth to Gower, where Swansea was put to flames.[43] Three years later, in 1215, Rhys Gryg's nephew, Rhys ap Gruffydd advanced again to Gower. Although its custodian was then the formidable William Marshal, earl of Pembroke, Rhys took all the castles of Gower within a few days.[44] The chronicles name but few of these: first came Loughor and Talybont (MR 4; MO 6), which were burned; next came Swansea, where the garrison had burned the town to aid their defence of the castle, followed by Oystermouth, where both castle and town were destroyed (Vol. III, Part 1b, LM 12, 18). Shortly before this devastating campaign, as his troubled reign drew to its close, and beset by far wider problems, King John, in May 1215, had granted the Braose lands in Wales to Giles, the bishop of Hereford and son of William de Braose the elder. As Rhys ravaged Gower, Giles and his brother Reginald were busy securing the Braose lands in central Wales. Within days of obtaining John's grant of the Braose patrimony Giles had aligned himself with the baronial opposition and with Llywelyn ab Iorwerth. Giles was dead before the end of 1215, but the alliance with Llywelyn was sealed by the marriage of his brother Reginald with the prince's daughter, Gwladus Ddu. Thus it was that Reginald was able to secure the lordship of Gower despite its total subjection to Rhys ap Gruffydd.

Reginald de Braose (1215–1217) resisted all attempts by King John to regain his allegiance, knowing full well that the continued tenure of his Welsh lands was far more dependent on his alliance with his princely father-in-law. After John's death on 19 October 1216, Earl William Marshal, former custodian of Gower and regent during the minority of Henry III, finally persuaded Reginald to make his peace with the Crown. Reginald's earlier misgivings were justified, for his defection swiftly brought Llywelyn ab Iorwerth to Gower, and he had no option but to yield Swansea Castle to him. Llywelyn conveyed the castle to Rhys Gryg who then proceeded to subjugate the entire lordship.

Rhys Gryg (1217–1220) destroyed Swansea Castle and then turned his attention to all the other castles in the lordship which were also devastated in an awesome campaign of the utmost ferocity.[45] Anglo-Norman settlers were driven from Gower and Welshmen took over their lands. Llywelyn ab Iorwerth soon acknowledged Rhys Gryg as the lord of Gower, with Morgan Gam, the lord of Afan, receiving the manors of Landimôr and Kilvey. A later record identifies at least one English lord expelled from Gower in 1217, and presumably one of the castles destroyed. In 1241 Henry III ordered that Penmaen (CR 18) was to be restored to Philip Hareng, whose father had been dis-

[41] *Ann. Camb.*, p. 57.
[42] Beverley Smith, *Glam. Co. Hist.*, III, p. 218 and notes 73, 74, p. 617.
[43] *Ann. Margam*, p. 32.
[44] *Bruts: B.S., Pen 20, R.B.H.*
[45] J. Beverley Smith, *Glam. Co. Hist.*, III, pp. 222–3; *Bruts: B.S., Pen 20, R.B.H.*

seized during the war with Llywelyn ab Iorwerth.[46] Philip's father was clearly expelled by Rhys Gryg. It is of interest that 1217 is the terminal date ascribed to the pottery recovered during excavations at the castle at Penmaen.

Though Rhys Gryg's determined and thorough effort to achieve a Welsh resettlement of Gower in 1217 coincided with the terminal date of the present survey, it must be added that Gower was soon restored to English rule. After Llywelyn ab Iorwerth returned to the fealty of the king in 1218, Rhys Gryg long delayed his similar homage. Eventually, in 1220, Llywelyn was compelled to lead a force to Deheubarth to compel Rhys to surrender Gower and his other conquests and do homage to the king. Llywelyn's son-in-law, Reginald de Braose, remained out of favour, but the previous year the prince's daughter, Margaret, had been married to the rightful heir of the Braose lands. So it was, in 1220, that Gower was conveyed to Llywelyn's second Braose son-in-law, John, son of the William who had been put to death in Windsor Castle in 1210. For our purposes, however, English rule was far less securely established in Gower than it was in Glamorgan at the end of our 'early' period.

The Early Castles of Gower, 1107–1217 (Figs. 7 and 8)

Part 1a describes ten early castles in Gower. In addition, there were early castles at Oystermouth and Swansea, but their impressive later masonry requires their inclusion in Part 1b (LM 12, 18). Taking these two important castles into account the twelve early castles in Gower comprised two mottes, eight castle-ringworks, one early stone castle, and one extraordinary earthwork attributed to the Welsh. All except the last site (Cae-Castell, UW 2), which lies isolated in the northern uplands, were Norman foundations. The two mottes were that which survives at Talybont (MO 6) and another which formerly existed at Swansea; both lay in Border Gower flanking the neck of the peninsula and respectively placed on the rivers Llwchwr and Tawe. Swansea, the *caput*, understandably developed substantial later masonry works; an uncertain late record might indicate a stone tower at Talybont, but the surviving remains betray no trace of this. With one exception the eight castle-ringworks all occupy the Gower peninsula, and six of them did not come to possess masonry defences.[47] The six are Bishopston, Cil Ifor, Mountyborough, North Hill Tor, Norton, and Penmaen (CR 1, 5, 14, 15, 16, 18).

The other two ringworks at Loughor and Pennard (MR 4, 6) both developed masonry defences; in both cases it required excavation to demonstrate their original form. Loughor is the only ringwork found in Border Gower, on the Llwchwr a short distance S. of the motte at Talybont; its siting within a Roman fort at a river crossing on the main Roman road recalls the castles similarly sited in the lordship of Glamorgan.

The only castle with surviving early masonry in Gower is Oystermouth (Vol. III, Part 1b, LM 12), where a rectangular first-floor hall of Norman character has been identified upon an elevated rocky outcrop, but is now hemmed in by an impressive and complex series of 13th-century and later structures. These later additions defy any attempt to discern the nature of the primary defences enclosing this Norman hall, but the topography of the site prompts comparison with the more complete early masonry castles surviving at Dinas Powys (EM 1) and at Chepstow (Mon.). It is probable that early masonry strengthened the motte of the lords of Gower at Swansea before 1217, but no surviving fabric appears to be much earlier than the late 13th century.[48] Even with Swansea admitted as a probable early stone castle, two such castles represent a very low proportion in comparison with the ten early earthwork castles. In the larger but far more densely castled Glamorgan lordship, comparable figures indicate eleven or twelve early stone castles and forty-five earthworks with no masonry. This modest but distinct difference in the proportions of early stone castles in Gower and Glamorgan, respectively and approximately 13 per cent. and 17 per cent. of their totals, might demonstrate D. J. C. King's paradox of castle-building: danger called for castles, but these could only be built strongly in masonry in conditions of peace.[49] The constant pressures exerted on Gower by the princes of Deheubarth, with serious and destructive Welsh incursions in 1116, 1136, 1151, 1189, 1192, 1212, 1215 and 1217, allowed few periods

---

[46] Clark, *Arch. Camb.* (1893), p. 303.

[47] We exclude the dry-stone revetments recorded in excavation at Bishopston and Penmaen (CR 1, 18) and that noticed during survey at North Hill Tor (CR 15).

[48] What remains of Swansea Castle has just been surveyed in detail for Part 1b. Initial impressions suggest that the square tower accommodating the 18th-century debtor's prison is the earliest surviving fabric. Whether it might be deemed an 'early' tower awaits further consideration.

[49] King, *Cast. Ang.*, I, p. XXXIX and *Bryncheiniog*, VII (1961), p. 73.

of peace and stability, particularly after the death of Earl William of Warwick in 1184, when five of these invasions and the same number of changes of tenure would occur by 1217 in just that period when stone castles were proliferating in other areas.

Two maps serve primarily to chart the staged conquest of Glamorgan lordship as indicated by the castles known to have been founded under its first two Norman lords. No Gower castles are plotted on the first of these maps (Fig. 6) which covers the period up to the death of Fitzhamon in 1107; it was only in that year that Henry de Beaumont arrived in Gower and no castle is recorded there until 1116. The second of these maps (Fig. 7) adds those Glamorgan castles known to have been established during the tenure of Earl Robert of Gloucester, who died in 1147, but also plots those known to have been built in Gower by that date. A third more detailed map (Fig. 8) plots all castles identified as early foundations in Gower, Glamorgan and the small segment recently annexed from Gwynllŵg, including those lacking documentary or archaeological evidence to indicate the date of their foundation.

We have identified twelve early castles in Gower, including the primary castles at Swansea and Oystermouth. Six of these must certainly have been founded well before 1147 and are therefore plotted on Figure 7. *Swansea Castle* (Vol. III, Part 1b, LM 18) was no doubt established by Henry de Beaumont on his arrival in Gower in 1107. There is also reason to believe that he established a castle at *Pennard* (MR 6) as the centre of the demesne manor he certainly held there, and he enfeoffed Henry de Villers at *Loughor* and *Talybont* (MR 4; MO 6). De Villers probably founded the castles at those places and one of them must have been the un-named castle in Gower which was destroyed by Gruffydd ap Rhys ap Tewdwr in 1116 as he advanced from the W. upon Swansea, which repulsed his attack although he took its bailey.[50] *Pennard Castle* appears to have been equally early. When Earl Henry founded a cell of the Norman abbey of St Taurin of Evreux at Llangennydd his endowments to it included the church at Pennard ('Pennart') which lies very close to the demesne castle there, which it probably served.[51] There is also evidence to suggest that William de Londres of Ogmore assisted Earl Henry in the conquest of Gower and that he was granted *Oystermouth* (Vol. III, Part 1b, LM 12). Before Oystermouth became a possession of the chief lords of Gower it was certainly held by the de Londres family. William's son, Maurice, granted the church

there to St Peters, Gloucester, when he founded Ewenny Priory as its cell in 1141, though it is possible that he was merely confirming its earlier grant to the abbey by his father.[52] As at Pennard, the existence of a church close to Oystermouth castle before 1141 is strong evidence for the early foundation of that castle. *Swansea*, *Pennard*, *Loughor* and *Talybont* may be confidently ascribed to the early years of the conquest of Gower by Henry Beaumont, and probably *Oystermouth* also.

Near Pennard, across Three Cliffs Bay, the castle-ringwork at *Penmaen* (CR 18) must also have been founded before the death of Henry I in 1135. One of the fees of the old enfeoffment, established by 1135 and declared as such by Earl William of Warwick in *Liber Niger* and *Liber Rubeus*, was held by Terricus Hareng who may be identified as the ancestor of the Hareng expelled from Penmaen by Rhys Gryg in 1217, whose son Philip recovered seisin in 1241 on the instruction of Henry III.[53] The Harengs appear to have been followers of the Beaumonts in Dorset, and they also appear in Pontefract, Yorkshire. Precise dating of the 12th-century pottery recovered in the excavation at Penmaen is not possible, but it would not preclude a very early foundation.

A seventh castle is also plotted on Figure 7 as a further early-12th-century foundation, although in this case it is archaeological rather than historical considerations which permit its inclusion. This castle is the ringwork at *Mountyborough*, Penrice (CR 14). It lies immediately adjacent to the parish church of St Andrew, which may well have been an early 12th-century foundation; it was certainly granted by Robert de Penres to the Knights Hospitallers during the episcopate of Peter de Leia (1176–1198). Like Pennard and Oystermouth, Mountyborough was surely established along with the church. It is only the third largest Gower castle-ringwork in area (after North Hill Tor and Norton, CR 15, 16), but by far the most massively embanked example in the lordship; as with mottes, the largest ringworks are often the earliest foundations.[54] Mountyborough is also one of twelve 'ancient

---

[50] *Bruts: B.S., Pen 20, R.B.H.*

[51] David Crouch, *BBCS*, CCI (1984), pp. 134–5, appendix II, p. 141.

[52] J. Conway Davies, N.L.W. Journal, III (1943–44), pp. 120, 124–5.

[53] Clark, *Arch. Camb.* 1893, p. 303.

[54] In the lordship of Glamorgan, for example, the eight largest castle-ringworks include only one of uncertain date and seven founded before 1135 (see Fig. 45, p. 80).

knights' fees' held by military service which are listed in an important charter of 1306. This list, discussed below, must be treated with great reserve; where they may be identified, those knights' fees pertaining to holders named in *Liber Niger* and *Liber Rubeus* are a far more reliable indication of original Norman settlement. In the case of Mountyborough, however, its designation in 1306 as an 'ancient knights' fee' may be accepted.

Liber Niger and *Liber Rubeus* proved to be of considerable help in elucidating the original settlement of Glamorgan. In Gower they have only permitted us to identify one castle, at *Penmaen*, as a foundation before 1135. Earl William's returns name only two other holders who might be identified with Gower. One ancient fee was held by Lucas, but the Lucas family of Stout Hall in Reynoldston is not known there before modern times and it has no castle (though it was an 'ancient fee' listed in 1306). The other holder, under Earl William, William de Turberville, also had one fee of the old enfeoffment. Turberville is not difficult to identify as the lord of Landimôr, the large manor extending along the N. coast of the Gower peninsula. Before 1165 this William de Turberville had granted the churches at Rhosili, Landimôr and Llanrhidian (with its chapel of Walterston) to the Knights Hospitallers.[55] Within the territory of Landimôr we might consider the castle-ringworks of *Cil Ifor* and *North Hill Tor* (CR 5, 15) as works which may have been associated with William de Turberville. Neither is impressive nor significantly sited beside a church, so this interesting speculation does not induce us to accept either site as an early foundation to be plotted on Fig. 7.

To summarize, we have accepted *Swansea*, *Pennard*, *Loughor*, *Talybont*, *Oystermouth*, *Penmaen* and *Mountyborough* as castles of the early 12th century, and found it impossible to attribute *Cil Ifor* and *North Hill Tor* with any confidence to a particular period in that century, though a foundation by 1165 is worthy of further consideration. There remain three further sites of early type or characteristics for which there is no evidence whatsoever which would lead us to attribute any one of them to a specific date before 1217. These three are the castle-ringworks at *Bishopston* and *Norton* (CR 1, 16) and the strange earthwork in the northern hills at *Cae-Castell* (UW 2), which must be a Welsh site.

The 1306 list of twelve 'ancient knights' fees' which were held by military service, and mentioned above in connection with Mountyborough, is found in the charter of liberties granted by William de Braose in that year to the English and Welsh of his English county (*comitatus*) of Gower.[56] The context of this charter gives reason to doubt that very many of these fees were of the old enfeoffment, founded before 1135, though Seyler accepted them as such.[57] William de Braose prepared this charter at a time when he was required to demonstrate to King and Parliament his title to marcher rights in Gower. Hearings concerning this suit were conducted from 1300 to 1306, and the list of supposed ancient fees would no doubt have bolstered his claims. Two of these 'ancient fees' we have admitted on the basis of other evidence: Penrice (*i.e.* Mountyborough) and Penmaen. Unlike these, the remaining ten fees listed lack both 12th-century documentary evidence and early castles. These ten are Port Einon, Oxwich, Henllys, Weobley, Scurlage Castle, Reynoldston, Knelston, Nicholaston, Stembridge, and Fernhill. Most of their lords were indeed prominent in Gower from the late 13th century, but none of them may be accepted as early foundations.

It remains only to add that the four knights' fees we have accepted as ancient (*Loughor*, *Talybont*, *Penmaen*, and *Mountyborough*) would have been held by knight-service at the lord of Gower's castles at *Swansea* or *Oystermouth* (or perhaps at his castle at *Pennard*), where they would also attend his courts. As well as his demesne manors at Oystermouth and Pennard, the chief lord also possessed the independent demesne manor of Kilvey, strangely isolated from Gower on the E. side of the Tawe. This small manor might recall the lord of Glamorgan's separate administration of his lordship of Gwynllŵg. Unlike Gwynllŵg, however, there were no castles in the smaller manor of Kilvey, and beyond the observation that much of it appears to have been taken up by woodland and bog we need not comment further.

In 1217, as we have seen, the Norman conquest of the lands between the Llwchwr and the Rhymni, the future historic county, was far from achieved. Gower, its castles demolished and the Anglo-Normans expelled, was firmly controlled by Rhys Gryg. Glamorgan had suffered less catastrophic crises and a strong Norman hold had been maintained over the

[55] *Epis. Acts* I, pp. 362–5; Rees, *Order of St John*, pp. 29, 116; *Glam. Co. Hist.*, III, pp. 212, 616 n. 4; *Arch. Camb.* 1897, pp. 101–2, 105–6, 204.

[56] Clark, *Cartae*, III (dcccli), pp. 990–1000 (the list of fees, p. 995); *Glam. Co. Hist.*, III, p. 210. Seylor, *op. cit.* (n. 32) provides a most detailed discussion of this charter, with map.

[57] Seyler, *op. cit.* (n. 32), p. 314.

coastal areas, but even there the first de Clare lord inherited a disgruntled and virtually independent Welsh population in the *Blaenau*, soon to vent its anger in support of Morgan Gam of the house of Iestyn ap Gwrgant, who was intent on recovering Newcastle. The ultimate English conquest, as it should be termed after 1204, is a subject for Part 1b.

Despite the administrative and racial duality exhibited in the Glamorgan of 1217, and the total if temporary collapse of alien rule in Gower, the 12th-century Norman settlements in both lordships had established an enduring administrative framework that would long outlive the Middle Ages. As a conclusion to this survey of that turbulent century we may cite a most interesting 16th-century manuscript in Cardiff Public Library as a demonstration of the lasting foundations laid in these lordships in that century. This document is 'a survey of all the Knights' fees in the county (*comitatus*) of Glamorgan, as well *in Capite*, as castle guard and Knights Service, made in the 8th day of January, *anno Dom*: 1546'.[58] Undertaken so soon after the Acts of Union (1536–43) which merged Gower and Glamorgan in the new county, and despite the anachronism of its terminology so long after the general commutation of castle-guard and knight-service, this survey clearly reveals the survival of Norman territorial arrangements. In Glamorgan many original knights' fees remained intact as 'Mannours and Lordships Held of the King as of his Castle of Cardiff, by castle guard and knights service (paying yearly for wardsilver at St Andrews day)'. These included the four fees of Penmark (Sir John St John paying 26*s*. 8*d*.), the fee of St Fagans (the heirs of David Mathew paying 6*s*. 8*d*.), the fee of Llandow (Thomas ab John paying 6*s*. 8*d*.), and the half-fee of Llantrithyd (Sir Rice Mansell paying 3*s*. 4*d*.). Although no families returned in the 1262 Extent of Glamorgan survived, their successors paid the same wardsilver at the rate of a noble (6*s*. 8*d*.) per fee. Other original fees had been divided by subinfeudation, but again the total wardsilver payment received at Cardiff remained the same. Another section of this survey listed those holding by knight-service and castle-guard at the Duchy of Lancaster castle of Ogmore. The tenants of Henry, earl of Worcester, as lord of Gower, were also enumerated. As in Glamorgan, the families had changed but ten of the twelve 'ancient knights' fees' of 1306 were listed; Scurlage and Penmaen are missing: by 1546 sand had engulfed the castle and vill of Penmaen. This late survey merits detailed study for the information its contains in regard to subinfeu-

dation and the creation of entirely new manors in the 13th century and later. Sub-fees and manors of late creation form the bulk of the entries in this survey, but they only serve to emphasize the remarkable continuity represented by the ancient fees of the 12th century.

IV   The Early Castles Discussed

This section considers general aspects of the fifty-seven early castles included in Part 1a together with the other early castles identified but treated in Part 1b for reasons given in Section I of this Introduction. These castles have been classified into seven categories: Mottes without Masonry (Section MO); Castle-Ringworks without Masonry (Section CR); Unclassified, probably Welsh Castles (Section UW); Vanished Early Castles (Section VE); Masonry Castles built over Mottes (Section MM); Masonry Castles built over Castle-Ringworks (Section MR); and Early Masonry Castles (Section EM). For a discussion of each of these categories, taking into account known or suspected examples to be treated in Part 1b, the reader may turn to the preambles to each section. The longest preamble is that to Section UW, dealing with the very few early castles which may be regarded as Welsh works. Throughout Wales, Anglo-Norman castles outnumber those which may be regarded as Welsh foundations, an important fact well worthy of detailed discussion in the light of the Glamorgan evidence. This aspect need not be pursued further here. The preambles to Sections MO and CR both briefly notice the importance of glacial drift in regard to distribution within the county; this 'glacial factor' became apparent during the Commission's survey and it is explored in more detail below. Similarly, there are general aspects relating to early masonry castles which call for more consideration, since these are treated in three separate sections, each with its own preamble.

The general aspects of the early castles pursued here are arranged in such a way that a broadly chronological progression of topics is considered. These aspects are: A. *Distribution*, considering the general distribution of sites in regard to the geography of the county as a whole and such factors as communications and pre-existing settlement; B. *Siting*, which turns to localized aspects of topography which governed the choice of sites for castles and dependent settlements;

---

[58] Cardiff Public Library MS. 3.464, fols. 135–137.

C. *Glacial Drift*, in regard to the siting of mottes and castle-ringworks, and considered separately as an especially interesting aspect of the early castles of Glamorgan which is yet to be demonstrated in other areas; D. *Early Masonry Castles*, noticing the characteristics of the early stone castles of Glamorgan; E. *Excavations*, outlining the considerable contribution of archaeology to the present study; and finally, F. *Later Masonry*, at castles which are fully described in this Part (1a), is noted in an annotated list to assist those concerned more with the later castles of Glamorgan.

A The Distribution of the Early Castles

The general concentration of the overwhelming majority of all castles on the fertile coastal areas, and particularly in the Vale Proper and Gower Proper, has been sufficiently emphasized in Section II of this Introduction. If the concentration of manorial exploitation and the concomitant castles in these agriculturally rich areas requires no explanation or comment, another aspect noticed in the section dealing with the geographical background does deserve further consideration. We have noticed the importance of the main Roman E.–W. road between Caerleon and Carmarthen in the Norman conquest and settlement of Glamorgan and Gower (Fig. 9). The Conqueror no doubt advanced to St Davids along this route in 1081, founding Cardiff Castle and its mint on his return journey. In 1093 this route is by far the most probable means by which Fitzhamon advanced to assume lordship in Glamorgan. We have suggested that Rumney castle, beside the Rhymni River and overlooking the Roman crossing, was founded by Fitzhamon, if not by William I's followers before him. Beyond Rumney and Cardiff, further castles were set close to the Roman road, three at St Nicholas, one at Bonvilston and others at Llanquian, Penllyn and Stormy, before we come to Kenfig, Earl Robert's castle at another river-crossing on the line of the road, and others similarly sited at Aberafan, and on both sides of the Neath River crossing. We have given reasons for attributing at least nine of these thirteen castles to the periods of primary settlement under Fitzhamon and Earl Robert; of the other four, Stormy was founded in the 1150s, but there is no evidence for the dating of Llanquian and two near St Nicholas at Cottrell and Coed-y-Cwm.

Maritime communications have also been associated with the Roman road in Section II, where we noted major demesne castles at Rumney, Cardiff, Kenfig and Neath, all within or probably very close to Roman forts sited at river-crossings and on or just above estuaries and with adjacent harbours.

Turning to the smaller lordship of Gower, with fewer castles, the strategy of conquest appears to have been the same. There, the Normans approached from Carmarthen to the W. The main Roman road crossed the Llwchwr, to enter the territory at Loughor on its E. bank. There, within the Roman fort, Henry de Villers established a castle, supplemented by another further up the river at Talybont, where there is reason to suspect a further river-crossing on the line of a subsidiary Roman road. Further E. Henry de Beaumont chose another estuarine site at Swansea for his *caput*, this again close to the Roman road and matching Loughor, on the Tawe, the E. boundary of the lordship. There can be no doubt that the main Roman road provided an essential artery which was utilized to the full in the appropriation and subsequent Norman settlement of the lowlands of Glamorgan and Gower.

A further aspect of the distribution of the early castles in the lordship of Glamorgan noticed above is again worthy of further notice, though without adding further to what has already been suggested in Section III A of this Introduction (pp. 10–11). The recent recognition of a primary Norman settlement in the Cardiff area, established in 1081 by the Conqueror, has permitted us to speculate that an arc of mottes to the N. of the castle at that place may well represent the outer limits of the lands appropriated at that date, and before the arrival of Fitzhamon in 1093. Similarly, Section III (pp. 10 and 21) adds the speculation that Rumney and the lowlands of Gwynllŵg (Wentloog) may also have been settled at this early date along with Cardiff. The lack of any manorial context for the mottes to the N. of Cardiff at an early date (and much later at only two of them) is the reason for this speculation. We have already named the sites in question, and plotted their distribution in relation to Cardiff (Fig. 5, p. 11).

B The Sites of Early Castles

Though entering Gower and Glamorgan at different dates and from opposite directions, the earliest Norman settlers appear to have followed the ancient Roman road, and the earliest castles in both lordships were established on its line. Understandably, the leaders of the Norman advances into both areas,

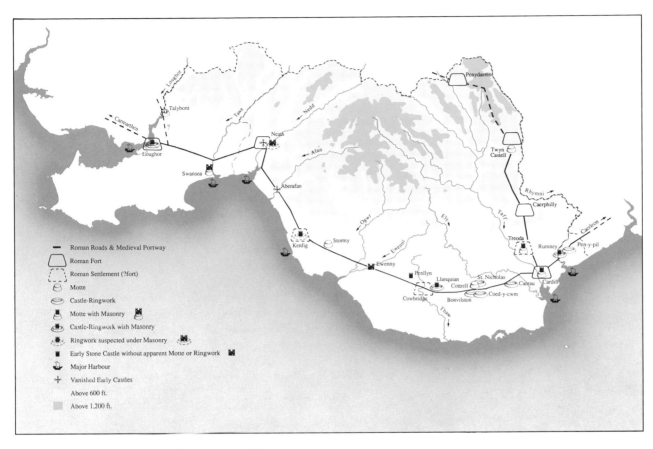

Fig. 9. Early Castles sited on or near Roman roads and forts.

Henry de Beaumont in Gower, and Fitzhamon and his successor Earl Robert in Glamorgan, selected the most obvious and suitable sites for their own castles: Fitzhamon at Rumney and Cardiff (where the Conqueror had preceded him); Earl Robert of Gloucester at Kenfig, and his constable, Richard de Granville at or near the Roman fort at Neath; and Henry de Villers, steward of Henry de Beaumont, at Loughor. All these castles were on prime sites previously chosen by the Romans. Lesser Norman settlers in both lordships were forced to seek less obvious sites for the castles needed to assure their personal safety and subdue and administer the lands granted to them. We turn now to the types of sites that were favoured by these followers of the conquerors.

The terrain of the lowlands of Gower and Glamorgan did not furnish sites with a full circuit of impressive natural defences. In fact only three of our early sites lie on the tops of high, isolated hills, all of which lie within Iron Age hill forts. Even these (the motte at Ruperra and the castle-ringworks at Caerau and Cil Ifor, MO 4; CR 4, 5) occupy only tiny areas of far larger entrenched plateaux and therefore constitute very elevated scarp-edge sites. The rest are all low-lying, with no particularly noticeable preference for any of the five common types of site: (i) scarp-edge sites with one flank naturally protected, (ii) blunt promontory sites (often embraced between steep natural scarps and lesser re-entrants), (iii) sites on level ground beside rivers or small streams which may have provided wet defences or marshy approaches usually no longer apparent, (iv) sites on very slight elevations affording a good outlook but negligible defence, and finally (v) sites on entirely neutral ground. There are very few strong promontory sites with only one limited flank permitting easy approach; Dinas Powys Ringwork and North Hill Tor (CR 7, 15) are perhaps the only true examples, though we could add the masonry castles of Dinas Powys, Llangynwyd and Oystermouth (EM 1; MR 2; Vol. III, Part 1b, LM 12). Many sites display several of the five characteristics listed above: Brynwell (CR 3) is sited on a very slight and modest scarp above a marshy hollow; Rumney (MR 7) lies above a precipitous fall to the

33

Rhymni river, yet an insignificant re-entrant could demand its classification as a blunt promontory site. Leaving aside such sites, the following are the best examples to illustrate the five types:

(i) *Scarp-edge sites*: Bishopston, Coed-y-Cwm, and Howe Mill (CR 1, 6, 10) and the masonry castles of Newcastle, Penllyn and Penmark (EM 3, 4; Vol. III, Part 1b, LM 14).

(ii) *Blunt promontory sites*: Penmaen, Pen-y-Pil, Llanquian, and Pennard (CR 18, 19; MR 3, 6).

(iii) *Level sites beside rivers or streams*: Felin Isaf, Morganstown, Bonvilston, Walterston, and Ogmore (MO 2, 3; CR 2, 21; MR 5).

(iv) *Modestly elevated sites*: Cottrell, Talybont, Llandow, Llanilid, Mountyborough, St Nicholas, and Coity (MO 1, 6; CR 11, 12, 14, 20; MR 1).

(v) *Sites on neutral ground*: Stormy, Tomen-y-Clawdd, Twmpath (Rhiwbina), Gelli-garn, and Pancross (MO 5, 7, 8; CR 8, 17).

One further aspect of the siting of early castles is worthy of notice. Twelve of them were sited *immediately alongside medieval churches*: at Ystradowen (MO 12); Caerau, Llanilid, and Mountyborough (CR 4, 12, 14); Aberafan, Llangewydd, and Oldcastle (VE 1, 3, 4); Treoda (MM 2); Coity and Loughor (MR 1, 4); and Newcastle and Sully (EM 3, 6). Fifteen were very close to churches, including the now besanded sites at Penmaen and Pennard (CR 18; MR 6), where the church sites have been located and excavated, and Llandow (CR 11), where scrutiny of air photographs of fields around the church led to the discovery of this all but erased castle-ringwork.

C   Glacial Drift as a Factor Influencing the Segregated Distribution of Mottes and Castle-Ringworks in Glamorgan

In 1969 D. J. C. King and Leslie Alcock demonstrated the seemingly irrational distribution of castle-ringworks in England and Wales, identifying thirteen concentrations forming localized groups to the virtual exclusion of mottes.[59] Two of these groups were in Glamorgan, one in Gower, the other in the Vale of Glamorgan. No certain explanation was discerned, though it was considered that the personal preference of certain lords might account for such groups. In Glamorgan, however, a geological determinant is apparent, with the presence or absence of glacial drift dictating which of these early castle-types was built in a particular area.

In the lordship of Glamorgan castle-ringworks form an entirely exclusive group in the Vale Proper, with mottes concentrated further north. During survey it was ascertained that almost all of these mottes were apparently formed of glacial material. In the lordship of Gower the earthwork castles display a similar segregation. Two mottes, at Swansea and Talybont, are to the N., flanking Border Gower; S.W. of these lie the eight castle-ringworks within the lordship, all on the Gower peninsula. Sixteen mottes have been identified in the county (including four with later masonry): the two in the lordship of Gower and fourteen in the lordship of Glamorgan. When these mottes are plotted in relation to the known southern limit of the drift in south Wales it is clear that they all lie to the N. of this limit. As regards the twenty eight certain castle-ringworks, five of the eight known in Gower and all but three of the eighteen in Glamorgan lie S. of the drift (Fig. 10). A geological determinant was clearly apparent; in all but a few cases the presence or absence of drift appears to have determined whether a lord built a motte or a castle-ringwork.

To explore this thesis more closely, given the small scale of drift maps available, the valued advice of R. A. Walters of the British Geological Survey was sought. He was able to confirm from his unpublished work on drift that only two of our fourteen mottes were sited on drift-free pockets, and even these were within the limits of the drift. These are the motte at Ruperra (MO 4), which was built on intractable nodular limestone, and the motte suspected at Castell Coch (Vol. III, Part 1b, LM 4), which lies on Carboniferous limestone. Both mottes in Gower were confirmed as sites upon drift.

Turning to the ringworks S. of the limits of the drift, it was not possible to ascertain a common geological factor to explain the eight found on the Gower peninsula; there we find irregular scattered deposits of drift as well as large areas of Carboniferous limestone which at least may be cited as the basis for many of them (*e.g.* North Hill Tor, Norton and Penmaen, CR 15, 16, 18). In Glamorgan, however, the geological evidence was not confused in this way. There it was possible to prepare a drift map covering the Vale Proper and the Border Vale (Fig. 11), an area embracing most of the castles of the lordship (ten of its fourteen mottes and sixteen of its eighteen certain

[59] D. J. Cathcart King and Leslie Alcock, 'Ringworks of England and Wales', *Château Gaillard*, II (1969), pp. 90–127 (particularly pp. 99–106).

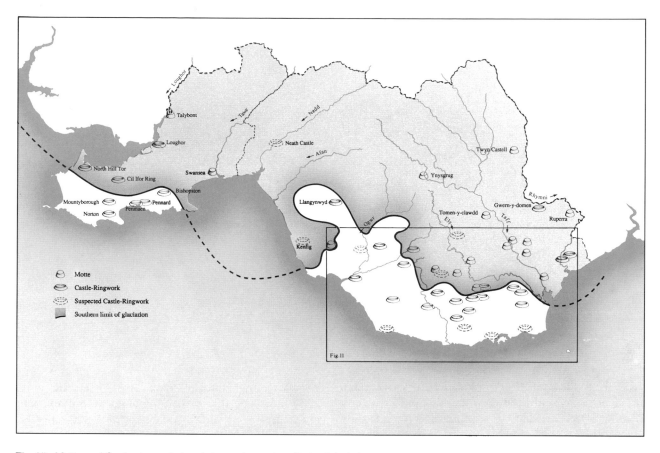

Fig. 10. Mottes and Castle-ringworks in relation to the southern limit of glaciation as plotted by D.Q. Bowen (1977).

castle-ringworks), as well as the two ringworks in Gwynllŵg, to the E. of Cardiff. Of the sixteen Glamorgan ringworks plotted on this map, fourteen lie S. of the drift, seven on Lias limestone, four on Carboniferous limestone and three on Triassic rock. This broad expanse of shallow fertile soils also has four of the seven masonry castles with plans suggesting them as the sites of primary ringworks. Only three ringworks are found on the drift, at Gwern-y-domen, Llanilid and St. Nicholas (CR 9, 12, 20), the first of these just beyond the area of the map, near Caerphilly.

We may make two broad conclusions regarding mottes and ringworks in Glamorgan. Mottes were generally raised in those areas where pre-existing glacial formations provided sites easily adapted for the purpose, or on level ground where they could be raised without difficulty with the upcast of their ditches. Ringworks, on the other hand, generally occupy the flat plateaux of the Vale, lacking in the abrupt outcrops or elevations found to the N., and with a thin soil rarely as much as 1m thick over consolidated rock which is for the most part Lias limestone. On such ground, it appears, it was not feasible to create mottes with the great quantities of rubble which would have been produced from the deep ditches required.

There is no evidence that there was any question of status in the feudal hierarchy playing a part in the choice of castle-type. Although the chief lords had mottes at their *capita* at Cardiff and Swansea, the first lord of Gower had a castle-ringwork at Pennard, Fitzhamon had another at Newcastle and Earl Robert would raise another at Kenfig (and probably at Neath, beneath the later stone castle). There is a hint that the first castles raised in Glamorgan under the Conqueror, as we suspect, were mainly mottes lying to the N. of the motte at Cardiff. This appearance of a chronological factor, however, may not be taken too far; the local geology of Cardiff furnished the glacial drift suited to motte construction.

It remains to notice that in 1947 the late E. Neaverson, geologist and antiquarian, observed the importance of glacial drift in regard to the many mottes found in north Wales to the almost total exclusion

35

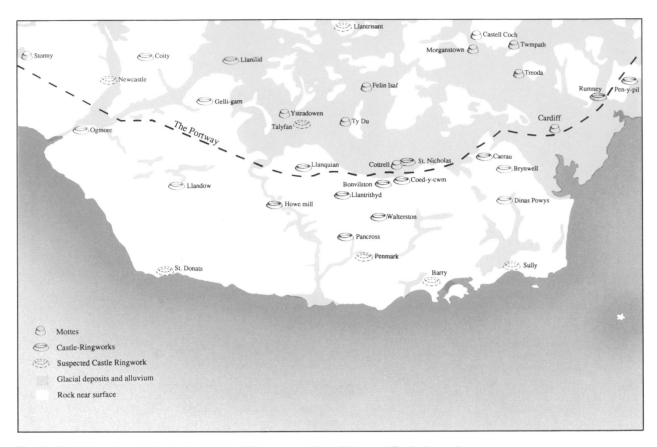

Fig. 11. Glacial deposits and alluvium in the Vale of Glamorgan, with the Mottes and Castle-ringworks.

of castle-ringworks, which, being then hardly recognised as castles, were not considered by him.[60] His comments on mottes, however, are worth noting:

'The Drift deposits (including the alluvium) are important ... because they comprise the only non-consolidated rock-material in North Wales, and they obviously determine the distribution of the artificial mounds on which early Norman castles were built.'

'The construction of these strongholds requires the presence of a suitable substratum which could be rapidly fashioned into conical mounds. Hence the distribution of Norman castles is limited in general by the presence of Drift deposits, the only non-consolidated rocks in North Wales.'[61]

Finally, it should be noted that while drift favoured the erection of mottes, it was also most suitable for ringwork construction. Unfortunately, few areas seem to display the abrupt and distinct separate zones of drift and shallow soils over rock which we find in Glamorgan. In consequence, no other areas present such a clear geological pattern so readily related to isolated groups of ringworks. This question has been

provisionally considered in relation to the mottes and ringworks of Wales as a whole, but more intense study of groups of ringworks like those in Pembrokeshire and mid Monmouthshire is required.[62]

D   Early Masonry Castles

Early masonry has been identified at twelve* of the fifty-seven castles described in Part 1a, and at four others which are described in Part 1b on account of their more significant later fabric. The sixteen* sites in question are plotted on Fig. 12 and treated in four

---

[60] E. Neaverson, *Medieval Castles in North Wales; a Study of Sites, Water Supply and Building Stones*, Liverpool University Press (1947).

[61] Neaverson, *ibid.*, pp. 6, 17.

[62] C. J. Spurgeon, 'Mottes and castle-ringworks in Wales' in John R. Kenyon and Richard Avent (eds.) *Castles in Wales and the Marches; Essays in Honour of D. J. Cathcart King*, University of Wales Press (1987), pp. 23–49 (geology and earthwork castles, pp. 32–6).

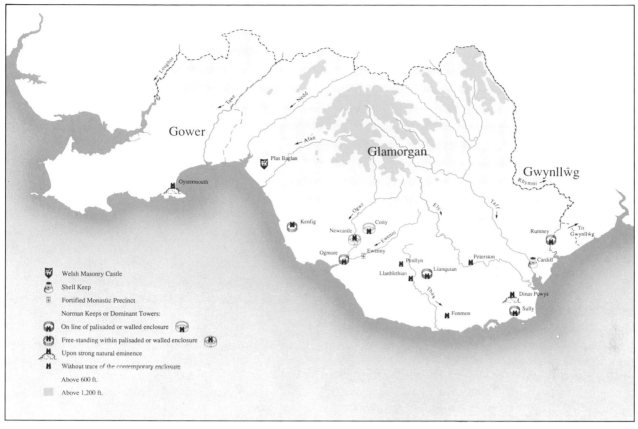

Fig. 12. The Early Masonry Castles.

sections of Part 1a (UW, MM, MR and EM) and one section of Part 1b. (LM):

Part 1a	UW	5	Plas Baglan
Part 1a	MM	1	Cardiff Castle
Part 1a	MR	1	Coity Castle
Part 1a	MR	3	Llanquian Castle
Part 1a	MR	5	Ogmore Castle
Part 1a	MR	7	Rumney Castle
Part 1a	EM	1	Dinas Powys Castle
Part 1a	EM	2	Kenfig Castle
Part 1a	EM	3	Newcastle, Bridgend
Part 1a	EM	4	Penllyn Castle
Part 1a	EM	5	Peterston Castle
Part 1a	EM	6	Sully Castle
Part 1b	LM	5	Ewenny Priory
Part 1b	LM	6	Fonmon Castle
Part 1b	LM	7	Llanblethian Castle
Part 1b	LM	12	Oystermouth Castle

* Loughor Castle (MR 4) may now be added.
See postscript to the site account.

Only Oystermouth (in Gower) and Rumney (in Gwynllŵg) lay beyond the bounds of the lordship of Glamorgan, and even these were respectively the castles of a leading Glamorgan tenant (de Londres of Ogmore) and that lordship's chief lord. Three sites, however, require individual consideration on account of their particular form and ownership: Plas Baglan, Cardiff Castle and Ewenny Priory. The remaining thirteen may be treated together as small or medium-sized early stone castles, each characterized by its square or rectangular keep or dominant tower, though there are discernible variations in their layout, siting and development. First, however, it is necessary to explain the allocation of these sites to the various sections of this inventory and to notice the condition and extent of their Norman fabric.

Section UW includes the extraordinary early masonry castle of Plas Baglan, along with four un-classified earthworks, all attributed to the Welsh. Cardiff Castle, with its motte, is described in Section MM. Section MR, describing seven masonry castles raised upon castle-ringworks, includes three which incorporate 12th-century fabric (Coity, Ogmore and Rumney) and tiny Llanquian which might well be equally early. Each of the six castles included in Section EM has Norman masonry; three of these were perhaps stone castles from the outset (Dinas Powys, Penllyn and Peterston), while at the others the masonry appears to have either supplemented a palisaded ringwork (Kenfig and Sully), or to have entirely replaced such a primary work (Newcastle). The four castles assigned to part 1b, Section LM, are those at Ewenny, Fonmon, Llanblethian and Oystermouth, where 12th-century masonry may be discerned along with far more substantial later fabric.

The impressive roll of sixteen early stone castles must be qualified in that limited vestiges of early fabric survive at many of them. Two, indeed, have now made way for recent housing developments (Rumney and Sully), though both were excavated before they vanished. Substantial Norman fabric is visible and freely accessible to the public only at Cardiff, Coity, Ogmore and Newcastle. Excavations at Dinas Powys, Kenfig, Peterston and Llanblethian would probably reveal substantial remains of keeps now largely buried in their own debris, and would be most informative at the little castle of Llanquian and the early Welsh site at Plas Baglan; relatively undisturbed, these six sites merit the most stringent protection. Comparable archaeological potential is lacking at Penllyn, Ewenny Priory, Fonmon and Oystermouth; their Norman fabric is encased in later work.

Plas Baglan (UW 5), which like Cardiff and Ewenny demands individual consideration, is distinguished by its simple plan and as the solitary Welsh stone castle known in the county.[63] Its vestiges indicate a square walled enclosure set upon a scarped platform with a rectangular first-floor hall or tower set in one angle and ranging along the strong natural scarp to the W., opposite the entrance. Traces of two splayed embrasures pierce the curtain, one within the basement of the hall. Its location, simple plan and the crudely fan-tooled dressings found loose on the site, all suggest a foundation in the 12th century by the Welsh lords of Afan. Morgan ap Caradog (*ca.* 1147–*ca.* 1207) is regarded as its probable founder. Welsh masonry castles of the 12th century are extremely rare.[64] In Deheubarth scant vestiges survive of the masonry probably raised by the great Rhys ap Gruffydd at Ystrad Meurig (Cards.), Dinefwr (Carms.) and Castell Nanhyfer (Pembs.), and nothing of that which he certainly added at Cardigan Castle. Elsewhere, and confined to Gwynedd, there are only the indeterminate

stone footings excavated on the rocky outcrop of Tomen Castell (Caerns.), not far from the later Dolwyddelan Castle, the equally indeterminate fragments of Carn Fadryn (Caerns.) and Penrhyndeudraeth (Mer.), and the stone-revetted 'motte' at Cwm Prysor (Mer.). Plas Baglan, therefore, presents a uniquely intact and comparatively undisturbed early Welsh masonry castle of quite individual plan, though the presence of loose 13th-century mouldings suggests later additions which could only be identified by excavation.

Cardiff Castle (MM 1) is by far the largest early castle in the county, but it stands apart for three significant aspects of its structural development. First, it is the only site in the county with masonry attributed to the late 11th century, when its walled inner ward incorporated refurbished sections of the Roman fort wall. Second, it is the only early masonry castle in the county which incorporated a motte. Third, that motte was of sufficient size to accommodate its 12th-century shell-keep which also stands alone. The late-11th-century masonry at Cardiff, attributed to William I (1081), is preceded in Wales only by William Fitzosbern's work at Chepstow, Mon. (1067–71), which also incorporated reused Roman building materials, though not on their original site. Porchester (Hants.) Exeter (Dev.) and the Tower of London furnish other near contemporary examples of the refurbishment of Roman walls seen at Cardiff. Turning to the great motte which also distinguishes Cardiff, the great polygonal shell-keep which crowns it is attributed to Earl Robert of Gloucester (*ob.* 1147), and is characterized by the alternating ashlar quoins of Sutton stone at its angles and the profusion of putlog holes which pierce its facets of mixed rubble and glacial pebbles. In a far less regular form the polygonal nature of the Cardiff shell-keep is reflected in the layout of the curtain-walls of many of the lesser early castles discussed below. These walls in some cases display similar quoining, putlog holes and masonry, features which were perhaps derived from Cardiff Castle, where their lords, as tenants, performed their feudal duties. Carisbrooke Castle on the Isle of Wight has a very similar but less regular polygonal shell-keep, broadly contemporary with that at Cardiff, if it is correctly ascribed to 1136.[65]

---

[63] Only the 13th-century Morgraig Castle (Vol. III, Part 1b, LM 9) has been claimed authoritatively as another, if later, Welsh stone castle in the county, though this view is rejected here. See preamble to Section UW, p. 138.

[64] Spurgeon, op. cit. (n. 62), pp. 26–7.

No other shell-keeps are known to have existed in the county. Swansea Castle (Part 1b, LM 18), the *caput* of Gower, also formerly possessed a large motte supporting masonry, but nothing to suggest a shell-keep was observed during clearance in 1909–13. Vague 19th-century records mention masonry which crowned a mound at Aberafan (VE 1) and an undoubted motte at Treoda (MM 2); both are now vanished, and no walling remained at the latter when it was excavated prior to development. Finally, there are two 14th-century records indicating a 'tower' at the fine motte at Talybont (MO 6), but no traces of masonry survive there to indicate its nature or location. The Cardiff shell-keep is certainly the finest and most intact example of its type to survive in Wales, where very few are found; mottes are very common, but generally far too small to support such structures. Lesser remains of polygonal shell-keeps in Wales are confined to those at Brecon, Crickhowell and Tretower (all in Brecknock), and at Wiston (Pembs.); another, of indeterminate form, is suggested by stone rubble and mortar on the motte at St. Clears (Carms.).

Ewenny Priory (Part 1b, LM 5) is the third early masonry site requiring individual consideration. The impressive 13th-century precinct walls and gatehouses of this Benedictine priory, though confined to the western part of the enclosure and a work of prestige rather than serious fortification, are worthy of full discussion in part 1b. Here we must notice the vestiges of the primary 12th-century precinct wall and its two Norman gateways.[66] The priory was founded in 1141 by Maurice de Londres, the second Norman lord of Ogmore. A simple unfortified precinct wall which first enclosed the priory now survives only on the vulnerable E. side, where it was never modified. Towards the close of the 12th century elaborate gateways were added which are now encased in the more massive North and South Gatehouses of *ca.* 1300. Only vestiges of the Norman gateways are now discernible, but sufficient to indicate that these were identical rectangular blocks which both contained a vaulted passage of two bays divided at the roll-moulded jambs and arch of a central gate. These gates opened back within the inner bays and each was protected in front by a portcullis. Externally, the long walls were buttressed at each end and in the centre in line with the jambs of the gate. The inner bay of the N. gateway was removed when the later North Gatehouse was built, but its footings were recorded and surveyed in 1913. More substantial remains of the early S. gateway survived incorporation in the later South Gatehouse,

which largely consisted of an added rectangular flanking tower on its E. side. This later tower, like the front of the reconstructed North Gatehouse, projected boldly forward from the line of the curtain. At the gates this curtain was rebuilt and battlemented along with the gatehouses, and presumably replaced the primary precinct wall which appears to have been set back only slightly from the fronts of the early gateways.

The Norman gateways at Ewenny are described more fully in Part 1b (LM 5). They are paralleled in Glamorgan only by the modest early-13th-century gatehouse at Ogmore (MR 5), though that structure lacks a portcullis. Only Newcastle, Bridgend (EM 3), retains another 12th-century gateway; despite its finely enriched decoration, that gate is a simple opening in the curtain protected only by a projecting square tower on one flank. Dinas Powys (EM 1) formerly displayed a simple early gateway like that at Newcastle (and retains a postern of this type), and another probably existed beside the keep at Coity until it was replaced by the later gatehouse of the 14th century.

The remaining thirteen early castles to be considered are all Norman works characterized by their possession of a dominant tower or keep of square or rectangular form (Fig. 13). 'Keep' is an exaggerated term for many of the towers in question, but in each case this tower constitutes the dominant structure of a small or medium-sized early castle. All of them are ruinous; only Coity, Ogmore and Penllyn retain any vestiges of their upper floors. At Llanquian, Dinas Powys, Kenfig, Peterston, and Llanblethian only the remains of the basements of such towers survive, now largely concealed by their own debris. The keeps at Fonmon and Oystermouth are encased in later fabric, while those at Rumney and Sully are now vanished after recent rescue excavations. Rumney, Kenfig and Newcastle were castles of the chief lord; the rest were those of tenants-in-chief, except for Llanquian and Fonmon which appear to have been respectively sub-tenancies of Llanblethian and Penmark.

Surviving evidence at Coity, Ogmore, Dinas Powys, Kenfig, and Newcastle, and the information gained from excavation at Rumney and Sully, is sufficient to identify three forms of stone castle which

[65] Stuart Rigold, 'Recent Investigations into the Earliest Defences of Carisbrooke Castle, Isle of Wight', *Château Gaillard*, III, 1966, pp. 136–7.

[66] C. A. Ralegh Radford, *Ewenny Priory* (Official Guidebook, 1976), pp. 18–23; *Arch. Camb.*, 1913, pp. 27–45.

evolved in Glamorgan in the 12th century. Excluding the special case of Cardiff, with its shell-keep and even earlier masonry, these castle-types may be defined in relation to the siting of their keep or dominant tower:

1. The keep flanking the entrance, with or without a stone curtain to replace a pre-existing palisaded enclosure.
2. The keep free-standing within a palisaded or walled enclosure, and opposite its entrance.
3. The keep set back from the entrance on a strong eminence within the enclosure on particularly elevated sites.

Of the seven sites for which there is sufficient evidence, only Dinas Powys Castle (EM 1) falls within the third category. The only site lacking clear evidence for a primary castle-ringwork beneath its masonry, though it replaced an abnormally complex example of that type nearby, its keep was set on the most elevated point of a steep-sided promontory well beyond the entrance. The keep encased in later work at Oystermouth (Part 1b, LM 12) is similarly placed on a natural rocky eminence crowning a hill. The Dinas Powys keep is the earliest masonry on the site, possibly raised before 1150; its walled ward was not added until *ca.* 1200.

In category 1, with keeps flanking the entrance, we have Coity (MR 1), Ogmore (MR 5), Rumney (MR 7), and possibly Llanquian (MR 3), and vanished Sully (EM 6). The keep and the stone curtain at Coity were raised together in the late 12th century. Ogmore, in contrast, possessed its keep from the early 12th century, but this was integrated with a palisaded enclosure until the stone curtain was built in the early 13th century. Rumney Castle similarly retained its palisaded enclosure after its keep was inserted, probably in the late 12th century. The keep at Sully is thought to have been raised before 1150, and again it accompanied a palisaded enclosure until the site was drastically remodelled in the 13th century. In all cases these keeps straddle the defences of the enclosure, but with only modest projection to the field.

Category 2 castles, with free-standing internal keeps, are less numerous. We may only cite Kenfig and Newcastle (EM 2, 3). The early-12th-century keep at Kenfig, though reduced to its lower levels, was clearly of classic form. It nevertheless stood within a palisaded enclosure as late as the Welsh attack of 1232, and possibly until the further attack of 1295, before its stone curtain was built. Research for this volume disclosed the previously unsuspected former existence of a free-standing keep within the walls of Newcastle. This keep was described and sketched in unpublished notes by G. T. Clark in the early 19th century. The 12th-century date of this keep may be presumed, and historical grounds would suggest that it could only have been earlier than or, more probably, contemporary with the fine flanked curtain-wall attributed to Earl William (1147–83) or to Henry II while he had custody of the lordship (1183–89). The large square tower flanking the fine Norman gateway at Newcastle has sometimes been seen as a keep, on analogy with the much more formidable structures similarly placed at the nearby castles at Ogmore and Coity. This tower, however, is rather smaller than the identical tower flanking the W. side – and Clark's early account settles the issue. The enigmatic and finely-constructed masonry basement termed the 'cellar' at Ogmore should be mentioned in this context. Sufficiently massive to support a tall free-standing tower, possibly of timber at higher levels, this structure was added in the late 12th century. Thus interpreted, along with the earlier keep flanking the entrance, it produced a castle combining the attributes which define categories one and two.

In four cases it is not possible to allocate early stone castles to the categories defined above. These are Penllyn (EM 4), Peterston (EM 5), Fonmon, and Llanblethian (Part 1b, LM 6 and 7). The interesting vestiges of the undoubted keep at Penllyn are all that survive of the castle. The early keeps emphatically suggested by masonry protruding above large mounds of rubble at Peterston and Llanblethian are both now free-standing within the walled enclosures of much later castles, but these are far too rectilinear to suggest that they represent earlier 12th-century lines of defence. Finally, at Fonmon, there is no evidence to relate the keep encased in later fabric to any early enclosure.

No chronological significance emerges from the three categories of keep-castle defined. Ogmore and Kenfig, which may be confidently claimed as two of the earliest keeps in Glamorgan on structural and historical grounds, are respectively defined as castles of categories 1 and 2. Archaeological and historical reasoning respectively suggest an early-12th-century date for keeps at the category 3 castles at Dinas Powys and Oystermouth. Similarly, stone castles of the later 12th century may be of category 1 (Coity) or category 2 (Newcastle). Irrespective of categories, there is an understandable tendency for a more complete fortification in masonry as the early period advanced. In

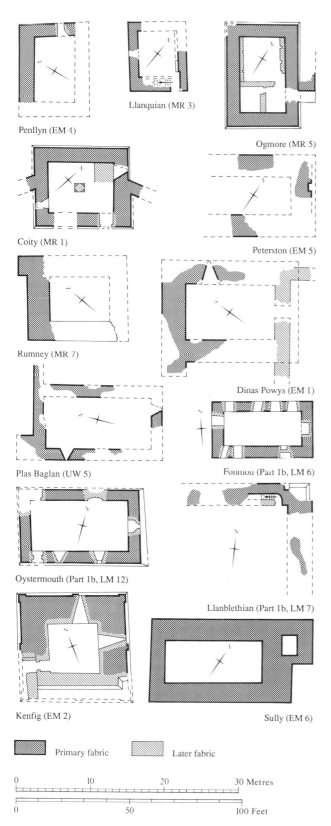

Penllyn (EM 4)

Llanquian (MR 3)

Ogmore (MR 5)

Coity (MR 1)

Peterston (EM 5)

Rumney (MR 7)

Dinas Powys (EM 1)

Plas Baglan (UW 5)

Fonmon (Part 1b, LM 6)

Oystermouth (Part 1b, LM 12)

Llanblethian (Part 1b, LM 7)

Kenfig (EM 2)

Sully (EM 6)

Primary fabric   Later fabric

0   10   20   30 Metres

0   50   100 Feet

the latter half of the 12th century, Coity, and probably Newcastle, were both given curtain-walls along with their keeps as they were converted to stone castles. In contrast, the earlier stone keeps at Ogmore and Kenfig retained their palisaded enclosures until the 13th century.

Newcastle (EM 3), like Cardiff, merits particular attention. Despite the loss of its keep, it is the most significant example of Norman military architecture in Glamorgan, precocious in its incorporation of two boldly salient mural towers, and quite exceptional in its lavish ashlar masonry. It is attributable either to Earl William before 1183, or to King Henry II between 1183–89, the latter possibility giving added historical significance. The inventory account discusses factors which would favour either of these attributions. Earl William possessed Sherborne Old Castle, Dorset, which is cited as a possible model on account of its similar mural towers, plan and details, all built before 1135 by Roger, Bishop of Salisbury. For Henry II, however, a compelling historical context for his authorship is outlined, and, despite the omission of any mention of such royal works at Newcastle, his castle at Orford, Suffolk, is cited as another possible model.

Newcastle is also exceptional as a 12th-century stone castle entirely lacking any later modifications or additions, excepting very minor internal domestic works. This rare survival of a purely Norman castle is explained by its acquisition in 1217 by the Turberville lords of nearby Coity. They and their successors maintained Coity as their principal residence, and there they undertook extensive works of a defensive and domestic nature. Absentee lords may also have curbed any major works after the early 13th century at Ogmore (MR 5) and Dinas Powys (EM 1), where earlier structures presumably sufficed for their stewards.

Ground plans of the keeps or dominant towers ascribed to the 12th century are assembled for comparison in Fig. 13, excluding only the long-vanished central keep of unknown dimensions at Newcastle. In size they range from the massively-built Kenfig, with walls 14m square and 3.7m thick above its stepped and battered plinth, to little Llanquian, at 9m by 8m and with walls only 1.5m thick. Comparable measurements of the keep at Dinas Powys (18m by 13m; 3m), as assumed on strong surviving evidence, would sug-

Fig. 13. Early Keeps and dominant towers (Sully after G.T. Clark and G. Dowdell; Rumney after K. Lightfoot).

gest a structure of even greater size than that at Kenfig. Llanblethian was another very large keep; the extent of the mound of rubble there suggests dimensions well in excess of the 12m lengths of visible walling, over 3m thick, which form one of its angles. Keeps at Sully (19m by 11m; 3m), and Peterston (11.5m by at least 17m; 3m) were also large. The rest are rather smaller, with average dimensions of 13m by 10m and walls consistently about 2m thick. For comparative purposes the special case of Plas Baglan is also shown in Fig. 13. This unique Welsh example, clearly inspired by Norman prototypes, is surprisingly large at about 17m by 10m, though its walls are only 1.5m thick. Like all but the square keep at Kenfig, Plas Baglan is rectangular.

Dinas Powys, Sully and Plas Baglan keeps all incorporated square turrets set at one angle which probably housed latrines, as is suggested by the square presumed cess-pit at the base of the turret at Sully. A similar undoubted latrine turret at Kenfig (not shown in Fig. 13) was a 13th-century addition. Classic external Norman embellishment is in evidence only at Kenfig with its fine stepped plinth and its clasping and pilaster buttresses, all in ashlar. The Sutton stone dressed quoins at the angles of Coity and Ogmore were no doubt common, and might be sought at the buried remnants surviving at Dinas Powys, Peterston and Llanblethian. General masonry was of random uncoursed rubble of a mixed nature, as at Coity, Ogmore and Kenfig, though at Peterston randomly laid squared blocks of Lias limestone were intermittently brought to levelled courses, a feature shared with the contemporary curtain-walls at Newcastle and Dinas Powys. Glacial pebbles form a large proportion of the random masonry of Cardiff shell-keep and are also prominent in the keep at Ogmore. The red Triassic conglomerate forming a high proportion of the Norman walling at Coity differentiates the early work from the many later additions at that complex site. The Roman brick and tile incorporated in the keep at Kenfig is another interesting feature discussed in the account of that site. Herringbone masonry is prominent at Penllyn, and was suspected in the lower courses surviving at Rumney.

The internal arrangements of Norman keeps and towers in Glamorgan are not clear. Vestiges of upper floors can be studied only at Coity, Ogmore and Penllyn; elsewhere, these structures are either masked in later fabric, or reduced to their basements, which are largely buried in their own rubble. The general characteristics are nevertheless apparent. As first con-structed, only the small tower at Llanquian appears to have had a vaulted basement, though late-18th-century descriptions of the keep at Dinas Powys might suggest a vault existed there. The vault over the basement at Kenfig was not inserted until the late 13th century; the more elaborate vault at Coity dates from the 14th century.

Internal arrangements are seen most clearly at Ogmore where one wall survives to its full original height, lacking only its early crenellations, which were removed when a second-floor chamber was subsequently added above the first-floor hall. There are no original openings at basement level; entry to the first floor was gained by an external stone stair rising upon the foundation set against the inner wall on the E. side. At first floor level the Ogmore keep was transversely sub-divided by a partition set against a modest ashlar buttress visible on the surviving W. wall. This buttress marks a step in the floor level; the larger and higher S. chamber was lit by two round-headed embrasures of fine Sutton stone ashlar, but the finest surviving feature is the Norman fireplace serving the lesser N. chamber. This fireplace retains three voussoirs of a projecting round-headed hood and vestiges of the round columns and cubical capitals which carried it, all rendered in Sutton stone. Traces of another Norman embrasure of finely-jointed ashlar survive on the stub of the N. wall, this opening enlarged as a door to provide access to the later curtain-wall. A most modestly gabled original roof is indicated by a longitudinal slot in the W. wall, and access to its protecting parapet was presumably in the N.W. angle, where a newel-stair was inserted to reach the later upper floor and latrine.

Scant evidence survives for the internal arrangements and details of other early keeps and towers. Slight but predictable evidence of an original first-floor entry is recorded at Kenfig, where an attached carved capital of Sutton stone vouches for a first-floor of quality to match its fine external ashlar. Sufficient survives at Ogmore and Coity, and is recorded at Sully, to assert that those keeps had no original ground-level access, and Penllyn retains its first-floor round-headed entrance and traces of a fore-building. Of the rest, where the entire trace of ground plans is incomplete, only Llanquian appears to have a lower entrance (and a vaulted basement). Another uncommon feature of Llanquian is the straight-flight mural stair opening from its lobby. Only Llanblethian keep is known to possess a similar mural stair between basement and first floor, though there without comparable ground-level access. On present evidence, it appears that basements were usually reached through trapdoors. A first-floor latrine is indicated by the outfall recorded at Peterston; another is attested by the cesspit set in an outshut at Sully, and may be indicated by similar projections at the angles of the keeps at Dinas Powys and Plas Baglan. Original splayed embrasures lighting basements are recorded at Coity, Oystermouth and Plas Baglan; only those at Coity retain traces of ashlar dressings.

The vanished keep at Newcastle was no doubt a fine structure to judge from the quality of its surviving curtain wall, towers and gateway. The fine enriched carving of the Newcastle gateway is reflected in the re-used dressings recorded at Ogmore, where such dressings may be related to the upper floors of the keep or the 'cellar'. The early fan-tooled ashlar recorded at Plas Baglan might also derive from its keep; such tooling is confined to this exceptional Welsh site and the 12th-century priory at Ewenny.

Norman square or rectangular keeps are not common in Wales. The Glamorgan examples, together with the lesser but dominant towers, constitute the greatest concentration of such early masonry in the Principality, illustrating the paradox of castle-building: danger inspired the building of castles, but to build strongly in stone demanded conditions of peace.[67] They demonstrate the secure and enduring Norman hold on the Glamorgan lowlands, where even a solitary Welsh stone castle was tolerated. A smaller group in Gwent includes the notable keep of William Fitzosbern at Chepstow (1067–71), which was soon followed by the keep at Monmouth, and later by those at Usk and White Castle. Elsewhere, examples are few and far between. To the W., in Pembrokeshire, there is a strong square early tower at Manorbier, and the foundations of another at Haverfordwest; a re-used Norman capital is taken as evidence for another at Kidwelly (Carms.). In the central marches we may cite only the early square towers at Dinas and Hay, both in Brecknock. In the N. no such early Norman work survives, but Robert of Rhuddlan's late-11th-century castle at Deganwy (ca. 1088) is thought to have been a stone keep and bailey. For the Welsh keep or tower at Plas Baglan, the only parallels are the scant vestiges of Rhys ap Gruffydd's keeps at Ystrad Meurig (Cards.) and Castell Nanhyfer (Pembs.), and perhaps the masonry footings discovered at Tomen Castell, near Dolwyddelan (Caerns.).

The keep tradition outlived the Norman period in

Glamorgan. The account of Loughor Castle (MR 4) describes its modest square keep of the late 13th century; excavations suggested that this may have replaced a 12th-century stone tower. Other late keeps, both square and round, are described in Part 1b. When Bishop's Castle (LM 2) was built at Llandaf in ca. 1300 the N.E. tower housed a first-floor hall over a vaulted basement. The mid-13th century Morgraig Castle (LM 9) possessed an even more keep-like rectangular tower, set at its highest point and dwarfing four other horseshoe-shaped towers flanking the curtain. At Penlle'r Castell (LM 13), a late-13th-century castle of the lords of Gower, there are superficial indications of the stumps of two large free-standing square towers, one at each end of the site. The Prison Tower surviving at Swansea (LM 18) is large and possibly earlier than the fine late-13th and 14th-century first-floor hall adjacent; its location in what was a lesser ward of the vanished 'Old Castle', however, leaves room to doubt that it ever dominated the site. Finally, there is the large square S.W. tower at Weobley (LM 20), of keep-like character but lacking any detail to date it earlier than the 13th century; and the stump of an undated free-standing rectangular tower (PC 9) on a rocky knoll close to the much later Oxwich Castle. Five tower-houses of the late Middle Ages are described in Section TH; one of these, at Llanmaes (TH 3), has sometimes been regarded as a keep. Round keeps of the 13th century occur at Llantrisant and Penrice (LM 8, 15), and another is suspected at Talyfan (LM 19), while Morlais Castle (LM 10) retains a notable vaulted polygonal undercroft pertaining to a massive keep of the 1290s.

At one site excavation might well reveal the base of a further Norman keep. Penmark Castle (LM 14) was the *caput* of the large and rich Umfraville holding from the earliest years of the conquest; no surviving visible masonry is earlier than the 13th century, but large overgrown mounds of rubble could mask an early keep, particularly as the Umfraville's tenants at nearby Fonmon boasted such a structure.[68]

E   Excavations

Pioneering work by W. Ll. Morgan at the castle-ringwork at Bishopston (CR 1) in 1898 was the first

---

[67] D. J. Cathcart King, *Brycheiniog*, VII (1961), p. 73 and *Cast. Ang.*, I, p. xxxix.

[68] A sketch of Penmark Castle on a map of 1662 by Evans Mouse features a prominent internal tower. (Fonmon Collection, Glamorgan Record Office).

of nine major archaeological excavations at early castles in Glamorgan. There have also been five excavations on a lesser scale at another five early castles, and at eight others information of interest has been recorded during fortuitous disturbance of the remains. Relevant site accounts summarize the evidence derived from all these excavations, citing published reports. For convenience these excavations may be listed here, along with two major and four lesser excavations at later castles described in Part 1b:

i. *Mottes*

Major Excavation:	MM 2	Treoda
Minor Excavation:	MO 8	Twmpath, Rhiwbina
Observed Disturbances:	MO 2	Felin Isaf
Observed Disturbances:	MO 6	Talybont Castle
Observed Disturbances:	MO 11	Ynyscrug
Observed Disturbances:	MM 1	Cardiff Castle
Observed Disturbances:	LM 18	Swansea Castle

(No information was obtained regarding excavations noticed during survey at Tŷ Du (MO 10) in 1980.)

ii *Castle-Ringworks*

Major Excavation:	CR 1	Bishopston Old Castle
Major Excavations:	CR 7	Dinas Powys Ringwork
Major Excavations:	CR 13	Llantrithyd Ringwork
Major Excavations:	CR 18	Penmaen, Castle Tower
Major Excavations:	MR 4	Loughor Castle
Major Excavations:	MR 7	Rumney Castle
Major Excavations:	EM 2	Kenfig Castle
Major Excavations:	EM 6	Sully Castle
Minor Excavations:	CR 5	Cil Ifor Ring
Minor Excavations:	CR 6	Coed-y-cwm
Minor Excavations:	CR 19	Pen-y-pil
Minor Excavations:	MR 6	Pennard Castle
Observed Disturbances:	CR 11	Llandow
Observed Disturbances:	CR 14	Mountyborough
Observed Disturbances:	CR 21	Walterston

iii *Early Masonry Castles*

Excavations listed above at Cardiff, Rumney, Kenfig and Sully disclosed early masonry. There were also indications of a 12th-century tower preceding the surviving tower of the late 13th century at Loughor Castle.

iv *Later Masonry Castles*

Major Excavations:	LM 9	Morgraig Castle
Major Excavations:	LM 11	Neath Castle
Minor Excavations:	LM 1	Barry Castle
Minor Excavations:	LM 2	Bishop's Castle
Minor Excavations:	LM 10	Morlais Castle
Minor Excavations:	LM 18	Swansea Castle

(At Ogmore (MR 5) excavations disclosed a lime-kiln of *ca.* 1300. At Cardiff (MM 1), already listed, the foundations of internal buildings of the late Middle Ages have been revealed.)

It is relevant to notice the fourteen castles in Glamorgan which have been cleared, consolidated and made accessible to the public. Eight of these are in state guardianship: Coity (MR 1), Loughor (MR 4), Ogmore (MR 5), Newcastle (EM 3), Caerphilly (Part 1b, LM 3), Castell Coch (Part 1b, LM 4), Weobley (Part 1b, LM 20) and parts of Ewenny Priory (Part 1b, LM 5). The other six are in the care of local authorities: Cardiff (MM 1), Barry (Part 1b, LM 1), Bishop's Castle, Llandaf (Part 1b, LM 2), Oystermouth (Part 1b, LM 12) and, with restricted access, Neath Castle and Swansea Castle (Part 1b, LM 11, 18).

Not all excavations have been adequately published, and some not at all. Significant reports are available for work at Bishopston, Dinas Powys Ringwork, Llantrithyd, Penmaen, and Loughor, and those on Rumney and Sully were generously furnished in advance of publication.* For the important demesne castle and deserted borough of Kenfig only one of the many interim reports is illustrated and reasonably detailed.

Particular attention has focused on the castle-ringworks in the county. In most cases this was intentional, though at Loughor, Rumney and Sully the discovery of underlying ringworks was fortuitous, while that at Kenfig is now suspected after consideration of the remains and the available records of the excavations there. Excepting Morgan's major excavation at Bishopston (1898) and his minor excavation at Cil Ifor (1910), Richard's work at Kenfig (1924–32), and the significant observation recorded at Mountyborough (1927), all other archaeological work at Glamorgan castle-ringworks has been carried out since the 1950s. Interest was aroused in these earthworks by Professor Leslie Alcock's work at the complex multivallate site at Dinas Powys (1954–58). He followed this with further excavations at Penmaen and Pennard (1960–61), and inspired those undertaken at

* For Sully, now see B.B.C.S., XXXVII (1990), pp. 308–60.

Llantrithyd (1960–69), Coed-y-cwm (1963–65) and Pen-y-pil (1965). During this spate of activity the first hints of a primary ringwork were revealed at Sully (1963–69), and further significant work followed at Loughor (1968–71, 1973) and at Rumney (1978, 1980–81).

The nature of the defences of castle-ringworks has been investigated with particular success at several sites. At Bishopston and Dinas Powys there was evidence for double rows of timber uprights rising through their ramparts; these are believed to have supported timber fighting platforms now known in more detail at Hen Domen (Monts.). Two vertical upright posts accidentally exposed within the rampart at Mountyborough may denote similar timberwork. Single rows of posts suggesting more simple external timber palisades or revetments are recorded at Rumney and Pennard. At Rumney a rear timber revetment of the bank was even more clearly indicated, and another was suspected at Llantrithyd. At Bishopston a step on the counterscarp of the ditch was interpreted as the emplacement for a row of stakes. Although a palisade is recorded at Kenfig in 1183/4, and again in 1232, when it formed the outer defence of the keep, no trace of this was observed during the excavations. At Dinas Powys ringwork the sophisticated timberwork founded within the inner rampart was further strengthened with a vertical dry-stone revetment, a feature repeated on the two ramparts immediately fronting it, but which was applied only to the rear of the fourth and outer rampart. Similar dry-stone outer revetment is still visible at North Hill Tor, and was recorded in the excavations at Sully, while at Coed-y-cwm and at Penmaen it was applied to the flanks of their gate-passages. At Penmaen this revetment was secondary, replacing a remarkable timber gate-tower, 6m square, which had been destroyed in a fire. A similar timber gate-tower protected the entrance of the primary phases at Rumney; rebuilt, again in timber, this access was eventually blocked and replaced in another position by a simple stone gate-tower. A most exceptional gate of Iron Age character at Dinas Powys ringwork is only one of several individual features noticed at that multivallate site.

The interior of the castle-ringwork at Bishopston was levelled up by about half a metre. At Rumney, Loughor and Kenfig, however, this process was taken further and their ramparts were raked back to create elevated level platforms; even without excavation this process is clearly in evidence in the area of the 'cellar'

at Ogmore, and may be deduced at Coity.

Internal domestic buildings of the 12th century have been identified in excavations at seven castle-ringworks. In four cases (at Llantrithyd, Penmaen, Loughor, and Sully) it was found that primary timber-framed buildings were replaced by dry-stone structures before the close of the 12th century; the same sequence was also discerned at Pennard, differing only in the use of mortar for its secondary stone hall. At Rumney timber buildings were not replaced in stone until the 13th century, and at Coed-y-cwm no more than slight traces of timber buildings set on sole-plates were observed. The secondary dry-stone buildings of the 12th century at Llantrithyd, Penmaen, Loughor, and Sully, and that with mortared walls at Pennard, were all characterized by their rounded angles. Twelfth-century buildings of this type are also recorded beyond the confines of castles at the medieval settlements at Barry, Burry Holms, Cosmeston, Highlight, Mynydd Bychan, and Rhosili. This distinctive house-type common in S.E. Wales has been discussed by David M. Robinson, who considers their possible cultural origins and the probable characteristics of their vanished superstructures.[69] The largest of them is the double-aisled hall within Llantrithyd Ringwork, a building securely dated to the early 12th century by the important coin hoard sealed in its destruction layers. Another very large hall of timber, with a single aisle, was raised in the early-12th century within Rumney Castle, and was replaced later in the century by an equally imposing unaisled timber hall.

The addition of masonry defences ensured the continued occupation of at least sixteen castle-ringworks beyond the 12th century (including such suspected cases as Kenfig and Penmark). Excavations have shown that Dinas Powys Ringwork and Llantrithyd were abandoned before 1150, and that occupation ceased at Penmaen and at Bishopston very early in the 13th century. Dinas Powys Ringwork was replaced by the nearby stone castle of the same name. Mountyborough was presumably retained until it was replaced by the nearby stone castle of Penrice in the 13th century. Without changing sites, the conversion of castle-ringworks to fortified manorial centres was carried out at Rumney and Sully; the latter conversion was particularly notable for its complete disregard of the earlier defences, which were levelled and ignored in

[69] 'Medieval Vernacular Buildings Below the Ground: A Review and Corpus for South-East Wales', *Glamorgan–Gwent Archaeological Trust Annual Report*, 1981–82, pp. 94–123.

the new and greatly extended layout. The lack of any 13th-century or later artefacts from the minor excavations at Coed-y-cwm and Pen-y-pil suggests that these were deserted before the 13th century. Conversely, the brief trowelling of fortuitous soil disturbances during survey at Llandow and Walterston clearly demonstrated the continued occupation of those sites; in each case sections of the buried foundations of substantial mortared halls were observed. These buildings were of a type common to the late 13th or early 14th century and matched that disclosed at Rumney Castle. The foundation at Llandow sealed rubbish deposits containing 12th-century sherds; that revealed at Walterston was associated with a sherd of the 13th century.

The mottes of Glamorgan have not been so systematically tested by excavation. The only detailed published report available is the commendable account of the rescue excavation of the truncated remains of the motte at Treoda (1966), though this was only able to disclose an underlying Bronze Age barrow forming a convenient core for this low-lying site, recalling the mottes at Rûg (Mer.) and St. Weonards (Herefs.), and Roman sherds sealed between the barrow and the superimposed motte. These sherds add further credence to other indications suggesting that this motte was placed within a Roman fort, as outlined in the Inventory account. No trace remained of superimposed masonry recorded in the 19th century. Morgan's published observations of the removal of the motte at Swansea in 1913 merely confirm its large dimensions, its location, as shown in an 18th-century panorama by the Buck brothers, and the presence of substantial masonry upon it. Fortuitous exposures at Ynyscrug have shown that the motte was raised over a moraine and confirmed the nature and approximate extent of its bailey; similar exposures have also confirmed the bailey at Felin Isaf. More notable are Clark's record of the wooden piles of an early bridge disclosed in the motte ditch at Cardiff when it was opened up again in the 1880s, and the three post-holes recorded in an exposure on the flank of the large motte at Talybont. These post-holes were ranged along the lower slope of the motte; their position in relation to the bailey does not suggest that they represent a bridge support, but rather that they may have supported a palisade encircling the base of the motte (see Fig. 30, p. 66). The scant information published regarding the trench cut to the centre of Twmpath, Rhiwbina, in 1849 is uninformative.

In 1980, during survey, a neatly pegged and infilled trench across the ditch was noted at the presumed Welsh site at Briton Ferry. Despite full inquiry the identity of the excavator remains unknown and no information regarding the work has been gleaned. Any such information which might emerge could be significant; Briton Ferry is one of five sites placed in Section UW, as presumed Welsh castles in Glamorgan, and the only one to have been excavated.

Few of the later masonry castles treated in Part 1b have been excavated. The most extensive and significant investigation was that which unexpectedly exposed the entire plan of Morgraig Castle and showed that this strange site was never completed and only briefly occupied. The publication of this work in 1906 was a collaborative effort of enduring value. The full publication of more recent excavations at Neath (1970–74) and Bishop's Castle, Llandaf (1971) is still awaited; the work at Neath disclosed strong indications that the curtain-wall was set into a pre-existing ring-bank. Bishop's Castle and Barry Castle were excavated before being laid out as public amenities. An excavation at Morlais Castle in the early 19th century disclosed the remarkable multangular vaulted undercroft, but no report was published, though G. T. Clark fortunately described and surveyed the site at the time. Later masonry has also been disclosed in the excavations at the early castles founded at Cardiff, Ogmore and Swansea.

F Later Masonry Fully Described in Part 1a

Section I of this Introductory Survey explains the division of the material between parts 1a and 1b of Volume III. This division necessitated the subjective allocation of certain sites to one of those parts on the basis of the perceived greater significance of either their early or their later remains. In consequence each Part incorporates some full accounts of fabric or history more appropriate to the other Part. To assist the reader the Introductory Survey opening each Part concludes with an annotated alphabetical list of all such sites which they fully describe. Here we notice those sites included in Part 1a which incorporate later fabric or for which there are records suggesting vanished later masonry.

Aberafan Castle (VE 1)
Vanished site. Briefly recorded in the mid-12th century. Antiquarian records suggest former existence of later masonry, some possibly crowning a motte.

Cardiff Castle (MM 1)

Large castle with great motte within re-used Roman defences. Shell-keep. Much substantial later fabric is described, notably the keep-gatehouse and fore-building, cross-wall and Black Tower (13th-14th century); the Western Apartments (early-15th century, with significant additions and modifications in the 16th, 18th and 19th centuries). An account of the neo-Gothic and neo-Roman restoration (1868–1927) is also given.

Coity Castle (MR 1)

Castle-ringwork and bailey with late-12th-century keep and curtain (I and II). Substantial later additions: (III) Vaulting in keep and adjacent annexe, middle gatehouse, domestic block with service rooms and projecting latrine-tower, outer ward walls with three towers (all 14th-century); (IV) Rebuilt N. curtain of inner ward and integrated N.E. gatehouse, chapel, and in the outer ward the tithe-barn, W. gatehouse and conversion of south towers to a postern and a gatehouse (all 15th-century); (V) Added upper floors of keep and its annexe and the refurbishment of the domestic block (16th century).

Dinas Powys Castle (EM 1)

Keep of 12th century with curtain of *ca.* 1200. Loose dressings and documentary evidence indicate 13th- and early-14th-century occupation.

Kenfig Castle (EM 2)

Keep and castle-ringwork of early 12th century (I). Later developments include: (II) Latrine-turret and basement embrasures added to keep in mid-13th century; (III) S. wall of keep rebuilt and vault inserted, the interior ground level raised, and a curtain wall with gatehouse added, all in the late 13th century; (IV) Keep entrance modified and south building added against curtain in the early 14th century. Sand encroachment thereafter progressively overwhelmed castle and borough which were virtually abandoned by 1500.

Llandow (CR 11)

12th-century castle-ringwork. Occupation in the late 13th or early 14th century indicated by the foundations of a centrally-placed building of mortared masonry.

Llangynwyd Castle (MR 2)

Suspected castle-ringwork of the 12th century. Imposed Great Gatehouse attributed to Gilbert de Clare in the 1260s on account of its close resemblance to the main gatehouse at Caerphilly and as a response to the destruction 1257. A three-quarter-round tower, also added to the crude curtain of uncertain date, may predate the gatehouse.

Loughor Castle (MR 4)

Primary castle-ringwork of 12th century gradually infilled to create a level platform. Curtain-wall added *ca.* 1200. A small square keep of the late-13th century appears to have replaced an earlier tower similarly set well out from the line of the curtain and over the scarp.

Newcastle, Bridgend (EM 3)

Substantial remains of a late-12th-century stone castle raised over a primary ringwork. Minimal later additions comprise the fragmentary North Building and an extension to the East Range, both of the 13th century or later, and minor 16th-century modifications to the South Tower.

Ogmore Castle (MR 5)

Early-12th-century castle-ringwork and bailey with keep and enigmatic 'cellar'. Curtain-wall, gateway and bridge-pit of the Inner Ward added in early 13th century. Hall and offices in Inner Ward followed later in that century. The bailey never walled, but received a stone building in *ca.* 1300. A lime-kiln raised over the ruins of this building was in turn abandoned when the abutting 'Court-house' was raised in the 14th century.

Oldcastle, Nolton (Bridgend) (VE 4)

Vanished site. Antiquarian records and surviving re-used dressings suggest the former existence of 13th-century masonry.

Pennard Castle (MR 6)

Primary 12th-century castle-ringwork with stone hall. Masonry defences with twin-towered gatehouse and half-round turret added *ca.* 1300. Large square western tower the only subsequent addition.

Peterston Castle (EM 5)

A presumed 12th-century keep is suggested by vestiges largely buried in a great mound of rubble. This lies within a rectilinear enclosure now retaining only the fragments of two rectangular angle-towers and probably of 13th- or 14th-century date.

Plas Baglan (UW 5)

Rare Welsh stone castle of the 12th century. The presence of loose 13th-century moundings suggests later additions not discernible on the surface.

Rumney Castle (MR 7)

A castle-ringwork with a complex structural development (I and II), even before a stone keep was added in the late 12th century (III). In the first half of the 13th century a new timber hall (the third of its type) and a timber kitchen were built (IV), followed by a re-sited entrance protected by a simple stone tower (V) replacing the original gateway with its timber tower. Finally, in the late 13th century (VI), the site was levelled up and a fortified manorial centre was built. The keep survived, but a new stone hall was added before final destruction in 1295.

Sully Castle (EM 6)

Castle-ringwork of 12th century with stone keep. In the early 13th century a new and extended layout entirely disregarded the earlier defences to create a rectilinear walled enclosure retaining only the earlier keep. A new domestic block was incorporated on the S.W.

In the late 13th or early 14th century the domestic accommodation was modified and a large additional stone hall was built.

Talybont Castle (MO 6)

Motte with no trace of masonry, but records of a tower in 1319, and of a castle in 1353, suggest the former existence of masonry at this castle.

Treoda (MM 2)

Vanished motte. An early 19th century unpublished record indicates the former existence of masonry incorporating a portcullis upon the motte. Even then it was said to have gone, and no trace was found in rescue excavations in 1966. This masonry may well have been the 'fortelletum' newly-built at Whitchurch in 1317, and was surely the ruinous castle noted by Leland *ca.* 1539.

Walterston (CR 21)

Fragment of a 12th-century castle-ringwork. Against the tail of the surviving length of rampart the foundations of a substantial mortared building of 13th-century date have been recorded.

* * * * *

The Early Castles

Section MO: Mottes without Masonry

Monuments MO 1 to 12

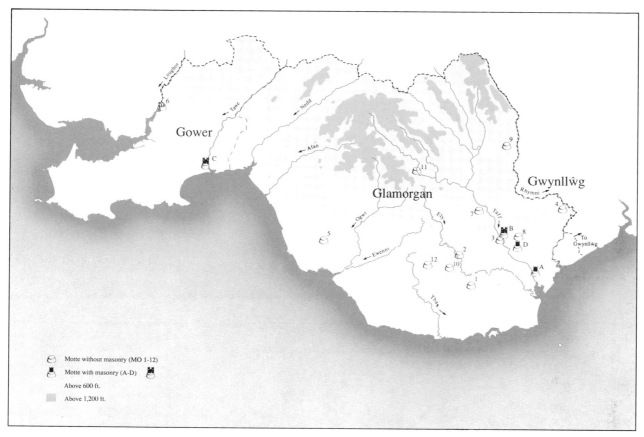

Fig. 15

1 Cottrell Castle Mound.	10 Tŷ Du.
2 Felin Isaf.	11 Ynyscrug.
3 Morganstown Castle Mound.	12 Ystradowen.
4 Ruperra Motte.	
5 Stormy Castle.	*Mottes with Masonry*
6 Talybont Castle.	A Cardiff Castle (MM 1)
7 Tomen-y-clawdd.	B Castell Coch (LM 4) ⎫ Volume III
8 Twmpath, Rhiwbina.	C Swansea Castle (LM 18) ⎭ Part Ib
9 Twyn Castell, Gelli-gaer.	D Treoda (MM 2)

Section MO describes twelve mottes with no surviving traces of masonry, though record evidence suggests that Talybont (MO 6) may have been converted to stone. Four other mottes which had masonry imposed upon them are to be described in other sections; these are listed above and included on the map (Fig. 15, A–D). Of the sixteen mottes identified, two lie in Gower and fourteen in the lordship of Glamorgan. The total is modest; only the five counties of N. Wales have fewer mottes, ranging from the single example in Anglesey to the thirteen in Flintshire. In the remaining counties to the S. totals range from eighteen (Pembs.) to thirty-three (Monts.). Despite this comparatively small number of mottes, Glamorgan still

Fig. 14. (*Opposite*) Stormy Castle (MO 5); aerial view from the north-west.

presents the greatest number of earthwork castles when account is taken of its twenty-seven and more castle-ringworks which far exceeds the number in any other county in Wales. The mottes and ringworks, together with other early castles, are discussed together in the Introduction (pp. 10–48). Here it is only necessary to summarize matters raised there which concern the mottes.

The distribution of the mottes in the county of Glamorgan is essentially a lowland one, with only two (MO 9 and 11) found in the northern uplands. The

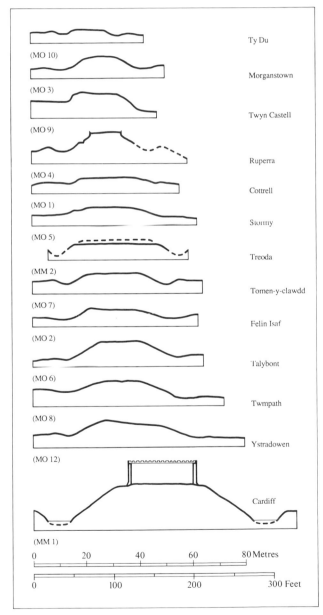

Fig. 16. Profiles of Mottes in Glamorgan and Gower.

rest, however, are not in the fertile Vale of Glamorgan, where there are only ringworks, but in that intermediate area termed the Border Vale. The mottes cluster most thickly to the E. of this zone, where they form a close-set group to the W., N.W and N. of the chief lord's castle at Cardiff, with its huge motte. In discussing distribution (pp. 34–36), it is noted that there is a strong correlation between the mottes and the area of glacial drift in the county. Excepting Ruperra (MO 4) and the motte at Castell Coch (B), all lie on drift. The drift extends southwards to a line approximating to the Port Way, the main Roman and Medieval route through Glamorgan, with Cottrell Motte (MO 1) upon its southernmost fringe. South of the drift is the shallow but fertile soil of the Vale laid over hard rock, predominantly Lias Limestone, and there only ringworks are found. Gower presents a similar segregation of the two types of earthwork castle: ringworks lie on the peninsula of Gower, while the two mottes are to the N. flanking its landward base.

A further aspect of the distribution of our mottes, also noted (pp. 10–11, 32), is their concentration in the vicinity of Cardiff, nine lying between 6.5 and 13.5km of the great motte there. The conventional account of the Norman conquest and settlement of Glamorgan makes it difficult to explain seven of the ten mottes in and near Cardiff. These lie in the southern parts of the hill commotes of Meisgyn and Senghennydd, which were not annexed to the chief lordship until the mid 13th century (Fig. 8, pp. 22–3). Historians have occasionally pondered the possibility of an early, limited and temporary advance into the hill commotes; the archaeological evidence of the mottes appears to support this. The distribution and individual siting of the seven mottes in question, together with the extreme rarity of mottes in the rest of the uplands strongly suggests that this screen of sites around Cardiff was Norman in origin. This matter is discussed further in the Introduction (pp. 10–11) and, individually, in some site accounts. A related factor is the evidence which attributes the building of Cardiff Castle to William I, in 1081; the revived acceptance of a mint of the Conqueror in Cardiff is particularly significant in this respect.

The mottes of Glamorganshire vary greatly in size. Cardiff, as one would expect, is clearly the largest and most impressive example, and the finest in Wales, with a basal diameter, excluding its ditch, of 69.50m. The evidence from Swansea for the vanished motte there suggests that the *caput* of Gower possessed another large motte about 52.00m in basal diameter. The diagram (Fig. 16, p. 52) shows the gradation of those mottes for which profiles are available, with little Tŷ Du at a mere 17.68m in diameter dwarfed by the others.

With the exception of Ynyscrug (MO 11) and Twyn Castell (MO 9) it is not easy to identify any other mottes as possible Welsh works. A few exceptional earthworks in the Welsh commotes have been identified as probable Welsh medieval castles (Section UW), two of them displaying a vague resemblance to mottes (UW 2, 3). Castell Bolan (UW 3) has certainly been regarded as a motte, despite eccentric features, along with the embanked glacial mound at Gwern-y-domen

(CR 9) which is here classed as a castle-ringwork. A motte is also reputed to have formerly existed at the vanished site at Aberafan (VE 1).

A bailey is known to have existed at only four of the twelve mottes without masonry described in this section (MO 2, 3, 6, 11). The twelve compare with the thirteen similarly classed by D. J. C. King (*Cast. Ang.*, I, pp. 159–75). To arrive at his total King has included Castell Bolan (UW 3) and Gwern-y-domen (CR 9) but excluded Tŷ Du (MO 10), which he regards as no more than a possible miniature motte. Most of these sites are alphabetically listed under different names by King; where necessary, his preferred name is given in the reference that follows each account.

MO 1   Cottrell Castle Mound

A motte (Figs. 17 and 18) lies in former parkland S. of the vanished Cottrell House, which house incorporated 16th-century fabric reasonably attributed to Rice Merrick (Vol. IV, (i) No. 52). Lying at 800m to the W.N.W. of St Nicholas, the motte is one of

three castle earthworks clustered W. of that village: Y Gaer ringwork (CR 20) is at 400m on its N.E.; Coed-y-cwm (CR 6) is at 820m S.S.E. on the other side of the Port Way, which here approximates to the southern limit of a broad expanse of glacial drift

Fig. 17. Cottrell Castle viewed from the west.

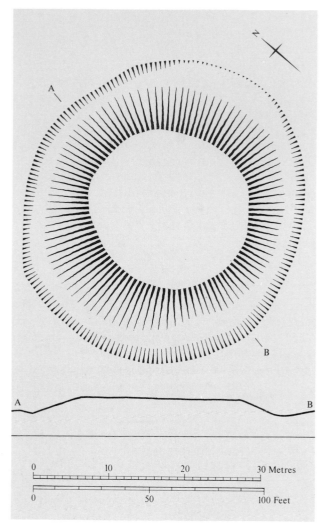

Fig. 18. Cottrell Castle Mound.

(Fig. 11, p. 36). On this drift, the motte crowns a low rounded hill and is exceptional for its low broad profile and narrow ditch, a form perhaps explained by an 1862 record of the levelling and planting of its top.[1] The level summit is between 20m and 21m in diameter and elevated 1.7m above the surrounding level. A shallow surrounding ditch is only absent for a short section to the E., where its line is marked by a shelf. There is no evidence for a bailey, though natural scarps to the S. have been mistaken for one.

Cottrell motte is not recorded, but it was within the manor of Tre-hill, which probably constituted one of the three knight's fees of St Nicholas, held by sub-tenants of William Corbet in the Extent of 1262,[2] the others presumably being represented by the two ringworks mentioned above. The name Cottrell de-rives from the family first recorded in the Despenser survey of 1320, when Roger Cottrell held three ploughlands in this vicinity.[3] Rice Merrick's father, Meurig ap Hywel, acquired Cottrell Manor in 1546, and Rice records the scant remains of Cottrell Court, the medieval manor house of Trehill.[4]

King, p. 169 (St Nicholas No. 2).

St Nicholas.
ST 07 S.E. (0809–7450)   11 vi 80   XLVI N.E.

[1] G. T. Clark, *Arch. Camb.* 1862, p. 100. See Treoda (MM 2) for another account of the landscaping of a motte.
[2] Corbett, *Glamorgan Lordship,* pp. 223–4.
[3] Merrick, *Morg. Arch.,* p. 73; Pierce, *Dinas Powys,* p. 280.
[4] Merrick, *Morg. Arch.,* p. 138; T. J. Hopkins, *Morgannwg,* VIII (1964), pp. 5–13.

MO 2   Felin Isaf

In pre-Norman times Meisgyn was seemingly bounded to the S. by the Ely River, between its emergence from the mountains to the W. of Llantrisant and its final turn south-eastwards to the sea between St Fagans and Llandaf. An early and permanent Norman encroachment to the N. of this boundary was made with the creation of the le Sore fee of St Fagans and Peterston.[1] The Clun, a tributary joining the Ely just S. of Llantrisant, gave its name to the manor of Clun, recorded from the early 14th century, after the annexation of Meisgyn by Richard de Clare in 1244–45. The full extent of Clun is uncertain, but it was probably centred on the area lying S. of Llantrisant and contain-ing Miskin and Felin Isaf. Here, the Ely River divides Meisgyn from the lordship of Talyfan to the S.W., while at 4.8km to the S.E. of Llantrisant the tributary, Nant Coslech, marks the W. boundary of the le Sore fee of St Fagans and Peterston, and within the angle between these waters lies the mutilated motte and bailey of Felin Isaf (Figs. 19 and 20).

The site occupies the tip of a south-pointing finger of glacial drift protruding into the flat alluvial plain of the Ely, which flows by on the S.W. side. A railway

[1] Corbett, *Glamorgan Lordship.* p. 241; Nicholl, *Normans,* pp. 53–5; R. Griffiths, *Glamorgan Historian,* III (1966), p. 164.

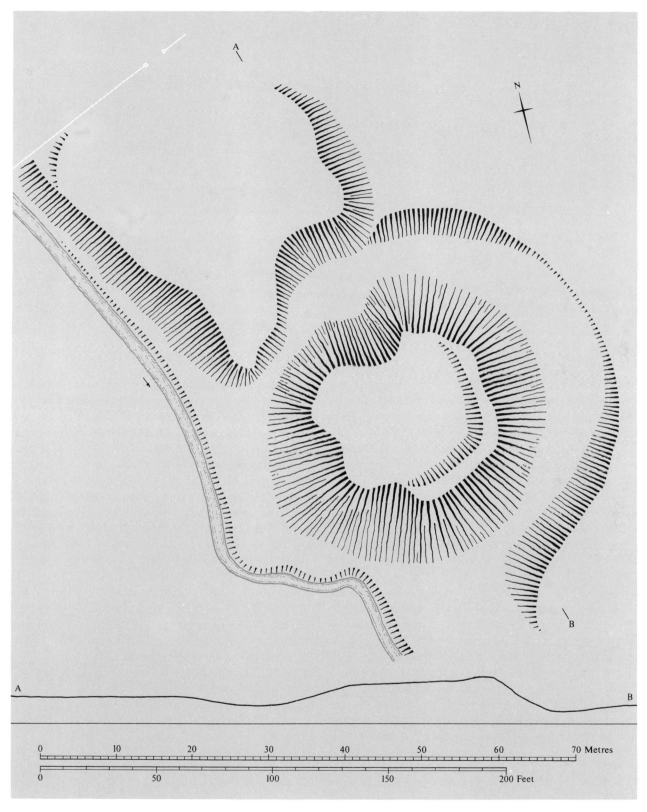

Fig. 19. Felin Isaf.

Fig. 20. Felin Isaf viewed from the east.

line between motte and river has not damaged the earthworks, which occupy the field to the S. of Felin Isaf farmhouse. The position possesses negligible natural defence; a slight natural scarp falls towards the river along the S.W. side. The motte is set against this scarp and retains traces of its encircling ditch in other directions. The small bailey lies to the N.W. and is only faintly perceptible, defined by the natural scarp to the S.W. and faint and incomplete scarps to the N.W. and S.W. The hedge-line bounding the field to the N. has eliminated traces of the perimeter and probable entrance. The bailey measures approximately 28m by 32m.

The motte is mutilated and has a summit of uneven height, being 3.4m above the level beyond the ditch to the S., but only 2.0m above the bailey on the N. The perimeter of the summit has also been eroded irregularly, but would have had a diameter of about 21m. The surrounding ditch averages 0.8m in depth.

No documentary evidence is known for this castle. As a presumed 12th-century site, its location in territory generally regarded as Welsh until the annexation in 1244–45 in itself poses problems presented by other mottes in this and the neighbouring territory of Senghennydd. Felin Isaf, with other mottes to the N. of Cardiff (MO Nos. 3, 4, 7 and 8), might represent Welsh works, though it seems more probable that they indicate an initial and temporary Norman encroach-

ment into the southern parts of these hill commotes. These problems are discussed in the Introduction (pp. 10–11). For Felin Isaf it should be noted that an early Norman settlement of Clun has been tentatively suggested,[2] and that would explain the record of a most substantial Norman church that formerly existed at Llantrisant (see Vol. III, Part 1b, LM 8). As a demesne manor, as it was after the annexation of Meisgyn, Clun was almost indistinguishable in its economy and social structure from St Fagans by 1307, with extensive arable and meadow and its customary tenants.[3]

Postscript: A Bosch factory is to be established in the immediate vicinity of the motte. On 25 May 1989 the site was revisited during clearance. The farmhouse to the N.W. had been demolished and the ditch defining the N.W. extremity of the bailey was clearly exposed during grading. It was 4m wide and apparently V-shaped, running from the natural scarp 170ft beyond the former hedge-line shown on Fig. 19.

King, p. 165 (Llantrisant No. 2)

Llantrisant.
ST 07 N.E. (0606–7926)   25 v 89   XLII N.W.

---

[2] Corbett, *Glamorgan Lordship,* pp. 40–42, 63, 245.
[3] *Glam. Co. Hist.,* III pp. 313–14

MO 3   Morganstown Castle Mound

This low-lying motte occupies an alluvial river terrace near the W. bank of the Taff at 7½km to the N.W. of Cardiff. Just to the N. the river emerges from the narrow defile above Tongwynlais. To the W. of the river the steep slopes of the Little Garth divide the Glamorgan uplands from the more congenial undulating lowlands to the S. Morganstown motte is well situated for surveying traffic along the W. bank into

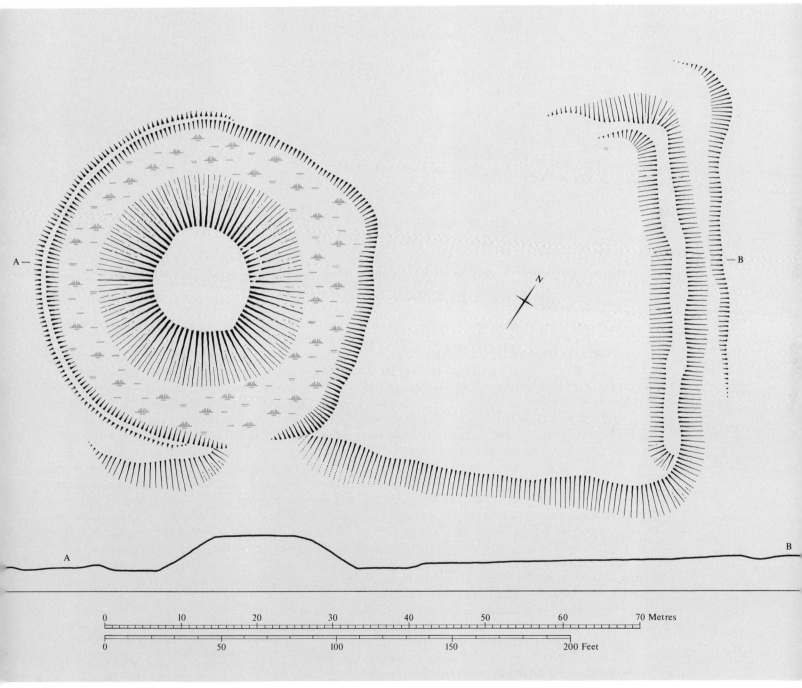

Fig. 21. Morganstown Castle Mound.

Fig. 22. Morganstown Castle Mound from the south-west. Castell Coch (LM 4), background left.

and from the uplands, and is overlooked by Castell Coch (Vol. III, Part 1b, LM 4) on the hillside opposite, which could command movement on that side of the river.

The motte (Figs. 21, 22) is small but steep-sided and its ditch is wet. The summit is 3.8m above the surrounding level and measures 13.4m N.–S. by 12m E.–W. An adjoining bailey of rectilinear form is vaguely outlined by scarps to the E. of the motte. This earthwork was formerly in the grounds of nearby Tŷ-Nant House, and at the turn of the century its ditch was re-cut, an operation no doubt accounting for the slight counterscarp bank around the W. side. At the same time 'slight excavations' yielded 'fragments of ancient pottery'.[1] More recently, a sherd of south-western French polychrome ware has been reported from the site.[2] Trees and overgrown shrubs now mask the motte.

There is no historical reference to this site. Like other mottes and one ringwork clustered to the N. and N.W. of Cardiff, its presumed foundation in the late 11th or early 12th century, long before the mid-13th-century annexation of the upland commotes of Meisgyn and Senghennydd, is of some interest.[3]

Morganstown motte lies at the N. extremity of the small manor of Radur which forms the S.E. portion of Meisgyn. The manor is not recorded until the early 14th century, but there are grounds for the suspicion that it may have been established before the annexation of the whole of Meisgyn in 1244–45, not least the siting of this, its only castle.[4] The manor and parish of Radur occupied a strip of land some 1.6km wide and extending for 4km along the W. side of the Taff, bounded to the S. by Clawdd Constable,[5] its boundary with Llandaf, and to the N. by the abrupt lower slopes

[1] Charles Morgan, Trans. Cardiff Nat. Soc., LVII (1924), p. 20.

[2] ex inf. E. J. Talbot.

[3] See Introduction, pp. 10–11. The other mottes are MO Nos. 2, 4, 7 and 8; the ringwork CR 9. In addition the masonry castles MM 2 & LM 4 are raised upon mottes.

[4] Corbett, Glamorgan Lordship, pp. 40–42, 63, 247.

[5] Cardiff Records, V, p. 354; Trans. Cardiff Nat. Soc., LVII (1924), p. 16; Rees, Map.

of Little Garth, immediately N. of the motte. The siting of the motte at the S. termination of Taff gorge would seem most appropriate to a Norman foundation intended to protect the more fertile lands of the manor to the S. in the vicinity of the parish church and village (Vol. III, Part 2, DV 16). There is slight evidence that this southern settlement was in existence by the late 11th century in the record of *villa aradur,* situated 'between Llandaf and the woods'. Although this reference concerns the life of the 6th-century St. Cadog, it was written in the late 11th century and could be taken as a statement applicable to that period.[6] The dedication of the church to St John the Baptist might also be early Norman, though it first appears in the Norwich Taxation of 1254.

King, p. 168 (Radyr).

Radur.
ST 18 S.W. (1281–8189)   24 ii 81   XXXVII S.W.

---

[6] J. B. Davies, *B.B.C.S.,* XXVII (1977), p. 312.

MO 4   Ruperra Motte (Castell Breiniol; Castell y ddraenen)

From the Taff Gorge at Tongwynlais to Coed Craig at Ruperra, a distance of 11km, a line of hills and ridges abruptly divides the lowlands of Cibwr from the uplands of Senghennydd. Three castles lie upon this high ground: to the W. on a lofty shelf of Fforest Fawr, the 13th-century Castell Coch (Vol. III, Part 1b, LM 4), its masonry masking an earlier motte; further E., on Craig Llanishen, Castell Morgraig (Vol. III, Part 1b, LM 9), another stone castle of the 13th century; to the E., on the summit of Coed Craig above the River Rhymni, Ruperra motte. After the conquest the greater part of Cibwr formed the lordship of Cardiff which, at the centre, extended to the ridges of Craig Llanishen and Cefn Onn. To the E. and W., however, enclaves of territory to the S. of the natural divide remained in dispute with the Welsh at Whitchurch and Llanfedw until the definitive annexation of the mid 13th century, though mottes in these areas could indicate that there had been an initial Norman advance to this natural line of high ground (see Introduction, pp. 10–11, Fig. 5).

Ruperra motte crowns the summit of Coed Craig ridge at 575ft above O.D. The ridge is composed of nodular limestone within red mudstones. The hill is thickly wooded, and during survey the motte was found to lie within a large unrecorded multivallate hill-fort of Iron Age type.[1] This particularly elevated situation within a hill-fort is paralleled at Twmbarlwm, 6.3km to the N.N.E., in the neighbouring Monmouthshire lordship of Gwynllŵg. Below the hill to the S.W. lies the shell of the early-17th-century castellated mansion of Rhiwperra (Vol. IV, Part 2, No. 30) while at 270m S.E. of the motte is the plough-levelled site of Llanfedw church.[2] Iolo Morgannwg,

---

[1] Discovered too late for inclusion in *Glam. Inventory,* Vol. 1, Part 2; *Arch. in Wales,* 20 (1980), pp. 26–7.

[2] At ST 2258 8656; Rees, *Map.*

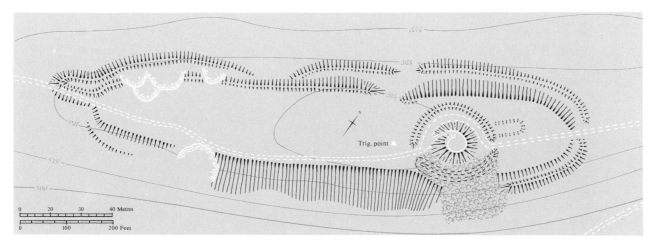

Fig. 23. Ruperra Motte, with sketch-plan of surrounding hill-fort.

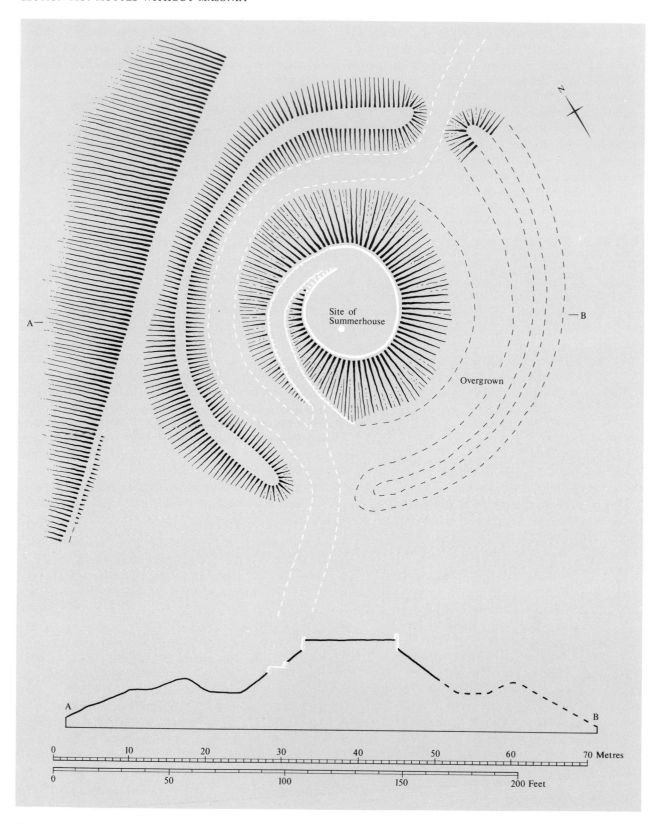

Fig. 24. Ruperra Motte.

ca. 1800, noticed the site as '*Castell Breiniol, commonly called now Castell y ddraenen*', names no longer current.[3]

The hill-fort is long and narrow, defined by eroded bivallate defences to the N.W., and by the steep natural scarp to the S.E. (Fig. 23). The motte lies to the N.E. end of this earlier enclosure, set against the S.E. scarp. With its surrounding ditch and counterscarp bank, it occupies the full width of the hill-fort, perhaps intentionally isolating a suitably confined area at the N.E. end as a ready-made bailey. The motte stands 6.0m above the level of the ridge and has a summit diameter of 12.0m. A modern track along the ridge has broken through the counterscarp bank to the N.E. and S.W. and followed the ditch around the N. side. To the S.E. impenetrable vegetation masks both ditch and counterscarp bank; it is uncertain whether they continue unbroken, or terminate on each side against the steep natural fall.

A square two-storeyed summer-house and surrounding wall had been raised upon the motte by the Rhiwperra family before 1764, when annotations to an estate survey surmised the former existence of a palisaded timber castle on the site.[4] No summer-house was recorded here by Clark in 1875.[5] There remains a stone-revetted path to the summit around the W. face of the motte and the enclosing stone wall, but nothing of the summer-house. A low spreading bank 3.5m wide which encloses a rectangular area 17m by 10m, abutting the counterscarp bank to the N.E., may have outlined an equally recent tennis court or bowling green.

There is no known historical record of the motte, but only of Llanfedw, in which it lay. By 1307, on the death of Countess Joan, this was a 'member' of the castle and town of Caerphilly.[6] This record suggests that Llanfedw was part of the Welsh territory annexed at the time of the foundation of Caerphilly Castle (Vol. III, Part 1b, LM 3). The motte would no doubt have been obsolete by then, and if of Norman foundation could only have been held briefly in the initial period (see Introduction, pp. 10–11).

King, p. 169.

Michaelston-y-Vedw (E), Llanfedw (C)
ST 28 N.W. (2233–8670)   25 ii 81   XXXVII N.E.

---

[3] Iolo Morganwg MSS., N.L.W., MS. 13089 E, p. 128.
[4] *Country Life*, Oct. 23, 1986, pp. 1277–9. A letter of Rev. W. Watkins, *ca.* 1762, records the bizarre discovery of an erect skeleton in a room 2.5m square during the digging of the foundations of a summer-house at Ruperra (*Catalogue of MSS Relating to Wales in the British Museum,* ed. Edward Owen (1922), IV, p. 847).
[5] *Arch. Camb.* 1875, pp. 68–9.
[6] *Cardiff Records,* I, p. 273; *Glam. Co. Hist.,* III, pp. 312–3.

MO 5   Stormy Castle

The mutilated remains of the motte of the Sturmi family occupy the E. tip of a low ridge of glacial drift in the wide and shallow valley of Nantfforwg Brook on the N. side of Stormy Down.[1] The Port Way crosses the Down at 0.7km to the S.W., and the site is about halfway between the chief lord's castles at Kenfig and Newcastle, Bridgend (EM 2 and 3). No castle is recorded here, but the site must indicate the location of Sturmieston (*villa sturmi*) established by Geoffrey Sturmi on previously unploughed waste before 1154 (see below and f/n 3). The eroded mound (Figs. 14, 25) is 35m in diameter and 3m high, with a summit diameter between 15m and 18.00m. No trace survives of its ditch or of a bailey, and it has been disturbed by a hedge-bank and two pits to the W. and N. Immediately to the S., former buildings are represented by scarps and grass-grown banks. Though traces of a well and a scatter of 18th- and 19th-century sherds suggest recent occupation here, the surviving fragment of the E. gable of the southernmost building appears to be medieval. Another settlement lies nearby: within an enclosure 200m to the S.E., at the foot of Stormy Down, are the remains of three medieval buildings (Vol. III, Part 2, MG 31). Before 1183 Margam Abbey had obtained the entire holding of the Sturmis to form a grange which was eventually divided into Magna and Parva Stormy, a division perhaps represented by the two clusters of buildings at and near the motte.

William Sturmi, along with William de Londres of Ogmore, witnessed a charter at Kidweli before 1115,[2] but he is not known in Glamorgan. Geoffrey Sturmi next appears as founder of the vill of Sturmi '*in a lonely place, on land which no one had ploughed*

---

[1] For the Sturmi family, see Clark, *Cartae,* II, pp. 494–5; Gray, *Kenfig,* pp. 253–68; Nicholl, *Normans,* pp. 137–41.
[2] Nicholl, *Normans,* pp. 137, 174, 182 (citing Dugdale, *Monasticon,* IV, p. 64, No. 1).

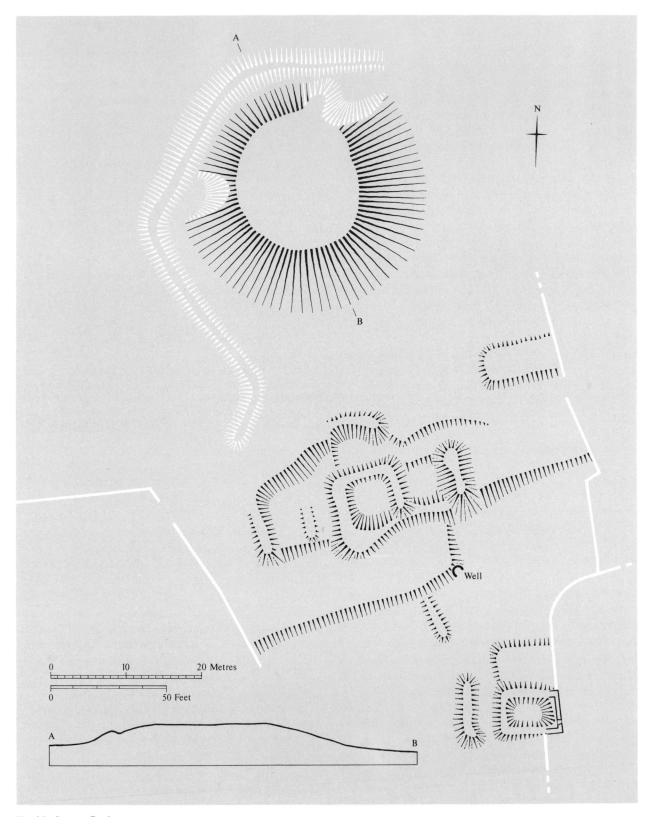

Fig. 25. Stormy Castle.

Fig. 26. Stormy Castle viewed from the north-east.

previously'.[3] Geoffrey established a church at his vill and thereby occasioned a dispute over its tithes, which was settled by Archbishop Theobald of Canterbury in 1154.[4] Before 1166 Geoffrey had disposed of portions of his lands at Stormy to Margam, and later his son and heir Roger conveyed to the same abbey the whole residue of Sturmieston, including his wife's dower of eighty acres, for a perpetual rent of half a mark.[5] This agreement was confirmed by Earl William (*ob.* 1183), to whom Roger and his heirs still owed service for this 'land' in the Earl's 'fee' of Margam, and received half a mark annually from the Abbey.[6]

Though possessing six carucates of arable and thirty-six acres of meadow, Sturmieston was on land of poor agricultural quality. The Sturmis, like the neighbouring Scurlages at Llangewydd (VE 3), ceded their lands to Margam and re-appeared in the lordship of Gower. It is not clear why Sturmieston was never regarded as a knight's fee like Llangewydd. Both had a castle and a church, and Sturmieston's perpetual farm to the monks for half a mark, or 6*s.* 8*d.*, was

the equivalent of the wardsilver payment owed by Llangewydd and other Glamorgan fees.[7]

King, p. 170 (Tythegston Higher)

Tythegston (E), Tythegston Higher (C)
SS 88 S.W. (8458–8153)   11.ii.80   XL N.W.

---

[3] Clark, *Cartae,* I (clii), p. 151; *Epis. Acts,* II, L154, p. 654.

[4] Clark, *Cartae,* I (cxxxix), pp. 138–9; *Epis. Acts,* II, L130, p. 647; Patterson, *Glouc. Charters,* p. 10; *Glam. Co. Hist.,* III, pp. 116–7. The site of the church is unknown. A font found in 1909 at Stormy Farm, W. of the motte, was removed to Margam church (*Arch. Camb.* 1909, pp. 373–4).

[5] Clark, *Cartae,* I (cxiv; cxxxiv), pp. 14, 131–2; *Epis. Acts,* II, L149, pp. 652–3; Patterson, *Glouc. Charters,* No. 134, p. 124. The rent is cited in a later deed by Roger's wife, Gunnilda (Clark, *Cartae,* I (cxlii) pp. 140–1; *Epis. Acts,* II, L185, p. 663).

[6] Clark, *Cartae,* I (cviii; cl), pp. 109, 149–50; VI (mdcix; mdcx; mdcxii), pp. 2331–5; *Epis. Acts,* II, L306, p. 697; Patterson, *Glouc. Charters,* Nos. 126, 134, pp. 118–9, 123–4.

[7] The rent was quit claimed to the abbey by Roger Junior in 1234 (Gray, *Kenfig,* p. 261; Nicholl, *Normans,* p. 138).

MO 6   Talybont Castle (Castell Du; Castell Hu; Banc-y-Rhyfel)

Talybont is the only surviving motte in the lordship of Gower, and like Loughor Castle (MR 4), at 5km to the S.S.W., it stands on the W. border of the lordship beside the Afon Llwchwr, which forms the boundary with neighbouring Carnwyllion. Though the main Roman road crossed the river at Loughor, an ancient crossing is also indicated at Talybont by the name, which is pre-Norman : the nearby church had a predecessor, named 'Lan Teliav Talypont', mentioned in the *Book of Llandav*.[1] The present church, now abandoned, lies on the bank of the river at 410m to the N.W. of the motte. Another motte, Ystum Enlli in the neighbouring lordship, lies on the opposite bank of the river and strengthens the probability of a crossing here (Fig. 27).[2]

Talybont Castle (Fig. 28) crowns a low rounded hill of glacial drift overlooking the crossing, from which it is now separated by the M4 cutting. The motte retains its surrounding ditch and rises 6m above the surrounding level. Though uneven, the summit betrays no indication of masonry as is suggested by late references to Talybont tower (1319) and castle (1353).[3] The bailey to the S. has been subject to ploughing, which has also diminished the motte ditch, except to the N.E. beyond a modern hedge-bank which crosses the motte. Eroded scarps define a spade-shaped bailey with the strongest indications of an entrance gap to the S. A slight mound upon the termination of the E. scarp against the motte ditch probably represents the only remaining vestige of the bailey bank. Two rectangular structures were recorded as cropmarks set against the E. scarp in 1972.[4] A recent cutting into the S.W. flank of the motte was examined during survey and section X-X recorded across the toe of the motte (Fig. 30). Three post-holes were visible cutting into the undisturbed natural gravel and ranged across the lower slope some 3m within the line of its present base. The S. post-hole yielded two sherds, one being a rim of probable 13th-century date. A bridge support or more probably a palisade around the base of the motte may be represented by these features.

Henry de Beaumont, Earl of Warwick, was granted Gower in or soon after 1106 on the assasination of Henry I's ally, Hywel ap Goronwy.[5] The castles of Loughor and Talybont were established by Henry de Villers as the respective centres of two fees held of

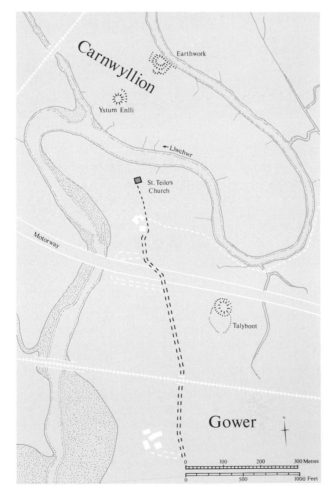

Fig. 27. Talybont Castle: location map.

Fig. 28. *(Opposite)* Talybont Castle.

[1] *Liber Land.*, p. 140.

[2] *Carms. Inventory*, No. 327; Morgan, *East Gower*. pp. 8–9, with discussion of surrounding topography.

[3] *Turrym de Talebont* held by Petro de Alta Ripa in 1319, Clark, *Cartae*, III (dcccxciii), p. 1066; *Villa de Talband in qua sunt unum castrum et unum feodum militum* (1353, cited in a suit of 1396), Clark, *Cartae*, IV (mlxxi), p. 1391.

[4] A. Ward, M4 Survey, Carmarthen Museum (1972), p. 3.

[5] For Hywel's grant of Gower in 1102, *Bruts : B.S., R.B.H.* and *Pen. 20;* Henry de Beaumont's arrival in Gower is unrecorded, but before 1115 he had granted land at Llangenydd to the Abbey of St Taurin, Evreux. *Glam. Co. Hist.*, III, p. 207.

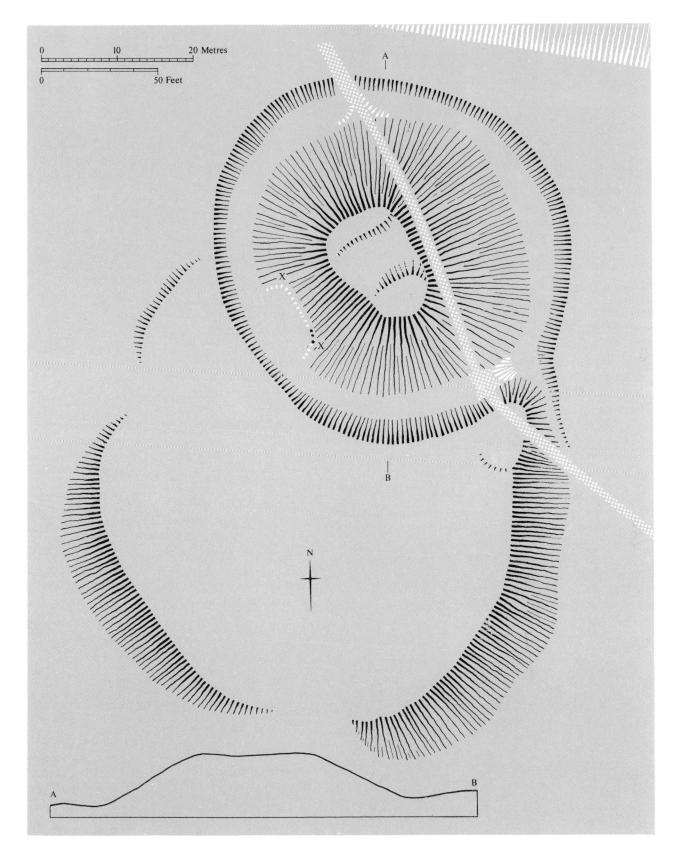

Fig. 29. Talybont Castle viewed from the south-east.

the chief lord who established himself at Swansea. Swansea castle withstood an attack by Gruffydd ap Rhys of Deheubarth in 1116, but an un-named castle in Gower, probably Loughor or Talybont, was burnt and many of its garrison slain.[6] Later, Henry de Villers granted an area of his fee of Talybont to Neath Abbey soon after its foundation in 1129. The land so granted lay to the S. of the castle and formed the grange of Cwrt-y-carnau (Vol. III, Part 2, MG 1), the transaction having the consent of 'Henry de Warwick'.[7] Uprisings or savage incursions are recorded in Gower in 1136, 1151, 1189 and 1192, but Talybont Castle is not mentioned. In 1215 the castle, then held by Hugh de Meules, was destroyed in Rhys Ieuanc's fierce campaign in alliance with Llywelyn ab Iorwerth.[8] The *turrym de Talebont* (1319) and the 'castle and knight's fee' (1353), noted above with references, must relate to this site. It would appear that before 1319 Talybont had become part of the chief lord's demesne, for the tower and 34 acres of land were listed then among the many alienations made by William de Braose in Gower. The castle of 'Liman', mentioned in a royal licence of 1322, was probably Talybont, for in the 16th century Rice Merrick noticed at Llandeilo Talybont '*the castle of Lean, now scarce the ruin to be seen*' and also referred to it as 'Llyan'.[9] Despite these late references, no signs of masonry survive, and of the *villa de tulband* of 1353 only the castle earthworks and the derelict church remain, the latter soon to be re-erected at the Welsh Folk Museum, St Fagans.

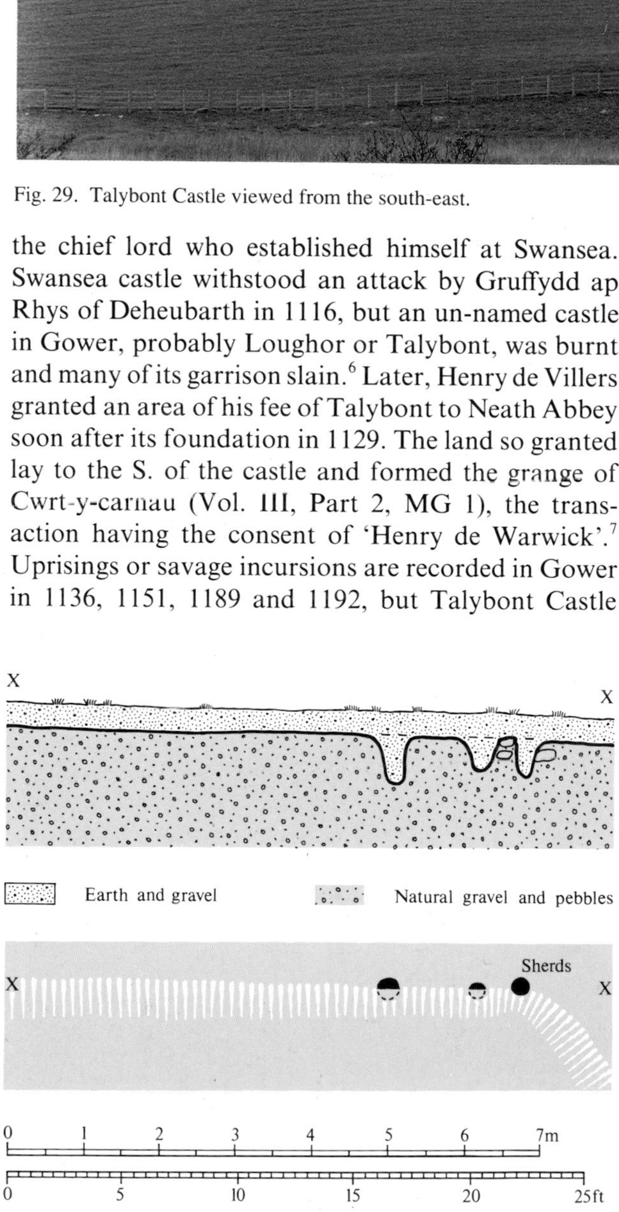

King, p. 165 (Llandeilo Talybont)

Llandeilo Tal-y-bont.
SN 50 S.E. (5860–0267)   12 i 76   VII S.W.

X ———————————————————— X

☐ Earth and gravel   ☐ Natural gravel and pebbles

X ——— Sherds ——— X

0   1   2   3   4   5   6   7m
0   5   10   15   20   25ft

Fig. 30. Talybont Castle: exposed section of motte recorded in a recent disturbance on the south-west flank.

[6] *Bruts: B.S., Pen. 20*, and *R.B.H.*

[7] Clark, *Cartae*, I (clvii), p. 155; II (cccxviii), p. 316; *Epis. Acts*, I, D264, pp. 297–8. This Henry was the youngest brother of Earl Roger of Warwick, more usually styled Henry du Neubourg, as on his coins struck at Swansea before 1141. He ruled Gower *ca.* 1138 to 1166+ (see David Crouch, *B.B.C.S.*, XXXI (1984), pp. 131–41).

[8] *Bruts: R.B.H., Pen 20, B.S.*

[9] Clark, *Cartae*. III (dccccvii), pp. 1100–01; Merrick, *Morg. Arch.*, pp. 116, 120.

Fig. 31. *(Opposite)* Talybont Castle: (a) view from the south-west; (b) aerial view from the north-east

MO 7   Tomen-y-Clawdd

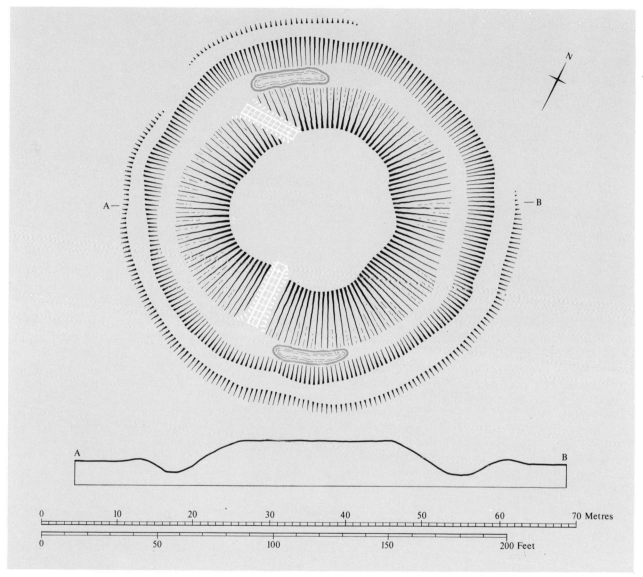

Fig. 32. Tomen-y-Clawdd.

This motte (Fig. 32) survives unharmed as an amenity in the heart of a recent housing development at Tonteg. Houses face it on all sides across an encircling road, set beyond the counterscarp bank outlining its well-preserved ditch. Three reliable observers agreed on the absence of any traces of a bailey before the encroachment of housing.[1] The motte is 4.2m high above the bottom of its ditch, or 3m above surrounding ground. The summit is flat and 21.5m in diameter. The ditch retains water in places, and a counterscarp bank is present for most of the circuit. The site lies at 350ft above O.D. on flat ground with no natural protection, though a small rill rising immediately N.E. ran around the E. and S. sides before the encircling road was built. St Illtud's, the parish church, is 1km to the W., on higher ground.

There is no historical reference to this castle. It

---

[1] W. Ll. Morgan, *Arch. Camb.* 1913, p. 111; N.M.W., Fox MSS, I, p. 36; N. V. Quinnell, O.S. Records.

Fig. 33. Tomen-y-Clawdd viewed from the south-west.

lies in Meisgyn, 13km to the N.W. of Cardiff, and is an outlying example of the seven mottes which cluster to the N. and W. of the chief lord's castle there (see Introduction, pp. 10–11). No hint of masonry is present to explain the former local name for the site: Coed-y-tŵr (Tower Wood).[2] Two flights of wooden steps set into the slope of the motte expose a make-up of sandy soil.

King, p. 166 (Llantwit Vaerdre).

Llantwit Fardre.
ST 08 N.E. (0916–8647)   8 x 80   XXXVI   N.E.

---

[2] Morgan, *ibid.*

MO 8   Twmpath, Rhiwbina

Twmpath is one of two mottes in the lordship of Whitchurch, which occupied the N.W. part of Cibwr commote, within the angle formed by the River Taff, to the W., and the commotal boundary along the steep ridge of Cefn (or Craig) Cibwr, to the N.[1] From Thornhill, near Castell Morgraig (Vol. III, Part 1b, LM 9) on Cefn Cibwr, a secondary ridge named Twynaugwynion, better known as Coed y Wenallt, thrusts southwards, and, after rising to 750ft, it terminates in a confined plateau at 300ft above O.D. This ridge is flanked by the passes of Cwm Nofydd to the W., and Briwnant to the E., whose streams unite S. of the motte which lies on the terminal plateau, being well-placed to control movement along the passes or along Heol-y-Wenallt, the ridgeway northwards to Cefn Cibwr. Cardiff is 6.4km to the S.S.E., and the other motte in Whitchurch, Treoda (MM 2), is 1.8km to the S.[2]

---

[1] E. L. Chappell, *Old Whitchurch, The Story of a Glamorgan Parish,* Cardiff 1945, provides the best account of the lordship, with map.

[2] No exact line could be suggested for the Roman road from Caerphilly to Cardiff (*Glam. Inventory* I, Part 2, No. 754). The possibility of an unsuspected Roman Fort at Treoda (MM2) is an added factor suggesting a line passing close to Twmpath, as well as Treoda.

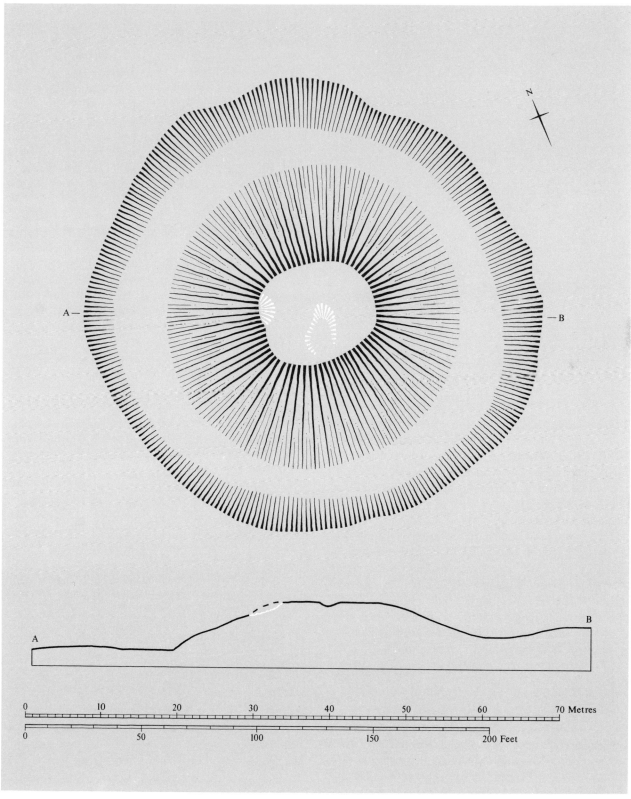

Fig. 34. Twmpath, Rhiwbina.

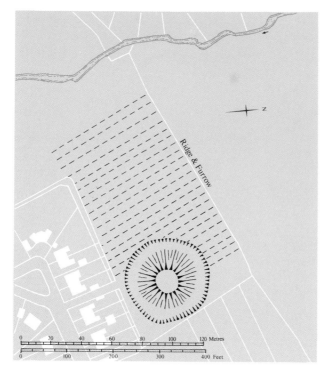

Fig. 35. Twmpath, Rhiwbina: location map showing presumed medieval ridge and furrow.

Twmpath motte (Fig. 34) is well-preserved, and of those in Glamorgan only Cardiff and Ystradowen (MM 1; MO 12) exceed it in size. Its summit is 15m in diameter and up to 6.40m, to the W., above its ditch. The motte was trenched to the centre in 1849, and a black peaty layer 0.60cm thick was noted, together with traces of grass and broom on the old ground surface.[3] It stands on a southern terminal spur of a wide expanse of glacial drift, and recent small pits cut into the top show a make-up of earth, gravel and small stones. No traces of a bailey are present, and none are recorded on the land immediately S.E. where houses have recently been built. Presumed medieval ridge and furrow 4.88m wide is visible over most of the field in which the motte stands (Fig. 35).

This abuts the motte ditch around the W. side and extends for almost 100m south-westwards towards Cwm Nofydd.

No historical record is known of Twmpath motte, nor of the neighbouring motte at Treoda until that site had received its 13th-century masonry. Early Norman activity in the vicinity is indicated by the settlement of a dispute between Earl Robert and Urban, Bishop of Llandaf, concerning lands in Whitchurch and elsewhere.[4] By this settlement, made at Woodstock in the King's presence in 1126, the chapel at Whitchurch (*stuntaf*) was recognized by Earl Robert as a chapelry of Llandaf, as it continued until the creation of Whitchurch parish in 1845, the Bishop receiving the tithes of the vill and of the lands given by the Earl to the chapel. There is further evidence of Norman activity in the area soon after 1141, with the recent discovery of a hoard of over a hundred coins, in Coed-y-Wenallt to the N. of the motte.[5] Twmpath would seem to represent early Norman settlement in this part of Cibwr, though later, perhaps in 1158 at the time of Ifor Bach's abduction of Earl William, it may have returned to Welsh ownership. By his exploits Ifor repulsed encroachments made upon his territory, and in compensation received undefined additional property.[6] Only in 1267 was Whitchurch manor (as *album monasterium*) formally established by the chief lord, following the annexation of the hill commotes.[7]

King, p. 171 (Whitchurch).

Whitchurch (E), Cardiff (C).
ST 18 S.E. (1538–8220)   11 vi 80   XXXVI S.W.

---

[3] *Arch. Camb.* 1849, pp. 301, 317–18.
[4] Chappell, *op. cit.*, pp. 8, 40–41; *Liber Land.*, pp. 27–9; Clark, *Cartae*, I (1), pp. 54–6; *Epis. Acts.*, II, L45, pp. 620–1; Patterson, *Glouc. Charters*, No. 109, pp. 106–08.
[5] Boon, *Welsh Hoards*, Part II, pp. 37–82.
[6] *Glam. Co. Hist.*, III, pp. 33–34.
[7] Rees, *Cardiff*, p. 19.

MO 9   Twyn Castell, Gelligaer

Twyn Castell lies at 700ft above O.D. and 150m to the S.E. of the annexe of Gelligaer Roman fort.[1] Gelligaer church is on slightly higher ground to the W., overlooking the motte (Fig. 36). Though weakly sited in this direction, the ground falls away to the E., and some measure of protection was provided by a small re-entrant dingle on the S. side, though this has now been largely masked by a recent road embankment. The site (Fig. 37) consists of a very steep-sided mound

---

[1] *Glam. Inv.*, Vol. I, Part 2, No. 737, and inset to Fig. 53 showing site of motte.

with a flat top of roughly oval shape and a maximum surviving diameter of 18m (E.–W.), a lesser N.–S. diameter being partly the result of erosion to the S. This summit is 6.60m high on the E. side, but only rises 3.20m to the W. facing rising ground. There are no signs of masonry, and no remains of a surrounding ditch or of a bailey. Erosion on the steep sides of the motte exposes earth and large boulders. It lies in the garden of one of the adjacent terraced cottages, its sides overgrown, and during survey its top served as a chicken run. A small stream flows along the S. side.

This small and crude motte, lacking the usual symmetry, has been attributed to the Welsh rulers of the mountain commotes of Senghennydd. It is in Uwch Caeach commote, where it is the only castle, except for the massive and much later masonry castle raised by Gilbert de Clare at Morlais, near Merthyr (Vol. III, Part 1b, LM 10). It has been suggested that Twyn Castell was the *Castrum Cadwallon* mentioned in the *Pipe Roll* for 1197–98, and the seat of Cadwallon, the son of Ifor Bach, which was fortified by Hywel of Caerleon for the King during a period when Cad-

wallon was often leading Welsh contingents in Normandy.[2] Following annexation of the Welsh commotes of Senghennydd in 1267, Gelli-gaer became one of the demesne manors of the chief lord, as a 'member' of Caerphilly, though Llywelyn Bren, heir of the native dynasty, still held lands in the vicinity in 1315.[3]

King, p. 164 (Gelligaer).

Gelli-gaer.
ST 19 N.W. (1368–9694)　　　20 x 80　　　XX S.W.

---

[2] *Pipe Roll,* 9 Richard I, 194; *Glam. Co. Hist.,* III, pp. 25 and 35.
[3] *Glam. Co. Hist.,* III, pp. 74, 312, 314.

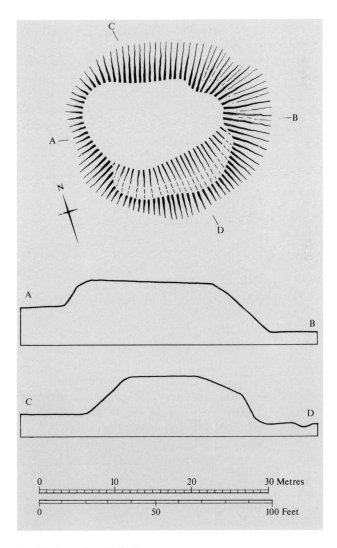

Fig. 36. Twyn Castell, Gelligaer, viewed from the east.

Fig. 37. Twyn Castell, Gelligaer.

MO 10   Tŷ Du

This diminutive moated circular mound is so low and narrow that one hesitates to term it a motte, but for others as small; that at Wotherton in Shropshire, for example, is even smaller.[1] Tŷ Du also has some uncertain indications of a bailey, and its encircling ditch, fed by the adjacent brook and still marshy, could have made a strong obstacle.

Tŷ Du is at 2.48km to the E. of Talyfan Castle (Vol. III, Part 1b, LM 19), and in the E. part of the lordship of that name. The linear boundary dyke, Clawdd Coch, is 650m to the E., and Tŷ Du is outside the large area of the Ely Valley enclosed by that dyke and possibly identified with 'the park of Talyfan' recorded in 1296 (Vol. II, Part 2, MI 64). Pendoylan village lies within the line of the dyke, 1.40km to the E.S.E.

Tŷ Du (Fig. 38) lies on a level area of glacial drift and is set against the narrow marshy fringe on the N. side of a small tributary brook of the Nant Tre-Dodridge. It is overlooked from the S. from ground rising steeply on the opposite side of this brook. Its flat-bottomed and wet ditch is open towards the stream, except for one length of counterscarp bank which continues the outer line of the ditch some way across the marsh. This short counterscarp bank, and two other isolated stretches to the N., must represent ditch scouring; there is no indication that they were formerly part of a continuous defensive bank.

In diameter the mound is between 17m and 19m overall, and 12m to 13m across its level top; it rises only 1.40m above the surrounding ditch. A rough pit has been dug at the centre, and a more regular excavation undertaken on the W. side, neither being in-filled; the spoil from the latter, forming a bulge into the ditch, may soon give the erroneous impression of a bridge abutment.

To the N.E., within an angle formed by the stream, two features offer uncertain indications of a bailey. A curving scarp defines the limits of the marsh. Further N. a low bank with slight north-facing ditch partially defines a narrow area of drained ground against the scarp. It must be stated that the bank is of the proportions of a hedge-bank, and the scarp

Fig. 38. Ty Du. The smallest Motte in the county. There is no record of the two recent pits dug into its summit.

[1] *Arch. Camb.* 1965, pp. 47–76 and Fig. 3 (2).

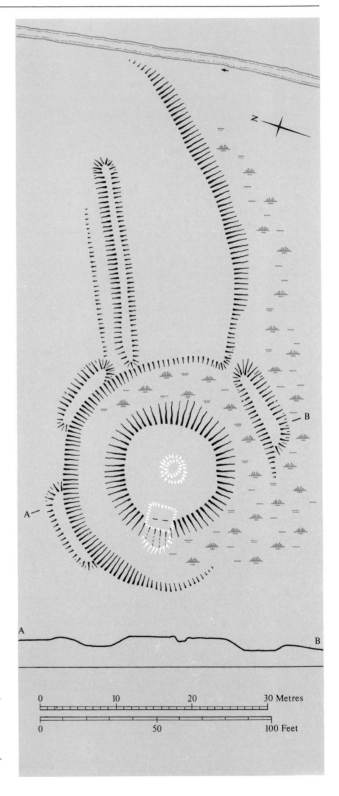

Fig. 39. Ty Du viewed from the west.

may represent the former line of the stream, but this is certainly the most suitable area for a bailey, and the tiny area defined by the bank is of dubious agricultural value.

King, p. 173 (Pendoylan, as possible castle).

Pendeulwyn.
ST 07 N.W. (0461–7705)　　　12 vi 80　　　XLII S.W.

MO 11　Ynyscrug

On the E. bank of the Rhondda River at Trealaw, opposite the confluence with the Clydach, is the last mutilated fragment of a large mound (Fig. 40). During the construction of the Taff Vale Railway (T.V.R.) in about 1855 most of the mound was removed. The surviving W. segment presents a steep and eroded section for 31m along the now disused railway track, above which it rises 3.8m centrally, and 4.6m above the narrow river terrace on the W. The vanished upper part of the mound rose considerably higher. To the

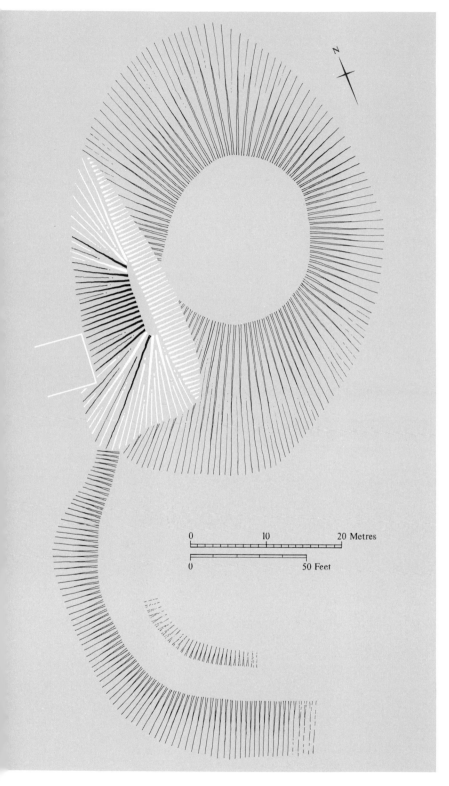

Fig. 40. Ynyscrug. Motte restored from tithe map; bailey scarps as observed in 1986.

S., in 1980, a bailey was indicated by a curving scarp rising 1.9m to the W., and with a slight inner fall on the S. side; its E. side had been obliterated by the railway. In July 1986 these vestiges of the bailey were levelled during road construction, when it was seen that its enclosing bank was formed of upcast gravel. The still surviving motte fragment was shown to be composed of undisturbed glacial gravel and boulders surmounted by loose redeposited earth and gravel derived from its former ditch.[1]

In 1903 the bard and local historian Morien (Owen Morgan) described and sketched from memory the former appearance of Ynyscrug.[2] Shorn of his fanciful theories of bardic origin, his description offers valuable information which is the more credible for his evident ignorance of the nature and true significance of mottes. Morien states that the surviving vestiges are but a small fragment, less than one sixth, of what existed before the construction of the T.V.R. between Dinas and Treherbert. Significantly, he identified similar 'sacred mounds' in the mottes at Whitchurch (? MO 8), Ystradowen (MO 12) and Tonteg (MO 7).[3] Above all, despite the absurdly exaggerated height stated in the caption (30.5m), and the bards depicted upon the mound, his sketch shows a perfectly typical motte. Such a mound is also suggested by the depiction of a large oval tree-clad feature here on the tithe map of Ystradyfodwg, which predates the building of the railway.

The site lies in the centre of Glynrhondda commote which was annexed by the chief lord, along with Meisgyn, ca. 1245, though an unidentified portion of it was still retained by two sons of Morgan ap Cadwallon, of the princely line, according to the Extent of 1262. Morien notes that the manorial court of Glynrhondda met in the adjacent Pandy Inn, though this was seemingly a late and post-medieval practice.[4] Following the 13th-century annexation of Glynrhondda, its court met at Llantrisant.

King, p. 168 (Rhondda).

Ystradyfodwg (E), Rhondda (C).
SS 99 S.E. (9948–9278)   2.vii.86   XXVII N.E.

[1] H. J. Thomas and D. Clayton, *Morgannwg*, XXX (1986), pp. 74–5.
[2] Morien, *History of Pontypridd and Rhondda Valleys*, (Pontypridd, 1903), pp. 239–42, and figure facing p. 239.
[3] Morien, *ibid.*, pp. 29–30.
[4] *Cardiff Records*, III, pp. 274, 276; *Glamorgan Historian*, II (1965), pp. 80, 86.

MO 12 Ystradowen

Fig. 41. Ystradowen viewed from the east.

This unfinished motte (Fig. 42) is at a little over 200ft above O.D. on the W. side of Ystradowen church, on ground sloping gently to the S.E. The road running N. from Cowbridge passes close on the E. side, and here crosses the watershed on the saddle between the modest elevations of Mynydd y Fforest on the N.W. and Pen Tal-y-fan to the S.E., the latter crowned by Castell Tal-y-fan (Vol. III, Part 1b, ML 19), a little over a kilometre distant. Approached from the road to the S.E., Ystradowen appears a typical motte; in fact, it consists of the reshaped S.E. end of a glacial ridge, which has been scarped and ditched around its extremity. To the N.W. the ditch was never cut through the natural ridge to isolate the intended motte. The scarping and ditching was also unfinished: to the N.E. the ditch is at its widest and incorporates

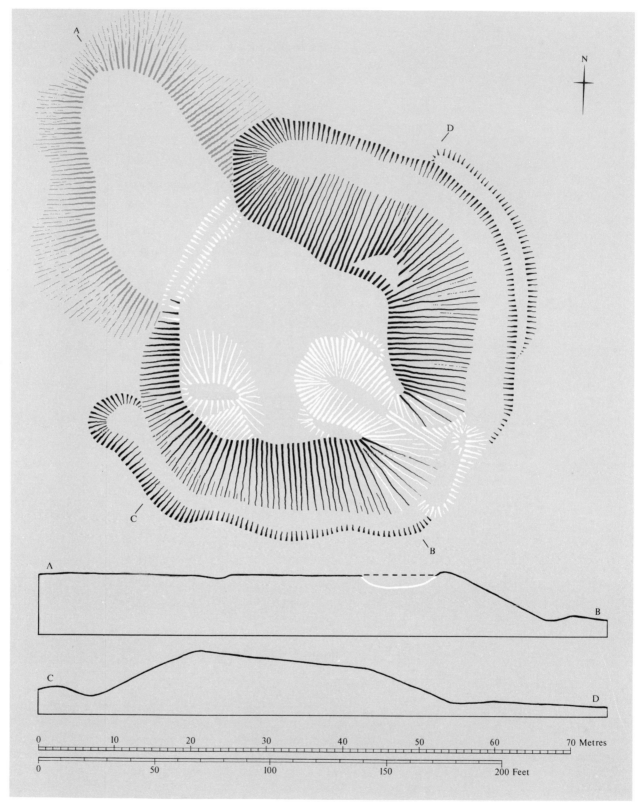

Fig. 42. Ystradowen.

a long stretch of counterscarp bank, but to the S. the ditch is much narrower and more irregular, and without a counterscarp bank. Between these two stretches of ditch, modern treasure-seekers have cut into the mound and masked the adjacent ditch with their upcast, inspired no doubt by the tradition that this was a royal burial mound or druidic 'sacred mound'.[1] The summit is uneven, falling eastwards from a dump of spoil to the W. (Fig. 42, profile C–D). This dump is not easily related to the robber trench to the S., and suggests the original intention of raising the whole summit higher, to bring it above the level of the ridge to the N.W. (profile A–B showing the need for this). To the N.W., where the ditch was never dug, a low modern bank and ditch probably represents the 'restoration' and fencing of 1894.[2] Beyond this, the natural ridge continues at the same level as the top of the unfinished motte and would have provided the obvious area for a bailey, though there are no indications to suggest that one was ever begun.

Ystradowen, measured at the base of its scarp on profile C–D (Fig. 42), is 47m in diameter, a size in Glamorgan second only to Cardiff motte, which is 72m. Its summit, assuming an intended height at least equal to the higher W. side, would have been about 20m in diameter.

Ystradowen lies in Talyfan lordship, within sight of Castell Talyfan, *caput* of the St Quintins who accompanied Bishop Odo of Bayeux at the Conquest and were in Glamorgan by 1102.[3] The St Quintins came to hold the member lordships of Llanblethian and Talyfan, quite probably by 1126, when Richard St. Quintin attested the important agreement between Earl Robert and Bishop Urban of Llandaf, with other Glamorgan magnates, at Woodstock,[4] though the date

of their acquisition is not on record. Ystradowen might represent an initial attempt to establish a castle, soon abandoned in favour of nearby Castell Talyfan, which from the trace of its vestigial walls may well have begun as a castle-ringwork. In Ulster, Piper's Fort, Farranfad, is a less certain unfinished motte; the motte at Downpatrick is a more probable parallel to Ystradowen.[5]

Postscript: The chapel of *cherleton* listed as a possession of Tewkesbury Abbey by Bishop Nicholas (1148–1183) has now been identified with Ystradowen by David Crouch (*Llandaff Episcopal Acta*, S. Wales Record Society, Vol. V, pp. (1988) 28–9 and note on p. 30). This identification suggests that the abortive motte was the intended *caput* of a Norman lordship of 'Charlton' rather than the base first chosen by the St Quintins.

King, p. 171.

Ystradowen.
ST 07 N.W. (0108–7765)   18 xii 80   XLI S.E.

---

[1] Morien, *History of Pontypridd and Rhondda Valleys*, (Pontypridd, 1903) p. 29; In the *Western Mail*, 19.iv.33, it was claimed to be the burial place of 'King Owen', which had been restored and fenced in 1894; Evans, *Glam. Hist. and Top.*, 1944, pp. 446–7. Following one tradition, the trees upon the mound are called Druids Grove on some O.S. maps.

[2] see note 1.

[3] Herbert St Quintin witnessed a Fitzhamon charter in this year: Clark, *Cartae*, I (xxxv), p. 38; Lloyd, *Hist. Wales*, II, p. 441, n. 153.

[4] Clark, *Cartae* I (1), pp. 54–6; *Epis. Acts.*, II, L45, pp. 620–21; Richard is also mentioned in the foundation charter of Neath Abbey (1129): Clark, *Cartae*, I, (lxvii), pp. 74–6.

[5] *An Archaeological Survey of County Down* (H.M.S.O., 1966), No. 787, pp. 118, 1956, and No. 408.2, pp. 202–03.

Section CR:
Castle-Ringworks without Masonry

Monuments CR 1 to 21

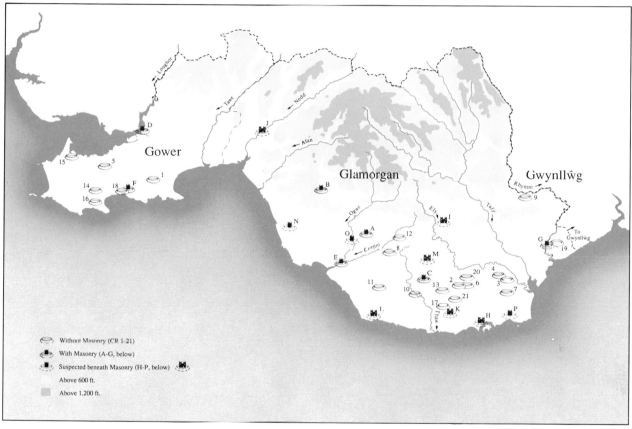

Fig. 44

1	Bishopston Old Castle.	15	North Hill Tor.	F	Pennard. (*MR*-6)
2	Bonvilston.	16	Norton.	G	Rumney. (*MR*-7)
3	Brynwell, Leckwith.	17	Pancross, Llancarfan.		
4	Caerau, Ely.	18	Penmaen, Castle Tower.	*Suspected:*	
5	Cil Ifor Ring.	19	Pen-y-pil, St Mellons.	H	Barry. (*LM*-1)
6	Coed-y-cwm.	20	St Nicholas Gaer.	I	Llantrisant. (*LM*-8)
7	Dinas Powys Ringwork.	21	Walterston.	J	Neath Castle. (*LM*-11)
8	Gelli-Garn Ringwork.			K	Penmark. (*LM*-14)
9	Gwern-y-domen.	*Castle-Ringworks with masonry:*		L	St Donats. (*LM*-16)
10	Howe Mill Enclosure.	*Known:*		M	Talyfan. (*LM*-19)
11	Llandow.	A	Coity. (*MR*-1)	N	Kenfig. (*EM*-2)
12	Llanilid.	B	Llangynwyd. (*MR*-2)	O	Newcastle. (*EM*-3)
13	Llantrithyd.	C	Llanquian. (*MR*-3)	P	Sully. (*EM*-6)
14	Mountyborough, Penrice.	D	Loughor. (*MR*-4)		
		E	Ogmore. (*MR*-5)	*Volume III Part 1b.	

Fig. 43. *(Opposite)* Caerau, Ely (CR 4): aerial view from the north-east *(Committee for Aerial Photography, Cambridge University).*   79

Section CR describes twenty-one castle-ringworks without trace of masonry. Sixteen masonry castles which are certainly or possibly built over primary ringwork-castles are described and illustrated in later sections, but listed and mapped above (Fig. 44, A–P). Four previously unknown ringworks were found during survey, all severely eroded sites (Brynwell, Howe Mill, Llandow and Pancross, Nos. CR3, 10, 11, 17).

Even excluding the seven certain, and nine possible, ringworks known or suspected at masonry castles, the twenty-one inventoried here constitute the largest county group in Wales, well above the sixteen in Pembrokeshire and the seven in Cardiganshire. It might be added that in England the two largest county totals are the sixteen in Shropshire and the eleven in Yorkshire.

Within the county of Glamorgan, ringworks outnumber mottes, which total only sixteen, including the four with later masonry (Section MO). Gower lordship has two mottes, but, including two with later masonry, eight ringworks (CR 1, 5, 14, 15, 16, 18; D, F). In the lordship of Glamorgan, which has fourteen mottes, there are the remaining fifteen ringworks of earth and four certain and nine possible sites at later masonry castles. In both Glamorgan and Gower, the distribution of the ringworks shows an emphatic and almost exclusive concentration in the southern lowlands (Fig. 44). In Gower not one lies in areas that were in Welsh hands in the 12th century, and all are situated on the peninsula of Gower. In Glamorgan all but two lie in the 12th-century Norman lordships to the S. The exceptions are the possible earthwork that may have preceded the 13th-century stone castle at Llantrisant (I), and the hybrid 'ring-motte' of Gwern-y-domen (CR 9), which may well be related to the many mottes in their vicinity and, with them, reflect Norman activity in the early years of the conquest. All other ringworks occur to the S. or W. of these mottes.

The almost complete segregation of the castle-ringworks from the mottes in the lordship of Glamorgan is discussed in the Introduction (pp. 34–36, Figs. 10, 11). It appears that geological factors largely dictated the type of castle that could be built. In the Vale of Glamorgan and the adjacent foothills it is certain that all but two mottes lie on glacial drift, which extends as far S. as a line approximating to the Port Way (Fig. 11, p. 36). To the S. of this line there are only ringworks on the fertile but shallow soils of the Vale, and the bed-rock, predominantly

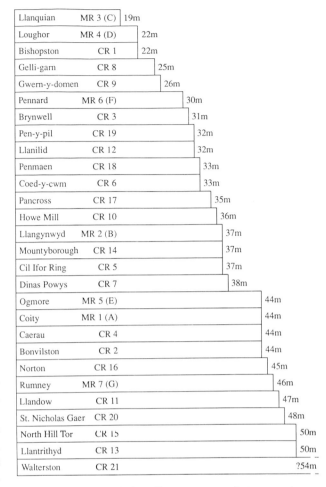

Llanquian	MR 3 (C)	19m
Loughor	MR 4 (D)	22m
Bishopston	CR 1	22m
Gelli-garn	CR 8	25m
Gwern-y-domen	CR 9	26m
Pennard	MR 6 (F)	30m
Brynwell	CR 3	31m
Pen-y-pil	CR 19	32m
Llanilid	CR 12	32m
Penmaen	CR 18	33m
Coed-y-cwm	CR 6	33m
Pancross	CR 17	35m
Howe Mill	CR 10	36m
Llangynwyd	MR 2 (B)	37m
Mountyborough	CR 14	37m
Cil Ifor Ring	CR 5	37m
Dinas Powys	CR 7	38m
Ogmore	MR 5 (E)	44m
Coity	MR 1 (A)	44m
Caerau	CR 4	44m
Bonvilston	CR 2	44m
Norton	CR 16	45m
Rumney	MR 7 (G)	46m
Llandow	CR 11	47m
St. Nicholas Gaer	CR 20	48m
North Hill Tor	CR 15	50m
Llantrithyd	CR 13	50m
Walterston	CR 21	?54m

Fig. 45. Castle-ringwork sizes: diameters measured at presumed palisade positions and averaged for oval or irregular sites.

Lias Limestone, is seldom far from the surface. There are two or three ringworks on the drift but mottes, it would appear, could not be raised to the S. where a suitably workable substratum was lacking.

Regarding the form of Glamorgan's ringworks, the complete ring-bank predominates, even at some sites which have very strong natural defence to some sides (e.g. Caerau and Coed-y-cwm, CR 4, 6). There are only five partial ringworks, where penannular banks protect only the vulnerable flanks on strong promontory or scarp-edge sites (Bishopston, North Hill Tor, Norton, Walterston and Llanquian; CR 1, 15, 16, 21 and C). The five exclude Howe Mill and Pen-y-Pil (CR 10, 19), where recent levelling has created partial ringworks, and Dinas Powys and Penmaen (CR 7, 18), where missing sections of ramparts are believed to have slipped over steep slopes at the tips of their promontories. Equally rare are ringworks with baileys, which are found at only four sites: Bishopston, Gelli-garn, Pancross and Ogmore (CR 1, 8, 17 and E). A fifth may have been started, but never finished, at Dinas Powys (CR 7), while Walterston (CR 21) has a very large embanked outwork, certainly too large for a bailey, but possibly an enclosed village.

In size, these ringworks range in diameter from 19m at Llanquian (C) to around 50m at Llantrithyd, St Nicholas and Walterston (CR 13, 20, 21; see Fig. 45). Within this range of sizes, no sub-groups form clusters at particular segments of the range; they rise fairly evenly from smallest to largest. Several interesting points arise, however, not least the fact that castles as important as Ogmore and Coity were equalled or exceeded in size by eight ringworks which, unlike them, never became masonry castles. Furthermore, the two smallest ringworks, at Loughor and Llanquian, both had masonry, as did Pennard, which is little larger. Regarding the eight largest sites, one is a castle of the chief lord at Rumney (G), one the centre of a Norman member lordship, held with full regality, at Coity (A), while at least five were castles of knight's fees. Of the rest, two appear to have been episcopal castles: Bishopston (CR 1) and Caerau (CR 4); two others passed to monastic houses: Gelli-garn (CR 8) to Neath and Bonvilston (CR 2) to Margam.

It is clear that the vast majority of the ringworks, perhaps all, were Norman castles. Only Llanilid (CR 12) and Gwern-y-domen (CR 9) might be claimed as Welsh sites, though there are reasons for favouring a Norman origin even for these. In general, the attribution of sites to the Normans is almost entirely dependent upon detailed historical and documentary research that has been undertaken for Glamorgan, particularly the work of Clark, Corbett, Nicholl, and Patterson. The medieval records of this county are more readily available in print that those of any other Welsh county. Manorial records are particularly vital,

since very few ringworks are specifically mentioned in any context. Ogmore Castle (E) is named in 1116, and Loughor (D) in 1151. For the rest, we may only assume the existence of a castle at each of the many documented manors, and particularly at those held by knight-service. To these may now be added the last faint vestiges of the de Winton castle (CR 11) at their fee of Llandow. Before this was found Llandow was the only knight's fee returned in 1166, and suspected to be in Glamorgan, for which no manorial centre of any date was known, though some of these centres retain no 12th-century earthwork or masonry.

Many excavations have been undertaken on Glamorgan ringworks, beginning with the pioneering work of W. Ll. Morgan at Bishopston (CR 1) in 1898. He also dug at Cil Ifor (CR 5) in 1910, but without results of note. More recently, major excavations have been carried out at Dinas Powys, Llantrithyd and Penmaen (CR 7, 13, 18), as well as on the stone castles over ringworks at Loughor and Rumney (D, G). Excavations on a smaller scale have been undertaken at Coed-y-cwm, Pen-y-pil and Pennard (CR 6, 19 and F). Summaries of the results of these excavations are given in the relevant accounts.

Only fifteen of the twenty-one castle-ringworks without masonry described here were similarly classified and listed by D. J. C. King in 1983 (Cast. Ang., I, pp. 159–75). To correlate these figures, note that King places Pen-y-pil (CR 19) under its former county of Monmouthshire; Howe Mill and Llandow (CR 10, 11) are subsequent additions to known sites; and that he regards Gwern-y-domen (CR 9) as a motte, Cil Ifor (CR 5) as a 'possible castle', and rejects North Hill Tor (CR 15) as a prehistoric hill-fort. Finally, he adds the strange earthwork of Cae-castell (UW 2) to his list of ringworks. References to King's list follow the site accounts, his site-names given only where they differ from those preferred here.

CR 1   Bishopston Old Castle (Barland Castle)

This partial ringwork, with bailey, lies 0.7km to the N.E. of Bishopston church, at about 170ft. above O.D., on the crest of the S. side of a ravine above Bishopston Brook (Fig. 46). A penannular bank, set against the natural scarp, defends a modestly raised oval interior, 22m long from N.E. to S.W. by 15m. The flat-topped bank has no original gap for an entrance, that to the S. probably marking one of the

sections cut in 1898. To the W. of this narrow gap are traces of an internal stone revetment, probably related to those excavations, for no such feature was recorded. There is an external ditch. About 23m S.E. of the ringwork, a length of faint and ploughed-down bank runs S.W. from the edge of the ravine, marking the end of the bailey, though its former extension to link with the main work along the S.W. side is now

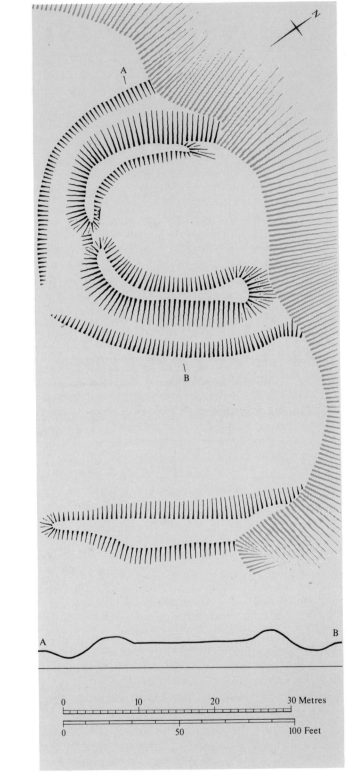

Fig. 46. Bishopston Old Castle (Barland Castle). Pioneering excavations here in 1898 by W.Ll. Morgan recognised the medieval date of such earthworks.

obliterated. The faint bank of an old hedge-line some 38m further to the S.E. is not illustrated. A sparse cover of trees and bushes is confined to the ringwork.

Excavations undertaken here in 1898 by Lt.-Col. W. Ll. Morgan were a significant contribution to castle studies.[1] Morgan, at that early date, attributed the site to the Normans, and identified a group of similar sites in Gower; he was also able to postulate the nature of the timber defences of the ringwork from the sockets of decayed posts within the bank.[2] Three cuts were made across the defences, revealing a V-sectioned ditch, originally up to 2.5m deep; in the body of the rampart, below its flat top, two rows of post-sockets were identified (Fig. 47). These were 1.83m apart, and the front line had consisted of posts between 6.4 and 11.4cm in diameter, and averaging 30cms apart. The rear line of posts was less regular. A step halfway up the counterscarp of the ditch may have carried another row of stakes. The interior had been artificially raised to between 45 and 60cms above the old ground surface. No structures were identified in the interior, but finds included a bronze buckle, the soles of leather shoes, and pot-sherds of late-12th

---

[1] Alcock, *Dinas Powys* pp. 83–87; King and Alcock. *Château Gaillard*, III, 1966 (1969), pp. 91–2.

[2] *Arch. Camb.* 1899, pp. 249–58: Morgan. *East Gower*, pp. 180–83; *Swansea Scientific Society Report*, 1989.

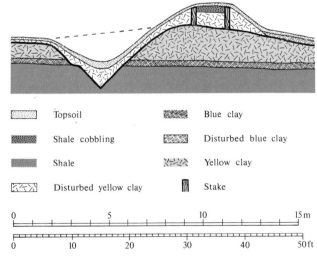

	Topsoil		Blue clay
	Shale cobbling		Disturbed blue clay
	Shale		Yellow clay
	Disturbed yellow clay		Stake

Fig.47. Bishopston Old Castle: section of the defences (Morgan, 1898). Redrawn from *Arch. Camb.*, 1899. Two further sections similarly identified the palisade. Finds demonstrated a Norman date, previously attributed to a ringwork only at Caesar's Camp near Folkestone, excavated by Pitt-Rivers in 1878.

or early-13th-century date.

Old Castle is not recorded. It lies within the episcopal manor of Bishopston (Llandeilo Ferwallt).[3] This ecclesiastical centre of pre-Norman foundation was the only property within Gower that was retained by Llandaf after dispute with St Davids in the time of Bishop Urban (1107–34).

King, p. 161

Bishopston.
SS 59 S.E. (5820–9001)   11.iii.81   XXIII S.W.

[3] Clark, *Arch. Camb.* 1893, pp. 11–3; *Glam. Co. Hist.*, III, p. 93; Morgan, *East Gower*, pp. 170–3.

CR 2   Bonvilston

Bonvilston, a village on the Port Way, seven miles W. of Cardiff, is named after the Bonville family that settled here by the mid-12th century. Its Welsh name, Tresimwn, though not recorded before the 16th century, is probably derived from Simon de Bonville, who occurs in mid-13th-century records.[1] The Bonville castle (Fig. 49) lies isolated at 850m S.E. of the village, on low-lying and marshy ground in the angle between converging minor contributory streamlets of Nant Carfan, a location confirmed by the descriptions of Merrick and Lhuyd.[2] It consists of a well-preserved castle-ringwork, roughly oval, but distinctly right-angled to the N., and measuring, at the crest of its bank, 51m N.–S. by 37m E.–W. The surrounding bank is broken for a gap to the E., probably representing the entrance, for on each side the bank is increased in height, and a slight causeway partly fills the adjacent ditch. This ditch is everywhere wet or marshy, being fed by the brook which flows along its course to the S. The site is completely overgrown with small trees and brambles. Where cleared, to facilitate survey, no trace of masonry was observed, though Merrick stated that stone from decayed walls was carried off or burned in a lime-kiln erected on the site. During survey, a fragment of a hand-quern, with parallel striations, was found in the next field to the N.

The marshy ground flanking the stream to the E. of the castle is traversed, some 60m upstream, by an embankment, best preserved to the S., where it has a ditch on its E. side (Fig. 48). This earthwork does not connect with the castle, and it embraces an area rather too large and marshy for it to have enclosed a bailey. It is more probably associated with the subsequent exploitation of the manor by the monks of Margam (Vol. III, Part 2, MG 39). A house platform abuts its N. extremity, and a wood a further 110m to the E., now Coed yr Aber, but formerly Coed yr Abad (Abbot's Wood), recalls Lhuyd's 'Abbot's Castle', his name for the ringwork.[3]

Bonvilston was a sub-manor of Wenvoe, held from

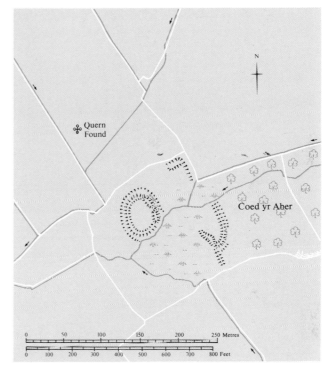

Fig. 48. Bonvilston: the site and surroundings, showing associated earthworks.

the Sully lords of Wenvoe and Sully by service of half a knight. There is no medieval record of the castle, but the Bonvilles, who also held lands in Devon and Somerset,[4] were certainly here by the mid 12th century, if not earlier. Two parts of the tithes of Bonvilston were granted to Tewkesbury Abbey, a grant comparable with those of such early Norman settlers as de Somery, Turberville, and de Londres, and which,

[1] Pierce, *Dinas Powys* pp. 12–13.
[2] Merrick, *Morg. Arch.*, pp. 64, 138; Lhuyd, *Parochialia*, III, p. 21.
[3] Pierce, *Dinas Powys* p. 14; Lhuyd, *Parochialia*, III, p. 21.
[4] Pierce, *Dinas Powys* p. 12; Clark, *Cartae*, II, p. 537, n.

with these others, was confirmed by Bishop Nicholas (1153–83).[5] The earliest de Bonville recorded in Glamorgan is Roger, who witnessed a deed of the same bishop.[6] Before the close of the 12th century the family had granted 40 acres at Caerwigau to the Knights Templar, whose subsequent transfer of these

40 acres to Margam Abbey, together with additional grants of land in Bonvilston by John de Bonville, was confirmed by Countess Isabel (1189–99), by Pope

[5] Clark, *Cartae*, I (cxxxvi), pp. 133–5.
[6] Clark, *Cartae* I (cxxxv), pp. 132–3.

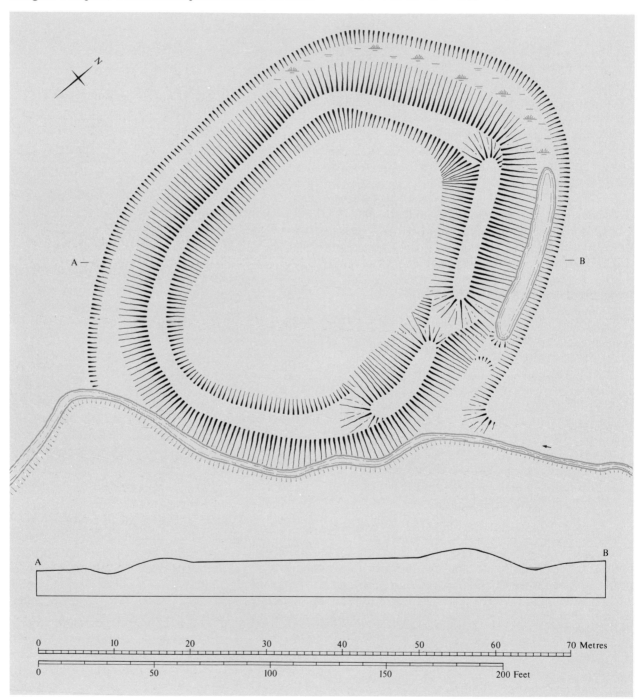

Fig. 49. Bonvilston.

Fig. 50. Bonvilston viewed from the north-east.

Innocent III (1203) and by King John (1205).[7] Early in the 13th century the Bonvilles made further grants to Margam.[8] Then, *ca.* 1250, Robert de Bonville conveyed the whole of Bonvilston to the Abbey for an annual payment to him of three marks, the abbot thereafter assuming the feudal responsibility of rendering to the lord of Wenvoe the service of half a knight, a transaction witnessed by Reymund de Sully and confirmed in his own separate charter.[9] For the token annual rent of half a pound of wheat to Margam, the Bonvilles retained some land at Bonvilston, and Simon de Bonville witnessed the important Extent of 1262.[10] No attempt was made by the monks to destroy the secular settlement and its castle, as they did earlier at Llangewydd (VE 3).[11]

King, p. 161

Bonvilston.
ST 07 S.E. (0706–7336)   19 xi 80   46 N.W.

---

[7] Rees, William, *Order of St. John*, pp. 53–4; Patterson, *Glouc. Charters*, No. 137, pp. 126–7 (her later confirmations of the same: Nos. 140, 144–5, 148–9); Clark, *Cartae*, II (cclxxxvii), pp. 291–2 and (cclxiii), p. 261.

[8] Clark, *Cartae*, II (cclx, cclxii), pp. 259–60; Rees, *ibid.*

[9] Clark, *Cartae* II (dxxxii, dxliv), pp. 542, 572–3.

[10] Clark, *Cartae*, II (dxxix, dcxv), pp. 539–40, 649.

[11] F. G. Cowley, *The monastic order in South Wales, 1066–1349* (Cardiff, 1977), pp. 90, 239; R.C.A.M., *Glamorgan Inv.*, Vol. III, Part 2, MG 34, pp. 287–9.

CR 3   Brynwell, Leckwith

Vestiges of this eroded castle-ringwork were discovered during survey in the rickyard immediately S. of Brynwell Farm. It is the only castle identified within the lordship of Leckwith, a demesne manor of the chief lords of Glamorgan for most of the Middle Ages, and it lies on high ground to the W. of the Ely River, some 3.5km S.W. of Cardiff. Leckwith is now a parish, but its church of St James was anciently a chapel of Llandough, and along with that church and the chapel of Cogan it was granted to Tewkesbury Abbey early in the 12th century.[1] Brynwell Farm lies 1km to the W. of the former chapel, and on a modest elevation to the S. of a tributary of the Bullcroft Brook. The name Brynwell first appears in 1830; before then, from 1393, the place was known as Barnwell.[2]

The N. part of the castle-ringwork (Fig. 51) has

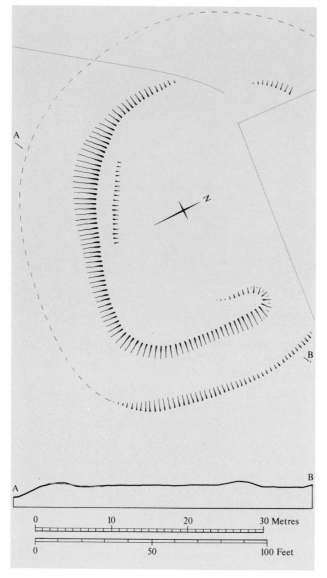

A   B

| 0 | 10 | 20 | 30 Metres |

| 0 | 50 | 100 Feet |

Fig. 51. Brynwell, Leckwith.

been levelled beyond the hedge bounding the rickyard, but to the S. it is defined by a bold scarp with faint traces of a crowning bank and external ditch, which define an enclosure some 30m in diameter. There is a pronounced angle to the S.E. (*cf.* CR 2, 9). Further N. the adjacent farmhouse, which incorporates a trefoil-headed lancet and roof trusses of late-medieval type, may occupy the site of a former bailey (Vol. IV, Part 2, No. 92).

No castle is recorded at Leckwith. The manor remained a possession of the chief lords throughout the 12th century, though *ca.* 1179 Gruffudd ab Ifor Bach of Senghennydd vainly laid claim to it when he granted lands there to Margam Abbey, though with a proviso promising alternative lands in Senghennydd if he were unable to fulfil the gift.[3] When the lordship of Glamorgan reverted to the Crown on Earl William's death (1183), Leckwith figures in the accounts of the *custos*, Maurice de Berkeley.[4] It passed to John, count of Mortain, on his marriage with the heiress Isabel in 1189. In the mid-13th century Richard de Clare (1243–62) granted the whole of his manor of Leckwith to Nicholas de Sandford for a quarter knight's fee.[5] Fulco de Sandford held the quarter fee in the Extent of 1262.[6] Between 1295 and 1307 Leckwith reverted to the chief lord, and thereafter remained a demesne manor.[7]

King, p. 164 (Leckwith)

Llandough, Cogan and Leckwith (E), Leckwith (C). ST 17 S.W. (1468–7439)   11.iii.82   XL N.W.

[1] Clark, *Cartae*, I (cxxxvi), p. 133.
[2] Pierce, *Dinas Powys* P. 53; *Cardiff Records*, I, p. 156.
[3] Clark, *Cartae*, I (clix), p. 159; Corbett, *Glamorgan Lordship* p. 214; *Glam. Co. Hist.*, III, p. 35; *Cardiff Records*, II, p. 35; *Epis. Acts*, II, p. 698.
[4] *Pipe Roll* 1184–85 (Clark, *Cartae*, I (clxxi), pp. 170, 173).
[5] Clark, *Cartae* II (dxv), p. 521.
[6] Clark, *Cartae*, II (dcxv), p. 651 & p. 656, n.
[7] Corbett, *Glamorgan Lordship*, p. 215; I.P.M. Joan de Clare, *Cal. I.P.M.* (Edw. I), No. 435, pp. 322–4.

CR 4 Caerau, Ely

The undocumented castle-ringwork at Caerau, on high ground at 3.75km W. of Cardiff, and 1.4km N.W. of Brynwell (CR 3), is of interest for three aspects of its siting: it lies within the N.W. angle of a large multivallate hill-fort (Figs. 43, 52, and Vol. I, Part 2, No. 673) from which it derives its name 'forts' in Welsh; the abandoned and ruinous church of St Mary's abuts its defences on the S.W.; and, finally, it lies in the south-western part of the medieval episcopal manor of Llandaf. Its elevated situation, at 230ft

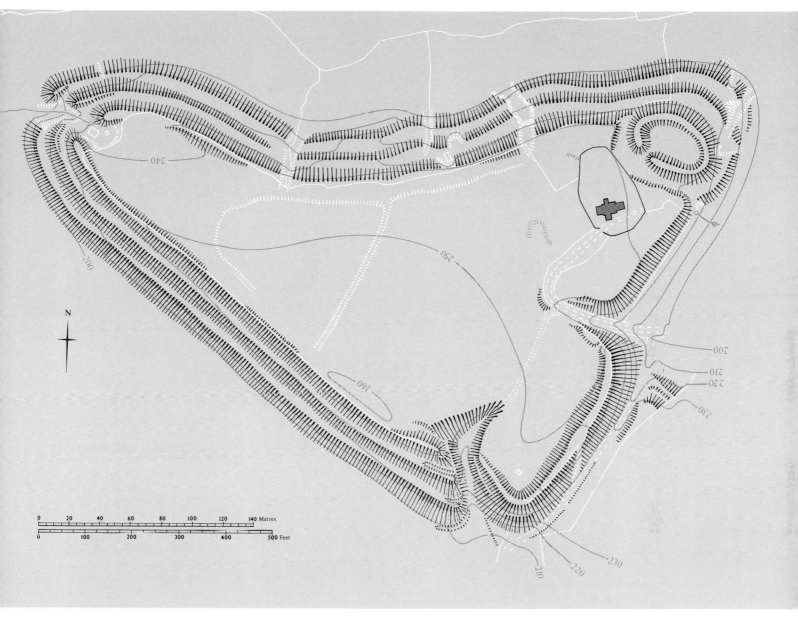

Fig. 52. Caerau, Ely: the hill-fort and later castle-ringwork.

above O.D. within a hill-fort, may be compared with that of Cil Ifor ringwork (CR 5) and Ruperra motte (MO 4). The siting of early castles beside a church is not uncommon, but here, St Mary's, though it became a parish church after the Reformation, was originally a chapel of Llandaf.[1]

The ringwork (Fig. 53) is well-preserved, its strong and noticeably flat-topped bank defining an oval area 52m by 34m, with a gap for the entrance to the S.W., in which direction the site is further protected towards the level interior of the fort by a strong penannular

ditch. The bank on the N. side of the entrance is built higher than the rest, and has a very broad and level top (cf. CR 2, 14, 18). To the N.E. the bank has been raised over the eroded inner line of the fort. There are no traces of a bailey, or of buildings within the ring, though one sherd of 12th-century date is reported.[2]

There is no historical record of the castle, and in

---

[1] *Cardiff Records*, II, p. 36; Rees, *Cardiff*, p. 97, n. 69.
[2] Alcock, *Dinas Powys*, pp. 89, 91, 215.

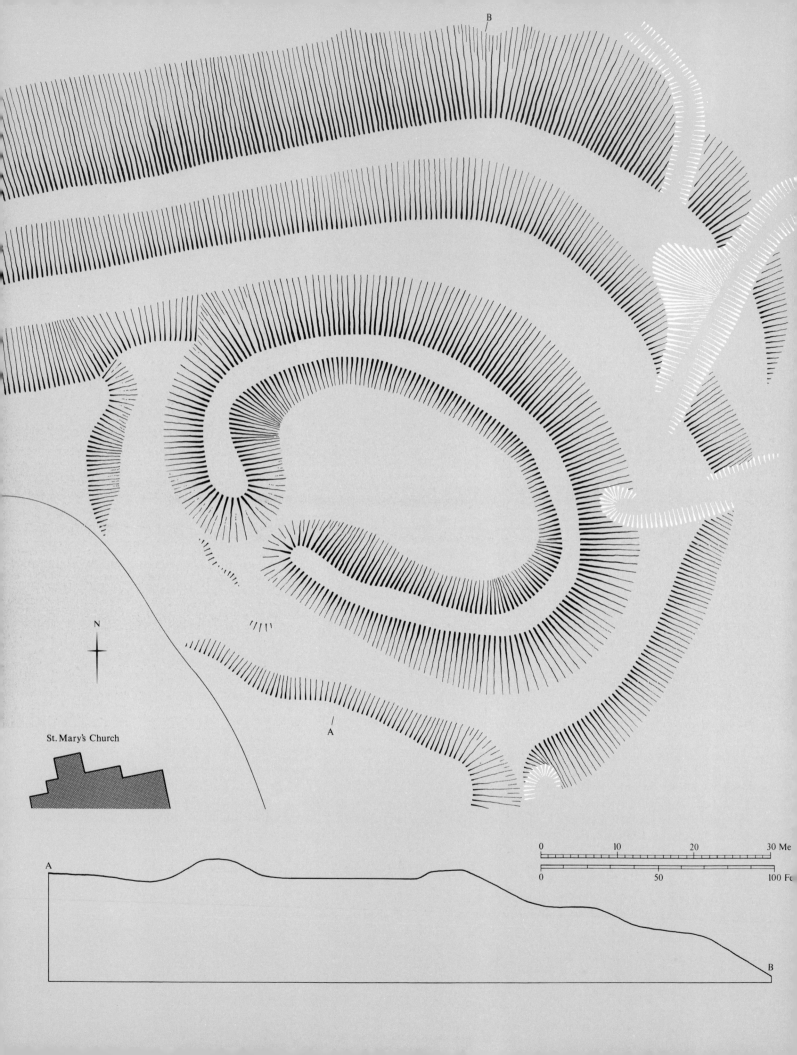

B

N

St. Mary's Church

A

A

0   10   20   30 Me

0   50   100 Fe

B

Fig. 54. Caerau Castle-ringwork viewed from the church tower to the south-west. Cardiff lies on the distant plain beyond.

the absence of any evidence suggesting an early lay manor here, it seems probable that this was an episcopal castle, like that at Bishopston Old Castle (CR 1). The Bishop of Llandaf was a lord marcher, in right of his manor of Llandaf, the temporalities of which, in 1291, were worth almost twice the spiritualities of the entire diocese.[3] By the close of the Middle Ages Caerau (*Kayre* or *Cayre*) was held by the Malefants of the bishop, as of his manor of Llandaf.[4]

King, p. 161

Caerau (E), Michaelston-le-Pit (C).
ST 17 N.W. (1354–7509)   26.iii.81   47 N.W.

---

[3] Taxation of Pope Nicholas IV; C. N. Johns, *Glamorgan Historian*, X, 1974, pp. 187–8; *Cardiff Records*, II, p. 22.

[4] *Cardiff Records*, I, pp. 297–8, and III, pp. 56–7; Merrick, *Morg. Arch.*, p. 94.

Fig. 53. *(Opposite)* Caerau, Ely: the castle-ringwork.

CR 5   Cil Ifor Ring

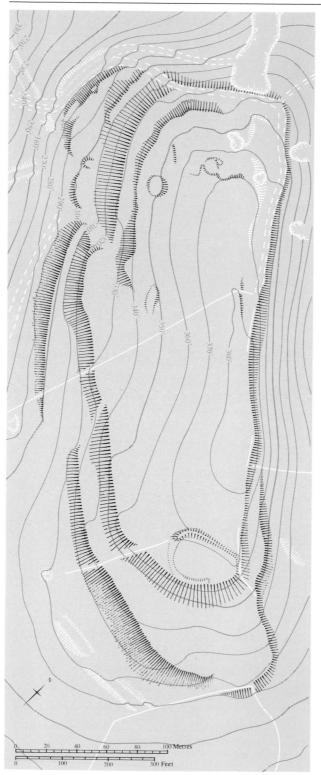

The summit of the isolated ridge of Cil Ifor Top, commanding wide views over the Loughor estuary to the north, is enclosed by the defences of a large multivallate hill-fort (Vol. I, Part 2, No. 665). An oval castle-ringwork (Figs. 55 and 56) has been inserted within the S.E. end of the fort, at a height of 113m above O.D., and overlooking the village and parish church of Llanrhidian, which lie 1km to the W. The ringwork encloses almost 0.1 ha, and measures 41m E.–W. by 30m N.–S., its S.E. side following the inner fort rampart, as at Caerau, Ely (CR 4). Ploughing has almost obliterated the ring-bank to the S., though an arc to the N. is better preserved and stands up to 1.5m high, having been utilized as part of a recent field boundary. An external ditch is marked in places by a lush growth of grass; there is no trace of an entrance. A trench cut across the ringwork in 1910 by W.Ll. Morgan yielded no significant evidence.[1]

There is no record of this castle, but its early manorial associations appear to be with Landimôr, and the Turberville family. In 1166 the tenants of the earl of Warwick, lord of Gower, listed in both *Liber Niger* and *Liber Rubeus*, include William de Turberville who held an unlocated fee of the old enfeoffment (*i.e.* established by 1135). The location of this fee may be indicated by the donations made to the Knights Hospitallers *ca.* 1165 by William de Turberville, and confirmed by Bishop Peter de Leia (1176–98).[2] William granted the Knights the churches at Rhosili, Landimôr and, close to Cil Ifor Ring, Llanrhidian, with its chapel of Walterston. These grants suggest a wide 12th-century holding, mainly centred along the northern coast of the Gower peninsula, between Landimôr and Llanrhidian, and probably including Weobley (Vol. III, Part 1b, LM 20) which lies between those places. Though Weobley is named as one of the ancient knights' fees, held by military tenure, in William de Braose's charter of liberties (1306),[3] it was only two years earlier that John Turberville granted

Fig. 55. Cil Ifor hill-fort and castle-ringwork. See Caerau, Ely (CR 4) and Ruperra Motte (MO 4) for other Early Castles within hill-forts.

[1]   *Arch. Camb.* (1911), pp. 47, 51.
[2]   *Epis. Acts.*, pp. 362–5; *Arch. Camb.* 1897 pp. 101–2, 105–6, 204; Rees, *Order of St. John*, pp. 29, 116; *Glamorgan Co. Hist.*, III, pp. 212, 616 n.4.
[3]   *Glamorgan Co. Hist.*, III, p. 240.

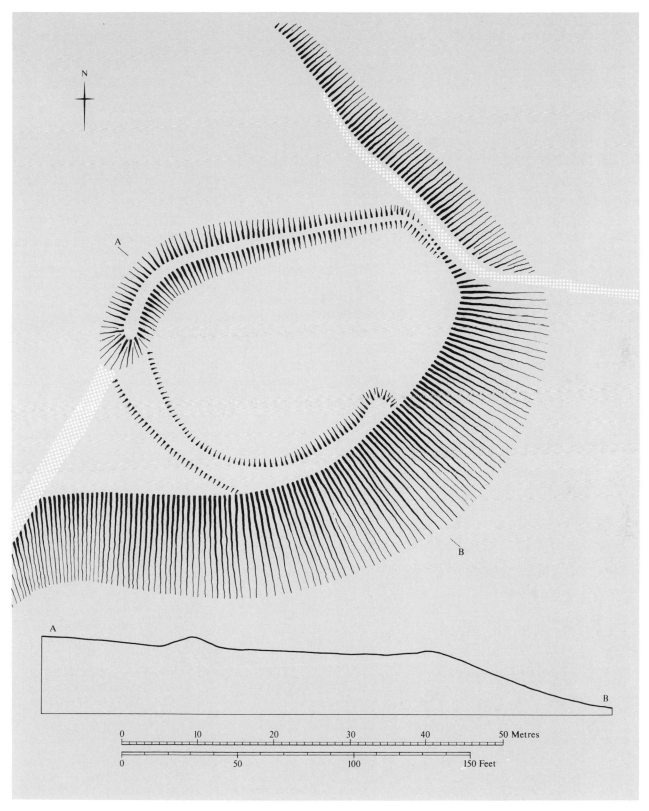

Fig. 56. Cil Ifor Ring.

land at Leyston, in Weobley, to David de la Bere.[4] This is the first recorded mention of the Beres in Weobley, where they began to construct a stone castle at about this time.[5] What remains of Landimôr Castle is of even later date (SH 1). The only known castle sites which might relate to the Turberville holdings in Gower in the 12th century are Cil Ifor Ring and the very strange ringwork at North Hill Tor (CR 15).[6]

King, p. 173 (Llanrhidian No. 2)

Llanrhidian (E), Llanrhidian Lower (C).
SS 59 S.W. (5069–9222)   6.iii.81   XXII S.E.

---

[4] *Arch. Camb.* 1866, pp. 282, 285–86; Nicholl *Normans*, p. 168, n.
[5] W. G. Thomas, *Weobley Castle*, Official Guidebook, 1971.
[6] The bailey of a motte, said to have survived at 'Leyston' (*Arch. Camb.* 1920, p. 315) has not been confirmed. Indeterminate traces of a rock-cut ditch at Leason (SS 488925) are probably the site in question, but the remains are not certainly those of a castle.

CR 6   Coed-y-cwm

Coed-y-cwm (Fig. 58) lies 900m S.W. of St Nicholas, on level ground in woodland at the edge of a ravine which skirts the N.E. side. Across the Port Way, a short distance to the N., lie Cottrell Motte (MO 1) and St. Nicholas Gaer (CR 20), respectively 800m W.N.W. and 1km E.N.E. These three early castles may well represent the three knights' fees of St Nicholas, held of William Corbet in 1262. Coed-y-cwm ringwork is circular, 33m in diameter at the top of its bank, with an external ditch and, to the N.E. a counterscarp bank. Rather exceptionally the bank and

ditch are continued undiminished around the N. side to the very edge of the steep fall to the ravine, where a false impression of a further section of counterscarp bank is created. There is a modern break through the defences to the N.E., opposite the original entrance, which is marked by a wider gap in bank and ditch. The featureless interior slopes slightly from the N.W to the S.E. A modern field bank lies upon the outer lip of the ditch to the S.E.

The site was excavated by J. B. Akerman (in 1963) and E. J. Talbot (in 1964–65).[1] It was found that the

Fig. 57. Coed-y-cwm viewed from the south-east.

entrance passage was flanked by dry-stone piers (*cf.* Penmaen, CR 18), and metalled with surfaces of two periods. The piers were possibly secondary. The defences, sectioned on the S.E, side, proved un-expectedly formidable: the top of the bank had been capped with stone slabs, and though much eroded, was still over 3m above the flat bottom of the ditch. No traces of a timber revetment were found. Trenches within the defences, to the N. and the S., disclosed

much daub, associated with burnt timbers which were tentatively interpreted as sole-plates. Potsherds of 12th-century character were sparse, but compared well with wares dated before 1150 A.D. at Llantrithyd (CR 13) and Penmaen (CR 18). Some of these sherds

---

[1] *Morgannwg*, VIII (1964), pp. 69–70 and IX (1965), p. 95; *Arch. in Wales*, 1963, No. 42, p. 17; 1964, No. 44, pp. 17–18; 1965, No. 61, p. 30.

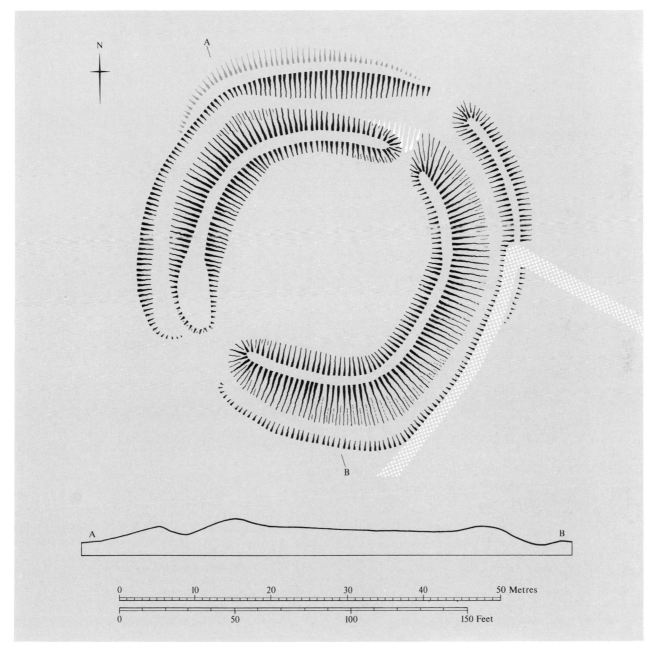

Fig. 58. Coed-y-cwm.

were sealed between the successive metalled surfaces at the entrance; others lay on a cobbling within.

Though all three earthwork castles at St Nicholas are undocumented, it seems significant that in 1262 William Corbet held three fees there of the chief lord, and even more, that the Extent in question states that the three were held of him by others.[2] No Corbet figures in the Gloucester returns of 1166 in *Liber Niger* and *Liber Rubeus*, and discussion of its subinfeudation and early tenure has been confused and contradictory.[3] The identification of the three early castles at St Nicholas clarifies the inadequate documentary sources. St Nicholas Gaer is by far the most likely *caput* of the first tenant-in-chief, who was probably a Corbet (see CR 20). Cottrell, by 1320, and probably much earlier, was sub-enfeoffed to the Cottrells (see MO 1). Coed-y-cwm ringwork is surely the *caput* of a fee subtenanted to the Mitdehorguill family by the mid-12th century. This is suggested most strongly by the location of lands granted to Margam Abbey in two deeds of 1186–91 by Milicent, daughter and heiress of William Mitdehorguill, who also granted '*common pasture of her whole fee of St Nicholas*'.[4] The lands granted were located to the W. of Coed-y-cwm, near the boundary with Bonvilston (Fig. 59). Both deeds refer to Milicent's father, William de Mitdehorguill, who occurs *ca.*1151 as a witness to another Margam deed, by which date he may be presumed to have obtained his fee at St Nicholas.[5] Rather later in the period in which Milicent made her grants to Margam (1186–91), she recurs as wife of Adam de Somery, who confirms her grants.[6] The later tenure of the Mitdehorguill fee is uncertain.

Doghill, the name now applied to Worleton (Vol. III, Part 2, MS 9), a medieval moated manor-house of the bishops of Llandaf situated 2km S.S.E. of Coed-y-cwm, may furnish further confirmation of the Mitdehorguill association with this part of St Nicholas. Its medieval name is obsolete, but Doghill, which first appears in 1540 and survives as a farm name, has been interpreted as a corruption of de Horguill.[7]

King, p. 169 (St Nicholas No. 3)

St. Nicholas.
ST 07 S.W. (0828–7366)   23.ii.81   46 N.E.

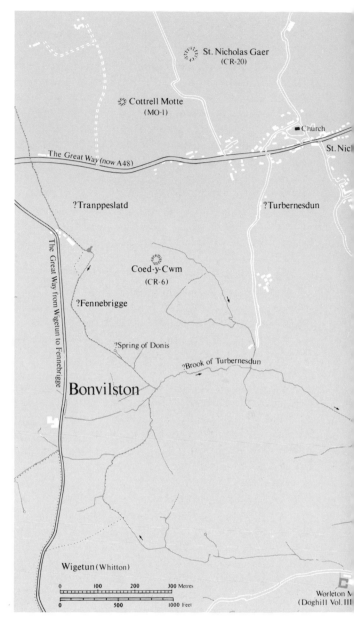

Fig. 59. The St. Nicholas area: the village, three early castles, and moated site. Other names shown figure in grants made in the Mitdehorguill sub-fee in 1186-91.

fees (p. 119), was later inclined to favour the Mitdehorguills (p. 224, n.). Nicholl, *Normans* (pp. 8, 46) favoured the Somerys, with the improbable assertion that St Nicholas itself was but one fee, the others being Bonvilston and St Georges.

[4] *Epis. Acts*, II, L224, p. 675 and L225, pp. 675–6; Clark, *Cartae*, II (cccxcv and cccxcvi), pp. 389–91.

[5] *Epis. Acts*, II, L127, p. 646

[6] Clark, *Cartae*, I (clxxiii), pp. 177–8; *Epis. Acts*, II, L217, pp. 672–3.

[7] Pierce, *Dinas Powys*, pp. 281–3; Evans, *Glam. Hist. and Top*, pp. 418–9.

[2] Corbett, *Glamorgan Lordship* pp. 34–35, 119, 223; Clark, *Cartae*, II (dcxv), p. 650.

[3] Corbett, (*Glamorgan Lordship*) having first presumed the de Somerys to have been the earliest holders of the three St Nicholas

CR 7   Dinas Powys Ringwork

The castle-ringwork near Dinas Powys, 5.5km S.W. of Cardiff, is the most complex and unusual example of its class in Wales. Professor Leslie Alcock identified six phases of occupation during his important excavations of 1954–58.[1] Of these, the last two phases witnessed the development of an elaborate multivallate castle-ringwork in the late-11th and early-12th centuries. The recent myth that the castle re-used an Iron Age fort must be dismissed.[2] There was no evidence for defences related to the Iron Age occupation; fortifications, in the form of a single bank and ditch, were not erected until Phase 4, when they protected a Welsh princely seat of the 5th–7th centuries A.D. Then, after a long period of abandonment, ca. 1100, the castle-ringwork of Phases 5 and 6 re-used, but greatly elaborated, the Dark Age defences. There had been no continuity of occupation, despite the adoption of the enigmatic *Dinas Powys* as the name for the Norman lordship established in the area, and for its later stone castle and village. The siting of the ringwork can be compared with that of other early castles in Glamorgan, which utilized earlier, long-deserted fortifications, both of the Iron Age (*vide* Ruperra, MO 4; Caerau, CR 4; Cil Ifor, CR 5), and of the Roman period (*vide* Cardiff, MM 1; Loughor, MR 4; and, possibly, Treoda, MM 2).

Dinas Powys ringwork (Figs. 60 and 61) lies in Cwrt-yr-ala Park, 670m N.W. of the masonry castle of the same name, on the N. side of Dinas Powys village and in the neighbouring parish of Michaelston-le-Pit. Just N.W. of the isolated eminence occupied by the stone castle, is a whale-back hill of Carboniferous Limestone, running N.W. and bounded to the S.W. by the steep-sided defile of Cwm Gorge. The top of this hill rises gently, reaching its highest point at a blunt promontory to the N., where the ringwork is sited, 140m beyond the Iron Age Southern Bank A, and a presumed siege-work, Southern Bank B, thought to be contemporary with the ringwork. Steep falls provide natural defence, except to the S., where four lines of bank and ditch were drawn across the neck of the northern promontory. Within the rampart, the roughly oval enclosure measures 40m N.–S. by 25m E.–W., and covers about a quarter of an acre. These defences are best described in chronological order, following the excavator's numbering, which ran outwards from the innermost line, Bank I and Ditch I.

The earliest defences (Fig. 61), of the 5th and 6th centuries (Phase 4) comprised Bank II and Ditch II.[3] These are markedly slighter than the other lines. The clay and rubble Bank II was of simple dump construction without the dry-stone revetment which characterized the other ramparts. It was fronted, without a berm, by a V-shaped, rock-cut ditch. These defences covered the vulnerable S.E. front, terminating to S.W. and N.E. with inturns drawn parallel to the natural scarps. The entrance was to the N.E., where the ditch was not continued to the head of the scarp. Beyond the terminations of the Bank II, the remaining perimeter of the enclosure may have been protected by a fence. Within were traces of at least two dry-stone houses. Material associated with this defended settlement constitutes the largest Early Christian assemblage from Wales and the Marches.

Bank I and Ditch I, built in the late-11th or early-12th centuries, after the site had been deserted for three of four centuries, represent the next phase of the defences (the excavator's Phase 5).[4] Bank I was set well within the line of the decayed Bank II, greatly reducing the area enclosed. It survives as an exceptionally broad and low penannular earthwork facing S. Originally it continued around the northern perimeter, along the steep northern cliffs, where it is believed to have fallen away on the collapse of an outer revetment founded a little way down the slope. The excavations disclosed a remarkable sequence in the construction of this bank. Freshly-quarried limestone from the ditch furnished material for the strong revetted front of the bank. Next, earlier refuse littering the site was heaped against the back of the rubble bank. Finally, the weathered masonry from the collapsed Early Christian houses was used to form a stone capping to the top and rear of the bank, which stood up to 1.80m in height and was 9.15m wide. Bank I

---

[1] Alcock, *Dinas Powys* (those sections describing the Dark Age occupation are now reproduced in the same author's *Economy, Society and Warfare among the Britons and Saxons* (Cardiff 1987), chapters 2, 5–9, with supplementary discussion in chapters 1, 3, 4).

[2] For the excavator's rejection of this myth, see *Antiquity*, 1980, pp. 231–2 and his *Economy, Society and Warfare ...*, 1987, pp. 7–9.

[3] Alcock, *Dinas Powys*, 27–8, Fig. 10.

[4] *Ibid.*, pp. 73–79 (and *Economy, Society and Warfare ...*, 1987, pp. 9–17).

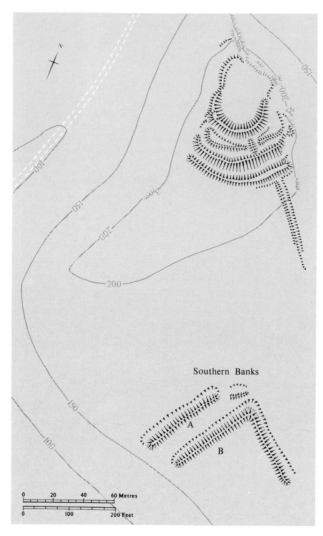

Fig. 60. Dinas Powys Ringwork and the Southern Banks.

was distinguished by two constructional features: its front dry-stone revetment, and a reinforcement of vertical timberwork represented by some 30 or more post-holes cut into the bed-rock (Fig. 61). These were mostly found along the northern cliff edge, beneath the line of the vanished bank in that sector, but others were identified to the W., S. and E. From these post-holes it was inferred that a double row of timbers rose up through the body of the rampart to support an elevated fighting-platform. The bank is higher and wider at the S.W. angle where the timber defences may have incorporated a tower, though large trees prevented the investigation of this possibility.

The entrance was to the N.W. where a sloping quarried entrance passage was contrived between the hilltop and a rock spur. A hornwork set against this spur

compelled a staggered approach, and at the upper end of the passage a pair of large post-holes marked the position of a gate which was probably incorporated in the timberwork of the perimeter.

Ditch I converged with the rear of the earlier bank on the S.E., but was set back from it to the S. and E., isolating small areas of the former enclosure. The W. slopes were scarped, a strengthening not required to the N.

The third and final phase of the defences (the excavator's Phase 6) followed soon after the completion of the inner ringwork, when the vulnerable S. front was strengthened by adding Banks III and IV and their respective ditches.[5] At the same time, these new defences were linked to the ringwork by a roughly revetted causeway, structurally joined to Bank III, but butted against Bank I, and carried across the disregarded primary Bank II, which provided some of its material. These additional defences followed an arc immediately beyond the Early Christian defences, with some encroachment into its ditch. In construction and scale they were similar to Bank I, though some qualification is needed in respect of Bank IV. While Banks I and III were externally revetted in dry stone, Bank IV presented a peculiar inversion of this normal arrangement. There, the outer scarp sloped gently into its ditch, which was feeble and irregular where tested, and the dry-stone revetment was applied to the internal face. This inversion was tentatively explained as either a booby-trap, or as the desperate continuation of building, sheltered from harassing fire by the unfinished outer bank.[6] Bank IV is much larger to the E. than to the W., which, taken with the feeble nature of its ditch, suggests that the outer-most line was never completed. An aborted programme of building is further suggested by Bank V. From a point near the N. end of Ditch IV, this bank runs S.E. for some 45m, beyond which it weakens, to fade out completely 15m further on. There is a ditch along its N.E. side, and one untested hypothesis views this outwork as the E. side of an unfinished bailey,[7] and envisages a withdrawal of the work-force to the shelter of Bank IV, where the internal revetment was built under fire. This theory is bolstered by the suggestion that the

Fig. 61. *(Opposite)* Dinas Powys Ringwork, showing excavated areas and post-holes of its defensive timberwork.

---

[5] *Ibid.*, pp. 79–83.

[6] *Ibid.*, p. 81.

[7] *Ibid.* p. 83.

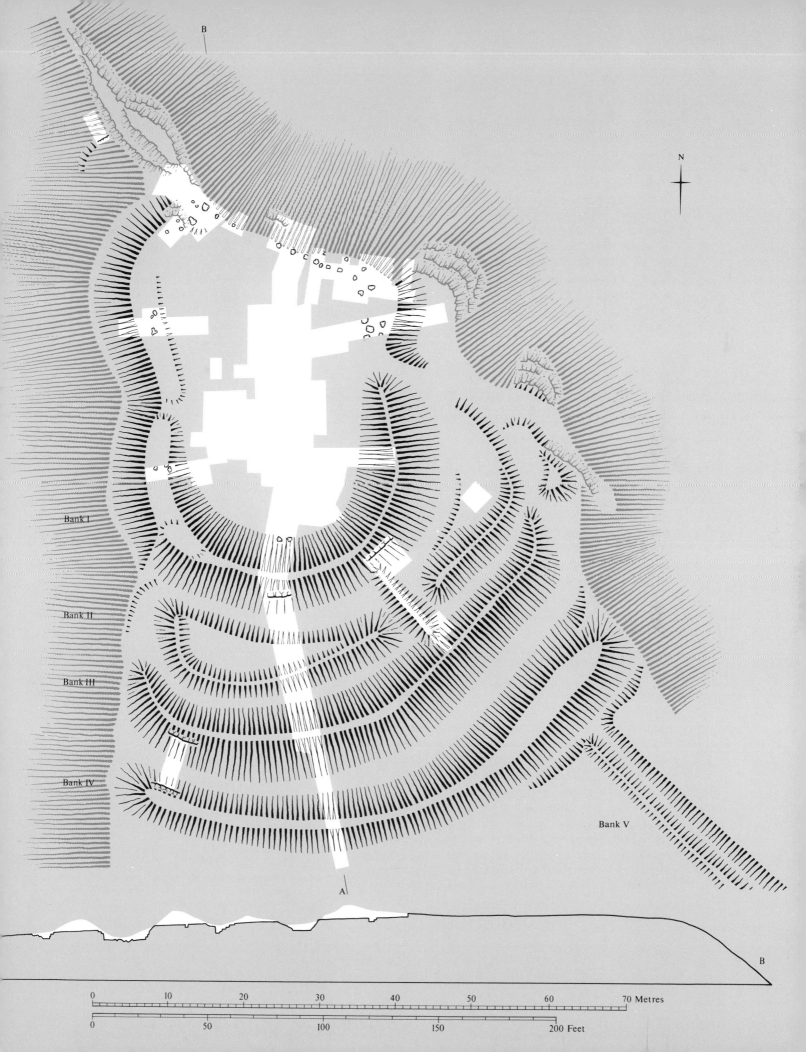

Bank I

Bank II

Bank III

Bank IV

Bank V

N

B

B

A

A

B

| 0 | 10 | 20 | 30 | 40 | 50 | 60 | 70 Metres |

| 0 | 50 | 100 | 150 | 200 Feet |

nearby Southern Bank B was a siege-work.

Southern Bank B is an L-shaped earthwork, its ditch to the N., facing the ringwork, from a distance of 140m down the gentle slope to the S.[8] Its W. arm abuts the western slope of the hill, but on the E. the earthwork fades out on the gently sloping hill-top. The bank had a dry-stone front revetment, and was fronted by a rock-cut, V-shaped ditch. A parallel un-revetted bank, Southern Bank A, lies 10.5m N. of the W. arm; this was shown to be earlier than Southern Bank B, and was assigned to the Iron Age. Though not confirmed by finds, Southern Bank B was tenta-tively explained as a siege-work raised against the nearby ringwork.

The detailed structural information yielded by the defences was not complemented by any evidence for internal arrangements, or by related finds. For dating the ringwork, there were four 'Norman' sherds, prob-ably from one vessel, sealed in the stone capping of Bank I, and assigned to the late-11th or early-12th centuries.[9] Unexpectedly, no contemporary domestic structures were discovered within the massively-built defences, nor any finds to indicate residential occupa-tion. The ringwork was seemingly a short-lived mili-tary strong-point of the invasion period, and was never developed into the normal fortified residence of a lord.[10] An epilogue to the history of the site was recorded archaeologically: its defences were not aban-doned to slow decay, but were subjected to systematic slighting.[11] This was interpreted, in the context of the assumed siege-work nearby, as the 'vengeful destruc-tion' of the besieging force. It is also conceivable that this slighting might have been carried out by the lord himself to deny its strong defences to any hostile force after he had replaced it with a new castle to the S. This alternative would imply a move to the nearby stone castle (EM 1) well before 1150. This stone castle has not been excavated, but its remains are not in-consistent with such an early foundation, and similar pre-emptive slighting is thought to account for the mutilation of ringworks at Castell Madoc (Brecs.) and Ystum Enlli (Carms.), though in these instances the ringworks were replaced by nearby mottes.[12]

Besides the sparse but crucial ceramic evidence dating the ringwork to *ca.* 1100, its structure presents many features comparable to other demonstrably con-temporary sites, which were undoubtedly Norman works, as well as two highly individual characteristics. The building of a complete ring-bank on a site with some flanks strongly protected by nature is not univer-sal, but may be observed in Glamorgan at Caerau

(CR 4) and Coed-y-cwm (CR 6). Coed-y-cwm also provides a parallel for the stone capping of the ram-part. The dry-stone revetments at Dinas Powis are possibly paralleled at North Hill Tor (CR 15), and certainly at the gateways at Penmaen (CR 18) and Old Aberystwyth (Cards.).[13] Slabs in the ditch-fill at Penmaen also suggested a possible perimeter revet-ment there. The extra height and width of the inner rampart at the S.W. angle at Dinas Powys may be compared with the clubbing of one of the rampart ends at entrances at Caerau, Mountyborough, Pen-maen, Pen-y-pill and St. Nicholas ringworks (CR 4, 14, 18, 19, 20), and with the heaping up of one angle of the newly-discovered rectilinear earthwork of Cae-castell, in upland Gower (UW 2). Above all, the timberwork of the inner rampart at Dinas Powys pro-vides a significant feature of the defences, and affini-ties with the double row of timber uprights recorded by Morgan at Bishopston (CR 1), and with those recently identified within the bailey bank at Hen Domen (Monts.).[14] Less elaborate or indeterminate timbering is also recorded at the ringworks at Mounty-borough (CR 14) and Pennard (MR 6), and suspected at Penmaen (CR 18), where it would have linked with a strong timber gate-tower.

The two exceptional characteristics at Dinas Powys are the siting and form of its entrance, and the multi-vallation and complexity of its southern defences. Where entrances are apparent at other strongly-sited castle-ringworks, they usually face the most level approach (*e.g.* Caerau, CR 4, and Penmaen, CR 18), and none display the Iron Age characteristics of the staggered and sloping entrance, with hornwork, at the northern tip of Dinas Powys. The impressive multi-vallation to the S. is also of archaic character, while the causeway and inner revetment of the outer bank are unparalleled. It is rare to find even a counterscarp bank, as at Old Aberystwyth, and, in Glamorgan, at North Hill Tor (CR 15), where a dry-stone revetment is also visible.

Before outlining the scant early historical records

---

[8] *Ibid.*, pp. 4–6, 21–2 and 81–2, Fig. 3.

[9] *Ibid.*, pp. 73, 90–1, 147–8 and Fig. 32. (*Economy, Society and Warfare* ..., 1987, pp. 12, 17).

[10] *Ibid.*, pp. 79, 93.

[11] *Ibid.*, p. 82.

[12] D. J. C. King and Leslie Alcock, *Château Gaillard*, III, 1966 (1969), p. 100.

[13] C. H. Houlder, *Ceredigion*, III (1957), pp. 114–7.

[14] P. Barker and R. Higham, *Hen Domen, Montgomery. A Timber Castle on the English-Welsh Border*, Vol. I, 1982, pp. 29–31, Fig. 16.

Fig. 62. Dinas Powys Ringwork: the inner bank and ditch, looking west.

of Dinas Powys, a traditional context for the castle should be dismissed. A late tradition, perpetuated by the Elizabethan, Rice Merrick, in his account of the conquest of Glamorgan, claims that Dinas Powys was a seat of Iestyn ap Gwrgant and that it was captured by the Norman invaders.[15] Certainly the archaic features of its entrance, its multivallation, the continued use of the Welsh name Dinas Powys, and the archaeological evidence for a final siege and destruction, might all be taken as confirmation of the tradition. This tradition, however, is demonstrably false

in many of its assertions, and worth little credence.[16] Iestyn ap Gwrgant is known only from two grants in the *Book of Llandav*, and from the lordship exercised by his 12th-century descendants in the northern commotes.[17] No acceptable text relates him to Dinas

[15] Merrick, *Morg. Arch.* pp. 12, 23; Alcock, *Dinas Powys*, pp. 89–90.

[16] R. Griffiths, 'The Norman Conquest and the Twelve Knights of Glamorgan', *Glamorgan Historian*, III (1966), pp. 153–69.

[17] *Glamorgan Co. Hist.*, III, pp. 7–9.

Powys, and those commotes ruled by his descendants furnish no fortification as sophisticated, but only four ill-assorted and far weaker sites (UW 1–4). On balance, Dinas Powys ringwork, despite its peculiarities, is best seen as the initial *caput* of the Norman lordship. The continued use of the name Dinas Powys, which may have derived from the earlier site, need not surprise us. It may well have come to designate the territory around, in which case its adoption by the Normans would have its parallels at such castles and lordships as Builth, Pembroke and Brecon.[18]

Dinas Powys was a large and fertile lordship, comprising the entire parishes of St Andrews, Merthyr Dyfan, Michaelston-le-Pit, Highlight, and perhaps Cogan and parts of others. In the 'Spenser Survey' of Glamorgan in 1320 its value of £60 was equalled only by Ogmore and Penmark, and its fertility, registered by its 32 ploughlands, only by the latter.[19] The lordship was acquired by the Somery family, later the lords of Dudley, Staffs., in the earliest years of the conquest of Glamorgan. Roger de Somery appears in 1102 as witness to a charter approved by Fitzhamon,[20] and Dinas Powys was surely his un-named lordship from which two parts of the tithes were conceded to Fitzhamon's foundation at Tewkesbury.[21] In 1166 both *Liber Niger* and *Liber Rubeus* name Adam de Somery as the holder of seven fees of the old enfeoffment, under the Earl of Gloucester. Of these, three-and-a-half fees were accounted for by Dinas Powys, a valuation known from the Extent of 1262, when Robert de Somery was the holder.[22] This valuation is little less than that of those valued at 4 fees and held by de Londres at Ogmore, Nerber at St Athan, and Umfraville at Penmark. Dinas Powys and these three lordships, all on the best coastal land, were clearly the most generous holdings bestowed by the chief lord.

Roger de Somery seems the probable builder of Dinas Powys ringwork, where the negligible traces of Norman occupation material, and the lack of domestic quarters, suggest a briefly-used strong-point which was quickly replaced by the nearby stone castle (EM 1). Such early changes of site are known or suspected in the area. The St Quintins seemingly abandoned an unfinished motte (MO 12) for a better site nearby (LM 19),* and at Penrice the change of site was probably much later in the 12th century, or early in the next (CR 14 to LM 15). The stone castle at Dinas Powys has been regarded as a late-12th-century work, and it is certainly not recorded before *ca.* 1200. Nevertheless it incorporates a large rectangular keep,

and other features, which are not inconsistent with a much earlier date. Excavation here might serve to complement that at the ringwork.

Dinas Powys ringwork lies in the ancient parish of Michaelston-le-Pit and the coterminous sub-fee of Michaelston, successively held in the 13th century by the Reigny and Ralegh families. Joan de Ralegh's extent of Michaelston dated 1307, preserved in the Somerset Record Office, appears to have noticed the then long-deserted ringwork as a prominent topographical feature termed 'the old castle' (*yoldecastel*), and near it 'the old castle way' (*yoldecastell[w]eye*).[23] These names refer to features in Michaelston where the ringwork is the only castle and there is no earlier hill-fort which might have been so-named.[24] 'Old Castle Way' may be equated with one of two old tracks which may be traced respectively for 320m S. and 310m S.W. from points SS 1475–7309 and SS 1520–7283 on the stream skirting Michaelston village. Their projected lines converge close to the N. end of Cwm Gorge, with Dinas Powys village and its stone castle as their obvious destination, after passing in that defile directly beneath the ringwork. That ringwork was surely the nearby 'old castle' of the 1307 extent, a name that might imply an understanding of its former function and replacement by the 'new' stone castle further S.

King. p. 163 (Dinas Powys No. 2)

Michaelston-le-Pit.
ST 17 S.W. (1482–7224) 26.iii.81 47 N.W.

---

[18] For a general discussion of this aspect, see King, D. J. C., 'Castles and the Administrative Divisions of Wales: A Study of Names', *Welsh History Review*, X (1980–81), pp. 93–6. There is no record of a commote of Dinas Powys, but these lesser Welsh divisions are not know for lowland Glamorgan.

[19] Merrick, *Morg. Arch.*, pp. 72–5.

[20] Clark, *Cartae*, I (xxxv), p. 38.

[21] Confirmed by Bishop Nicholas (1148–83): Clark, *Cartae*, I (cxxxvi), pp. 133–5; *Epis. Acts*, II, L170, p. 659. Roger must be numbered with the un-named 'Barons of Robert Fitzhamon', whose tithes were confirmed to the abbey by Henry I (*ca.* 1107): Clark, *Cartae*, I (xxxvi and xxxvii), pp. 39–40; *Epis. Acts*, II, L25, p. 614.

[22] Clark, *Cartae*, II (dcxv), pp. 649–50.

[23] Somerset Record Office, DD/WO 47.1; transcribed and discussed by M. Griffiths, *B.B.C.S.*, XXXII, 1985, pp. 173–201 (the relevant place-names, pp. 180, 192).

[24] *cf.* Marcross Grange (*Glam. Inventory*, Vol. III, Part 2, MG 15) and Stormy Castle (MO 5) for hill-forts so-named in medieval boundary descriptions. The castle within a hill-fort at Caerau (CR 4), though now within the civil parish of Michaelston-le-Pit, was not within the medieval parish and sub-fee of that name.

* But now see postscript, p. 77.

CR 8   Gelli-garn Ringwork and Bailey

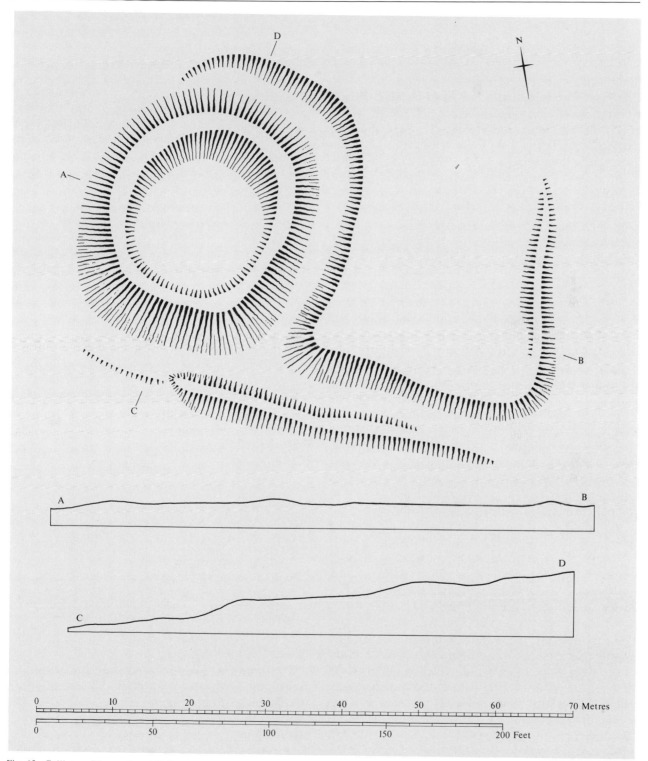

Fig. 63. Gelli-garn Ringwork and Bailey.

Though much eroded, and one of the smallest in the county, this castle-ringwork is of interest as one of five castles in Glamorgan that were the centres of manors granted to monastic houses (see also, Stormy, MO 5; Bonvilston, CR 2; Granville's Castle, VE 2; and Llangewydd, VE 3). Gelli-garn was, by the mid-12th century, a sub-fee held of St Fagans by the Hawey family. Its castle lies at about 76m above O.D. on the gentle slopes to the S. of St Mary Hill Down. Further down this slope lie the hamlet of St Mary Hill, 150m to the S., and the Neath grange of Gelli-garn at 360m to the S.W. (Vol. III, Part 2, MG 16). The parish church lies higher, 670m to the W.N.W. The castle (Fig. 63) lacks natural defences and is overlooked from the N., though it has extensive views in other directions. It has been greatly eroded by ploughing and is now defined by a low bank surrounding a slightly depressed interior. At the crest of its scarp it measures 26m N.–S. by 25m E.–W. An arc of its ditch, much infilled, survives around the eastern side, but as recently as 1963 its whole circuit was complete, except for a gap of 9m to the S.W. To the E.S.E. are vestiges of a bailey, roughly rectangular, and defined by a denuded bank to the E. and a scarp to the S., but retaining no trace of its N. line. To the S. there is a line of ditch and counterscarp bank partly fronting both ringwork and bailey. The site lies in pasture, periodically ploughed to improve herbage.

The sub-fee of Gelli-garn (*Kilticar, Kiltecar, Kylthykarn* etc.) occupied the southern part of the parish of St Mary Hill, and comprised the southernmost component of the territory and member lordship of Rhuthin. The larger northern part of Rhuthin contained another ringwork at Llanilid (CR 12), at 3km N.E. of Gelli-garn. The N. boundary of Gelli-garn is not certain, but to the W. Afon Ewenni formed its boundary with Coity, and its tributary, Nant Ganna, divided it on the S. from Ogmore. To the

W. was Talyfan, beyond the parish boundary. Nant Ganna flows in a broad-bottomed valley some 700m to the S. of the castle.

There is no documentary reference to Gelli-garn Castle, but its military use was certainly terminated by an agreement of the period 1154–83, by which Samson de Hawey (*Allweia*) gave the sub-fee of Gelli-garn to Neath Abbey in exchange for the abbey's vill of Littleham, near Bideford, Devon. This exchange was made with the consent of the chief lord, Earl William, and that of John le Sore of St Fagans, Samson's overlord, and was finalized before Henry II's court by Samson's son, William.[1] Rice Merrick's account of the exchange, citing the cartulary of Neath Abbey, now lost, confirms details known from extant records, thereby giving credence to his further similarly attributed claims regarding Gelli-garn which are not recorded elsewhere.[2] The cartulary, he claimed, showed that Samson de Hawey's father, Richard (or William) Pincerna, was the first lord of Gelli-garn, which he had held of Odo le Sore of St Fagans, and that the exchange of the fee with Neath had been occasioned by Samson '*being disgraced and spoiled by the Welshmen, his neighbours of Rhuthin, and so brought to extreme poverty*'. The grange, with its 10 carucates of arable, became one of Neath's most valued possessions.

King, p. 169 (St Mary Hill)

St Mary Hill.
SS 97 N.E. (9603–7869)   26.ii.81   XLI S.W.

---

[1] Patterson, *Glouc. Charters*, Appendix, No. 245, p. 172; Dugdale, *Monasticon*, V, p. 259. Recapitulated in a confirmation by King John (1208): Clark, *Cartae*, II (cccxviii), pp. 315–6, and IV (dccccxliii), pp. 1200–1.
[2] Merrick, *Morg. Arch.*, pp. 58, 64.

CR 9   Gwern-y-Domen

Gwern-y-domen, 'the marsh of the mound, motte', is aptly named. It occupies a boggy patch at 68m above O.D., 300m S. of the Rhymni River and 2km to the N.E. of Caerphilly Castle (LM 3). No documentary reference explains its location at the southern extremity of Senghennydd Is-caeach. Here it lies in Welsh territory not annexed by the chief lord until 1267, shortly before work began on Caerphilly Castle. There can be no connection between the two castles,

and the ringwork must represent a far earlier settlement.

The site (Fig. 64), one of the smallest castles in the county, is founded on a glacial mound of gravel and pebbles rising some 4m above the marsh. The flanks of this mound have been scarped, and its top was doubtless levelled to receive the D-shaped ring-bank raised around its summit. Across its bank this defended area measures 26m N.–S. by 25m E.–W. A

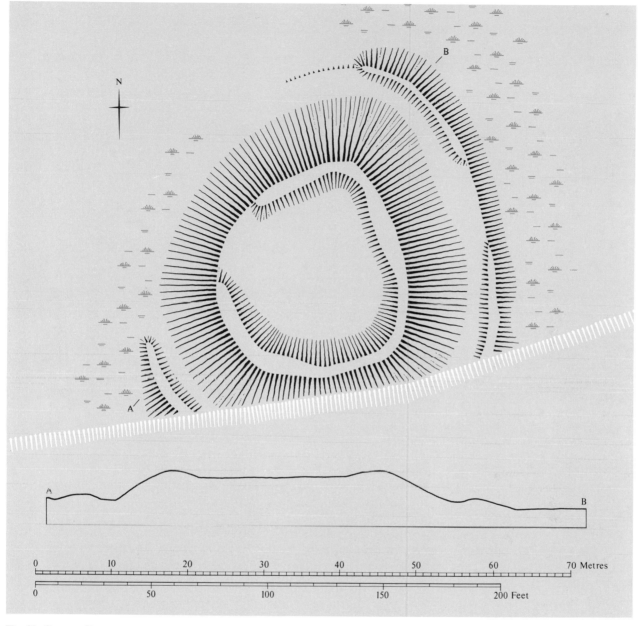

Fig. 64. Gwern-y-Domen.

gap in the bank to the N.W. is presumably the site of an entrance. To the N. the bank forms a right-angle, and to the S., where it faces gently rising ground, it is strongest. A ditch and counterscarp bank cover the E. and S.W. sides, and before the construction of the railway cutting, which clips the S. side, these were probably continuous. There is no bailey; irregular hummocks beyond the railway track to the S. are modern spoil-heaps.

This ringwork raised upon an elevated mound has posed problems of classification. It has been termed a border line case, a hybrid motte-and-ringwork,[1] and most recently it has been adjudged a motte.[2] The mound, however, is clearly a natural feature, and the ring-bank the most prominent artificial feature. It is therefore classed here as a ringwork. Other less elevated hybrid sites, raised like this upon natural

[1] Alcock, *Dinas Powys*, p. 214.
[2] King, *Cast. Ang.*, Vol. I, p. 170.

Fig. 65. Gwern-y-Domen from the east.

mounds, are to be seen at Llanilid (CR 12), Cefn Bryn-talch (Monts.) and Castell Cynfal, near Tywyn (Mer.).

Gwern-y-domen is 11.3km to the N. of Cardiff Castle, but only 2.7km N. of Cefn Onn, the high ridge which formed the N. boundary of the lordship of Cardiff.[3] The site is best explained as one of a group of castles raised by the Normans in the earliest years of the conquest to protect the northern approaches to the chief lord's castle at Cardiff. Other possible military strong-points of the invasion period have been suggested, all similarly unknown in the records, and lying close on the N. side of Cardiff (see Introduc-tion, pp. 10–11 and MO 3, 4, 7, 8; MM 2). Such castles of the conquest might well have been short-lived, as excavations have demonstrated at Dinas Powys ringwork (CR 7).

King, p. 170 (Van)

Bedwas (Van hamlet) (E), Van (C).
ST 18 N.E. (1751–8789)   12.vi.80   XXXVII N.W.

[3] W. Rees, *Trans. Cardiff Nat. Soc.*, LXIII (1930), p. 18–34 and map facing p. 18.

CR 10   Howe Mill Enclosure

This ringwork (Fig. 66) is now so mutilated that its classification as a medieval castle might be doubted. When first inspected in 1961, however, an unbroken crescentic bank continued to the steep natural fall on the N., rising to 1.0m in height to the E., where its line has now vanished. Traces also survived of a bank along the crest of the escarpment, and there were two low outer banks to the S.E. Rejected as a work of the Iron Age, but deemed to be medieval, it was not surveyed until 1980, when only the illustrated vestiges had survived ploughing. These consist of a denuded line of scarp to the E., which continues as a low spread bank at the centre; nothing survives of the W. sector of the bank, nor of the low outer banks or of that

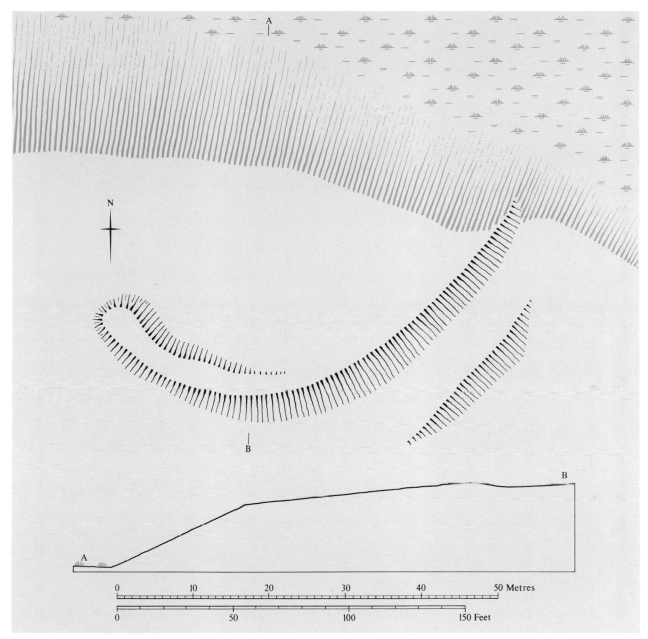

Fig. 66. Howe Mill Enclosure.

formerly crowning the N. escarpment. At its best, to the S., the ploughed-down line is no more than 0.60m high on its outer scarp.

The site lies in the parish of St Mary Church which was part of the medieval fee of Llandough, held from the early-12th century by the Walsh family.[1] Their late medieval fortified manor-house, Llandough Castle (TH 2), set beside the parish church 660m to the S.S.W., betrays no early medieval fabric, and no hint of any early earthwork defences. Howe Mill Enclos-

ure, as the only other presumed castle site in the fee of Llandough and St Mary Church, was possibly the 12th-century *caput*.

The River Thaw, skirting the foot of the escarpment to the N., separates Llandough from the lordship of

---

[1] *Liber Niger* and *Liber Rubeus* (1166), when the son of Richard Walsh was holder; Corbett, *Glamorgan Lordship*, pp. 33–4, 118; Nicholl, *Normans*, pp. 60–2, 75–7.

Llanblethian, where 350m down stream on a similar and facing escarpment is Beaupre (Vol. IV, Part 1, No. 1), a fine gentry house incorporating fabric of *ca.* 1300.

King (not listed).

St Mary Church (E), Llanfair (C).
ST 07 S.W. (0050–7212)   9.x.80   45 S.E.

CR 11   Llandow

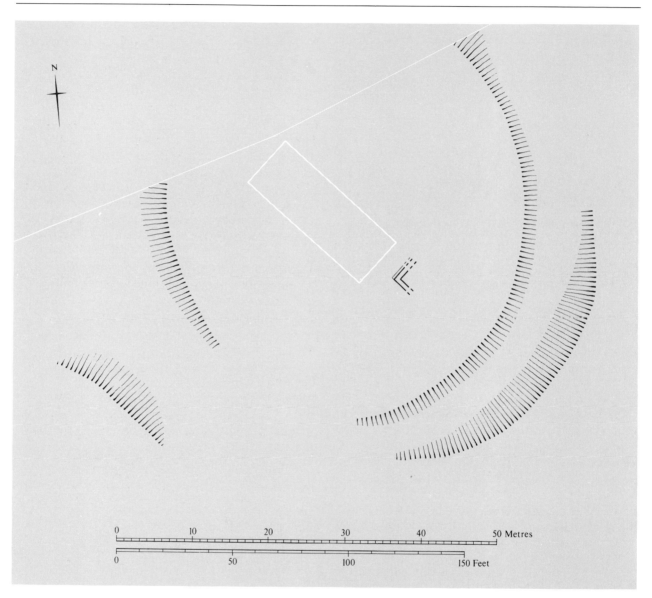

Fig. 67. Llandow: the eroded castle-ringwork.

This castle-ringwork (Fig. 67), almost obliterated by the plough, was sought and discovered during fieldwork in a predictable position, only 100m S.W. of the parish church at Llandŵ. An air photograph had vaguely indicated a circular plough-mark at the spot and, despite long cultivation, its general form is still just discernible on the ground. Finds from the site have confirmed 12th- and 13th-century occupation. A castle was expected here because Llandow was the only Glamorgan knight's fee deduced from *Liber*

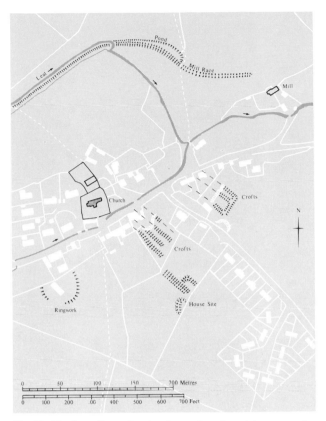

Fig. 68. Llandow village, showing the castle and surviving traces of the medieval settlement.

well-mortared building of late-13th- or early-14th-century date. More significantly, this building overlay rubbish deposits which yielded sherds of 12th-century pottery.

In searching for the castle, traces of the medieval settlement were also discovered (Fig. 68). The remains of crofts and at least one house site are centred 180m to the N.E. of the castle at SS 9437–7330, while a leat, mill-pond and mill-race are well-marked to the N. of the village. These earthworks were discovered too late for inclusion in Volume III, Part 2.

Llandow was held of the earl of Gloucester by service of one knight at Cardiff Castle.[1] The fee was established before 1135, as deduced from *Liber Niger* and *Liber Rubeus*, which list the holder in 1166 as 'Rogerus de Wintonia' (Winchester). Roger de Winton, or successive Rogers, are recorded in various deeds of the late 12th and early 13th centuries. In the period 1148–83 Roger de Winton held land at Penarth of Hubert Dalmary, paying two sparrow-hawks.[2] Roger also witnessed three deeds dated to 1180, 1193–98 and 1202.[3] At the Extent of 1262 Llandow was held by William de Winton.[4] The Wintons reputedly held the sub-fee of Llanquian, in Llanblethian lordship, where there is a ringwork with a small stone tower or hall (MR 3) and where the family was said to have still survived, as the Wilkins, in the late 19th century.[5]

King (not listed).

Llandŵ (Llandow)
SS 97 S.W. (9418–7321)   21.v.82   XLV N.W.

[1] Corbett, *Glamorgan Lordship* pp. 34, 118; Nicholl, *Normans*, pp. 62–3.
[2] Patterson, *Glouc. Charters*, No. 16, p. 41 and n.
[3] Respectively: *Epis. Acts*, II, L192, pp. 666–7 (=Clark, *Cartae*, I (clx), pp. 160–61); *Epis. Acts*, II, L242, p. 680 (=*Cartae*, II (ccxx), pp. 225–6): *Epis. Acts*, II, L254, p. 683 (=*Cartae*, II (cclxxii), pp. 269–70).
[4] Clark, *Cartae*, II (dcxv), p. 650.
[5] Clark, *Cartae*, I, p. 161, note.

Niger and *Liber Rubeus* in 1166, and founded before 1135, for which there was no known castle or acknowledged manorial centre of any date.

Llandow ringwork lies on level ground, but is very slightly elevated above the village and surrounding area. It enjoys no natural defence. A circular scarp, 46m in diameter, surrounds an isolated modern barn, a segment having been destroyed to the N.W. by recent housing. Faint traces of a former ditch are just perceptible to the S.E. and S.W. Immediately S.E. of the barn the farmer had recently uncovered traces of walling, and these were explored during survey. It was clear that the walling represented the W. angle of a

CR 12   Llanilid

This strong and well-preserved castle-ringwork, 53m above O.D. and beside Llanilid parish church (St Ilid and St Curig's), is presumably the 12th century *caput* of Rhuthin, a member lordship in the debatable lands between the Shire Fee on the fertile lowlands to the S., and the Welsh commotes to the N. This lordship

lay in the parishes of Llanharan, Llanilid and St Mary Hill. The southern part of the latter parish was taken from Rhuthin early in the 12th century, to form the Hawey sub-fee of Gelli-garn, centred on Gelli-garn ringwork (CR 8), 3.2km to the S. of Llanilid. Rhuthin was flanked to the W. by Coity, and to the E. by

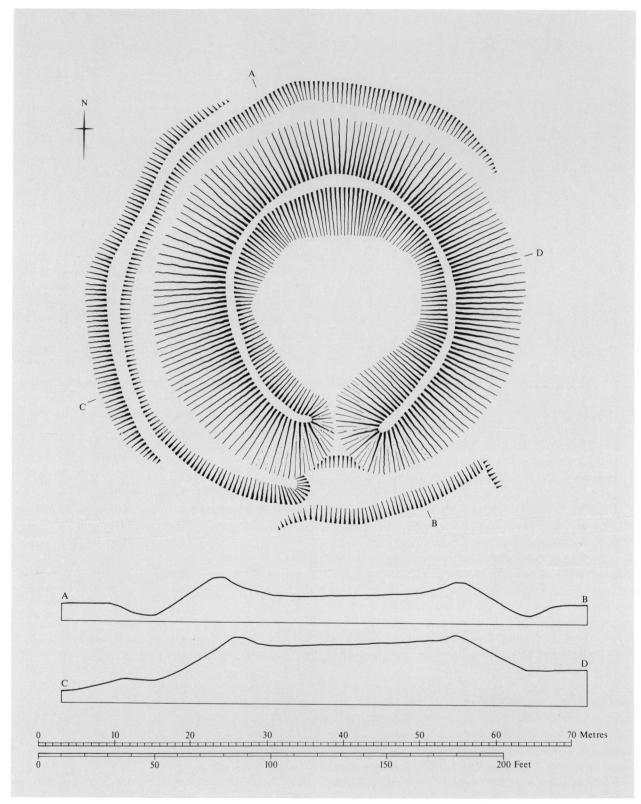

Fig. 69. Llanilid.

Fig. 70. Llanilid from the north-east.

Talyfan, both Norman member lordships, held respectively from an early date by the Turbervilles and the St Quintins. To the N. was the Welsh member lordship of Glynrhondda. The moated site of Gadlys (Volume III, Part 2, MS 5), at 200m S.S.E. of the ringwork, may represent a change of administrative centre on the annexation of Rhuthin by the chief lord in 1245.[1] Another moated site, Felindre (Volume III, Part 2, MS 4), lying 770m to the W.S.W., probably marks the administrative centre of the Hospitaller manor of Milton. The road from Llanilid to Felindre follows the medieval Heol Porth-mawr.

The ringwork (Fig. 69), one of the best in the county, shares a low and probably glacial eminence with the parish church. It is defined by a strong bank, from the crest of which the internal diameter E.–W. is 30m and slightly more N.–S. The bank is strongest to the N., facing a confined area of level ground. An entrance gap to the S. faces the church which is immediately adjacent. A well-marked ditch is only lacking to the E. There is a counterscarp bank to the W. The church may occupy a bailey, but there is no certain trace of one. The site is wooded, and its interior is

4m higher than the external level to E. and W., and 1.3m above the ground to the N. and S. Its elevation suggests that the ringwork was sited on the highest part of the glacial hillock, and needed only scarping, levelling and the addition of the ring-bank.[2]

Rhuthin, like the flanking member lordships of Coity and Talyfan, may well have been a pre-Norman commote, though a small one by Welsh standards. Despite the early loss of the small area of Gelli-garn to the Hawey sub-fee, the remainder seems to have been retained by the Welsh for some time after the conquest, and held by Rhys, the son of Iestyn ap Gwrgant.[3] Rhys ab Iestyn certainly granted the church and land of Llanilid to Neath Abbey.[4] This grant, made soon after the foundation of Neath Abbey in

---

[1] A similar change of site is suggested at Llantrithyd (CR 13).

[2] Gwern-y-domen (CR 9) is a similarly elevated ringwork upon a glacial hillock.

[3] Clark, *Arch. Camb.* (1878), pp. 12–13 and *Land of Morgan*, p. 31; Corbett, *Glamorgan Lordship*, p. 73; Merrick, *Morg. Arch.*, p. 39; *Glam. Co. Hist.*, III, p. 25.

[4] Clark, *Cartae*, II (cccxviii), p. 316.

1130, is known only from King John's confirmation to the abbey in 1208. There is no record of a grange at Llanilid, and despite King John's confirmation it would appear that Llanilid and the remainder of Rhuthin fell to the St Quintins, of neighbouring Talyfan, very soon after Rhys's grant. The well-preserved state of the ringwork suggest that it was probably raised by the St Quintins after some undocumented arrangement with the abbey; other earthwork castles on lands granted to the Cistercians are either much mutilated (*cf.* Stormy, MO 5; Gelli-garn, CR 8), or completely gone (*cf.* Llangewydd, VE 3), reflecting the 12th-century application of their rule in regard to castles, though this had been relaxed by the 13th century, when Margam obtained Bonvilston (CR 2). The St Quintin presence in Rhuthin, though not documented, is made most probable by the lordship exercised there by the Siwards in the 1240s. The Siwards seem to have obtained the St Quintin lands by marriage, and these included Rhuthin, as well as Talyfan and Llanblethian.[5] In 1245 these lands were confiscated by Earl Richard de Clare. Despite an appeal *Coram Rege* by Richard Siward they remained thereafter in the hands of the lords of Glamorgan.[6] As suggested above, the moated site nearby may well have replaced the castle at Llanilid after 1245, under the chief lords, as the house and court of their stewards.

King, p. 165.

Llanilid
SS 98 S.E. (9778–8132)   9.ii.81   XLI N.W.

---

[5] Corbett, *Glamorgan Lordship*, p. 227.

[6] Corbett, *Glamorgan Lordship*, pp. 73–6; *Glam. Co. Hist.*, III, pp. 50–1, 340.

CR 13   Llantrithyd Ringwork

This early castle, in the de Cardiff half-fee of Llantrithyd, is of two-fold interest: it is the earliest of three neighbouring sites which seem to have been the successive seats of the lords of the manor; and excavations have produced significant finds and structural evidence relating to occupation in the early 12th century. Horseland moated site (Volume III, Part 2, MS 7), which probably succeeded the castle, is 600m to the S.W., while 170m to the W. lies the shell of the fine 16th-century mansion of Llantrithyd Place (Volume IV, Part 1, No. 17), the final manorial seat. The parish church of Llantrithyd, St Illtyd's, just to the N.E. of the mansion, has herringbone masonry in the N. wall of the nave, and contains a Romanesque cross-base. A broad and shallow valley separates the castle from the church and mansion.

The ringwork (Fig. 71) is pear-shaped, measuring 56m N.–S. on its largest internal diameter. To the W. its defences have been destroyed by modern quarrying; so reduced, the surviving portion of the interior measures up to 45m E.–W. The defences comprised a bank and external ditch which survive to the N. and E. To the S. only the ditch remains, and even this is obliterated to the S.W., leaving a gap of 16m between its present termination and the quarry. Presumably the entrance occupied part of this gap. Natural defence was negligible, with but gentle external falls to the N, W. and S., and level ground to the E. which soon begins to rise. The site lies upon Carboniferous Limestone, with a soil cover averaging only 30cm in thickness.

Excavations were undertaken between 1960 and 1969 by Mr T. F. R. Jones and Mr P. J. Green, for the Cardiff Archaeological Society, and the results published in 1977.[1] The excavations suggested that the rampart may have had a rear timber revetment, and that it was deliberately slighted, to fill in its rock-cut ditch, prior to ploughing which left only a curtailed line of shallow ditch to the S.[2] Buildings in the interior were found to represent three phases of occupation during the period *ca.* 1100 to *ca.* 1150.[3] The first phase was represented by *Building 4*, a timber-framed structure at the S. end of the site, marked by six post-pits.[4] This was tentatively equated with some form of tower protecting the entrance thought to lie to the S., but it seems rather withdrawn from the line of the S. rampart to fulfil this purpose adequately. In the second phase the extraordinary buildings 1 and 3 were raised.[5] Both were set into the inner part of the rampart to a degree which leaves doubt that the defences remained tenable. *Building 1*, to the N., was a strange

---

[1] *Llantrithyd, A Ringwork in South Glamorgan*, Cardiff Archaeological Society, 1977.

[2] *Ibid.*, pp. 4–5, Figs. 5, 6.

[3] *Ibid.*, pp. 13–14.

[4] *Ibid.*, pp. 10–11, 17–18, Fig. 11.

[5] *Ibid.*, pp. 5–10, 16–20, Figs. 7, 9.

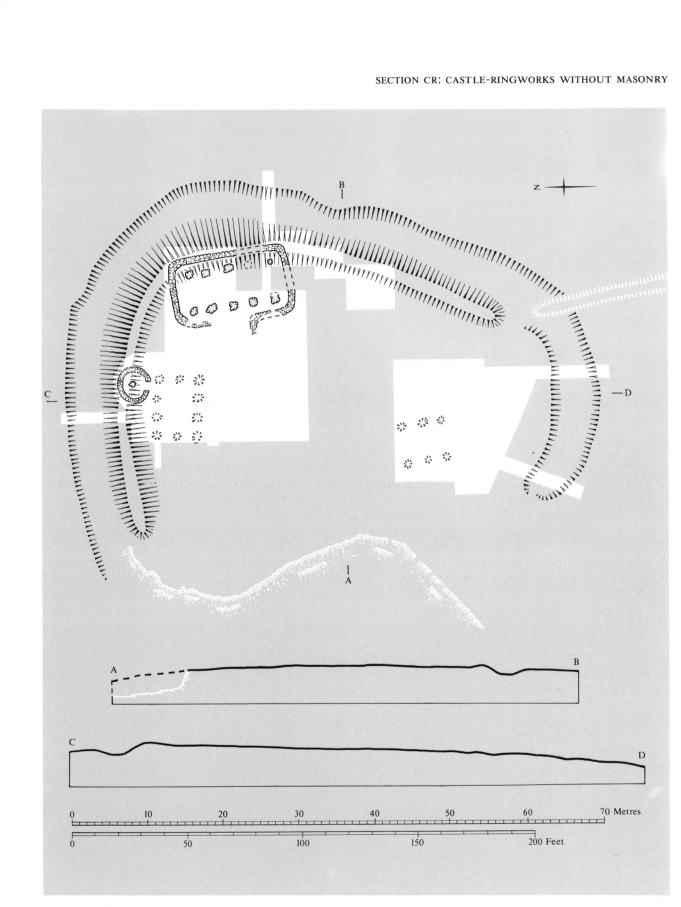

Fig. 71. Llantrithyd Ringwork, showing excavated areas and structures.

Fig. 72. Silver penny of Henry I's Type XI; minted at Cardiff and recovered from the hall at Llantrithyd. *(Now in N.M.W.)*

circular dry-stone structure with an external diameter of 4.57m and a narrow door to the S. facing the interior. Finds suggested that it may have been a detached kitchen. *Building 3*, to the E., was a very large aisled hall of six bays, marked by five pairs of internal post-pits, and contained within a well-built dry-stone wall, which was 90cm thick and had rounded corners (*cf.* Penmaen, CR 18; Sully, EM 6; and Pennard, MR 6). It measured 16m by 10m externally, and was probably thatched, with its rafters set on a low external wall. The entrance was to the W. and may have been reached through a porch. A coin hoard showed this building was standing between 1122 and 1124. The final phase saw the erection of *Building 2*, a timber-framed structure 7.35m E.–W by 5.20m, defined by ten post-pits.[6] This lay immediately in front of the entrance to the circular Building 1, at the N. end of the site, and it was built after the aisled hall went out of use around the mid-12th century. It represents the final occupation of the site, which finds suggest was short-lived.

There was a residual scatter of Roman and prehistoric finds over the whole site, and much medieval pottery and metalwork. Of special interest is the coin hoard from the aisled hall. Nine silver coins of the first quarter of the 12th century from the N.W. corner of the hall were interpreted as a hoard deposited between 1122 and 1124, probably lodged in the roof structure.[7] The coins were all of Henry I (1100–1135), and two were from a mint in Cardiff, dissipating previous doubts about the existence of a mint there (Fig. 72).

The de Cardiff family obtained a half knight's fee in Wales before 1135, as indicated by *Liber Rubeus* (1166), when William de Cardiff was the holder. This half-fee, held of the earl of Gloucester by service at Cardiff Castle, was surely Llantrithyd, on the evidence from the ringwork excavations. The de Cardiffs are known to have been in Glamorgan under Fitzhamon, and may well have received Llantrithyd before his death in 1107, as the first de Cardiff on record is a William, who as sheriff witnessed a deed sponsored by Fitzhamon in *ca.* 1102.[8] The same William, or a successor of that name, was mandated by Pope Calixtus II in 1119 regarding complaints by the Bishop of Llandaff,[9] and in the subsequent agreement between Bishop Urban and Earl Robert, in 1126, a mill that he had built was granted to the Bishop.[10] An early-13th-century mainprise of another William de Cardiff, dating at the latest to 1231, guarantees the good behaviour of his Welsh tenants in *Landrired*, furnishing the earliest clear indication of the proprietorial rights of his family in the sub-fee.[11] Other members of the family are frequently encountered in records of the 12th and 13th centuries, and they obtained further lands at St Hilary and at Newton, near Kenfig. Yet another William de Cardiff held Llantrithyd at the Extent of 1262. The line ended in an heiress in the 14th century, and the subsequent descent of the fee is confused.[12] By the late 15th century it had come to the Bassetts, builders of Llantrithyd Place.

King, p. 166.

Llantrithyd
ST 07 S.W. (0455–7273)   23.vi.81   XLVI N.W.

[6] *Ibid.*, pp. 7, 17–18, Fig. 7.

[7] Michael Dolley: *Ibid.*, pp. 52–56 and *Brit. Numis. Journ.*, XXXI (1962), pp. 74–9 and XXXIII (1964), pp. 167–71.

[8] Clark, *Cartae*, I (xxxv), p. 38.

[9] Clark, *Cartae*, I (xliv), p. 48; *Epis. Acts.*, II, L30, p. 616.

[10] Clark, *Cartae*, I (1), p. 54; *Epis. Acts.*, II, L45, p. 620.

[11] J. Conway Davies, *N.L.W. Journal*, III (1943–44), pp. 126, nn. 157, 133–4 [mis-dated *ca.* 1126 in Clark, *Cartae*, I (li), p. 57]. For the place-name see Pierce, *Dinas Powys*, pp. 121–4.

[12] J. Barry Davies, in *Llantrithyd, a Ringwork in South Glamorgan*, (*op. cit.*, n. 1) p. 75; for another descent, involving tenure by the Bawdrips, see Lewis, *Breviat*, pp. 128, n. 7; 132, n. 5; 140, n. 2; and Corbett, *Glamorgan Lordship*, p. 234.

CR 14   Mountyborough (Mounty Brough)

Mountyborough, the 12th-century castle of the knight's fee of Penrice, is a ringwork, later superceded by the stone Penrice Castle (LM 15), which lies on another site 850m to the N.E. The association of Mountyborough with the initial Norman settlement here is suggested by its location only 80m S.W. of the parish church of St Andrew's, with which it shares the summit of a low glacial hill at 64m above O.D. (Fig. 74). It commands extensive views in all directions, though the near view is somewhat limited to the N.E., along the hill-top towards the church.

The site is entirely overgrown with thorn, bramble and gorse, and survey was possible only after much selective clearance.[1] The plan (Fig. 73) records all

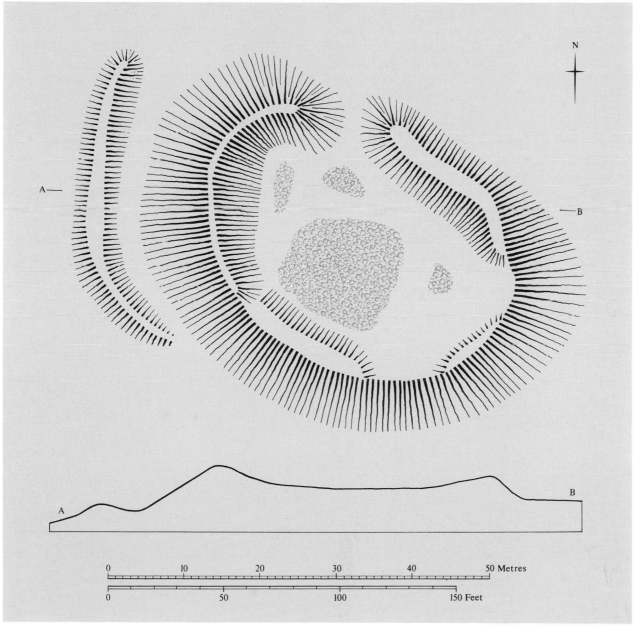

Fig. 73. Mountyborough.

113

surviving traces of the surrounding defences. Internally, no structures were located in clearing survey lines; areas not cleared and inspected are indicated on the plan. The ringwork occupied the highest part of the hill-top, its interior being slightly higher than the ground to the N.E., around the church (*cf.* Llanilid, CR 12). The S.W. end of the hill was scarped down to a ditch, and a ring-bank formed to enclose an oval area 42m by 31m. The bank is highest to the W., where a segment of the ditch and a counterscarp bank survive outside. Such outer features have been destroyed by ploughing to the N., S. and S.E., and by abutting gardens to the N.E.[2] The ring-bank is much lower to the S. and E., with two gaps left above the steep scarping. The entrance is to the N., marked by a break in both bank and scarping. The top of the bank on the E. flank of the entrance is wider than elsewhere, a feature noted at other Glamorgan ringworks, and perhaps devised to accommodate a timber tower, or lesser structure, to protect the gate (*cf.* Caerau, CR 4; Penmaen, CR 18; Pen-y-pil, CR 19 and St Nicholas, CR 20). The termination of the opposed bank to the W. is of exceptional steepness, possibly maintained by a buried dry-stone revetment like that revealed in excavations at Penmaen (CR 18). In about 1927, an intrusion made into the outer face of the rampart from one of the gardens to the N.E., revealed the remains of one, or possibly two vertical timbers set in the old ground surface and rising

through the bank,[3] suggesting the presence of timber-work like that recorded at the ringworks at Bishopston and Dinas Powys (CR 1, 7). Eroded areas of the main scarp show the hill to be composed of glacial gravel, sand and pebbles.

There is no certain trace of a bailey, which could only have been placed towards the church to the N.E. In that direction there is certainly a rise in the ground at the far side of the village green, near the S.W. corner of the churchyard. This quite indeterminate feature is situated where it might betoken the N.E. end of such a bailey, 64m distant from the ringwork, but only excavation could confirm this.

Penrice (Pen-rhys) gave its name to the Penres family, who granted the adjacent church of St. Andrew to the Slebech Commandery of the Knights Hospitallers at some time during the episcopate of David, bishop of St Davids (1147–76). This grant was confirmed *ca.* 1180 by John de Penres, and *ca.* 1200 by Robert de Penres.[4] There is no reason to doubt the inclusion of Penrice in the list of 'ancient knight's fees', established before 1135, in William de Breos's

---

[1] Clearance kindly permitted by Mr Christopher Methuen Campbell of Penrice Castle Mansion.

[2] The ditch was still visible all round, except in the gardens to the N.E., when the site was first inspected in 1967.

[3] *Ant. Journ.*, XLVI (1966), p. 207.

[4] Rees, *Order of St. John*, p. 26; *Arch. Camb.* 1897, pp. 98, 102, 107, 205.

Fig. 74. Mountyborough from the south-west.

charter of Liberties of 1306.[5] It would seem probable that the family which was named after this place, where there is an early castle, and where they have documented associations in the 12th century, was indeed among the earliest Norman settlers in Gower. They survived here until the early 15th century, when an heiress took Penrice to the Mansels. No fabric of the much larger masonry castle (LM 15) to the N.E. may be dated earlier than the mid 13th century.[6] It should be noted, however, that the S.W. end of the castle, incorporating its earliest structure, the round keep, is separated from the rest by a scarp, and that Norman mouldings were claimed to have been unearthed in this area during unpublished excavations mentioned by Clark in 1866.[7] Only further excavation

might show whether this scarp defines an earlier and more limited occupation of the site in the 12th century by the Penres family on their desertion of Mountyborough.

King, p. 168 (Penrice No. 2).

Penrice
SS 48 N.E. (4922–8786)   29.x.82   XXXI N.W.

---

[5] Clark, *Cartae*, III (dcccli), p. 995; *Glam. Co. Hist.*, III, p. 210; *Arch. Camb.* (1924), p. 314.
[6] D. J. C. King and J. C. Perks, *Arch. Camb.*, CX (1961), pp. 71–101.
[7] King and Perks, *ibid.*, p. 101; Clark, *Arch. Camb.*, (1866), p. 280 and *Med. Milit. Arch.*, II, p. 356.

Fig. 75. Mountyborough from the north-east.

CR 15   North Hill Tor

Fig. 77. North Hill Tor: the interior viewed from the summit, looking south-eastwards.

This extraordinary partial ringwork (Fig. 78) lies at the W. end of a large coastal area of north Gower, stretching from Landimôr to Llanrhidian, which had fallen to the Turbervilles by the mid-12th century. The site occupies a rocky headland, 740m N.N.E. of Cheriton parish church (St Catwg's), and high above the extensive Landimôr salt marshes to the N., with wide

Fig. 76. *(Opposite)* North Hill Tor: aerial view from the east.

views beyond over the Loughor estuary. Landimôr Castle (SH 1), a late medieval strong-house of the Johnys family, is 1.25km to the E.S.E. Further along the coast to the E. are the late-13th-century Weobley Castle (LM 20) and Cil Ifor Ring (CR 5), respectively 2.7km and 5.5km to the E.S.E., which are both within the territory held by the Turbervilles.

The limestone headland utilized for the castle rises to its maximum height at its north-western tip, as a

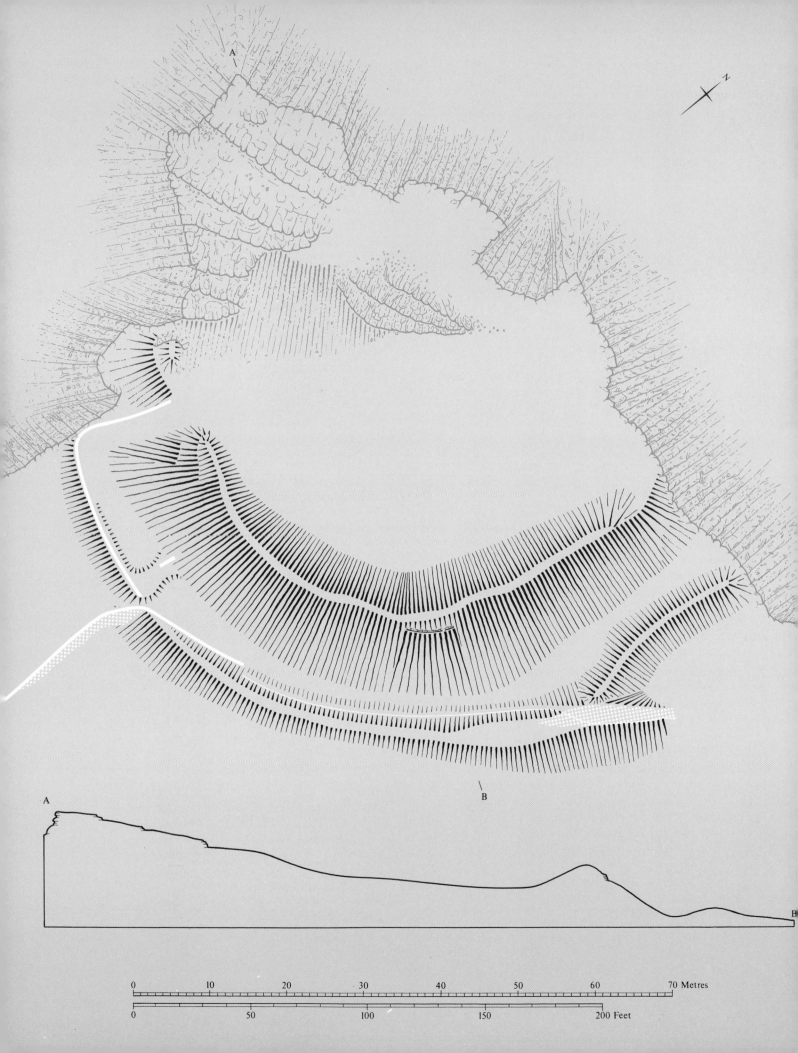

A

B

A   B

0   10   20   30   40   50   60   70 Metres

0   50   100   150   200 Feet

Fig. 79. North Hill Tor: the interior viewed from the summit, looking eastwards.

rocky eminence over 40m above O.D., with precipitous falls to the W. and N. From this quite un-
inhabitable height, the ground slopes back gently to
the S.E., on which flank a massive crescentic bank,
up to 7m in height above its ditch, is drawn across
the promontory. Beyond the bank is an external ditch
and counterscarp bank. Towards the centre of the
main bank, traces of dry-stone revetment are visible
for a distance of 6.5m along the upper part of its outer
scarp (*cf.* Dinas Powys, CR 7). To the W., the inner
bank stops well short of the cliff, to continue, after
a gap of 6.75m, as a short length of much lesser bank
linking with the cliff. This large gap is the only feasible
position for the entrance.

Within the defences an arc of almost level ground
provides an habitable belt, averaging 23m in depth,
immediately to the rear of the defences; there are no
traces of habitation on this area. Externally, the
ground slopes away gently to the S.E.

There is no medieval record of a castle at this place.
The Turberville connection with the area, however,
is undoubted. William de Turberville held one Gower
fee of the old enfeoffment, established by 1135, of
the earl of Warwick, as listed in both *Liber Niger*
and *Liber Rubeus* (1166). Neither of these sources
names the fee listed, but other records show it to be

Fig. 78. *(Opposite)* North Hill Tor.

in North Gower. About 1165, William de Turberville
granted the Knights Hospitallers of the Slebech Commandery '. . . the church of Llanrhidian with its chapel
of Walterston, and the church of *Llandunnor*, and the
church of Rossilly . . .'[1] *Llandunnor* appears to be a
misreading of Landimôr (the church by the sea), the
vanished predecessor of the existing parish church of
Cheriton, which is thought to have replaced the older
church after 1291, when Landimôr church is last
recorded in Pope Nicholas's Taxation.[2] William's
grant was confirmed by Bishop Peter de Leia (1176–
98), and the Turbervilles were still lords well after
the 12th century. In 1335 Gilbert de Turberville issued
a charter as lord of Landimôr.[3] It seems possible that
North Hill Tor may have been the castle of the Turbervilles in the early 12th century, though Cil Ifor (CR
5) is an alternative within their territory.

King, p. 174 (Cheriton; rejected as a castle)

Cheriton
SS 49 S.E. (4530–9381)   6.iii.81   XXI N.E.

[1] Rees, *Order of St. John* pp. 29, 116; *Epis. Acts.*, pp. 362–65;
Arch. Camb. (1897), pp. 101–2, 105–6, 203; *Glam. Co. Hist.*, III
p. 212.
[2] *Arch Camb.* (1897), pp. 203, 211 n. 53, 211; (1920), pp. 316–18.
[3] *Arch. Camb.* (1866), p. 283.

CR 16   Norton Camp

At Norton a partial ringwork (Fig. 81) occupies a blunt E.-facing spur at about 69m above O.D., and 860m N.W. of Oxwich Castle (Vol. IV, Part 1, No. 2), a 16th-century mansion that may incorporate late medieval fabric. Norton lies in the manor of Oxwich, reputed to be one of the ancient knight's fees of Gower, and recorded as such by William de Braos in his charter of liberties in 1306.[1] Its early history is little known. It has been suggested that the de la Mares were the first holders of Oxwich, and that it passed to the Penres family, of neighbouring Penrice, by marriage to an heiress in the first half of the 13th century.[2] In like manner it passed to the Mansel family, along with Penrice, in the late 14th century. The early earthwork castle of Penrice lies 1km to the N. at Mountyborough (CR 14).

Norton ringwork relies on natural slopes to the N.E., E. and S.E. sides. The only artificial defences are to the W., facing level ground, where a bowed line of bank cuts off the spur. This bank is unbroken, but its N. and S. extremities have been mutilated by modern quarrying; no entrance is apparent, nor is there a surviving trace of any ditch. Within the bank a clearly marked house-platform occupies the highest point of the interior, in the N.W. quarter. The remainder of the interior slopes quite steeply towards the S.E., an exception to the more normal level interior, and paralleled only at North Hill Tor (CR 15).

King, p. 167 (Oxwich No. 2).

Oxwich
SS 48 N.E. (4915–8677)   8.vii.81   XXX N.W.

---

[1] Clark, *Cartae*, III (dcccli), p. 995; *Arch. Camb.* (1893), pp. 300–1; (1924), p. 314 n.; *Glam. Co. Hist.*, III, pp. 210, 240.
[2] *Arch. Camb.* (1961), p. 73.

Fig. 80. Norton Camp: aerial photograph from the west.

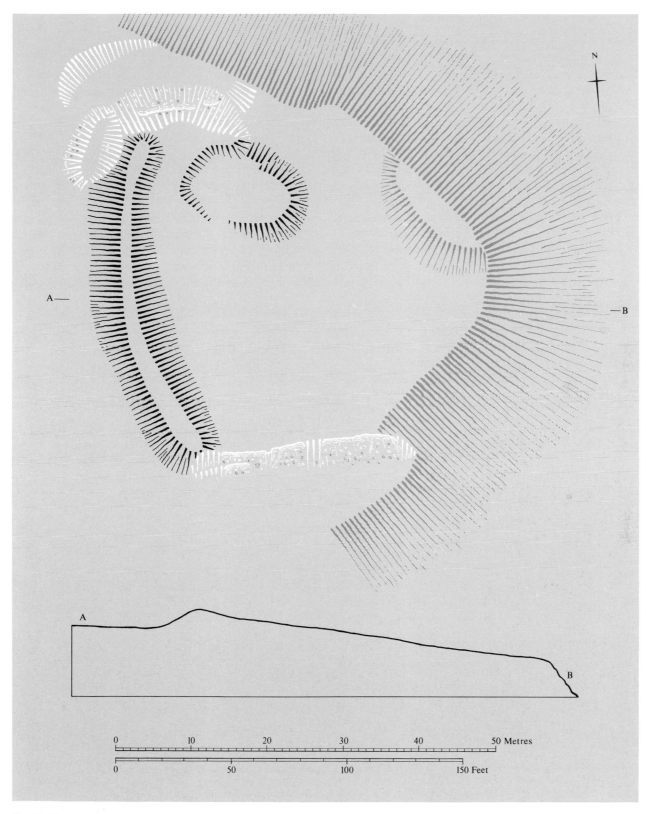

Fig. 81. Norton Camp.

CR 17   Pancross, Llancarfan

The much mutilated vestiges of this ringwork and bailey were discovered during field survey. They lie at 61m above O.D., on the level plateau to the W. of the steep-sided valley of Nant Carfan. The village and church of Llancarfan are hidden from view in this valley, 500m to the E.N.E. Crosstown (Vol. III, Part 2, MH 11), a late medieval hall-house, lies 110m to the W.S.W., while the farm and cross-roads of Pancross lie 300m to the S.S.E.

The mutilated vestiges indicate a ringwork approximately 30m in internal diameter, with a bailey on its W. side (Fig. 82). By itself, what little remains of either component might have been classed as an unidentified earthwork; together, however, they strongly suggest

an earthwork castle. The remains of the ringwork occupy the E. end of a small rectangular field enclosure of recent date. To the S. and E. of this enclosure the hedges have been grubbed out, and it has been joined to the adjacent field, but to the N. and W. its hedge-banks survive intact. The irregular mounds and scarps which define the ringwork defy description, but the slight elevation of its area, and the indications of an internal depression are clear enough. The earthwork seems to have been robbed to raise the modern hedge-banks, and further damage has been caused by ploughing on the S., since the removal of the hedge on that side, its line surviving only as a scarp. At the S.E. angle and E. side of the former field enclosure,

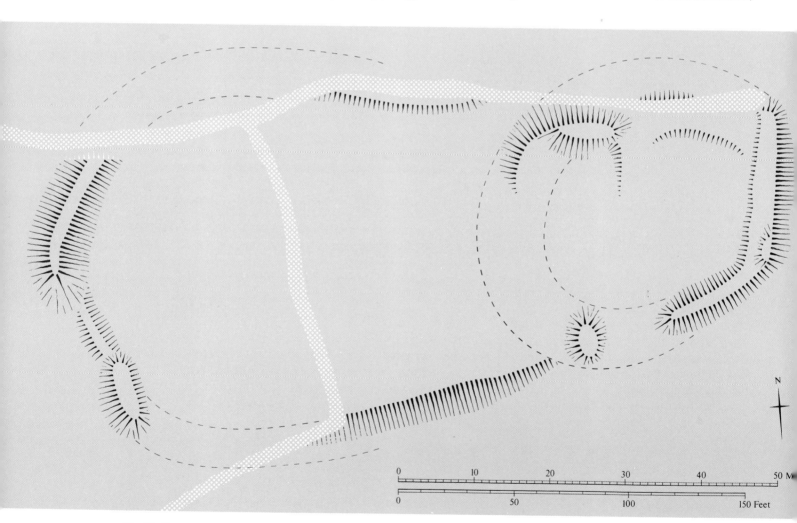

Fig. 82. Pancross, Llancarfan.

the hedge-line survives as a particularly thick hedge-bank, presumably raised with material from the adjacent bank of the ringwork.

The bailey survives as a low curving fragment of bank, much reduced by ploughing, about 52m from the ringwork in the next field to the W. A gap towards its centre may mark the entrance. To the N., its continued line has been ploughed out beyond the hedge, but it reappears, incorporated in the N. hedge bank of the E. field, to terminate 5m short of the N.W. side of the ringwork, where a ditch would have intervened. To the S., it may only be surmised that the line of the bailey followed the scarp marking the line of the former hedge.

There is no record of a castle in this vicinity, discounting the anomalous motte-like 'round tumulus like a fort', on which was erected 'Cadog's Kastil', according to the *Life* of that Dark Age saint.[1] Another mutilated and unrecorded castle in Llancarfan lies just over 2km to the N.E. at Walterston (CR 21). Both castles may be connected with 12th-century Normans, Walter at Walterston, and Payn at Pancross. The prefix 'Pan' derives from the personal name Payn, the remaining element from either the nearby crossing of old roads, or a standing cross.[2] The latter is more likely, perhaps a wayside or boundary cross, on the evidence of a grant of land by Henry de Umfraville in 1186–91. This land was *'next the cross which is situated on the road which leads from Llancarfan to Llantwit, between the two valleys, from the great way to the water of Carfan'*, a description that clearly refers to Pancross.[3] It may also indicate a possible Umfraville interest in the castle site. The Umfraville lords of Penmark, who were among the greater lords of Glamorgan, certainly obtained extensive areas of Llancarfan, particularly in the Llanvithyn area, where they were major donors of the lands which formed a Margam grange (Volume III, Part 2, MG 38). Presumably, a certain Payn was a sub-tenant of Umfraville at Pancross. In the late 13th and early 14th century there was a Philip Payn associated with Wrinston and Michaelston-le-Pit, a customary tenant of some status. His antecedents are unknown, but his successive overlords, the Reignys and the Raleghs, possessed the manor of Llancarfan, and a William de Reigny witnessed the late 12th-century Umfraville deed, already cited and concerning lands near Pancross.[4]

King, p. 164 (Llancarfan)

Llancarfan
ST 07 S.W. (0467–7001)   27.x.76   XLVI S.W.

[1] A. W. Wade Evans, *Vitae Sanctorum Britanniae et Genealogiae*, 1944, p. 47.
[2] Pierce, *Dinas Powys*, pp. 94–5.
[3] *Epis. Acts.*, II, L227, pp. 676–7; Clark, *Cartae*, II (ccccli), p. 441; *Arch. Camb.* 1865, p. 356.
[4] *B.B.C.S.*, XXXII (1985), pp. 180–2; *Arch. Camb.*, 1865, pp. 356–7 and 1868, p. 356.

CR 18   Penmaen, Castle Tower

Penmaen is listed as one of the ancient knight's fees of Gower, in William de Breos's charter of 1306,[1] and excavations have confirmed 12th-century occupation of the castle there. This castle, clearly the *caput*, lies at about 43m above O.D., in a strong position at the point of a promontory, on the W. side of Three Cliffs Bay. Penmaen Burrows, a large besanded area, occupies the land on the W. side of the castle, and dunes cover the site of the former settlement beside the castle. Foundations of buildings have been observed in the dunes, and the ruins of the church, excavated *ca.* 1861, are still to be seen at 280m to the W.N.W. of the castle.[2] The settlement was abandoned late in the Middle Ages, and a new village and church were founded on higher ground about 700m to the N.[3] On the fringe of the dunes, 46m W. of the castle, is a pillow mound, though, unlike nearby Pennard Castle (MR 6), Penmaen has no medieval record of a rabbit warren.

Castle Tower (Fig. 83) is defended by a strong crescentic bank and ditch, facing W. and isolating the tip of the headland. The flanks to the N. and S. were originally embanked to a lesser degree, but slight traces of these banks survive only to the S. There is a break in the main bank to the N.W., marking the entrance. The ditch was cut into the Carboniferous

[1] Clark, *Cartae*, III (dcccli), p. 995; *Arch. Camb.* (1924), p. 314; *Glam. Co. Hist.*, III, p. 210.
[2] *Arch. Camb.* 1861, pp. 362–3; 1920, pp. 279–98. Near to this church is a chambered tomb (Volume I, Part 1, No. 35).
[3] *Glam. Co. Hist.*, III, p. 401. Similar encroachments of sand engulfed Rhosili, Pennard (across Three Cliffs Bay from Penmaen) and, most dramatically, the chief lord of Glamorgan's castle and fortified borough of Kenfig.

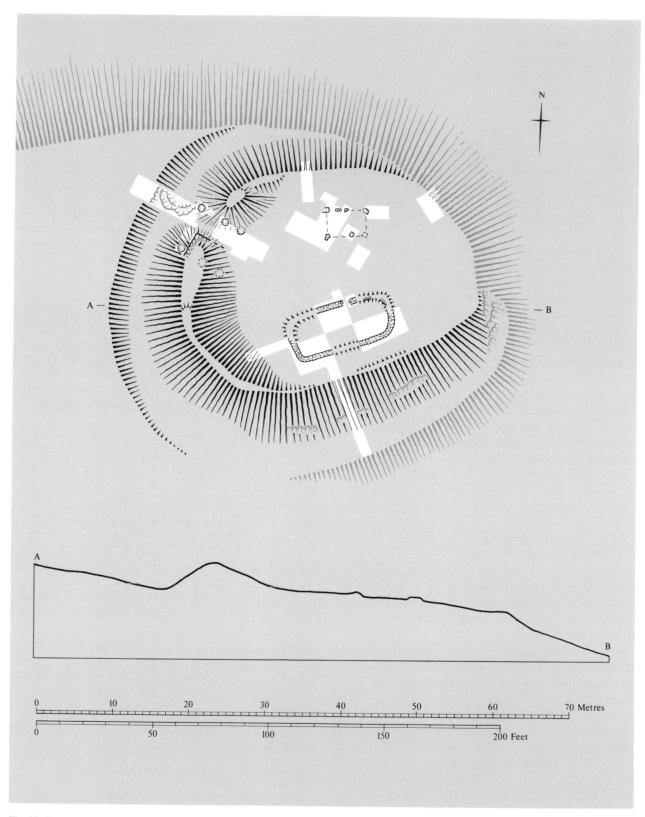

Fig. 83. Penmaen, Castle Tower, showing excavated areas and structures.

124

Fig. 84. Penmaen, Castle Tower: aerial photograph from the west.

Limestone bed-rock. Measured from the crest of the lunate rampart, the oval interior is 39m E.–W. by 27m N.–S. Within, to the N., is a confined area which has been levelled to accommodate buildings. The remainder of the enclosure slopes unevenly to the E. and S.

The site was excavated in 1960 and 1961 by Professor Leslie Alcock.[4] Two main structural phases were identified, the first characterized by buildings of timber, the second by dry-stone buildings. There was associated pottery of the 12th and early-13th centuries.

In Phase I, the castle was dominated by a massive square gate-tower of timber, forming both the entrance and the keep of the palisaded enclosure (Fig. 85). The evidence was sufficiently clear to attempt to trace its ancestry and suggest parallels both in Roman and Carolingian gate-towers and in early Norman stone gatehouses in England.[5] At the entrance, a causeway was left across the rock-cut ditch. Limited investigation upon the rampart furnished no evidence for a timber palisade and fighting-platform, but by analogy with Bishopston and Dinas Powys (CR 1, 7), and given the strong timber gate-tower, such surrounding timberwork is most probable. In the small area excavated on the E. perimeter, above the steep fall at the end of the promontory, no trace was found of a rampart, or of post-pits for a palisade; here, it

appears, the bank has slipped down the slope.

The timber gate-tower was 6m square, and outlined by two parallel rows of three massive post-pits set against the flanking rampart ends.[6] Two of these post-pits on the S. are assumed, having been masked by later Phase II blocking of this side. The timbers held in these pits were of sufficient size to support a bridge and living accommodation, surmounted by a fighting-platform.

In the interior, two buildings of phase I were located on the levelled area to the N.[7] This limited provision of accommodation in the interior may only in part reflect the uneven nature of the ground, and strengthen the view that the gate-tower incorporated ample living quarters for the lord. The excavator's Building T/i was 5m by 3.6m, and outlined by rock-cut post-pits. It was interpreted as a substantial timber-framed hall of two bays. Close on its S.W. was Building T/ii, of similar construction, and possibly a detached kitchen (cf. Llantrithyd, CR 13).

Phase II followed a conflagration which destroyed the gate-tower. The gate-passage was then narrowed, and faced with a dry-stone revetment. At the same time, the bank was heightened, and to the S. of the entrance its top was widened, possibly to accommodate a small tower to protect the gate (cf. Caerau, CR 4; Mountyborough, CR 14; Pen-y-Pil, CR 19; and St Nicholas, CR 20). The dry-stone revetment of the narrowed gate-passage was strengthened or revetted in timber. This reduced passage was about 2m wide, and above it there was no doubt a bridge and fighting-platform. Beyond the gate, the ditch was deepened, and the causeway narrowed.

The second phase also saw the construction of a dry-stone round-cornered hall to the S.[8] To level its site, refuse and rubble were heaped against the tail of the lesser S. rampart, and a shelf was cut in the rock to take its upper long wall. This hall was crudely built, and measured 12.5m by 5m internally. There was an entrance in the N. long wall. The small quantity of fallen rubble suggested a low wall, directly supporting the rafters of the hipped roof, a crude structure in comparison to the aisled hall, also round-cornered, at Llantrithyd (CR 13).

The pottery from the excavation was broadly date-

---

[4] Alcock, *Ant Journ.*, XLVI (1966), pp. 178–210.

[5] *Ibid.*, pp. 187–90.

[6] *Ibid.*, pp. 183–7, Plate XXXVI, Fig. 4.

[7] *Ibid.*, pp. 190–2, Figs. 6, 7.

[8] *Ibid.*, pp. 192–95, Fig. 8.

Fig. 85. Penmaen, Castle Tower: Reconstruction drawing of the Phase I castle by Alan Sorrell (by kind permission of Mr. Mark Sorrell).

able to the 12th and early 13th centuries, but did not furnish evidence for dating the two phases.[9] Some of the wares were comparable with those found at Llantrithyd, Ogmore and Pennard (CR 13, MR 5, 6).

Historical evidence for Penmaen in the 12th century is limited to its inclusion in the late (1306) list of the ancient knight's fees of Gower that were established before 1135.[10] In 1166 one fee of the old enfeoffment was held, under the earl of Warwick, lord of Gower, by Terricus Hareng (*Liber Rubeus*) or Harang (*Liber*

Niger). This fee may well have been Penmaen, for in 1241 Henry III instructed the lord of Gower to restore Penmaen to Philip Hareng, whose father had been disseised during the war between the King and Llywelyn ab Iorwerth.[11] Penmaen, therefore, was clearly numbered among 'all the castles of Gower'

---

[9] *Ibid.*, pp. 199–206, Figs. 10, 11 (E. J. Talbot).
[10] See note 1.
[11] Clark, *Arch. Camb.* (1893), p. 303. No source is quoted.

that were destroyed by Rhys Gryg, ally of Llywelyn the Great in 1217, when the English population was allegedly expelled from the land.[12] The Harengs would appear to have been the first lords of Penmaen, and to have possessed it until their expulsion in 1217. It seems that during the subsequent re-establishment of English suzerainty in Gower a certain John Blancagnel, previously recorded at Walterston (Gower) and Porteinon, managed to obtain the devastated Penmaen fee, for before 1239 he had granted Penmaen church to the Hospitallers.[13] Whether the order of 1241 enabled Philip Hareng to supplant this intruder is not known. Probably not, for in 1320 another John

Blancagnel granted lands in the fee of Penmaen, though an Adam Hering was still a land-holder there.[14] What is certain, however, is that the castle was never restored after 1217.

King, p. 168.

Pen-maen
SS 58 N.W. (5341–8804)   23.ii.82   XXXI N.E.

[12] *Brut* (*R.B.* and *Pen 20*). Two years earlier, Rhys Ieuanc had already taken 'all the castles of Gower' (*R.B.*).
[13] *Arch. Camb.* (1920), pp. 143–4.
[14] Clark, *Cartae*, III (dcccxcvii), p. 1080.

CR 19   Pen-y-Pil, St Mellons (Cae'r Castell)

Fig. 86. Pen-y-Pil, St. Mellons, from the north-west.

Pen-y-Pil lies 1km S. of the Monmouthshire village of St Mellons and its parish church, but in that part of the parish that was incorporated into Glamorgan in 1950. Historically, its Monmouthshire connection is more relevant, for with Rumney Castle (MR 7), a castle ringwork with superimposed masonry, 2km to the S.W. and also brought into Glamorgan, it lies in the S.W. portion of the lordship of Gwynllŵg. This lordship was based on Newport to the E. It fell to Fitzhamon in the late 11th century, along with

Glamorgan, but though it remained with the lords of Glamorgan thereafter, it was always separately administered from Newport's successive castles. While Rumney is well documented, being a castle of the chief lord, Pen-y-Pil is not on record.

The site (Fig. 87) is only 200m S.E. of the main Cardiff–Newport highway, the continuation of the ancient Port Way through Glamorgan, and broadly the line of the Roman road heading E. to Caerleon. Now in the grounds of a recently-built secondary

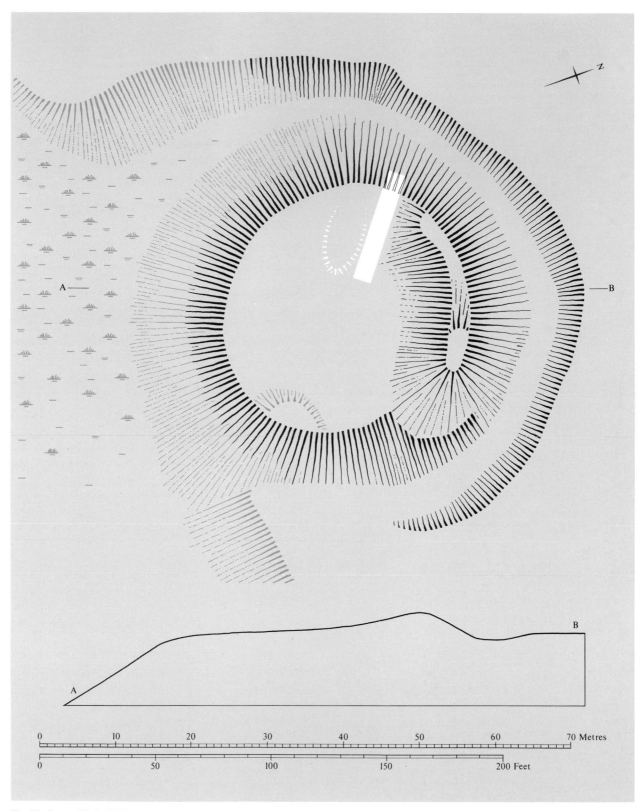

Fig. 87. Pen-y-Pil, St. Mellons.

school, it is protected to the S. by a steep-sided dingle with marshy floor, and to the S.W. by a re-entrant from this. The re-entrant, from its upper end, had been continued as a wide ditch, which described a semicircular course to terminate 15m short of the edge of the ravine on the S.E. A lunate bank, broad and eroded, backs this ditch on the most vulnerable N. side, facing level ground. The circular area thus enclosed measures 33m in diameter, and is elevated above the level ground to the N. and E. Some recent levelling-up has taken place, for plans of 1913 and 1957 show a full ring-bank, broken only for an entrance to the E., at the present termination of the ditch.[1] Above this termination, the surviving bank to the N. of this former entrance is clubbed and raised higher than the rest, a feature of other ringwork entrances in the county (cf. Caerau, CR 4; Mountyborough, CR 14; Penmaen, CR 18 and St Nicholas, CR 20). There is no trace of a bailey.

A section was cut across the rampart on the N.W. side in 1965 by Mr E. J. Talbot.[2] This showed the bank had been raised in two phases; firstly a bank of green marl was raised, then this was widened internally, and heightened by about 60cm, by the addition of red marl. No traces of timberwork were located on or within the bank, but timbers on a different alignment below the green marl bank may represent the burnt posts of an earlier structure of unknown date. Pottery of the 12th century was found.

As stated, the site is undocumented, but it should be noted that Norman fabric has been recorded at St Mellon's church.[3]

King, p. 288 (St. Mellons; listed under Monmouthshire).

St. Mellons, part of (formerly in Monmouthshire)
ST 28 S.W. (2270–8035)   4.vii.80   XLIIIa N.W.

[1] *Arch. Camb.* (1913), p. 85; O.S. Records, 1957.
[2] *Arch. in Wales* (1965), p. 32; *Med. Arch.* X (1966), p. 196; *Morgannwg*, IX (1965), p. 95; *Ant. Journ.*, XLVI (1966), p. 207.
[3] *Arch. Camb.* (1857), pp. 267–9; (1913), p. 84.

CR 20   St Nicholas Gaer

This castle-ringwork is the best-preserved example of its class in the county, and one of the largest. Though reputed baileys have been discounted, as natural features, its interest is enhanced by the proximity of two other earthwork castles, the motte at Cottrell (MO 1), and the ringwork at Coed-y-cwm (CR 6). Cottrell Motte is 400m to the S.W., Coed-y-cwm 1km to the S.S.W. (Map, Fig. 59, p. 94). The latter site is to the S. of the Port Way, the others to the N. of it, while the village and church lie on this ancient route, 620m S.E. of St Nicholas Gaer. The three sites all lie in the parish and lordship of St Nicholas, which was held of the lords of Glamorgan by the Corbets, by service of three knights at Cardiff Castle. St Nicholas Gaer, being the nearest of the three to the church, and the most impressive of them, may be reasonably accepted as the castle of the Corbet tenant-in-chief, the others those of sub-tenants. Lands around Coed-y-cwm were held by the Mitdehorguill family by the mid 12th century, while Cottrell motte was seemingly the *caput* of the sub-fee of Tre-hill, linked with the Cottrell family, though they are not on record there until 1320.

The bounds of St Nicholas lordship are uncertain, but to the W. they shared a common limit with the parish and fee of Bonvilston. To the S.E., partly within St Nicholas parish, the episcopal manor of Worleton (Vol. III, Part 2, MS 9) separated the lordship from the Sully fee of Wenvoe, while to the N. and S. respectively, its bounds are believed to have extended into the parishes of St Georges and Llancarfan.[1]

The castle (Fig. 89) is oval and measures, at the crest of its rampart, 52m E.–W by 44m N.–S., dimensions in excess of those of such important stone castles as Newcastle, Coity and Ogmore (EM 3, MR 1, 5), which all began as ringworks. It lies on a low hill, in a commanding position, with a wide outlook to the S. over the Port Way and the Vale of Glamorgan. Alleged baileys to the N. and S.E. sides must be rejected.[2] That claimed to the N. is probably an old hedge-line, while the platform to the S.E. is a glacial terrace with no visible indication that it was ever adapted as an outer enclosure. The interior of the ringwork is elevated above external ground, suggesting that its strong bank crowns a scarping of the top of the hill (cf. Gwern-y-domen, CR 9; Llanilid, CR 12; and Mountyborough, CR 14). The top of the bank is flat and wide, broadening considerably each side

[1] Corbett, *Glamorgan Lordship*, p. 224.
[2] *Glam. Co. Hist.*, III, p. 446; *Château Gaillard*, III, 1966 (1969), p. 114.

Fig. 88. St. Nicholas Gaer from the east.

of the entrance, particularly to the W. This entrance is to the S.W., where a clear gap is fronted by a causeway. The thickening of the flanking rampart ends is a feature of other ringworks in the county (Caerau, CR 4; Mountyborough, CR 14; Penmaen, CR 18; and Pen-y-pil, CR 19). The ditch is well-marked all round, except for a short stretch to the N.E. which has been filled in. There is a short length of counterscarp bank to the E. There are no traces of habitation within the enclosure, which is now rough pasture. The rampart is overgrown with bushes and fern.

There is no reference to any castle at St Nicholas, and discussion of the early tenure and subinfeudation of the lordship has been contradictory and confusing.[3] The suggestion that the lordship was one of the three-and-a-half de Somery fees of Dinas Powys is erroneous.[4] A Robert Corbet was certainly active in the service of Earl Robert, witnessing his charter to St Peter's, Gloucester, and his treaty with the earl of Hereford, both in the period 1140–47.[5] Though not proof of a Corbet lordship of St Nicholas, this early presence in Glamorgan is important, for no Corbet is listed in the 1166 returns in *Liber Niger* and *Liber Rubeus*, yet in 1262 William Corbet answers for the three fees of St Nicholas, which were by then all held of him.[6] It seems probable that St Nicholas was in wardship in 1166, and so excluded from the lord of Glamorgan's returns, for in the *Pipe Roll* of 1202 Roger Corbet payed 8 marks for an un-named fee to King John, then lord of Glamorgan.[7] As to the subinfeudation of the whole of St Nicholas by 1262, two presumed sub-fees have been treated above. The

third was surely centred on St Nicholas Gaer, the presumed Corbet *caput* of the lordship. William Corbet was not slow to assert his rights after this subinfeudation, for in 1280 he sued Earl Gilbert concerning the wardship and marriage of Adam le Someri, his tenant, presumably the heir to the old Mitdehorguill holding around Coed-y-cwm.[8] The sub infeudation of the three fees no doubt accounted for their specific exclusion from William's residual holdings in the lordship, when these were granted to his daughter, Hawisa, on her marriage to Lawrence de Sandford in 1254.[9] Serious Welsh attacks may well have prompted the Corbets to give up their personal administration of almost the whole of their lordship. In 1226 the Margam chronicler claims that St Nicholas was burnt, and in 1229 it was destroyed again by Hywel ap Maredudd of Meisgyn.[10] Another William Corbet is named as lord in inquisitions *post mortem* in 1307 and 1314, and the name recurs in the Despenser Survey of 1320.[11]

[3] Corbett, *Glamorgan Lordship*, pp. 119, 224 n.

[4] Nicholl, *Normans*, pp. 8, 46. The Somery interest stemmed from a marriage to an heiress of the Mitdehorguill sub-fee located in the area of Coed-y-cwm. Adam de Somery contracted this marriage in the late 12th century (Clark, *Cartae*, I (clxxiii), pp. 177–8; *Epis. Acts*, II, L217, pp. 672–3).

[5] Patterson, *Glouc. Charters*, No. 84, p. 87 and No. 95, pp. 95–6.

[6] Corbett, *Glamorgan Lordship*, pp. 34–5, 223–4; Clark, *Cartae*, II (dcxv), p. 650.

[7] Clark, *Land of Morgan*, 1883, p. 68.

[8] J. Conway Davies, *The Welsh Assize Roll, 1277–1284*, 1940, pp. 182, 283, 304.

[9] C.F. Shepherd, *St. Nicholas, A Historical Survey of Glamorganshire Parish*, 1934, p. 50; Corbett *Glamorgan Lordship*, p. 224 n.

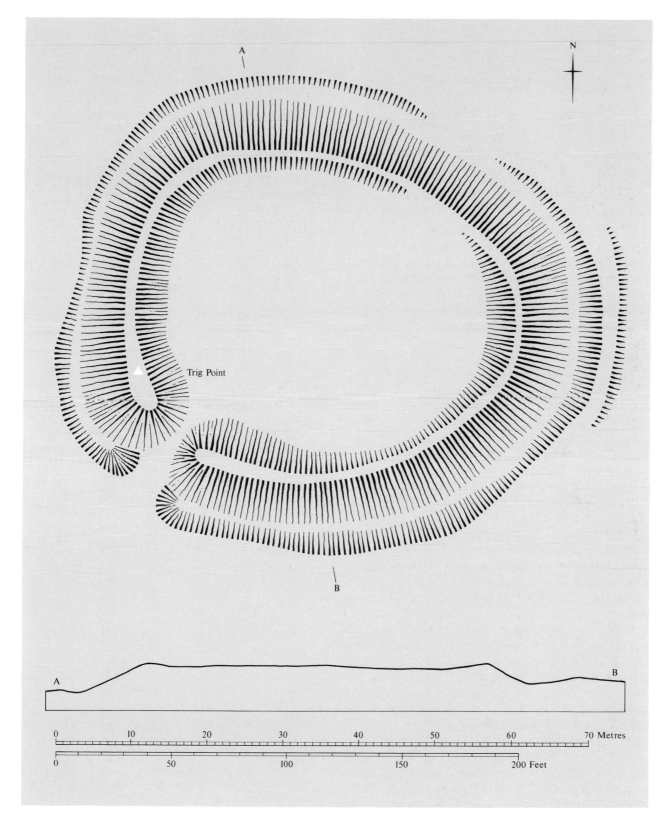

Fig. 89. St. Nicholas Gaer.

131

The main fee, probably based on Y Gaer and the village, seemingly came to the Flemings of St Georges, as a sub-fee, and then to their successors, the Malifants.[12]

The Corbets were probably the initial Norman settlers at St Nicholas, the builders of Y Gaer, and among the earliest to arrive, for the gift of a portion of the tithes there to Fitzhamon's foundation at Tewkesbury was confirmed by Bishop Nicholas (1148–83).[13]

King, P. 169.

St Nicholas
ST 07 S.W. (0846–7476)   23.ii.81   XLVI N.E.

[10] Clark, *Arch. Camb.* (1862), p. 101; *Glam. Co. Hist.*, III, p. 47.
[11] *Cardiff Records*, I, pp. 272, 281; for the Despenser Survey: Merrick, *Morg. Arch.*, p. 72.
[12] Clark, *Arch. Camb.* (1862), p. 102
[13] Clark, *Cartae*, I (cxxxvi), pp. 133–5; *Epis. Acts.*, II, L170, p. 659.

CR 21   Walterston, Llancarfan

The remnant of a partial ringwork at Walterston has suffered further maltreatment since survey (Fig. 91), much rubble and rubbish having been dumped in the W. half of its ditch. Walterston is a hamlet of Llancarfan, lying 2km N.E. of the parish church, and on the E. side of the little Ford Brook. To the W. side of the brook a crescentic bank and ditch enclosed an indeterminate area against the modest protection furnished by its waters and fringing marshy ground. The surviving remnant of this earthwork, to the N., consists of a slightly bowed stretch of strong bank, 50m in length, its E. end abutting the slight natural scarp to the brook. To the W. it has been severed, and its continuation destroyed, to accommodate a large cattle-store. There are no artificial defences along the scarp to the brook which offers little serious defence. Assuming a constant curve in the bank, the enclosure would have been D-shaped, measuring 60 to 70m on its straight side, to the S.E., and about 50m at its greatest width.

During survey a 12th-century rim-sherd was recovered from the severed end of the rampart on the W. This was securely stratified at the base of the rampart near its centre. To the rear of the bank mortared masonry was observed in section, and followed, as far as possible, by trowelling the much-disturbed ground surface within. This revealed the footings of the W. end of a substantial mortared building, its N.W. angle set against the tail of the bank, and its W. gable measuring 5.80m. A sherd of 13th-century pottery was found in its debris.

There are clear traces of a large outer enclosure to the N. and N.W. of the ringwork (Fig. 90). Its perimeter follows the boundary of the field, and is marked to the W. by a low earthen bank, and to the N. by a scarp, both running parallel to but within the field boundary. This enclosure is too large for a

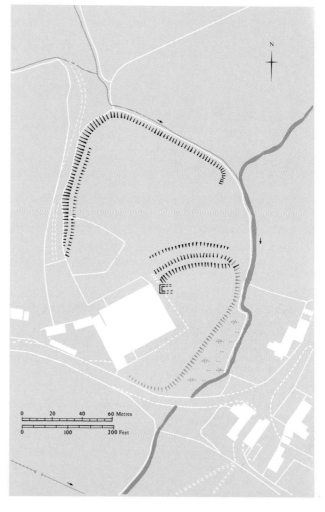

Fig. 90. Walterston, Llancarfan: the castle-ringwork and outer enclosure.

bailey, but it might represent the position of an enclosed vill. Lesser traces of a similar large and embanked enclosure survive beside the stone castle

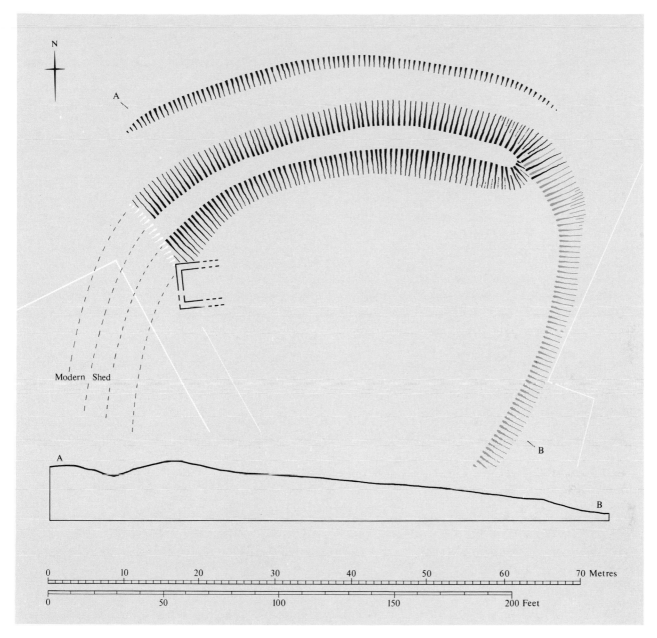

Fig. 91. Walterston, Llancarfan.

at Penmark, only 2.5km to the S.S.W., where it appears to have enclosed part of the village and its church (Vol. III, Part 1b, LM 14). The form of that castle also suggests that it lies upon a primary ringwork, and its lords, the Umfravilles, certainly possessed lands in adjacent Llancarfan.

There is no record of the castle at Walterston. Its first lord may have been the A. de Waltervilla who witnessed a Fitzhamon charter to Tewkesbury *ca.* 1102.[1] This is the earliest form of the place-name.[2]

Walterston is claimed to have been a sub-fee of the Sully fee of Wenvoe.[3]

King, p. 170.

Llancarfan
ST 07 S.E. (0682–7123)   9.ii.81   XLVI S.W.

[1] Clark, *Cartae*, I (xxxiv), p. 37.
[2] Pierce, *Dinas Powys*, p. 103.
[3] Corbett, *Glamorgan Lordship*, p. 181; Lewis, *Breviat*, p. 101 n.

Section UW:
Unclassified, probably Welsh Castles

Monuments 1 to 5

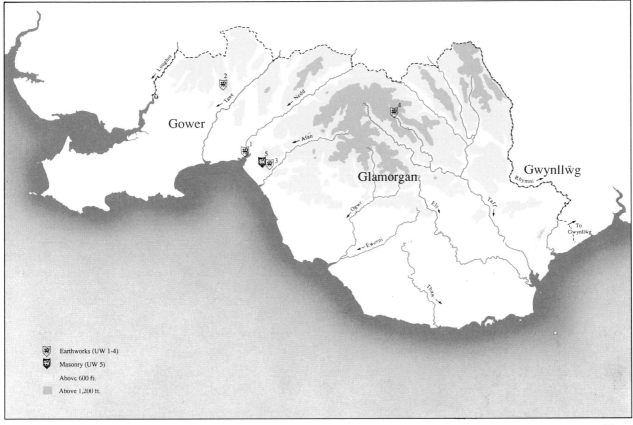

Fig. 93

1	Briton Ferry (Hen Gastell).	3	Castell Bolan (Cwm Clais).	
2	Cae-castell, Rhyndwyglydach.	4	Castell Nos, Aberdâr.	5 Plas Baglan.

Section UW describes five sites (Fig. 93) which do not fall easily within any recognized classes of castles. They do not form an homogeneous group, all being exceptional. That they were castles is postulated from their compactness and the strength of their natural or artificial defences. Two were discovered during field-work for this volume (Briton Ferry and Cae-castell, UW 1 and 2); another was previously regarded as a late medieval domestic ruin (Plas Baglan, UW 5). Only Castell Bolan (UW 3) is clearly intended to be a motte, though it is so aberrant as to be better placed in this section. Even more aberrant reflections of the motte are vaguely suggested by the raised and thickened rampart at an angle of Cae-castell (UW 2), and by the citadels formed by the economical scarping of natural outcrops at Briton Ferry and Castell Nos (UW 1 and 4). The square walled platform of Plas Baglan (UW 5) in no way resembles a motte, but it does dominate a subordinate lower shelf which may have constituted a bailey; it is also the only one which is of masonry. The other four are earthworks, though this term fits ill with the rocky sites at Briton Ferry and Castell Nos (UW 1 and 4).

The exceptional nature of each of these sites is one

Fig. 92. *(Opposite)* Castell Nos (UW 4) viewed from the south-east.

135

reason for suspecting that they are Welsh and not Anglo-Norman works. Their locations strengthen this suspicion; with one exception, all lie in territory indisputably Welsh until the mid 13th century or later, while the exception, Briton Ferry (UW 1), may be identified as a Welsh mid-12th-century castle of Morgan ap Caradog ab Iestyn, lord of Afan. The only other documentary reference which might be related to any of these castles is less specific; it concerns the castle of Morgan Gam (lord of Afan *ca.* 1217 to *ca.* 1241), mentioned in 1245 and relating probably to Plas Baglan (UW 5).

Of the five sites, only one lies in the lordship of Gower. This site, Cae-castell (UW 2), is remotely set in the uplands of Gower Wallicana, and is the only castle in the lordship that can be attributed to the Welsh. Of the other four sites, all in the lordship of Glamorgan, Castell Nos (UW 4) stands apart in the northern uplands of the commote of Meisgyn, and so seems Welsh. The remaining three sites lie near the coast, not far from the estuaries of the Nedd and Afan rivers, but must all be works of the Welsh lords of Afan. These are Briton Ferry (UW 1) in Neath Ultra and both Castell Bolan and Plas Baglan (UW 3 and 5) in Afan. Taken with the two castles at Neath (VE 2 and LM 11) and that at Aberafan (VE 1), these form a most interesting group of crucial relevance to any understanding of the ill-recorded Norman settlement of this western extremity of the lordship of Glamorgan. This group of castles is plotted on Fig. 94. The castles at Neath are the vanished Granville's castle (VE 2), to the W. of the river, and Neath Castle (LM 11), the castle of the lords of Glamorgan on the E. bank. Aberafan Castle (VE 1), another vanished Castle, lay near the mouth of the Afan.

The valuable but largely mythical account of the Norman conquest of Glamorgan related in the 16th century by Llwyd, Stradling, Powel and Merrick is particularly unreliable in regard to the territories of Neath and Afan.[1] Robert Fitzhamon, they claimed, bestowed Neath on Richard de Granville, and Afan on Caradog, son of the vanquished Prince of Morgannwg, Iestyn ap Gwrgant. Although these early historians utilized documents now lost to us, as well as others which survive confirming some of their claims, much is fable and the chronology unsupported. There is nothing to confirm any Norman influence in Neath and Afan in the time of Fitzhamon.[2] By the time of his death in 1107 it is only certain that his dominion extended over the coastal plain as far as the Ogmore valley, and marginally beyond that

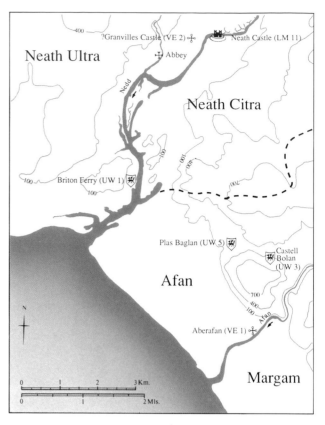

Fig. 94. Castles in the Neath-Aberafan area.

river only in the vicinity of Newcastle, Bridgend (EM 3), a castle he had established by 1106. Expansion further W. was undertaken in the time of Earl Robert of Gloucester, after his marriage to the heiress, Mabel, *ca.* 1114. Earl Robert brought with him to Glamorgan the commander of the knights of his household, his constable, Richard de Granville.[3] At some time between 1114 and 1130 de Granville established himself at Neath, on the W. side of the river, where he built a castle (VE 2) that was probably within or near the Roman fort (Vol. I, Part 2, No. 734). This advance must have been undertaken in concert with Earl Robert when he established Neath Castle (LM 11) on the E. bank of the river, opposite de Granville's castle. Neath Castle survives as a 13th-century stone structure, but its circular plan betrays an earlier castle-ringwork on the site. In establishing these castles at Neath between 1114 and 1130, Earl Robert and

---

[1] R. A. Griffiths, *Glamorgan Historian* III (1966), pp. 153–69, for detailed discussion of the traditional accounts.

[2] For recent analyses of the evidence, see *Glam. Co. Hist.*, III, chapter I; *Morgannwg*, II (1958), pp. 9–37.

[3] See VE 2, p. 156, note 2.

Richard de Granville were no doubt following up the foundation of the demesne castle at Kenfig (EM 2), which is attributed to this period. In their advance W. to Neath they would have followed the Roman road along the confined coastal strip between the Afan and Nedd rivers, traversing the commote of Afan. This commote was certainly held at that time by Caradog ab Iestyn, though not by any grant by Fitzhamon, as 16th-century historians claimed. Having established their castles at Neath, the Normans could not have ignored the vital importance of their narrow line of communication with the Glamorgan heartlands along the Afan coastal tract (Fig. 94). The very creation of the demesne lordship of Neath appears to be a clear encroachment upon the ancient commote of Afan, which was surely bounded by the two rivers. To hold this annexed land it seems inconceivable that the coastal strip was not also annexed, a view strengthened by the single 12th-century reference to the castle at Aberafan (VE 1), which contradicts the usual claim that Aberafan was a castle founded by the Welsh lords of Afan. In 1153 the *Bruts* notice the destruction of that castle, with great slaughter, by Rhys ap Gruffydd of Deheubarth, brother-in-law of Caradog ab Iestyn. Caradog had died before this, but it must be noted that Rhys attacked Aberafan after a wide-ranging campaign against Norman castles in West Wales, and that Caradog's son and successor is recorded as a staunch adherent of his uncle. The Aberafan Castle destroyed in 1153 was surely a Norman base on the vital route serving Neath and its frontier settlers, particularly as there is some evidence of lands in its vicinity having been given to a certain William Fitzhenry by Earl William (1147–83).[4] There is no evidence to suggest that the Welsh lords of Afan had established themselves at Aberafan after the 1153 attack and the 1262 Extent names their territory Baglan, not Afan, implying that Plas Baglan was then their administrative centre. It was perhaps only after the foundation of their borough at Aberafan by Leisan ap Morgan Fychan *ca.* 1304 that the 12th-century castle was rebuilt, apparently in masonry. Thereafter, Aberafan would have been the obvious administrative centre of the lords of Afan, by then thoroughly anglicized and styled *de Avene*, while Plas Baglan had certainly passed to a cadet branch soon after.

With the annexation of the coastal strip, along with Neath Ultra and Neath Citra, between 1114 and 1130, only the adjacent hill country was left to Caradog ab Iestyn. Initial arrangements did not long survive, for in 1130 de Granville granted his castle and lands

in Neath Ultra to the abbey he then founded there. It was perhaps to bolster his now unsupported frontier castle at Neath that Earl William granted lands on the coastal strip to William Fitzhenry. Meanwhile, in their truncated commote, Caradog and his son Morgan presumably ruled from Plas Baglan, while neighbouring Castell Bolan must have been in their possession or that of a close follower. The lost cartulary of Neath Abbey, quoted by Rice Merrick, informs us that Morgan ap Caradog, who succeeded to Afan *ca.* 1147, built the recently identified castle at Briton Ferry (UW 1), in order to control the river-crossing, and by implication the traffic along the coastal strip. If we are correct in believing that the Aberafan Castle destroyed by Rhys ap Gruffydd in 1153 was Norman, this event perhaps gave Morgan the opportunity of extending his influence to the coast, though with Neath still in the hands of the chief lord, a degree of reluctant acquiescence in this Welsh advance must be assumed, particularly as Briton Ferry was a possession of Neath Abbey; the W. bank, where the castle was built by Morgan, had been part of de Granville's gift, while the E. bank (Llansawel) was the gift of Earl Robert. Morgan certainly held authority over the ferry and coastal route in 1188, when as 'prince of those parts' he conducted Gerald and Archbishop Baldwin along the coast and over both rivers.

Morgan's ambitions were far from achieved with his advance to the coastal highway. On the death of Earl William in 1183 he was soon in arms, and attacked Neath, Kenfig and Newcastle, Bridgend. As a result of these ventures Newcastle was ceded to him, and remained with his successors for several decades, but no concessions were made at Neath, and no further adjustments to the territorial arrangements in Neath-Afan are discerned before the Welsh lords of Afan finally exchanged their lands with the chief lord in the late 14th century.

* * * * *

The five sites described here make up the only Section entirely devoted to castles thought to be Welsh. Apart from these there are very few other castles in the county which may also be Welsh, and they fall into other recognized classes and are therefore described in the relevant Sections. Before noting these,

---

[4] Patterson, *Glouc. Charters*, No. 221, p. 171 (see VE 1, notes 12, 13).

a general statement on Welsh castles is necessary.

In all parts of Wales, Welsh castles are greatly out-numbered by those of the Anglo-Normans. A recent study has identified 319 earthwork castles in Wales, made up of 242 mottes and seventy-seven castle-ringworks.[5] Of the 319 earthwork castles, only eighty-five furnish any evidence for the date and circum-stances of their foundation (sixty-three mottes and twenty-two castle-ringworks), and only eleven of the eighty-five were Welsh. Welsh masonry castles are even rarer: before 1200 there were records of only the four or five stone castles of the Lord Rhys of Deheubarth (the scantiest of vestiges surviving of only two) and three or four crude masonry structures in Gwynedd. Welsh stone castles of the 13th century, most notably the eleven raised by the two Llywelyns of Gwynedd,[6] are even more clearly outnumbered by English works.

In Glamorgan, the rarity of Welsh castles is particu-larly evident. Section MO describes twelve mottes and notes four others underlying later masonry castles. Of these only two might be attributed to the Welsh, namely the remnant of a motte at Ynyscrug (MO 11), in Glynrhondda commote, and Twyn Castell (MO 9) at Gelli-gaer, in Senghennydd Is-caeach commote. Set deep in the uplands, both sites are surely Welsh, especially Twyn Castell, an unusually small motte which may be the castle of Cadwallon, son of Ifor Bach, recorded in the *Pipe Rolls* of 1197–98. Ynyscrug, a mere fragment of a much larger motte, has no known record. Much further to the S. seven other mottes form an arc to the N. of Cardiff, but although in Meisgyn or Senghennydd Is-caeach on land held by the Welsh until the mid-13th century, these are likely to be temporary Norman castles of the earliest years of the invasion (Introduction, pp. 10–11 and p. 52).

Section CR describes twenty-one castle-ringworks and notes fifteen others known or suspected beneath later masonry castles. It is most unlikely that any of these were built by the Welsh. Only at Llanilid (CR 12) is there a slight hint of a Welsh origin: the church beside this fine castle-ringwork was granted to Neath Abbey soon after 1130 by Rhys ab Iestyn, brother of Caradog, lord of Afan. The grant, however, men-tions no castle, and this well-preserved site appears to be the *caput* of the St Quintin fee of Rhuthin, which was established in the area soon after Rhys's grant. Mention should also be made here of the castle-ringwork, strictly a hybrid 'ring-motte', at Gwern-y-domen, near Caerphilly (CR 9). This lies in Senghen-

nydd Is-caech but is to be regarded as a Norman site of the invasion period, part of that screen to the N. of Cardiff and the only site among them which was not a normal motte.

Four vanished early castles are described in Section VE. Of these, only Aberafan (VE 1) has been held to have been a Welsh castle from its foundation, but for reasons given above seems to have originated as a Norman castle, probably a motte, that was certainly destroyed in a Welsh attack in 1153, but was eventually rebuilt in stone by the Welsh lords of Afan when they founded the borough of Aberafan *ca.* 1304.

Masonry castles in Glamorgan are overwhelmingly Anglo-Norman. Excluding tower-houses, strong-houses and the many possible stone castles in-corporated in later domestic work, there are thirty-seven undoubted masonry castles in the county. The only certain stone castle of the Welsh surviving in the county is Plas Baglan (UW 5), described in this section, to which we might add the late stone castle of Aberafan (VE 1), mentioned above. Otherwise, only the uncompleted Morgraig (LM 9) has been seriously or authoritatively considered as a Welsh castle.[7] Morgraig lies on the ridge which dominates Cardiff from the N., and it has been argued that it was a castle of the last Welsh prince of Senghennydd, built in the mid 13th century in the unsettled period before Gilbert de Clare annexed Senghennydd and reinforced his Conquest by raising the giant Caer-philly a little to the N., thereby rendering the unfi-nished Morgraig obsolete. This period for the construction of Morgraig seems certain. Its nature is certainly quite extraordinary, favouring the Welsh attribution, but its size, strength and bold siting, totally dominating Cardiff, make it difficult to envis-age as a native castle permitted by the Clare earls.

One Norman masonry castle deserves mention here, as for a period it became a Welsh castle. New-castle, Bridgend (EM 3) was founded by Fitzhamon before 1106 and rebuilt in masonry *ca.* 1184. It is noteworthy as a major castle ceded to a Welsh prince

---

[5] C. J. Spurgeon, 'Mottes and Castle-ringworks in Wales', in *Castles in Wales and the Marches, Essays in Honour of David Cath-cart King*, Cardiff, U.W.P., 1987, pp. 23–49.

[6] R. Avent, *Castles of the Princes of Gwynedd*, H.M.S.O., Cardiff, 1983 gives an illustrated account of Welsh stone castles in North Wales and a brief discussion of Welsh earthwork castles.

[7] King, *Cast. Ang.*, I, p. 163; *Trans. Cardiff Nat. Soc.*, XXXVIII (1905), pp. 20–58, reports excavations that showed it to be un-finished; C. N. Johns, *Caerphilly Castle* (Official Guidebook, 1978), p. 4.

and retained for 30 years or more. This success was achieved by Morgan ap Caradog, lord of Afan, who directed the Welsh uprising following the death of Earl William in 1183. The castle, apparently only recently refurbished in stone, was presumably ceded in some settlement of hostilities. It passed to his heir *ca.* 1207, but was never conveyed to his younger son who succeeded *ca.* 1214.

Four castles are traditionally claimed to have been Welsh in origin. Merrick claims Cardiff Castle (MM 1) and Dinas Powys Castle (EM 1) were strongholds of Iestyn ap Gwrgant. Others have regarded Coity Castle (MR 1) and Castell Coch (LM 4) as castles first raised by Welsh princes, the latter usually being attributed to Ifor Bach of Senghennydd. No evidence supports any of these traditions. It is probable that Cardiff Castle was founded by William the Conqueror in 1081, while Dinas Powys was certainly the work

of the Somerys, replacing the nearby ringwork of the same name (CR 7) which was probably the primary castle in their fee. Coity Castle can only be reasonably ascribed to the Turberville lords of Coity, and Castell Coch is a 13th-century stone castle of the Clares, perhaps overlaying a Norman motte of the invasion period.

To sum up, only the mottes at Gelligaer and Ynyscrug (MO 9, 11), and the vanished 14th-century masonry castle at Aberafan (VE 1) might be considered as purely Welsh Castles to add to the five described in this section. These eight castles are small and of simple if varied form, with only two of stone and four clustered together in Neath-Afan to the W. Compared with these, the larger and altogether more accomplished masonry castle of Morgraig (LM 9), despite its abnormal features, is not easily viewed as a Welsh work.

UW 1 Briton Ferry (Hen Gastell)

Morgan ap Caradog ab Iestyn, Welsh lord of Afan throughout the second half of the 12th century, is said to have built a castle on a steep hill in Cadoxton-juxta-Neath (Llangatwg Nedd) and close to the dangerous crossing of the Nedd at Briton Ferry, which focus of coastal communications it was to control. The authority for the building of this Welsh castle is the Register of Neath Abbey, now lost but cited by Rice Merrick.[1] The unrecorded vestiges of defences here described agree with the lost Register in their location and are of a character best ascribed to the Welsh. The testimony of Gerald of Wales endorses Morgan's reputed control of the ferry, for in March 1188 the archdeacon and Archbishop Baldwin made the hazardous crossing of the Nedd with Morgan ap Caradog, 'the prince of those parts', as their guide and leader.[2] The ancient ferry, *passagium de Briton* (1289) or *passagium aquae de Bruttone* (1307), was a valued asset of later lords of Glamorgan.[3] It was sited 1km above the mouth of the river and just S. of the modern road viaduct. At this point the river is flanked by two isolated hills. Warren Hill, on the E. bank, is crowned by vestiges of an Iron Age hill-fort (Vol. I, Part 2, No. 628). The hill on the W. side is a smaller but more abrupt and equally elevated outcrop of Pennant Sandstone, rising to over 30m from the dunes, which are now utilized as a golf course, and its confined summit, dominating the site of the ferry, has been fortified.

The vestiges of fortification (Fig. 95) consist of a lunate scarping and ditching of the S.W. flank of the summit and the levelling of part of the area thus isolated. Precipitous falls in other directions required no improvement. There is no doubt that the short length of rock-cut ditch is artificial, and in 1980 a neat trench across it had recently been infilled; unfortunately no information about this seemingly careful excavation has yet come to light, despite enquiry. The summit, 7m above the bottom of the ditch, is 28m E.–W by 21m N.–S. Its surface is fairly level and for the most part bare rock with little vegetation. A central area, slightly raised, seems to have been levelled over an area measuring 4m by 8m. To the N.E. a segment of the summit has been destroyed by a modern quarry. Nothing suggests that the uneven and confined rocky ridge to the S. of the ditch served as a bailey.

The simplicity of this fortification supports its attribution to Morgan ap Caradog, particularly as its

---

[1] Merrick, *Morg. Arch.*, p. 109 (for the reliability of his citations from the Neath cartulary, pp. xxi and xxviii and *Arch. Camb.* 1887 pp. 88–94); Lhuyd, *Parochialia*, III, pp. 123–4, transcribes Merrick, adding the name '. . . een castle', *i.e.* Hen Gastell. See also Phillips, *Vale of Neath*, pp. 61, 134.

[2] Giraldus, *Itin. Kamb.*, p. 72

[3] In 1289: Clark, *Cartae*, V (mccxx), p. 1685. In 1307: *Cal. I.P.M.*, IV, No. 435, pp. 322–34. See also Phillips, *Vale of Neath*, pp. 134–5.

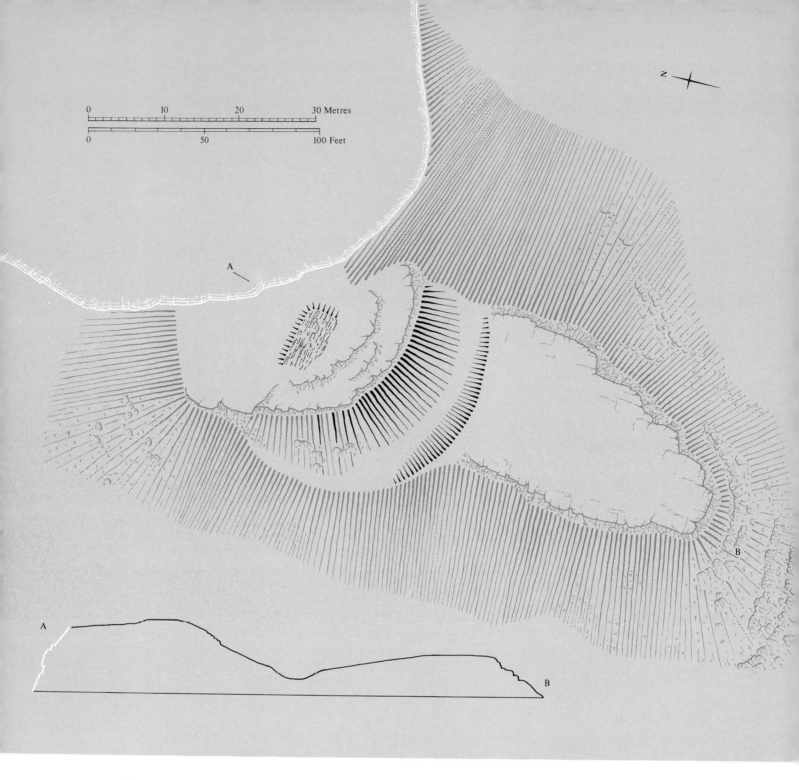

Fig. 95. Briton Ferry (Hen Gastell).

closest parallel is Castell Nos (UW 4), a similarly fortified rocky eminence that is remotely situated in Meisgyn, the territory of his brother Maredudd. It is also known that Morgan held lands W. of the Nedd, for it is recorded that he granted Neath Abbey common of pasture between that river and the Tawe.[4] Also, it was claimed by Merrick that the Neath Regis-

ter proved that his father, Caradog ab Iestyn, enjoyed certain lands between those rivers.[5] This area had fallen to Richard de Granville before 1130, in which

[4] Clark, *Cartae*, II (cccxviii), p. 316 and IV (dcccclxiii), p. 1201; *Arch. Camb.* 1867, p. 8.

[5] Merrick, *Morg. Arch.*, p. 39.

140

Fig. 96. Briton Ferry viewed from the north-east.

year he granted it, along with his now vanished castle (VE 2), to the abbey he founded at Neath. By 1130 Earl Robert had established a demesne lordship on the E. bank of the Nedd, centred on a castle some 4km upstream from Briton Ferry (LM 11), but the records do not explain how Caradog and Morgan were able to outflank this western outpost of the chief lord to gain lands formerly held by de Granville. Morgan succeeded Caradog as lord of Afan in about 1147, the year in which Earl William became chief lord. Morgan is known to have been in rebellion against Earl William, but the date and details are lacking.[6] It is reasonable to suspect that Morgan's uncle, Rhys ap Gruffydd of Deheubarth, was acting on his behalf in 1153, when he destroyed a presumably Norman castle at Aberafan (VE 1).[7] If this is so, the

castle at Briton Ferry was most probably raised by Morgan between that year and 1188, when Gerald of Wales, without noting the castle, was led by him across the Nedd. The broader historical context of the castles of Neath and Afan is considered in the introduction to this section (pp. 136–37)

King, p. 173 (possible castle).

Cadoxton-juxta-Neath (Llangatwg Nedd) (E), Coed-ffranc (C)
SS 79 S.W. (7315–9403)   29.iii.84   XXIV N.E.

---

[6] Clark, *Cartae*, II (cccxlvii), p. 348.
[7] *Bruts* (*R.B.H.*, *Pen 20*, and *B.S.*).

UW 2 Cae-castell

This small square earthwork (Fig. 98) was discovered when investigating the possible significance of the name 'cae-castell' (castle field) in the tithe apportionment. It lies 200m S.E. of Llechart-fach farm at 183m above O.D. and on the W. edge of a deep ravine running N.–S. A short distance S., this ravine joins the deeply-incised Nant Llwydyn valley, which in turn links with the Clydach at Pont Llechart. The small size and fresh appearance of the site suggest a medieval date.

The ground abutting the ravine slopes gently from N. to S. and influences the nature of the defences;

Fig. 97. Cae-castell: the north bank and ditch.

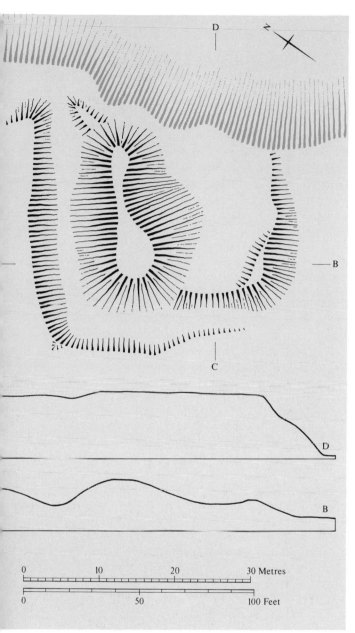

Fig. 98. Cae-castell.

these are strongest facing the rising ground to the N. They define a roughly square area set against the ravine, where no artificial work was required. There is a well-marked ditch to the N. and W., but only a line of scarping to the S. A low modern hedge-bank follows the counterscarp of the ditch. The area within the ditch is approximately 21m square, but almost half of this is occupied by the large and irregular N. bank. This disproportionately large bank forms a bulbous termination at the N.W. angle where its top is 5m wide and rises to 4.7m above the ditch. Towards the E. this northern bank narrows and decreases in height before terminating against the ravine, where a short subsidiary bank from its base partly closes the E. end of the ditch from the steep natural fall. A short stretch of bank of more normal proportions exists at the S.W. angle.

This quite singular earthwork might have slight affinity with the motte and bailey, if the elevated N.W. angle were taken to be the intended strong-point of the site. Its square form virtually discounts any possibility that it represents an unfinished motte; square mottes are extremely rare in Britain.

No record of this site is known, but its high altitude and remote situation, deep in Gower Wallicana and far from any known manorial centre, suggest it was the work of a medieval Welsh lord. No clear parallel can be cited, but two other Welsh castles, both in Afan, might be noted. Plas Baglan (UW 5), though of masonry, is founded on a small square platform at the edge of a ravine; Castell Bolan (UW 3), on one interpretation, might be seen as an aberrant motte and bailey, though not with any likeness to Cae-castell.

King, p. 168 (Rhyndwyclydach).

Llangyfelach (E), Rhyndwyglydach (C)
SN 60 S.E. (6941–0473)   3.xii.81   VIII S.W.

UW 3 Castell Bolan (Cwm Clais)

Castell Bolan occupies the top of a spur at 124m above O.D. on the N. flank of Mynydd Dinas. To the N. it overlooks Cwm Clais, which constitutes the eastern end of a pass between Baglan to the W. and the Afan valley at Cwmafan to the E. Plas Baglan (UW 5) lies at the W. end of this pass, 1.2km W.N.W. To the S. Mynydd Dinas rises to 258m and obstructs visibility

towards Aberafan, where a castle (VE 1) formerly existed on the narrow coastal plain 2km to the S.S.W It is possible that Plas Baglan, Castell Bolan and the Iron Age hillfort of Pen-y-castell (Vol. I, Part 2, No. 679) are the three castles respectively recorded in this vicinity by Edward Lhuyd as 'castell y wiryones', 'y Castell' and 'ben y Castell'.[1]

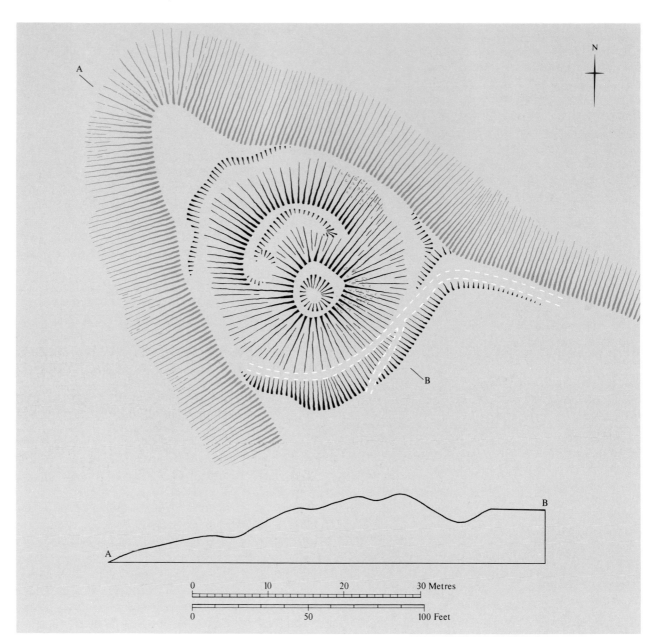

Fig. 99. Castell Bolan (Cwm Clais).

Castell Bolan (Fig. 99) is a motte of extraordinary form. It occupies the full width of the N.W. extremity of a spur, with steep natural falls to the W., N.W. and N.E. sides. To the S.E. level ground soon slopes upwards towards the summit of Mynydd Dinas; only in this direction could a bailey have been accommodated, though there is no trace of one. A wide crescentic ditch on this vulnerable S.E. side isolates the spur and is linked by shelves along the flanks with a lesser ditch that excludes the confined and dropping tip. The motte is oval, 26m by 28m at its base, and its regular lower slopes present the outward appearance of a typical motte, particularly from the S.E. side. Its upper part, however, is quite exceptional. Towards the S.E. it rises to a cratered D-shaped summit measuring 6m by 7m, with a central depression 1m deep. At a lower level to the N., mid way down the slope of the motte, a curving bank contains a con-

---

[1] Lhuyd, *Parochialia*, III, p, 28

144

Fig. 100. Castell Bolan viewed from the south.

fined lunate shelf. This crescentic bank, like that around the summit, has a regular and purposive appearance not to be explained as an unfinished motte, or one which has been mutilated by treasure-seekers (*cf.* Ystradowen, MO 12). The possibility that these features represent the remains of collapsed stone structures is equally improbable; no mortar and very little rubble is present on the motte or in its ditch. Two other explanations suggest themselves. Firstly, it might perhaps represent a quite aberrant motte in which the summit, facing the vulnerable side, shelters a small subsidiary living area on its northern slopes like a tiny bailey. Secondly, the claim that the motte served as a firing-point for the Volunteers in the 19th century, if confirmed, would offer a plausible explanation for the features described.[2]

Pending excavation, it may be reasonably assumed that this site was a castle of the 12th-century Welsh lords of Afan, or one of their followers. If a Welsh castle, as seem likely from its situation, and despite possible aberration, it clearly imitates the Norman motte. There is no certain historical record of the site, though it has been suggested that it might have been 'the castle that once belonged to Morgan Gam' (*fl.* 1217–41) where, on an adjacent slope, Herbert Fitzmatthew was slain by the Welsh in 1245.[3] The general historical context of the early castles of Neath and Afan is discussed above at the start of this section (pp. 136–37).

King, p. 160 (Baglan No. 2).

Baglan (E), Port Talbot (C)
SS 79 S.E. (7679–9202)   3.viii.80   XXV S.W.

[2] A. J. Richards, *B.B.C.S.*, VII (1933–35), pp. 223–4 and *Trans. Neath Antiq. Soc.*, IV (1933–34), pp. 101–3.
[3] *Ann. Camb.*, *s.a.* 1246; Clark, *Land of Morgan*, p. 109; A. L. Evans, *Trans. Port Talbot Hist. Soc.*, No. 3, II (1974), p. 28. It should be added that this reference more probably applies to Plas Baglan (UW 5).

UW 4 Castell Nos, Aberdâr

Fig. 101. Castell Nos, Aberdâr, viewed from the east.

Castell Nos lies remote in the northern uplands of Meisgyn on an abrupt and rocky eminence on the E. bank of the Rhondda Fach, which river marked the western boundary of Meisgyn and divided it from the neighbouring commote of Glynrhondda. A steep and craggy slope on the E. side of the site falls to a marshy hollow which isolates the eminence from the higher ground of Castell y Waun. Only 80m E. of the site runs the ancient ridgeway of Cefn Ffordd (or Heol Adam), which follows the high ground E. of the Rhondda Fach from near its confluence with the Rhondda Fawr to Hirwaun Common on the border with Brycheiniog.[1]

The site (Figs. 92, 102) crowns the S.E. end of an isolated eminence rising to a level summit about 380m above O.D. and measuring 35m N.–S. by 12m E.–W.

It has no artificial defences above the steep falls to the E., or along the edge of the precipitous cliff to the S., but to the N. and W. the summit has been scarped down to a ditch of modest proportions. There are no traces of internal structures; the square pit at the S. end is a recent disturbance. The ruins of a square dry-stone building which lie across the ditch to the N. are probably those of a shepherd's hut of no great age. Beyond the ditch to N. and W. the ground slopes gradually to the abrupt flanks of the hill. On this lesser slope to the N.W. is an isolated 12m stretch of possible ditch (not shown) that has been interpreted as an

---

[1] Merrick, *Morg. Arch.*, p. 129 and *Rees's Map*; For other medieval routes in Glamorgan named Cefn Ffordd (near Neath) and Heol Adam (near Gelli-gaer) see Vol. III, Part 2, RO 4 and RO 6.

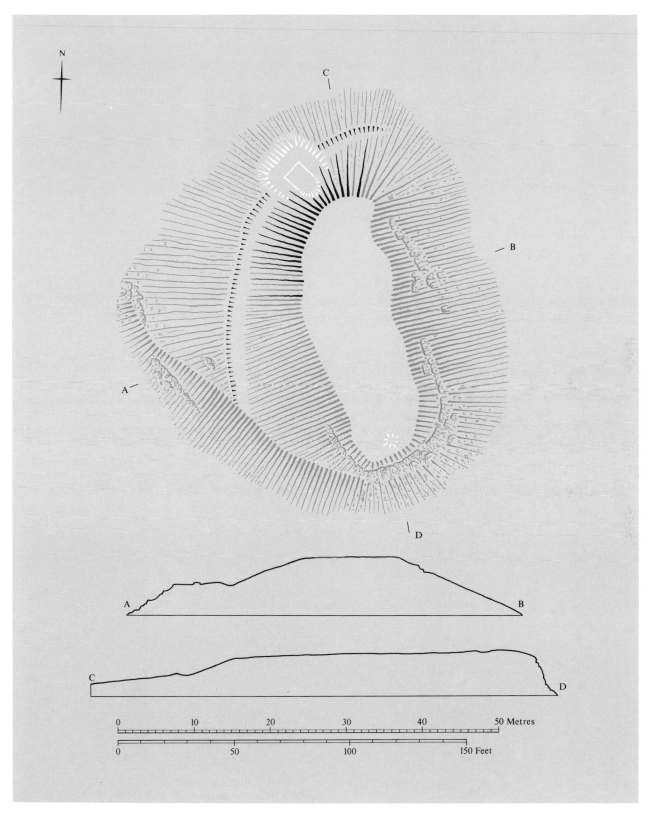

Fig. 102. Castell Nos, Aberdâr.

Fig. 103. Castell Nos, Aberdâr: aerial photograph from the north.

unfinished bailey.[2] The scarped summit might represent a medieval Welsh attempt to create a motte-like fortress from this naturally strong position. Its form and compactness certainly have more affinity with medieval than with prehistoric fortification.

There is no medieval record of the site, but as 'Castell Nose' on its ' ...high stony creg...' it was noted by Leland, who also noted its vicinity as an area then producing barley, oats and a little wheat. The closest parallel for Castell Nos is Briton Ferry (UW 1), the late 12th-century castle of Morgan ap Caradog ab Iestyn, whose brother Maredudd then ruled Meisgyn. Maredudd seems the probable builder as it is unlikely that it would have been built on the

very western boundary of Meisgyn after 1229, when his successor, Hywel ap Maredudd, annexed Glyn-rhonndda to the W. of the adjacent river, let alone after *ca.* 1247, when the chief lord, Earl Richard de Clare, annexed both commotes.[3]

King, p. 172 (Aberdare; possible castle).

Aberdâr
SN 90 S.E. (9651–0016)　　10.vi.80　　XVIII N.W.

---

[2] N.M.W. Fox Notebook, II (1935), pp. 87–8; O.S. Record Card SN 90 S.E. 1.

[3] *Ann. Margam, s.a.* 1227; *Glam. Co. Hist.* III, pp. 47, 50–1

UW 5　Plas Baglan

Plas Baglan, despite its name, 'Palace', or 'Mansion of Baglan', and its genteel literary associations of the 15th and 16th centuries, is a strongly fortified site, a castle rather than a moated site. Its vestiges and location indicate a Welsh masonry castle that certainly existed by the 13th century, and was probably founded in the previous century. It lies secluded on the eastern edge of the precipitous ravine of Cwm Baglan, at 2.3km N.N.W. of Aberafan Castle (VE 1) and 1.2km W.N.W. of Castell Bolan (UW 3). The 16th-century house of Blaen Baglan (Vol. IV, Part 1, No. 23) is on higher ground near the head of the cwm and 430m to the N.E., while 300m to the W., across the ravine, is St Baglan's church for which two Early Christian sculptured stones suggest a pre-Norman foundation (Vol. I, Part 3, Nos. 886, 961).

The castle (Fig. 104) occupies a strong position at 53m above O.D. within the angle formed by Cwm Baglan to the W. and a deeply incised re-entrant dingle to the S.; to the N. and E., facing rising ground, it is protected by a right-angled ditch which defined a platform 21m square. Traces of a mortared wall survive around this platform, particularly to the N., where there are clear indications of a square projecting turret on the W. and a buttress or stepped plinth towards the centre. To the E. the wall is marked by a stoney bank, but stone-robbing and erosion have removed all traces to the S. Incorporated within the N.W. angle of this perimeter wall are the ruins of a rectangular tower or first-floor hall. Set N.–S. along the greater part of the W. side of the enclosure, this structure has walls 1.52m thick and measures externally 17.37m by 10.06m. There are the remains of

two splayed embrasures, one to the W., the other to the S. in the only surviving portion of that wall. The northern half of the building is defined by intermittent visible parts of the walls which must survive to a height of some 1.5m within the stoney banks which follow their lines. The projecting turret to the N. presumably served a latrine on the vanished first floor. This dominant structure occupied the greater part of the W. half of the platform. Remains of lesser buildings in the N.E. quarter may be marked by its slight elevation, isolated scarps and an isolated wall fragment. The entrance was probably at the gap between the S. end of the stoney E. bank and the dingle to the S.

The southern end of the eastern ditch is infilled, probably as a result of recent stone-robbing to provide material for the now abandoned Ty Newydd Farm. This farm of 18th- or early 19th-century date lies 110m S.E. of Plas Baglan. Its outbuildings and yard walls re-use much ashlar matching that which occurs in the rubble on the site. Mainly honey-coloured Oolitic Limestone, this ashlar also includes grey Pennant Sandstone. The Oolitic Limestone dressings include at least four jamb stones from doors or windows, all with a plain broad chamfer; one found on the scarp immediately below the W. wall of the tower, was internally rebated and grooved for a shutter. Five plain squared blocks of the same stone, re-used at the farm, are distinctly and crudely fan-tooled; small similarly tooled fragments are present at the site and might suggest a 12th-century date for some of the fabric, though later work is indicated by diagonally straight-tooled stones. Among the grey Pennant Sandstone is a roll-moulded door jamb.

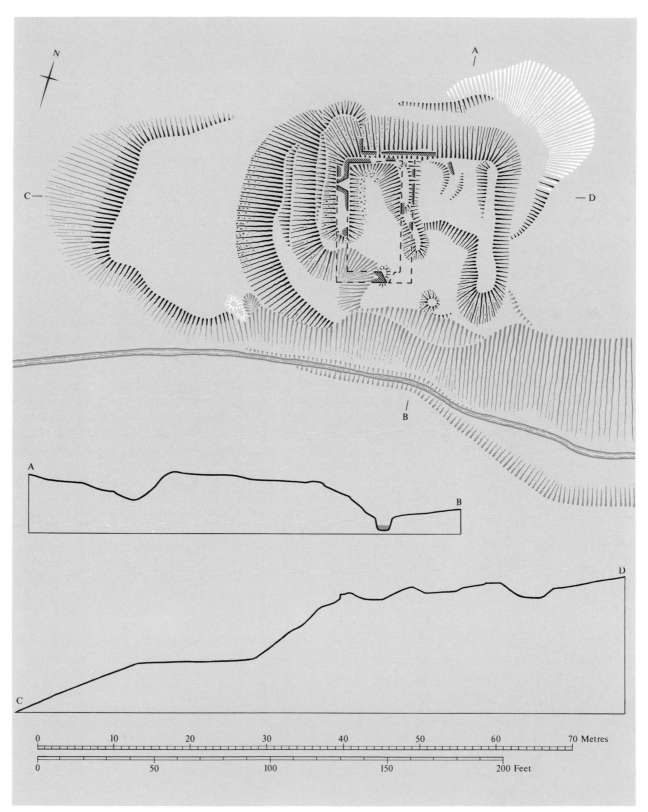

Fig. 104. Plas Baglan.

Fig. 105. Plas Baglan, viewed from the north-east.

To the W. side of the platform a steep rubble-strewn slope falls to a level shelf 9m below. Two parallel and more gently-sloping berms along this slope suggest

Fig. 106. Seal of Morgan Gam, lord of Afan (*fl.* 1217-41), drawn from a photgraph provided by *The British Library*.

that is has been artificially scarped to strengthen the main upper platform. The irregular shelf below is a natural feature, roughly equal in area to the upper platform and ideally suited to accommodate a bailey, and it has possibly been scarped about its perimeter for this purpose, but there are no traces of structures upon it.

Documentary evidence for the castle of Plas Baglan is lacking, but its singular form and secluded location, close to the ancient church of St Baglan, suggest it was a stronghold of the Welsh lords of Afan. This probability raises the question of its status in relation to the two nearby castles of Aberafan and Castell Bolan (VE 1, UW 3 and map, Fig. 94, p. 136). It is usually assumed that the Welsh lord of Afan built the now vanished castle at Aberafan, 2.3km to the S.S.E., and that this was their *caput*. Both assumptions are questionable; although they may have held the coastal strip after the Norman castle of Aberafan was destroyed by Lord Rhys in 1153, they did not make that castle their *caput*, certainly not before the foundation of their borough there *ca.* 1304. Probably they administered the territory from Plas Baglan, as it is named *Bagelan* in the Extent of 1262, which states that Morgan Fychan (*ob.* 1288) owed no service except a heriot of a horse and arms at death.[1] Both Plas Baglan and the nearby Castell Bolan (UW 3) lie in Baglan

---

[1] Clark, *Cartae*, II (dcxv), p. 651 and n., p. 656.

parish; either might be considered as 'the castle that once belonged to Morgan Gam' (*fl.* 1217–41) near which Herbert Fitzmatthew was slain by the Welsh in 1245.[2] His death occurred on an adjacent slope, a topographical feature lacking at the low-lying Aberafan site. Plas Baglan would appear more significant than Castell Bolan, not only for its proximity to the church and its masonry, but also for its late-medieval association with the princely family. Two cadet branches of the Welsh lords of Afan survived at Baglan long after the lordship passed in exchange to the chief lord, Edward Despenser, at some time between 1359 and 1373.[3] Both branches descended from Rhys, younger brother of Lleisan ap Morgan Fychan, and

Fig. 107. Seal of Lleisan ap Morgan Fychan, styled *de Avene*, who founded Aberafan borough *ca* 1304 (after *Arch. Camb.* 1867, p.27).

established important lineages at Blaen Baglan and Plas Baglan, the latter represented in the 15th century by the celebrated gentleman-bard Ieuan Gethin ab Ifan ap Lleisan ap Rhys (*ca.* 1400–80).[4] The Plas came by marriage to the Thomas family, and was no doubt the 'Courte Baglan' of 1570, which was seemingly

abandoned early in the 17th century.[5] The tower of Plas Baglan is perhaps alluded to in the farm-name of Ty'n-y-Twr, 200m N.W. across the cwm, and in the tenement of *Tir y Ture*, which was leased by the Crown in this locality in 1632.[6]

The primitive tooling of some of its ashlar, its dominant tower or hall and its lower platform vaguely reflecting a motte and bailey plan, might all favour a late-12th-century foundation, though a recent opinion favours a 13th-century date.[7] If it was founded before 1200, its builder may have been Morgan ap Caradog, lord of Afan *ca.* 1147–*ca.* 1207, founder of the castle at Briton Ferry (UW 1). Though less massively-walled, the tower at Plas Baglan is larger that the Norman keeps at Ogmore (MR 5) and Penllyn (EM 4), and only marginally smaller than others at Sully (EM 6) and Dinas Powys (EM 1). Threatened on his eastern flank by the Norman keeps of the chief lord at Kenfig (EM 2) and Newcastle (EM 3), Morgan could not have ignored the merits of such structures, particularly as he managed to obtain possession of the latter as a result of his leading role in the revolt of 1183–84, passing it on to his heirs who lost it before 1217. The eclipse of Plas Baglan, it may be surmised, began with the foundation of the Welsh borough at Aberafan, *ca.* 1304, and the rebuilding of the 12th-century castle there as a more convenient centre for administration, the more remote site being ceded to a cadet.

Plas Baglan might be the '*Castell y wiryones*' westernmost of the three castles noted in Baglan parish by Edward Lhuyd, but this name is not otherwise recorded.[8]

King, p. 160 (Baglan).

Baglan (E), Port Talbot (C).
SS 79 S.E. (7562–9230)   6.ix.77   XXV N.W.

[2] *Ann. Camb., s.a.* 1246.

[3] A. Leslie Evans, *Trans. Port Talbot Hist. Soc.*, No. 3, II (1974), pp. 37–9. See also G. T. Clark, *Arch. Camb.* 1867, p. 15 and Phillips, *Vale of Neath*, p. 363.

[4] *Glam. Co. Hist.*, III, pp. 497–9; Phillips, *Vale of Neath*, pp. 471–9.

[5] A. Leslie Evans, *Trans. Port Talbot Hist. Soc.*, No. 2, I (1965), pp. 56–7; Phillips, *Vale of Neath*, pp. 364, 374; Lhuyd, *Parochialia*, III, p. 122; Merrick, *Morg. Arch.*, p. 107.

[6] Clark, *Cartae*, VI (mdvii), pp. 2197–8; Phillips, *Vale of Neath*, p. 264.

[7] King, *Cast. Ang.*, I, p. 160.

[8] Lhuyd, *Parochialia*, III, p. 28. Lhuyd's 'y Castell' may be the nearby Castell Bolan (UW 33), and the third the hill-fort of Pen-y-castell.

Section VE: Vanished Early Castles

Monuments 1 to 4

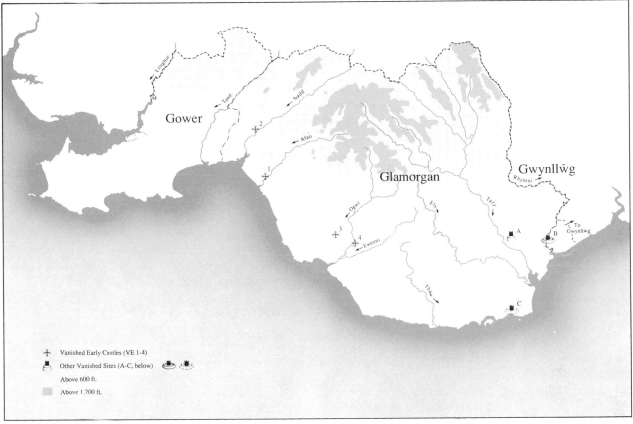

Fig. 108.

1   Aberafan Castle.
2   Granville's Castle, Neath.
3   Llangewydd Castle.
4   Oldcastle, Nolton (Bridgend).

Other Vanished Sites:
A   Treoda (MM 2)
B   Rumney Castle (MR 7)
C   Sully Castle (EM 6)

The four castles included in this section are not the only vanished castles in the county, but those for which we have no information on which they might be reliably classified. Others, noted below, include some which were equally early, but these are more recent losses for which there is sufficient information to place them in their relevant sections.

Of the four sites in this section, three are known from records of the 12th or early 13th century (Aberafan, Granville's Castle and Llangewydd; VE 1, 2 and 3), and the last from consistent antiquarian references and its suggestive name (Oldcastle, VE 4).

The precise location of Aberafan and Oldcastle is not in doubt, but only the approximate locations of Granville's Castle and Llangewydd Castle may be suggested. The four were no doubt earthwork castles, and 19th-century records suggest that Aberafan had a motte. It might also be conjectured that Granville's Castle was a motte, and that Llangewydd and Old-castle were castle-ringworks, these assumptions being based on their respective locations on glacial drift or shallow soils over rock (See Introduction, pp. 34–6).

The disappearance of Granville's Castle and Llan-gewydd Castle is not surprising; they were respectively abandoned to Neath and Margam Abbeys in 1130 and 1202–18, when the latter was certainly dismantled and levelled. Late records of the unrecorded castle at Oldcastle suggest it survived long enough to be furnished with masonry. Similarly at Aberafan, while the single medieval reference to it in 1153 must refer to the suspected motte, late accounts suggest this also became a stone castle, probably after *ca*. 1304.

Vanished castles described in other sections should also be noted here, as well as those which are so vestigial as to be almost vanished.

Three castles have been lost in recent years, fortunately only after the surviving remains were excavated in advance of destruction. These are Treoda (MM 2), a motte with strong evidence for superimposed masonry; Rumney (MR 7), a castle-ringwork with later masonry; and Sully (EM 6), a suspected castle-ringwork with a 12th-century keep and later masonry. Treoda was excavated in 1966 before its site was cleared for development; no trace of the recorded masonry had survived. Rumney was excavated between 1977 and 1981, before its remnants were destroyed; an early castle-ringwork was identified beneath a complex of later masonry defences and internal structures. At Sully, excavations in the 1960s, before housing development, largely confirmed and supplemented unpublished plans made by G. T. Clark during excavations in the last century.

The remains of five other earthwork castles are so vestigial as to be almost vanished, though sufficiently marked to be classified as a motte and four castle-ringworks. The vestigial motte is Ynyscrug (MO 11). The vestigial castle-ringworks are Howe Mill Enclosure (CR 10), Llandow (CR 11), Pancross (CR 17), and Walterston (CR 21).

Mention might also be made here of the motte that formerly existed at Swansea (LM 18); its remnants were cleared away in 1913, but there remains the substantial masonry of its adjacent S. ward, so this castle is far from vanished. The tower-house at Tythegston (TH 5) is invisible if not vanished, built up in a large 18th-century mansion.

Finally there is the list of possible castles in Vol. III, Part 1b, Section PC, which includes sites retaining but slight vestiges of an uncertain nature, or antiquarian records which might indicate castles. These include the sites of such possible early castles as Castleton (PC 2) and Wenvoe (PC 11), neither recorded, but both at the centres of significant early Norman lordships.

VE 1   Aberafan Castle

The last vestiges of Aberafan castle were levelled a century ago and houses built over its site. It lay at 8m above O.D. beside the parish church of St Mary and 180m W. of the River Afan. The 1st edition of the O.S. 25-inch map (1876) shows a large rectangular enclosure measuring 55m by 46m internally and defined by a ditch averaging 13.5m in width (Fig. 109). There was no bank, but near the centre a small un-ditched mound 9m in diameter was no more than a former cockpit.[1] The enclosure was named 'Beili y Castell' (O.S.), 'Baily'r castell' (tithe schedule, 1843), or 'Bailey Castell' (1831–31).[2] Consistent antiquarian accounts suggest the former existence of masonry. Merrick, in the 16th century, noted ' … an old castle now in ruin', and in 1715 the will of William Seys bequeathed ' … that castle or scite of a castle called Castle Aberavon', together with its lands, tenements and mills.[3] 'Ruins' and 'foundations' were respectively noted in 1811 and 1813.[4] It has also been claimed that there was a motte crowned with masonry at the castle, as suggested by the reminiscences of persons living before the site was cleared in the late 19th century.[5] While the cockpit mound was far too small and improbably sited for a motte, and might well have prompted some of these reports, it is nevertheless quite probable that a motte may have once stood beside this particularly large bailey. Before 1897, when the 2nd edition of the O.S. 25-inch map was published, the terraced houses of Castle St., St. Mary Place and St. Mary St. had been built over the site of the bailey (Fig. 109), and one record claims that in clearing the motte in 1895 a mass of masonry and rubble was disclosed.[6] Many of the houses overlying the E. side of the bailey were recently cleared to make way for an

---

[1] *Arch. Camb.* 1861, p. 173 (see Neath Castle (LM 11) for another cockpit built within a castle).

[2] The last, in Margam Estate rent roll of 1831–32, reproduced in *Glamorgan Historian*, VI (1969), facing p. 24.

[3] Merrick, *Morg. Arch*, p. 107; J. A. Bradney, *A History of Monmouthshire*, III, Part 2 (1923), p. 199.

[4] Carlisle, *Top. Dict.* (1811) and Lewis, *Top. Dict.* (1833).

[5] Armitage, *Norman Castles*, p. 296; A. Leslie, Evans, *Trans. Port Talbot Hist. Soc.*, No. 3, Vol. II (1974), pp. 19–20.

[6] Evans, *ibid.*, p. 20

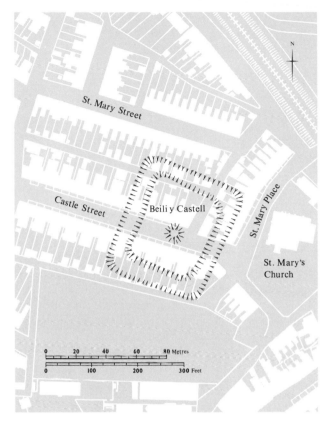

St. Mary Street

Castle Street

Beili y Castell

St. Mary Place

St. Mary's Church

N

| 0 | 20 | 40 | 60 | 80 Metres |
| 0 | 100 | 200 | 300 Feet |

Fig. 109. Aberafan Castle: the location of vestiges recorded in 1876 on the O.S. 25-inch map.

elevated access road to the M4.

The adjacent parish church, appropriated to Margam Abbey in 1383, was completely rebuilt in about 1859.[7] Two late-medieval tomb-slabs are preserved in the S. porch, and there are two cross-bases in the churchyard. One tradition claims that the church was formerly encircled by a moat.[8]

While the character of Aberafan Castle remains uncertain, the significance of its location is clear. It lies at the S.E. end of the narrow coastal plain between the Nedd and Afan estuaries, well-placed to observe the crossing of the latter river by the main E.–W. route following the Roman road through Glamorgan, the *via maritima* of Gerald's *Itinerary* of 1188, when the crossing was by a ford. The site at Briton Ferry (UW 1) served a similar function at the Nedd crossing, 5km to the N.W. It is the accepted view that the coastal strip between these sites was retained in Welsh hands as part of the member lordship of Afan, the lordship which Robert Fitzhamon reputedly bestowed on Caradog ab Iestyn, and that Caradog founded the castle at Aberafan.[9] This opinion is not easily recon-

ciled with the single medieval reference to the castle in 1153, when Rhys ap Gruffydd of Deheubarth, with his brother Maredudd, burnt the castle and houses at Aberafan and slew the garrison.[10] Caradog ab Iestyn had married Rhys's sister Gwladys, and by 1153 their son Morgan had succeeded to Afan. If Rhys's fierce attack on Aberafan was directed against a castle of his nephew, and one who was soon his staunch ally, it fitted ill with the rest of his campaign of that year, which was aimed at Norman settlements in the S.W., including Tenby and St. Clears (Ystrad Cyngen), and followed his earlier attacks on Gower.[11] There are also other facts to suggest that the attack on Aberafan was not another example of the frequent hostilities between related Welsh princes. It is known that Earl William, who succeeded Earl Robert Consul in 1147, granted lands in Afan to William Fitzhenry.[12] Though the date of this grant is uncertain, it is very probable that the lands granted were in the vicinity of Aberafan. Fitzhenry granted to Tewkesbury the chapel of St Thomas which lay in the Afan lands the earl had given him.[13] The site of this chapel has been identified with The Croft, a farmstead formerly located 130m S.E. of Aberafan Castle, where a cross-inscribed slab and a piscina were recovered during its demolition in 1869.[14] If this identification of the chapel of St Thomas is correct, it is most probable that Fitzhenry built the nearby castle and that this was the castle destroyed in 1153. Thereafter it was probably long abandoned; there is certainly nothing to suggest that Morgan ap Caradog or his princely

[7] *Arch. Camb.* 1859, p. 153.

[8] Evans, *op. cit.*, p. 19.

[9] Merrick, *Morg. Arch.*, p. 107; Lewis, *Top. Dict.* (1833); Clark, *Land of Morgan*, p. 30; Corbett, *Glamorgan Lordship*, p. 41; *Arch. Camb.* 1847, p. 18; Lhuyd, *Parochialia*, III, p. 122; Lloyd, *Hist. Wales*, II, pp. 440, 504.

[10] *Bruts (R.B.H., Pen 20* and *B.S.).*

[11] Lloyd, *Hist. Wales*, II, pp. 503–5.

[12] Patterson, *Glouc. Charters*, Appendix, No. 221, p. 171. William Fitzhenry is an intriguing figure, and otherwise only recorded in Glamorgan when, with Earl William of Gloucester, he consented to Samson de Halweya's exchange of his fee of Gelligarn (*vide.* CR 8) for Neath's vill of Littleham in Devon. It is tempting to wonder whether William Fitzhenry might have been a brother of Earl Robert Consul, Earl William's father and a base son of Henry I.

[13] Dugdale, *Monasticon*, II, p. 67; Clark, *Cartae*, I (cxxxvi), p. 134; *Epis. Acts*, II, L170, p. 659; *Arch. Camb.* XCVI (1941), p. 195.

[14] Walter de Grey Birch, *A History of Margam Abbey*, 1897, pp. 116–7, 224; *Arch. Camb.* 1925, pp. 424–5; *Glam. Inventory*, Vol. I, Part 3, No. 884, p. 42.

successors re-occupied the site before the late 13th or early 14th century. Their lands are termed Baglan, not Afan, in the Extent of 1262, and their continued occupation of Plas Baglan (UW 5) is likely until the founding of their borough at Aberafan in *ca.* 1302. Then, perhaps, Aberafan Castle was rebuilt in stone to become the administrative centre of the lords of Afan, while Plas Baglan, on its elevated shelf 2.3km to the N.N.W., certainly passed to a cadet branch.

After the acquisition of Afan by the Despenser lords of Glamorgan by exchange in the period 1359–73,[15] it is probable that Aberafan Castle was neglected,

though it survived to be granted to Sir William Herbert by Edward VI in 1550.[16] (See pp. 136–37, for a discussion of the early castles of Neath and Afan.)

King, p. 171.

Aberafan (E), Port Talbot (C)
SS 79 S.E. (7622–9012)   11.x.88   XXV S.W.

[15] A. Leslie Evans, *Trans. Port Talbot Hist. Soc.*, No. 3, Vol. II (1974), pp. 37–9; see also G. T. Clark, *Arch. Camb.* 1867, p. 15 and Phillips, *Vale of Neath*, p. 363.
[16] *Arch. Camb.* 1853, p.166.

VE 2   Granville's Castle, Neath

This long-vanished castle was built before 1130 by Richard de Granville as the *caput* of lands he had acquired on the W. side of the Afon Nedd, Neath Ultra, where it probably lay within or near Neath Roman fort (Vol. I, Part 2, No. 734). A chapel of St. Giles, which incorporated Norman fabric and formerly stood of the W. bank of the river only 180m N.E. of the fort, has been equated with the castle chapel known from the records.[1] For a brief period this castle constituted the westernmost stronghold of the lordship of Glamorgan, set some 500m in advance of the chief lord's castle (Neath Castle, LM 11) on the E. side of the river in Neath Citra (Fig. 110). These two castles were probably built soon after *ca.* 1114, when Robert Consul was granted seisin of the lordship of Glamorgan.[2] Richard de Granville was Robert's constable, the commander of the knights of his household, an honoured rank enjoyed before his lord became Earl of Gloucester in 1121/22 and retained at least until 1130.[3]

In 1130 Richard de Granville granted his castle and all his lands between the Nedd and Tawe rivers to the Abbey he founded at Neath in that year. His foundation charter and two subsidiary charters constitute the only contemporary record of his castle. The foundation charter granted the abbey the chapel of his castle.[4] The castle itself was ceded to the abbey by Granville's two subsidiary charters known only from the long and involved *inspeximus* and confirmation of Richard Neville, Earl of Warwick (1468).[5]

Richard de Granville was seemingly childless, but the surrender of his Neath fee and his presumed retirement to his Devon manors is usually seen as the reaction to difficulties encountered in holding this remote outpost against a resurgent Welsh power.[6] Despite

unrest inspired by Caradog ab Iestyn of Afan and his brothers in 1127,[7] however, it is difficult to view the withdrawal as a surrender to Welsh hostility, not only because Richard acted with the express consent of Henry I and Earl Robert and his heir, William, but also because Glamorgan was unique in being quite unaffected by the widespread Welsh uprisings after the King's death in 1135.[8] Neither is there any evidence to support the assertion that Richard's constableship related to Earl Robert's castle at Neath, or that he remained in office there for a while after the abbey was founded.[9] In fact, he disappears from Glamorgan, and his castle on the W. bank was probably dismantled by the monks; it was seemingly no more by 1207, when King John, as lord of Glamorgan, confirmed to the

[1] *Arch. Camb.* 1861, p. 344; Phillips, *Vale of Neath*, pp. 86–7. The chapel was dismantled in 1863 to make way for the low-level station at Neath. Some of its Sutton Stone dressings were reset in a boundary wall of the station.
[2] Patterson, *Glouc. Charters*, No. 166, p. 152, n.
[3] Patterson, *Glouc. Charters*, No. 152 for writ of 'R(obertus) regis filius', witnessed by 'Ric(ardo) constabulario' (1120–21); Richard was still Robert's constable in 1130: *Cartae*, V (mccxx), *inspeximus* Ab, p. 1680. There is no evidence that his constableship was ever linked to any castle, as became the practice later in the century.
[4] Clark, *Cartae*, I (lxvii), pp. 74–6; Phillips, *Vale of Neath*, pp. 556–8. (Confirmed by King John, 1208: *Cartae*, II (cccxviii), p. 315; by Edward III, 1336: *Cartae*, IV (dccccclxiii), p. 1200; and by Richard Neville, 1468 – see n. 5 below.)
[5] Clark, *Cartae*, V (mccxx), pp. 1677–90 (*Ab* and *Ac*, pp. 1680–1).
[6] e.g. *Glam. Co. Hist.*, III, p. 24; Clark, *Land of Morgan*, p. 31; *Arch. Camb.* 887, pp. 93–4.
[7] *Ann Margam*, p. 12; *Epis. Acts*, II, No. L46, p. 621.
[8] *Glam. Co. Hist.*, III, p. 30.
[9] *Arch. Camb.* 1887, p. 90.

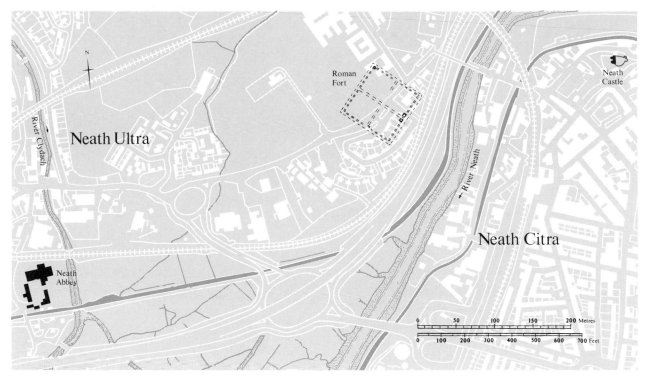

Fig. 110. Granville's Castle, Neath: location map. The castle was probably within or near the Roman fort.

Abbey ... *locum ubi castellum Ricardi de Granavilla quondam fuit ...*[10].

Since the transitory Granville association with Glamorgan was entirely under the patronage of Earl Robert Consul, it is necessary to dismiss the persistent but erroneous view that Richard de Granville was a brother of Robert Fitzhamon, who is claimed to have granted him his fee at Neath well before his death in 1107.[11] This mythical relationship with Fitzhamon stems largely from 17th-century interpolations into Rice Merrick's text by a Granville Earl of Bath intent on bolstering his claims to Glamorgan.[12]

The existence of two castles, both named Neath Castle, one on each side of the river, was correctly discerned from the records by Merrick, and argued in an important paper by David Lewis in 1887,[13] but there is no evidence to support Merrick's belief that the surviving castle on the E. bank was a 'new' castle replacing Granville's to the W. (*vide* Neath Castle, LM 11).

King, p. 171 (Neath No. 2)

Cadoxton-juxta-Neath (E), Neath (C).
SS 79 N.W. (near 7480–9780)   22.vi.64   XVI S.W.

[10] Clark, *Cartae*, II (cccvii), p. 309. For other castles given up to Neath or Margam see Stormy (MO 5), Bonvilston (CR 2), Gelli Garn (CR 8) and Llangewydd (VE 3).
[11] Phillips, *Vale of Neath*, p. 656; Clark, *Cartae*, I, p. 76, n. and *Land of Morgan*, p. 31; Nicholl, *Normans*, pp. X and 14; Corbett, *Glamorgan Lordship*, p. 67; Lloyd, *Hist. Wales*, II, p. 440.
[12] Merrick, *Morg. Arch.*, pp. 27, 52–4, 106, and especially nn. 50, 55 (p. 175), n. 111 (pp. 177–8). See also Patterson, *Glouc. Charters*, p. 77, n.
[13] Merrick, *Morg. Arch.*, pp. 53, 106; *Arch. Camb.* 1887, pp. 86–115, especially pp. 89–94.

VE 3   Llangewydd Castle

The vanished castle of Llangewydd doubtless stood near the former church of St Cewydd, sited in *cae'r hen eglwys*, old church field, 470m S.E. of the Margam grange of Llangewydd (Vol. III, Part 2, MG 34). This church stood 500m E. of an important intersection of ancient routes (Fig. 111). Running N. from

157

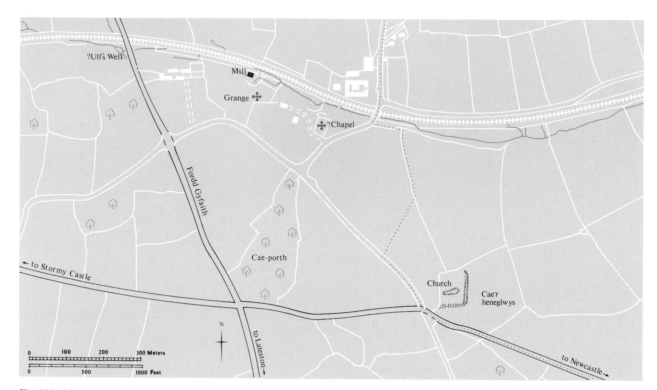

Fig. 111. Llangewydd Castle: location map. The castle probably stood beside the E-W road between Stormy and Newcastle, and close to the church in *Cae'r hen eglwys* or the nearby intersection with Ffordd Gyfraith running N-S.

Laleston, 1km to the S., was Ffordd Gyfraith, the 12th century ... *strate publice (sic) que vadit de Lagelst' in directum ad montana per fontem Ulfi.*[1] Ulf's Well is perhaps that now rebuilt at SS 8679–8155. At Llangewydd this route is crossed by the E.–W. road linking Stormy Castle (MO 5), 3½km to the W., with Newcastle (EM 3), 3¼km to the E. The former existence of a castle at Llangewydd was deduced by F. G. Cowley from a vivid passage by Gerald of Wales in his *Speculum Ecclesiae*.[2] Written *ca.* 1218, this relates the extreme measures taken by the monks of Margam Abbey in the hope of improving the terms of their lease of a knight's fee. To this end, they dismantled and levelled the castle, destroyed the church by night, and expelled the parishioners. Subsequent litigation by the knight failed, and the abbey maintained its lease. The fee and its knight are not named, but Llangewydd is the only knight's fee in Glamorgan that was held by Margam, and one for which numerous contemporary deeds confirm the gist of Gerald's text.[3] Cae-porth, a wooded enclosure W. of St Cewydd's Church and in the N.E. angle of the cross-roads (Fig. 111), was suggested by Cowley as the possible site of the castle; this wood certainly marks an area of disturbed ground in a most suitable location, but

the pits and mounds are the result of quarrying and nothing suggestive of a castle is discernible.

The knight's fee of Llangewydd was held by the Scurlage family from the mid 12th century until 1202, when it was leased to Margam. This enfeoffment, carved from the demesne lordship of Newcastle, was after 1135, as no Scurlage held a fee of the 'Old Enfeoffment' up to that date, as given in *Liber Niger* and *Liber Rubeus*. The fee was held by the service of one knight at Cardiff Castle, or the commuted payment of 6s. 8d. as wardsilver. William Scurlage the Younger is the first holder in the records; between 1153 and 1166 he granted the grange of Llangewydd to Margam.[4] William was succeeded by Herbert,

---

[1] Clark, *Cartae*, I (cix), p. 110; Patterson, *Glouc Charters*, No. 129, p. 120.

[2] Giraldus Cambrensis, *Opera*, IV, 134–6; F. G. Cowley in *Arch. Camb.*, CXVI (1967), pp. 204–6; *Morgannwg*, XI (1967), pp. 15–16; *Glam. Co. Hist.*, III, 1971, p. 102; and *The Monastic Order*, pp. 80–1, 182–3.

[3] Corbett, *Glamorgan Lordship*, p. 36; neighbouring Stormy (MO 5), obtained by Margam in 1183, was never styled a knight's fee; Bonvilston Castle (CR 2) and its manor only rated half a knight's fee, and was not possessed by Margam until *ca.* 1230. The sub-fee of Gelli-garn (CR 8) was obtained by Neath Abbey.

whose son, David Scurlage, by an agreement of 1202, leased the whole fee of Llangewydd to Margam Abbey for a complicated series of payments in cash and kind and an annual rent of 3 marks, the monks rendering service to the earl.[5] The church of Llangewydd was also conveyed to the abbey,[6] and the way prepared for the events described by Gerald. In corroboration, other deeds suggest that David attempted to rescind the agreement, presumably outraged at the monks' behaviour; his claim to have been under age at the time of the agreement was rejected, however, and Margam retained the fee.[7] Llangewydd became its most profitable grange, with 8 carucates of arable and 83 acres of meadow, and figured in numerous confirmations obtained by the abbey from Countess Isabel before 1217.[8] The abbot answered for the fee in the Extent of 1262, when William Scurlage held one quarter of a knight's fee at Llanharry valued at 40s.[9] This William was constable of the chief lord's castle at Llangynwyd (MR 2) in 1258, and his holding at Llanharry was centred on Trecastell (SH 3). Others of the family settled at Scurlage in the Gower parish of Llanddewi.

King, p. 171.

Laleston
SS 88 S.E. (near 8755–8092)   23.vi.81   40.N.W.

---

[4] Clark, *Cartae*, I (cxxxiv), pp. 131–2; *Epis. Acts*, II, No. L149. Confirmed by Earl William, Henry II and Popes Urban III and Innocent III: Clark, *Cartae* I (cviii), p. 109; (cix), p. 110 and (clviii), p. 157; *Epis. Acts*, II, Nos. L167, L184, L202 and L259; Patterson, *Glouc. Charters*, No. 126, p. 118 and No. 129, p. 120.
[5] Clark, *Cartae*, II (cclxxii), pp. 269–70, (cclxxiii), pp. 270–1 and (ccccl), pp. 438–9; *Epis. Acts*, II, Nos. L254 and L255.
[6] Clark, *Cartae*, I (ccxi), p. 216 and VI (mdlxx), p. 2301; *Epis. Acts*, II No. L301.
[7] Clark, *Cartae*, I (ccxv), p. 220, II (ccccxliv), pp. 432–3, VI (mdcvi–mdcvii), pp. 2328–29; *Epis. Acts*, II, L282 and L320.
[8] Clark, *Cartae*, II (cccxxvi and ccxlii) pp. 326, 342, and VI (mdcv), p. 2327; *Epis. Acts*, II, Nos. L280, L281; Patterson, *Glouc. Charters*, Nos. 137, 139, 140, 142, 143–9.
[9] Clark, *Cartae*, II (dcxv), p. 651.

VE 4   Oldcastle, Nolton (Bridgend)

Consistent post-medieval antiquarian accounts and slight surviving vestiges suggest that there was once a castle at Oldcastle, or Nolton, a hamlet that was the ancient nucleus of Bridgend.[1] Nolton lies in the parish and former lordship of Coity on a level ridge of gravel fronting the E. bank of the Afon Ogwr. Newcastle (EM 3), at 610m to the N.N.W., crowns a high escarpment on the opposite bank, while between the two places an old and a new bridge mark the position of the ancient ford that was a focus of traffic in medieval and earlier times.[2] As early as 1106, Robert Fitzhamon had established a castle and settlement at Newcastle, a fact which has complicated consideration of Oldcastle, since the two sites are now both within the urban confines of the comparatively late town of Bridgend. While the alternative names of Nolton (Old Town) and Oldcastle have been understandably correlated with Newcastle, the early date of the latter makes this localized sequence highly doubtful; if the names have any chronological meaning they more probably relate to Coity Castle (MR 1), 2.8km N.E., the *caput* of the lordship which embraced the E. bank of the Ogwr and the site in question. All that is certain is that by the close of the medieval period a settlement had grown up at Oldcastle, served by a chapel of Coity and soon to be merged with the town which developed to the N., on the E. side of the stone bridge first noticed by Leland.[3]

There is firm evidence for a castle at Nolton in the 16th century, both from Leland, who notes the name '*Hene castelle*', and from Merrick who notes '*. . . a castle now in decay, whereof that hamlet took its name.*'[4] The ruins were again noticed in the late-18th-century edition of Camden, and even as late as 1811 Carlisle recorded that the inhabitants of Bridgend attended divine service at Oldcastle chapel, near the ruins of an old castle which had been partly built over by a tithe-barn.[5] Malkin (1804), Rees (1815) and Lewis (1833), all made similar observations.[6] It is said that stone foundations of great strength have

---

[1] H. J. Randall, (*Bridgend: the Story of a Market Town*, 1955, p. 15) rejects the castle, disregarding Tudor writers here cited in notes 3–4.
[2] Randall, *ibid.*, p. 6.
[3] Leland, *Itin. Wales*, pp. 28–9.
[4] Merrick, *Morg. Arch.*, p. 104 (and Lhuyd, *Parochialia*, III, p. 127).
[5] Camden's *Britannia*, ed. Gough, 1789, p. 501; Carlisle, *Top. Dict.* (1811), *s.n.* Bridgend.
[6] B. H. Malkin, *The Scenery, Antiquities and Biography of South Wales*, 1804; T. Rees, *A Topographical and Historical Description of South Wales*, 1815; Lewis, *Top. Dict.* (1833), *s.n.* Bridgend.

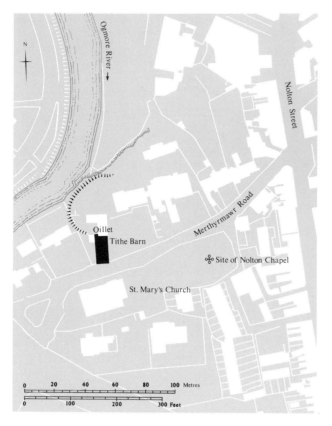

Fig. 112. Oldcastle, Nolton (Bridgend): location map. The tithe-barn retains features relevant to persistent antiquarian allusions to a castle here.

been encountered in the grounds behind the barn.[7]

The tithe-barn survives, its S. gable set to the N. side of Merthyr Mawr Road and directly opposite St Mary's Church, the modern successor of the late medieval chapel of ease (Fig. 112) Only the external walls of the barn survive, the interior having been gutted and new floors inserted. It nevertheless retains interesting features, particularly at the N. end. Here a lower recent building has been added in line, but above this, high in the N. gable, is the presumably re-used base of a cross-oillet. A door on the W. side re-uses medieval quarter-round mouldings of Sutton Stone and further fragments of the same are built in higher up the wall. The N.E. angle of the barn is dressed with good sandstone quoins, while westwards the N. gable, at its lower level, projects for a short

distance beyond the W. lateral wall, confirming the re-use of earlier ruins in the construction of the barn. Its E. wall is much patched and of irregular line, and it is known to have an arched doorway below the present ground level.[8]

The N. gable of the barn stands about 33m from a low but precipitous cliff above the river. The intervening ground is level, as it is to the E. where stands a former hospital. To the W., however, the cliff curves inwards from the river to form a blunt low spur set some 5m above the level of the adjoining property. While nothing remains to suggest this curving scarp has been used in fortification, the strength it offers to W. and N. is suggestive, particularly as its line would naturally follow on beneath the N. end of the barn, beyond which only excavation could now locate any ditch which might have isolated the spur.

The only medieval records which might relate to Oldcastle, Nolton, are three entries in the *Fine Rolls* concerning a lawsuit of 1199–1201 between Payn de Turberville, lord of Coity, and Walter de Sully.[9] They disputed ownership of a knight's fee in Coity and the 'Old Town'; the fee has been identified with Coychurch, 3.4km to the E. of Oldcastle. King John was then Lord of Glamorgan, but the outcome of the hearing in his court is not known; the fee of Coychurch certainly remained with de Sully, though it had reverted to Turberville by the 14th century.[10] Nothing further is heard of 'Old Town', which has also been tentatively identified with Oldcastle, Nolton, perhaps so named in relation to Coity Castle (MR 1).[11]

King, p. 171 (Bridgend Old Castle).

Coity (E), Bridgend (C)
SS 97 N.W. (9053–7951)   24.ii.81   40.N.E.

[7] M. R. Spencer, *Annals of South Glamorgan*, Carmarthen, 1913, pp. 8–9.

[8] *Ex inf.* Lt.-Col. J. A. R. Freeland. For plan of barn, see *Glam. Inventory*, Vol. IV, Part 2, p. 547, No. 3.

[9] Clark, *Cartae*, II (ccxix–ccxxx), pp. 235–6 and *Limbus Patrum*, p. 452.

[10] Clark, *Arch. Camb.*, 1877, p. 8 and 1878, p. 118; Corbett, *Glamorgan. Lordship*, pp. 35, 111, 120; Nicholl, *Normans*, pp. 30–1, 162.

[11] Nicholl, *ibid*; Clark, *Cartae*, II, p. 236 n.

Section MM:
Masonry Castles built over Mottes

Monuments MM1 and 2

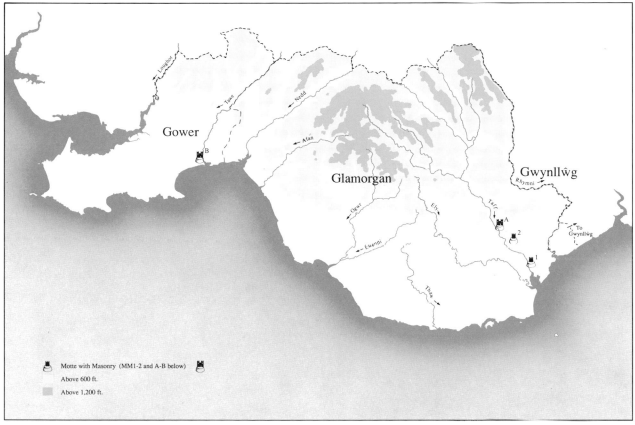

Fig. 113

1 Cardiff Castle
2 Treoda (Whitchurch)

Other Mottes with Masonry:
A Castell Coch (LM 4) ⎫ Volume III
B Swansea Castle (LM 18) ⎭ Part 1b

The mottes at Cardiff Castle and Treoda (Whitchurch) described in this section are two of four mottes in the county which were given masonry defences; the other two, at Castell Coch and Swansea, are included in Vol. III, Part 1b (LM 4, 18). This apparently illogical separation is justified on consideration of the most significant known or surviving remains at each site. Cardiff and Treoda are best included with the early castles; the first, for its great and historic late-11th-century motte, and despite substantial later fabric; the second, now vanished, because the scant information

regarding its masonry would contribute little to the comparative study of later castles in Part 1b. Conversely, surviving later masonry at Castell Coch and Swansea is of greater significance than the minimal information respecting their mottes, which may be summarized here.

Castell Coch (LM 4) is a small but powerful restored 13th-century castle entirely masking the motte, its masonry even cladding the steep slopes to the bottom of the ditch. Its ground profile no doubt distorts and exaggerates the underlying motte, but suggests it was large, rising from a basal diameter of about 34m to a summit perhaps 24m across and about 8m above the bottom of the ditch. These dimensions are too approximate for their inclusion on the diagram illustrating the profiles of Glamorgan mottes, but they are sufficient to conclude that it may well have been exceeded in size only by the great motte at Cardiff (Fig. 16, p. 52) and that which formerly existed at Swansea. There is no record of Castell Coch before the masonry castle was built in the late 13th century. It is one of the group of early mottes to the N. of Cardiff thought to have been raised by the first Normans to arrive in the area in the late 11th century, most of which were soon abandoned (Introduction, pp. 10–11).

The motte at Swansea (LM 18) was clearly portrayed by the Buck brothers in the 18th century, but what survived, including imposed masonry foundations, was cleared away in 1913. It appears to have been another large motte, about 52m in diameter at its base, and apparently only exceeded in size by the motte at Cardiff, as befitted its status as the *caput* of the lordship of Gower. It was founded *ca.* 1106 and withstood a Welsh assault in 1116. Surviving fabric is limited to a large square tower and the adjoining 13th-century curtain-wall defining the S.E. angle of a ward to the S. of the former motte. Within this angle is set an impressive 14th-century domestic block rising upon a series of vaulted cellars and incorporating a fine and rare arcaded parapet surmounting the earlier curtain wall.

Mottes, including those with masonry, are discussed in the preamble to Section MO and in the Introduction (pp. 10–48), noting aspects of their distribution and comparative rarity in the county, particularly in relation to castle-ringworks. The preamble to Section MR (pp. 217–18) observes that the wealth and status of respective owners, rather than the size and strength of primary earthworks, was the most relevant factor in raising stone castles over ringworks. Both factors appear relevant in the case of the four mottes which were rebuilt in masonry. The three in

the lordship of Glamorgan, at Cardiff, Treoda and Castell Coch, were all castles of the chief lord. Similarly, Swansea was the *caput* of the lord of Gower. Regarding size and strength, Treoda was only of medium size, but Castell Coch and Swansea appear to have been those closest in size and strength to our fourth site, the huge motte at Cardiff. Cardiff motte was seemingly protected by masonry defences from its foundation, with the refurbishment of the western defences of the Roman fort; the shell-keep on the motte followed in the 12th century. Castell Coch and Treoda were probably given their masonry in the late 13th century, but that on the vanished motte at Swansea is not securely dated.

Four other sites claimed to be mottes with masonry upon them may be rejected, and another two noted, although they are described in other sections for lack of certainty. At Kenfig (EM 2) a measured profile (Fig. 234, p. 321) excludes the possibility that the keep stands upon a motte; it was probably within a ringwork. At Loughor and Rumney (MR 4, 7) primary ring-banks were truncated and their interiors raised when walls replaced their palisades in the 13th century; the consequent large low mounds no more constituted mottes than the similarly infilled ringworks at Coity and Ogmore, which retain their walls and have therefore avoided such mistaken classification. The final site rejected in this context is the eccentric motte-like mound of Castell Bolan (UW 3), where a cratered top lacks the stone content required for the acceptance of its interpretation as a collapsed tower.

The two sites less easily discounted, but lacking evidence sufficient to include them here, are Talybont (MO 6) and Aberafan (VE 1). Talybont motte betrays no surface indication to suggest that it once supported the tower recorded in the 14th century, though no excavations have explored this possibility. Finally, at Aberafan, only the discovery of lost records, plans or photographs could now confirm unsubstantiated and inadequate reports of a motte supporting masonry at this long-vanished site.

MM 1   Cardiff Castle

The late-Roman fort chosen as the site for Cardiff Castle was described in an earlier Inventory (Vol. 1, part 2, 1976, No. 735). To supplement this earlier account, recent evidence from excavation is briefly summarized. Cardiff Castle was founded by William

I in 1081, twelve years before it became the *caput* of the lordship of Glamorgan established by Robert Fitzhamon. It occupies the entire area of the late-Roman fort, on a glacial terrace on the E. bank of the Taff. The fort defences were adapted to Norman require-

Fig. 114. Cardiff Castle viewed from the top of the Pearl Assurance Tower, looking west.

ments, at the lowest river-crossing, and served by the Roman road running E.–W. across the county (the medieval Port Way). Another Roman road ran N. into the uplands, and the river was navigable southwards for 2.5km to the broad Taff-Ely estuary. As elsewhere, Roman surveyors had chosen a position that proved irresistible to their successors.[1]

The glacial terrace accommodating castle and fort extended over 600m to the S. and there a borough was established by 1102; palisaded by 1184, it was later enclosed by a stone wall first mentioned in 1349 (Vol. III, Part 1b, TD 1). Beyond the South Gate of the town the gravel terrace gave way to the heavy clays of the waterlogged moors which characterized the seaboard between the Taff-Ely and Rhymni estuaries. Uncongenial for habitation and an effective impediment to traffic until embanked and drained by later medieval folk, but then valuable agricultural land, these moors dictated the siting of the castles at Cardiff and Rumney (MR 7, 3.9km to the N.E.), and of the Roman road that linked them.[2]

Cardiff lies within Cibwr, the small southern commote of Cantref Senghennydd lying between the Taff and Rhymni rivers, and extending from the sea to the lower ridges of Caerphilly Mountain to the N. Most of this commote was retained by Fitzhamon as the demesne lordship of Cardiff, with an important manor at Roath (Vol. III, Part 2, MS 13) exploiting the fertile lowland plain E. and S. of Cardiff. Further N., on higher ground, lands were granted to the abbeys of Keynsham, Tewkesbury, Margam and Llantarnam, but the tenurial descent of Whitchurch and its castle (MM 2) remains obscure before the late 13th century.[3]

The Roman forts at Cardiff

The Inventory account cited was written before systematic excavation within the fort, though finds had suggested the prior existence of a fort of the 1st century. Between 1974 and 1981 excavations enabled Mr Peter Webster to suggest a sequence of four overlapping forts.[4] A large *Neronian fort* first occupied the site ca. 55–80/90 A.D.; extending beyond the walls of the final fort, it covered 12 hectares on the evidence of the siting of its presumed *principia* in the N.E. quarter of the castle. *The second fort* occupied about one-fifth of the first, retaining parts of its N.–S. axial road and northern defensive line; occupied briefly in the late 1st century, it largely lies beyond the N. wall of the stone fort. *The third fort* closely followed the

lines of the second, though marginally advanced to the S. and reduced to the N.; it was occupied until its earth and timber defences were levelled to make way for the stone fort.

The late-Roman stone fort alone is relevant; its defences dictated the lines of the medieval castle. The name, quadrangular form, and location of the castle led G. T. Clark to suspect a Roman origin as early as 1862.[5] Only in 1889, however, was the Roman wall accidentally identified on the E. side, deep within the earthen bank outlining most of the castle perimeter.[6] Between 1889 and 1923 intermittent excavation disclosed the entire circuit of the Roman walls.[7] The E. half of the S. wall and the E. and N. walls survived to heights of between 3.66m and 5.18m, while the foundations defined the W. front for 27m southwards from the N.W. angle. The rest of the W. front, and the W. half of that to the S., was defined by the medieval curtain bounding the outer flanks of the Inner Ward of the castle. Excavations and observations at widely separated locations, three to the W. and two to the S., demonstrated that these curtain-walls exactly followed and incorporated the Roman fabric at lower levels.[8]

[1] See Introduction, pp. 15, 32, and Loughor (MR 4), Treoda (MM 2), Kenfig (EM 2), Granville's Castle (VE 2), Twyn Castell (MO 9) and Rumney Castle (MR 7). Donald Moore discusses the correlation of Roman and Norman military sites in Wales in *Akten Des XI Internationalen Limes Kongresses*, Akademai Kaido, Budapest, 1978, pp. 19–34.

[2] G. C. Boon discusses medieval drainage and embankment of the coastal levels in F. H. Thompson (ed.), *Archaeology and Coastal Change* (Soc. Antiq. Lond., 1980), esp. pp. 32–4.

[3] William Rees provides a detailed account of the lordship of Cardiff, with map, in *Trans. Cardiff Nat. Soc.*, LXIII, 1930, pp. 18–34. The map also appears in Rees, *Cardiff* (Plate IV) along with further discussion of the lordship. See also *Glam. Co. Hist.*, vol. III pp. 14–15.

[4] Interim reports in *Arch. in Wales, Morgannwg* (1974–81) and in *Britannia* (Vols. VI–XIII, 1975–82). Final interim reports in *Archaeology in Wales* (1981, pp. 42–45) and *Morgannwg* (XXV, 1981, pp. 201–11) include a plan illustrating the sequence of forts. See also Mr Webster's chapter in *Glam. Co. Hist.*, II, 1984, pp. 277–313.

[5] *Arch. Camb.*, 1862, p. 252 (reprinted in *Med. Milit. Arch.*, 1884, I, pp. 337–38). The name derives through early forms (e.g. *Cairdif, Kayrdyf*) from *Caer* (*Castrum*) on the Taff (G.O. Pierce *Glam. Co. Hist.*, II p. 459).

[6] *Arch. Camb.*, 1890, pp. 283–92.

[7] John Ward, *Archaeologia*, LVII, 1901, pp. 335–52; *Arch. Camb.*, 1908, pp. 29–64 and 227–28; 1913, pp. 159–64; 1914, pp. 407–10 and in *Trans. Cardiff Nats. Soc.*, XLVI (1913), pp. 85–89. See also R. E. M. Wheeler, *Antiq. Journ.*, II (1922), pp. 361–70.

[8] Ward, *ibid.*, 1913 (both papers).

The Roman wall, with variations at the S.E. angle, was of constant form and dimensions. Above a plinth set on boulder footings, it was 3.2m thick to a height of 2.28m, where four internal offsets of one course reduced its thickness to 2.59m. It was backed by an earthen bank and enclosed an area of 3.7 hectares, measuring 185m by 200m to its outer faces, beyond which projected evenly spaced polygonal towers, two flanking a central gateway on the N., which no doubt matched another on the site of the present South Gate. The medieval ditch beyond the wall had removed all traces of the Roman ditch.[9]

After clearance, the Roman circuit was reconstructed, except those parts incorporated in the medieval curtains to W. and S. A course of red Radyr Stone separates ancient from modern walling, but an improbable mural passage, projecting over the Roman bank in totally inauthentic fashion at the approximate level of the Roman wall-walk, gives excessive height to an otherwise commendable restoration.

Cardiff Castle in the records

The Roman walls were faced with square blocks of Lias Limestone, the core being of glacial boulders set in iron-hard cement. The singular hardness of this cement leaves little doubt that much of the Roman masonry was still standing in the late 11th century. This probability is germane to strong evidence suggesting that William the Conqueror raised Cardiff Castle in 1081.[10] William built large mottes at Warwick, York, Lincoln, Huntingdon, and Cambridge, all within pre-Norman rectangular fortifications;[11] within the Roman fort at Cardiff is one of the largest mottes in Wales.[12] For long the claim by three Welsh chronicles that William founded the town of Cardiff in 1081 has been discounted, and the castle attributed to Robert Fitzhamon's undoubted acquisition of the area in ca. 1093.[13] Recent numismatic studies by Mr George Boon now confirm the existence of a mint of the Conqueror at Cardiff; five of its coins have been identified, the earliest from the castle.[14] It is reasonable to assume that William raised the motte at Cardiff Castle in the context of his pact with Rhys ap Tewdwr at St Davids in 1081. On his return, the King founded Cardiff and, presumably, its mint. Numismatic opinion has reverted to the long-disputed identification of a mint of the Conqueror at St Davids, 'signing' DEVITUN (Dewi's, or David's Town). These mints presumably enabled Rhys to render his annual tribute of £40 to the king, which Domesday

records, for the Welsh minted no coins. The King's choice of Cardiff is also credible; Rhys had won supremacy in south Wales earlier in the year by defeating Caradog ap Gruffydd, the king of Glamorgan, who is now seen to have been a vassal of the crown from 1072, when he had won Glamorgan with Norman help.[15]

In 1093 Rhys ap Tewdwr fell in battle with the Normans near Brecon. There is no doubt that Robert Fitzhamon's singularly undocumented 'Conquest' of Glamorgan was prompted by Rhys's death, during the general and well-recorded advances into Wales by other Norman lords. From the foundation of Cardiff in 1081 to 1093 the Conqueror's coins attest a Norman presence at Cardiff, and suggest that Fitzhamon's coming may well have been the simple assumption of control in an area long overawed by a strong Norman enclave at Cardiff.

Fitzhamon's tenure (ca. 1093–1107) is well-attested, and his grants to Tewkesbury Abbey included *capellum de castello de Cairdif*, the first record of the castle.[16] His followers held their fees by service of castle-guard at Cardiff. From the outset the limited area initially annexed, the *shire-fee*, was administered from Cardiff; as early as ca. 1102 a deed is witnessed by William, *Vicecomes Kard'*, the first recorded sheriff of Cardiff.[17] As *caput* of Glamorgan,

---

[9] Ward, *op. cit.* (n. 7), 1908, p. 52, n. 1; M. G. Jarrett, in *Roman Frontier in Wales*, 2nd Edn., 1969, p. 70.

[10] The evidence is discussed by C. J. Spurgeon in J. R. Kenyon and R. Avent, (eds.) *Castles in Wales and the Marches; Essays in Honour of D. J. Cathcart King*, Cardiff, 1987, pp. 38–42 and in *Château Gaillard*, XIII, 1986 (1987), pp. 204–05. See also David Crouch, *Morgannwg*, Vol. XXIX, 1985, pp. 20–41.

[11] D. F. Renn, *Château Gaillard*, I, 1962 (1964), pp. 130–31; Renn, *Norman Castles* p. 30; *Hist. King's Works*, I, 1963, pp. 19–32.

[12] D. J. Cathcart King, *Château Gaillard*, V, 1970 (1972), p. 104, n. 12.

[13] *Ann. Margam*, p. 4; *Breviate Ann* (printed in *Arch. Camb.*, 1862, pp. 272–73); *Brut., B.S.* p. 83 (*Sub anno* 1080); J. E. Lloyd discounted these chronicles in *Hist. Wales* (I, pp. 393–6, 402) and in *Trans. Soc. of Cymmrodorion* 1899–1900, pp. 160–64. His pre-eminence as a Welsh historian has generally stifled further consideration of these texts.

[14] Boon, George, *Welsh Hoards*, pp. 40–48 and notes 35–37 (pp. 66–67).

[15] Caradog's relations with the Normans are discussed by Crouch and by Spurgeon, (*op. cit.* n. 10). Paul Courtney (*Morgannwg*, XXX, 1986, pp. 65–69) accepts the foundation of Cardiff in 1081 by William, but makes the improbable suggestion that Rhys ap Tewdwr established its mint.

[16] Clark, *Cartae*, I (xxxvii), p. 40 and *Epis. Acts*, II, L25, p. 614 (a confirmation of 1148 names Fitzhamon's chaplain as Robert: Patterson, *Glouc. Charters*, No. 179, pp. 161–2).

the castle housed the *comitatus*, or county court, the *exchequer*, the *chancery* and the *prison*, where the lord's authority was imposed by his officers, headed by his sheriff and including a receiver, a constable and an auditor. The *mint* established by the Conqueror was surely within the castle. No evidence exists from it for the reign of Rufus, but it is well-attested in the reigns of Henry I and Stephen; its last known coins were issued by Earl Robert, during Stephen's reign, in the name of the Empress Maud.[18]

The castle also provided for the discharge of spiritual and feudal duties. The *chapel* granted by Fitzhamon to Tewkesbury functioned until the Reformation and seems to have stood in the Outer Ward against the tail of the E. rampart.[19] *Houses* in the Outer Ward were assigned to the knights of the shire to facilitate the discharge of their duties of castle-guard and attendance at the monthly court; though these houses were owned by the lord, the knights were obliged to repair and maintain them.[20] They are mentioned by Leland and Merrick in the 16th century, though only one was intact when the latter wrote (*ca.* 1580).[21]

Few records of the feudal administration at Cardiff survived the savage baronial assault of 1321, when at Cardiff, and other castles, a particular objective was the destruction of Hugh Despenser's charters and muniments.[22] Further losses might be attributed to the capture of the castle by the forces of Glyndŵr in 1404. A series of largely external records furnish an uneven history of the castle. There were frequent and often protracted periods of royal control, with the wardship of minors or heiresses under Henry I (1107–?1113), Henry II (1183–89), Henry III (1230–43 and 1262–63), Edward II (1314–17), Edward III (1349–57), and Edward III/Richard II (1375–94). In addition, John was lord of Glamorgan 1189–1214 (as king from 1199), Richard 1472–85 (as Richard III from 1483), and Prince Henry Tudor (Henry VIII from 1509) inherited the lordship in 1495 and it remained in the possession of the Crown until 1550.

Robert Fitzroy, illegitimate son of Henry I and the first earl of Gloucester (from 1121–22), acquired the Honours of Glamorgan and Gloucester by his marriage with Mabel, heiress of Fitzhamon, probably in 1113.[23] In 1126 Cardiff Castle was secure enough for the custody of the King's brother, Duke Robert of Normandy, who was held there until his death in 1134.[24] In 1126 the castle also figures in the Agreement of Woodstock, between Earl Robert and Bishop Urban of Llandaff; a clause stipulates that trials by combat involving their men shall be carried out *in*

castello de Kardi.[25] Earl Robert probably built the keep towards the end of his life. His authority in Glamorgan was challenged during the Welsh uprising which followed the death of Henry I in 1135. This crisis may have inspired the building of the keep, though Robert's leadership of Empress Maud's movement against Stephen from 1138 furnishes another incentive.

Earl William succeeded in 1147. The castle witnessed a celebrated raid in 1158, when Ifor Bach, lord of Senghennydd, alienated by encroachments into his lands, abducted the earl and countess and their infant son, and held them until his demands were conceded. This daring enterprise was undertaken at night, Gerald of Wales adding the significant gloss that it involved the scaling of very high walls that fortified the castle.[26] Gerald's evidence is credible since he recorded this event on a visit to the castle only thirty years later. He also notes that Henry II passed a night at Cardiff on his return from Ireland in 1172.

When Earl William died in 1183 Glamorgan passed into the custody of the Crown, pending its expected

---

[17] Clark, *Cartae*, I, (xxv), p. 38; J. Beverley Smith, *Morgannwg*, II (1958), p. 15 and *Glam. Co. Hist.*, III, p. 16.

[18] Boon, *Welsh Hoards*, pp. 41, 46, 48-49 and p. 68 n. 4. The note dismisses the mistaken attribution of three coins to a Cardiff mint of Earl William under Henry II (Rees *Cardiff*, p. 11, n. 10 and *Industry Before the Industrial Revolution*, I, p. 38, n. 53).

[19] The chaplain's annual salary was 100s. in 1393 (*Cardiff Records*, I, p. 159), and in 1535 106s. 6d. was paid 'by ancient custom' (*Valor Ecclesiasticus* – *Cardiff Records*, V, p. 298). T. J. Hopkins, *Glamorgan Historian*, I (1963), p. 161 (and facing Plate) publishes Francis Grose's sketch plan (British Museum, Add. MS. 17398); this locates the chapel on the central E. side.

[20] See King John's writ of 5 March 1208, cited in f/n. 30. Castle-guard was computed on the basis of 40 days service for each 100 acres held (see Patterson, *Glouc. Charters*, No. 97, p. 98 and n.).

[21] Leland *Itin. Wales*, pp. 34–35; Merrick *Morg. Arch.*, p. 89. Foundations of these houses were recorded in the 19th century (Clark, *Arch. Camb.*, 1890, p. 285) and again in 1974–81 (see f/n. 4). The decay of these houses no doubt accelerated from the 13th century with the commutation of castle-guard by the payment of 6s. 8d., ward silver for each fee.

[22] J. Conway Davies, 'The Despenser War in Glamorgan', *Trans. Royal Historical Society*, Third Series, IX, 1915 (pp. 21–64), p. 55.

[23] Patterson, *Glouc. Charters*, No. 166, p. 152, n.

[24] *Ann. Margam*, p. 13; *Ann. Theokes.*, s.a. 1133; *Breviate Ann.* (*Arch. Camb.* 1862, p. 273); *Ann. Camb.* and *Brut, B.S.* err in claiming he died at Gloucester (where he was buried).

[25] Clark, *Cartae*, I (1), pp. 54–6; *Epis. Acts*, II, L45, pp. 620–21; Patterson, *Glouc. Charters*, No. 109, pp. 106–08.

[26] *Breviate Ann.* (*Arch. Camb.*, 1862, p. 274); *Ann. Margam*, p. 15; Giraldus Cambrensis, *Itinerary*, I, 6; *Glam. Co. Hist.*, III, pp. 34 and 336.

conferment on John, Count of Mortain, who was betrothed to the heiress Isabel. The royal officers, however, were soon confronted by a serious Welsh uprising led by Morgan ap Caradog of Afan and directed mainly against the demesne castles to the W., but the town of Cardiff was also burnt.[27] A force was dispatched to Cardiff from Bristol, and though hostilities ended in July 1184, Cardiff and other castles maintained strong garrisons. The Pipe Rolls record expenditure of 66s. 6d. on the castle and houses, and 19s. 9d. on two mills and the gates and palisade of the town. Henry II retained control of Glamorgan until his death in 1189; at the castle, the repair of its houses cost £4. 12s. 11d. in 1187–88.[28]

John of Mortain married Isabel in August 1189, soon after the king's death, obtaining possession of the lordship of Glamorgan. He remained in possession until 1214, as king from 1199, although he divorced Isabel in that year. Custody was granted to William de Braose in 1202. He was succeeded in 1207 by Fawkes de Bréauté, who by 1209 had repaired the castles of Cardiff, Neath, and Newport at a cost of £81. 8s. 6d., with a further £58. 18s. 6d. being expended for works by Geoffrey of Cardiff, Gilbert Palmer, and the masters William the Carpenter and Eli of Neath.[29] On 5 March 1208 King John ordered his barons and knights to repair *his* houses in the castle bailey at Cardiff (*Kaerdif*), as they were obliged to do, the better to discharge their castle-guard as they valued their fees. This writ disposes of the claim that the knights' houses were an antiquarian fabrication.[30]

In 1214 John's former wife, Isabel, married Geoffrey de Mandeville, earl of Essex, and Fawkes de Bréauté was ordered to grant her seisin of Glamorgan and its castles. Her death in 1217 settled the inheritance on Gilbert de Clare, earl of Hertford, the son of her sister Amice.

The de Clares were lords of Glamorgan for almost a century (1217–1314). Cardiff Castle is unnoticed in the time of Earl Gilbert I (1217–30), but figures in the records of the minority of his son, Richard, who did not obtain seisin until 1243. Hubert de Burgh was initially the royal *custos* of Cardiff Castle and the Honour of Glamorgan, but after his fall in 1232 he was replaced by Peter des Riveaux. This appointment provoked serious baronial opposition under Richard Marshal, earl of Pembroke, in alliance with Llywelyn ab Iorwerth and the Welsh lords of the Glamorgan uplands. In 1233 Marshal and his allies moved against Glamorgan and Gwent, taking Cardiff and other castles and forcing the dismissal of Peter des Riveaux.[31] Cardiff (variously *Caerdyf, Kirdive, Kerdif*), alone of the castles taken, was spared destruction, although its seizure was resisted by the king's garrison, and Warin Basset was slain.

Under Earl Richard (1243–62) there is one possible and inconsequential reference to Cardiff Castle in Richard Siward's unsuccessful appeal in 1247 to the *curia regis* for the recovery of Talyfan and Llanblethian, confiscated for his treason. The earl's castle of *Kydif* mentioned in these proceedings is surely Cardiff.[32] Earl Richard died in July 1262. His heir, Gilbert, was only nineteen years old but he obtained seisin in August 1263. During this brief minority Humphrey de Bohun, earl of Hereford and Essex, and Walter de Sully were successive custodians. De Bohun accounted for expenditure of £62. 14s. 6d. at Cardiff Castle for the constable, with three horses, three valets without horses, a warder, gatekeeper, cook, washerwoman, two watchmen and five footmen.[33] The important Extent of Glamorgan of 1262 furnishes no information on Cardiff Castle.

Gilbert II, the 'Red Earl' (1263–95), was the leading magnate of the realm, but Cardiff Castle is rarely mentioned in the records. It figured briefly as the prison of Gruffydd ap Rhys in 1267, following Earl Gilbert's annexation of his patrimony of Senghennydd. Gilbert's great new castle in the annexed territory at Caerphilly (LM 3), built before the wars with Llywelyn ap Gruffydd, and only about 10km N. of Cardiff, no doubt spared the *caput* from any Welsh attack. Following the wars, however, Edward I halted at Cardiff on 15–16 December 1284 during his triumphal progress through Wales.

---

[27] *Hist. Kings Works*, Vol. II, pp. 650–51; *Glam. Co. Hist.*, III, p. 37; *Ann. Margam, s.a.* 1185, p. 18.

[28] *Pipe Rolls*, 30 Henry II, 1183–84, pp. XXVII and 110; 31 Henry II, 1184–85, pp. XXVI-XXVII and 5–7; and 34 Henry II, 1187–88, p. 8; Clarke, *Cartae*, I (clxxi), pp. 170–72.

[29] *Rot. Litt. Pat.*, i, pp. 19, 68; *Pipe Rolls*, 9 John, 1207–08, p. 221 and 10 John, 1208–09, p. 24; *Rot. Litt. Claus.*, i, p. 92 (Clark, *Cartae*, II, cccxii), p. 312); Clark, *Cartae*, II (cccliii), p. 354 (wrongly dated to *ca.* 1216).

[30] *Rot. Litt. Pat.*, i, 79; Clark *Cartae*, II (cccxxi) pp. 320–21. *Glam. Co. Hist.*, III, p. 288 disregards the clear import of this writ.

[31] Altschul, *The Clares*, pp. 64–5; *Glam. Co. Hist.*, III, p. 48; *Bruts: B.S., Pen. 20, R.B.H.; Ann. Camb; Cron. Wallia; Ann. Theokes.*

[32] *P.R.O.*, KB 26/159, M2; misread *Kidis* in Clark, *Cartae*, II (dxxxv), p. 551 and *Arch. Camb.* 1878, p. 244 (both transcribed from a corrupt MS. and wrongly dated – see *Glam. Co. Hist.*, III, pp. 50–51 and n. 31, p. 588).

[33] Clark, *Land of Morgan*, pp. 123–25; *Glam. Co. Hist.*, III, pp. 52–3. *Cardiff Records*, I, p. 104 (Ministers Accounts).

Fig. 115. Cardiff Castle: the Motte and Shell-keep viewed from the south.

Earl Gilbert II died on 7 December 1295, his heir Gilbert being a minor. Royal custody was averted, for his wife, the king's daughter, Joan of Acre, was jointly enfeoffed and retained possession. Joan's secret marriage to Ralph de Monthermer so enraged Edward I that her lands were briefly seized, and Richard Talbot was granted custody of the castle and vill of Cardiff (*Kerdyf*) on 14 July 1297.[34] The king soon relented, and Joan and Ralph had joint livery of the estates until the countess died in 1307.

Earl Gilbert III, the last Clare lord (1307–14), was still a minor on his mother's death, but although the custody of Cardiff Castle was successively granted to Henry de Llancarvan and Ralph de Monthermer, he seems to have obtained seisin before the end of 1307.[35] His precocious career ended on the field at Bannockburn in 1314, when he was but twenty-three years old. His inquisition *post mortem* records his castle at *Kaerdif*, where £12.5s. was rendered as ward silver for 36½ knight's fees.

Between 1314 and 1317 Glamorgan was in royal custody, pending a partition of the de Clare estates among the three sisters of the late earl. This period was disturbed by two insurrections, the first soon after the earl's death and the second, and more serious, in 1316.[36] The first revolt had begun before the tenure of Bartholomew de Badlesmere as royal custodian (Sept. 14 1314–July 8 1315). He pursued a policy of conciliation, and at Cardiff Castle he expended 12s. 9d. on the re-roofing of the houses with shingles, £1.1s. 3d. on the repairs or fittings to the larder, gates, prison, and walls, and further sums for victuals and the wages of the doorkeeper, two watchmen and the constable.[37]

Payn de Turberville, lord of Coity, who succeeded Badlesmere as custodian (8 July 1315–20 April 1316), instigated a more repressive policy and provoked the more serious revolt. Led by Llywelyn Bren of Senghennydd, this raged from January to March 1316. The outbreak was expected: in December the king had ordered Turberville adequately to victual and garrison Cardiff and the other castles in the lordship.[38] The ferocity of the uprising exceeded expectations. Neath, Kenfig and Llantrisant Castles were attacked, and, nearer to Cardiff, Caerphilly was besieged and entrenchments were constructed on the intervening ridge overlooking Cardiff to impede any relieving force from that place. On 10 February John Giffard of Brimpsfield was given charge of Cardiff Castle, and from there, on 12 March, 150 men-at-arms and 2,000 footmen advanced to relieve Caerphilly, heralding

Llywelyn's surrender on 18 March. On 20 April Giffard was appointed custodian of the lordship in place of Turberville.

John Giffard was *custos* until May 1317. His accounts record widespread damage and diminished receipts attributed to Llywelyn Bren's rebellion, even at Cardiff. At the castle 32s. 11d. was expended on re-roofing the Black Tower and the houses, and repairing a furnace and the bridge towards the keep, and a further 73s. 0¼d. on the outer wall of the bailey and repairs to the houses. The work on the houses was carried out by two carpenters who used shingles made in the lord's wood; a plumber and his man used lead, tin, and pitch for the roof of the Black Tower. The castle gatekeeper received 3d. a day and two watchmen each received 2d. a day.[39]

Hugh Despenser the younger acquired the lordship of Glamorgan in 1317, when the Gloucester lands were divided between the three heiresses. His wife, Eleanor, was the eldest sister of the last Earl Gilbert. Hugh embarked on a policy of ruthless encroachment into the lands settled on his brothers-in-law, Hugh Audley and Roger Damory, and by dubious means he attempted to acquire the lordship of Gower. These unscrupulous plans of aggrandizement, compounded by his envied intimacy with the king, provoked the baronial reaction of 1321, which has been called 'The Despenser War in Glamorgan'.[40] The barons began hostilities at Newport on 4 May 1321. Although Hugh was forewarned and his castles were 'guarded and victualled for all eventualities',[41] the rebels were irresistible. First, Newport was taken, and then Cardiff Castle fell on 9 May to a force of 800 men-at-arms, 500 light cavalry, and 10,000 footmen, and within a few weeks they had stormed and sacked all Hugh's castles from Newport in the E. to Dryslwyn

[34] Altschul *The Clares*, p. 157; Clark, *Land of Morgan*, p. 147; *Cardiff Records*, III, p. 13; Moor, *Knights of Edward I*, Harleian society, IV (1931), p. 31 and V (1932), p. 2.

[35] *Cardiff Records*, III, pp. 13–14; Clark, *Land of Morgan*, pp. 150–51.

[36] J. Beverley Smith, *Glam. Co. Hist.*, III, pp. 72–86.

[37] *Cardiff Records*, I, pp. 108, 114–5; Clark, *Land of Morgan*, p. 155.

[38] *Cal. Anc. Corr.*, pp. 172–3; *Cardiff Records*, III, pp. 14–15.

[39] Giffard's accounts, wrongly dated to 1281, are transcribed by Clark, *Cartae*, III (dccxlii–dcxlix), pp. 813–48. For the castle and town of Cardiff: dccxliii, pp. 813–5 (translated in *Cardiff Records*, I, pp. 132–3).

[40] Conway Davies, *op. cit.* (f/n. 22), pp. 21–64; see also T. B. Pugh, *Glam. Co. Hist.*, III, pp. 167–71.

[41] *Cal. Anc. Corr.*, pp. 219–20.

in the W., including eight in the lordship of Glamorgan.[42] Though Despenser was condemned and exiled by Parliament in August, his lands and exalted position were restored after the royalist victory at Boroughbridge in March 1322. Before the close of April he requested the delivery to Cardiff Castle of the rebel, Thomas of Usk, together with a springal that had been captured at Cardiff and taken to Berkeley Castle.[43] Despenser's recovery was brief. The fugitive king joined him at Cardiff Castle 26–28 October 1326, before his final despairing wanderings in Glamorgan. From Cardiff the king made the first of several appeals for the levying of troops among the Welsh of Glamorgan and Gwent.[44] Captured near Llantrisant in November, he abdicated in January 1327, two months after Despenser's execution at Hereford.

Leniency was shown to Despenser's widow, Eleanor, who recovered her inheritance in 1328 and was succeeded by her eldest son, Hugh, Lord Despenser (1337–49). There is no record of Cardiff Castle during this period, nor during the lordship of Edward Despenser (1357–75), who inherited after a minority. The castle re-appears in the records following Edward's death, during the long minority of his son Thomas (1375–94).

In 1376 Thomas Broun, the king's receiver in Glamorgan, accounted for his wages at 12d. a day as constable of the castle of *Kerdyf*, the gatekeeper Peter John receiving 2d. a day; £11. 18s. 4d. was rendered as ward-silver from 35¼ knights' fees; a rabbit-warren yielded 6s. and the issues of the mills, fisheries and tolls were worth £26. 13s. 4d. by the year.[45] In January 1377 Broun was succeeded by William Walsh, who by June had expended £87. 16s. 11½d. on repairs at four castles, eight mills, and to sea-walls. The castles were Cardiff, Llantrisant, Kenfig, and Neath and two of the mills were at Cardiff.[46] In 1393 Roger Panter, surveyor of the churches of Tewkesbury Abbey, recorded the annual salary of the chaplain of the castle of *Kerdif* as 100s.; wine for Cardiff church, and chapels at Roath and in the castle, had cost 3s. 2d.[47]

Thomas, the last Despenser lord, had seisin in 1394. A favourite of Richard II, his career was ruined by the revolution of 1399 which brought Henry IV to the throne. He was executed at Bristol in 1400, having supported the futile bid to restore the deposed king. His lands were seized by the crown, but restored to his widow, Constance of York, in 1401, who retained them until her death in 1416. In July 1400, six months after Despenser's execution, Constance gave birth to

his eventual heiress, Isabel, at Cardiff Castle.

The rebellion of Owain Glyndŵr began in 1400, shortly before Glamorgan was restored to Constance. In August 1403 Glyndŵr led a force against Glamorgan and Gwent, attacking Cardiff and Newport. Orders were given in September to provision these castles. By October Cardiff Castle was in imminent danger when Henry IV instructed the earl of Devon to lead a force sufficient to avert its fall but, despite this, the castle appears to have fallen to Glyndŵr in 1404.[48] The town was burnt and the castle sacked, according to the one authority for this event; as late as 1492 the bailiffs recorded murage tolls for the repair of the walls 'which were greatly damaged in the time of the rebellion of Wales', noticing also many vacant burgages 'destroyed, laid waste and burned by the rebel Welsh many years ago'.[49]

A fragmentary account of William Rye, preserved in the public records, is the only testimony to the apparently futile efforts made at Cardiff in 1403–04 to repulse the insurgents.[50] Decipherable items emphasize the desperate situation at the castle. An undetermined sum was released to the mayor for the wages of 138 men and 435 archers, respectively paid 12d. and 6d. a day. In addition, the garrison included 24 men-at-arms whose wages amounted to 400s., at 12d. a day each. Twice the accounts record the payment of 22s. 6d. for nine sheaves of arrows. Two guns were purchased for 8s., together with 4lb of gunpowder worth 8s., an iron pestle for loading the guns worth 2d., 40 'gadds' for the guns at 2s. 6d., and 56 'gun stones' (i.e., cannon balls) at 24s. Rye also accounts for works on the fortifications of the town and castle; 79 sailors received 4d. a day for divers works 'for issue from siege'. Provisions listed included

---

[42] Conway Davies, *op. cit.* (f/n. 22), pp. 54–7; Pugh, *op. cit.* (f/n. 40), pp. 170–71.

[43] *Cal. Anc. Corr.*, p. 185.

[44] Clark, *Cartae*, VI (mdcxxxi), pp. 2361–2.

[45] *Cardiff Records*, I, pp. 150–52 (Ministers Accounts).

[46] Exchequer Accounts Various, Foreign Accounts (L.T.R.), 51 Edward III (E.101/487/12); further details of this account follow in 2 Richard II (E.364/22).

[47] *Cardiff Records*, I, p. 159.

[48] *Cal. P. R.*, Henry IV, ii, pp. 296 and 439; Clark, *Cartae*, IV (mxciv), p. 1454; Lloyd, *Owen Glendower*, Oxford, 1931, pp. 54, 74, 76, 89–90, 152; *Glam. Co. Hist.*, III, pp. 183–85.

[49] *Eulogium Historiarum* (ed. F. S. Haydon, Rolls Series, 3 vols., 1858–63), III, p. 401; *Cardiff Records*, I, pp. 174–5, 180 (Ministers Accounts); Rees, *Cardiff*, p. 14.

[50] *P.R.O.*, E.101/44/5, Exchequer Accounts Various, 5–6 Henry IV (30 September 1403–29 September 1405).

quantities of flour and salmon, 4 pipes of red and white wine at £10, and 3 barrels of salt fish at 53s. 4d. Internal section totals of £102 and £28. 5s. 5d. are legible, the latter for victuals and artillery, but overall expenditure is unclear.

In February 1405 Constance, Lady Despenser, was frustrated when attempting the treasonable abduction of the young Edmund Mortimer from Windsor. Apprehended at Cheltenham, she had intended to conduct Edmund, a potential claimant to the throne, to Cardiff, probably to convey him to the rebel forces then installed there.[51] This conspiracy against Henry IV is hard to comprehend, given the king's leniency in re-instating her in 1401; following hard on the collapse of English authority in her lordship and the capture of Cardiff by the rebels, however, her conduct may reflect despair at the royal assistance extended to her. Whatever her motive, her treason was again forgiven and her lands restored to her in 1406. Edward, duke of York, her brother, was deputed to restore the situation in Glamorgan, and accounts of 1409 record his household expenses at Cardiff Castle.[52] By then the crisis was over. Constance died in 1416 and Glamorgan passed to Isabel, the Despenser heiress, and her husband, Richard Beauchamp, earl of Worcester. He died in 1422, and in 1423 Isabel married his namesake, Richard Beauchamp, earl of Warwick.

To Richard of Warwick (1423–1439), tradition attributes much of the surviving fabric of the Western Apartments. The male line of the Beauchamps terminated with the death of Earl Richard's son, Henry, in 1445. His daughter and heiress died a minor in 1449, and the inheritance passed to Richard Nevill, husband of Beauchamp's sister, Ann. He was created earl of Warwick, and, like the Beauchamp lords before him, he was preoccupied with great territorial interests in England, and with the struggles of the Wars of the Roses. Earl Richard, 'the Kingmaker', was killed in arms at Barnet in 1471. He left two daughters, Isabel and Ann Nevill, whose husbands, themselves brothers, disputed the succession. In an eventual partition enforced by the King in 1474, Ann's husband, Richard, duke of Gloucester became the last medieval marcher lord of Glamorgan. Richard, like his father-in-law, was entirely preoccupied with his interests in England, and the political convulsions that would lead him to the throne. From 1477, or earlier, his agent in Glamorgan was Sir James Tyrell, reputed murderer of the Princes in the Tower, who was his sheriff and steward of Glamorgan, and constable of Cardiff

Castle, offices he held until Richard's death at Bosworth in 1485. The few surviving records of Richard's tenure include two charters retaining seals of the Cardiff chancery.[53]

In 1486 Glamorgan was granted to Jasper Tudor, duke of Bedford and uncle of the new king. He was another absentee ruler, Sir Richard Croft, of Croft Castle, Herefordshire, serving as his sheriff of Glamorgan, steward of Morgannwg and constable of Cardiff Castle, at an annual salary of £100. The lordship reverted to the crown in 1495, on Jasper's death, and was settled on his infant great-nephew, Henry, the future Henry VIII, but farmed to Charles Somerset, later earl of Worcester. On his accession to the throne in 1509, Henry VIII granted Charles Somerset tenure for life. Administration was devolved to his deputy-sheriff, Sir Mathew Cradock, whose grandson, George Herbert, succeeded to that office in 1524. Cradock's accounts as receiver in 1515 record the daily wage of 3d. paid to Sir Robert Jones as gatekeeper at Cardiff Castle. The deputy-gatekeeper, Owen Vayne, accounts for 9s. 4d. expended on the customary 7d. a week diet of three named felons, imprisoned before their hanging. A further 115s. 1d. was charged for the wages of a tiler and his labourer, and the tiles, shingles, shingle-nails, and lime used to tile the great hall and other houses in the castle. In 1519 the same materials, together with nails, ironwork, and locks were purchased and used for the repair of houses, a stable and chambers in the castle. On this occasion Owen Vayne charged 14s. for the custody and hanging of another two felons.[54]

In the late 1530s Leland described Cardiff Castle as '. . . a great thing and a strong, but now in sum ruine.' He noticed two gates. The larger or Shirehall Gate was near a '. . . great large tour caullid White Tour: wherin is now the Kinges armary.' Leland's 'White Tower' is the Keep; the Shirehall Gate presumably stood on the line of the cross-wall between the Keep and the Black Tower. Leland's lesser gate, his 'Exchequer Gate', was presumably that communicating with the town and beside the Black Tower on the S. which he termed the 'Dungeon Tower'. Leland also noticed the knights' houses in the outer ward.[55]

---

[51] Clark, *Cartae*, IV (mxcvi), pp. 1456–7; *Glam. Co. Hist.*, III, p. 182.

[52] *Glam. Co. Hist.*, III, p. 184 and n. 136, p. 609.

[53] Clark, *Cartae*, V (mccvi), pp. 1649–53 and mccxliv, pp. 1723–5 (seals illustrated pp. 1650–1, 1724).

[54] *Cardiff Records*, I, pp. 200–3 (Ministers Accounts).

[55] Leland, *Itin. Wales*, pp. 34–35.

In 1551 Edward VI granted Cardiff Castle and the lordship of Glamorgan to William Herbert, who was created earl of Pembroke and Lord Herbert of Cardiff. During the tenure of his son, Earl Henry (1570–1601), an extensive programme of rebuilding was undertaken, particularly in the area of the domestic apartments against the W. wall. By ca.1580 Merrick was able to note that Earl Henry had '... repaired and translated the form of all the rooms within the castle'. Two adjacent friaries in Cardiff provided stone for these works, and more were carried out between 1588 and 1590. Henry Martyn accounts for works in 1588–89. Materials included five cart-loads of freestone from the 'Fryers', and works were undertaken on the kitchen, pantry, exchequer, Shire-hall, the lord's chamber, the dining chamber, the great chamber and the hall. New chimneys, hearths, and stairs are also mentioned and the kitchen windows were glazed. In 1590 works in the Keep are indicated; the lodging in the 'mownte' is mentioned, new floors were inserted in 'Mr. Babyngton's decayed chamber in the Kepe', and a 'Great Arch of Stone' replaced the drawbridge at the entrance to the Keep – presumably spanning the moat. Elsewhere, the wardrobe, the Black Tower, and the South Gate were also repaired. The restored apartments were lavishly furnished. Inventories of 1581 and 1585 record many-coloured curtains of taffeta, silk, velvet, and satin, some embroidered; also listed were quilts, carpets, leather hangings with the lord's arms, and tapestries including sets depicting the story of Bacchus and 'poetical fancies'.[56]

Merrick describes the castle at this period. He entered by a 'fair gate' on the S., noting the knight's houses, all decayed except for that of Sir Edward Mansel, and the Shire-hall. The Black Tower, on the W. side of the South Gate (Leland's 'Dungeon Tower'), housed prisons in its two basements, the 'stafell yr oged' ('room of the harrow') and 'stafell wen' ('white room'). Two gates pierced the internal cross-wall between the Black Tower and 'Iestyn's Tower' (the keep; Leland's White Tower). The apartments against the W. wall, with their 'very fair and stately front' with bay windows, and the external angular (Beauchamp) tower, he wrongly ascribes to Lady Eleanor or Elizabeth Despenser. The Keep was then reached through two gates, one at each end of a bridge spanning the moat, both defended by a portcullis. A planked walk had replaced the drawbridge set upon this bridge, now reconstituted much as Merrick described it; curiously, he regarded the pit beneath it as the prison that had held Earl Robert

of Normandy in the early 12th century. Merrick also provided evidence for the location of gardens and the wood-yard, and describes the general layout of the western apartments.

Philip Herbert, fourth earl of Pembroke, espoused the Parliamentary cause shortly before the outbreak of the Civil War. The king seized his estates, and appointed Sir Anthony Mansel as his governor at Cardiff Castle. Mansel was killed in the first Battle of Newbury (1643), and was succeeded in rapid succession by William Mayo, Sir Nicholas Kemys, and Sir Thomas Tyrrell, before the strategic value of the castle drew hostilities to its walls.[57] As many as 7,000 men had been arrayed for the king at Cardiff in 1642, and following his defeat at Naseby in 1645, Charles attempted to rally further support in the area. He was at Cardiff Castle on 16 July, and again from 29 July to 5 August, appointing Sir Richard Bassett as governor there in place of Tyrrell. On 17 September 1645 Bassett was forced to deliver the castle to a Parliamentary force, though permitted to march thence with 16 pieces of ordnance and his provisions, powder and arms. Edward Pritchard of Llancaeach, Parliamentary governor of the castle, was besieged in February 1646 by defectors led by Edward Carne. A small fleet under Vice-Admiral Crowther sustained the garrison until the arrival of a strong force under Major-General Laugharne. Carne withdrew to the N. of Cardiff, where he was engaged and defeated with heavy losses on 18 February. Parliament maintained a garrison at the castle and in June 1647 it was supplied with match, bullets and 20 barrels of powder. Further threat to it ended with the royalist defeat at St Fagans, 6km to the W., in May 1648. In 1649 Parliament chose not to demolish the castle.

A survey of 1666 described the castle as 'partly demolished and out of repair'. An inventory of 1673 indicates a number of rooms still in use, including the Mayor's Room, the Receiving Chamber, the Round Tower Chamber, the Audit Room, Mr Herbert's Chamber, and the Hall.[58]

[56] Merrick, *Morg. Arch.*, pp. 89–92; N.L.W., Bute MSS., 7231, 7265–67; *Arch. Camb.*, 1913, p. 134; Rees, *Cardiff*, pp. 118–9; *Glam. Co. Hist.*, IV, pp. 123–24, 130; J. P. Grant, *Cardiff Castle; its History and Architecture*, 1923, p. 29.

[57] *Glam. Co. Hist.*, IV, pp. 258–61, 264 and 271–74; J. R. Phillips, *Memoirs of the Civil War in Wales and the Marches* (2 Vols. London, 1874), I, pp. 231, 319, 357, 389; *Cardiff Records*, IV, pp. 146–53; *Calendar of State Papers, Domestic, 1649–50*, p. 264 (for order sparing castle from demolition).

[58] *Cardiff Records*, II, p. 88; N.L.W., Bute MSS, 845.

Charlotte Herbert, daughter of Philip, the seventh earl of Pembroke (*ob.* 1683), conveyed the castle and Glamorgan estates to Thomas, Viscount Windsor, whom she took as her second husband in 1704. In 1766 Charlotte's granddaughter and heiress, also Charlotte, married John, Viscount Mountstuart, the son of the Prime Minister, the third earl of Bute. Lord Mountstuart acquired the Glamorgan estates, *iure uxoris*, on the death of Lady Windsor in 1776, and estates in Scotland and Bedfordshire in 1792, when he succeeded as the fourth earl of Bute. In 1796 he was made a marquess.

Cardiff Castle witnessed unparalleled changes during the tenure of the marquesses of Bute, which terminated in 1947 when the fifth marquess presented it to the city. Extensive works by the first, third and fourth marquesses produced an incomparable neo-gothic restoration, incorporating and augmenting the surviving Roman, Norman, Medieval, and Tudor fabric. The second marquess (1814–48) embarked on the staggering development of Cardiff as a major port.[59]

When John, Lord Mountstuart, acquired Cardiff Castle in 1776 it had not been a frequented residence of its lords since the 16th century. Its crumbling fortifications sheltered only the modest dwelling of the Bird family, hereditary agents. John embarked on a programme of clearance, landscaping, and reconstruction, abandoned before its completion on the death of his son and heir in 1794. Plans submitted for this work by Robert Adam survive, but a scheme devised by Capability Brown was chosen.[60] Brown demolished the cross-wall between the Black Tower and the Keep, including the crenellated fore-building of the latter, with its lower gatehouses. The Shire-hall and lesser buildings in the outer ward were removed, the moat around the motte was filled in, and the interior was landscaped. Henry Holland was engaged to reconstruct the Western Apartments, adding a new south wing to balance a restored Herbert wing to the north, the whole crenellated and incorporating symmetrically disposed sash and neo-gothic windows. A new tower achieved a symmetrical western front centred on the Beauchamp Tower. These apartments were unfinished when work was abandoned in 1794.

John, the second marquess (1814–1848), grandson of the first, employed Sir Robert Smirke to complete the Western Apartments, seemingly before 1818, but expenditure on his grand scheme to develop the port of Cardiff curbed further expenditure on the castle, where only four full-time servants were employed.[61]

The third marquess, also John (1848–1900), was only six months old when he succeeded to the title. During his minority his mother, Lady Sophia Bute, resided for long periods in the castle until her death in 1859. She restored the Black Tower for use as estate offices, adding the external stone stairs masking the severed S. end of the cross-wall.[62] The third marquess came of age in 1868. He confessed to 'a considerable taste for art and archaeology and, happily, the means to indulge them'. At Cardiff Castle and Castell Coch, in happy collaboration with the eccentric genius, William Burges, he created incomparable neo-feudal dream castles. Even before Bute's coming of age, Burges had submitted a report on the redevelopment of the S.W. angle of Cardiff Castle. Work began soon after the minority came to an end and was to continue, with few intervals, until the 1920s. The inspiration throughout was that of Burges; after his death in 1881 successive directing architects respected his master-plan, combining careful investigation (sometimes by excavation) and restoration of ancient fabric, with a free and brilliant recreation in the richest neo-gothic style, clearly differentiated from the old. These successors were William Frame (1881–1905), H. Sesom-Hiley (1905–1921), and, from 1921, John P. Grant.

Burges began by raising the *Clock Tower*, completed by 1873; a work of sheer fantasy, it presented a dramatic first impression at the western entry to the town, soaring high above the S.W. angle and linked to the Black Tower by a refaced section of the S. curtain, which was given a neo-Norman crenellated and roofed wall-walk.

In 1872 a scheme was drawn up for the *Western Apartments*. By Burges's death in 1881 this was completed, except for a proposed grand stair and the lavish interiors of a few chambers. Holland's castellated *East*

---

[59] For the Butes at Cardiff, two works are indispensable: John Davies, *Cardiff and the Marquesses of Bute*, Cardiff, 1981; J. Mordaunt Crook, *William Burges and the High Victorian Dream*, 1981 (pp. 253–79 for the third marquess' work at Cardiff Castle). Rees, *Cardiff*, pp. 344–9, for a useful appendix on the castle restoration. See also Mark Girouard, *Country Life*, 1961 (I, 6 April, pp. 760–3; II, 13 April, pp. 822–5 and III, 20 April, pp. 886–9); D. B. Hague, *Glam. Co. Hist.*, III, pp. 426–9.

[60] Works cited in f/n. 59; Mordaunt Crook, p. 260; Davies, p. 80; Rees, p. 344; and Girouard, I, pp. 761–2.

[61] Mordaunt Crook, *op. cit.* (f/n. 59), p. 260; *Plans and Prospects*, Welsh Arts Council, 1975, No. 6; Davies, *op. cit.* (f/n. 59), pp. 90–1.

[62] Grant, *op. cit.* (f/n. 56), pp. 30–31; *Arch. Camb.* 1862, p. 265 and 1913, p. 134. The restoration was by Pritchard of Llandaff. 18th and early-19th-century prints attest the accuracy of the restoration.

Front was partially retained, but the entry returned to the S. end, where a fifth angular bay was added. *The Hall*, subdivided by Holland, was thrown open again to create a fine library over the largely undisturbed medieval vaulted basement. Bedrooms on the floor above made way for a large *Banqueting Hall*. The 15th-century *Beauchamp Tower* was redesigned; the Octagonal Stair was inserted, and above it the Chaucer Room, the whole being crowned with a striking timber spire modelled on that at Amiens. The 16th-century *Herbert Tower* and Holland's tower to the N., renamed the *Bute Tower*, were heightened. Burges's projected grand staircase in the entrance lobby was never executed, but beyond this, domestic apartments and kitchens were rebuilt, incorporating the new *Guest Tower*. To unite these towers, old and new, to the two great chambers in the central block, further mural passages were cut in the massive western curtain. A private oratory was also created in the little annexe S. of the Beauchamp Tower, where the second marquess had died in 1848.

The third marquess's taste for art and archaeology is proclaimed by the architectural and decorative magnificence of the redesigned Western Apartments, and in less well-recorded aspects of the long programme of work. Before restoration began, G. T. Clark published an account of the castle, and his unpublished papers and comments in subsequent publications show how closely he observed the operations and furnished advice throughout.[63] During excavations in 1872 he sketched a 'recently discovered' drawbridge pit and foundations, and by 1884 the motte ditch had been opened up again, and flooded, 'with great attention to its original dimensions', an operation revealing the wooden piles of an early bridge and the stone arch of a later one, with the base of a gateway at the foot of the motte, close to a well. Stone steps were uncovered on the slope of the mound. Clark also noted the foundations of the cross-wall between the Keep and the Black Tower, and their restoration at ground level. Excavations in 1873 uncovered the footings of the Shire-hall and adjacent buildings in the Outer Ward; too imperfect for restoration, these were recorded on plans still conserved at the castle (Fig. 128).

From 1881 William Frame continued to execute Burges's plans, initially preoccupied with unfinished interiors in the Western Apartments. In 1889, however, the unforeseen discovery of the substantial E. wall of the Roman fort beneath the rampart presented the opportunity of adding a classical dimension to Burges's master-plan. By 1890 most of the E. front of the Roman wall was laid bare. At intervals thereafter the entire course of the Roman wall under the rampart was exposed, culminating in Grant's clearance of the E. half of the S. wall in 1922–23. Before 1900 Frame began to reconstruct the vanished Roman superstructure, and by 1914 Sesom-Hiley had largely restored the E. wall and was well advanced on the N. wall and gateway. The Roman restoration was completed by raising a wall over the foundations that survived at the N. end of the W. front, and a further section over the substantial remains E. of the South Gate disclosed by Grant. By then, in five widely-separated investigations (1908–12), Sesom-Hiley had demonstrated that the medieval curtain-wall defining the S.W. angle, from the South Gate to the N. end of the Ladies Walk, rose directly upon substantial remains of the rest of the Roman circuit.

The inserted mural gallery, improbably based on Aurelian's wall at Rome, was regrettable; commendably, however, care was taken to conserve and display the Roman fabric. Externally, to display Roman core rising higher than its facing, niches were provided in the new wall above the marker-course. Internally, a tunnel from the S. gate to a large chamber at the S.E. angle exposed a fine stretch of Roman walling. Viewing points with access from the mural gallery were inserted at the central E. tower, the N.E. and N.W. angles, and at the Roman gate, which was also accessible at ground level through its original rear doors.

Romanists may regret the inserted mural gallery and the consequent excessive height of the restored Roman wall, but internally this ensured complete restoration of the medieval bank. Minimal cuts disturbed this bank, sufficient to expose and restore the Roman wall; refilled, they leave the interior hardly changed – except for the restored Roman N. gate, previously hidden within an unbroken rampart.

The Roman restoration was the major contribution of the fourth marquess (1900–47), but lesser works were concentrated on the medieval fabric. He rebuilt the South Gateway, and at the N. end of the Ladies' Walk he added the small square turret to embrace the severed end of the medieval curtain rising from

---

[63] G. T. Clark, *Arch. Camb.* 1862, pp. 249–71, reprinted, with additions, in *Med. Milit. Arch.*, 1884, I, additions pp. 16–7, 143, 340–41); *Arch. Camb.* 1890, pp. 283–92. Clark's last contribution to archaeology, concerning Cardiff Castle, appeared in the *South Wales Echo*, 28 January 1898, three days before his death; see also Clark Papers, *N.L.W.*, Welsh Castles II, 5198 E.

its Roman base, and to mark the junction with the restored Roman wall beyond. Between this turret and the keep, he partially restored the N. cross-wall spanning the motte ditch. The keep itself was consolidated, and floors restored to its gatehouse; fortunately, this substantially Norman edifice, the finest shell-keep in Wales, was never converted to the great domed structure contemplated by the third marquess.[64] In 1921 Grant restored the West Gate of the town, adjacent to the Beauchamp Tower, and in 1927 he built the present entrance hall to the Western Apartments, where Burges had intended to place his grand staircase.

Since the castle was given to the city in 1947 it has been well-maintained as an impressive public asset. The grounds and most of its buildings are now open to the public, including the tunnel giving access to the Roman wall. A military museum has long been established in the Black Tower, and another has recently been set up in the Roman Mural Gallery. The castle archives are maintained, and preserve much Burges material. Generous assistance was given during survey by the city authorities and their staff at the castle.[65]

The structural development of the castle[66]

After three major post-medieval programmes of rebuilding, culminating in the comprehensive work of the Butes, it is not possible to determine with cer-

tainty a complete structural sequence. We may, nevertheless, identify seven significant periods of construction, four of them in the Middle Ages:

This sequence of building periods is illustrated in four simplified overall plans (Fig. 116, a–d). These depict the castle in: (a) the late 11th and 12th centuries, *Periods I* and *II*; (b) the 13th and 14th centuries, *Period III*; (c) the early 15th century, *Period IV*; and (d) in 1923, *Periods V* to *VII*. The Shire Hall and other buildings disclosed by excavations in the Outer Ward are not shown, but they appear on the detailed plan (Fig. 128). There is no specific documentary evidence for the four medieval structural phases identified. Minor repairs and buildings works are noted in the preceding

Fig. 116. *(Opposite)* The Structural Development of Cardiff Castle. The Shell-keep of Period II is the only addition shown to the primary Inner Ward of masonry on plan (a). The final plan (d) portrays the existing remains following the clearance and restoration of most of the Roman walls in Period VII.

[64] Mordaunt Crook, *op. cit.* (n. 59), p. 268.
[65] Particular thanks are extended to J. R. C. Bethel and D. St. J. Griffiths of the South Glamorgan Architects Department for furnishing photographs and a copy of their survey of the West Apartments; to Mrs P. Sargent, late of the castle archives; and to Mrs Patricia Eylcs, Mr G. Gray, Mrs Molly Stone, and Mr Peter Eriksen for their generous assistance during survey.
[66] Clark (*op. cit.* f/n. 5 and 6: 1862, 1884 and 1890) and Grant (*op. cit.* f/n. 56, 1923) furnish good accounts of the castle. Ward's reports on the late-Roman defences (*op. cit.*, f/n. 7, 1901, 1908, 1913 and 1914) provide crucial evidence for the nature of the primary castle.

I	*Late 11th century*	Motte; Walled Inner Ward; large Outer Ward enclosed by earthen bank raised over Roman wall (William I, 1081).
II	*12th century*	Stone shell-keep on motte (probably by Earl Robert, *ca.* 1140).
III	*13th–14th century*	Black Tower; Keep Gatehouse and integral hall; Keep fore-building with stone bridge and lower gatehouses; gate on cross-wall (mostly by de Clare earls, 1217–1314, some perhaps by Despensers in 14th century).
IV	*Early 15th century*	Western Apartments, with Beauchamp Tower (Richard Beauchamp, earl of Warwick, 1423–39), and other lesser additions.
V	*Late 16th century*	Western Apartments refurbished and extended (Henry Herbert, 2nd earl of Pembroke).
VI	*Late 18th century*	Western Apartments reconstructed and extended (Henry Holland); Cross-wall, Keep fore-building and buildings in Outer Ward removed, motte ditch filled and interior landscaped (Capability Brown for John, 1st marquess of Bute, 1776–94).
VII	*Late 19th/Early 20th century*	Comprehensive restoration and neo-gothic/neo-Roman reconstruction (3rd and 4th marquesses of Bute, 1868–1927).

a) Late 11th & 12th Centuries

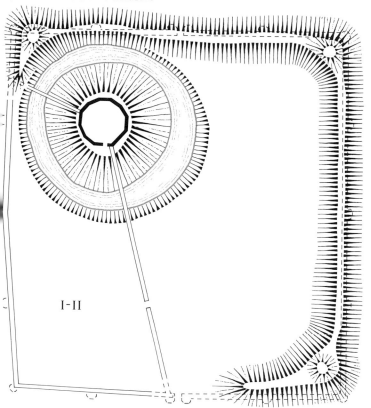

I-II

(b) 13th & 14th Centuries

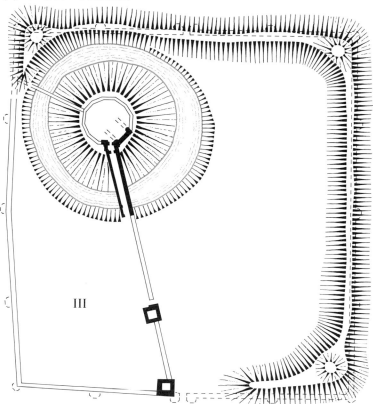

III

c) 15th Century

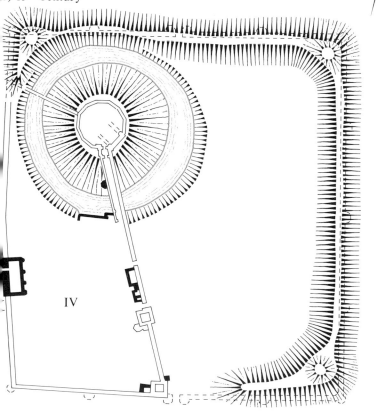

IV

(d) 16th-20th Centuries

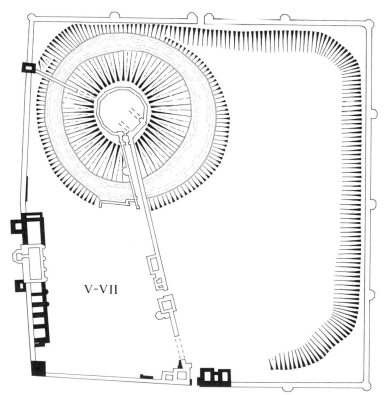

V-VII

N

Roman numerals indicate relevant building periods

Additions in each period/s portrayed

section. Of these, only the re-roofing of the Black Tower in lead in 1316 is significant, suggesting it was of some age by that date. Archaeological and architectural criteria are essential to the definition of the four significant medieval programmes of building that are discernible.

Period I: The Primary Castle

(Fig. 116, a).

The huge motte at Cardiff dominated the castle from its foundation. Evidence already outlined strongly suggests that it was raised in 1081 by William I. Archaeological evidence recorded during the clearance of the Roman defences is crucial in considering the nature of the primary castle. These defences clearly defined the perimeter of the castle, though largely buried deep within the massive earthen rampart that was raised over them to the N. and E. To the S.W., between the ends of this rampart, the Roman wall appears to have been restored to define the external flanks of an Inner Ward to the S. of the motte. The rampart is shown to be contemporary with the motte by its slight outward deviation from an otherwise straight N. line, respecting the N. lip of the motte ditch. To the S.W., however, investigations at five points have demonstrated that the medieval curtain-walls embracing the Inner Ward rise directly upon substantial remains of the Roman wall.[67] The suggestion that the medieval rampart extended around the entire circuit of the primary castle is hard to sustain. This presupposes that it was later entirely removed on the S.W., together with the lesser bank of the Roman defences incorporated within it, an undertaking difficult to envisage, involving the removal of 250m of rampart 29m wide and 8m high. More probably, as archaeological evidence suggests, the Roman walls embracing the Inner Ward to the S.W. were reconstructed at the outset, re-using the outer facing from the rest of the perimeter, where the superimposed rampart was intended for the protection of the outer bailey (see below, p. 190).

The Inner Ward of the early castle was surely completed in stone on the lines of the internal cross-walls illustrated in early prints and now marked by modern walls raised on their foundations. Palisades, which may well have linked with the timber defences crowning the motte, were presumably replaced by walls in the 12th century when the keep was built. There is no recorded evidence for the timber defences on the motte or on the rampart enclosing the outer ward.

No ditch fronted the main N.–S. cross-wall. Such a ditch, linked with the main outer ditch, would have precluded the re-use of the Roman S. gate as the only external entrance to the castle, and no ditch has been recorded in excavation close to this cross-wall.

At Porchester Castle, Hampshire, the Mauduits enclosed an inner ward in the N.W. angle of a Roman fort, again retaining the remainder of the enclosure as a large outer ward, though there the entire circuit of Roman walls was refurbished to protect the castle. Roman walls were also re-used at the Conqueror's castles at Exeter and the Tower of London.

Period II: The 12th-century castle

(Fig. 116, a).

The 12th-century polygonal shell keep is the most impressive medieval structure remaining at the castle. Its polygonal form and ashlar quoining are paralleled by the shell-keep on the motte at Carisbrooke, which is thought to have been built by 1136. Though this dating is early for such structures, it is consistent with the attribution of the Cardiff example to Robert of Gloucester (*ob.* 1147), perhaps in response to the general Welsh uprising of 1136. This revolt preoccupied Earl Robert in Glamorgan in that year, and if his keep was not begun then, his leading role in support of Empress Maud from 1138 was a further factor that may have inspired him to strengthen the castle; in Glamorgan he recruited troops, and in the castle he minted coins for the empress.

Period III: 13th–14th century

(Fig. 116, b).

Fabric attributable to this period is aligned along the E. wall of the Inner Ward, from the Keep to the Black Tower. A gatehouse was added to the shell-keep, and at the same time the adjacent facet of the shell wall was rebuilt as the S.E. gable of a hall that straddled the interior. Also integrated with the new *Gatehouse* was a massive *Fore-building*, raised over a stone stair built down the slope of the motte and carried across the ditch on a stone bridge, which now replaced that of timber. This fore-building, at its lower end, incorporated two further gatehouses, one at each end of the bridge. Further S. a square tower was added to flank the S. side of the gateway between the wards, and the *Black Tower* was added at the S.E. angle of

---

[67] Ward, *op. cit.* (f/n. 7), both 1913 papers cited.

the Inner Ward, flanking the main South Gate but not communicating with it.

It is probable that these additions were completed by the early 14th century, and that they were the work of the de Clare earls (1217–1314). The *Black Tower*, excluding its later annexe, appears to be the oldest addition of this period. It is a 13th-century structure first recorded in 1316, when it was re-roofed with lead. The *square tower*, similarly flanking the left-hand side of the internal gate between the wards, may be contemporary with the Black Tower, though it differed in having a door opening from the passage. It was demolished in the late 18th century and modern dwarf walls now outline its foundation.

The *Fore-building* of the Keep was also demolished in the 18th century, but it is portrayed in detail by earlier artists (Fig. 134a). Again, its foundations are now marked by modern dwarf walls. Here, however, traces of the original fabric are still visible, and toothing low down on the external face of the keep gatehouse show that at least the lower levels of the fore-building were contemporary with it. The recently cleared fore-building at Sandal Castle, West Yorkshire, is a complex, phased structure quite different in its parts, but similarly incorporating strong fortified entrances at its lower end; in concept and general appearance it has much in common with that at Cardiff.

The *Gatehouse and Hall* inserted in the Norman Keep may be ascribed to the de Clares, though later in their period of lordship. Surviving details in the gatehouse are consistent with work of *ca.* 1300, and the chamfered outer angles, though lacking basal spurs, reflect the style of the towers of the gatehouse at Llanblethian (Vol. III, Part Ib, LM 7), which was under construction in 1314. The only remaining wall of the hall is clearly contemporary with the gatehouse.

Period IV: Early 15th century

(Fig. 116, c).

The central core of the *Western Apartments* against the W. curtain, together with the adjacent *Beauchamp Tower* projecting externally, are attributed to Richard Beauchamp, earl of Warwick (1423–39). The architectural style and detail of these earliest components of the block accord with this attribution. The Beauchamp Tower, in particular, is appropriate to a work of Earl Richard, being a fine octagonal machicolated structure comparable to the much larger Guy's Tower at Warwick Castle, completed in 1394. The central

hall block is also consistent with a date in the early 15th century. The elaborate vaulting of the bays, or turret-recesses, was heavily restored when the hall became the library. Before this, in 1862, Clark identified the arms of Isabel Despenser and Earl Richard of Warwick on an original heraldic boss in the southernmost bay.[68] The strong Beauchamp Tower clearly served to protect the adjacent West Gate of the town, a sensible precaution after the Welsh assault of 1404.

Lesser additions of this period abut the cross-wall between the Wards, or pre-existing structures on its line. Three of these additions were angular turrets; two housed newel stairs at internal angles of the Black Tower and the tower beside the inner gate, and the third enclosed a well set against the fore-building of the keep, towards the base of the motte. The stair turrets were clearly additions, so similar that they were surely contemporary. Their angular form reflects that of the four turrets of the Beauchamp hall, two of which also housed newel stairs. Together with the well-turret, they may reasonably be ascribed to the 15th century. Three other additions may be assigned to this period: the building encroaching upon the motte ditch and abutting the outer gatehouse of the fore-building; the range of rooms abutting the cross-wall to the N. of its gate; and the annexe added to the Black Tower in the angle formed on its W. side with the curtain. All post-date work attributed to Period III.

Period V: Late 16th century

(Figs. 116d, 117–19).

Merrick's description of the castle in *ca.* 1580, and other records cited, specify extensive building and repair at the castle under Henry Herbert, earl of Pembroke (1570–1601),[69] using stone from the nearby friaries. They indicate widespread refurbishment, with new floors, stairs, and hearths or chimneys. Works were undertaken in the keep, the Black Tower, the Exchequer, the Shire-hall, the Wardrobe, the South Gate and the Western Apartments. Little of this work has survived later restoration. Surviving Tudor fabric is limited to the much restored Herbert Tower of the Western Apartments, and the weathered square-headed windows that remain in the Black Tower, and the Keep Gatehouse and adjacent Hall gable on the motte.

[68] Clark, (*op. cit.* f/n. 5), 1862, pp. 261–2 and 1884, p. 343. Grant, (*op. cit.* f/n. 56), p. 37, seems to ignore this boss, excluding the turrets as a later addition by Jasper Tudor.
[69] See f/n. 56

a

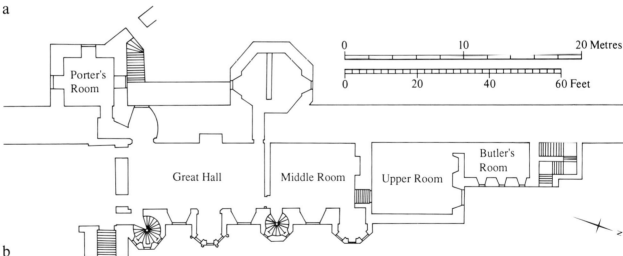

b

Fig. 117. Cardiff Castle: the Western Apartments of Period V before extensive rebuilding by Henry Holland (Period VI, 1776-94): (a) the east Front in 1775 by S. Sparrow *(National Library of Wales);* (b) tracing of plan matching Sparrow's engraving.The original, dated 1826 by J. Wheeler, clearly portrays the building before 1776 *(Cardiff Castle Archives).*

An accurate plan and an engraving, both earlier than the restorations of 1776–94, make known most of the vanished Tudor additions to the Western Apartments (Fig, 117, a & b). The plan is conserved in the archives at Cardiff Castle.[70] Marked as a plan by J. Wheeler, Architect, it is dated 1826, but this cannot be accurate. It clearly delineates additions to the 15th-century block which were demolished by 1794, and

replaced by Henry Holland's flanking wings shown in depictions of *ca.* 1800 and 1815. This is confirmed by an engraving of 1775, which depicts the lay-out, fenestration, and arrangements of Wheeler's plan, which are again depicted with less clarity or detail

---

[70] Cardiff Castle, Bute/Burges archives, SR1/2. A scale confirms its accuracy in regard to surviving fabric.

178

Fig. 118. Cardiff Castle from the west as it appeared in Period V. Engraving by Samuel and Nathaniel Buck, 1741, before the removal of the Fore-building of the keep and Holland's addition to the Western Appartments in Period VI, 1776-94 *(National Library of Wales)*. For a more detailed portrayal of the Fore-building, see Fig.134 (a).

in a painting and another engraving of the castle before the removal of the central cross-wall by Capability Brown.[71]

The 1775 engraving and Wheeler's plan, taken together, make clear the original form of the central 15th-century nucleus of the apartments, and of the vanished Tudor wings to N. and S. The internal arrangements of the apartments are clear. To the N. Herbert added a large storeyed block, matching the medieval hall in height, width, and castellated parapet. It lacked fenestration towards the court, being lit only by a window in its N. wall against a narrower block added beyond. This smaller block was of similar height and crenellation, but its lower or 'Butler's' room was generously lit by three windows towards the court. The northern extension was completed with a commodious stair-block entered direct from the court and leading to the upper floors.

The extent of the Herbert additions to the S. is uncertain. The 18th-century plan and engraving depict the ruins of a formerly enclosed lobby against the S. wall of the primary block; the kitchen and 'other necessary houses' noted in this area by Merrick had already vanished. The ruined lobby was reached from the court by a short flight of steps and through a door

in its truncated E. wall. To the right, three doors led from the lobby to the main block, the first broken through to the newel stair in the adjacent stair-turret. The other two doors led directly into the 'Great Hall'.

The primary central block was sub-divided by a transverse partition demarcating a reduced 'Great Hall' and Wheeler's 'Middle Room', the 'fair dining chamber' noticed by Merrick. This dining chamber was furnished with a fireplace in the N. wall, close to a door broken through to the N. extension. The reduced main hall was provided with a lateral fireplace, set into the great curtain-wall and surely a feature of Beauchamp's hall. Merrick noticed a buttery and pantry in the lower part of the hall; these were presumably screened off, together with the entry from the stair turret. Beyond the curtain, the Beauchamp Tower was sub-divided at this level, and a window was inserted in the curtain near the S.W. corner of the hall. Merrick's description suggests that this window was at first set in a projecting angular

---

[71] Grant, *op. cit.* (f/n. 56), facing p. 38, reproduces the engraving of 1775. He also reproduces the painting (no longer in the castle) and the comparable engraving, attributed to Sandby in 1756 – these facing pp. 32 and 22. The painting is also reproduced in *Cardiff Records*, V, p. 281.

Fig. 119. Cardiff Castle: the Western Appartments of Period V, west front, portrayed in 1775 by Paul Sandby. The West Gate of the town, bottom right *(National Library of Wales).*

bay. Shortly afterwards, however, it appears that an angled passage was broken through the curtain from the S. flank of the deep recess of this window. This passage gave access to the Herbert Tower, then added externally. Since Merrick makes no mention of this tower, its construction probably necessitated the removal of the bay window he described.

Merrick furnishes further details of the castle in the late 16th century which may be noticed here. A lesser gate had been inserted in the main cross-wall between the wards, and the Inner Ward had been sub-divided by a cross-wall of indeterminate date, running E.–W. This wall separated a quadrangular 'Middle Court' to the S. from an irregular 'Inner Court' set against the ditch of the motte. The ruins of this secondary cross-wall are portrayed on depictions of the 18th century (Fig. 134a). Merrick also notes a postern gate through the W. curtain, next to the N. wall of the Western Apartments, presumably blocked when the northern extensions were raised soon after he wrote. He also records a walled wood-yard on the S. side

of the 'Middle Court', flanking the access road to the Black Tower along the rear of the main cross-wall. To the W., it adjoined a kitchen garden in the S.W. corner of the court, the 'chiefest garden' before the earl's restorations, when two new pleasure gardens were laid out further N. One of these fronted the hall-block in the Middle Court; the other was in the Inner Court, below the 'Ladies Walk'.

In the Outer Ward, Merrick noted the Shire-hall and the house of Sir Edward Mansel, the sole remaining house of the Glamorgan knights. Elsewhere were gardens and orchards, all enclosed by a decayed wall upon the rampart, which was a flimsy and late structure.

Period VI: Late 18th century

(Figs. 116d, 120–24).

The ruinous condition of the Herbert extensions to the Western Apartments by the mid 18th century has been noticed. After long neglect the first marquess

Fig. 120. Cardiff Castle: the Western Appartments, east front, as refurbished and extended in Period VI by Henry Holland, 1776-94: (a) in *ca.* 1800 *(National Library of Wales);* (b) in 1815 by Buckler *(British Library).*

Fig. 121. Cardiff Castle: the Western Appartments, west front, as restored by Henry Holland in Period VI, 1776-94. Painting of *ca.* 1800 formerly in Cardiff Castle (Repr. from *Cardiff Records,* Vol. 5).

of Bute undertook an extensive programme of clearance, landscaping, and rebuilding between 1776 and 1794, when it was aborted on the death of his heir. The clearance involved the complete removal of the Herbert extensions to the N. and S. of the Beauchamp hall-block. The fore-building of the keep and the crumbling internal cross-walls were also erased, and the ditch around the motte filled, clearing the interior for landscaping by Capability Brown. He retained the great motte and its Norman keep as a perfect picturesque feature.

The reconstruction of the *Western Apartments* was entrusted to Henry Holland, rather than Robert Adam, who also submitted a most elaborate scheme in 1777.[72] Holland erased what remained of the Herbert wings, raising in their place symmetrical two-storeyed blocks, each with a lesser terminal wing. Beyond the curtain he achieved a symmetrical western front, centred on the Beauchamp Tower, by adding a northern tower to balance the Herbert Tower (the sole Tudor structure to survive), and by the recessed and balanced infilling of the spaces between the three towers. To integrate the extended apartments, the massive intervening curtain was honeycombed with passages. Holland's scheme was largely completed when work was abandoned. In 1802 Sir Richard Colt

Hoare described this castellated classical creation as '*so thickly beset with sash windows that little of its ancient character can be perceived ...*', adding that it remained in an unfinished state.[73] Holland's work was almost entirely erased during the comprehensive redevelopment carried out by the third and fourth marquesses.

The external appearance and internal arrangements of the late-18th-century apartments are largely known from excellent detailed depictions, plans, and a section. The internal eastern front is clearly delineated on an engraving of *ca.*1800, and a drawing of 1815 (Fig. 120, a,b). The Western Front is well-portrayed in a painting of *ca.* 1800, and a further drawing of 1815 (Figs. 121, 122). Clark's plan of 1862 largely confirms plans of 1830 thought to be those of Sir Robert Smirke (Fig. 123, a,b). Finally, there is an original section across the apartments, measured by Burges in 1872–73, before he began his comprehensive

---

[72] Mordaunt Crook, *op. cit.* (f/n. 59), p. 260. Adam's abortive scheme envisaged a three-winged semi-hexagonal house (Soane Museum, XXXVII, 47–50).

[73] M. W. Thompson (ed.), *The Journeys of Sir Richard Colt Hoare through Wales and England 1793–1810*, 1983, p. 209. The foundations of Holland's addition between the Herbert and Beauchamp Towers were exposed by drainage work in February 1988.

Fig. 122. Cardiff Castle: the Western Appartments, west front, as restored by Henry Holland in Period VI, 1776-94. Drawing of 1815 by Buckler *(British Library)*.

restoration in this area (Fig. 124).

Depictions of Holland's *Eastern Front* show that he mirrored the surviving central block in the height and crenellation of his wings. In this he followed the Elizabethan architect, whose work he replaced, but accentuated this symmetry by providing the upper floor of each wing with three pointed and traceried windows matching those he restored after their original form in the central block. On the lower floor Holland abandoned this archaism, replacing two of the three small two-light windows between the bays with tall sash windows, these balanced by three larger examples in each wing. Incongruously, however, these sash windows were set beneath Tudor-style labels. The third two-light Tudor window between the northernmost bays of the central block was now broken through, providing a new main entrance set below a further label. This entrance, together with the faithfully restored southern stair-bay, now presented the only irregular features of an otherwise symmetrical façade, further balanced by lesser matching wings at the ends, by a string-course carried unbroken as labels over the half-basement, and by the removal of the newel stair from the third projecting bay from the

S. and its refenestration to match that of the flanking bay windows. Previously, this had been plain, like the still surviving stair-turret on the S. end of the primary block.

Beyond the curtain, the *Western Front* was similarly transformed into a castellated symmetrical front by the addition of the square northern tower, equally-spaced from the now central Beauchamp Tower (Figs. 121, 122). The flanking towers were of equal height and similar dimensions, and their castellation was continued inwards to the Beauchamp Tower upon matching recessed additions built between the towers. As Colt Hoare remarked in 1802, only the greater height and bulk of Beauchamp's octagonal tower conveyed any impression of the ancient structure.[74] Fenestration enhanced the symmetry, with balanced tiers of sash windows to each flank, varied only with the introduction of pointed windows on the upper floors of the flanking square towers – these repeating the treatment given at this level along the entire interior facade. Both fronts, indeed, introduced neo-Gothic features to differing degrees, ingeniously merging quite different

---

[74] See f/n. 73.

a

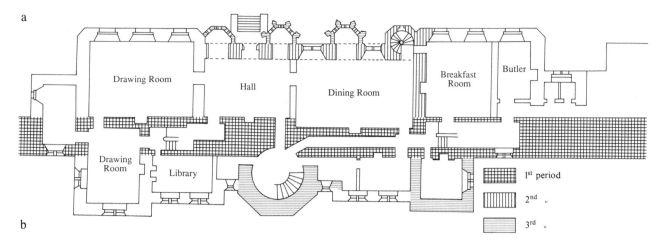

b

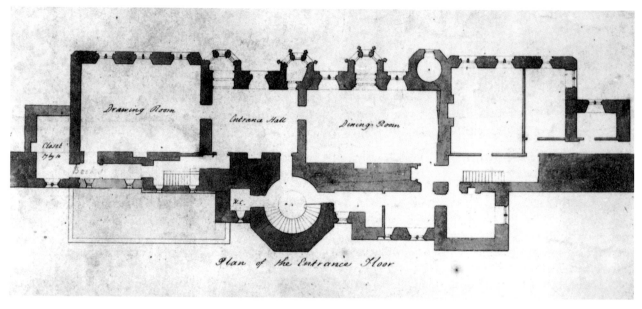

Fig. 123. Cardiff Castle: the Western Apartments, main floor, as restored by Henry Holland in Period VI, 1776-94: (a) plan of 1830, attributed to Sir Robert Smirke (by permission of the *National Museum of Wales*); (b) plan of 1862 (after G.T. Clark, *Arch. Camb.*, 1862).

medieval central masses to new classically symmetrical facades.

The internal arrangements of Holland's restored apartments are made clear in the plans of 1830, attributed to Smirke and largely confirmed by Clark in 1862 (Fig. 123, a,b). Smirke is known to have completed the unfinished interiors within about three years of the succession of the second marquess in 1814.[75] The ancient central Hall was still divided; to the S. the proportions of the 'Dining Room' were improved by removing 1m from the inner face of the curtain. N. of this the Tudor 'Middle Room' now became the 'Entrance Hall'. The lord's private apartments occupied the new N. wing and adjacent additions beyond

the curtain. Two chambers were ingeniously integrated by opposed encroachments into the curtain sufficient to accommodate a party door. Elsewhere, many passages were cut through the curtain. The new south wing was subdivided into the 'breakfast room' and a lesser chamber for the butler. The medieval vaulted basement was partitioned to accommodate two cellars and a passage, with access to the servants' hall and a kitchen, respectively placed beneath the new N. and S. wings. Further cellars were added beyond the cur-

---

[75] Mordaunt Crook, *op. cit.* (f/n 59), p. 260. Smirke had designed the enormous castellated Eastnor Castle, Herefs., begun in 1812.

tain, and bedrooms were partitioned off on the upper floor.

The ingenuity of Holland's successful merger of ancient and modern on his exteriors, and the remarkable integration achieved within, did not impress contemporary opinion. Before Colt Hoare's strictures of 1802, noted above, Lord John Byng had complained in 1787 that the expenditure of '... *much money with so ill-taste ... destroyed it of all appearance*'. The third marquess was equally unimpressed. Before engaging Burges to replace most of Holland's work, he was 'painfully alive to the fact that (Cardiff) Castle is very far indeed from setting anything like an example in art', and degenerated into a 'Picturesque seat'. No authority seems to have appreciated the merits of Holland's design, though an abortive proposal for a Gothic-style extension to Penllyn Castle (EM 4), possibly by Sir Matthew Digby Wyatt, incorporates a huge octagonal tower clearly inspired by that integrated in the Cardiff apartments.[76] Elsewhere in Glamorgan a similar classical conversion of a medieval castle was less successfully achieved at Fonmon (LM 6).

Period VII: Late 19th/Early 20th Century

(Figs. 116d, 125–27).

The restoration of the Black Tower during the minority of the third marquess has been noticed. Eighteenth-century depictions attest the accuracy of its refurbishment between 1848 and 1859 by the dowager marchioness. The third marquess's distaste for the late-18th-century restoration brooked no delay in remedial action when he attained his majority in 1868. Already acquainted with the 'soul-inspiring Burges', and having limitless resources, he embarked on the creation of the neo-feudal castle he craved. He and his successor largely achieved this aim. Their efforts are easily dismissed as 'the ultimate in nostalgic escapism', but it should be emphasised that the Butes collaborated with leading antiquarian authorities. They excavated and clearly marked the last vestiges of the internal cross-wall and keep fore-building; discovered, cleared, and carefully reconstructed most of the Roman wall; consolidated the keep and opened up its surrounding ditch. These and lesser acts of discovery and conservation go far to counter criticisms of their excessive reconstruction in other areas. The Cardiff restoration stands as a splendid creation in its own right, ranking high among the few celebrated European 19th-century restorations or fantasy castles.

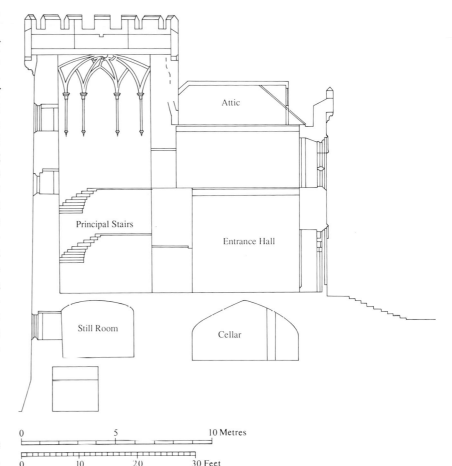

Fig. 124. Cardiff Castle: the Western Apartments and Beauchamp Tower: cross-section by William Burges, 1872-73, before his alterations in Period VII. Traced from the original in the *Cardiff Castle Archives*. For the existing cross-section, see Fig.140.

This aspect is given exhaustive and authoritative treatment by Mordaunt Crook, who regards Cardiff as unique in Victorian Britain, 'matchless in its obsessive exoticism ... a dream-castle implanted in a city'.[77]

The chronology of the phases of restoration has been outlined. It remains to detail the impact of this comprehensive and protracted programme of work on the castle. The aim was to re-create a Gothic castle fit for the richest man in the world, sweeping away the detested 'picturesque' contribution of Holland and Brown, and restoring a medieval aura to an Inner

[76] Lord Byng is cited in Rees, *Cardiff*, 1969, p. 344 n.; for the third Marquess' views, see Mordaunt Crook, *op. cit.* (n. 59), p. 260; the abortive Penllyn design is illustrated in *Plans and Prospects; Architect in Wales 1780–1914*, Welsh Arts Council, 1975, p. 16.

[77] Mordaunt Crook, *op. cit.* (f/n. 59), pp. 278–9.

Fig. 125. Cardiff Castle: the Western Appartments, existing east front.

Ward symbolically re-created with the partial re-construction of the cross-wall on foundations which had been lost to sight since the landscaping. Work began on the W. side of the Inner Ward, where the extraordinary Clock Tower at the S.W. angle, completed in 1873, gave a striking vertical accent at the entry to the town. The assault on the 'picturesque' concentrated on the Western Apartments. Excepting only the main component of Holland's N. wing and his adjacent North Tower, all 18th-century additions were demolished (compare Figs. 123 and 138b). A Gothic western front was restored, a podium that would ultimately support a truly theatrical neo-medieval superstructure. The 'foundation stone' of the North Tower, renamed the Bute Tower, was laid on 24 April 1873, but its external masonry clearly betrays the survival of Holland's structure at lower levels. Divested of its crenellations, and refenestrated in Gothic style, its walls of small local lias stones were surmounted by two ornate storeys, executed in large alien ashlar blocks and served by an added stair-turret. The Beauchamp Tower was crowned with its striking Amiens steeple, but otherwise undisturbed beyond wholesale refacing and refenestration. The Herbert Tower, like the North Tower, was increased by two storeys, though less incongruously in local lias stone.

Yet further S., within the line of the curtain, the huge Guest Tower was raised in fine ashlar above the new S. wing. Flanked by the three pre-existing towers and the new Clock Tower, the Guest Tower completed the matchless Cardiff skyline, 'a High Victorian fantasy, a belligerent rejection of Georgian harmony, balance and coherence' (Mordaunt Crook).

Internally, the Guest Tower dominated the rebuilt S. wing of the apartments. Its angular stair-turret simulated the four medieval bays of Beauchamp's hall-block, later complemented by a replica bay-window added alongside by Grant when he reconstructed the entrance hall in 1927. In the central block, and the surviving part of the 18th-century N. wing, the fenestration facing the court retained the forms bequeathed by Holland, but within them mullions, transoms, and tracery diminished these vestiges of the Georgian design.

The curtain walls enclosing the Inner Ward were not neglected. The great outer curtain, its Roman substructure not yet perceived, was lavishly treated. With the erection of the Clock Tower, and the demolition of abutting external properties, it was possible to restore the curtain as far as the Black Tower. There, and between the Clock Tower and the apartments on the W., Burges re-created a 'Norman Curtain', complete with roofed wall-walks, hinged crenel-flaps, and

Fig. 126. Cardiff Castle: the Western Appartments, existing west front. Restored West Gate to the town, bottom right.

(formerly) a section of external covered hoarding, all based on Continental survivals. The wall was refaced, and only later was it found to stand upon the substantial remains of the Roman wall, incorporating its core, which rises well above the 2.28m of surviving but buried internal facing in one sector. North of the apartments the W. curtain-wall was not restored. There, the external face retains irregular rough patching proclaiming its antiquity. At the S. end of this unrestored wall an ornate rustic bridge formerly crossed the moat from a door at the foot of the Bute Tower, providing access to the friary in the adjacent park, excavated and laid out by the third marquess.

The reconstruction of the Roman wall begun by Frame in the 1890s, continued under Sesom-Hiley (1905–21) and Grant (from 1921). Between 1907 and 1912 Sesom-Hiley investigated the outer curtain of the Inner Ward at five points, demonstrating that the Norman masonry rose directly upon substantial remains of the Roman wall, to its full thickness of 3.05m on the W., but internally narrowed to 2.44m on the S. These investigations, reported by Ward,[78] were at the Black Tower and close to the Clock Tower, on the S., and in the kitchens, near the Beauchamp Tower, and at the N. end of Ladies' Walk on the W. Excavation had previously disclosed the Roman foundations closing the short interval between the Ladies' Walk and the N.W. angle. Reconstruction of the N. Roman wall had been completed in 1922, when further clearance of external buildings, E. of the South Gate, enabled Grant to disclose and reconstruct its last unexplored section, introducing his ingenious tunnel to display the well-preserved inner face. Grant now confronted the problem of successfully merging the reconstructed Roman wall with the medieval wall on the W. and S. sides. To the S. he demolished a simple and probably Tudor gateway beside the Black Tower, together with a late porter's lodge on its E. side. These he replaced in neo-Gothic style, the lodge as a crenellated square tower, and all constructed in glacial pebbles with ashlar quoins. This new masonry matched the adjacent Black Tower, its quoins blunting an abrupt vertical junction with the western limit of the reconstructed Roman wall. To the W., a small square turret at the N. end of the Ladies' Walk served the double purpose of enclosing the severed end of the thick medieval curtain (which intrudes into the greater area of both floors and displays Roman corework), and suitably marking the junction with the reconstructed Roman wall running N. Eastwards from this turret, Grant partially reconstructed the wall

Fig. 127 Cardiff Castle: external south front. The South Gate and Black Tower, centre; Burges's restored 'Norman Curtain' and Clock Tower, left; restored Roman wall overriding original fragment, right.

crossing the motte ditch to the keep.

Externally, Grant cleared and rebuilt the West Gate of the town, and the short length of wall that had formerly linked it to the castle beside the Herbert tower. Within the Western Apartments he completed work by constructing the plain entrance hall, with its new bay-window, where Burges had intended his truly grand staircase. In the 1930s the restoration of the Keep was begun. The turret was rebuilt on the gate-tower, and the fenestration of the adjacent hall-gable was restored; the wall-walk of the Keep was paved, but only a short stretch of its crenellations had been restored before work was halted for the last time under the Butes.

Description of the architecture and earthworks

Surviving remains are described in a broadly chronological sequence, beginning with the motte and earthen rampart, and continuing with the masonry structures in the presumed order of their first construction, though describing later development in each area.

---

[78] See f/n. 7 (Ward, 1913, both papers).

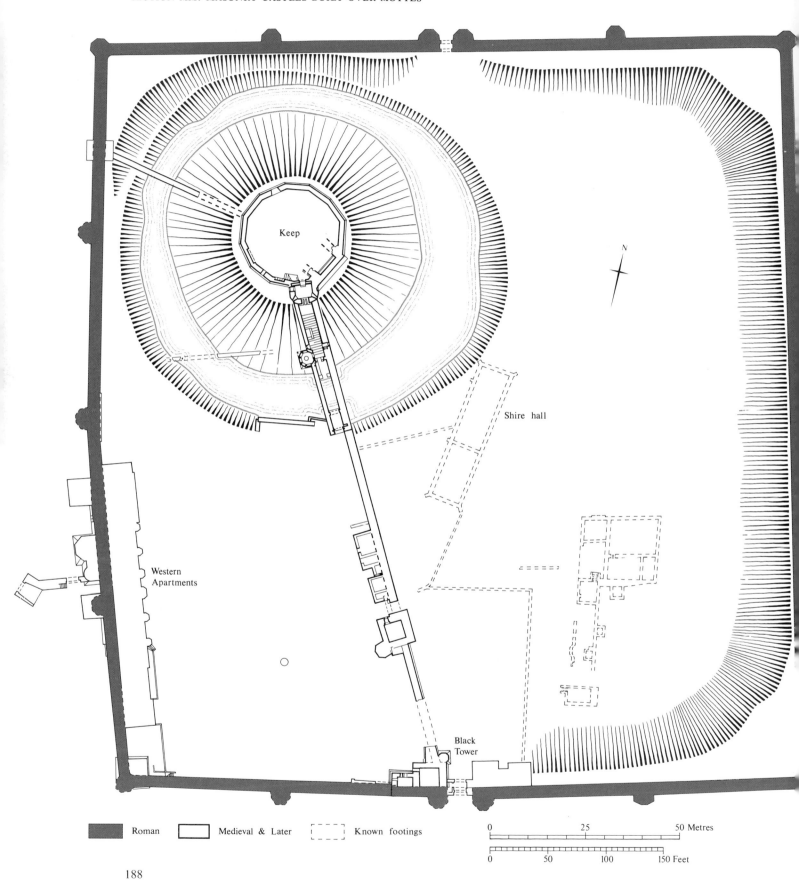

Keep

Shire hall

Western
Apartments

Black
Tower

Roman   Medieval & Later   Known footings

0   25   50 Metres

0   50   100   150 Feet

Fig. 129. Cardiff Castle: the Motte and Shell-keep from the Beauchamp Tower, looking north-east. The restored Roman wall and modern civic centre, beyond.

The Motte and Earthen Rampart

(Figs. 114, 116, 128–30).

The Motte and its ditch fill the N.W. quarter of the late-Roman fort. As befits a motte attributed to the Conqueror, it is the largest in Wales. It rises 10.67m above ground to a summit 33m in diameter. The surrounding ditch was restored to its original dimensions in the last century, when its permanent flooding was ensured by cutting a subterranean culvert to tap the mill-leat flowing down the western external ditch. The motte was entirely artificial and created from glacial boulders and gravel derived from its ditch. No traces of its original timber structures have been recorded, though the piles of a timber bridge were recorded by Clark near the reconstructed stone bridge when the ditch was re-opened.

Fig. 128. *(Opposite)* Cardiff Castle: general plan of existing structures and location of foundations disclosed during excavavions. Less determinate footings encountered in the Inner Ward and on the bank in the south-east angle of the Outer Ward are not shown.

The *Earthen Rampart* that defined the outer perimeter of the Inner Ward now only survives internally. Its original form and dimensions are shown on Fig. 116a–c. This massive bank ran unbroken from the N. termination of the Ladies' Walk (now marked by Grant's turret) to the porter's lodge on the E. side of the South Gate. Internally it was much thickened at the three angles it formed, its inner scarp falling directly to the motte ditch within the N.W. angle. Beyond this, the entire bank was bowed outwards to respect the curve of the ditch on the N. side of the motte. With the removal of the outer part of the bank this outward deviation is less apparent, but remains an emphatic indication that the motte and rampart were envisaged and raised together. The rampart was between 20m and 27m wide at its base, excluding greater widths at the angles, and it rose up to 8.20m above the Roman ground level (7m above that of the present surface). The Roman wall was entirely buried beneath this bank, generally a little in advance of its centre line. Ward concluded that the wall had suffered centuries of gradual robbing and decay before the medieval bank was raised, but his published sections, and photographs in the Commission's archives (Ministry of Works Collection) permit an alternative interpretation. Of three clear photographs of sections cut across the débris fronting the wall, only one displays a single, squared, lias facing block. With this minor exception, the debris is entirely composed of small stones and glacial pebbles derived from the Roman core-work. The debris is everywhere very limited in volume, and invariably coincides in height with the surviving courses of facing at the external base of the wall, suggesting that the facing was robbed for re-use by the builders of the primary castle, immediately before they raised the earth rampart. Had the exposed core of the ancient wall remained exposed to the elements for any length of time, its erosion would have raised the level of the debris well above the facing which survived at its foot. The re-use of Roman facing stones by the primary castle-builders to enclose the walled Inner Ward favours this re-interpretation of Ward's evidence.

Evidence is lacking for the primary palisade crowning the rampart, and for the wall recorded in 1316. The flimsy boundary wall cleared away from its crest in the late 19th century was only 1.83m high and 0.61m thick.[79] Three mounds which formerly surmounted the rampart, one in each of its angles, were probably late landscaping features. These were erased, along with a tunnel and external bridge cut through the defences N. of the motte by the second marquess, which were not needed when the adjacent Roman gate was restored.

The W. and N. ditches now channel the respective waters of the old mill leat and the feeder for the docks. To the S. and E. the ditches are filled in and grassed.

The Curtain Walls of the Inner Ward

(Figs. 116a–d and 128).
Four walls define the Inner Ward, with the keep at its N.E. angle. Substantial remains of these walls survive only on the W. and S. sides, largely refaced, and rising upon the Roman walls. Modern walls which now define the internal cross-walls to the N. and E. were raised on medieval foundations. Available evidence suggests that the Inner Ward was walled when the castle was founded by the Conqueror in 1081. The size of the Roman enclosure would have demanded a concentration of the main defences around only part of this area. Three aspects of the

archaeological evidence indicate that the Inner Ward was walled from the outset:

(i) Where the founders raised their great earthen rampart over the Roman wall, this wall had been stripped of its outer facing. The re-use of these dressed stones in the vicinity may be assumed.

(ii) Ward, without grasping the implications in regard to the primary castle, demonstrated that the medieval curtain on the W. and S. sides of the Inner Ward rose directly upon the Roman wall and concluded that '... *when the medieval builders appeared on the scene, the Roman enceinte ... was standing to a considerable height, and ... they utilised and restored it for their own purposes'.*[80] Here, surely, they re-used lias blocks robbed from the ancient wall on other fronts.

(iii) Negative evidence suggests that the internal cross-wall on the E. flank of the Inner Ward was a primary feature. On the reasonable assumption that the Inner Ward was defined on the line of this wall, it is difficult to envisage a primary palisade in the absence of any trace of an external ditch in excavations along its E. side.

The *West Curtain* is built to the full thickness (3.05m) of the underlying Roman wall. Its Roman core is visible at the N. end of the Ladies' Walk in Grant's turret. Within the apartments it is claimed that the Roman core survived to an average height of 7.90m in the kitchens in the S. basement. Modern patching of the inner face now masks this core and inhibits the easy recognition of undisturbed Roman facing recorded there, though re-used Roman lias blocks appear to be incorporated in medieval work on the upper part of the wall in this area.

The Western Curtain may be divided into three sections. The N. section is 82m in length between the apartments and Grant's turret. It supports the wall-walk known as the Ladies' Walk, a broad path battlemented on both faces with modern ornamental merlons. This section rises about 6m above the present internal level. Irregular patching is most evident externally, together with randomly surviving putlog holes. A further 78m are largely incorporated in the Western Apartments, where its thickness has permitted the construction of many mural passages. Finally, there is a short free-standing section linking

---

[79] G. T. Clark, *op. cit.* (n. 5), 1862, p. 253 and 1884, p. 338; Ward, *op. cit.* (n. 7), 1908, p. 33, Fig. 1. For repair of the wall in 1316: *Cardiff Records*, I, pp. 132–3.

[80] *Trans. Cardiff Nat. Soc.*, XLVI (1913), p. 6.

with the Clock Tower. Reconstructed and refaced with split pebbles, this section, like that to the N., is close to its original height. It incorporates a roofed 'neo-Norman' wall-walk, which continues into the apartments as far as the Guest Tower.

The *South Curtain* differs from the last in being only 8ft thick (2.44m). This reduction was made by raising the inner face within the line of that of the Roman wall, which was found to survive intact to a depth of 2.28m below the present surface. An internal continuous bench now marks the position of the Roman face. Like the S. part of the West Curtain, this wall has been restored and refaced with split pebbles; its roofed 'Norman' wall-walk and crenel-flaps survive, but a stretch of external hoarding has vanished, its position towards the centre indicated by beam-holes between the holes draining the walk. Restored at its original height, its wall-walk communicates with the Black Tower through an upper door in that building.

Except for a gap at its S. end, the *Cross-wall* defining the E. side of the Inner Ward is marked by Bute's dwarf wall raised over foundations he exposed. Its nature is also known from 18th-century depictions. It was 1.80m thick above a batter on both faces, and rose 6m above the present level to a wall-walk battlemented on both faces, as Merrick noticed in 1580. This wall-walk communicated with the Black Tower through the surviving first-floor door now reached by the modern external stair. An entrance 40m N. of the Black Tower pierces the cross-wall, flanked to the S. by a square tower of similar dimensions to the Black Tower. Like that tower, it has an angular turret added to one of its inner angles. It differs only in its modest projection beyond the outer face of the curtain and its door communicating with the passage. Its structural relationship with the cross-wall cannot be ascertained, but it is probably an insertion. Both towers flank simple entrances, recalling 12th-century parallels at Coity (MR 1), Newcastle (EM 3) and Ogmore (MR 5); here, however, the pointed vault in the Black Tower would indicate a later date, and both were probably inserted by the de Clares in the first half of the 13th century. The range of narrow buildings against the inner face, immediately beyond the entrance, were apparently butted against it in the late Middle Ages. A postern formerly pieced the wall just N. of these buildings. At its N. end the cross-wall is continued up the face of the motte to link with the keep, but here it was incorporated with the fore-building, described below.

Little may be said of the *Northern Cross-Wall* joining the keep to the adjacent West Curtain at its N. termination, across the intervening ditch. It was partially rebuilt on its foundations by Grant, but work halted before it closed with the keep, which betrays no scar at the point of junction.

The Keep

(Figs. 130–34).

The 12th-century polygonal shell keep is the finest of its type in Wales. A regular polygon of 12 sides, its wall is set well back from the edge of the motte, and rises on a batter to a crenellated wall-walk 8.20m above the berm. Its faceted wall, 1.60m thick excluding the batter, encloses an area 23.40m in diameter. Its medieval fabric is of two periods. The ten plain facets are ascribed to the mid 11th century; the southernmost facet, incorporating the entrance, and that adjoining it to the E., are of the late 13th or early 14th century.

The *Norman Fabric* is characterized by its masonry of small Lias Limestone blocks, with an uneven but general admixture of glacial pebbles and red Radyr Sandstone; by the alternating quoins of Sutton stone at its angles; and by its profusion of regularly-spaced putlog-holes. Much of the batter has been patched, and some of the upper quoining on the N. is renewed, but the ten facets are largely Norman work, including the eroded stumps of the merlons. These facets are described running clockwise from the gatehouse.

The first two facets W. of the Gate tower incorporate the upper part of a steep and narrow (0.60m) stair to the wall-walk. Clearly original, its lower part was removed when the later gate-tower was added, rendering it obsolete. Its oblique run up the internal faces of the wall was achieved by narrowing the wall at this point. The second facet also incorporates a small impractical doorway, now blocked and set about a metre above the internal level. Its outer dressings are entirely modern and it is merely the decorative treatment of a ragged breach shown in a painting of 1789.[81] The third facet incorporates a more problematical feature on its internal face. A recess 3.80m wide narrows above, like a chimney, but lacks a flue, being inexplicably open up to the wall-walk where it is covered by modern paving. The painting of 1789 shows the feature much as it survives today. Grant believed it was merely an effort to pre-

---

[81] Formerly in the Castle, this painting by Julius Caesar Ibbetson is reproduced in *Cardiff Records*, V, facing p. 2.

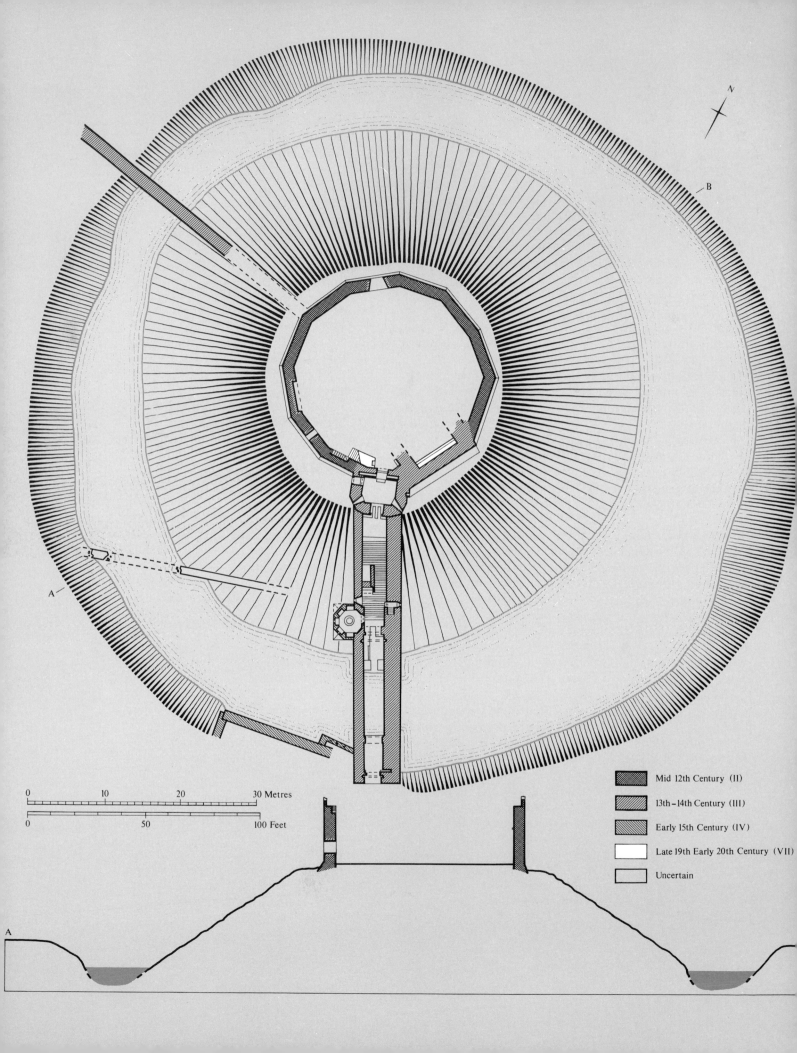

N

B

A

	Mid 12th Century (II)
	13th–14th Century (III)
	Early 15th Century (IV)
	Late 19th Early 20th Century (VII)
	Uncertain

0   10   20   30 Metres

0   50   100 Feet

A

Fig. 131. Cardiff Castle: the Shell-keep from the Beauchamp Tower, looking north-east. The modern civic centre beyond, City Hall clock tower, right. The distant ridge marked the southern limit of the Welsh commotes of Senghennydd, annexed by Gilbert de Clare in 1267.

serve the wall by making good another breach. Alternatively, it may be the last remnants of a chimney in a wing of the vanished hall within the keep. The fourth angle from the Gate Tower, where the projected line of the N. cross-wall closes with the keep, shows no evidence of this former junction; the cross-wall must have butted against the keep. Just before the fifth angle, at about 6.0m above the base, an inexplicable corbel protrudes from the external face of the wall. A further breach in the sixth facet has been made good, in recent times, by the insertion of a segmental-headed window-like opening. At first-floor level the seventh facet is pierced by two evenly spaced windows, now lacking dressings, and blocked on the outer face. These windows, together with internal corbels, are the last traces of indeterminate buildings formerly ranged around the interior. The tenth and

Fig. 130. *(Opposite)* Cardiff Castle: the Motte, Shell-keep, and Forebuilding. Ground plan and profile.

final surviving Norman facet, closing against the E. side of the later work, is distinguished by the reconstruction of its two western merlons. No other crenellations on the Norman wall had been restored when Grant's work was terminated in the 1930s.

The fabric of the remaining two facets on the S. is clearly integrated, and of one build, though later altered and refurbished. One facet incorporates the *Gate Tower*; the other, integrated on its E. side, the S. gable of *The Hall* which formerly straddled the interior, where it is now vanished.

The *Gate Tower* (Fig. 132) projects to the outer edge of the berm around the summit of the motte. Built flush with the inner face of the keep, its angular projection has seven faces. The masonry of this tower and the adjoining gable is better-coursed in larger blocks of Lias Limestone and Radyr stone, with sandstone quoins, but few glacial pebbles so characteristic of the Norman fabric. Three chambers are carried on renewed timber floors above the entry. The dressings of the door in the external face refurbish a ragged gap portrayed in 1828. Within the ground-floor lobby narrow loops pierce the walls flanking the door, their sandstone dressings largely restored. A small door gives access to the berm around the motte on the W. side; its external dressings are modern, but the lower internal jambs are original. The pointed inner door retains deep draw-bar holes.

The first floor is reached by a stone stair set against the inner face of the tower, and masking the lower steps of the narrow Norman stair to the wall-walk of the shell keep. The secondary stair rises to a renewed pointed doorway at the W. end of the rear wall. Within the chamber, irregularly disposed narrow loops pierce the side walls. A wider opening in the outer face gave access to this level of the vanished fore-building. It retains its draw-bar hole and socket, but its dressings and relieving arch are modern. The toothing of the vanished structure survives on the outer face, E. of this door. The internal angles of the wall on the W. side of this chamber retain their original limestone quoins, but those dressing the inner angles of openings are renewed. The loop in the E. side is set well forward, to accommodate the door to a short, straight, mural stair leading N.E. to the vanished contemporary hall. A slanted recess at the lower end of this passage contains a latrine in the thickness of the wall, served by a projecting chute set on corbels in the external angle. The walls flanking the stair retain ancient plaster scored with *graffiti*, the earliest being '1691 D. Shelard'. A second recess at the top of the stair housed another latrine, immediately within the door from the first floor of the hall, and served by a similarly projecting and corbelled-out chute set in the adjoining facet. The door to this stair-passage within the tower chamber is modern, its flat lintel enigmatically inscribed '128–', while its N. jamb blocks one side of an equally modern segmental-headed door with a voussoir inscribed '13—'. There was no internal communication with the second floor from this chamber.

The second floor chamber is now reached by a modern wooden stair, rising from the external stone stair to the lower floor. Formerly, the only access was from the hall on a squinch set across the angle made with that building and now almost vanished. The dressings of the pointed door into the tower are renewed, except for the lower half of the E. jamb, which is plain-chamfered with a straight-cut stop. There is a draw-bar hole within. Five irregularly dis-

posed narrow loops pierce the walls, two abutting on the S.W. side. That to the front has been enlarged. Most of these loops retain original limestone quoins at their inner angles. A newel stair, entered from the short passage from the external door, rises to the next floor.

On the third floor, deep offsets carry the floor, providing a much larger chamber at this level. The door from the stair is set across the inner E. angle. A second door, at the inner W. angle, leads to a short flight of steps down to the wall-walk of the shell keep. This door retains its draw-bar hole. The internal angles of the chamber retain original quoins. Three narrow loops survive, one blocked. In addition, there are four windows with Tudor dressings, most or all inserted in former loops. The largest and best-preserved, set in the E. wall, was of three square-headed lights, set beneath a relieving arch (Fig. 133). The jambs and mullions are plain-chamfered, without glazing rebates. The other Tudor windows were two-light windows of similar form and date, all attributable to Henry Herbert in the late 16th century. The newel stair leading to this floor continues to the battlements.

The restored battlements dominate the castle and surrounding area. The newel stair is now continued upwards within an entirely modern turret raised in the 1930s by Grant, who also restored the crenellations of the main tower upon their original corbel-table.

The Hall raised within the keep adjacent to the gatehouse has been entirely swept away, except for its S. gable, which replaced the adjoining facet of the Norman wall. This gable was made thicker, being advanced externally and set upon a more massive batter. Its internal face retains beam-holes which supported two upper floors. The second floor is pierced by a wide three-light Tudor window matching that on the third floor of the gatehouse and set within a segmental-headed rear arch. There are sockets for two bars in each light. In the W. angle a door opens into the latrine in a recess in the gable, served by the projecting corbelled chute already noticed. The window was recessed to the floor level. The first floor formerly displayed a Tudor window identical to that above. In the 1930s Grant laterally widened this opening to restore two narrow splayed loops that had been blocked in the 16th century when the window was inserted between them. Restoring the masonry dis-

Fig. 132. *(Opposite)* Cardiff Castle: the Gate Tower of the Keep and intergrated surviving gable of the Hall: (c) ground floor; (b) first floor; (a) second floor; (e) third floor; (f) parapet level; (d) section A-B.

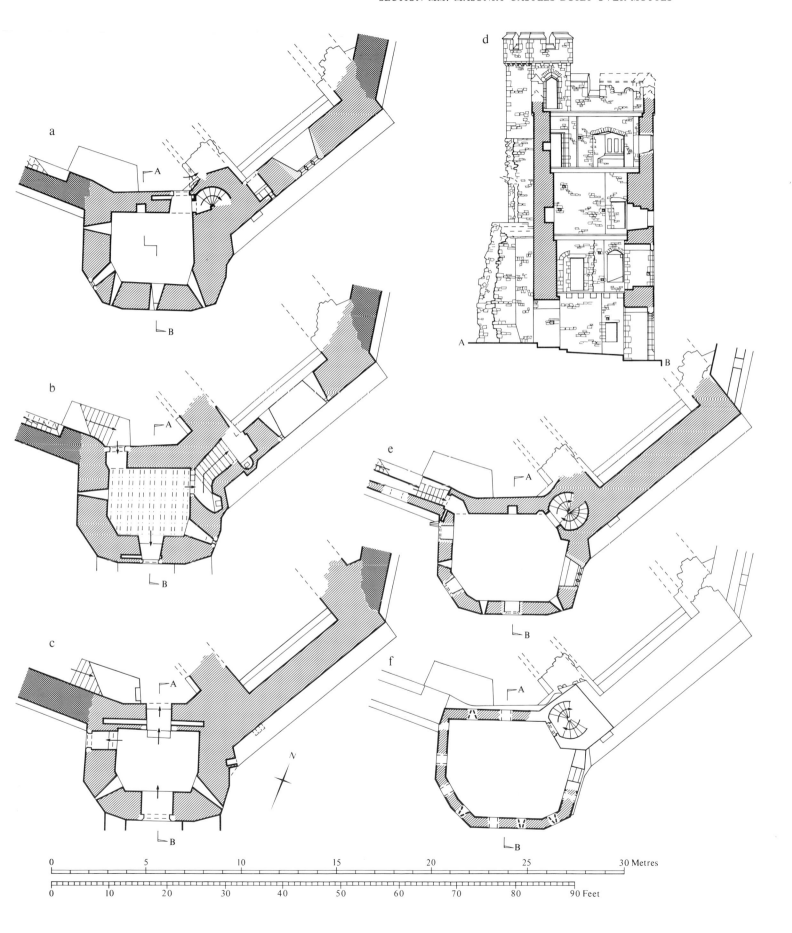

SECTION MM: MASONRY CASTLES BUILT OVER MOTTES

a

b

c

d

e

f

0   5   10   15   20   25   30 Metres

0   10   20   30   40   50   60   70   80   90 Feet

N

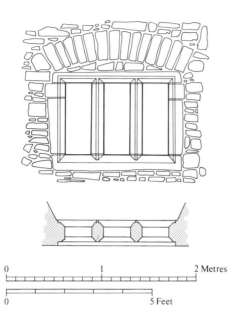

Fig. 133. Cardiff Castle: Tudor Window, third floor chamber of Keep Gate Tower, east wall. Attributed to Henry Herbert's works in the late 16th century (Period V).

placed by this window, Grant reconstructed the nearer splays of the loops to each side, to match their opposed original splays. A complete run of beam-holes defines the floor level, and a door to the W. marks a recessed latrine sharing its chute with that above. This latrine is that noticed at the head of the straight mural stair from the first floor of the gatehouse. The gable at basement level is now masked by a modern internal buttressing, though Grant recorded a further window set high in the wall, now masked externally by a patching of lias blocks. The composite double-roll-moulded corbels supporting the latrine chute are renewed, but match eroded original corbels on the adjacent chute in the angle, serving the gatehouse.

The Keep Fore-building

The barbican or fore-building protecting the entrance on the S. side of the keep was a most impressive structure. It was described by Merrick in the late 16th century:

'... on the right-hand side, is a fair broad way, mounting upward, leading to the keep ... in the entry of which stand two strong gates about [ ] foot distant. Between these gates was a deep, dark dungeon, covered with a bridge of thick boards, wherein it is supposed that Robert Courthose ... was detained .... In every of these gates was a place for a portcullis. Near the inner gate, on the left hand, is a well of great depth .... In both sides this entry be chambers, not so fair as strong. And on the left hand is a stair leading to the upper rooms, and so to a tower higher than all the rest within this castle, being leaded and embattled'.[82]

This illuminating description, discounting the absurdity of the dungeon beneath the bridge, is demonstrably accurate. At ground level, the dwarf walls raised over the foundations exposed by the third marquess, and avowedly reflecting them, entirely conform to Merrick's description. To appreciate its dominating visual impact, and affirming this early account, there are good 18th-century depictions showing the fore-building before its demolition by Capability Brown. The engraving of 1775 reproduced here is the most detailed view (Fig. 134a). By that date the crenellation on the fore-building had largely crumbled, together with the upper part of the angular turret housing the well, which had risen even higher to a corbelled parapet when depicted on the Bucks' panorama of 1748. Despite this erosion, in 1775 it remained an impressive structure, thrust out to bestride the moat to the full height of the shell keep. The 1775 view shows cross-oillets on the well-turret. This great barbican was integrated with the defences of the Inner Ward. Large doors were set high up on the fronts of the two lower gatehouses placed on each side of the moat, the outer one opening directly upon the wall-walk of the cross-wall leading to the first floor of the Black Tower. From this outer gatehouse an upper-level drawbridge of some sort may be envisaged, communicating with the upper door shown on the face of the Middle Gatehouse at the foot of the motte. This upper 'gallery' was surmounted by a further floor, at which level a Tudor three-light window had been inserted in the outer face of the Middle Gatehouse, to supplement cross-oillets and a window on the flanks at this level. Originally crowned by a large battlemented platform, this outwork was immensely strong. Artists' depictions do not reveal the internal defensive arrangements of the approach from the ward through the ground-level gates and up the enclosed stone stairs on the face of the motte. For this approach, however, we have the evidence of the lower walls, as reconstructed by the third marquess.

The fore-building projects 35m beyond the outer face of the keep gate-tower and is just over 6m wide

---

[82] Merrick, *Morg. Arch.*, p. 89–90.

196

Fig. 134. Cardiff Castle: the Shell-keep shortly before and after the removal of the Fore-building. Engravings of: (a) 1775, by S. Sparrow for Grose's *Antiquities;* (b) 1823, by W. Woolnoth after H. Gastineau *(National Library of Wales).*
For another portrayal of the Fore-building see Fig.118.

197

overall, excluding the projection of the well-tower. Its walls are of unequal thickness. That to the E. is 2m thick, almost twice that of its counterpart to the W., for this flank carried the defences facing the Inner Ward, which were continued to the Black Tower. At lower levels both walls were bonded into the face of the keep gate-tower, where toothing rises above the reconstructed level. The long passage within is 3.20m wide on the slope of the motte, narrowing to 2.60m at the lower gatehouses and bridge. It is probable that this passage was vaulted above, like Gilbert de Clare's

stairs linking the Great Hall to the southern water-gate at Caerphilly, situated on a slope beneath the Transverse Block inserted in the 1270s (Vol. III, Part 1b, LM 3). The cramped gallery above would have permitted murder-holes to survey the lower stair.

The Outer Gate displays the grooves of a portcullis fronting the projecting jambs of its door. Its inner end projects into the moat. Beyond this, the broader defensive wall to the E. continues unbroken across the moat to the Middle Gatehouse. The lesser W. wall incorporates a broad arch open to the moat which

Fig. 135. Cardiff Castle: the Black Tower and South Gate, internal north front, in 1775. The cross-wall to the right was soon to be demolished in the works of Period VI (see Fig.136, opposite). Aquatint by Paul Sandby *(National Library of Wales)*.

is bridged, as in Merrick's time, by transverse boards. At the inner end, before the Middle Gate, the passage is narrowed beside a pit to receive the inner end of a turning bridge. In an unpublished note and sketches of 1872, G. T. Clark records the arrangements of this bridge and the recovery from the pit of one end of its cylindrical wooden axle which retained a stout iron gudgeon.[83] Portcullis grooves again front the jambs of the Middle Gate beyond, within which the stone steps commence. A door on the left opens into the angular spurred well-turret at this point. A second door, on the right, provided access to the upper levels by a reversed mural stair with a narrow splayed light at its foot. A similar light pierces the opposite wall to the W. Beyond the Middle Gate, and half way up the stair, an inexplicable pit on the W. side narrows the passage and incorporates some original masonry. Fronting the gate-tower of the keep, there is a draw-bridge pit, which also displays original masonry. Two slots run from this pit under the entrance; they presumably served in some way when raising or securing the bridge, though they were not deep enough to house counter-balances.

At the foot of the fore-building, abutting its W. side, are remains of buildings set into the outer scarp of the moat. A thinner, right-angled wall abuts the Outer Gatehouse. Its lower part is original, marked out by red tiles, and it descends without a batter into the water. Its other end butts against a thicker wall with a bold batter, also descending into the moat. This wall is also original at its lower levels. Its W. termination overlaps a further short wall fragment at right angles to it. For no good reason, these fragments have been described as 'barracks'.

The Black Tower and South Gate

(Figs. 135–37).

The Black Tower (*Blaketour*) is first recorded in 1316, when it was re-roofed with lead. By the 16th century it was the 'Dungeon Towr . . . large and fair' noticed by Leland, a designation confirmed in *ca.* 1580 by Merrick, who observed that 'in the lowermost rooms were very strong prisons, the one called *Stafell yr Oged*,[84] the other *Stafell Wen*,[84] respectively translated 'the room of the harrow', 'the white room'. It stands at the S.E. angle of the Inner Ward, and at the S. end of the battlemented cross-wall which furnished protected and elevated communication with the keep. Though a prison by the 16th century, its primary function was as a strong defensive feature of the inner

perimeter, dominating the simple main entrance to the castle. It closely resembled the tower flanking the main gate on the cross-wall, and both were probably built in the early 13th century, to judge from their square form, flanking simple entrances, and the pointed vault in the Black Tower. A reliable restoration in the mid 19th century is proved by earlier depictions of the tower (Figs. 135, 136). The angular stair-turret was refaced in Lias Limestone; the main body of the tower and its annexe were less thoroughly refaced, their fenestration was faithfully restored, and tolerable crenellations were added to a surviving corbel-table. It now houses the Museum of the Welch Regiment.

The Black Tower is made up of two parts: a primary tower and a lesser annexe added to the W. The South Curtain forms the S. wall of both parts. The secondary nature of the annexe is indicated by a contrived inter-

---

[83] See f/n. 63 (Clark Papers).
[84] See f/n. 82.

Fig. 136. Cardiff Castle: the Black Tower in the early 19th century, internal north front. The cross-wall (Fig.135, opposite) has been demolished, though a prominent stub marks its junction with the Black Tower (*Cardiff City Library*). The missing crenellations were to be restored *ca.* 1850 by Lady Sophia Bute.

locking of quoins rising upwards from the first-floor level at the point of junction on the external S. wall, and by the differing floor levels in the separate parts (Figs. 127 and 137f). The lowest interlocking quoins presumably indicate the height of the curtain when the tower and annexe were successively raised against it. The Lias Limestone quoins at the flanking angles on this front are renewed, but the corbel-tables supporting restored crenellations are original, and square headed late-Tudor windows inserted in the upper floors retain most of their original plain-chamfered frames. These windows are set beneath relieving arches. The three in the main tower are mullioned and transomed; two lesser two-light windows without mullions suffice for the first and second floors of the annexe, with a plain, square, dressed frame for a yet smaller window on its upper floor.

On the E. front, the outer half of the tower is now masked by the modern gate. Within the gate, however, there are three restored plain-framed square windows, one to each upper floor. A smaller square-framed opening close to the lowest of these windows lights a plunging shaft serving the basement. At the N.E. angle the lower part of the angular stair-turret retains some original facing, and rises on spurs from a square

base. Renewed facing above this incorporates restored cross-oillets, small and decorative rather than functional, but vouched for by early prints.

On the N., beyond the turret, simulated toothing on the outer end of the modern external stair-block indicates the position of the cross-wall as it closed with the tower. Lias quoins survive near the base of the N.W. angle. The Lias masonry is of irregularly-coursed small stones. The corbel-table is original, but crenellations and fenestration are restored, including a pointed window on the second floor.

The main tower measures 9.3m by 9.0m externally, and rises to three floors above a vaulted basement. The stair-turret, like the annexe, is an addition. The lower vaulted chamber is 5m square, its lofty pointed vault rising 4.35m above the floor and set parallel to the curtain. This curtain is 2.50m thick; the E. wall, flanking the gate-passage, is 2.25m thick, but the remaining internal walls are both thinner. There is no communication with the gate-passage or the floor above; the only access is by the door in the W. wall, which retains original quarter-round moulded jambs beneath a renewed pointed head. Minimum ventilation and a flicker of light were provided by a small plunging vent high in the E. wall, at the point of the

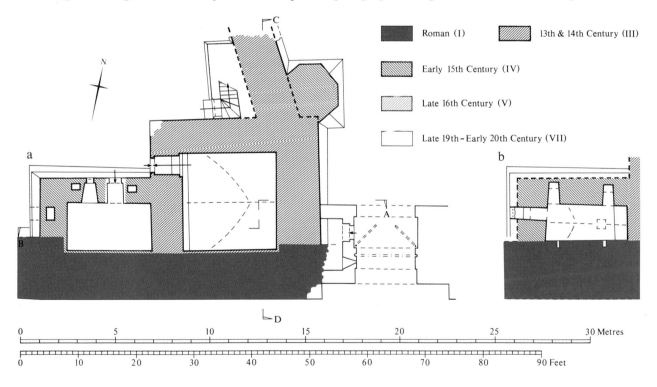

Fig. 137. Cardiff Castle: the Black Tower and its Annexe, as existing, *above:* (a) ground floor, and; (b) cess-pit beneath Annexe. *Opposite:* (g) first floor; (e) second floor; (c) third floor; (d) section C-D; (f) section A-B.

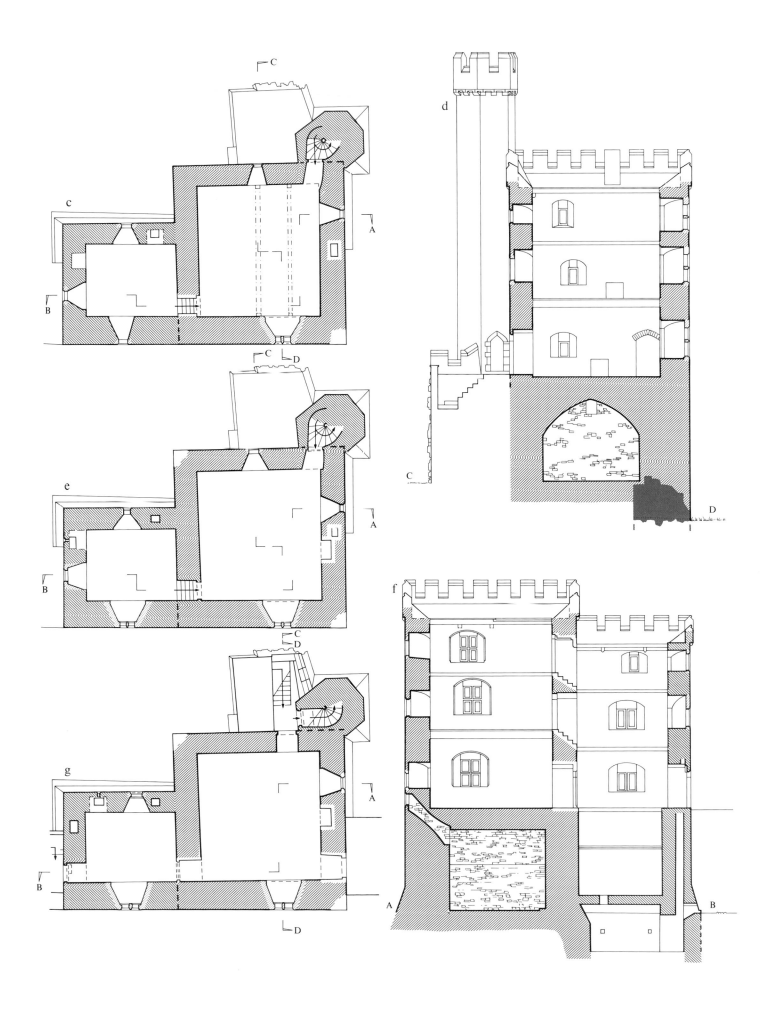

vault. This grim chamber may have been conceived as a prison cell from the outset, as it certainly was by the 16th century. Its floor is now slightly below external ground level; before landscaping in the 18th century this area of the ward was about 1m higher. Adjacent trees on mounds mark isolated areas retained at their original level.

The first floor is reached by the modern external stone stair masking the stump of the cross-wall. The door at the top of this is original, but it formerly communicated only with the wall-walk on the cross-wall. A second door entered at this level from the wall-walk of the South Curtain, approached through the annexe. At this level, corresponding with that of the wall-walks, the tower walls were narrowed to provide larger upper chambers measuring 6.8m by 6.4m. The first floor was lit by a late-Tudor two-light window, with mullion and transom, and set in a splayed recess with segmental-headed rear arch. A lesser, splayed single light pierces the E. wall, above the entrance, and a modern door is broken through at the S.E. corner to provide access to the portcullis chamber of the modern gate. A fireplace is set between these features. The second floor was reached by a door from the wall-walk into the stair-turret, adjacent to that into the tower. The first floors of both tower and annexe are at the same level, but the second and third floors of the tower are above equivalent levels in the annexe, which are reached down steps in the passages cut through the W. wall of the tower (Fig. 137f, Section A–B).

From the newel stair in the turret a slanted passage is cut through to the second floor chamber at its N.E. corner. The nature of this passage, and its equivalent on the floor above, together with the superior masonry of the turret and its spurred base and angled form, leave no doubt that this stair was a later addition to the tower. The second floor chamber has an additional splayed light in its N. wall, but otherwise its fenestration matches that on the floor below. Doors to the stair and to the annexe retain parts of their original quarter-round moulded frames. A fireplace is again situated in the E. wall. The third floor has no fireplace, but is otherwise identical and retains corbels supporting renewed ceiling beams.

The Annexe added on the W. side of the Black Tower in the angle made with the S. curtain rose on a batter set on a narrow plinth. It enclosed a deep vaulted cess-pit, excavated to a depth of 3m below the medieval ground level and narrowed to the S., where it had encountered the buried inner face of the

Roman wall identified here by Sesom Hiley in 1913.[85] The pit was further reduced by a buttress added to its E. end to maintain the adjacent wall of the Black Tower, leaving a chamber measuring 3.60m by 1.90m. Access is provided through a small opening in the pointed vault. The Roman wall to the S. is refaced with pebbles and Lias blocks, but its core is still exposed in two niches and a gap left towards the haunch of the vault.

Three latrine outfalls discharge into the cess-pit in deep recesses, one at each end of the N. wall and a third at the N. end of the W. wall. These outfalls rise through the walls, bypassing the ground floor chamber, one serving each of the upper chambers. A small opening at the foot of the W. recess may be an original outlet; traces of a relieving arch are visible externally.

The chamber above the cess-pit, now a public lavatory, was formerly at ground level but is now reached up several modern steps at its door on the N. side. An inspection cover in its renewed flooring replaces a trap-door noticed in 1923 by Grant, who suggested that the pit was one of the two dungeons recorded by Merrick. This view may be discounted; the cess-pit was a functional adjunct of the apartments above, comparable with that under the annexe added to the keep at Coity (MR 1). Bypassed by the latrine chutes, the ground-floor chamber was surely the second dungeon in the Black Tower. At this level the medieval S. curtain had been stepped back from the Roman inner face, giving larger internal dimensions to this and the chambers above. The dressings of the pointed door and splayed light on the N. are renewed.

Identical chambers above are all without fireplaces. Their inserted Tudor windows correspond in detail to the larger ones in the main tower, and though set at a lower level the renewed crenellations are similarly set upon an original corbel-table. On the first floor, opposed doors in the E. and W. walls permitted circulation through the annexe and tower between the adjacent wall-walks to the W. and N. A square recess in the N. wall accommodated the lowest of the three latrines served by the cess-pit. It was lit by a small square light, now blocked. There is a two-light late-Tudor window in the S. wall. The second-floor fenestration repeats that below, adding a third window in the W. wall and with the small latrine-light moved to a recess corresponding with the W. outfall in the pit, but now boarded up at the N. end of the same

---

[85] *Trans. Cardiff Nats. Soc.*, XLVI (1913), p. 87.

wall. In the S.E. corner, steps lead up to the main tower. Similar fenestration and access to the main tower are provided on the third floor. At this level, however, there is no trace of the third latrine evidenced in the cess-pit. The remaining shaft is now blocked well below this level and there is no indication externally of a latrine light or recess. Its assumed location is plotted in relation to the known outfall below, which would place it at the E. end of the N. wall.

The Black Tower no doubt housed the gatekeeper or his deputy in the apartments above the ground-floor dungeons. As gatekeeper in 1376, Peter John received 2d. a day. By 1515 Sir Robert Jones was gatekeeper for life; his deputy was the keeper of the prison.

The Western Apartments

(Figs. 138–42).
Detailed description is confined to the area of the 15th-century primary central block. Its subsequent development in three post-medieval periods of building (V–VII) has been outlined (pp. 177–87 and Figs. 117–26). Here, more detailed plans and sections illustrate the surviving fabric of all periods. Only the long section is extended to include the full extent of the final period of building, including the Clock Tower. The ornate and colourful late-19th-century interiors have been authoritatively described and well illustrated by Mordaunt Crook.[86]

On the *main internal front* to the E., the primary block is embraced by four angular bays. The southernmost of these is the plainest and least disturbed. It contains a newel stair, and is built with well-coursed Lias blocks. The outer facet is pierced by a door, and above this are two small stair-lights, all largely 15th-century work. The door is of segmental-pointed form, set beneath a hood-mould of the same shape, with plain angled terminals. The stair-lights are cusped, beneath square hood-moulds. A projecting plinth is finished above and at ground level with a course of moulded ashlar. Ornamental crenellations rise above the general level of the front, which is similarly battlemented.

The three bays further N. are superficially identical and all much restored. The first of these preserves an especially ornate form; the next is smaller and was originally a plain stair-turret, like that last described, before its conversion to a window bay in the late 18th century. Only the second and fourth bays originally

served as windows. The second bay has slender buttresses applied to each of its angles, each supporting a moulded pinnacle. The buttresses are carried down on the plinth, and the pinnacles rise to a moulded string-course at which the bay is reduced in girth. This embellishment was recognized as original by Clark in 1862, and it is discernible as a feature unique to this bay on the pre-Holland depiction and plan cited above (Fig. 117 a and b). The pointed windows of this bay were renewed by Holland, following their original form. This turret is also battlemented, and given decorative cross-oillets. When Holland removed the newel stair in the third and smallest bay he refenestrated and embellished it to match the last-described ornate bay in every detail, including its buttresses and pinnacles. The final N. bay lacks the buttresses and pinnacles.

Holland's North Wing laps over the N.E. angle of the primary central block, and retains his crenellations and fenestration (pointed above, sash below), though now containing neo-Gothic tracery. Holland's matching fenestration in the intervals between the bays of the original block was similarly gothicised, and a new window of his form has replaced the entrance he inserted between the northernmost bays.

South of the primary block, Grant's entrance hall (1927) was given another matching bay-window, and the entry was placed between this and the angular stair-turret of the late-19th-century Guest Tower dominating the internal front.

The general features of the external western front of the apartments have been described. Only the massive *Beauchamp Tower* calls for detailed description. This angular tower rises on a square base with semi-pyramidal angle-spurs. Its masonry is of squared and well-coursed Lias Limestone. Restored crenellations are carried upon machicolations with ornately moulded brackets. Alternate merlons are pierced with cross-oillets, and below the machicolations two tiers of small windows pierce each facet. The windows are much restored, with inserted cusped frames and square hood-moulds. Despite restoration, this tower is largely as it appears in depictions of the 18th century. Burges's ornate spire is a striking modern addition. Modern refacing has masked all trace of an improbably-sited door, with pointed head, which was shown at the foot of the outer face of the tower in depictions of *ca.* 1800.

The Lias masonry of the lower part of the *Bute*

---

[86] Mordaunt Crook, *op. cit.* (f/n. 59).

Tower, to the N., is a survival of Holland's late 18th-century work. Below the Beauchamp Tower on its S. side, the restored town wall joins the castle from the adjacent West Gate. The Beauchamp Tower was clearly sited to dominate this entry to the town. Further S., within the town wall, is the greatly heightened 16th-century *Herbert Tower*, beyond which a section of Lias masonry approximates to the level of the curtain before Bute superimposed the ashlar-faced *Guest Tower* upon it.

The restored *Central Block* is of three storeys, at present designated the Basement, the Library, and the Banqueting Hall, all undivided and with internal dimensions of 19.50m by 5.50m. The only remaining original entry to this block is the modest door at the foot of the southern stair-bay. This gives to a newel stair leading both down to the basement and up to the Library (and former Hall). This cramped and awkward entry could only have served as a secondary or service approach. The main entrance probably entered through the S. wall, as it did before the 18th-century rebuilding, and does today through Grant's new entrance hall.

The *Basement* is set partly below the external level, but less so than formerly. It has a pointed vault, constructed of good, tooled Lias blocks. The tooling is mainly diagonal, sometimes pock-marked. Below the haunches, 1.64m above the floor, these vertical walls are of similar but untooled Lias blocks. All doorways and the three windows to the court are restored. These windows are set above steeply stepped internal cills. Two passages are cut through the thick curtain to the W. and other doors are set in the end walls to communicate with adjacent cellars.

The Hall, now the Library, is modestly elevated above the court. In the important engraving of 1775 (Fig. 117a), it is the upper floor, the present 'Banqueting Hall', which displays large traceried windows

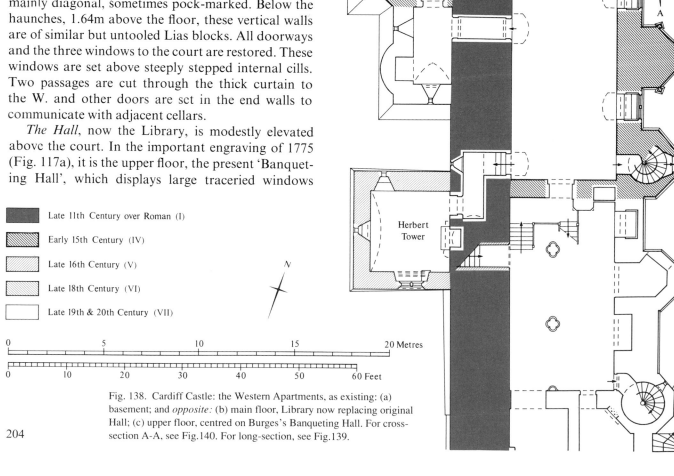

Late 11th Century over Roman (I)

Early 15th Century (IV)

Late 16th Century (V)

Late 18th Century (VI)

Late 19th & 20th Century (VII)

N

| 0 | 5 | 10 | 15 | 20 Metres |

| 0 | 10 | 20 | 30 | 40 | 50 | 60 Feet |

Fig. 138. Cardiff Castle: the Western Apartments, as existing: (a) basement; and *opposite:* (b) main floor, Library now replacing original Hall; (c) upper floor, centred on Burges's Banqueting Hall. For cross-section A-A, see Fig.140. For long-section, see Fig.139.

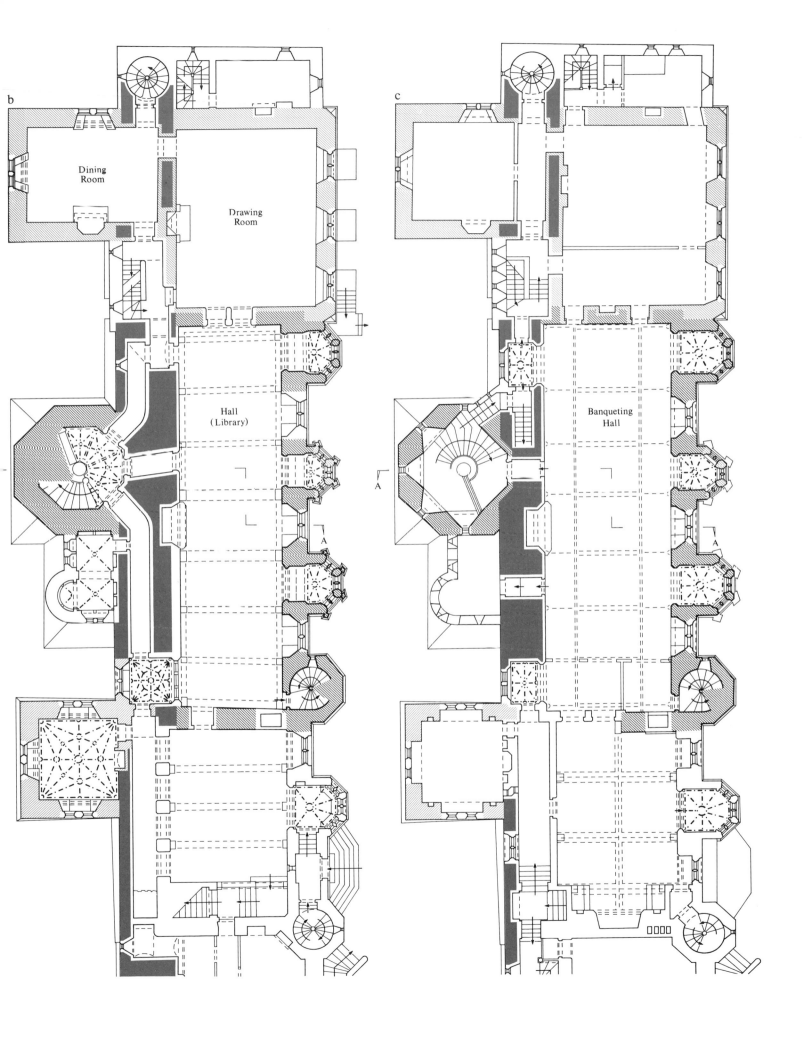

b

Dining
Room

Drawing
Room

Hall
(Library)

A

A

A

c

Banqueting
Hall

A

A

between the bays; those below are smaller two-light Tudor windows less befitting the great hall. As all other evidence favours a lower hall, it must be suspected that the Tudor windows had been inserted within former traceried windows. Besides the designa-

Fig.139. Cardiff Castle. The Western Apartments as existing, including the Clock Tower added by Burges. Long section looking west (resurveyed to update J.P. Grant's section of 1927, provided by *South Glamorgan County Council*).

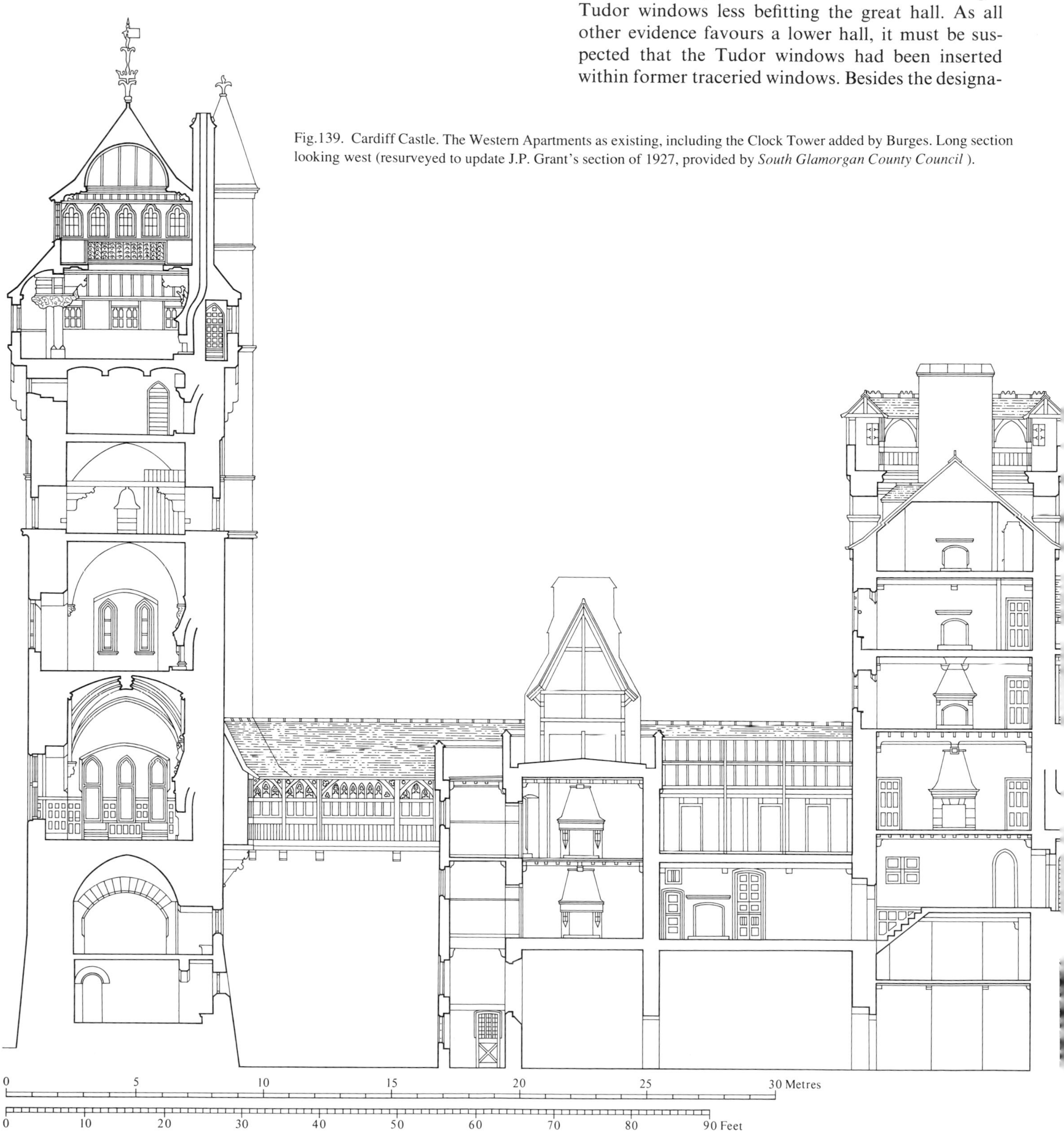

tion 'great hall' given to the S. chamber of the then divided lower level on the contemporary early plan, this also showed a deep lateral fireplace inserted in the curtain to the W. Suitably medieval in its siting, this fireplace was also directly opposed to the uniquely ornate bay-window on the internal E. front, with its special external embellishment confined to the lower level. In the 16th century, Merrick noticed the hall at the lower level: '*Being above ground*', as this level is, '*a broad easy pair of stairs . . . directeth to the entry*

Early 15th Century (IV)　　Late 18th Century (VI)　　Late 19th & Early 20th Century (VII)

Late 11th Century over Roman (I)

Early 15th Century (IV)

Late 19th Century (VII)

0   5   10   15 Metres

0   10   20   30   40 Feet

in the lower part of the hall (where there) is a buttery and pantry; and in the lower rooms very fair and great cellars for wine and beer'. The newel stair at the S.E. angle was a suitable service stair, furnishing direct access to the cellars below. Screened off at the S. end, it would conveniently have served Merrick's buttery and pantry, jointly enclosed in this area. His 'broad and easy' stair would fit that depicted in 1755, leading to a lobby and doors into the hall at the S. end. Clark regarded the present Library as the hall, adding a further suitable embellishment to the ornate bay that seems to have marked the dais, noting that its internal vaulting incorporated an heraldic boss displaying the arms of Isabel Despenser and Earl Richard Beauchamp of Warwick, the presumed builders of the primary block.[87]

The former hall was refurbished by Burges as the *Library* (Fig. 142). Receiled and lavishly decorated, its most striking addition was the fireplace in the W. wall. North of the fireplace a door with an ornately-moulded frame leads through the W. curtain to the *Beauchamp Tower*, where an elaborate staircase replaced that installed by Holland. At the N. end of the library two more ornate doors give access to Holland's *Drawing Room*. On the W. this room communicates with the *Dining Room*, its nearer end encroaching into the thickness of the curtain, as it had done as a chamber of Holland's North Tower, now heightened and renamed the Bute Tower.

A small private *Oratory*, in the S. angle between the curtain and the Beauchamp Tower, replaces a small room where the second marquess died in 1848. South of this, the first floor chamber of the Herbert Tower was refurbished as the *Arab Room*, the last to be decorated by Burges.

The *Banqueting Hall*, like the Library below it, was opened up to the full dimensions of the primary central block, replacing three bedrooms. Its lofty roof is of elaborate vaulted hammer-beam construction, copied from the parish church at Framlington, Suffolk, or from St Peter's, Norwich, in flamboyant Perpendicular style. It was furnished with a Screens Passage and Minstrels' Gallery to the S., and a richly sculpted chimney-piece depicting scenes at Cardiff Castle in the time of Earl Robert of Gloucester. Inspired by a chimney-piece in the Hotel Jacques Coeur at

Fig. 140. Cardiff Castle. The Western Apartments and Beauchamp Tower as existing: cross-section A-A as indicated on Fig.137. For the same cross-section by Burges before his reconstruction, see Fig.124.

[87] See f/n. 68.

Fig. 141. *(Opposite)* Cardiff Castle. The Western Appartments: the Banqueting Hall on the upper floor.

Fig. 142. Cardiff Castle. The Western Appartments: Library, formerly the Hall, on the main floor.

Bourges, it forms the centrepiece for huge murals likewise depicting the exploits of Earl Robert.

The 19th-century range to the S. of the primary block is dominated by the massive Guest Tower, and incorporates lesser apartments, kitchens, a vaulted wine cellar tunnelled out under the court, and Grant's entrance hall of 1927. These recent additions, replacing Holland's smaller South Wing, are less lavishly executed. Beyond them, however, Burges's roofed 'Norman' wall-walk leads to his remarkable Clock Tower.

The *Clock Tower* is a unique and extraordinary structure, Burges's first and dramatic overture at Cardiff (Fig. 139, Section A–B). Completed by 1873, it is 7.62m square and rises seven storeys to a height of 40m. The two lower chambers were designed as the gardener's residence and closed to those above, which were reached by the 'Norman' wall walk from the Western Apartments. The five chambers rising from this level provided a complete suite of rooms for the lord, including two fitted out with great magnificence. These were the *Winter Smoking Room* on the third floor, entered from the wall-walk, and the *Summer Smoking Room* on the topmost floor. Two bedrooms and the room housing the clock mechanism occupied the floors between. The Winter Smoking Room is richly decorated with themes derived from Norse and Saxon mythology, classical allusions, and astrological motifs, all related to time and its passing. In the Summer Smoking Room an Upper Gallery affords panoramic views, and through it is suspended a magnificent gold chandelier representing the sun. Rich decoration again mixes classical, astrological, and other themes.

General comments on the medieval masonry defences

The masonry castle at Cardiff was effectively limited to the walled Inner Ward. The keep, with its strong and complex fore-building, was fully integrated with the ward curtain, which was battlemented to each side of its broad wall-walk. The early-15th-century *Beauchamp Tower* was apparently the only salient tower on the enceinte, and there is no twin-towered gate-house. No traces of towers were found at the western angles of the ward, and the tower flanking the gate on the cross-wall projects only slightly into the field. These deficiencies might appear surprising in the main castle of the lordship, for 32 years the *caput* of Earl Gilbert the Red, founder of the matchless Caerphilly, only 10.7km distant and so illustrative of the massive 'Edwardian' flanking drum-towers and keep-gate-houses of the late 13th century. Caerphilly was but the most spectacular enterprise of a programme of castle-building undertaken by the later de Clare earls. They raised new stone castles at Caerphilly, Castell Coch, and Morlais, and greatly strengthened Llanblethian, Llangynwyd, Talyfan, and other castles held by them.[88] Given this great programme of peripheral and offensive castle-building, it is perhaps not surprising that they expended less effort on the more secure lowland castle at Cardiff.

The *shell-keep* is the finest of a very small number of its type in Wales.[89] The vanished Treoda (MM 2), on the N. outskirts of Cardiff, may have been the only other example in Glamorgan. The polygonal Cardiff keep is best compared with that at Carisbrooke, Isle of Wight. Its fore-building recalls that at Sandal, West Yorkshire; a less distant parallel may be indicated by the twin-towered gatehouse recorded at the foot of the large motte at Caerleon, Monmouthshire, though there the form of the keep on the motte is uncertain.[90]

The large Outer Ward was not defended in masonry, excepting its simple gate to the S., beside the Black Tower. Walling that has been recorded by antiquaries suggests no more than a flimsy wall, not intended for defence. This outer enclosure accommodated the Shire Hall and houses of the knights owing castle-guard, and served as a gathering-ground for forces in times of trouble. The un-walled earthen bailey beside the stone castle at Ogmore (MR 5) is a lesser parallel. Another might be the great outer enclosure at Llangynwyd (MR 2), unless that was merely a pre-existing Iron Age work.

Excavations: the evidence for the castle

Roman evidence from excavations has been summarized and cited above in relation to the nature of the primary castle defences. Here we summarize the contribution that excavations have made to a wider understanding of the medieval castle.

There have been four phases of excavation at the castle. First, there was the clearance of the motte ditch and excavation to reveal the foundations of the cross-wall, and of buildings in both wards. This work, in 1872–73, preceded the partial restoration of the cross-wall; lesser foundations within the wards were too decayed for similar restoration, but they were surveyed. Secondly, after 1889, the newly-discovered Roman fort wall was cleared, yielding vital information regarding the castle defences.[91] A third and very limited excavation by Dr M. G. Jarrett in 1960, W. of the South Gate, showed that the Roman ditch had been completely removed by the larger medieval ditch.[92] The fourth phase of excavation (1974–1981) was undertaken in the Outer Ward by Mr Peter Webster.[93] Only those excavations concentrated on the Roman walls have been published in detail.

The unpublished excavations undertaken for the third marquess in the late 19th century are known only from incidental references, especially those by G. T. Clark, and from the surviving plans of foundations in the castle archives (shown on Fig. 128, with minor additions revealed by Webster). The stated opinion of Clark permits us to accept the details reconstructed above ground on the fore-building, cross-

---

[88] C. J. Spurgeon, *Château Gaillard*, XIII (1986), 1987, pp. 213–18 and Map 5, p. 221.

[89] At Brecon, Crickhowell, and Tretower in Breconshire, and at Wiston in Pembrokeshire. Others may have existed at Builth (Brecs), Carmarthen, Llandovery and St Clears (Carms), Treoda (Glam, MM 2), and Langstone Court (Mon).

[90] Jeremy K. Knight, *The Monmouthshire Antiquary*, I (1963), pp. 71–72 (misprinted 23–24). A similar twin-towered fore-building has recently been reported at Crickhowell motte, Brecs.

[91] See f/n. 7.

[92] See f/n. 9.

[93] See f/n. 4.

wall and adjacent structures. Furthermore, the unpublished 19th-century plan of the foundations in the Outer Ward has been largely confirmed by Webster. The piles of a timber bridge were recorded in the motte ditch and fragments of a drawbridge were recovered at the adjacent Middle Gate. These and other aspects of the early excavations are cited in the discussion of the respective components of the castle.

Evidence derived from work on the Roman fort defences, and from the limited exploration by Jarrett, relates to the defences of the castle perimeter, particularly in its primary phases, and requires no further comment. Webster's recent work, however, contributes to a wider understanding of the castle and its development, not least by confirming the foundations previously recorded in the Outer Ward and adding a few details to them. He also found no evidence for occupation between the end of the Roman period and the founding of the castle by the Normans, contradicting the view that robbing of the Roman wall was carried out in the Dark Ages (Vol. I, No. 735, p. 93). This negative evidence furthers the suggested robbing of much of the Roman wall to provide the Norman founders of the castle with material for a primary walled Inner Ward.

The foundations re-excavated in the Outer Ward were all of late-medieval date. Evidence of occupation in the early Middle Ages was limited to rubbish pits. From this it was postulated that buildings of the early castle phases were of timber. The Shire Hall was explored, confirming that it was a long and narrow building strengthened with buttresses applied to its angles and side walls. It was roofed with stone tiles and some slate, and it seems to have stood until the 18th century. Late-medieval buildings S.E. of the Shire Hall were also confirmed by Webster, who dis-

covered an additional cellar and a cess-pit. Indications of their date varied, probably due to post-medieval refurbishment. Some cellars had not been filled in until the late 18th century, suggesting that buildings survived until Capability Brown's landscaping. A wall enclosing these buildings corresponded with that illustrated by Speed in 1610.

Landscaping was claimed to have lowered the level of the N.E. quarter of the castle. It was also concluded that the main axial Roman road running N.–S. had created an appreciable division between a more elevated E. side and a lower W. side. This is not easily reconciled with a general reduction in the level of the S. part of the Inner Ward after landscaping, as shown by early engravings and aspects of the surviving Black Tower. The evidence for a lowering of the level of the E. half, however, was emphatic and presumably matched that to the S.W. Further work is needed to explore this aspect, and the suggestion that landscaping involved the dumping of material in the W. part of the castle.

Sundry loose dressed stones have been noted within the castle, a few appropriate to elaborate tracery. The castle chapel that formerly lay against the E. rampart has not been located, but it would be unwise to suggest that such mouldings derived from that structure, or anywhere else in the castle, since it is known that stone from the nearby friaries was used in the late-16th-century restoration. The most significant chance find within the castle is undoubtedly the coin of William the Conqueror's Cardiff mint, fully discussed above.

King, p. 162

Cardiff, St John (E), Cardiff (C)
ST 17 N.E. (1808–7659)   14.xii.88   XLIII S.E.

MM 2   Treoda (Whitchurch)

The vanished motte of Treoda in the parish and demesne manor of Whitchurch (*Album Monasterium; Blancminster*) retained traces of medieval masonry until it was truncated early in the 19th century. What remained was finally removed during redevelopment in 1966 after excavations had revealed no trace of the masonry, but had disclosed a Bronze Age barrow forming the core of the motte (Vol. I, Part 1, No. 421). There is also evidence to suggest the Treoda stood within a Roman enclosure.

The motte stood immediately S. of Treoda man-

sion, within its grounds. This house of the early 19th century, also destroyed in 1966, stood on the site of a house regarded as ancient in the 16th century.[1] About 60m E.S.E. of the motte stood the medieval church, a chapelry of Llandaf, that gave both ancient and modern names to the parish, castle and manor. Superseded in 1885 by the present church of St Mary's, further S.W., its footings were consolidated as an ame-

[1] Merrick, *Morg. Arch.*, pp. 93, 98. R.C.A.M., Glam. Inventory, Vol. IV, Part i, No. 87, p. 345.

nity in 1973, when Roman sherds were found in the graveyard.[2] Roman material was also recovered from the surface of the barrow and beneath the motte built over it, as we notice below. The proximity of the castle and church permits no doubt that the former was the administrative centre of the lordship. At 30m above O.D. and 1.6km E. of the River Taff, it was 4.5km N.N.W. of Cardiff Castle, and one of a cluster of three or four mottes within or just beyond the N.W. portion of the commote of Cibwr, the southernmost division of Senghennydd which was appropriated by the chief lords at an early date. Twmpath, Rhiwbina (MO 8) is 1.9km to the N., and also within Whitchurch. To the N.W., Morganstown Castle Mound (MO 3) is 3.1km distant, on the far bank of the Taff in the neighbouring manor of Radyr. Finally, a fourth motte is strongly suspected beneath the masonry of Castell Coch (Vol. III, Part 1b, LM 4), three quarters of a kilometre N. of Morganstown and 3.5km N.W. of Treoda. These sites form the closest concentration in an arc of eight or more mottes to the N. and N.W. of Cardiff, quite possibly indicating an early, limited, and largely temporary Norman advance into the hill commotes (Introduction, pp. 10–11).

It is conceivable that Treoda was built within a Roman fort and on the line of the Roman road running N. from Cardiff. The excavations of 1966 identified Roman sherds on the surface of the Bronze Age barrow, sealed by the motte.[3] We have noted further Roman sherds found in the adjacent graveyard in 1973. Unpublished notes and sketches made by G. T. Clark at Treoda on 14 September 1848 show that the castle stood within the N.E. quarter of a large playing-card shaped enclosure (Fig. 143):

"The mound, house, a field, the road and the church and churchyard stand within a bank or dyke of earth or loose stones of considerable size. I rather think of rectangular figure, now considerably ploughed down and made indistinct. It may be Roman from its figure ... at Rhiwbina 1½mls E. is a road called by tradition Roman ..."[4]

Transposing Clark's sketch plan upon the 1st edition of the 25-inch O.S. map, an enclosure 195m by 160m is indicated; its area is little under 8 acres. Today 48m of spread bank towards the centre of the W. side is all that survives, this obscured by shrubs immediately beyond the former W. wall of the old churchyard. Too large for a medieval enclosure, Roman military occupation is more probable, although the proximity to Cardiff and its sequence of Roman forts is puzzling.

Historical and Manorial Context

Though the demesne manor of Whitchurch was not created until after Gilbert de Clare's annexation of the northern commotes of Senghennydd in 1267, the mottes within its bounds at Treoda and Rhiwbina indicate much earlier Norman settlement. Such settlement is indicated by one clause of the important Agreement of Woodstock between Earl Robert of Gloucester and Bishop Urban of Llandaf in 1126.[5] This conceded all claims the bishop had made against the earl's men in lands they claimed were not held of the bishop. These lands included the vicinity of Whitchurch, where the chapel of '*Stuntaf*' (*Ystum Taff*, the bend in the Taff) was granted to the bishop, along with lands donated to it by the earl. Now lost, the chapel lay near the river about a kilometre W. of Treoda, and the tithes of its vill were conceded, the parishioners worshipping at the cathedral at Christmas, Easter and Whitsun and burying their dead there. The later medieval foundation beside the motte at Treoda continued these arrangements, being a chapelry of Llandaf until 1845, when the parish was first created.[6] There is no further record of Whitchurch until the late 13th century, but the customary tenancies then recorded there indicate long-established settlement.[7]

The demesne manor created in the late 13th century was bounded on the W. by the River Taff between the Radyr ford and Tongwynlais to the N. Across the river lay the small manor of Radyr. To the N. the limit followed the Nant Gwynlais and the high ground of the border ridge of Cibwr, almost to Castell Morgraig (Vol. III, Part 1b, LM 9), abutting the commote of Senghennydd Is-caeach. The E. boundary at first ran S. down the Briwnant Brook, and then

Fig. 143 (*Opposite*) Treoda, Whitchurch: Map indicating the location of the Motte and suspected Roman enclosure, both now vanished. The map is based on the O.S. 25-inch sheet; the enclosure, confirmed by a fragment of the west rampart surviving in 1969, is based on a plan of 1848 by G.T. Clark in the *National Library of Wales*.

---

[2] *Arch. in Wales*, No. 13, 1973, p. 49.

[3] Jeremy Knight and Eric J. Talbot, 'The Excavation of a Castle Mound and Round Barrow at Tre Oda, Whitchurch,' *Trans. Cardiff Nat. Soc.*, XCV, 1968–70, pp. 9–23.

[4] G. T. Clark Papers ('Glamorgan Manors'), Vol. VII, *N.L.W.* MS 5215E.

[5] *Liber Land.*, pp. 27–9; Clark, *Cartae*, I (1), pp. 54–6; *Epis. Acts*, II, No L45; Patterson, *Glouc. Charters*, No. 109, p. 107.

[6] Edgar L. Chappell, *Old Whitchurch, the Story of a Glamorgan Parish*, Cardiff, 1945, pp. 8, 40–1.

[7] Corbett, *Glamorgan Lordship*, pp. 42, 58.

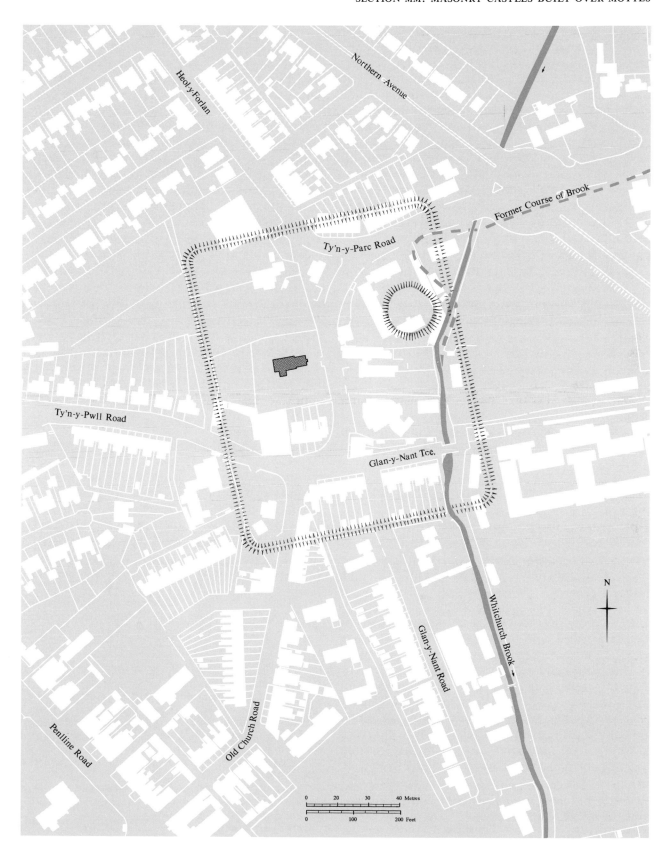

beyond, as far as modern Birchgrove, abutting the monastic manor of Roath Keynsham and a lesser grange of Margam. On the S. a circuitous course accommodated a northward extension of that part of the manor of the bishop of Llandaff that lay E. of the Taff, finally returning to the Radyr ford. These bounds did not comprise the full extent of the modern parish of Whitchurch.[8] Whitchurch is often claimed to be a southern extension of Senghennydd-is-Caeach. In the 14th century it certainly became a member of Caerphilly, in that commote, but this association is surely an administrative convenience adopted well after the foundation of that fortress in 1268, for the natural E.–W. ridge to the N. is by far the most logical line dividing Cibwr from the hill commote.

By the time of the death of Gilbert de Clare in 1295 the demesne lordship (*Album Monasterium*) was well established, with 300 acres of arable and a water-mill. Though there is no note of the castle in his inquisition *post-mortem*, it does record that the mill had been burnt in the revolt of 1294–95.[9] The manor had become a member of Caerphilly by 1307, when Gilbert's widow died; arable had increased to 345½ acres, but again no castle is recorded. It is of great interest that the restored mill was then leased out to Llywelyn ap Gruffydd, who would soon be leading the uprising of 1316 as the celebrated Llywelyn Bren, presumed son of the disinherited last Welsh lord of Senghennydd.[10] The last Clare earl, Gilbert III, died at Bannockburn in 1314, and his inquisition furnishes the first mention of a castle at Whitchurch (*Album Monasterium*), though it was worth nothing beyond reprise, having been burnt in the war.[11] It is uncertain whether this refers to the war of 1294–95, or, more probably, the revolt that followed soon after Gilbert's death.

The castle is next mentioned in a writ issued in 1315, during the period of royal custody before Glamorgan was finally granted to Hugh Despenser in 1317. The writ attempted to calm Welsh discontent at oppressions inflicted by crown officials in the lordship. One of the king's orders was that the newly built fort (*fortellettum in novo edificatum*) at Whitchurch (*Blaunk Moustier*) was to be delivered into the custody of Llywelyn Bren, though the mill leased to him there in 1307 was retained by the king.[12] The king's gesture was not sufficient to appease Llywelyn. Early in 1316 he destroyed Whitchurch mill, and probably the castle, before concentrating his followers in the hills and attacking Caerphilly Castle. John Giffard's accounts for the period following this brief but de-

structive revolt in early 1316 notice the mill, but not the castle.[13]

Further negative evidence suggests that the castle was destroyed by Llywelyn Bren in 1316, if it was scribal convention which accounts for its inclusion in the list of castles and manors ceded to Hugh Despenser in 1317. Had it been intact then, it is surely surprising that it escaped the attentions of the barons in 1321, when they ravaged its manor and sacked Hugh's eight other castles in Glamorgan and Gwynllŵg, including those surrounding it at Cardiff, Llantrisant, Caerphilly and Newport.[14]

The castle had been restored by 1349, when the inquisition after the death of Hugh Despenser II notices the ditch around it, and its annexed barton.[15] In 1440 a later inquisition specifies *Whitchurche* as an alternative name for the castle and manor, leaving no doubt over the identity of our site.[16] By the 16th century the castle was ruinous. Leland (*ca.* 1539) noticed '... vestigia of a pile or maner place decayed,' while Merrick (*ca.* 1578) twice records '... *an old castle or pile, now altogether in ruin, that the rubbish thereof can hardly be seen.*'[17] Merrick also remarks on the proximity of the church and the 'ancient house' of Treoda.

Description of the Castle

The truncated motte excavated before destruction in 1966 stood between 1.6m and 2.0m above the old ground surface and measured 40m in diameter at its

[8] Chappell, *op. cit.* (f/n. 6), pp. 14–5 and map facing p. vii.

[9] Chappell, *op. cit.* (f/n. 6), pp. 16–7; *Cardiff Records*, I, pp. 265–6; Corbett, *Glamorgan Lordship*, p. 58.

[10] *Cal I.P.M.*, Vol. III, 24 Edw. I, pp. 322–4; Clark, *Cartae*, III (dccclii), pp. 1000–04; Chappell, *op. cit.* (f/n. 6), pp. 18–9; *Cardiff Records*, I, p. 274. For the probable identity of Llywelyn ap Gruffydd: *Glam. Co. Hist.*, III, p. 74 and Chappell, *op. cit.* (f/n. 6), pp. 31–3.

[11] *Cardiff Records*, I, pp. 285, 288; Chappell, *op. cit.* (f/n. 6), pp. 19–20, 46.

[12] *Cal. C.R.*, 1313–18, pp. 161, 406; *Glam. Co. Hist.*, III, p. 74; Chappell, *op. cit.* (f/n. 6), pp. 31–3.

[13] Clark, *Cartae*, III (dccxlv), p. 822; Chappell, *op. cit.* (f/n. 6), p. 22; *Cardiff Records*, I, p. 144.

[14] Clark, *Cartae*, III (dccclxxxvi), p. 1051; J. Conway Davies, 'The Despenser War in Glamorgan', *Trans. Royal Historical Society*, Third Series, IX, 1915, pp. 24–5, 54–6.

[15] *Cardiff Records*, I, pp. 291–2; Chappell, *op. cit.* (f/n. 6), pp. 24, 46.

[16] *Inq. P.M.*, Isabella, countess of Warwick: Clark, *Cartae*, IV (mclviii), pp. 1566–7; *Cardiff Records*, I, p. 294; Chappell, *op. cit.* (f/n. 6), pp. 26, 46.

[17] Leland, *Itin. Wales*, p. 17; Merrick, *Morg. Arch.*, pp. 93, 98.

base.[18] The underlying barrow was 25m in diameter and centrally placed beneath the boulder clay imposed upon it to form the motte. Abraded Roman tile and sherds were recovered from the surface of the primary mound, together with four medieval sherds tentatively ascribed to the late 11th or early 12th century. The surrounding ditch was partially sectioned to the N., without discerning its full width or depth, but yielding sherds of 14th-century date. This ditch was probably linked with the brook skirting the E. side of the site. The excavator's conjecture that the motte had been lowered in the 19th century is now confirmed by the unpublished notes of G. T. Clark.[19] Visiting the site in 1848, he was informed by the owner, Mr Rowland, that he had removed about 5ft from the top of the mound to fill in the ditch, using stone and ashlar unexpectedly encountered to build his house (see text below). With this information, we may envisage a motte rising from its base, 40m across, to a height of about 3.60m, excluding its ditch, and with a summit about 28.0m in diameter. These dimensions are average for Glamorgan and very close to those of Cottrell, Stormy and Tomen-y-clawdd (MO 1, 5, 7).

The stone castle at Treoda is less easily discussed, particularly as Clark's many brief published comments are not easily reconciled with his own notes made over 30 years earlier. In print he consistently refers to a tower, usually round, but without giving any detail. In 1850, only two years after his visit, Treoda was '... the site of a tower'.[20] By 1883 it was 'the base of a tower (Early English)', and Earl Gilbert's '... circular tower, now destroyed ... enough remained ... a score of years ago to declare its date',[21] In 1884, 'at Whitchurch ... are, or recently were, the foundations of a detached round tower of considerable diameter, the base mouldings of which showed it to be of Early English date'; '... the low circular mound ... was the site of a tower of the time of Henry III.'[22] Finally, it is again regarded as a work contem-

porary with Caerphilly in 1886.[23]

The value of these various published notes is compromised by Clark's own hand-written notes made on the spot in 1848. These clearly demonstrate that he saw no masonry whatsoever, but relied entirely upon the word of Mr Rowland of Treoda regarding its nature. With a simple section showing the infilled ditch and an extra 5ft added in broken line on the top of the motte, Clark gives the following information:

'*The dotted outline is the original, but Mr. Rowland tells me he cut off about 5ft from the top, filled up the ditch and built his house and others with the stones, many of which were ashlar. He knew nothing of the stones till he began to work and commenced the cutting down to obtain ... of the ... across the mound. At the E. side he found some very well built and strong walling with what he thought a trace of a gateway with portcullis groove. He also found two silver coins of I think Edward I. The outline of the mound is perfectly regular and defined, no doubt rendered sharp after his excavations. There is no trace of the ditch.*'[24]

With this evidence to hand, Clark's round tower must be regarded with great caution. The mention of a gateway with portcullis on the E. side would discount any idea of a round keep, like Bronllys, as some have assumed.

King, p. 172 (as Whitchurch no. 2).

Whitchurch (E), Cardiff (C)
ST 18 S.E. (1560–8040)   29.xii.69   XLIII N.W.

[18] Knight and Talbot, *op. cit.* (f/n. 3), Fig. 2.
[19] See f/n. 4.
[20] G. T. Clark, *Arch. Camb.* (1850), p. 243.
[21] Clark, *Land of Morgan*, pp. 36, 134.
[22] Clark, *Med. Milit. Arch.*, I, pp. 150, 359.
[23] Clark, *Limbus*, p. 39.
[24] See f/n. 4.

Section MR:
Masonry Castles built over Castle-ringworks

Monuments MR 1 to 7

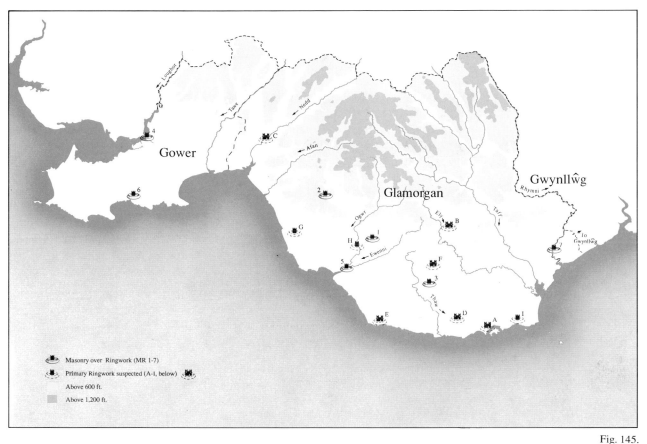

Fig. 145.

		Ringworks suspected:						
1	Coity Castle							
2	Llangynwyd Castle	A	Barry	(LM 1)	E	St Donats	(LM 16)	
3	Llanquian Castle	B	Llantrisant	(LM 8)	F	Talyfan	(LM 19)	*
4	Loughor Castle	C	Neath Castle	(LM 11)	G	Kenfig	(EM 2)	
5	Ogmore Castle	D	Penmark	(LM 14)	H	Newcastle	(EM 3)	
6	Pennard Castle				I	Sully	(EM 6)	
7	Rumney Castle							

*Volume III Part 1b

The castle-ringwork of earth and timber was clearly the predominant form of early castle in Gower and Glamorgan. The twenty-one described in Section CR were never strengthened by replacing their timber-work with masonry. To these may be added the seven which were certainly reinforced in this way, and a further nine suspected cases, giving a total of between twenty-eight and thirty-seven in the county. This section describes the seven masonry castles known to have been built over primary ringworks. These are listed and plotted above on Fig. 145, together with the nine suspected cases which are described in Section

Fig. 144 (*Opposite*) Ogmore Castle: the Norman keep; interior view of its west wall (*cf.* Figs 201, 202, 204, and 205).

EM or in Section LM of Part 1b.

Despite their imposed masonry, the castles at Coity, Llangynwyd, Llanquian and Ogmore (MR 1–3, 5) retain visible evidence of their primary earthworks, while excavations have confirmed their former existence at Loughor, Pennard and Rumney (MR 4, 6, 7). In all cases it appears that the layout of the masonry defences largely conformed to that of pre-existing timberwork, as proved at the excavated sites. Ogmore alone retains a well-preserved earthen bailey which was not refortified in stone along with its ringwork. The walls of the outer ward at Coity probably follow the lines of a similar bailey, while there is evidence to suggest that another example formerly existed at Rumney.

The size and strength of primary castle-ringworks do not appear to have been relevant in the eventual strengthening of some of them in masonry (see p. 81 and Fig. 45). Those refortified in this way include Llanquian and Loughor (MR 3, 4), the smallest ringworks in the county with respective internal diameters of 19m and 22m. Pennard (MR 6) was little larger, while even the important stone castles at Coity and Ogmore, both 44m in diameter, were equalled or exceeded in size by eight ringworks without masonry, and Rumney, at 46m, was exceeded by five. Except at tiny Llanquian, it was the status and wealth of respective owners which was of greater relevance. Llangynwyd and Rumney were castles of the chief lord of Glamorgan, Coity and Ogmore those of two of his major tenants. In Gower the chief lord held Pennard and had obtained Loughor before its masonry was built.

Masonry defences replaced timberwork at the seven sites described here in a series of full or staged conversions beginning with the early-12th-century keep at Ogmore and ending with the late-13th- or early-14th-century walls of Pennard. The early keep at Ogmore straddled the palisaded ring-bank until its curtain-wall was built in the early 13th century. The late-12th-century keep at Rumney is a similar case of the staged conversion also paralleled at Kenfig (EM 2), where a primary ringwork is suspected. Coity demonstrates a different process: there the keep and curtain-wall were raised together in the late 12th century in one programme of building; a unified conversion which is also suspected at Newcastle (EM 3). The curtain-wall at Loughor is now ascribed to c. 1200. It is not possible to date the scant vestiges of a ring-wall at Llangynwyd, though this displays at least two phases of imposed 13th-century masonry. Diminutive Llanquian is similarly reduced to scant vestiges, though when more intact it was ascribed to the 1220s by G. T. Clark.

MR 1   Coity Castle

Coity Castle stands beside the parish church of St Mary on a modestly elevated shelf on the N. side of Coity (Fig. 147). It enjoys a wide southern outlook towards the Vale of Glamorgan, but is overlooked from the N. by nearby ground rising away to the ridge of Cefn Hirgoed, 1.3km distant. At the same distance N.W. lies the moated site of Coity Higher (Vol. III, Part 2, MS 3), possibly a hunting lodge of the lords of Coity. No medieval houses survive in the village, but West Plas (Vol. III, Part 2, MH 18), a recently-demolished house of the late 15th century, stood beside the road 360m to the W. Newcastle (EM 3) and the vanished Oldcastle (VE 4) are both enveloped in the suburbs of Bridgend, the town centred 2.5km to the S.W. on the Afon Ogwr. Ogmore Castle (MR 5), near the mouth of that river, is 6.2km S.W. of Coity.

Coity Castle was the *caput* of the extensive lordship of Coity, held 'with royal liberty' by serjeanty of hunting. The Turbervilles were its lords from the early 12th century until the late 14th century, when the male line failed. It then passed in succession to Sir Lawrence Berkerolles and Sir William Gamage, the heirs of two sisters of the last Turberville lord. The Gamages retained Coity until 1584.

The lordship was contained within the angle formed by the Afon Ogwr and its tributary the Ewenni, which respectively defined its W. and S.E. sides, while a further tributary, the Ogwr Fach, defined its N. limit. The ecclesiastical parishes of Coity, Coychurch and St Brides Minor were embraced by these bounds, which abutted the lordships of Newcastle on the W., Ogmore on the S.E., Rhuthin and Newland on the E. and Glynogwr and Glynrhondda on the N.[1] The lordship, or 'Honour' of Coity as it was called in 1262, was not held by military service

---

[1] For the lordship and its bounds see G. T. Clark, *Arch. Camb.*, 1878, pp. 114–23; Nicholl, *Normans*, pp. 26–32, 160–6; Corbett, *Glamorgan Lordship*, pp. 70–72; *Rees's Map.*

Fig. 146. *(Opposite)* Coity Castle: the Keep, with gabled annexe, right, viewed from the south.

Fig. 147. Coity Castle viewed from the church tower on the north-east side.

but by serjeanty of hunting, though in 1317 its eastern constituent of Coychurch was listed as a knight's fee, and the whole serjeanty was deemed to equal four fees.[2] With minor exceptions the lower and more fertile lands to the S. constituted the Englishry (*Coity Anglia*), while the more sterile uplands of the northern part were the Welshry (*Coity Wallia*). Coity Castle and Oldcastle (VE 4), the only castles in the lordship, were both in the Englishry.

In the traditional account of the Norman conquest of Glamorgan related by 16th-century historians, Payn Turberville 'the Demon' (*Y-Cythraul*) was assigned the lordship of Coity by Robert Fitzhamon (*ob*. 1107).[3] Although no contemporary record supports this tradition it is credible. A *Payn Turberville* is well-attested in Glamorgan from 1126 when he witnessed Earl Robert's agreement with Bishop Urban.[4] His sons certainly held Coity, and it is hardly to be doubted that the subjugation of that territory was an essential preliminary to the establishment of Fitzhamon's Newcastle (EM 3) on the W. bank of the Ogwr, beyond Coity, by 1106. A further indication of early Norman settlement at Coity is the grant of two parts of its tithes to Tewkesbury Abbey; Payn Turberville was conceivably numbered with Fitzhamon's un-named 'barons of Wales', whose grants to that abbey, founded by their lord, were confirmed by Henry I in 1106 and 1107.[5] Payn's sons, Simon

[2] Extent of 1262: Clark, *Cartae*, II (dcxv), p. 651; Royal writ of 1317: *ibid*, III (dccclxxxvi), pp. 1053, 1055.

[3] Merrick, *Morg. Arch.*, pp. 27, 54 and appendix 2, p. 157; Clark, *Limbus*, p. 452 and *Arch. Camb.*, 1877, pp. 1 2; R. A. Griffiths analyses the traditional 'winning' of Glamorgan in *Glamorgan Historian*, Vol. III, pp. 153 ff., Coity pp. 167–8.

[4] Clark, *Cartae*, I (1), pp. 54–6; *Epis. Acts*, II, L45, pp. 620–1; Patterson, *Glouc. Charters*, no. 109, p. 106.

and Gilbert, who succeeded him in turn, granted lands they held in the neighbouring lordship of Ogmore to Ewenny Priory, founded in that lordship in 1141 by its lord, Maurice de Londres.[6] This close association with the lord of Ogmore increases the probability that Coity Castle was founded along with the de Londres castle at Ogmore (MR 5), first mentioned in 1116, and that the two castles existed by 1106 in support of Fitzhamon's Newcastle, the three marking the western limits of appropriations in his time.

Payn Turberville I witnessed the foundation charter of Neath Abbey in 1130,[7] four years after his first recorded appearance noted above, but the date of his death is uncertain. Ten Turberville lords succeeded him.[8] His sons *Simon* and *Gilbert I* were successively lords in the mid 12th century, jointly making grants to Ewenny Priory 1140–1148.[9] Gilbert I soon succeeded his brother, for before 1147 he alone joined Maurice de Londres in further donations to Ewenny, confirmed by Earl Robert.[10] Gilbert I's son, *Payn II*, succeeded before the death of Earl William (1183), under whom he witnessed various charters, including that chief lord's founding charter to Keynsham Abbey.[11] Payn II was actively engaged in suppressing the Welsh uprising following Earl William's death, being numbered with those receiving payments listed in the Pipe Rolls of 1184–85.[12] He was engaged in a lawsuit with Walter de Sully in 1199, probably concerning Oldcastle (VE 4), and witnessed a Margam charter in 1202 before his death in 1207, when his son Gilbert II received a writ of seisin, for which he rendered a fine of 50 marks and a horse.[13]

Gilbert II married a daughter of Morgan Gam, the Welsh lord of Afan, thereby acquiring Landimôr in the lordship of Gower. This marriage may also explain his acquisition of Newcastle (EM 3) in 1217, though this grant was disputed by his father-in-law, whose house had been granted this former demesne castle by John of Mortain in 1189. From 1217 Newcastle descended with Coity. At an unknown date, Gilbert was succeeded by his son, *Gilbert III*. Gilbert, father or son, was at war with Hywel ap Maredudd of Meisgyn in 1242,[14] but it was surely the younger Gilbert that held Coity in the Extent of 1262.[15] Gilbert III was dead by 1281 and his son, *Richard I*, is thought to have died two years later.

Payn III, son and heir of Richard I, was the provocative *custos* of Glamorgan in 1315–16, following the death of the last Clare earl at Bannockburn; his repressive measures largely fomented the revolt of Llywelyn Bren in 1316.[16] Payn answered for Coity

when Glamorgan was delivered to Hugh Despenser in 1317,[17] but he had been succeeded by his son, *Gilbert IV*, by 1319. This Gilbert recovered Landimôr in 1336 and served at Calais in 1346, but was dead by 1349.[18] His son, *Gilbert V*, soon died without issue and Coity passed to his uncle, *Richard II*, the younger son of Payn III.[19]

Richard II was the last Turberville lord of Coity. On Richard's death without issue, the inheritance passed to *Sir Lawrence Berkerolles*, son and heir of his eldest sister, Catherine Turberville. One charter suggests that Sir Lawrence had succeeded by 1384.[20] In 1404 and 1405 Sir Lawrence endured long and determined Welsh attempts to capture Coity Castle during the Glyndŵr rebellion, prompting two

Fig. 148. *(Opposite)* Coity Castle: reconstruction, as refurbished in the sixteenth century. The main ditch between the wards, shown open, was filled in some time in that century.

---

[5] Clark, *Cartae*, I (xxxvi – xxxvii), pp. 39–40. Later confirmed by Bishop Nicholas: *ibid*, I (cxxxvi), p. 134 and *Epis. Acts*, II L170, p. 659.

[6] J. Conway Davies, *N.L.W. Journal*, III (1943–4), pp. 114–16 and appendices pp. 129, 130, 133 and 136–7; Clark, *Cartae*, I, p. 103 and VI, pp. 2266–7; *Epis. Acts*, II, L117, p. 643 and L105, pp. 637–8; Patterson, *Glouc. Charters*, No. 68, p. 73.

[7] Clark, *Cartae*, I (lxvii), pp. 74–6.

[8] For the best genealogical analyses see Nicholl, *Normans*, pp. 32–8 and H. J. Randall in *Dict. Welsh Biog.*, p. 988. Very confused descents are given in G. T. Clark: *Limbus*, pp. 452–55 and *Arch. Camb.*, 1877, pp. 7–10, largely following Merrick, *Morg. Arch.*, pp. 54–6.

[9] Clark, *Cartae*, VI (mdxlv), pp. 2266–67; *Epis Acts*, II, L117, p. 643.

[10] Clark, *Cartae*, I (ci), p. 103; *Epis. Acts*, II, L105, pp. 637–8; Patterson, *Glouc. Charters*, No. 68, p. 73.

[11] Patterson, *Glouc. Charters*, Nos. 102–104, pp. 102–3 (Keynsham); Clark, *Cartae*, I, (cxxvi), pp. 122–3 and *Epis. Acts*, II, L186, p. 664 (Margam).

[12] Pipe Roll, 31 Henry III, 1184–85, p. 7; Clark, *Cartae*, I (clxxi) p. 172.

[13] Clark, *Cartae*, II (ccxxix – ccxxx), pp. 235–6, (the lawsuit); *Ibid*, II (cclxxii), pp. 269–70 and *Epis. Acts*, II, L254, p. 683 (the Margam Charter); Clark, *Cartae*, II (ccci), p. 305 (the writ).

[14] *Glam. Co. Hist.*, III, p. 50 (citing *Tewkesbury Annals*, pp. 124–5).

[15] Clark, *Cartae*, II (dcxv), p. 651.

[16] Clark, *Cartae*, III (dccxlii), p. 812 and (dccclxxv), p. 1035; *Glam. Co. Hist.*, III, pp. 75–6; *Cal. Anc. Corr*, pp. 172–3.

[17] Clark, *Cartae*, III (dccclxxxvi), pp. 1053, 1055.

[18] Clark, *Cartae*, IV (dccclxi), pp. 1195–6; Randall, *op.cit.* in f/n. 8.

[19] This follows Randall *op. cit.*, f/n. 8, and Corbett, *Glamorgan Lordship*, p. 72. Nicholl, *Normans*, p. 38, has Richard II as the brother of Gilbert V.

[20] Clark, *Cartae*, IV (mliv), p. 1356.

Dylan J. Roberts

expeditions to raise the siege, the first under Prince Henry and the second under the King himself.[21] Sir Lawrence Berkerolles died without issue in 1411.[22]

Following armed dispute at the castle and unrecorded litigation, Coity passed to *William Gamage*, grandson of Sarah Turberville, youngest sister of Richard Turberville II. William died in 1419, but was succeeded in the male line until 1584, when Coity and Newcastle passed to Robert Sydney, later Earl of Leicester, on his marriage to Barbara Gamage, heiress of John Gamage.[23]

Coity Castle in the Records

Despite its exposed position and especially privileged lords, Coity Castle is rarely mentioned in the records. No document of the 12th century mentions the primary timber castle raised by Payn Turberville I, nor the first masonry castle that replaced it before 1200. It is first recorded between 1207 and 1214 during the governorship of Falkes de Bréauté, King John's bailiff of Glamorgan, when a Margam document recorded an agreement made with Gilbert Turberville II concerning stray livestock of the abbey entering his lands. This mentions his castle (*castellum suum de Coitif*) and was drawn up in the presence of Falkes de Bréauté.[24]

The next mention is the uninformative notice that Payn Turberville III held the castle and manor of *Coytiff* on the death of Gilbert de Clare in 1314.[25] Two years later, Welsh tenants residing in the Englishry of Coity joined the uprising of Llywelyn Bren. Though the castle is not mentioned, it may be significant that after Llywelyn's surrender Payn removed the Welsh of the Englishry to the upland Welshry of Coity for the security of his lordship.

Owain Glyndŵr's revolt furnishes the most significant record of the castle. Briefly it figured in the national records.[26] Following Glyndŵr's appearance in Glamorgan in 1403 English power collapsed and even Cardiff may well have fallen to the Welsh. In 1404 Sir Lawrence Berkerolles was besieged at Coity by a strong rebel force, prompting a Commons plea to the King for a relieving force. This duly assembled under Prince Henry at Hereford in November, and may have brought temporary relief, but a second expedition was required in September 1405, under the King himself. This failed, its baggage train was plundered, and its confusion made complete by a violent storm and floods. There is no indication of the fate of the beleaguered garrison at Coity, but clear

indications at the castle bear witness to the ferocity of the Welsh assault. A large breach in the N. wall of the outer ward has clearly been rebuilt on the old line; an even greater breach on the N.-facing flank of the inner ward is indicated by the slightly withdrawn and rebuilt curtain replacing three or four facets of the original wall. These evident breaches on the vulnerable N. side, facing the rising ground which dominates the site, indicate the main thrust of the Welsh attack. On these northern slopes there are indistinct traces of entrenchments (Fig. 150), now largely levelled and confused by quarry-holes and former hedge-lines, which have been plausibly interpreted as earthworks thrown up by the Welsh in 1404–05.[27]

The castle (*castrum de Coityf*) next figures in the inquisition following the death of Sir Lawrence Berkerolles in 1411.[28] His death, without issue, occasioned another siege of the castle as rival claimants confronted each other in 1412. Although William Gamage, as grandson of Sarah Turberville, eventually triumphed in litigation regarding the succession, the castle was initially taken over by Joan, widow of Richard Vernon and heiress of Sarah's sister, Margaret Turberville. On 12 September 1412 William Newport and five others were instructed at Westminster '... *to go as quietly as they can to the castle and raise the siege* ...' mounted by William Gamage and others, '... *with no moderate multitude of armed men ... to expel Joan ... from her possession of it*'.[29]

---

[21] J. E. Lloyd, *Owen Glendower*, 1931, pp. 89 and 105–06; *Glam. Co. Hist.*, III, pp. 184, 300; Clark, *Cartae*, IV (mxcv and mxcvii), pp. 1455–7 (the former wrongly naming Sir Lawrence as Sir Alexander).

[22] Clark, *Cartae*, IV (mcvi), pp. 1466–9.

[23] Penry Williams, *The Council in the Marches of Wales under Elizabeth I* (1958), pp. 242–6; Clark, *Limbus*, pp. 390–1; *Arch. Camb.*, 1877, pp. 9–10 and *Cartae*, IV, p. 1469, n.; Nicholl, *Normans*, p. 39; Corbett, *Glamorgan Lordship*, p. 72.

[24] Clark, *Cartae*, VI (mdlxxxv), p. 2306. Falkes de Bréauté is the first witness: *Falc 'tunc vicecomite de Kaird'* ('*Kaird*', or Cardiff, being synonymous with Glamorgan).

[25] *Cal. I.P.M.*, 8 Edward II; *Cardiff Records*, I, p. 282.

[26] See f/n.21.

[27] G. T. Clark, *Arch. Camb.*, 1877. p. 6; the O.S. 25-inch map of 1899 portrays a strong ditch and counterscarp facing the N. flank of the castle and in line with the N. wall of the adjacent churchyard. This most likely evidence for a siege-work has now been levelled.

[28] Clark, *Cartae*, IV (mcvi), pp. 1467–8; *Limbus*, p. 454 and *Arch. Camb.*, 1869, p. 68.

[29] *Cal. C.R.*, Henry IV, iv, p. 407; *Cal. P.R.*, Sept. 16th, 1412; Nicholl, *Normans*, p. 39 (note); for Joan Vernon's claim see Clark, *Cartae*, IV (mcvi), p. 1488.

The outcome of this commission is unknown, but William Gamage won his suit according to law and custom, as ordered by the king in Chancery.

In 1414–15 William Rye was belatedly reimbursed by the king for £26. 13s. 4d. he had expended on grain sent to provision Coity Castle (*Castrum de Cortiff*).[30] This writ no doubt concerns supplies commissioned for the besieged garrison of Berkerolles in 1404–05. The castle (*Coytiff Castrum; Castro de Coitiff*) next appears in the inquisition on the death of William Gamage in 1419.[31]

Though the Gamages also possessed Newcastle, Coity remained their main residence and there they undertook major works. As their 'principal house' it is noticed by Leland (1536–39). '*This castell is maintainid ...*', he noted, while later in the 16th century Merrick described it as '*... a great old castle, most part kept up in good reparation*', and '*... a great strong castle ... which was and is maintained and repaired*'.[32] John, the last Gamage lord, also refurbished the South Tower at Newcastle (EM 3), but that castle, like Coity, did not enjoy such care and maintenance after they were acquired by Robert Sydney, later Earl of Leicester, on his marriage to John's heiress, Barbara Gamage, in 1584.[33]

The Sydneys held Coity until the 18th century, and although they were absentee landowners, the castle was still sufficiently maintained in the first quarter of that century to accommodate a younger son, Jocelyn Sydney, who settled there.[34] By 1811 it had come to Thomas Wyndham of Dunraven Castle (PC 6), whose daughter took it to the Earl of Dunraven by 1833, when it was described as 'extensive and magnificent even in its ruins'.[35] In 1869 it is recorded that the castle had '... lately been cleared out' by the dowager Countess of Dunraven, and in 1877 that Lord Dunraven had excavated the stair-passage between the hall and chapel.[36] The castle came into state guardianship in 1929.

General Description

(Figs. 147, 148, 150–53).
The castle consists of two wards, both walled. The circular inner ward on the E. clearly indicates a primary castle-ringwork; its ditch survives, much deepened, and strengthened by a strong counterscarp bank, except to the W. where these have been levelled within the walls of the outer ward. The roughly rectangular outer ward retains no trace of earthwork defences, but it is probable that it replaces a bailey

contemporary with the primary ringwork.

A faceted curtain-wall encloses the inner ward, except to the N., where this has been replaced by a secondary straight wall on a slightly withdrawn line. There are two gatehouses. The middle gatehouse communicates with the outer ward, flanked on its N. side by a square keep with a secondary annexed block. A projecting north-east gatehouse faces the church.

Fig. 149. Coity Castle: the North-East Gatehouse, internal front.

[30] G. T. Clark, *Arch. Camb.*, 1877, p. 9.

[31] Clark, *Cartae*, IV (mcxxiv), p. 1498.

[32] Leland, *Itin. Wales*, p. 33; Merrick, *Morg. Arch.*, pp. 104, 105.

[33] See f/n. 23.

[34] Philip Jenkins, *The Making of a Ruling Class; the Glamorgan Gentry 1640–1790*, (Cambridge University Press), 1983, p. 20.

[35] Carlisle, *Top Dict.* (1811); Lewis, *Top Dict.* (1833).

[36] G. T. Clark, *Arch. Camb.*, 1869, p. 69 and 1877, p. 5. Two large-scale unpublished plans surveyed in 1866 and 1867 demonstrate the progress of this clearance (G. T. Clark Papers, *N.L.W.*).

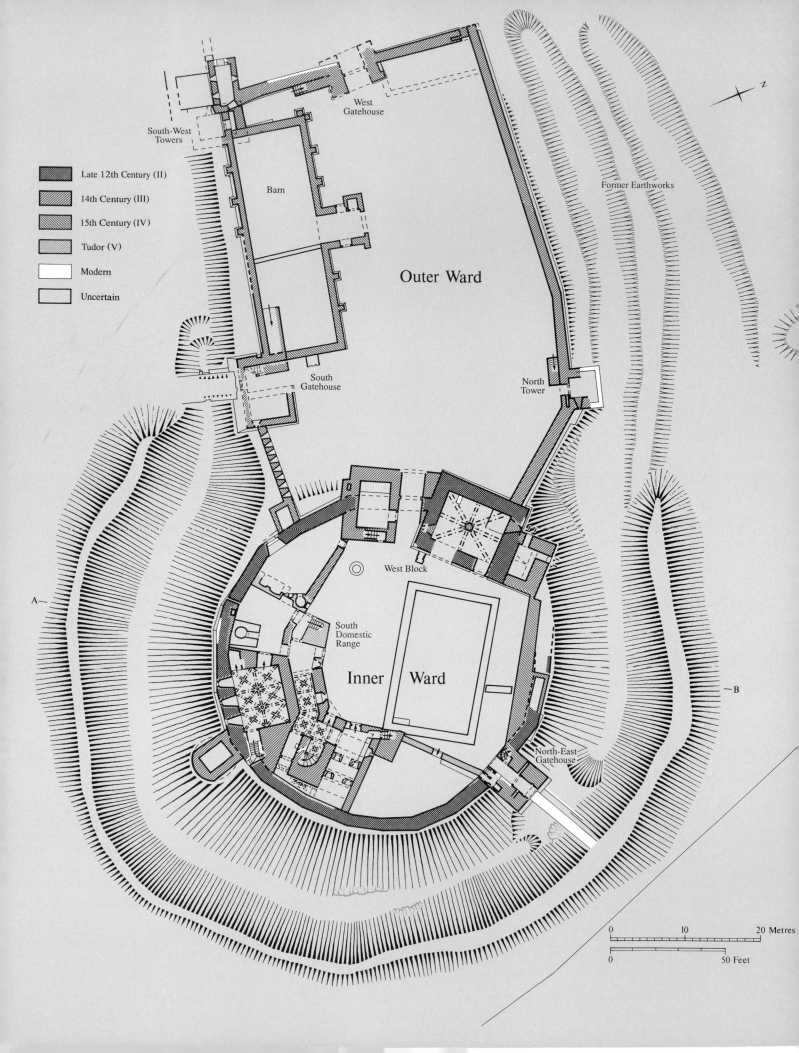

Late 12th Century (II)

14th Century (III)

15th Century (IV)

Tudor (V)

Modern

Uncertain

South-West Towers

West Gatehouse

Barn

Outer Ward

Former Earthworks

South Gatehouse

North Tower

West Block

South Domestic Range

Inner Ward

North-East Gatehouse

A

B

N

0   10   20 Metres

0   50 Feet

Well-appointed domestic quarters occupy a block ranged around the S. side, the hall flanked by a chapel to the E. and by service-rooms to the W. This block is well-provided with latrines housed in a projecting round tower added on the S. side.

Cross-walls connect the masonry of the two wards on the N. and S., between which the ditch separating them has been filled. Each cross-wall runs from a tower placed on the outer lip of the ditch, that to the S. having been later converted into a southern gatehouse. The main gatehouse to the outer ward lies at the centre of the W. side. At the S.W. angle there are scant traces of a third square tower projecting southwards; this was subsequently demolished and a postern gate inserted in its place on the line of the S. curtain, when a small rectangular turret was raised, projecting westwards from the angle. Within the outer ward, a large buttressed building against the S. wall possesses a large central porch. This was probably a barn, being conveniently placed adjacent to the secondary S.W. turret which appears to have been part of a mill.

Structural Development

The Buck brothers published a south view of the site in 1740 (Fig. 152). Two studies of the castle have been published, the first by G. T. Clark in 1877, the second by C. A. Ralegh Radford in 1946.[37] Sidney Toy described and illustrated the round south tower

of the inner ward in 1954.[38] Clark presumed that a primary earthwork castle had existed on the site, but failed to recognize the 12th-century origin of the keep. Radford proposed four main periods of construction in masonry:

(i) *Late 12th century*: The keep flanking the middle gate of the inner ward and, unconnected with this, the faceted curtain-wall around the S. and E. sides of the same ward.

(ii) *13th century*: The projecting round tower on the S. side of the inner ward.

(iii) *14th century*: In the inner ward, the middle gate, the renewed N. curtain (on a reduced line), and the domestic block, including the Chapel, around the S. side. In the outer ward, the west gate, walls and towers (the barn was not given a date, and the south gatehouse was not noticed).

(iv) *Tudor*: The annexe to the keep and lesser additions in the inner ward.

The present study both supplements and alters Radford's conclusions. His first period (12th century) is accepted, but supplemented by demonstrable evidence to show that the keep and faceted curtain-wall were integrated, the keep retaining stubs of this curtain to the N. and S. His second period (13th century)

[37] G. T. Clark, 'Coyty Castle and Lordship', *Arch. Camb.*, 1877, pp. 1–22 (reprinted, without supplementary historical matter, in his *Med. Milit. Arch*, I, pp. 487–91); C. A. Ralegh Radford, 'Coity Castle, Glamorgan', *Official Guide Leaflet*, H.M.S.O., 1946.

[38] Sidney Toy, *The Castles of Great Britain*, 2nd Edn., 1954, pp. 141–2.

Fig. 150. *(Opposite)* Coity Castle: general plan at ground level.

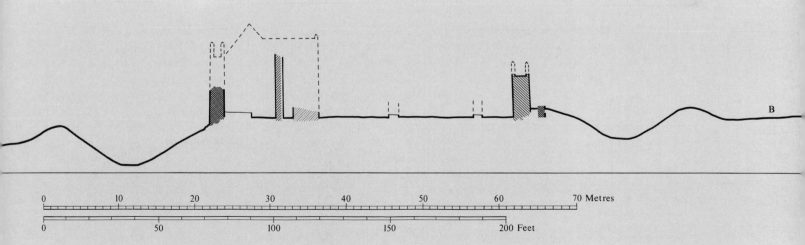

Fig. 151. Coity Castle: profile of Inner Ward (A-B on ground plan opposite). The truncated primary ring-bank is apparent to the N. (right), centred on the footings of the Norman curtain and in advance of the withdrawn 14th-century curtain which survives.

Fig. 152. Coity Castle: the south front in 1740. Line engraving by Samuel and Nathaniel Buck *(National Library of Wales)*.

may not be sustained; the round tower on the S. is now regarded as a work of the 14th century, pertaining to Radford's third period of work, seen by him as 'an almost complete rebuilding of the Castle'. While this is largely true, and the annexe raised against the keep (which he regarded as Tudor) may now be added to this work, some of the fabric he attributed to the 14th century is now seen as work of the 15th century. To this later period we may now ascribe the rebuilt N. curtain and the chapel in the inner ward, together with the barn and S.W. turret of the outer ward. Finally, Radford's fourth period of construction (Tudor) must exclude the annexe to the keep, now ascribed to the 14th century; only its third floor and some inserted details at lower levels are of the early 16th century.

Five main periods of construction may now be proposed, with four major phases of masonry work following an initial castle of earth and timber.

Period I – Ca. 1100:

A palisaded castle-ringwork, probably with a bailey on its E. side. This primary castle was surely raised before 1106, along with Ogmore Castle (MR 5), in support of Fitzhamon's Newcastle (EM 3) which was first recorded in that year. Payn Turberville I was the probable builder.

Period II – Late 12th century:

(*Ca.* 1183 or 1189).

The keep and faceted curtain of the inner ward replaced the palisade in the late 12th century. Two historical contexts for this conversion may be suggested. In 1183, following the death of Earl William, the Welsh rose in revolt and threatened the castles in the W. of the lordship. Payn Turberville II was active in countering this brief uprising, and during the wardship of Henry II (1183–89) it is possible that nearby Newcastle was converted to stone. If this brief revolt was not the motive for a similar conversion to stone at Coity, 1189 offered a second incentive. In that year John of Mortain, the future King, finally obtained Glamorgan on his long-delayed marriage to the heiress, Isabel. He seemingly bought peace by granting Newcastle to Morgan ap Caradog, the lord of Afan and leader of the 1183 revolt. If Payn II had not already improved his castle, this surely gave him an added incentive to do so, particularly as Newcastle must certainly have been rebuilt in stone by 1189. Payn II, to whom the primary stone castle may be confi-

226

dently ascribed, was lord of Coity before the death of Earl William in 1183 and survived until 1207.

Period III – 14th century:

Exceptionally, there is no evidence for 13th century additions to the primary stone castle at Coity. The 14th century, however, witnessed the most extensive programme of building at the castle. The inner ward defences were improved by the erection of the middle gatehouse, while the adjacent keep was internally rebuilt with vaulted floors, now served by a new annexe added on the N. side. New domestic quarters and service rooms were added around the S. side of the ward, these served by the round latrine-tower now raised against the outer face of the curtain. This period also saw the construction of the wall enclosing the outer ward, furnished with three square projecting towers on the N., S. and S.W. and an entrance of uncertain form to the W.

This extensive rebuilding of the 14th century was no doubt phased, but no sequence may be deduced. The ditch separating the two wards remained open during this period, and a cross-wall carried on relieving arches closed its vulnerable N. flank, facing rising ground. There is no evidence for a contemporary cross-wall closing this section of the main ditch on the S., where a palisade may have sufficed until the 15th century when the surviving wall was begun.

It is not possible to ascribe the works of this period to particular lords of Coity. Payn Turberville III (*ca.* 1283–*ca.* 1318) may have initiated them, and his son, Gilbert IV. (*ca.* 1318–*ca.* 1349), must certainly have contributed during his long tenure. Gilbert V, who next succeeded, did not long survive, while the last Turberville lord, Richard II, was elderly on his succession. Sir Lawrence Berkerolles, who appears to have inherited the lordship by 1384, could certainly have undertaken some of this work before his death in 1411.

Period IV – 15th century:

The work of this period, previously assigned to the 14th century, was concentrated in two areas, one of which was probably a response to severe damage sustained during the Welsh assaults of 1404 and 1405. These reparations and an improvement to the defences are concentrated on the vulnerable N. flank, facing the rising ground where siege-works were once recorded (Fig. 150).[39] A central section of the N. wall

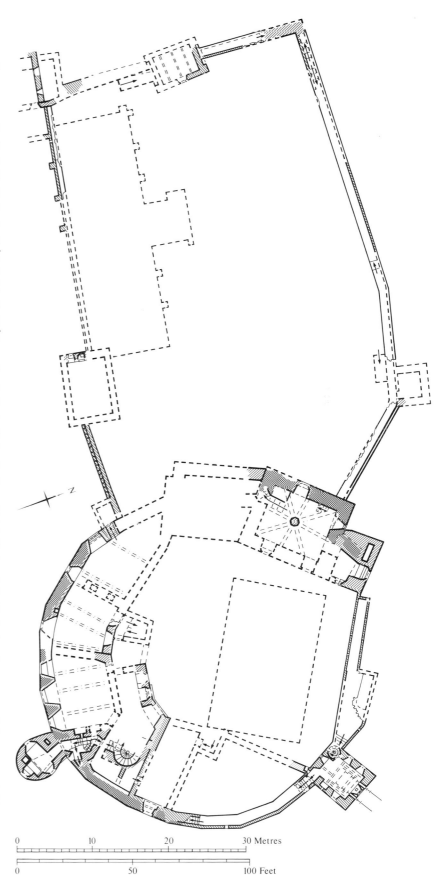

Fig. 153. Coity Castle: general plan at first floor level.

0   10   20   30 Metres

0   50   100 Feet

of the outer ward has been rebuilt, while an even greater breach seems to have been inflicted on the N. side of the inner ward. There, a new and slightly withdrawn straight curtain-wall replaced four or five facets of the earlier wall, its external parapet raised on corbels formed by reused newels from dismantled or demolished stairs. At the same time it is probable that the well-defended N.E. gatehouse was added at the E. end of this renewed N. curtain. The second area of works in this period was confined to the S. side, all demonstrably secondary to work of the previous period, but not closely dated or phased. The chapel must have been added early in the 15th century, for this period also saw its roof raised and its E. window enlarged. The southern cross-wall was also raised in this period, together with the large barn in the outer ward, its S. wall formed by the existing curtain, which required buttressing against a developed outward tilt before it could support the lateral thrust of the roof. The S. wall of the outer ward was further altered by the conversion of the S. tower into a gatehouse, while the S.W. tower was replaced by a simple postern and an adjacent turret erected out over the W. ditch (now filled). Finally, a simple square gatehouse was raised at the central entrance in the W. wall of the outer ward.

It may be assumed that Sir Lawrence Berkerolles must have undertaken the urgent reparations required on the N. soon after the damage inflicted by the Welsh in 1404–05. He may also have raised the N.E. gatehouse at this time, but as he died in 1419 most of the other 15th-century work was probably undertaken by his successors, the Gamages.

Period V – Tudor:

All surviving Tudor work identified is in the inner ward and is entirely devoted to improving the domestic arrangements of the castle. In the south block the upper floors were refenestrated and provided with new fireplaces, while a new service stair was added on the N. side of the service area, which was also given a new transverse range of ovens and fireplaces. The upper floors of the keep and its 14th-century annexe were similarly refurbished with new windows and fireplaces, and a new third-floor chamber with stepped gable was added to the latter. At this time a small postern door was cut through the N. wall of the keep, beside the projecting annexe, at mezzanine level between the basement and first floor. The Tudor dressings in the keep are identical to those found in the south block, and the universal use of arch-headed mul-

lioned windows with hollow mouldings points to a thorough refurbishment undertaken early in the 16th century. There are no square-headed, sunk-chamfered Elizabethan windows, such as those inserted at Newcastle by John Gamage. Of his immediate predecessors, it is possible that his grandfather, Sir Thomas Gamage, was responsible for the extensive Tudor rebuilding at Coity.

Architectural Description

A The Primary Earthwork Castle (Period I)

The castle believed to have been raised by Payn Turberville I in *ca.* 1100 is clearly reflected in the circular trace of the wall enclosing the inner ward. The reasonable assumption that this wall roughly follows the line of the primary palisade suggests that a castle-ringwork about 44m in diameter formerly existed. In size this would have been almost identical with contemporary local ringworks at Ogmore (MR 5; 44.5m) and Rumney (MR 7; 45m), and rather larger than that suspected at Fitzhamon's Newcastle (EM 3; 40m). Unlike Ogmore, Rumney and Kenfig (EM 2), Coity furnishes no visible evidence for the levelling up of its interior with material derived from the ring-bank at the time of conversion to stone. An indication of the survival of the truncated bank on the vulnerable N. side is apparent on the measured profile (Fig. 151, section A–B). The surviving penannular ditch has clearly been deepened and furnished with a strong counterscarp bank during subsequent masonry phases. Its western sector, within the outer ward, was probably filled in during the Tudor period. The deepened ditch averaged 16m in width and its depth ranges from 6m on the S. to 4m on the N. Its lower levels are cut through the rock on the W. and S., suggesting that its deepening furnished some of the local stone used in later building.

The rectilinear form of the outer ward and its present lack of any associated earthworks no longer indicate a bailey contemporary with the primary ringwork. It would be surprising, however, if the Turberville castle did not posses a bailey comparable with that raised by William de Londres at Ogmore, with whom Payn I was so closely associated in the settlement of Glamorgan in the early 12th century. It is also known that a ditch formerly fronted the

---

[39] See f/n. 27.

N. wall of the outer ward, linked with that of the inner work, and that this was further strengthened by a counterscarp bank integrated with that of the ringwork and fronted by a second ditch (Fig. 150).[40] It is also evident that a ditch formerly returned from this northern line to the edge of the natural shelf and fronted the W. wall of the ward; the S.W. turret functioned as part of a mill built out over this vanished ditch. These former earthworks leave little doubt that the outer ward occupies the site of a primary bailey.

B The Masonry Castle (*Periods II-V*)

The four main periods of construction in masonry are outlined above, and their probable historical contexts discussed. These successive works are so widely dispersed, and integrated one with the other, that it will facilitate the reading of the following descriptions if these periods are summarized here:

Period II:
Late 12th century (probably *ca.* 1183 or 1189).
Period III:
14th century (the most extensive programme of work).
Period IV:
15th century (reparations and additions).
Period V:
Tudor (early 16th century; domestic improvements).

Overall plans illustrate surviving masonry at ground- and first-floor levels (Figs. 150 and 153). More significant structures or ranges are illustrated at a larger scale, with additional plans of levels above the first floor and with sections and elevations. In the inner ward the *west block* (keep, its annexe and the in-

[40] These vanished earthworks are noted by Clark (*Arch. Camb.*, 1877, p. 6 and *Med. Milit. Arch.*, 1884, I, p. 490). They are also indicated on the O.S. 25-inch map of 1899, as indicated on Fig. 150.

Fig. 154. Coity Castle: the Inner Ward, external south front. The faceted Norman curtain shelters the later South Domestic Range, its salient Latrine-Tower to the right.

a

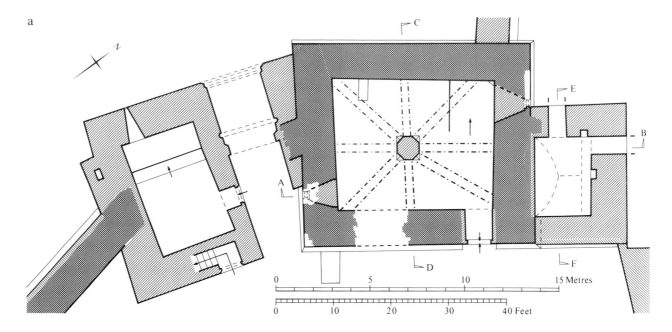

Fig. 155. Coity Castle. The West Block, Inner Ward: (a) ground plan (left to right: the Middle Gatehouse; the Keep; the Annexe); *below*, (b) Norman splayed light, N. wall, first floor of the Keep; and *opposite*, plans and details at upper levels: (i) plan at first floor; (e) plan at second floor; (d) plan at third floor; (c) Tudor fireplace on third floor of Annexe, N. wall.; (f) Tudor Window on E. side of above fireplace; (g) vestiges of inserted stair between first and second in the W. corner, mezzanine level; and (h) inserted stair between basement and first floor in the N. corner, mezzanine level.

tegrated middle gatehouse), *the south domestic range* (hall, latrine tower, chapel and services) and *the N.E. gatehouse* are given this detailed treatment; in the outer ward, *the barn and S.W. towers, the west gatehouse* and the *south gatehouse* are similarly treated.

The Inner Ward: West Block

(Figs. 146, 155–60).
The late-12th-century rectangular keep (Period II) is integrated on its N. and S. sides respectively with an annexe and with the middle gatehouse, both of the 14th century (Period III), forming a *western block*. The gatehouse is reduced to the lower courses of its ground floor, but sufficient survives of the ruined keep and annexe to reconstruct their basic arrangements on four floor-levels. Both the gatehouse and the annexe incorporate stubs of the late-12th-century curtain which bond with the keep, crucially demonstrating that the keep was raised along with the faceted curtain which survives impressively around the S. and E. sides. The gatehouse undoubtedly marks the position of a simple Norman gateway, probably similar to that surviving at Newcastle (EM 3), and of the entrance to the primary ringwork.

Above its batter, *the keep* measures 12.2m by 10.2m

externally. Its walls are 2m thick, and they are intact at ground level, except for two later breaches made through the E. wall facing the court. When the flanking gatehouse and annexe were added in the 14th century the massive ribbed vaults of the lower storeys

b

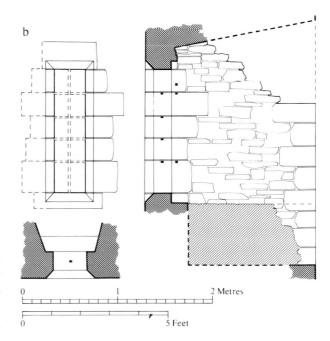

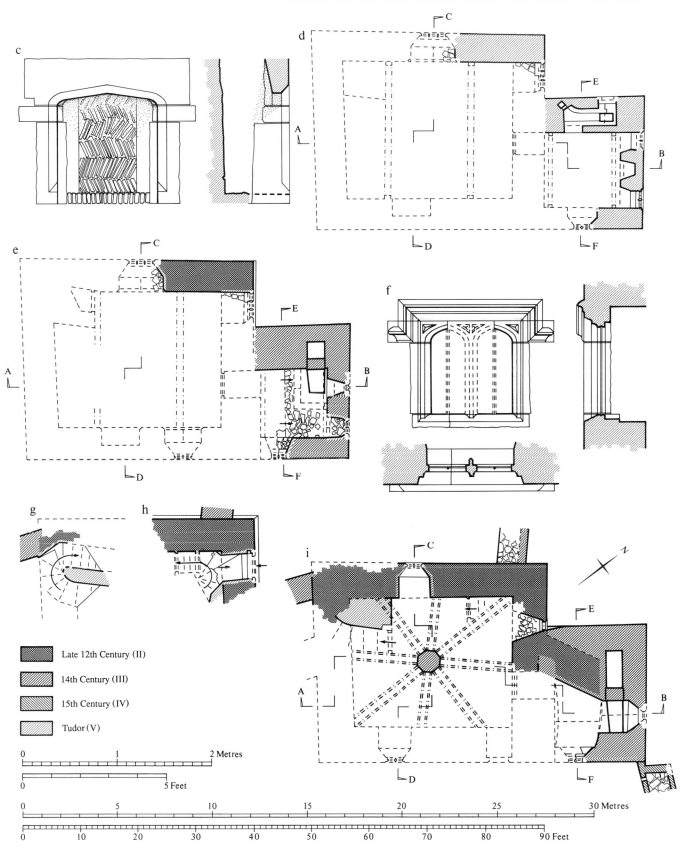

Late 12th Century (II)

14th Century (III)

15th Century (IV)

Tudor (V)

0 1 2 Metres

0 5 Feet

0 5 10 15 20 25 30 Metres

0 10 20 30 40 50 60 70 80 90 Feet

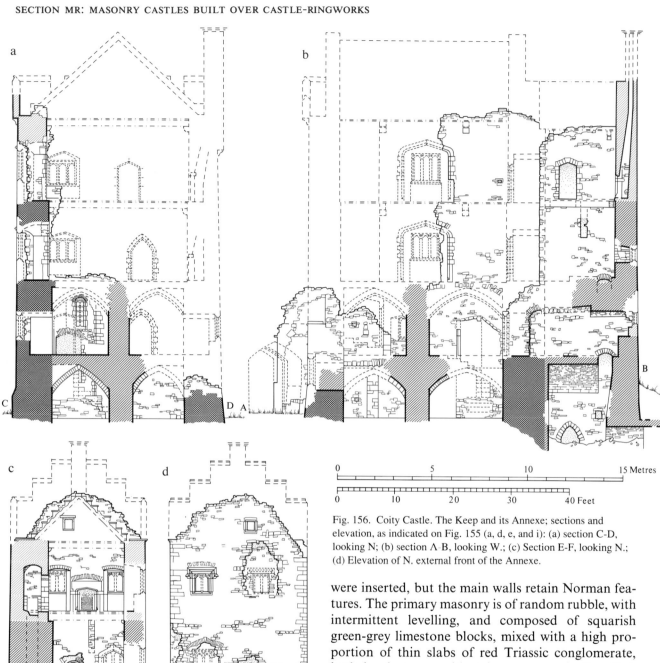

Fig. 156. Coity Castle. The Keep and its Annexe; sections and elevation, as indicated on Fig. 155 (a, d, e, and i): (a) section C-D, looking N; (b) section Λ-B, looking W.; (c) Section E-F, looking N.; (d) Elevation of N. external front of the Annexe.

were inserted, but the main walls retain Norman features. The primary masonry is of random rubble, with intermittent levelling, and composed of squarish green-grey limestone blocks, mixed with a high proportion of thin slabs of red Triassic conglomerate, both local stones evident in exposures in the ditch to the W. A particularly distinctive reddish colour is given to the Norman masonry by the predominance of Triassic rubble in the core of the walls.

The E. wall of the keep survives only at basement level, but its W. wall rises 16.5m high and displays features on three upper floors, with adjacent vestiges of the N. and S. walls rising as high as the first floor. The basement was originally surmounted by two upper floors, a third being added in the Tudor period (V) when a similar addition was added to the adjacent annexe. Before late breaches were made in the E. wall, entry was at first-floor level by a door at the N. end of that wall. This door was recorded in an unpublished sketch plan and elevation made by G. T. Clark in 1833,[41] which make possible the conjectural reconstruction (in broken line) of the missing parts of upper floors on the accompanying plans and sections. The keep rises from a strong batter with dressed Sutton Stone quoins at the angles, though these have been replaced at the S.W. corner during the building of the middle gatehouse.

The Basement: At this level a stub of the Norman curtain-wall projects obliquely from the external S. face, incorporated in the truncated wedge of masonry that survives of the N. side of the middle gatehouse. The stub, bonding with the keep, is clearly defined by straight joints and the reddish core of the Norman walling. A further straight joint on the E. side also defines the N.E. angle of the keep, where the annexe is butted against it. The larger ragged breach through the E. wall betrays no purpose, but that further N. was a doorway cut through the originally unbroken lower wall. On this side, the surviving lower courses of the wall have been refaced with ashlar, which includes a late-medieval dressing. The internal walls of the basement retain traces of two Norman loops. One is set in the S. wall against the S.E. corner and retains the lower parts of its internal jambs, which are outlined with dressed Sutton Stone blocks. This loop overlooks the area behind the presumed original gateway, and it was subsequently blocked. The other original loop lies diagonally opposite against the N.W. corner in the N. wall, giving outlook along the outer face of the adjacent curtain before the addition of the annexe. Only its E. jamb survives, but this retains internal Sutton Stone dressings which retain one springer of a former round-headed rear-arch. The W. jamb was damaged and the loop blocked when a Tudor stair was inserted in this corner, to give access to the upper floor and a postern that was cut at mezzanine level through the N. wall.

In the 14th century a ribbed vault, supported on an octagonal central column of sandstone ashlar, replaced an original floor that was probably of timber. The column survives, with broach stops at its base and retaining the springings of eight unchamfered ribs. The vault has fallen, except for a fragment to the W. which is underpinned by a modern buttress.

The inserted Tudor stair in the N.W. corner is marked by a rough block of masonry retaining traces of a stair that could only have functioned after the collapse or breaching of the vault above. Curving left,

Fig. 157. Coity Castle: the inserted 14th century columns and vestiges of the ribbed vaults they supported over the basement and first floor of the Keep.

around a vanished newel, this stair gave access to the first floor through a door marked by its surviving W. jamb set against the wall. Half-way up this stair, to the right, the N. wall was pierced to give access to a postern of the same period, now blocked.

The First Floor: Only the W. wall and attached vestiges of the N. and S. walls survive at this level. Presumably a hall, this chamber was originally reached through a door at the N. end of the E. wall,

---

[41] G. T. Clark Papers, *N.L.W.*

In the 14th century this chamber was also provided with a ribbed vault, supported on a further octagonal column of ashlar imposed upon that beneath. At this level the ribs were plain-chamfered, an elaboration absent in the basement and known here from one surviving springer on the column. From the base of this column to the W. wall vestiges of a good paving over the lower vault survive and continue into the deep recess of an inserted 14th-century window. This window was sufficient for a two-light opening, but its dressings have gone. Traces remain of a passage-stair, probably of Tudor date, in the S.W. corner.

A significant feature of the keep at first-floor level is the extraordinary survival of the stub of the contemporary Norman curtain, incorporated in the later annexe to the N., although the cess-pit on the lower level of this annexe has caused its removal below. Like that to the S., at ground level, this stub projects obliquely from the wall of the keep, and is again characterized by the reddish conglomerate rubble of its core. On its inner face it retains one jamb and the springer of a round-headed opening, now blocked and within the line of the N. wall of the keep; it may well have led to the original wall-walk (Plan, Fig. 155i; Section, Fig. 156b).

The Second Floor. Only the N. part of the W. wall survives at this level. This retains a beam hole and supporting corbel of a timber ceiling. The W. wall also retains the jamb of an inserted Tudor window. Its external dressings have gone, but internally the recess retains plain-chamfered dressings of sandstone, with an oblique stop, which support the springing of a rear arch of four-centred Tudor form. A large three-light window is probable. A similar window is evidenced in the N. wall against the N.W. corner, also lacking its dressings but retaining a sandstone label of Tudor style.

The Third Floor continues upwards on the surviving fragment of the floor below and represents an additional floor added in the early 16th century. This new chamber was fenestrated to the N. and W. by further recessed windows directly above the identical contemporary windows inserted below on the second floor. Again, the external dressings have gone, but similar identical sandstone dressings survive on the N. internal jamb of the W. window. Like the chamber below, this room also retains one beam hole and corbel of its timber ceiling. Externally, the surviving fragment

Fig. 158. Coity Castle: the vestiges of the Basement and first floor of the Keep, viewed from a higher level in the annexe.

known from Clark's sketches of 1833. A foundation of uncertain date, towards the S. end of the E. wall, may be connected with some form of external stair to this vanished upper door. The only surviving Norman feature at this level is a narrow square-headed light in the N. wall, directly above one of those below. Its external dressings are intact (detail drawing, Fig. 155b). These are plain-chamfered, and they retain the holes of an iron grill, behind which further holes indicate the position of a wooden shutter. The inner part of the rear arch has fallen, but one inner jamb retains the characteristic Sutton Stone blocks of the primary masonry work; the other jamb was destroyed by the insertion of the Tudor postern.

Fig. 159. *(Opposite)* Coity Castle: the Keep, shown as it may have appeared after refurbishment in the sixteenth century.

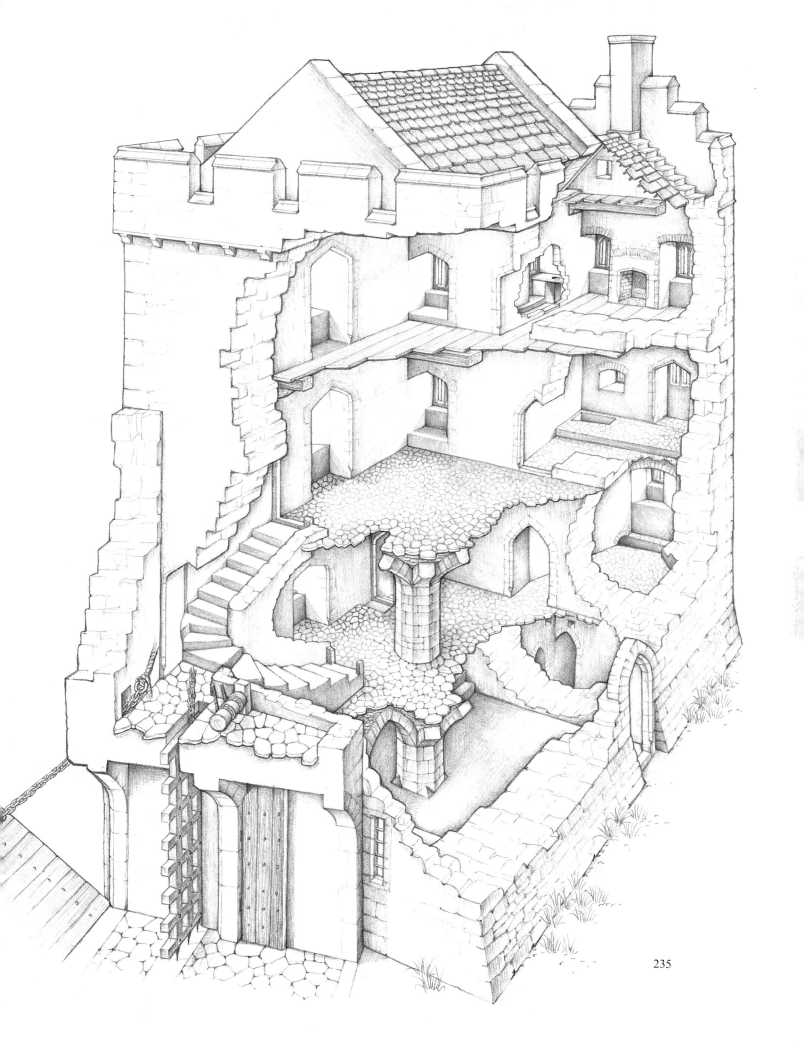

Fig. 160. Coity Castle: general view of the West Block from the S.

of the W. wall betrays the Tudor raising of the keep by a change in the quoins at the N.W. angle. The Norman work, with its reddish rubble and good Sutton Stone quoins, continues up to a level just above that of the floor of this upper chamber. Above this, the quoins are much smaller, and the Tudor masonry is of grey limestone rubble. At the top of the surviving masonry a short and truncated section of walling is carried forward on four concave-moulded corbels. An unexplained vertical straight joint separates this corbel-table from the adjacent angle. This fragment may represent the last remnant of a parapet surrounding the ridged roof that must have run N.–S. On the opposite E. wall, now fallen, Clark noted a corbelled-out Tudor chimney in 1833; this probably served fireplaces on the second and third floors.

The Keep Annexe

(Figs. 146, 155, 156, 160).

Formerly regarded as Tudor, it is now clear that the lower three storeys of this structure were raised in the 14th century; only its third floor, together with that added to the keep, was of the early 16th century. The lower floors are contemporary with the insertion of the two ribbed vaults in the keep. Together, these works represent a complete refurbishment and extension of the domestic provision of the primary stone domestic quarters. It is not obvious why this major work was carried out in the same period that saw the erection of the southern domestic block.

The annexe abuts the N. wall of the keep from its E. end as far as the Norman loops on this side on the two lower floors. Initially, it appears, these remained functional. The masonry of the annexe is of sandstone and limestone blocks, with more effort at coursing, and with dressed sandstone quoins. Straight joints mark its butting against the keep.

The Ground Floor consists of a cess-pit covered with a pointed vault pierced by a slot against the N. wall for a latrine above. Two arched openings, to the W. and N., pierce the base of the walls to drain the pit. The construction of this pit necessitated the removal of the lower part of the Norman curtain, which was underpinned by the inserted vault and survives above.

The first floor was of cramped and irregular form, due to the incorporation of the remaining upper part of the Norman curtain which crossed it obliquely. Despite this awkward shape, a depressed segmental vault was raised over it, running N. The small chamber was paved and lit by splayed lights in the N. and E. walls; neither retains its dressings. Within the N. window recess, a latrine was placed over one end of the slot in the vault below. No trace remains of the door communicating with the keep at this level.

The second floor of the annexe, like that of the keep, was refenestrated in the Tudor period, though it retained one single-light splayed window in its N. wall, near the N.W. corner. This corner of the room seems to have been screened off by a thin wall marked by toothings on the adjacent walls. Within this screened area a garderobe shaft pierces the floor to communicate with the cess-pit. A second window in the N. wall is set in a deep recess E. of the garderobe screen, and vestiges of another of similar form pierce the E. wall. Though lacking dressings, these windows are clearly Tudor insertions and their size indicates that they both once held two-light arch-headed frames like

that which is almost intact on the third floor. Again, this floor has lost its communicating door to the adjacent keep, but evidence for its beamed ceiling survives.

The added Tudor *third floor* is again furnished with a garderobe, this one housed in a mural closet in the W. wall, entered through a plain segmental-headed door and lit by a small window. The N. wall is best preserved and it retains a good central fireplace with a depressed segmental-headed lintel with oblique stops on its jambs (Fig. 155c); its recess is constructed in herringbone fashion with thin sandstone slabs. This fireplace is set between two identical recessed windows, that to the E. almost intact (Fig. 155f). The latter has lost only the central mullion dividing its two lights, but it retains its outer jambs which indicate segmental-arched lights with hollow chamfers beneath a surviving label. Vestiges of a third window of similar form survives in the truncated E. wall. This floor had a further timber ceiling supported on beams and corbels.

An attic is indicated beneath the N. gable of the annexe. This was lit by a small square light with a plain-chamfered surround. Above the roof steps run over this gable within a now much reduced parapet. (Section, E–F, Fig. 156c). A chimney that formerly crowned the gable served the fireplace on the third floor.

The Middle Gatehouse (Figs. 155a, 160) abuts the south side of the keep obliquely, the consequent alignment of its passage clearly dictated by the prior existence of a gateway through the angled facet of Norman curtain-wall joining the keep. This gatehouse is reduced to its lower courses, but these indicate its basic arrangements. To the N. its passage was defined by the narrowing wedge of masonry already described. A rectangular guard-chamber flanked the other side. Portcullis slots indicate the former existence of an upper chamber. The gatehouse, like the keep annexe, was an addition of the 14th century; together with the keep between them, these additions created the western block.

The gatehouse straddled the line of the curtain. Its front was carried out over the scarp of the former ditch, an encroachment facilitating the construction of the pit, 3.5m deep, at the forward end of the S. guard-chamber, its inner wall approximating to the outer face of the Norman curtain at this point. This pit cannot be connected with any garderobes above; a garderobe shaft exists in the adjacent S. wall, with an outfall discharging externally into the moat, and

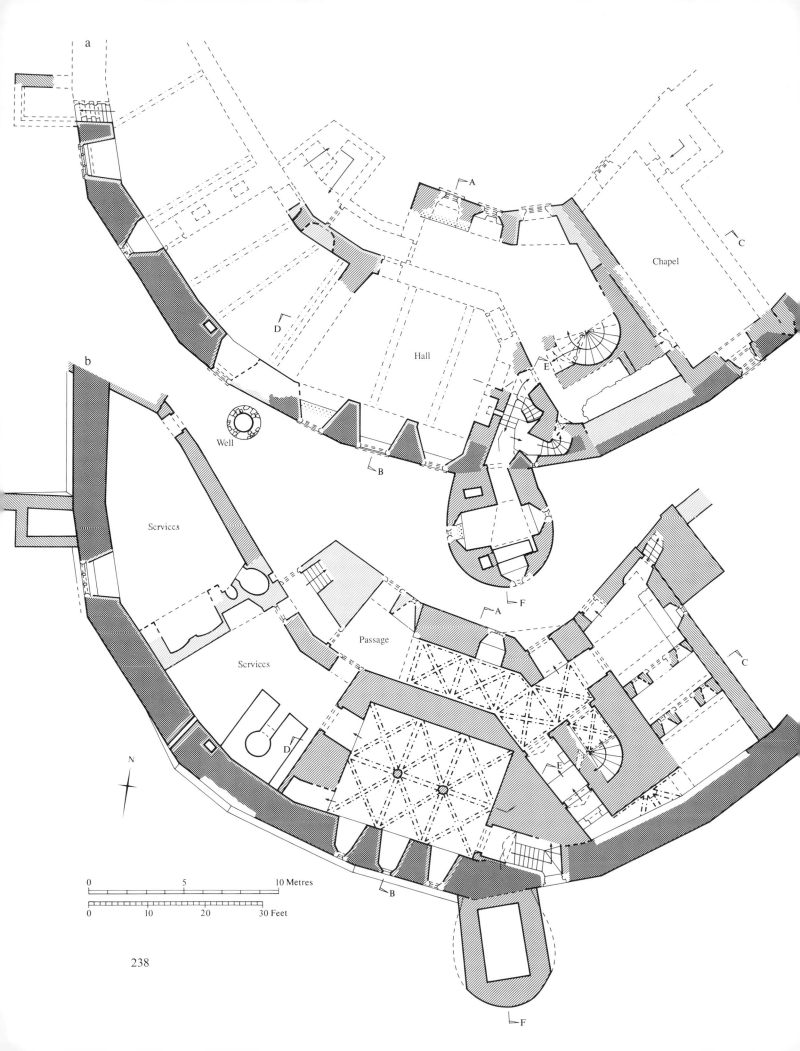

a

Chapel

A

C

D

Hall

E

B

F

b

Well

Services

Services

Passage

D

A

C

E

B

N

F

0　　　　　　　5　　　　　10 Metres

0　　10　　20　　30 Feet

the pit has no drainage provision like that beneath
the annexe. It was probably intended as a cistern. The
guard chamber was entered by a door from the passage, its dressings of Sutton Stone with a concave
chamfer-and-cushion stops below a bar. Access to the
upper chamber was by a mural stair entered through
another concave-chamfered doorway in the E. wall.
A narrow splayed loop in the W. wall, beyond the
pit, is the only other feature discernible in the
chamber.

The gate-passage is 10m in length. Its outer arch
has fallen, but its jambs are plain-chamfered and set
within a recess, also plain-chamfered at its angles, and
probably square-headed. A rebated stone may indi-

cate the provision of a drawbridge hinged within
recess, and a small square socket 1.5m above the
ground in the N. jamb could relate to a hand-rail
flanking the bridge. The grooves of a portcullis lie
3.0m within the passage, and behind them the projecting jambs of the doors, which are plain-chamfered
with broach stops.

The South Domestic Range

(Figs. 154, 161–71).
This complex range will be more readily understood
after a description of the late 12th-century curtain-
wall against which it was built. It has been noted that
this faceted curtain was built along with the keep,
which retains its previously unnoticed stubs on its N.
and S. flanks. It is possible to determine the full circuit
of this wall, which is completely vanished for only
a short distance eastwards from the keep annexe
before its footings are discernible in advance of the
rebuilt N. curtain of the 15th century.

Fig. 161. Coity Castle. Plans of the South Domestic Range; *opposite;*
(b) the ground floor; (a) the first floor; and *below:* (c) the second floor;
(d) the third floor of the Latrine-Tower.

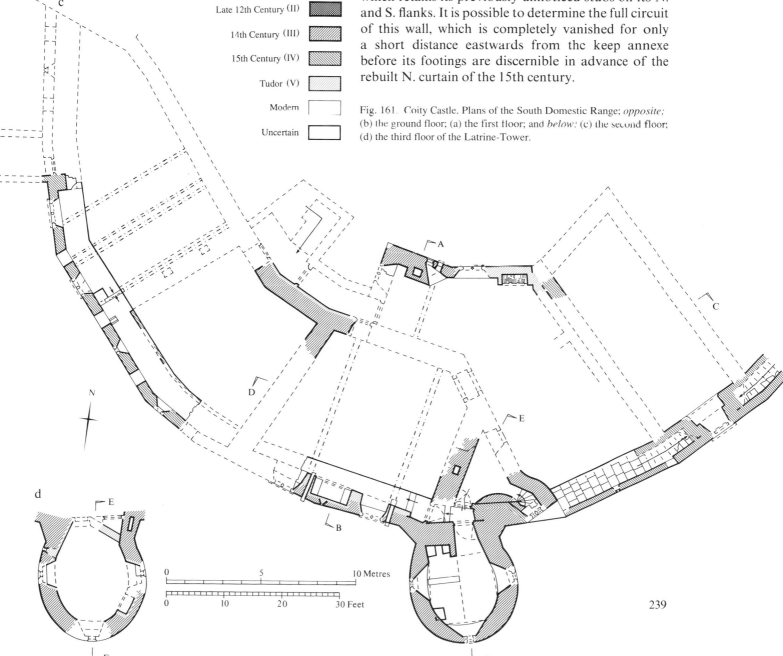

Late 12th Century (II)
14th Century (III)
15th Century (IV)
Tudor (V)
Modern
Uncertain

239

Fig. 162. Coity Castle. The South Domestic Range, sections as indicated on Fig. 161, a-d: *(above)* (a) long section C-D, looking S.; *(opposite)* (b) cross section A-B, looking E.; (c) section E-F of the Latrine-Tower, looking E.

Fig. 163. Coity Castle: general view of the South Domestic Range from the top of the Keep Annexe.

240

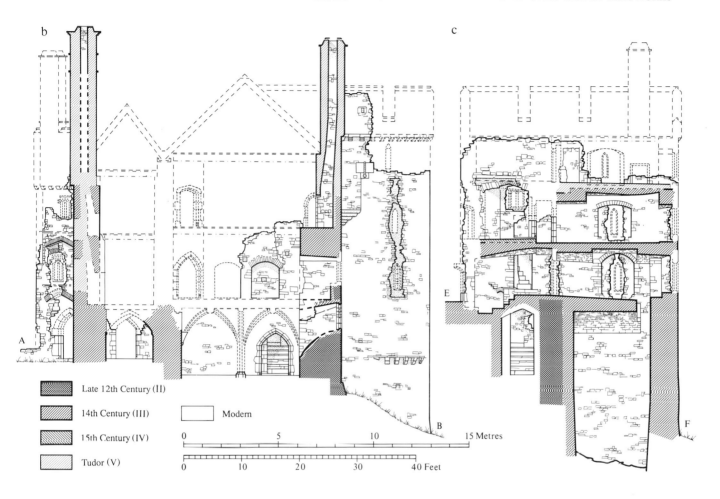

Late 12th Century (II)

14th Century (III)   Modern

15th Century (IV)

Tudor (V)

0   5   10   15 Metres

0   10   20   30   40 Feet

The multangular trace of this primary curtain-wall, which is 2m thick, describes a perfect circle. Later patching and refacing masks most of the surviving inner face of this wall, but externally its characteristic masonry is less heavily disturbed and, where exposed, its core exhibits the reddish colour characterizing Norman work at the keep. The external angles are formed with alternating quoins of Sutton Stone which are prominent around the S. and E. sides and very reminiscent of the treatment of the angles on the shell-keep at Cardiff. Viewed from these flanks the walls give every impression of being a similar shell-keep. The eastern section from the inserted N.E. gatehouse to the chapel displays the curtain at its original height, its wall-walk being 5m above the interior and retaining the lower part of its parapet, with traces of merlons. From the chapel to the middle gatehouse the S. curtain has been heightened, along with the abutting domestic range, but its original height is indicated by the alternating Sutton Stone quoins at the angles.

To the N.E. the wall is breached for the inserted 15th-century gatehouse, but although the N. curtain was rebuilt on a withdrawn line between this and the annexe, a remnant of the original curtain was retained. This remnant comprised the adjacent facet and part of the next, the latter being rebuilt to contain a deep pit or cistern against the front of the new N. curtain. Beyond the return wall of this cistern the footings of the next facet are discernible, and one further facet beyond this would have closed with that represented by the stub of wall incorporated in the fabric of the keep annexe.

The South Domestic Range was set against the inner face of the S. curtain. For the most part it was raised in the 14th century, though a *chapel* was added at the E. end in the 15th century, and extensive remodelling and refenestration, largely at upper levels, was undertaken in the early 16th century. The range includes a *central hall* over a vaulted undercroft, flanked on the N. by a vaulted passage leading to a grand newel stair, also vaulted at its entrance. *Service-rooms* lay to the W. of the hall, and a projecting round tower, added beyond the curtain, furnished generous latrine accommodation.

The Hall basement formerly possessed a rib-vaulted roof supported on two slender octagonal columns and multiple corbels in the wall (Fig. 164). The bases of these columns and most of the corbels survive. The basement was entered through a door on the W. from the service area. Another door set against the S.E. corner leads to a narrow stair now leading to the upper floor, but seemingly a modern insertion in what may have been a passage to a now vanished postern beside the round tower.[42] A lower step of the certainly renewed stairs reuses an altar-stone with incised crosses. The curtain wall is pierced for three windows to light the basement, one retaining a trefoil-headed lancet.

The passage and Grand Staircase: A vaulted passage runs along the N. flank of the basement leading to a similarly vaulted lobby flanked by no less than four wide doors. Two of these, in line to the S.E., are incorporated in a massive stair-block set obliquely against the E. end of the hall. The first door leads to a further vaulted passage with descending steps, seemingly intended to provide access to the lower floors of a projected chapel wing beyond the curtain that was never built. The second door gave on to a grand newel staircase to the upper floor (Figs. 2, 166). The other two doors flank the N. angle of the block, one opening towards the court, the other into the undercroft below the later 15th-century chapel. These doors all have pointed heads, complete or fragmentary, and have

Fig. 165. Coity Castle, South Domestic Range: conjectural reconstruction of the passage beside the Hall basement leading to the Grand Staircase.

plain chamfered jambs with ball stops, some with bars. The vaulting of the passage and lobby has fallen, but its nature is indicated by the triple corbels that remain in the walls. These indicate four bays, each with a quadripartite vault with plain-chamfered ribs. An identical vaulted bay covered the inner lobby at the foot of the grand newel stair. One splayed window in the N. wall lit the passage.

The Abortive Chapel Wing: The impressive vaulted passage leading under the grand newel stair has been mentioned as an intended access to a projecting wing that was never built. As well as the finely framed pointed arch from the lobby, this passage has a further fine pointed door at the foot of the steps within – yet it only leads to a very narrow area between the rear of the stair-block and the curtain. Its lower end is now partly blocked by modern masonry. A clear indication of the intention to build out beyond the curtain is given by a triple corbel, with three ribs like those already described, which projects from the rear

Fig. 164. Coity Castle, South Domestic Range: Conjectural reconstruction of the vaulted basement beneath the Hall.

[42] Clark claimed such a postern existed, but now only a ragged hole suggesting a former window survives. There is certainly a machicolation, set on a squinch above this angle, as Clark notes (*Arch. Camb.*, 1877, p. 5 and *Med. Milit. Arch.*, I, p. 489).

Fig. 166. Coity Castle, South Domestic Range: entry to the Grand Staircase.

wall of the stair-block. As it survives, this feature is absurd. It could only have functioned if the adjacent curtain had been breached and these ribs carried a structure built out over the external scarp. No breach was made, and the fact that a chapel was later added against the N.E. face of this stair block, also suggests that a projecting chapel wing had been originally intended, perhaps inspired by a chapel of this type added beyond the curtain at Kidwelly in the late 13th century.

The Hall on the first floor only retains is S. wall (the curtain) and portions of its E. wall and N.W. angle. Three deeply recessed windows pierce the curtain, these now having the remnants of inserted Tudor windows with labels and four-centred heads. A door gave access at the centre of the E. wall, and S. of

this the wall displays a curious segmental-headed recess, possibly a livery cupboard. The arch above is pierced by a small square vertical shaft, perhaps for a bell-rope to call servants or announce meals. The hall was ceiled by a wooden floor carried on large square beams. The position of the fireplace is uncertain. The main entrance, from a lobby at the head of the grand staircase, was presumably set across the vanished N.E. angle of the hall.

On the N. side of the hall a long narrow chamber with a segmental-headed fireplace and two recessed windows occupied the space above the passage, while a larger area above the lobby was later provided with a large Tudor window set on a squinch to the N.

The second floor above the hall retains emphatic traces of Tudor refurbishment in the S. wall. Here a deep fireplace and chimney stack survive, flanked by two wide and deeply recessed contemporary windows. The back of the fireplace is rendered in herringbone masonry like that used similarly in the keep annexe.

The Latrine-Tower (Figs. 161, 162, 167): This tower has been regarded as a 13th-century defensive addition. Its position and character do not support this. As the only tower flanking the curtain, its location on the naturally strongest side is odd. Above all, its construction over a cess-pit, with upper floors generously provided with latrines is an excessive concentration on sanitary arrangements for a defensive tower. As there is no indication that the adjacent hall-block was raised in the place of earlier domestic quarters, it must be assumed that this tower was built at the same time as the 14th-century block to serve its occupants. A similar latrine-tower of *ca.* 1300 exists at Swansea Castle (LM 18). The flanking corbel-tables of double convex corbels which carry a widened upper part of the tower, above the cess-pit, are also more appropriate to work after the 13th century.

At ground level, the base of the tower is cut down into the top of the scarp, the vaulted *cess-pit* being taken down well below the outside level and 8m below the floor above. A recorded outfall is no longer visible. Externally, straight side-walls are rounded outwards above on the double corbel-tables towards the first floor. The *first floor* is entered from the triangular block housing secondary stairways close to the E. end of the hall and the head of the grand stair. It is vaulted and has splayed lights to the flanks and a third to the front, the latter set in a recess occupied by a garderobe slot.

The second floor is reached from a newel stair in

Fig. 167. Coity Castle, South Domestic Range: external view of the Latrine-Tower and flanking walls.

the internal triangular block. Again vaulted, this chamber also has three splayed lights. Here there are two latrines, one set in an alcove in the N. wall, next to the entry, the other to the S.

The third floor of the tower only retains a few courses of its walling, but these still indicate three recessed windows matching those below, together with a fireplace to the S.E., and a loop, retaining the base of a cross-oillet, near the junction with the W. curtain. This curtain and that running E. retain stubs of the fallen walls of the tower, and show that it carried a parapet resting upon a corbel-table continuous with those on the curtains. At the lower level in the angles squinches were carried between wall and tower, that to the E. being broken for a large arched machicolation slot.

Services were accommodated in the irregular area between the hall undercroft and the middle gatehouse. This long narrowing area is now subdivided by a Tudor cross-wall incorporating fireplaces and ovens on both faces. The chamber nearer the hall contains the base of a large malting-kiln set against the curtain (Fig. 161a, 168). It is square with a circular chamber and a flue which is carried around the chamber with which it communicates through a series of vents. The date of this kiln is not certain. Near it, a drain pierces the base of the curtain. A fireplace was set in the

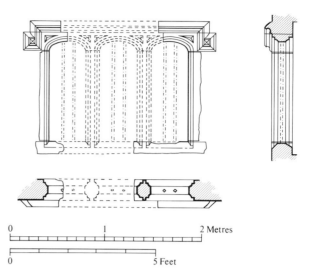

Fig. 168. Coity Castle, South Domestic Range: general view of the central Hall block and the adjacent part of the service area containing the Malting Kiln, bottom right.

Fig. 169. Coity Castle, South Domestic Range: Tudor window inserted in the curtain on the first floor above the Services.

inserted cross-wall on the W., and two doors on the N. led towards the court.

The second service-room to the W. was entered by a small door with chamfered jambs and bull-nose stops below bars. This door was at the W. end of the chamber close to the adjacent well. The cross-wall provides a large double fireplace and two adjacent ovens. A wide blocked window in the curtain is a Tudor insertion.

Beam holes mark the two floor levels of domestic apartments above these service rooms. These apartments were extensively remodelled in the early 16th century, but they are only known from the surviving details retained in the curtain-wall. Internally, the other walls are reduced to their lowest levels. The former arrangements are best seen externally. On the first floor there are the remains of two narrow late-medieval lights and, to the W., the jambs of a wide three-light Tudor window directly above another blocked below. It retains parts of its label. Above this again is another similar Tudor window set in the gable of a dormer. A second gable retains the remains of a rather smaller window, immediately E. of this. This window has caused the removal of the upper part of a dressed-stone arrow-slit, its lower oillet surviving beneath the cill. In this area a further loop is indicated and there are clear traces of the former late-medieval crenellations that were filled in when the Tudor second floor was built. The line of square drain-holes between the two floors marks the level of the medieval wall-walk. A Tudor crenellated wall-walk was added on the raised curtain.

The Tudor stair and extension. A further Tudor addition saw the raising of a stair-block and the extension of the vaulted passage on the N. side of the E. service-room. This stair provided a new service route to the hall through an extension of the upper long chamber to a door inserted at the W. end of the hall. Only the base and lower steps survive, but the S. jambs of Tudor four-centred doors survive at the E. ends of a ground-floor lobby and a first-floor landing. Beyond the landing door, to the right at the end of a passage, one jamb of an identical door entering the hall survives with vestiges of another above it on the second floor.

The 15th-century chapel is on the first floor of a secondary block lying N.W.–S.E. against the north-eastern flank of the 14th-century hall-block. This addition was substituted for the chapel-block originally intended but never achieved. The S.E. end of the chapel is incorporated in a facet of the curtain.

The ground floor is entered through a narrow door in the N.W. wall with rebated chamfer and cushion stops. Beyond this, on the right, is the formerly external, pointed N.E. door to the lobby of the main block, which has plain chamfers with bar-and-broach stops. It appears that this basement was adapted at some stage as a pantry or buttery by sub-dividing it into three compartments with the insertion of two cross-walls, both with central doors and flanked on the S.W. by small rectangular openings, formerly grilled, one retaining a finely-dressed slab as a cill suggestive of a serving hatch. The opposed sections of the cross-walls do not survive to this level. A splayed window is discernible in the N.E. wall of the outer compartment, above a stone bench, and Clark's unpublished plans show another, now vanished, in the same wall of the middle compartment.[43] The inner face of the curtain-wall at this level is much patched within the basement, but it retains one straight joint that may indicate a loop not noticeable externally. A stair-block has been added against the N.E. wall, reached by a door (with hollow chamfer and broach-and-bar stops), in the N. corner. This door existed before the stair block, which seems to represent an addition of the second phase of the chapel, providing access without recourse to the grand stair in the main block.

The chapel above was carried on what appears to have been a bipartite floor. Three rough and wide vaulted ribs traversed the basement, but did not wholly ceil it. These presumably supported a longitudinal timber floor. The ribs have fallen, but their positions are marked by surviving springers, those

Fig. 170. Coity Castle, South Domestic Range: external view, salient Latrine-Tower, left; tall first-floor Chapel window, right.

to the S.W. side inserted into the wall of the 14th century grand stair-block. The S.E. wall of the chapel rises to a gable added upon the curtain, over which steps carry the wall-walk from its original height on the N.E. This raised and stepped wall-walk over the gable retains the lower part of its parapet which incorporates the base of an oillet. A tall pointed window pierces the gable and retains some of its dressed-stone surround. This window is splayed from the inner sides of a recess, which incorporates the stump and opposed socket of a stone altar-table. The window is dressed with Sutton Stone ashlar and retains slots for a cross-beam in its jambs which may have served to suspend the pyx above the altar. This window belongs to the second phase of the chapel, for its upper part is built into a raising of the gable (incorporating the stepped parapet described). The earlier gable end is marked by lower flashing-courses on each side. An ornately moulded fragment of the cusped head of a window lying loose in the N. tower of the outer ward (Fig. 171e) may be from the chapel. The chapel served the lord and his retainers, who had direct access from the hall via a landing adjacent to the grand stair by a door faintly discernible in the S.W. chapel wall.

Fig. 171. *(Opposite)* Coity Castle, South Domestic Range: (a) the Chapel altar and window; (b) window piercing curtain, hall basement; (c) doorway, hall basement; (d) doorway to passage beside Grand Staircase; (e) tracery fragment, loose in North Tower (from Chapel?).

---

[43] See f/n. 36.

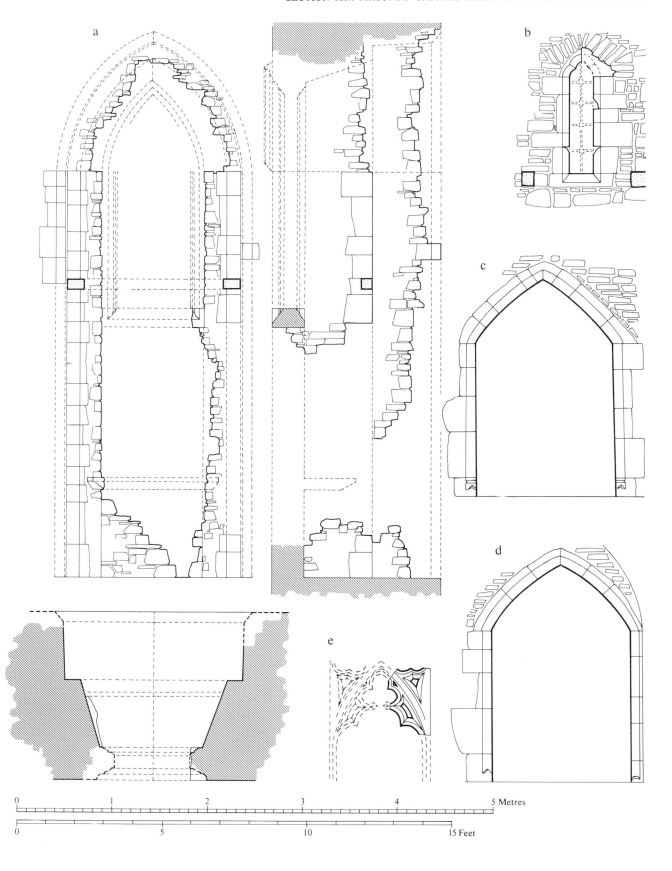

a

b

c

d

e

0   1   2   3   4   5 Metres

0   5   10   15 Feet

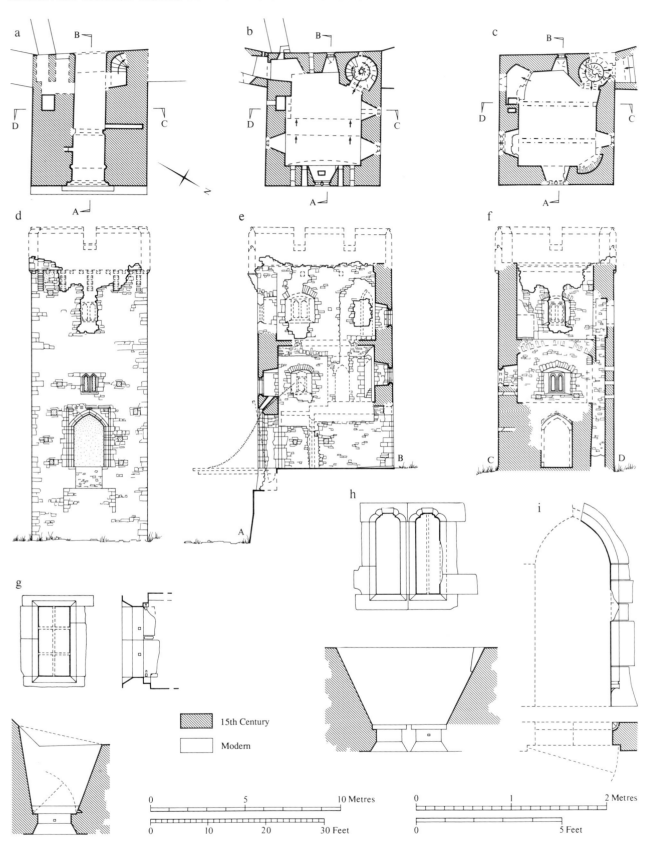

15th Century

Modern

0   5   10 Metres

0   10   20   30 Feet

0   1   2 Metres

0   5 Feet

The Court and Central Structure

The southern half of the court is grassed to the W., where the well is now furnished with a modern well-head, but towards the E. side traces of paving survive. Most of the northern part of the court is occupied by an enigmatic rectangular foundation measuring 17m by 10m internally and defined by the footings of a wall one metre thick. Except for a short bench-like internal feature at the S.E. corner and uncertain hints of a doorway adjacent to the N.W. corner, these footings are quite featureless. The proportions are unlikely, and the size excessive, for a hall. The only indication of its date is the partial overlapping of its S.E. angle by the secondary stair-block added to the chapel, presumably before the close of the 15th century.

The North Curtain and North-East Gatehouse

The renewed *North Curtain*, thought to have been raised after a breach made on this side by Glyndŵr's forces in 1404–05, runs in a straight line from the N.E. gatehouse to the keep annexe, abutting the N.E. angle of that structure most awkwardly with a narrow and vulnerable overlapping. This curtain follows a withdrawn line, excluding the northern facets of the Norman wall, though incorporating the two to the E. in a wide platform and a new cistern already described. The wall is built of random rubble and its wall walk was furnished with a parapet to each side, the outer one carried on a corbel-table formed of re-used newel-stones from a dismantled stair.

The North-East Gatehouse (Figs. 149, 172, 173), like the N. Curtain, was probably raised after the sieges of 1404–05. It consists of a square block built out over the scarp, its back flush with the old curtain. Its external face is built in coursed square-ish limestone and conglomerate blocks with ashlar quoins, though in the other walls more random rubble predominates. All walls are pierced by putlog holes. This modest gatehouse of three floors survives to the height of a fragmentary corbel-table that once carried a crenellated parapet. Its *ground floor* consists of a pas-

sage, formerly vaulted, between two thick piers of masonry. There are no guard-chambers, but at the inner end a tiny mural lodge was apparently incorporated in the S.E. pier. This is now blocked, but it was recorded by Clark.[44] It was entered by a door in the passage and seemingly lit by windows in the rear wall of the gatehouse, one of which is discernible. Opposite the blocked door of the lodge, another door in the passage leads to a newel stair to the upper floors, housed in the W. angle. The outer front, below the threshold, is boldly battered in sandstone ashlar. The outer arch is pointed and framed in plain-chamfered sandstone without stops. It is set within a square-headed recess, also framed in ashlar. Two holes in the upper angles of this recess obliquely pierce the wall upwards to provide chases for the chains of the drawbridge. A third hole more steeply angled above the centre of the arch is a spy-hole, opening in the cill of the window above. Within the arch the flanks of the passage retain the grooves of a portcullis, but the plain vault above is fallen. Towards the centre of the passage, evidence remains of the projecting jambs of the doors, with a deep draw-bar hole behind that to the N. This jamb survives at its base, which is of Sutton Stone, plain-chamfered with a diagonal stop. The arch at the inner end of the passage retains its jambs and the springing of a pointed arch. It is plain-chamfered, with broach stops, and set within a good relieving arch.

The *first-floor chamber* is reached at a cross-angle door from the newel stair, which continues to the upper chamber. The considerable narrowing of the massive piers below furnishes reasonable accommodation on these upper floors. The first-floor room, housing the portcullis, was amply fenestrated. Four single-light windows are disposed around its inner and side walls, while a double-light window pierces the outer wall above the entry. The single-light window in the inner wall retains its square frame of plain-chamfered ashlar with the socket holes of an iron grill and internal shutters. The outward-facing two-light window is restored but largely original. Its plain-chamfered jambs and mullion carry curious shouldered heads with modest side cusps. The spy-hole viewing the entry-point pierces the cill of this window which, like the lesser windows in the chamber, is set within a segmental-headed rear arch. The door to the stair in the W. corner was framed in sandstone with

Fig. 172. *(Opposite)* Coity Castle, the North-East Gatehouse: (a) ground floor plan; (b) first floor plan; (c) second floor plan; (d) external N.E. elevation; (e) section A-B, looking S.E.; (f) section C-D, looking N.E.; (g) window on second floor, S.W. wall, with evidence for grill and shutter.; (h) window on first floor, N.E. wall; (i) door to stair in W. corner of first floor chamber.

[44] Clark, *Arch. Camb.*, 1877, p. 3 and *Med. Milit. Arch.*, I, p. 488.

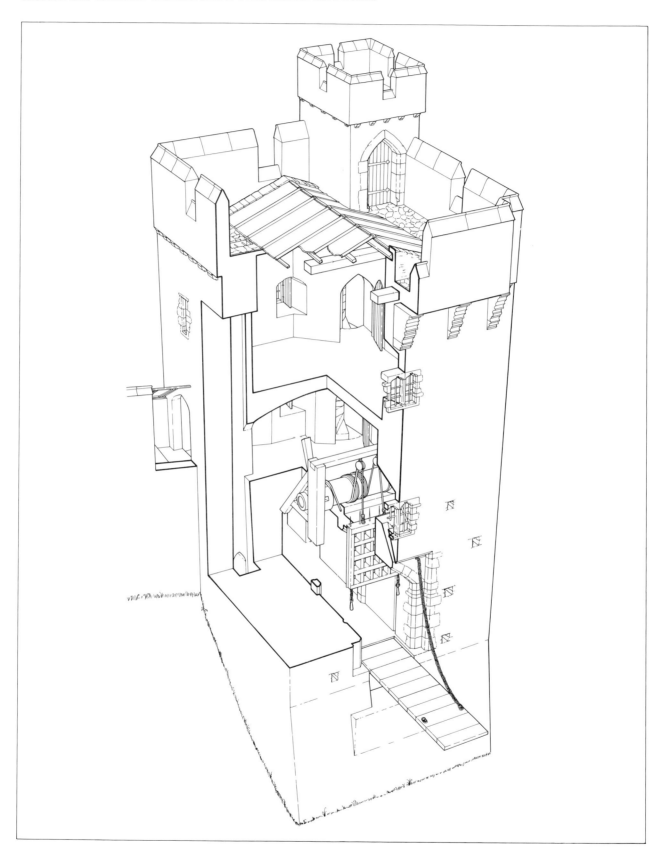

a pointed head and concave chamfer above cushion stops with bars. There was a latrine set against the S.E. wall, and close to this a lobby in the S. angle led to the wall-walk along the E. curtain. This chamber was spanned by a shallow segmental-headed vault which has largely fallen.

The *second-floor chamber*, reached by the continued newel stair, was ceiled in timber supported by two large beams indicated by a surviving socket and corbel. The stair door has hollow-chamfered Sutton Stone dressings with cushion-and-bar stops. There is a window in each wall. That in the inner wall of the gatehouse is a square-headed single light, identical to that in the same wall below, and also with evidence for its grill and shutter. A similar window in the N.W. wall lacks its dressings, as do the windows in the remaining walls which are larger and were designed to house two-light frames, no doubt matching that below already described. A recessed round-backed fireplace was set across the N. corner. Opposite this, in the S. corner, a recess housed a garderobe; the two outfall shafts exposed in this latrine indicate yet another garderobe above on the vanished wall-walk.

Before reaching the second floor, the newel stair gave access to the N. wall-walk through a door now destroyed. From the second floor it continued upwards to the roof and a crenellated wall-walk surmounting the gatehouse. The parapet, wall-walk, and upper part of the stair have fallen away, but the lower parts of several of the large enriched sandstone corbels that supported the machicolated parapet survive, but only one is complete. This projects 50cm from the S. end of the outer wall of the gatehouse and its face is ornately moulded with multiple hollows and cymas (both recta and reversa). On a modest scale, the form of this machicolated parapet reflects the great mid-15th-century Herbert castle at Raglan. This gatehouse, however, is more a prestigious entry facing the church, than a serious defensive structure, despite its portcullis. It has two of its three double lights facing the front, and its spy-hole above the gateway would have been blanked off by the raised drawbridge to deny its use as a murder-hole.

The East Yard

A tall, straight wall screened off a segment of the inner ward to the E. This Tudor insertion runs from the S. corner of the N.E. gatehouse to the stair outshut

Fig. 173. *(Opposite)* Coity Castle; the North-East Gatehouse.

of the chapel, abutting with a straight joint against both. The greater part of this wall is reduced to a height between 1m and 2m, but a substantial stub against the gatehouse shows that it rose to a height of 5.5m. It was 1m thick and had a central door, of which the lower jambs survive, with a stepped threshold to an irregular area confined between the curving E. curtain and the N. flank of the chapel. A bench footing runs along the internal face of the screen wall to the N., but the heavily patched inner face of the curtain betrays no sign of any structure in the form of corbels, toothing or creasing. It appears that this wall screened a mundane working area from the central court, perhaps a wood-yard like that which was screened off at Cardiff Castle (MM 1).

The Outer Ward

The outer ward is roughly rectangular and encloses a level court 55m by 37m, including the area of the infilled segment of ditch to the E. The evidence for its former earthworks, supporting the probability that the ward lies over a primary bailey, is discussed above. The medieval masonry of this ward is mainly of the 14th century (Period III), with additions of the 15th century (Period IV). There is no Norman or Tudor work, but merely a few modern reparations.

Cross-walls link the outer ward with the inner defences, originally spanning the ditch which separated the wards until the 16th century. A small square *North Tower* projected from the N. curtain, opposite a larger rectangular tower on the S., which was later converted into the *South Gatehouse*. The main entrance to the ward was the *West Gatehouse*, placed centrally in the W. wall. At the S.W. angle are the last scant vestiges of a *South-West Tower*, which was dismantled and replaced by the adjacent *South-West Turret*. The masonry of this ward is ruinous and only isolated fragments rise to first floor level. A significant building, the large buttressed *Barn*, represented by its footings on the S. side, is the only surviving internal structure. In the 19th century Clark recorded a long 'stable' in the N.W. corner, but this is now gone and its date uncertain. The entire circuit of the walls, with the exception of the S. cross-wall, is of 14th-century origin (Period III). When first raised this curtain incorporated the North Tower, the South-West Tower and the tower which later became the Southern Gatehouse. In the west wall there was an entrance of unknown form and a small postern door set against the N.W. angle. In the 15th century the S.W. turret replaced

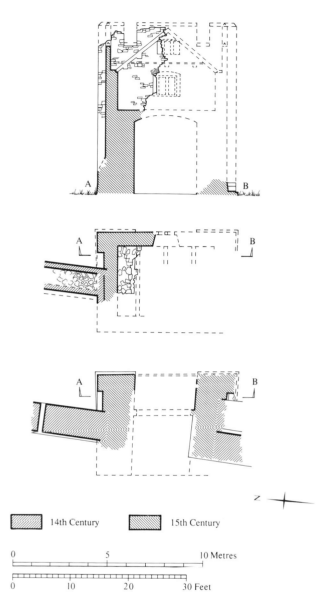

14th Century   15th Century

0   5   10 Metres

0   10   20   30 Feet

Fig. 174. Coity Castle, the Outer Ward: West Gatehouse.

tain. It is now reduced to its lowest levels and its outer half has gone, replaced by a thin rebuilt wall of modern date (existing in 1866). The door to the basement retains a draw-bar hole, and remnants of a splayed loop survive in the E. wall. The basement appears to have been vaulted, and access to the vanished upper floor was by an external stair butted against its south face beside the door.

The *North Curtain* is featureless, its masonry of roughly coursed red conglomerate slabs and square-ish blocks of grey-green limestone. A very evident rebuilding of a 6m section of the wall is apparent on both faces towards the centre. This is taken to represent damage suffered in the sieges of 1404–05. Above this rebuilding, a section of rebuilt parapet survives on the wall-walk. The small *N.W. Postern Door* set against the angle is now blocked. Its head is pointed and crudely formed by two plain-chamfered stones set on unchamfered jambs, all of sandstone. A draw-bar hole is present.

The West Gatehouse (Figs. 148, 174) is of the 15th century (Period IV). Very ruinous, it only survives to the first floor around its N.E. angle, and very mutilated there. Enough remains, however, to attempt a reasoned reconstruction (Fig. 148). A small square gatehouse, it straddled the curtain and no doubt replaced a 14th-century door at this point. A wide passage, certainly barrel-vaulted, was flanked by thick piers of masonry. One projecting jamb marks the position of doors. Access to the upper floor was from the pre-existing flight of stone steps set against the curtain to the immediate S., and through a door above, which has now vanished. The upper chamber upon the vault may be comprehended by the vestiges surviving of its inner E. wall (Section, Fig. 174). This shows evidence for a timber ceiling, carried on corbels and transverse beams. The surviving N. jamb of a splayed window is so placed, in relation to the dimensions of the room, to indicate a two-light window set beneath a depressed segmental rear arch. Above the ceiling a tiny attic occupied the space within a gabled roof running E.–W. This attic was lit by a small window represented by its N. splay. Above the roof, the walls rose to a crenellated parapet; the base of one crenel survives, and taking into account the position of the ridge of the roof, a matching crenel may be restored in the same position on the S. side. There was no access to the curtain to the N., which was provided with inner and outer parapets.

The W. curtain between the gatehouse and the S.W. corner is much refaced externally. At the corner the

the S.W. tower, the S. tower became the South Gatehouse, and the barn was built. The northern cross wall is contemporary with the adjacent 14th-century curtain, with which it is coterminous. The southern cross-wall is of the 15th century.

The *Northern cross-wall* extended the north curtain across the former open moat between the two wards to its full height. Its stability was ensured by broad relieving arches, three of which are still discernible at their heads just above the present ground level. The *North Tower* was raised on the outer lip of the dividing ditch, projecting northwards from the cur-

S.W. Tower (Fig. 176) was an original feature of the defences of this ward. It was rectangular and it straddled the W. end of the S. curtain, its greater part projecting outwards. This tower, contemporary with the 14th-century curtain that flanked it, was dismantled and a postern inserted in its place in the 15th century. The inner end only survives as footings, partly overlaid by the walls of the S.W. turret and barn. It appears that it was partly retained externally, perhaps as a porch to the new postern. The E. wall remains as a short stub, but a larger stub to the W. side retains one splay of a loop to the tower. Though termed a postern, it might be noted that the position of the door that replaced this tower is adjacent to the large barn, and it may have functioned primarily as a loading-door for grain.

When the S.W. tower was replaced by the postern, a small rectangular turret was raised, projecting out westwards over the scarp of the ditch, its inner wall overlying the footings of the inner W. corner of the tower. This *S.W. Turret* may have served as a mill. Its lower floor consisted of a cellar, now filled in; a small blocked opening with pointed arch visible externally in its S. lateral wall was evidently an outlet for water flowing S. along the ditch which formerly ran along this front and was to some extent dammed by this turret. The sluice incorporated in the stone bridge before the South Gatehouse, described below, is a further indication of works to control water in this area, presumably controlling the release of outflow into the moat of the inner ward. There were two small and crude cross-loops higher up in the S. wall; a third

Fig. 175. Coity Castle: Bridge with sluice fronting the South Gatehouse of the Outer Ward.

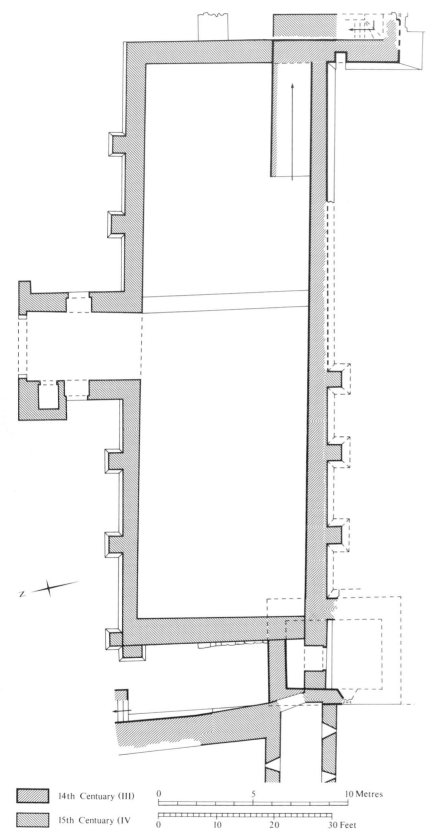

14th Century (III)

15th Century (IV

0   5   10 Metres

0   10   20   30 Feet

seems to have been broken through for a modern door in the outer W. wall, and another pierces the N. wall. The outfall arch is beneath the W. loop in the S. wall and below plan level. It is now perceptible only on the external face, blocked up, and clearly too large for a garderobe drain. There was a first floor which was lit by two plain rectangular lights in the S. wall. The entrance to this turret is marked by patching on the inner wall-face on the line of the curtain. A former post-medieval building raised against the S. face of the turret is indicated by the flashing for its gabled roof on this front, and this may have represented a continued use of the mill.

The Barn (Fig. 176) was built against the S. curtain, which formed its S. wall, in the 15th century. An outward lean is discernible on the inner face of this curtain. This probably explains the refacing of a long western section of its outer face, which incorporated three buttresses matching those which survive on the footings of the N. side of the barn. These buttresses all rise upon battered bases which extend between them on the lateral wall faces. A roomy porch at the centre of the N. wall had wide doors for easy entry and opposed lesser doors in the lateral walls, perhaps utilized to create sufficient draught when threshing grain. A small lodge occupies a thickening of the N.W. angle of the porch, conveniently sited for overseeing storage or distribution of grain. Internally an inserted cross-wall of indeterminate date sub-divides the barn. The E. gable wall abuts the masonry foundation of a stone stair set against the 14th-century curtain and incorporated within the later barn. This building seems to have survived intact in 1814. In that year Walter Davies noticed two noteworthy barns in Glamorgan, at Monknash and to the W. of Coity Castle, the latter described as 'the Westminster Hall of Coety Lordship'.[45]

The *South Tower* (and later gatehouse, Figs. 152, 177) was probably served on its upper floor by the stair incorporated in the adjacent angle of the barn. This structure is largely reduced to its foundations. It straddled the 14th-century curtain and its outer projection rose upon a strongly battered base. The only surviving feature of its original basement is the splay of a loop in the E. wall at the S.E. corner. The masonry survives on the first floor only at the S. end of the

Fig. 176. Coity Castle, Outer Ward: the Barn and South-West Towers.

[45] Walter Davies, *General View of the Agriculture and Domestic Economy of South Wales*, (London, 1814), Vol. I, p. 127.

W. wall, where it retains traces of a garderobe recess with an outfall placed beneath in the angle made with the curtain. South of this there is also evidence for a small splayed window. In the 15th century two transverse piers of masonry were inserted across the basement to flank a gate-passage serving a door broken through the external wall. Only the W. pier survives, and this incorporates the remnants of a stair to the upper floor. This gate was intact in the 18th century, when it was illustrated by the Buck brothers (Fig. 152) and by Sparrow. These artists indicate an off-centre entrance with a pointed arch set in a square-headed recess. On the first floor they illustrate two single trefoil-headed lights and above them a parapet carried on a corbel-table enclosed a gabled roof running E.–W. This building was set on the outer lip of the ditch separating the two wards.

A late medieval or Tudor stone bridge spanned the moat fronting this gatehouse. Its small vaulted arch incorporates a sluice on its W. opening to regulate the flow of water from the presumed mill at the S.W. angle into the main ditch.

The *South Cross-Wall* is of the 15th century at its lowest level, where it incorporates a range of eight cramped and curious cross-loops just above the level

0   5   10

0   10   20   30   40

Fig. 177. Coity Castle: the South Gatehouse of the Outer Ward. The reconstructed elevation is derived from eighteenth century descriptions by the Buck brothers (see Fig. 152) and Sparrow.

Fig. 178. Coity Castle; the South Cross-Wall: (a) external elevation; (b) internal elevation.

255

of the infilled ditch. These loops are crudely built and the cross-slits divided from the vertical shafts by small inserted wedge-stones. They seem to have served gunners rather than archers. At this level the wall was incorporated with a turret butted against the W. wall of the inner ward and containing a cess-pit serving garderobes of the inner ward's domestic block. This turret rose well above the level of a crenellated wall-walk that ran above the eight loops described. At a later date this wall-walk and its battlements were surmounted by a heightening of the wall. The straight joint against the turret marks this heightening, and the earlier crenels are clearly visible on the external wall. This heightening was effected with most irregular random rubble contrasting with the neater roughly-coursed rubble of the lower wall.

Miscellaneous Finds and Observations

No excavations have been undertaken at Coity, but during survey various loose moulded fragments of stone were recorded, some littering the site and others in the immediate vicinity. Other re-used dressings have been noted in the masonry that still survives. An ornately moulded tracery fragment, possibly from the chapel, lies in the N. tower, along with a well-carved boss from the intersection of the ribs of a vault. (Figs. 171e, 180). The four arms of this boss are moulded to receive ribs matching those of the north passage and undercroft of the hall-block. At the intersection, the boss is decorated with a multiple rose design.

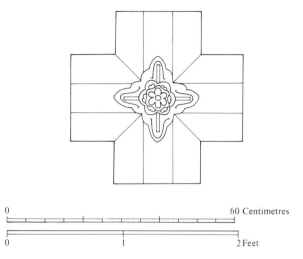

| 0 | | | | | | | 60 Centimetres |
| 0 | | 1 | | 2 Feet |

Fig. 180. Coity Castle: carved boss, possibly from the South Domestic Range, formerly placed at the intersection of the ribs of a vault. Now lying loose in North Tower of the Outer Ward.

Fig. 179. Coity Castle: loop with cross-slit in South Cross-Wall.

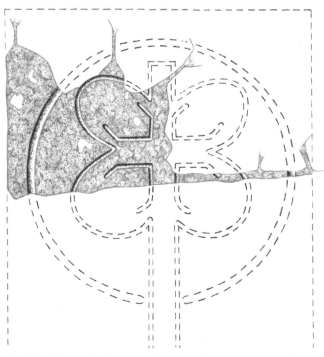

Fig. 181. Coity Castle: fragment of grave-slab re-used in Tudor stair addition of South Domestic Range.

Of special interest are three re-used tomb-slabs incorporated in masonry at the castle (Figs. 181, 182). An incised four-lobed outline cross, enclosed in a ring, is seen on a slab fragment incorporated in the Tudor stair addition to the hall-block. Another fragment, re-used as a step on the E. curtain, has the incised stepped base of an outline cross. Finally, there are two fragments of a finer and more detailed slab, re-covered and now held by the Ancient Monuments Inspectorate. These pieces were observed in the masonry of the truncated N. wall of the service block beside the hall. They bear the incised outline of a male in civilian dress beneath the trefoiled terminal of a

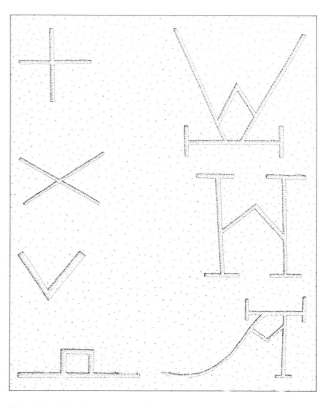

Fig. 183. Coity Castle: masons' marks on dressings of doorways and ribs of vaulting in the South Domestic Range. All relate to building work in the fourteenth century.

Fig. 182. Coity Castle: fragment of grave-slab re-used in walling of the South Domestic Block. Now recovered and held by Cadw.

Fig. 184. Coity Castle: plaque with arms of the Gamages, lords of Coity ca. 1412-1584. Now reset in wall of 'Pleasant View', a house facing the castle on the south side.

257

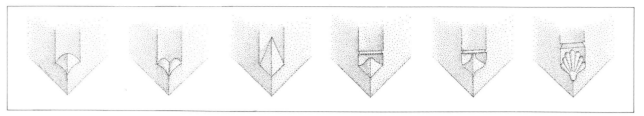

Fig. 185. Coity Castle: chamfer stops in the South Domestic Range.

probable cross. There is also a Roman 'X' and part of an incised shield with a bend. A fourth ecclesiastical fragment was also noticed in re-use as a step in the stair inserted in the passage from the S.E. corner of the hall undercroft. This step bears two small incised crosses which appear to indicate a re-used altar-slab. The adjacent parish church was almost entirely rebuilt in the early 14th century, but the dispersal of these fragments in masonry of so many periods does not reflect this rebuilding.

Loose fragments recorded include the segment of an octagonal chimney of sandstone and the base and part of the shaft of a multangular pilaster, besides many fragments of the dressings of windows and doors. Seven masons' marks have also been recorded on the dressings of the 14th-century hall-block, four marking doorways opening into or from the vaulted passage and lobby (Fig. 183) and three incised on the ribs of the vaulting.

One final piece worthy of record is an armorial plaque reset in the wall of 'Pleasant View', a house near the castle. This plaque bears the Gamage arms (argent, a bend lozengy gules on a chief azure three escallops of the first) and no doubt came from the castle. (Fig. 184).

King, p. 163 (Coyty)

Coety (Coity) (E), Coety Higher (Coity H.) (C)
SS 98 S.W. (9232–8149)   28.iv.87   XL N.E.

MR 2   Llangynwyd Castle

Llangynwyd Castle (Castell Coch) occupies a strong position on the tip of a promontory between the ravines of Nant y Castell and Cwm Cae-Lloi. On the vulnerable N.W. flank the promontory broadens and rises gently, and about 100m beyond the castle the northern half of a much eroded bank and ditch may denote a large bailey or an Iron Age fort. The southern half of this outer line has been destroyed in the vicinity of Castell Farm. The castle is isolated from Llangynwyd village, which lies 600m to the E.N.E., and ill-placed to observe movement along the Llynfi Valley, over 3km to the E. This isolation is surprising for a castle which constituted the administrative centre of Tir Iarll (Earl's Land), a lordship of the lords of Glamorgan. Secluded in the mountains S. of Maesteg, it was 8km N.E. of Kenfig Castle (EM 2) and almost 10km N.W. of Newcastle (EM 3), two other strongholds of the chief lords. While its tactical value was lacking, its strategic importance is clear: it constituted an advanced base against the threat posed by the troublesome Welsh lords of Afan.

The castle is not recorded before 1246, but Tir Iarll is thought to have been appropriated before the death of Earl Robert (1147), possibly during dissension between the four sons of Caradog ab Iestyn.[1] At least two phases of masonry are assigned to the 13th century, but the trace of the curtain suggests that a primary castle-ringwork of the previous century may have existed here. One indication of the early appropriation of Tir Iarll is the identification of Llangynwyd as a chapelry of St James of Kenfig, held by Tewkesbury Abbey, in the confirmation to that house by Bishop Nicholas.[2] An early castle at Llangynwyd would have represented the fourth stronghold established by the chief lords to secure their western flank, following Newcastle (EM 3; by 1106), and Kenfig and Neath (EM 2 and LM 11; by 1130). These castles posed a

[1] J. Beverley Smith, *Morgannwg*, II (1958), p. 20 and *Glam. Co. Hist.*, III, p. 31.
[2] *Capellam sti Cunioth de Leveni* (the chapel of Llangynwyd by the Llynfi), Clark, *Cartae*, I (cxxxvi), p. 134; *Epis. Acts*, II, L170, p. 659; *South Wales and Mon. Record Society Publications No 2*, 1950, p. 142; *Arch. Camb.*, 1941, p. 196.

threat to Afan, whose lord led determined assaults on the western castles in 1183–84, though Llangynwyd alone is not mentioned either then, nor in later Welsh attacks on Kenfig in 1228, 1232 and 1243.

The first mention of Llangynwyd Castle occurs in a Margam deed of 1246. This concerns restitution made to Margam by certain Welshmen for damages to the abbey; the bailiffs of Neath and Llangynwyd Castles were enjoined to compel observance of pledges made to the monks by these men.[3] In 1257 Llangynwyd Castle (*Langenau*) was taken by Llywelyn ap Gruffydd following his savage attack on Gower.[4] It is improbable that the castle was restored by the following year, when William Scurlage is recorded as its constable.[5] The lordship (*Langonydd*) had not recovered by 1262, when the extent following Earl Richard's death mentions no castle, but notes eighty houses destroyed there in the war.[6] During the brief custodianship of Humphrey de Bohun (1262–63) some reparations were carried out and twenty-eight men and eight horses maintained at the castle,[7] but it is to Gilbert de Clare that we must ascribe the major works of restoration soon undertaken, especially the great gatehouse.

During Madog's rebellion of 1294–95 Welsh insurgents in Glamorgan were led by Morgan ap Maredudd.[8] The inquisition following Earl Gilbert's death in 1295 records that Llangynwyd Castle had been burned during the uprising.[9] It appears that it was never restored. Tir Iarll was administered thereafter from Kenfig, and the record of 'the site of an ancient castle' at Llangynwyd in 1307 suggests its desertion.[10] Its abandonment is most clearly indicated by its absence from the roll of castles wilfully destroyed by the barons in their vengeful war against Earl Hugh Despenser in 1321: of ten of his castles sacked, seven were in Glamorgan.

The ruins were known by Merrick (*ca.* 1580) and Lhuyd (1696, as 'Castell y Llan'), but had been forgotten by the 19th century when G. T. Clark knew of no castle there.[11] Excavations by Fredrick Evans in 1906 cleared the remains of a strong twin-towered gatehouse and re-established the true nature of what was regarded locally as an 'ancient camp'.[12]

Postscript:

The Destruction of Llangynwyd Castle in 1257 by Llywelyn ap Gruffydd.

A Latin chronicle in the British Library (BL Royal 6B xi f. 108 v.) now furnishes a more detailed record of this attack. Recently noticed by Professor J. Beverley Smith, and seemingly of Cardiff provenance, the relevant entry for 1257 translates: "Lord Richard,

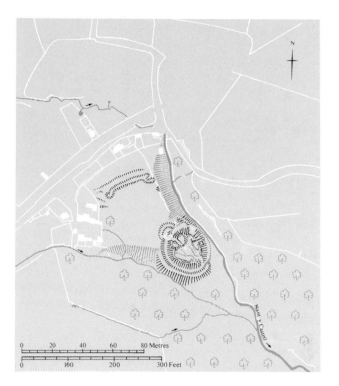

Fig. 186. Llangynwyd Castle: location map, showing the large embanked outer enclosure on the north-east side of the site.

Earl of Gloucester, came to Cardiff with a multitude of armed men. And Llywelyn was near Margam Abbey with a strong force. On the 13th July Llywelyn advanced upon Llangynwyd (*Llangunith*) and burnt the castle of the lord earl, killing twenty-four of the earl's men, the lord earl being then with a strong force at Llanblethian".

---

[3] Clark, *Cartae*, II (dxxvii), pp. 534–6; *Epis. Acts*, II, L438, pp. 727–8.

[4] *Bruts*: B. S., *Pen. 20*, *R.B.H.* (probably the unnamed castle noted by Matthew Paris, *Chronica Majora*, V, p. 642).

[5] Clark, *Cartae*, II (dxcv), p. 625; *Epis. Acts*, II, L491, p. 741; Patterson, *Glouc. Charters*, No. 129, n.

[6] Clark, *Cartae*, II (dcxviii), pp. 660–1.

[7] Altschul, *The Clares*, p. 246, Note 12; T. C. Williams, *Trans. Port Talbot Hist. Soc.*, No. 1, II, 1969, p. 60.

[8] For the rebellion in Glamorgan: Altschul, *ibid*, pp. 154–5 and *Glam. Co. Hist.*, III, pp. 59–60.

[9] *Cal. Inq. P. M.*, III, 24 Edward I, p. 244; Corbett, *Glamorgan Lordship*, pp. 40, 70; Nicholl, *Normans*, p. 150, n.

[10] *Cal. Inq. P. M.*, IV, 35 Edward I, No. 435, pp. 322–4.

[11] Merrick, *Morg. Arch.*, pp. 76, 102; Lhuyd, *Parochialia*, Part III, pp. 10, 18; Clark, *Arch. Camb.*, 1878, p. 123.

[12] These excavations are inadequately described in Frederick Evans, *Tir Iarll*, (Cardiff, 1912), pp. 50–6. Further information is given in *Minutes of Evidence to the Royal Commission on Ancient Monuments in Wales and Monmouthshire*, Vol. I, 1912, pp. 56–7.

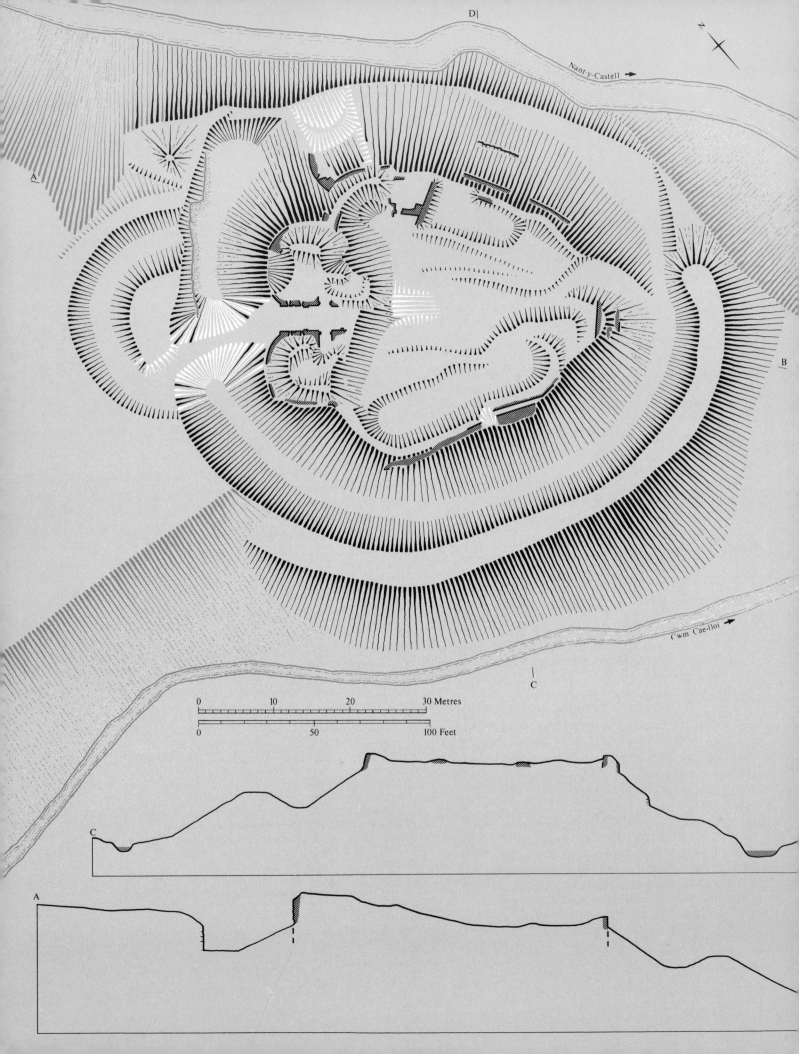

D|

N

Nant-y-Castell →

A

B

Nant-y-Castell →

Cwm Cae-lloi →

| C

0   10   20   30 Metres

0   50   100 Feet

C

A

Description of the Remains

The site consists of two parts: the outer work, questionably a large outer ward; and the inner work or castle proper (Fig. 186). The outer work is defined by the diverging declivities to the ravines and the vestiges of a bowed bank and ditch. The large roughly triangular area enclosed is now pasture and displays no surface features. The bank and ditch are very eroded and not superficially of medieval character. Where truncated centrally towards the farm, an uncertain hint of an inturn of the bank may suggest an entrance of prehistoric Iron Age type. Beyond this point the bank and ditch have been destroyed; the slight hollow-way entering the area is probably modern.

The main work (Fig. 187) on the tip of the spur is wooded and the remains are overgrown and much confused by spoil from the 1906 excavations. Steep scarping defines a pear-shaped enclosure 35m N.W.–S.E. by 37m N.E.–S.W. A strong ditch and counter-scarp bank protect the S. side and run on as an impressive rock-cut ditch, with vertical outer scarp, across the vulnerable N.W. flank. This rock-cut section is evidently a strengthened secondary re-cut, without counterscarp bank but fronted by a lunate ditch forming a barbican of sorts before the entrance. The oblique causeway confusing the nature of this outwork is known to be a work undertaken to facilitate the excavations in 1906. To the N.E. no ditch was required, but the scarping has left traces of a terrace on the steep natural fall.

Clear traces of the foundations of a curtain-wall intermittently define the enclosure. This curtain is of inferior construction and built of thin Pennant Sandstone slabs quarried at the site. It retains no trace of mortar, and there is a general internal fall suggesting that it might be seated upon a ring-bank. In places it appears to have been strengthened by the imposition of a battered external sheath of equally rough masonry. There is no evidence that this curtain originally possessed flanking towers.

The interior surface is irregular, but traces of dry-walling and scarps define two abutting sub-rectangular buildings set against the curtain on the N.E. side, the larger perhaps the hall. A third long rectangular building may be indicated by a hollow backing the wall along the S. side. The entrance on the N.W. side is flanked by two large mounds of building debris largely masking the substantial remains of a great

Fig. 187. *(Opposite)* Llangynwyd Castle: general plan and profiles.

gatehouse surviving almost to first-floor level and partially cleared in 1906.

The Great Gatehouse. In 1906 Evans tunnelled his way along the gate-passage and revealed its nature. It has subsequently suffered much erosion and vandalism, but the salient features of the gatehouse are clear. Clearly a secondary addition, its round-fronted towers flanked a structure rather larger than the main inner gatehouse at Caerphilly. It is constructed of Pennant Sandstone, no doubt derived during the deepening of the N.W. cross-ditch on this front. Sandy lime-mortar is used and dressings are of Sutton Stone. Sufficient survives of the gate-passage to establish its defensive arrangements. From without, these began with opposed loops fronting a portcullis, then further loops fronting double doors, side doors to flanking rooms and, finally, further doors closing against the interior and protected with an inner-facing portcullis. Although Llangynwyd lacks evidence for its vanished *assommoirs*, this sequence within the passage, together with the general form and proportions of the gatehouse, is enough to demonstrate its near identity with others at Caerphilly and Tonbridge. Using Jean Mesqui's code for gatehouse defences, Derek Renn has recently established the close similarities of Gilbert de Clare's work at Caerphilly and Tonbridge.[13] He shows that at these two castles, between inner and outer portcullises (H, for *herse*), the sequence of main doors (V, for *vantaux*), loops (.) and side-doors (,) is identical, their spacing almost exactly so. Applying this formula at Llangynwyd, symmetry is broken only by additional opposed loops beyond the outer portcullis (Fig. 188); in other respects sequence and spacing is again almost identical and sufficient to suspect that the hidden rear wall defines a gate-passage of similar length and incorporates stair-turrets at the inner angles. It is now clear that Llangynwyd was a third great gatehouse raised by Gilbert de Clare. We have seen that the castle was destroyed by Llywelyn ap Gruffydd in 1257 and was under repair in 1262–63. During the 1260s, which saw the start on Caerphilly in 1268, we may reasonably assume that Gilbert restored Llangynwyd.

The main doorways closing the gate-passage were of plain-chamfered Sutton Stone with bar stops similar to those of the first work at Caerphilly. The side doors to guard-rooms were also dressed with Sutton

---

[13] Derek Renn, 'Tonbridge and some other Gatehouses', *Collectanea Historica: Essays in Memory of Stuart Rigold*, 1982, pp. 93–103.

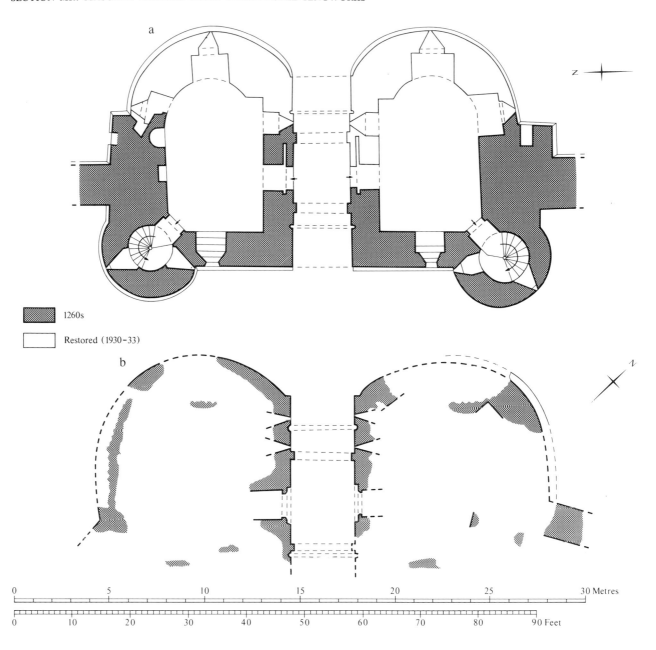

1260s

Restored (1930–33)

Fig. 188. Great Gatehouses: (a) Caerphilly (Part 1b, LM 3), the main inner Gatehouse; (b) Llangynwyd.

Stone, bull-nose or quarter-round in section, and one retained a fine fleur-de-lys stop illustrated by Evans, but now mutilated.[14] Traces are visible of three of the four portcullis grooves, all executed in Sutton Stone, as were the dressings of the loops. Three mouldings reset in the church porch at Llangynwyd probably derive from the gatehouse. One of these is an oillet, the others a plain-chamfered and stopped jamb and a jamb with a deeply hollowed keel moulding.

One further addition was made to the primary ring-

wall, but probably before the gatehouse was built. A three-quarter-round tower to the N. is clearly butted against the curtain. Only scant remains survive on one flank of a quarry that has largely removed most of its fabric. The surviving portion is of Pennant Sandstone laid in earthy mortar like that of the curtain. The tower had been seated well down the natural scarp and a solid platform of slabs levelled up its interior.

---

[14] Evans, *op. cit*, f/n. 12, p. 62, No. 3.

Upon this there were traces of a stone paving set over clay to floor the basement at a level 4.27m below the surviving upper course of the curtain. This tower may be explained as a necessary protection on this side – although the ravine here is deep, the opposite slope rises steeply to command the castle.

The condition of this castle is regrettable. The gatehouse, in particular, would yield much information if fully cleared and consolidated. The elements are causing constant erosion and, though remote, it has not escaped the recent attentions of treasure-seekers.

King, p. 165.

Llangynwyd (E), Llangynwyd Middle (C)
SS 88 N.E. (8516–8866)   9.x.85   XXXIV N.W.

MR 3   Llanquian Castle

The diminutive Llanquian Castle occupies a spur on the lower eastern slopes of Stalling Down at 90m above O.D. and 2km E. of Cowbridge. It is 500m N. of the A48, the medieval Port Way. The position is strong, except to the S.W. where the ground rises towards Hollybush Farm; in this direction, 85m from the castle, is the medieval chapel of St James of Llanquian, an early possession of Tewkesbury Abbey.[1] Between the chapel and the castle, earthworks mark the site of a medieval homestead (Vol. III, Part 2, LH 46). The chapel pertained to Llanblethian church, with which it was granted to the abbey in the early-12th century.

Llanquian, or 'Lancovian', was a sub-manor of the member lordship of Llanblethian, held from the 12th century by the St Quintin family until it passed soon

[1] Clark, *Cartae*, I (cxxxvi), p. 134; *Epis. Acts*, II, No. L170, p. 659. Its identity is betrayed by alignment and the stumps of arch-braced trusses in a humble cottage, now derelict. Plan and brief description in Vol. IV (2), No. 581.

Fig. 189. Llanquian Castle viewed from the south

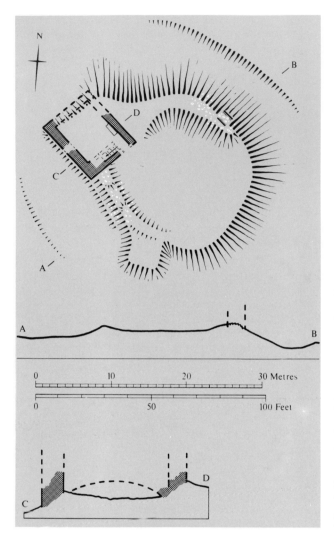

Fig. 190. Llanquian Castle: plan and profiles.

after 1220 to Siward of neighbouring Talyfan (Vol. III, Part 1b, LM 19), perhaps on marriage to the heiress.[2] In 1245 both Llanblethian and Talyfan were confiscated from Richard Siward by Earl Richard de Clare. It is only after this confiscation that we have any record of the sub-manor of Llanquian. In the 1262 extent of Glamorgan, Philip de Nerber of Castleton, St Athan (Vol. III, Part 1b, PC 2) was holding Llanquian as a quarter of a knight's fee, possibly enfeoffed by Earl Richard after 1245.[3] It remained with the Nerbers until the 16th century.[4] The tradition that Llanquian was at some time a castle of the de Wintons of Llandow (CR 11) has not been confirmed by any record.[5]

The castle (Fig. 190) consists of a slightly elevated circular knoll 20m in diameter with traces of a surrounding ditch to the S.W. and N.E. An irregular stony bank crowns the scarp of this mound, except on the S.E. side. On the N.W. a small rectangular stone building is awkwardly placed across the line of the bank and debris from its collapse may explain the thickening of the bank adjacent to it on the N. A much lesser bank runs S.E. from the building for 12m before fading out where a platform 4m square projects from the flank of the mound. Halfway between this platform and the building, the bank is reduced in height to suggest a possible entrance about 3m wide.

The rectangular stone building, 7.2m by 6.8m externally, survives to the level of the springing of the barrel vault of its basement (Fig. 190, section C–D), though it is largely masked by rubble which entirely covers its N. angle. The S.E. wall was 2.0m thick and accommodated a mural stair to the left of an entry at the E. corner. The S.W. wall is 1.2m thick, those to the N.W. and N.E. are 0.80m. The basement measures 6.2m by 5.6m internally and the springing of its vault survives for 2.0m along the N.E. wall, just above the level of the rubble filling it and masking any trace that may survive on the opposite side. These remains indicate a very small tower or first-floor hall.

A detailed description of the site was published by G. T. Clark in 1872.[6] At that date the remains were much better preserved. Its dry ditch, apparently then complete, was 2.44m deep, and a 'shell of masonry' outlined the whole perimeter upon the mound. Clark also observed the foundations of ruined chambers, including the surviving building, on the N.W. side, while he suspected a mural tower was concealed by a low mound to the N.E. (perhaps a mistake for our square 'platform' on the S.E.). Although the surviving rectangular building was then standing to a height of between 3.0m and 3.6m, no mention of its vault is recorded, a feature unlikely to have been missed by Clark – it was presumably masked at the time. He interpreted the structure as a small gatehouse, sufficient for such a small enclosure. Though

---

[2] Clark, *Arch. Camb.*, 1878, p. 15.

[3] Clark, *Cartae*, II (dcxv), p. 651; Corbett, *Glamorgan Lordship*, p. 36; Nicholl, *Normans*, p. 61.

[4] Clark, *Arch. Camb.*, 1867, pp. 376–80 and 1878, p. 17; *Cartae*, III (dccclxxxvi), p. 1053 and IV (mcxci-mcxcii), pp. 1628–30; J. A. Corbett, *Arch. Camb.*, 1889, pp. 73–4.

[5] Clark, *Cartae*, I, p. 161, n. and II, p. 655, n.; *Arch. Camb.*, 1872, p. 145 and 1878, p. 17, and *Med. Milit. Arch.*, II, p. 202.

[6] G. T. Clark, 'The Tower of Llanquian', *Arch. Camb.*, 1872, pp. 144–6 (reprinted in his *Med. Milit. Arch.*, II, pp. 201–3).

this may not be accepted, it is an interesting indication of the lack of any clear sign of an entrance at that date.

Excavations alone might discern the relationship of the rectangular tower with the ring-wall that must be accepted on Clark's evidence. Without his information the present stony bank only betrays slight traces of a wall 1.4m thick upon the ring-bank on the N.E. Neither Clark nor surface evidence indicate whether the ring-wall was of mortared masonry. If

a 12th-century castle-ringwork preceded it, beside an undoubted 12th-century chapel, it was the smallest in Glamorgan (Introduction, p. 80, Fig. 45). The date of the stone tower is uncertain, though Clark ascribed it to the reign of Henry III (1216–72).

King, p. 165.

Llanblethian
ST 07 S.W. (0189 7444)   9.iii.82   XLV N.E.

MR 4   Loughor Castle

Loughor Castle, established by Henry de Villers soon after 1106, was thought to be a large motte before the excavations carried out by Mr J. M. Lewis in 1968–71 and 1973.[1] He demonstrated that a primary castle-ringwork had been infilled, like that at Rumney (MR 7), in this case gradually, as successive phases of building were demolished and replaced. It also resembled Rumney in its location on the fringe of its lordship, near the mouth of a tidal river, at an important lowest crossing serving the main Roman road across South Wales.[2] The Afon Llwchwr marks the W. boundary of Gower lordship facing the commote of *Carnwyllion.* Talybont motte (MO 6), 5km N.N.E., protected another ancient crossing of the river. Swansea Castle (Vol. III, Part 1b, LM 18), *caput* of the medieval lordship of Gower, was 10.4km S.E. of Loughor near the mouth of the Tawe, and these castles flanked the root of the fertile peninsula where all but three of the lordship's castles are clustered.

Like the motte at Cardiff (MM 1), Loughor Castle lies within a Roman fort, *Leucarum* (Vol. I, Part II, No 733), which occupies the tip of a glacial promontory constricting the estuary where the south-flowing river turns W. to join the widening Burry Inlet. To the S. it overlooks extensive marshy flats flanking the meandering lower reaches of Afon Lliw, which joins the Llwchwr below the site.[3] Rail and road bridges now span the Llwchwr to an opposed promontory, but a ford about 60m above the latter bridge was negotiable for four hours at each tide in the early 19th century.[4] The location of the long-suspected Roman fort was only established in 1969 when its S.E. angle was disclosed beneath the S. and E. sides of the castle. Since the excavations at the Castle (and the account of *Leucarum* in Volume I of this Inventory), further work has greatly increased our knowledge of the extent and development of the fort.[5] Initially centred

on the site now occupied by the rebuilt church of St Michael, it was later reduced to exclude its S.W. third, retaining the ridge of greatest elevation occupied by both church and castle. In the Early Christian period continued use of the Roman road, and a hint of settlement, are indicated by a Roman altar reused in the 5th or early 6th century as a memorial inscribed with Oghams (Vol. I, Part 3, No. 845 and p. 21). The nature and duration of this settlement are uncertain, but when the castle was founded at the outset of the 12th century soil had formed over the ruins of the S.E. angle tower and the adjacent walls of the fort.

Loughor Castle was taken into state guardianship in 1946. In 1968 the main road to the N. was widened, cottages flanking the road were demolished, and the

---

[1] J. M. Lewis, 'Recent Excavations at Loughor Castle (South Wales)', *Château-Gaillard*, VII (1975), pp. 147–57. Mr. Lewis generously furnished detailed drawings of his excavations in advance of full publication and gave much valued advice. Mr Graham King, Planning Officer for West Glamorgan rendered further much-appreciated help by furnishing detailed drawings of the tower by his officer, Mr. Huw Daniel, which greatly assisted our survey and interpretations of the remains.

[2] Cardiff Castle (MM 1) is similarly sited on the river Taff, and Kenfig Castle (EM 2) on the now besanded estuary of the Cynffig, while the Roman crossing of the Nedd was flanked by Neath Castle (LM 11) and the vanished Granville's Castle (VE 2).

[3] Kenfig Castle (EM 2) might also occupy a Roman site. The vanished castle at Treoda (MM 2) was within a large rectangular enclosure of presumed Roman origin, while the unlocated Granville's Castle (VE 2) was in or near Neath Roman fort.

[4] Lewis, *Top. Dict.,* s.n. Loughor.

[5] R. and L. A. Ling, *Arch. Camb.,* CXXII (1973), pp. 99–146 (with account of Roman remains excavated at the castle by Mr. Lewis) and CXXVIII (1979), pp. 13–39. For a detailed interim report on later excavations by the Glamorgan-Gwent Archaeological Trust: H. S. Owen-John and D. R. Evans, *Glamorgan Gwent Annual Report*, 1983–84, pp. 66–115.

slope from the castle was landscaped. Exploratory trenching on the site of the demolished cottages produced Roman pottery and rampart material. There is no trace of the ditch to the N.W. and N., but its site is marked by a broad terrace to the E. and S., below a steep scarp rising up to 7.0m to a pair-shaped elevation measuring 29m by 23m and standing between 20m and 25m above the marshy flats to the S. Close to its apex on the S.W. a square stone tower, built out over the scarp, is the only upstanding masonry to survive. A slight bank around the perimeter marks the footings of the curtain-wall. Propitiously, a trench dug on the S.E. side of the presumed motte in the first full season of excavation (1969) identified the wall of the Roman fort towards the base of the mound, and within it the footings of the S.E. corner tower. Further trenches to the E. and S. soon defined the angle of the Roman fort. The castle-builders had capitalized on the natural elevation where it was augmented by the collapse and earthing over of this angle. This they isolated within a strong ditch and ring-bank in the first of five periods of building that were discerned:

Period I   (Ca. 1106–?1151):

The primary ring-bank survived to a maximum height of 2.0m, but retained no certain traces of its palisade. An insubstantial timber kitchen, 4.0m square and open to the W., was the only building asigned to this period. It lay on the E. side and was linked by a cobbled path to the vestiges of a circular oven set into the tail of the bank. On analogy with Penmaen (CR 18), it was assumed that the main residential quarters of this period were probably located in a timber gate-tower on the site of the later stone tower. The kitchen was destroyed by a fire that raged over the whole of the interior of the castle, a disaster which may well be related to a recorded destruction in 1151. Finds included decorated gaming counters, chessmen and plaques of bone, and carbonized unspun flax.

Period II   (?1151 to late 12th century):

In this phase the bank was extended inwards to furnish an elevated platform for timber buildings. These buildings were most clearly indicated to the N. and E. The N. building was 8.0m by 3m and defined by traces of the slots of its sill-beams and vestiges of a dry-stone W. gable. The E. building was indicated by parallel beam slots across the bank, the only traces

Fig. 191. Loughor Castle: aerial view from the east,

to survive. The floors of both buildings were of rammed gravel, and clay had been used to level the surface of the bank between them. A layer of mortar, predating the surviving tower and later curtain wall, suggested that the main accommodation in this period was in an earlier stone tower flanking the entrance to the E. This probability was strengthened by evidence that indicated that the surviving tower was raised on the site of an earlier stone building. Decorated gilt-bronze strips, pierced for application to wood or leather, were recovered from a midden that accumulated in this period over the lower central area.

Period III*   (late 12th to early 13th century):

Towards the close of the 12th century two or more stone buildings were raised over a sandy layer sealing the midden of Period II in the central area. Defined

Fig. 192. Loughor Castle: the Tower viewed from the interior.

by their footings and substantial cobbled floors, they had walls about 80cms wide and rounded angles. One was 4.5m by at least 8.0m externally and its siting required the prior demolition of the N. timber building of the previous period. The other was of uncertain width but at least 5.0m long.

Period IV* (?1220s to late 13th century):

A curtain-wall, ascribed to the 1220s, greatly strengthened the site at the outset of this period. Immediately below the turf, this wall survived to a maximum of about 1.5m on the N.E. and was almost

* See postscript for late revision.

267

2.0m wide. It had been frequently repaired and a sally-port 2.0m wide pierced it to the N. The only other structures related to this long period were two crude and small buildings raised on the sites of the timber buildings of Period II to the N. and E. sides. A green-glazed sherd of Ham Green ware sealed beneath the curtain and a crushed tripod-pitcher beneath adjacent building debris indicated a construction date in the first quarter of the 13th century.

Period V (late 13th century):

Towards the end of the 13th century the surviving square tower was inserted into the existing curtain wall. This was residential, but lacking in architectural embellishment. Its entire area was thrust out over the scarp from its inner N.E. wall on the line of the curtain, an arrangement designed to avoid encroachment upon the limited space available within, and probably over the vestiges of the tower of Period II. The adjacent W. ditch had been partly filled to ensure the stability of this tower (and probably that of its presumed prede-cessor). Its S.W. angle rose from a heavily stepped foundation, but where exposed towards the centre of the outer W. wall it rose directly from a flat masonry raft to suggest the incorporation of remnants of an earlier stone structure. These indications were largely confirmed within the tower where it was observed that the S. wall had been set in a trench cut through a pre-existing filling perhaps deposited to level the inter-ior of an earlier tower on the same site. A simple gateway pierced the curtain-wall beside the tower on the S.

Historical Background to the Periods of Building

Period I (ca. 1106–?1151):

Gŵyr commote was acquired by Henry de Beaumont, first Earl of Warwick, soon after the death of Hywel ap Goronwy in 1106.[6] By 1116 he had established Swansea Castle (LM 18) as *caput* of his new lordship of Gower, which castle withstood an assault in that year by Gruffydd ap Rhys of Deheubarth, who had first destroyed an un-named castle in Gower.[7] Only the castles at Loughor and Talybont (MO 6) could then have barred the western river-crossings and approach routes to Swansea; it was surely one of these that fell to Gruffydd in 1116. Both were granted by Earl Henry to his steward, Henry de Villers, who pro-

Fig. 193. Loughor Castle: entrance to the Tower.

bably founded Loughor soon after 1106 and seems to have acted as governor of Gower before the earl's death in 1119.[8] De Villers retained Loughor, but sub-enfeoffed Geoffrey Panchefot at Talybont.[9]

Following the death of Henry I (1135) the Welsh drove the Normans from Gower, inflicting a savage defeat on them between Loughor and Swansea on 1 January 1136.[10] Gower was soon recovered by Henry de Neubourg, youngest brother of Roger, 2nd Earl

---

[6] J. Beverley Smith, *Glam. Co. Hist.*, III, pp. 206–7; David Crouch, 'Oddities in the Early History of the Marcher Lordship of Gower, 1107–1166', *B.B.C.S.*, XXXI (1984), pp. 134–5. Gŵyr had been granted to Hywel by Henry I in 1102 (*Bruts*).

[7] *Bruts: B.S., Pen 20* and *R.B.H.*

[8] Crouch, *op. cit.* (n.6), p. 135.

[9] Clark, *Cartae*, I (clvii), pp. 155–6; *Epis. Acts*, I, D264, pp. 297–8 (being Bishop Peter de Leia's late-12th-century confirmation of (? a later) Henry de Viller's grant of land in Gilbert's fee to Neath Abbey, with the consent of Earl Henry. King John confirmed the same in 1208: *Cartae*, II (cccxvii), p. 316).

[10] *Gesta Stephani*, ed. K. R. Potter, Oxford, 1976, pp. 14–6; Lloyd, *Hist. Wales*, II, p. 470; Crouch, *op. cit.* (f/n. 6), pp. 136–7; Beverley Smith, *op. cit.* (n.6), p. 216. The battle is also recorded in the *Annals of Winchcombe* (Clark, *Cartae*, I (lxxxvii), p. 91).

of Warwick (1119–53), and thereafter this Henry ruled Gower until some date after 1166, issuing coins at Swansea before 1141, and probably exercising authority for his mother, Countess Margaret, who is thought to have held the lordship in dower from 1119.[11] Though Loughor is not mentioned, it would have been central to the Welsh invasion of 1136 and to Henry de Neubourg's campaign to recover the territory.

The conflagration that terminated the first period has been equated with the well-documented burning of the castle of *Aberllwchwr* by Maredudd and Rhys ap Gruffydd of Deheubarth in 1151.[12] This attack may well have terminated the interest of the de Villers in Loughor. Gower charters of *ca.* 1230 and *ca.* 1300 are witnessed respectively by Hugh and John de Villers,[13] but after 1151 the family is not recorded in association with Loughor.

Period II (?1151 to late 12th century):

There is evidence to suggest that Loughor was appropriated by Henry de Neubourg after the destruction of 1151 and was held by him until after 1166, when Gower finally reverted to his nephew William, the third Earl of Warwick (1153–84). This appears from his grant, in or after 1156, of the church beside the castle and a burgage in the town to the Knights of St John of Jerusalem.[14] The de Villers fee had become a demesne manor and a borough had been established, presumably within the vestiges of the Roman fort.[15] It is reasonable to attribute the rebuilding of Period II to Henry de Neubourg, assuming the validity of the ascription of the terminal conflagration of Period I to 1151 and accepting its consequent abandonment by de Villers. The strengthening of the ring-bank and the strongly suspected provision of a stone tower at the gate in this rebuilding would represent an appropriate response to the Welsh assault. Equally, finds such as the gilt-bronze strips in the midden, ornamental mounts once attached to wood or leather, and the first evidence for a borough, might be modest reflections of the prolonged period of tranquillity enjoyed by Gower during the reign of Henry II (1154–89), during which it passed into royal possession, for obscure reasons, on the death of Earl William in 1184.[16] The only mention of the castle from 1151 to the close of the century is a simple notice of its existence at the mouth of the Loughor by Gerald of Wales in his *Description of Wales*. It does not figure in the plundering of Gower by Rhys ap Gruffydd in 1189,

following the death of Henry II, nor in the records of the long siege of Swansea in 1192 and the consequent royal campaign to recover the territory.[17]

*Period III** (late 12th to early 13th century):

Two stone buildings raised over the midden in the central area are tentatively ascribed to this period (or to the outset of the next). Such limited and doubtful evidence may well reflect the spasmodic tenurial history of Gower in the early 13th century. Passing to King John on his accession in 1199, the lordship was granted to William de Braose in 1203, only to be repossessed by the king in 1208.[18] The sons of the discredited William de Braose (*ob.* 1211), Giles and Reginald, actively prosecuted claims to the lordship in an alliance with the Welsh princes, an alliance assured by the latter's marriage to a daughter of Llywelyn ap Iorwerth.[19] Swansea was burned by Rhys Gryg in 1212, and in 1215 Rhys ap Gruffydd took Loughor, Talybont, Oystermouth and 'all the castles of Gower'.[20] The consequent repossession of Gower by Reginald de Braose was brief, for in 1217 he came to terms with the new king, Henry III, and for this defection Llywelyn advanced on Swansea and installed Rhys Gryg, who proceeded to destroy the castles of Gower and apportion its lands among his followers.[21] Rhys Gryg was only dislodged from Gower by the armed intervention of Llywelyn in 1220, by then restored to royal favour, and it was finally bestowed on Reginald's nephew, John de Braose, in

---

[11] George C. Boon, *Welsh Hoards*, pp. 37, 49–50, 53–5, 77; Crouch, *op. cit.* (f/n. 6), 137–40.

[12] Lewis, *op. cit.* (f/n. 1), p. 152; *Bruts: B.S., Pen 20, R.B.H.*; *Ann. Camb*; Beverley Smith, *op. cit.* (f/n. 6), p. 216.

[13] Clark, *Cartae*, II (cccclxviii), p. 466; *Epis. Acts.*, I, D491, pp. 360–1; G. T. Clark, *Arch. Camb.*, 1868, p. 368.

[14] William Rees, *Order of St John*, p. 29 (incorrectly describing Henry as Earl of Warwick) and p. 38; *Epis. Acts.*, I, D499, p. 363; *Arch. Camb.* 1897, pp. 101, 204.

[15] Beresford, *New Towns*, pp. 556, 381 (n.3 questioning its burgality). Small and impoverished, Loughor never rivalled the only other borough in the lordship at Swansea. Merrick (*Morg. Arch.*, p. 145) notes its portreeve, annually elected by the burgesses and lord's steward.

[16] Beverley Smith, *op. cit.* (f/n. 6), pp. 218–19.

[17] *Ann. Camb.*, p. 57; Beverley Smith, *op. cit.* (f/n. 6), pp. 217–18.

[18] Clark, *Cartae*, II (cclxxxiii), pp. 287–8; Beverley Smith, *op. cit.* (f/n. 6), pp. 219–20.

[19] Beverley Smith, *op. cit.* (f/n. 6), pp. 221–2.

[20] *Ann. Margam*, p. 32; *Bruts: B.S., Pen 20, B.S.*; *Ann. Camb.* (s.a. 1214).

[21] *Ann. Camb.* (s.a. 1216); *Bruts: B.S., Pen 20, B.S.*

---

* See postscript for late revision.

that year.[22] The capture of Loughor Castle in 1215 is its only mention in this period; the modest (and questionable) structural development assigned to this period is not inappropriate for such turbulent times.

Period IV* (?1220s to late 13th century):

John de Braose (1220–1232) repaired Swansea Castle in 1221,[23] and the more settled conditions of this decade offer the probable context for the construction of the stone curtain-wall, a dating in accord with the ceramic evidence.[24] It seems probable that the primary stone tower, thought to have occupied the site of the surviving tower in Period II, was still standing on the line of the new plain curtain*. Without it accommodation it is hard to envisage the shabby little stone sheds on the N. as the only domestic buildings to be added in the refurbished castle. After an initial refortification, the archaeological evidence does not indicate a significant or active role for the castle, despite its strategic importance. The silence of the records accords with this. After a long minority, William de Braose II succeeded in 1241, and after assisting in the wars against Lleywelyn ap Gruffydd he entertained Edward I at Oystermouth Castle (LM 12) in 1284. This demesne castle, rather than Loughor, had become the lord's favoured alternative to Swansea.

Period V* (late 13th century):

The addition of the surviving stone tower, described below, terminates the structural history of the castle. Probably replacing an earlier tower of Period II, it was integrated with the earlier curtain wall on the N. and with the flank of a gateway in that curtain to the S. No architectural embellishment helps to date this simple structure, but its form is not inconsistent with the archaeological evidence for a date in the late 13th or early 14th century, after the Edwardian conquest of Gwynedd. Within these chronological limits there were two possible reasons for the final strengthening of the castle. One was the short-lived revolt of Rhys ap Maredudd in 1287, when Swansea and Oystermouth are known to have been attacked.[25] This episode left William de Braose II (1241–90) a few years in which he may have been inspired to improve the defences of his western outpost. The second possible context falls during the long rule of William de Braose III, though he might be an unlikely individual to be suspected of such constructive effort. A notorious profligate, he was forced to sell or give away countless estates, of which the castle, borough and manor of Loughor was the most striking alienation, and hardly an indication that he had expended any effort on it. In 1302 he granted Loughor to John Iweyn, his steward in Gower, who also received many lesser estates.[26] While the impecunious William is a most improbable castlebuilder during his tenure of Loughor from 1290 to 1302, its new lord may be regarded as one who may well have wished to improve his most estimable acquisition. Besides his stewardship of Gower, John Iweyn served as sheriff of Carmarthen in 1319, by which time he had become a leading official of Hugh Despenser, the despised lord of Glamorgan. He served Despenser at Dryslwyn and was appointed joint custodian of Neath where, during the baronial uprising against the lord of Glamorgan in 1321, he was captured and executed at Swansea.[27] This ambitious lord of Loughor may well have raised the tower when he acquired the castle in 1302.

Loughor reverted to the lords of Gower, despite petitions by Iweyn's heiress.[28] Subsequent notices of the 'castle and town' or 'castle and manor' in manorial deeds listing the possessions of the lords of Gower occur in 1322 (*Loghern*), 1396 (*Louchwarne*) and 1469/70 (*Lloughour*),[29] but these are uninformative. In the 1530s the castle is noticed by Leland, without his usual comment on its condition, but 'the ruinous walls of an old castle' are noticed by Merrick in 1587.[30]

Description and Discussion of the Remains

The pear-shaped eminence occupied by the castle is prominent on the S. side of the main road above a grassy landscaped slope (plan, Fig. 194). There is no surface evidence for the buried Roman fort angle. The

---

[22] *Cal. Anc. Corr.*, IV, 18, p. 24.

[23] *Bruts*: *B.S.*, *Pen 20*, *B.S.*

[24] Lewis, *op. cit.* (n.1), pp. 156–7.

[25] Beverley Smith, *op. cit.* (f/n. 6), p. 230.

[26] *Cal. Anc. Petitions*, No. 5449, p. 173 (n.) and No. 7975, pp. 269–70 (n.); Ralph A. Griffiths, *The Principality of Wales in the Later Middle Ages*, I, South Wales, (1972), pp. 258, 268; R. R. Davies, *Lordship and Society in the March of Wales, 1282–1400*, (Oxford, 1978), p. 100 (n.41); Clark, *Cartae*, III (dcccxciii), p. 1066.

[27] Griffiths, *ibid*; for his inquisition *post mortem*, see Clark, *Cartae*, III (dccccvi), p. 1096.

[28] His niece and heiress Alice petitioned for her inheritance, including the castle and town of 'Lochorne': *Cal. Anc. Petitions*, pp. 173, 269.

[29] For 1322: Clark, *Cartae*, III (dcccccvii), pp. 1100–1; for 1396, *Cartae*, IV (mlxxi), p. 1391; for 1469–70: *Inq. post mortem* of William Herbert, Earl of Pembroke, 9 Edward IV.

[30] Leland, *Itin. Wales*, p. 127; Merrick, *Morg. Arch.*, p. 145.

* See postscript for late revision.

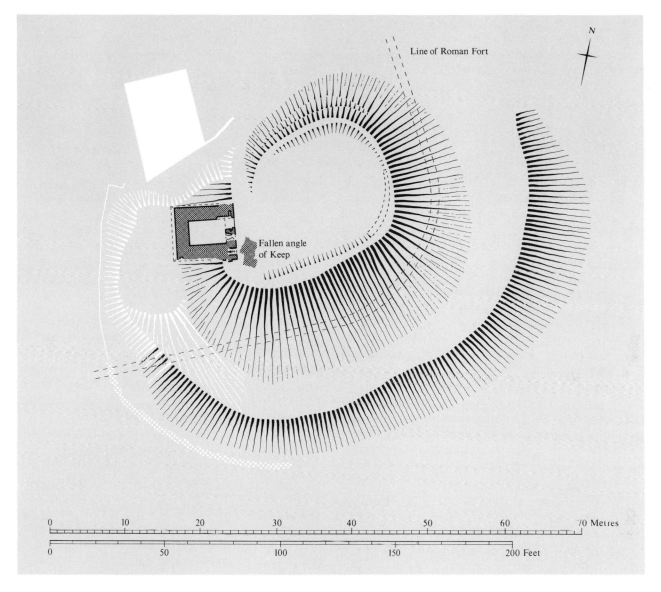

Fig. 194. Loughor Castle: general plan.

site and its immediate surrounds are similarly open and grassed, except to the N.W., where a former Gospel Hall lies partly over the line of the ditch. A continuous terrace marks the line of the ditch to the S. and E., skirting the foot of a steep scarp up to 7m high. The level summit has opposed diameters of about 29m and 23m; a low stony bank around its perimeter, marking the course of the curtain wall, is only absent towards the tower on the W.

The area enclosed upon this elevation is small; of the 27 certain castle-ringworks in Glamorgan only the little site at Llanquian (MR 3) is smaller (Fig. 45, p. 80). It is probable that a bailey formerly existed

along the ridge towards the site of the church which lies about 60m to the W. There are no certain traces of this, though attention has been drawn to the scarped churchyard perimeter.[31] In retrospect Loughor's identification as a motte was improbable; its low, broad summit, small for a castle-ring, is, nevertheless, roughly equal to that of the great motte at Cardiff (MM 1) and about double those of the next largest mottes in the county (Fig. 16, p. 52). Rumney (MR 7) was similarly misidentified as a motte before excavations showed the same broad structural deve-

---

[31] Derek Renn, *Norman Castles*, p. 231.

271

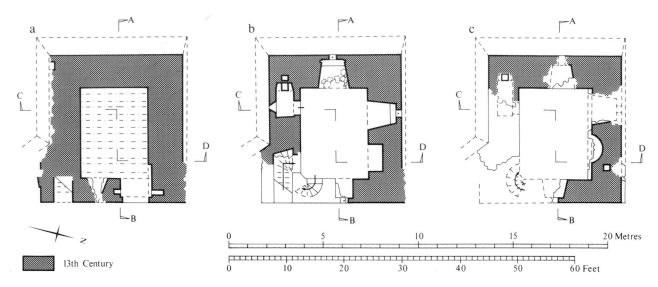

Fig. 195. Loughor Castle, the Tower: (a) ground floor; (b) first floor; (c) second floor.

lopment there as at Loughor.

The Tower of Period V (Figs. 192, 195–97) is the only upstanding masonry surviving on the site. Though small, it was the most substantial structure that existed here, unless rivalled by the earlier tower that it seems to have replaced. A residential tower with two floors above a basement, it survives to the level of the second floor where sufficient vestiges remain to establish the arrangements of that chamber, but nothing remains to indicate the form of the roof and battlements. The lower floors are intact, except for the greater part of a stair that occupied the S.E. angle. This fell away in the 1940s, but survives as one large prostrate block indicated on the general plan, and restored in finer lines on the detailed plans of

the tower (Figs. 194, 195). The masonry is of random slabs of Pennant Sandstone, intermittently coursed and set in lime mortar. There is no use of ashlar; the same rough slabs form the angles, and outline all openings, set as voussoirs for the arches and rear arches of the latter. Each of the upper floors was provided with a fireplace and latrine, but despite these necessary comforts the building was cramped, austere, and devoid of any architectural embellishment.

The inner E. wall was set in line with the pre-existing and now vanished curtain-wall of Period IV. At the N.E. corner five projecting horizontal toothing courses high on the N. wall show how the tower was integrated with the curtain. On the S. face an angled stub of the curtain survives high above faint surface indications of the side of a gate-passage; further S. an opposed termination of the earlier ring-work suggests that the entrance was always in this position alongside the later tower.[32] To the W. of this inner wall the tower was boldly thrust out over the ditch. To ensure stability the ditch had been partly infilled and the three outer walls were raised on battered lower courses. The briefly exposed indications of earlier masonry foundations incorporated at the base of the tower are no longer visible, and the robbing of the facing has left only the upper courses of the batter along these outer faces. This low-level robbing extends around the S.W. angle and along the S. wall, but the exposed core retains the inner part of a latrine outfall

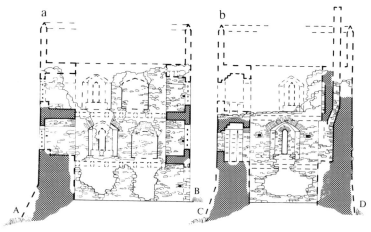

Fig. 196. Loughor Castle, the Tower: cross-sections A-B and C-D, as indicated on Fig. 195, a-c.

---

[32] Lewis, *op. cit.* (f/n. 1), p. 155 and *Med. Arch.*, XVI (1972), p. 186.

near the angle and serving both upper floors.

The construction of the tower over the scarp is a clear indication of the desire to avoid any encroachment on the limited area of the enclosed court. In the 12th century the Norman rectangular keeps at Clun (Shrops.) and Guildford (Surrey) were similarly raised on the scarps of mottes, as was the large D-shaped tower of the 13th century thrust out from the shell wall around the motte at Llandovery (Carms.). In Glamorgan a parallel at a castle-ringwork may be indicated by the scant vestiges of the keep unearthed at Rumney (MR 7), though that was insecurely founded with only one angle thrust out over the ditch.

Above the batter, present on three of its sides, the Loughor tower measures 8.0m by 7.0m externally. Though the building might be considered as a late example of the keep, its dimensions exceed only those of the little tower at Llanquian (MR 3: 7.2m by 6.8m) and approximate to those of the S. flanking tower at Newcastle (EM 3: 8.0m by 8.0m), where an internal free-standing keep is suspected. Others in the county are larger (see Introduction, pp. 39–43).

The ground floor was entered from the court by a wide door towards the N. end of the E. wall. A smaller second door at the S. end of this front, beyond a small loop, served a mural stair to the first floor in the S.E. angle, now fallen down but discernible in the adjacent prostrate block. The basement door retains its draw-bar holes, segmental-headed rear arch and a recess for its door on the right. The remaining internal walls were plain, and with only the small loop to the E. this chamber could only have served as a store. Its floor was levelled with that of the court, a levelling seemingly inherited from the previous stone structure in this position into which the bedding trench for the surviving S. wall was cut. The arrangements to bar its door from the inside may suggest that a trap door gave access through the floor above, which was supported on seven large transverse beams set in deep sockets.

The first-floor chamber was reached by a narrow angled stone stair from the smaller door at ground level in the E. wall. This stair was ceiled with well-layered alternating straight and chevron-set cross-slabs that are well preserved in the fallen fragment of masonry. The W. jamb of the upper door opening into the chamber remains *in situ*, the rest has fallen. To the W. of the entry, set in the S. wall, is a slab-roofed latrine-chamber, with seat and shaft, and lit by a tiny light to the S. Diagonally opposite the latrine in the N. wall is a recessed plain fireplace retaining

a few voussoirs of its former segmental head set flush with the wall. Alongside the fireplace in the N. wall, and centrally in the W. wall, are similar windows; the W. window is almost intact, but the other vestigial (Fig. 197). Both windows were set in wide splayed recesses, a little above floor level, and beneath segmental heads and rear arches. At their outer ends the recesses narrowed for small single lights which retain clear evidence for their iron grills. The best preserved W. window retains small bar-holes behind the outer jambs for securing shutters; a paving of slabs survives within the recess. In the E. wall one jamb survives of a third smaller unsplayed window serving this chamber, and S. of this was formerly the door for the stair to the upper floor, now evidenced in the fallen block below.

The upper chamber, reached by the last-mentioned newel stair, had its upper door directly over that to the first floor. Surviving masonry at this level makes clear that with minor differences the features of this chamber were identical and similarly disposed to those of the floor below. Indications of a latrine-chamber survive on the truncated wall top to the S., served by a chute with an outfall common to both floors.

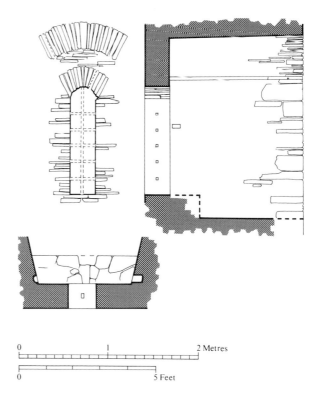

0   1   2 Metres

0   5 Feet

Fig. 197. Loughor Castle, the Tower: the west window on the first floor.

Here the fireplace opposite is set in a rounded recess. Finally, there are vestiges sufficient to indicate windows in the W. and N. walls matching those immediately below them. Only in the E. wall is the window different from its lower counterpart; here it is larger and splayed to match the W. and N. windows, and it has moved to a central position leaving no room towards the S.E. corner for a further stair to the battlements. This could only have occupied the vanished S. wall at this level.

Postscript:

Mr. J. M. Lewis is now preparing his final report on the Loughor excavation. Recent reappraisal of the evidence has resulted in a revision of the chronological scheme outlined above. The crux of the matter is that evidence for the extensive burning, formerly equated with the chronicled destruction of the castle in 1151, is now thought to relate mainly to the later destruction of 1215. Evidence for the fire of 1151 is present, but had been conflated with that of 1215. Further, it is now clear that the curtain wall, formerly assigned on grounds of historical probability to *c.* 1220, pre-dated the later fire, making it pre-1215, if the identification of the fire with the historical event of that year is valid. The consequent revision effects only periods III and IV above.

To summarise:

Period III (Late 12th/early 13th century–?1215): Building of the curtain wall, preceded by the demolition of the buildings on the bank; destruction in the interior involving a fire.

Period IV (?1215–late 13th century): Construction of dry-stone buildings in centre.

King, p. 166.

Loughor (E), Loughor Borough (C)
SS 59 N.E. (5642 9798)   1.iv.87   XIV S.W.

MR 5   Ogmore Castle

Ogmore Castle preserves the form of its primary castle-ringwork and bailey to an exceptional degree, despite the imposed masonry of its inner ward (Fig. 200). The castle was established by William de Londres by 1116, probably before the death of Fitzhamon in 1107. After the death of Thomas de Londres (*ca.* 1216) successive marriages of his heiress, Hawise de Londres, took it in turn to Walter de Braose (1223–34), Henry de Turberville (dead by 1240) and Patrick de Chaworth (1243–58). Hawise was finally succeeded by her sons Payn and Patrick de Chaworth (1274–78; 1278–83). In 1298, after a period of royal wardship, another heiress, Maud de Chaworth, carried Ogmore in marriage to Henry of Lancaster, and established a connection with the Duchy (as it was known from 1351) which endures to our times.[1] With the Duchy of Lancaster, the castle came to the crown on the accession of Henry IV in 1399.

The castle has been in guardianship since 1928 and its conserved remains reflect its tenurial history. The primary earthwork castle, the masonry defences of the inner ward, and most internal buildings may be attributed to the de Londres lords (*ca.* 1100–*ca.* 1216). The successive and brief tenures of Braose, Turberville and Chaworth are not securely reflected in the fabric, and only the lime-kiln and court-house in the outer ward may be attributed to Lancaster. Like Newcastle (EM 3), Ogmore preserves virtually intact the defences of an early stone castle which probably existed before 1216. After this, the exceptional lack of later 13th-century masonry is partly explained by the four changes of ownership during that century, particularly as the de Londres inheritance also included Kidwelly, a greater and more exposed castle where major works certainly pre-occupied the Chaworths,[2] no doubt to the neglect of this less vulnerable castle in Glamorgan.

Ogmore Castle lies on the E. bank of Afon Ewenni half a kilometre above its junction with the Afon Ogwr which joins the sea 2.2km to the S.W. From the S.E. the site is dominated by the steeply rising slopes of Ogmore Down, but this weakness was balanced by the double protection of the converging rivers to the N.W., the Ogwr being a mere 190m beyond the Ewenni across a flat marshy plain. Fitzhamon's castle on the W. bank of the Ogwr at Newcastle, Bridgend (EM 3), 3.7km to the N.E., is first recorded in 1106. There is reason to suspect that Ogmore was as early. The distribution of grants to the abbeys of Gloucester and Tewkesbury suggests strongly that the Ogwr Valley

---

[1] The best account of the lordship is by Professor R. R. Davies in *Glam. Co. Hist.* III, Chapter VI, pp. 285–311. See also H. T. Randall in C. A. Ralegh Radford, *Ogmore Castle* (Official Guide leaflet, 1971), pp. 1–2; Corbett, *Glamorgan Lordship*, pp. 77–8; Nicholl, *Normans*, pp. 77–84, 154–60.

[2] John R. Kenyon, *Kidwelly Castle* (Official Guidebook, Cadw, 1986).

marked the western limits of appropriation under Fitzhamon (*ob.* 1107).[3] By 1114, William de Londres was certainly serving at Kidwelly under Bishop Roger of Salisbury, who had been established there in 1106.[4]

Ogmore Castle is first mentioned in 1116. In that year William de Londres abandoned it, with 'all his cattle and all his precious wealth', when facing an attack by Gruffydd ap Rhys ap Tewdwr who had already ravaged Gower.[5] It is not known whether the attack materialized, but the wealth noted by the chronicler need not be doubted: Ogmore was the westernmost of four particularly large coastal lordships and was held by the service of four knights.[6] It contained the parishes of St Brides, Ewenny, Wick and the hamlet of Lampha, while its large detached Welshry of Glynogwr lay in the hills between the Ogwr and Garw Rivers, beyond Coity lordship. William de Londres

had been succeeded by his son Maurice by 1126. Maurice founded nearby Ewenny Priory (LM 5) in 1141, where his fine tomb survives.[7] By this date Maurice had also acquired the lordship and castle of Kidwelly, and perhaps that at Oystermouth (LM 12), where the church was among his generous endowments to the new priory.[8]

---

[3] *Glam. Co. Hist.*, III, pp. 14, 286; Ralph Griffiths, *Glamorgan Historian*, III (1966), p. 162; Randall, *op. cit.* (f/n. 1), pp. 1–2.

[4] Griffiths, *ibid*; Kenyon, *op. cit.* (f/n. 2), p. 4.

[5] *Bruts: B.S., Pen. 20, R.B.H.*

[6] *Liber Niger*; Clark, *Cartae*, II (dcxv), p. 650; *Glam. Co. Hist.*, III, pp. 288–9; Corbett, *Glamorgan Lordship*, pp. 34, 118; Nicholl, *Normans*, pp. 77, 82, 90.

[7] *Glam. Co. Hist.*, III, p. 287; C. A. Ralegh Radford, *Ewenny Priory* (Official Guide Leaflet, 1952); J. Conway Davies, *N.L.W. Journal*, III, (1943–44), pp. 107–37 (esp. pp. 120–2).

[8] Conway Davies, *ibid*, pp. 120, 124; Nicholl, *Normans*, p. 78.

Fig. 198. Ogmore Castle: the castle-ringwork viewed from the Outer Ward on its south-west flank.

Most documentation is late and of little assistance in interpreting the remains. A charter of Maurice de Londres, dating between 1139 and 1149, grants Ewenny rights of pasture alongside his castle of 'Hugemore'.[9] We also know of four mesne tenancies within the lordship which were held by knight service (Colwinston, Lampha, Dunraven and Pitcot), and of two dozen lesser tenants who performed ward of castle at Ogmore or Cardiff. Though only known from 15th-century rentals, this subinfeudation probably originated in the 12th century.[10]

Unpublished records of the Duchy of Lancaster show frequent expenditure on repairs and maintenance at Ogmore Castle in the late Middle Ages. Although new works were not significant, these records are of interest for naming various buildings within the castle, some of them now vanished.[11] In 1380–81 a carpenter was employed for fifty-three days building a *pantry* and *butchery* in the *hall* with timber brought from Neath.[12] Soon after Ogmore came to the Crown with the Duchy on the accession of Henry IV in 1399, Welsh rebels supporting Owain Glyndŵr spread devastation throughout the lordship in the years 1402–05.[13] The castle was not spared, for its 'Knighting Chamber' was burned by the insurgents and remained derelict until 1442–44 when it was restored at a cost of £10. 18s. 8½d. to accommodate the Duchy Council and their officers.[14] Welsh tenants of Ogmore were granted royal pardons in 1407 and 1410.[15] In the aftermath of the rebellion the Duchy accounts for the decade 1413–22 record the respective expenditures of £158 and £618 on the castles of Kidwelly and Carreg Cennen, with works undertaken in all but three of these years; in contrast, the meagre sum of £7. 12s. 3d. was expended at the less exposed Ogmore Castle, and that not until 1421–22.[16]

In 1429–30 the *bridge* fronting the castle gate at Ogmore was repaired, and crest-tiles were brought from Cardiff in 1441–42 to repair the roofs of the *chapel* and unspecified towers.[17] The restoration of the 'Knighting Chamber' in 1442–44 has already been noticed. Expenditure in 1445–46 included 10s. for a key for the 'Great Gate'. A total of £31. 10s. 1d. was expended on repairs during the 1450s. Repairs were made to the *exchequer*, the *chapel* and unspecified buildings; works costing £6. 4s. 1d. (1450–51) and £4. 8s. 0d. (1454–55) were undertaken on the 'Great Tower' (or Keep), and the *Court-house* in the outer ward was rebuilt for £2. 7s. 2d. (1454–55).[18] The latter sum was too small to account for the existing building within the outer ward. Further repairs were under-

taken in 1460–61, and finally the 'gable of the castle' was made good for £6. 3s. 4d. in 1511–12.[19]

In 1477 Ogmore was granted by Edward IV to his brother, Richard, Duke of Gloucester, in exchange for the castle and lordship of Elfael in Radnor, though it soon reverted to the Crown on the latter's accession in 1483.[20] The rentals suggest that castle-guard was still performed at Ogmore in the 15th century, and it was still '. . . meatly welle maintainid' when seen by Leland in the late 1530s.[21] By 1631, however, a detailed survey of the lordship noted that '. . . Ogmour Castle hath been in decay these many yeeres, and that there is one court house unto the same belonging which is now in sufficient reparacion . . .'. Courts leet were held at this court-house twice a year and courts baron monthly.[22]

Description: *The Primary Castle*

Despite later masonry, the nature of the castle raised in *ca.* 1100 by William de Londres is clear. It consisted of a castle-ringwork and spade-shaped bailey set against Afon Ewenni. The reasonable assumption that the curtain wall broadly follows the line of the original palisade indicates an oval ringwork enclosing an area 50m by 35m. The bailey betrays no indication that it was ever walled, the spur walls carried across the main ditch presumably linking with its palisade. This

Fig. 199. *(Opposite)* Ogmore Castle: reconstruction drawing depicting the site as it may have appeared in the early thirteenth century.

---

[9] Clark, *Cartae*, VI (mdxlvi), p. 2268.
[10] Davies, *op. cit.* (f/n. 1), p. 289; Nicholl, *Normans*, pp. 155–9.
[11] These records are cited by the *P.R.O.* call numbers, thanks to the kindness of Professor Rees Davies, historian of Ogmore (see f/n. 1), who furnished relevant extracts from his personal transcripts.
[12] D.L. 29/592/9445 m.4.
[13] Davies, *op. cit.* (f/n. 1), pp. 300–2.
[14] D.L. 29/593/9494–5; Davies, *op. cit.* (f/n. 1), p. 300; *Hist. Kings Works*, II, pp. 768–9.
[15] *Cal. P.R.*, 1408–13, p. 166; Clark, *Cartae*, IV (mci), pp. 1461–2.
[16] *Ex inf.* Professor Rees Davies; for Ogmore Castle: D.L. 29/732/12031/m.8.
[17] D.L. 29/593/9489 and 29/592/9493.
[18] D.L. 29/593/9499–9503; *Hist. Kings Works*, II, p. 769.
[19] D.L. 29/596/9558.
[20] Clark, *Cartae*, V (mccxxxi), pp. 1706–9; Davies, *op. cit.* (f/n. 1), p. 305; D.L. 37/46, no. 15.
[21] Leland, *Itin. Wales*, p. 28.
[22] Clark, *Cartae*, VI (mdiii), pp. 2177–93, esp. pp. 2182, 2188 and 2193, n.

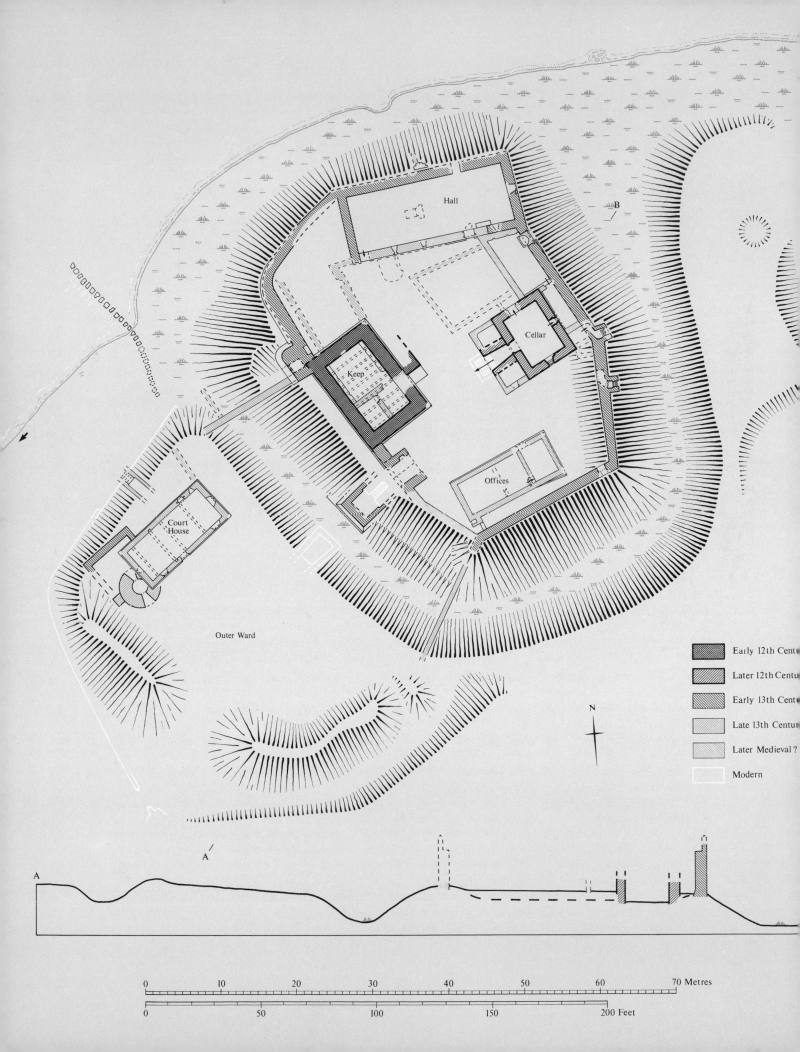

Hall

B

Cellar

Keep

Offices

Court
House

Outer Ward

Early 12th Centu...

Later 12th Centu...

Early 13th Centu...

Late 13th Centu...

Later Medieval?

Modern

N

A

A

A

| 0 | 10 | 20 | 30 | 40 | 50 | 60 | 70 Metres |

| 0 | | 50 | | 100 | | 150 | | 200 Feet |

followed the scarped river bank to the N., and continued along a strong curving bank which survives to
W. and S. A central break in this bank on the E.
marks the entrance, directly facing that to the
ringwork, now marked by the later stone gateway.
On thc W. a lane has destroyed the bailey ditch, fronting the entrance, but it survives to the S. This remaining segment of the bailey ditch ends high and dry
above the counterscarp of the much more massive
rock-cut ditch of the ringwork, which is still flooded
by high tides. It is probable that the main ditch was
originally little, if at all, deeper than that of the bailey;
it was no doubt deepened to strengthen the inner ward
and to furnish stone for building its curtain-wall. The
same process is equally apparent at Coity Castle (MR
1). When the inner ward was walled in the early 13th
century, its ring-bank was levelled and the material
used to raise the internal level by about one metre,
as demonstrated at the 'cellar', described below. The
slight inner fall on the S. and S.E. sides is more probably spoil redeposited during modern clearance than
vestiges of the ring-bank.

Description: *The Stone Castle*

The masonry of the Inner Ward, excepting minor later
additions, is all of the 12th or early 13th centuries.
It represents three periods of work. *The Keep* came
first, early in the 12th century. This was followed later
in that century by the *'Cellar'*. Finally, the *Curtain,
Gateway* and *Bridge-pit* were added very early in the
13th century, together with the *Hall* on the N., and
perhaps the *'Offices'* to the S.

(i) *The Keep* (Figs. 144, 201–05).

The substantial vestiges of a rectangular Keep of three
storeys flank the N. side of the entrance to the Inner
Ward. Externally it measures 14m by 9.7m, excluding
a battered base. Above this batter its walls are 1.8m
thick. The W. wall survives to a height of 12.50m and
discloses much of the arrangements of a Norman first-
floor hall, and some traces of a second floor which
was added later. The other walls only survive at basement level, except for a stub of the N. wall retaining
one side of a Norman opening on the first floor. The
Keep is built of irregular boulders, glacial pebbles,
and thin Lias Limestone slabs, all set in a brown mortar. The quoins are of roughly-dressed blocks at the
base of the S.W. angle, but of Sutton Stone ashlar
above. Sutton Stone is also lavishly used for the dress-

Fig. 200. *(Opposite)* Ogmore Castle: general plan and profile.

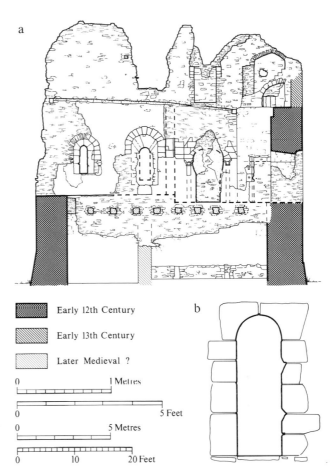

Fig. 201. Ogmore Castle, Keep: (a) cross-section, looking south-west;
(b) window on first floor, southern end of south-west wall.

ings of the windows and fireplace on the first floor;
the quarries of this widely-used stone were only 2.5km
distant, at Southerndown to the S.W.

The present entrance to the basement is inserted,
as are the walls defining a small chamber in its S.W.
angle and the benches, these last slotted for some form
of shelving. There were no original openings at this
level, the basement stores being reached by a trap door
in a floor indicated by beam holes in the W. wall.
First-floor access was by an external stair, probably
indicated by the square foundation set against the E.
wall.

The first floor seems to have been sub divided transversely, and its lesser N. end was heated by a fine
fireplace with a projecting round-headed hood (Fig.
205). Three voussoirs survive of the hood which was
carried on round columns with early cubical capitals.
The hearth was set in a curved recess and smoke-holes
pierced the back of the flue a little above the chimney
breast. Sutton Stone was used in the construction of

279

this fireplace and also for the two windows piercing the other half of the W. wall. Both retain much of the finely-jointed ashlar of their round-headed embrasures, particularly the northernmost, though its high cill has been lowered to floor level; original proportions are displayed by the other. Both embrasures splay to narrow external openings, the southernmost retaining its rounded head and jambs of Sutton Stone, the other only its head. Between the hood of the fireplace and the upper part of the northermost window a squared ashlar feature projects 0.3m from the wall. Its former downward continuation is indicated by the clear margin of the plaster extending towards the fireplace. It seems that this feature was set upon a step marking a raised floor level, served by the two windows, which was 0.6m above that of the lesser N. end. A timber partition might be suspected across the first floor at this point.

Fig. 202. Ogmore Castle; the Keep and Gateway; interior view from the north-east.

The only surviving feature of the S. wall, at this level, is a small patch of paving indicating a door leading out towards similar paving over the vault of the early-13th-century Gateway, and presumably an insertion of that time. In the opposite N. wall the upper part of the W. jamb and round head of an opening, dressed in ashlar, are retained on the surviving stub of the wall. This unsplayed opening appears to have been an original Norman window enlarged as a door to provide access to the wall-walk when the curtain was added, presumably by means of a short timber walk-way across the internal angle.

Fig. 203. Ogmore Castle, the Keep: (f) ground floor; (e) first floor; (d) second floor; (a) latrine turret, section A-B; (b) stair window, first floor; (c) latrine turret, south-east light of lower garderobe.

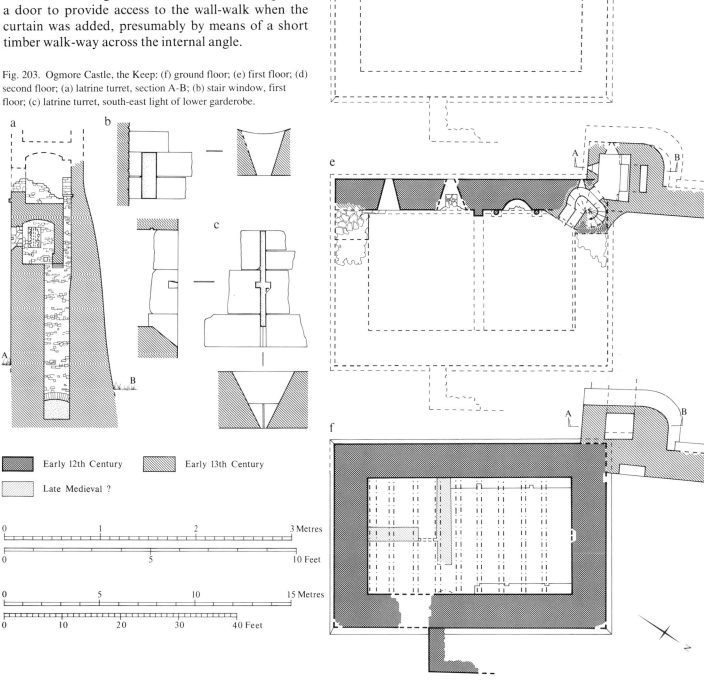

Early 12th Century
Early 13th Century
Late Medieval ?

| 0 | 1 | 2 | 3 Metres |

| 0 | 5 | 10 Feet |

| 0 | 5 | 10 | 15 Metres |

| 0 | 10 | 20 | 30 | 40 Feet |

Fig. 204. Ogmore Castle Keep: cutaway reconstructing the primary Norman work.

Originally the first floor was the upper floor of the Keep. Its gabled roof ran the length of the building and is marked by a longitudinal slot joining a beam hole at each end of the W. wall. Subsequently, a second-floor chamber was added, its masonry clearly marked externally, being set out slightly on the line of its lowest course at the level of the primary roof.

This added upper chamber was heated by a fireplace above that to the hall, and served by its chimney. The fireplace retains simple concave-moulded corbels which formerly held a modest projecting hood of indeterminate form.

When the stone curtain of the Inner Ward was added in the early 13th century it terminated against

Fig. 205. Ogmore Castle Keep: the Norman first floor fireplace reconstructed.

the N.W. angle of the Keep, incorporating an integral latrine turret clasping that angle. At the same time a newel stair was inserted in the angle, linking the upper chambers of the Keep and providing each of them with access to a latrine in the turret. This stair continued upwards from the second floor and the upper latrine-chamber to reach the wall top. Good ashlar quoins surviving on the angle of the second-floor chamber of the Keep at this point suggest that this chamber was first completed before the turret was itself heightened to serve it.

(ii) *The 'Cellar'* (Figs. 206, 207).

The 'Cellar' is a free-standing rectangular structure lying opposite the Keep on the E. side of the Inner Ward. It measures 9.55m by 7.50m externally, with walls 1.10m thick. Only its basement survives, this entered originally down three steps and a ramp within a barrel-vaulted passage to a door at the centre of its W. wall. This vaulted passage was butted against the building but is probably a part of the original design. The floor of the basement is 80cm below the assumed original level of the interior but its E. wall is founded at this height above the floor – suggesting that the structure was set against the inner tail of the ring-bank. When the material of the bank was used to level up the interior of the Inner Ward in the early 13th century, additional steps were added externally to those within the vaulted passage, increasing the depth of its basement to 1.6m (these steps are now retained within a modern revetment wall).

The building is constructed of roughly coursed rubble, but it has good squared quoins, and similarly dressed blocks are used for the main door and the internal walls of the sloping passage. The main door within this passage has lost its head, but the form of the abutting vault shows it to have been rounded. High windows pierced the end walls, that to the N. broken through for an inserted doorway; it presumably matched the S. window (Fig. 206e) which retains its boldly stepped cill and rear-arch and formerly held a small square frame with central bar. A small original door was set in the E. wall.

The placing of this 'Cellar' presents an interesting parallel to the keep at Kenfig and that vanished at Newcastle (EM 2, 3). Both of these were also free-standing within a ringwork. The 12th-century date of the 'Cellar' is not in doubt: it clearly precedes the construction of the early-13th-century curtain and its masonry is markedly Norman. Although its upper levels have vanished, traces of longitudinal slots where its walls are truncated may possibly indicate a timber superstructure. Radford presumed that the rather better masonry of this structure was later than that of the Keep, and that it was not built until late in the 12th century.[23] No dateable mouldings survive *in situ*, but two re-used dressings are built into the wall inserted between the rear wall and the E. curtain. These mouldings display sunk panels paralleled by the dressings of the gateway at Newcastle (EM 3), which are best seen as work of *ca.* 1180. If these came from the cellar they would confirm Radford's dating. The limited fenestration of this structure sug-

---

[23] C. A. Ralegh Radford, *Ogmore Castle* (Official Guide-Leaflet, 1971), p. 3.

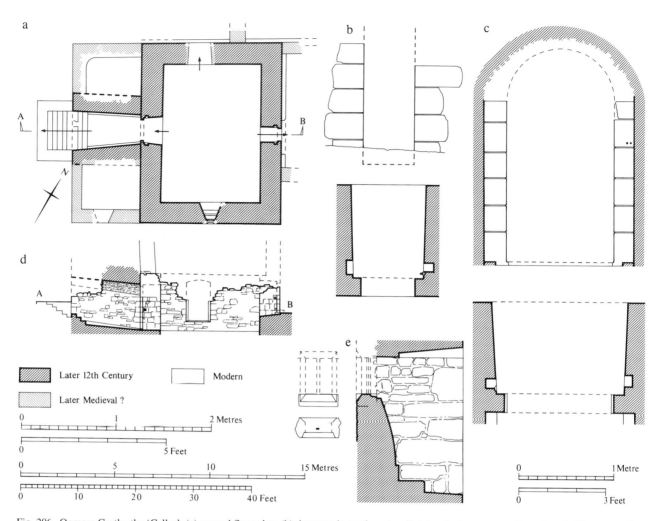

Fig. 206. Ogmore Castle; the 'Cellar': (a) ground floor plan; (b) doorway in north-east wall; (c) main doorway, south-west wall; (d) cross-section A-B; (e) window in south-east wall.

gests it served for storage. Its thick walls indicate a substantial vanished superstructure, possibly of timber and presumably of a domestic nature, unless this building housed the *exchequer* recorded in the 15th century.

(iii) *The Curtain, Gateway, Hall and Offices*

The remainder of the masonry of the Inner Ward is very largely of the early 13th century, the third period of building. This dating of the curtain is best demonstrated by the complete lack of flanking; not one mural tower was raised. The curtain also displays the faceted 12th-century construction seen at Coity (MR 1), Newcastle (EM 3) and at the Keep at Cardiff (MM 1), though lacking the bold alternating quoins of Sutton Stone at their angles. The curtain is between 5.0m and 5.5m high at its paved wall-walk, and where least eroded the parapet rises a further 1.60m on the E.

side. On the S. side the wall is 1.15m thick at base, narrowing slightly to its confined wall-walk (5.5m high and only 0.5m wide). A small postern existed in the E. curtain close to its junction with the S.E. angle of the contemporary hall. The plain-chamfered jambs of this door survive, but its head is gone. This postern was later blocked and its recess used for an inserted fireplace serving a small chamber contrived between the Hall and the 'Cellar'.

South of the postern a latrine was housed in a small turret adjacent to the S.E. angle of the 'Cellar'. This latrine-turret was matched by another of similar type a further 4.6m along the next facet and not previously noticed. To the W., wing walls crossed the ditch to link with the palisade protecting the bailey. Openings at the bottom of these walls permitted the entry of water from the river, a function now renewed at high

284

Fig. 207. Ogmore Castle: the 'Cellar'. Elevated view from the west.

tides since the clearance of the ditch during conservation.

The main gateway (Fig. 208) on the W., adjacent to the Keep, consisted of a simple vaulted passage between two inward projections of its flanking walls. That it constituted a most modest gatehouse is suggested by the paved floor above the vault. Its overall dimensions are 5.1m by 3.5m, the latter the depth of the passage. There was no portcullis or other protection; it was secured merely by double-doors which opened into recesses let into the vault above. The only parallels for this early gateway in Glamorgan are the vestiges of similar examples built up in the later gatehouses at Ewenny Priory (Vol. III, Part 1b, LM 5). A contemporary rectangular stone structure, boldly battered at its base, is set askew of the passage on the scarp of the ditch. An opposed structure on the counterscarp is modern, but presumably replaces an original abutment. A vanished superstructure on the inner abutment presumably housed the means of raising or sliding back the bridge that spanned the intervening gap.

The *Hall* (Fig. 209) on the N. was raised along with the curtain, which provided two of its walls. Internally it measures 21.00m by 7.70m with no traces of sub-division. Only its lower walls survive. That on the N., being also the curtain, is pierced by no original opening, a doorway to the river being an insertion. The shorter E. wall does retain a small splayed window, and as this pierced the curtain a deep-seated draw-bar provided a means of securing its shutters against an iron grill. Three similar small windows,

without barred shutters, lit this austere building from the S., where the wall also incorporated two doors. The main door was that to the E. which retains quarter-round moulded jambs and stops and a draw-bar socket (now blocked). There is no fire-place, but a central hearth was found during clearance. Nevertheless, this ill-lit chamber could hardly have constituted the hall, which presumably occupied the vanished upper floor, and was perhaps the '*Knighting Chamber*' rebuilt in 1442–44 long after destruction by the Welsh. The greater part of the surviving S. wall is narrower and later than its E. end, perhaps reflecting this rebuilding.

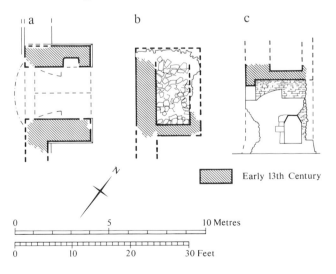

Fig. 208. Ogmore Castle, the Main Gateway: (a) ground floor; (b) first floor; (c) section, looking north-west.

285

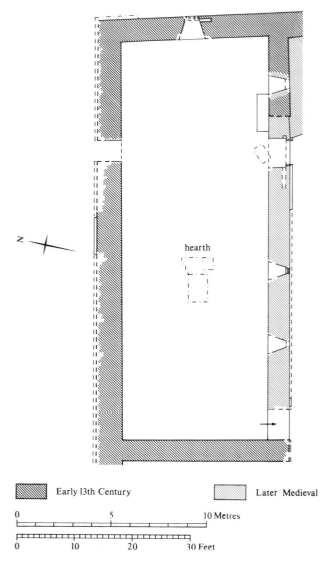

Early 13th Century   Later Medieval

```
0                5              10 Metres
0        10        20        30 Feet
```

Fig. 209. Ogmore Castle: the Hall in the Inner Ward.

The *Offices* on the S. side, a rectangular block 14.2m by 5.8m, are subdivided by two cross-walls, each with a door set against the S. wall. These doors retain vestiges of moulded jambs, one with the same quarter-round chamfer seen in the rebuilt S. wall of the hall. The function of this block is not clear.

The later inserted chamber with its fireplace contrived in the postern has already been noticed. To the S. of this two short walls define a small passage between the 'Cellar' and the curtain. These are the only visible remains of later additions to the Inner Ward. Footings of other walls which were revealed during conservation are now under grass, but they are shown on our plan (Fig. 200). It seems probable

that those on the N. side of the Keep marked the site of the kitchen, being well placed there for such an essential building which is otherwise lacking.

A replica of a pre-Norman inscribed stone is set up in the area of the suspected kitchen (Vol. I, Part 3, No. 926). This stone was found during clearance, built into a 19th-century lime-kiln erected within the 'Cellar'.

(iv) *Masonry Structures in the Bailey* (Figs. 210–12). The limited stonework of the bailey is confined to its N. side. Here a sequence of three overlapping structures has been identified by excavation.[24] The first, the fragmentary N. end of a rectangular building, 6.30m wide internally, is set against the scarp to the river. This building was abandoned by *ca.* 1300, when a circular lime-kiln with two opposed flues was built upon it. Finally, the kiln in turn was abandoned and its N.E. side demolished to make way for the S.W. gable of the *Court-house*, a building probably first erected in the 14th century but rebuilt in 1454–55.

The *Court-house* is 14.1m by 6.45m externally with walls 0.75m thick above a modest plinth. Its main door is slightly W. of the centre of the long S. wall. A second door, near the E. end of the N. wall, retains its Sutton Stone and sandstone dressings. These are plain-chamfered and stopped, with a pointed head. The building is without a fireplace, and there are indi-

---

[24] O. E. Craster, 'A Medieval Limekiln at Ogmore Castle, Glamorgan', *Arch. Camb.*, CI (1950), pp. 72–6.

Fig. 210. Ogmore Castle: the Court-house from the south; base of lime-kiln, left.

cations that it was divided into at least three bays by its roof trusses, while a later ceiling may be presumed from traces of the sockets of four beams and one corbel. Windows pierce each wall (Fig. 211). That in the W. gable is set high, its small rectangular frame of plain-chamfered dressed stone retaining the sockets of a grill. The E. window is also high in the gable, but of two lights and though similarly square-headed the frame and mullion were hollow-chamfered. Each

light was again provided with a grill. A small window like that in the W. gable was set in the N. wall close to the N.E. angle. Larger double-light splayed windows at each end of the main S. wall, facing the court, have lost their dressings, which probably matched those of the E. window.

This building is generally identified with the Court-house rebuilt in 1454–55 but at too little expense to account for the existing building.[25] The record of the Court-house being in good repair and regular use as late as 1631 must favour the traditional identification, particularly as the record of its rebuilding in the 15th century locates it in the outer ward (*exterioram wardam*). It may be added, however, that although its identification with the court-house is probable, the alignment and plan of this building would suit the liturgical arrangements of certain late-medieval chapels. Fenestration is especially concentrated at the E. end, with the E. window set high, while of those opposed in the adjacent long walls, that to the S. is far wider and could have accommodated a piscina no longer in evidence. A small door W. of the smaller

[25] *Hist. Kings Works*, II, p. 769, n. 3.

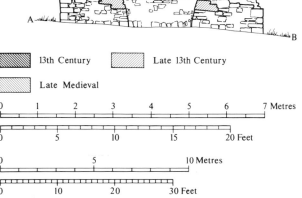

a

b

| | 13th Century | | Late 13th Century |
| | Late Medieval | | |

0   1   2   3   4   5   6   7 Metres

0   5   10   15   20 Feet

0   5   10 Metres

0   10   20   30 Feet

Fig. 212. *(Above)* Ogmore Castle: the lime-kiln.

Fig. 211. Ogmore Castle: (a) the Courthouse, lime-kiln, and rectangular primary stone building; (b) the lime-kiln, section A–B.

N. window could have served as a priest's door, while the main S. door would have been appropriate in a chapel, which designation is applied to this building on early O.S. maps.[26] Furthermore, the absence of a fireplace appears an unlikely omission for a late-medieval court-house, and no other building that remains may be identified as the chapel recorded in the 1450s.

The *Exchequer* and '*Knighting Chamber*' recorded in the 15th century were both no doubt within the inner ward, where tentatively they might be respectively identified with the vanished upper floors of the buildings here termed the '*Cellar*' and the *Hall*. There is an indication of the rebuilding of the greater part of the S. wall of the *Hall*, possibly reflecting the restoration of the '*Knighting Chamber*' in 1442–44, forty years after its destruction by the Welsh.

A duchy of Lancaster map of the lordship, dating to the reign of Elizabeth I, gives a delightful but highly imaginative view of Ogmore Castle.[27] This shows a cluster of buildings in what appears to be the outer ward; on closer examination these buildings are seen to be on the opposite side to the bailey, towards the 'King's Mill', which is clearly marked and may be identified with the former mill now serving as a tavern to the E. of the castle. The polygonal curtain is portrayed, but not the keep, and the impressive twin-towered gatehouse, ludicrously set centrally within the walls, deters further consideration of this interesting and early flight of fancy.

King, p. 166.

St Brides Major and Wick (E), St Brides Major (C)
SS 87 N.E. (8819–7698)   9.viii.86   XL S.W.

[26] The ruined chapel at Caswell, Bishopston, displays a similar undivided plan: Morgan, *East Gower*, pp. 174–7, p. 175 plan; O.S. 25-inch sheet XL 10, 1919 (surveyed 1875).

[27] *P.R.O.*, MCP. 49. Professor Rees Davies kindly furnished a copy of this map.

MR 6   Pennard Castle

Pennard Pill, a besanded estuary merging with Three Cliffs Bay on the S. coast of Gower, is respectively flanked to E. and W. by the high ground of Pennard and Penmaen Burrows. Penmaen castle-ringwork (CR 18) lies high on the edge of the western escarpment. A little over a kilometre N.E. of this ringwork, across the estuary, Pennard Castle occupies a similar position on a rocky bluff thrust out from Pennard Burrows, though in this case set back from the Bay and overlooking the point where Pennard Pill narrows and merges with a confined and steep-sided valley running N. Like Penmaen, Pennard Castle and its adjacent contemporary village is now besanded. The first Pennard Church (St Mary's) stood 100m E.S.E. of the castle; its footings are still visible, and those of houses in this vicinity have often been noticed in the dunes, one having been recently excavated.[1]

Pennard Castle, though impressive in situation, is crudely built and of modest strength. Its light walling defines an oval enclosure suggesting a primary castle-ringwork like that at Penmaen; this supposition was confirmed by excavation in 1961.[2] We have no record of the primary 12th-century ringwork. Pennard was certainly a demesne manor of the lords of Gower, and there is one sure indication that Henry de Beaumont, the first earl of Warwick, acquired it at the time of his conquest of Gower. Soon after his conquest, between 1107 and 1119, Henry established a cell of the Norman abbey of St Taurin of Evreux at Llangennydd in Gower; among his endowments to this foundation was the church of Pennard ('Pennart'), with its tithes.[3] It is not improbable that the ringwork, so close to the first St Mary's of Pennard, was already established at the time of this grant. Henry de Beaumont's successor, Roger, made further grants from the demesne at Pennard, these to Neath Abbey, founded in 1130.[4]

Very late in the 13th century, or early in the 14th century, Pennard Castle was fortified in stone. In 1317 William de Braose, Lord of Gower, granted his huntsman, William, rights in his warren of Pennard (Vol. III, Part 2, p. 323 (ii)), but our first record of the

[1] Glamorgan–Gwent Archaeological Trust, *Annual Report 1982–83*, pp. 75–6.

[2] Excavation by Leslie Alcock and Joan Jeffrey during more extensive work at Penmaen. Brief notes were published in *Med. Arch.*, VI–VII 1962–63, p. 326; *Morgannwg*, IV (1960), pp. 69–70 and V (1961), p. 81; *Arch. in Wales* (1961), p. 13. Mr. Bernard Morris has kindly furnished sketches, notes and plans made while assisting at Penmaen. Mr. Morris has also advised on many aspects of the castle and generously provided copies of old photographs and relevant extracts from his notes on the castle.

[3] David Crouch, *B.B.C.S.*, XXXI (1984), pp. 134–5. The text of the grant is given in full in appendix II, p. 141.

[4] Crouch, *ibid*, p. 135.

Fig. 213. *(Opposite)* Pennard Castle: view from the north-east.

castle is in 1322.[5] In the latter year a royal licence was granted to Hugh Despenser, lord of Glamorgan, permitting him to obtain by exchange the castles and manors of Swansea, Oystermouth, Pennard, Loughor and 'Liman' (probably Talybont, MO 6), these being the possessions of the widow of John de Burgo. These soon reverted to the lords of Gower, and the castle at Pennard is next mentioned in the lawsuit between Thomas Beauchamp, Earl of Warwick, and John de Mowbray in the 1350s.[6] In the 14th century there are also records of the court or *comitatus* of the lordship being held on occasion at Pennard, rather than at Swansea.[7]

When William de Braose granted hunting rights to his huntsman in 1317, he expressly excluded his rabbit warren in the sand dunes (*sandborghwys*) at Pennard. Within a century of the construction of the stone castle this early hint of sand encroachment heralded the end of the castle and its vill. As at Penmaen (CR 18), and more dramatically at the castle and walled borough of Kenfig (EM 2), it was necessary to build a new church further inland, and the old settlement was gradually abandoned.[8] By 1650 a survey of the manor records the castle as '*Desolate and ruinous, and soe long time unrepayred that scarsely there remayneth one whole wall . . . now compassed with much sand*'.[9] Deserted it may have been, but the survey exaggerates its dilapidation, to judge from the Buck print of 1741 (Fig. 214).

Architectural Description
(Figs. 216–221).

The form and dimensions of the *primary ringwork* at Pennard are indicated by the stone castle; a little of its detail is known to us from the limited excavations of 1961, already cited.[10] The castle enjoys the protection of steep natural slopes to the W. and N., and the primary ringwork was clearly a partial ringwork set against these natural scarps, its ring-bank and ditch following the curving trace of the walls to the S. and E. The enclosure thus defined, assuming its palisade followed the line of the curtain, measured 34m by 28m. The excavations disclosed evidence for a strong palisade along the cliff to the W., while to the S. it was deduced that the curtain had been inserted into an earthen bank, no doubt replacing the continuation of the palisade. Visible traces of the footings of a rectangular hall at the W. end of the enclosure were also excavated. This free-standing hall was found to be

---

[5] Clark, *Cartae*, III (dccclxxvii), pp. 1039–40; *Arch. Camb.* (1866), pp. 282, 288–9; *Cal. P.R.*, 16 Edw II, 176 (=Clark, *Cartae*, III (dccccvii), pp. 1100–1).

[6] Clark, *Cartae*, IV (mlxxi), p. 1391.

[7] e.g. Clark, *Cartae*, III (dccccxv), pp. 1112, 1114 and 1117, n.

[8] *Glam. Co. Hist.*, III, p. 401.

[9] *Surveys of Gower and Kilvey* (*Arch. Camb.* supplements 1861–70), p. 315.

[10] See note 2.

Fig. 214. Pennard Castle in 1741: engraving by Samuel and Nathanial Buck, looking south-west (*National Library of Wales*).

a hall predating the masonry fortifications of the castle, and it was probably built in the early 13th century to replace an earlier timber hall that is suggested by charcoal and burnt daub beneath it.

The *Stone Hall* was of irregular plan, tapering to a skewed N. end. Its median external measurements were 18.60m by 7.60m. The walls were well-mortared, 70cm thick, and built of red-purple conglomerate with white limestone dressings. Rounded external angles were squared within. The building was of three units. Towards the N. end opposed doors marked the lower end of the hall, the largest and central unit. A stone cross-wall N. of the passage retained the jambs of two rebated doors to a small service area, ultimately of one room since one of these doorways had been blocked. A second cross-wall at the S. end of the hall divided it from a private chamber. Footings of stone benches were found against this cross-wall and against the W. lateral wall, both facing a central hearth close to the cross-bench.

This detached hall of stone is of interest as one of a number of such buildings that are known to have existed within earth-and-timber defences.[11] More primitive dry-stone halls of this type are known at nearby Penmaen (CR 18) and Llantrithyd (CR 13), both in Glamorgan ringworks. There is a platform within Norton ringwork (CR 16) suggesting another, while masonry structures are noted within other ringworks never converted to stone at Llandow (CR 11) and Walterston (CR 21), though these last are of mortared masonry like that at Pennard. Outside Glamorgan, Grosmont in Gwent had a fine mortared hall within earthwork defences and another has been suspected from loose Norman carved detail at Kidwelly.

Before considering the stone defences, it should be added that the excavations also disclosed a small section of walling immediately within the curtain on the

---

[11] Leslie Alcock, *Morgannwg*, V (1961), p. 81.

Fig. 215. Pennard Castle: view from the north east (*cf*. Fig. 214).

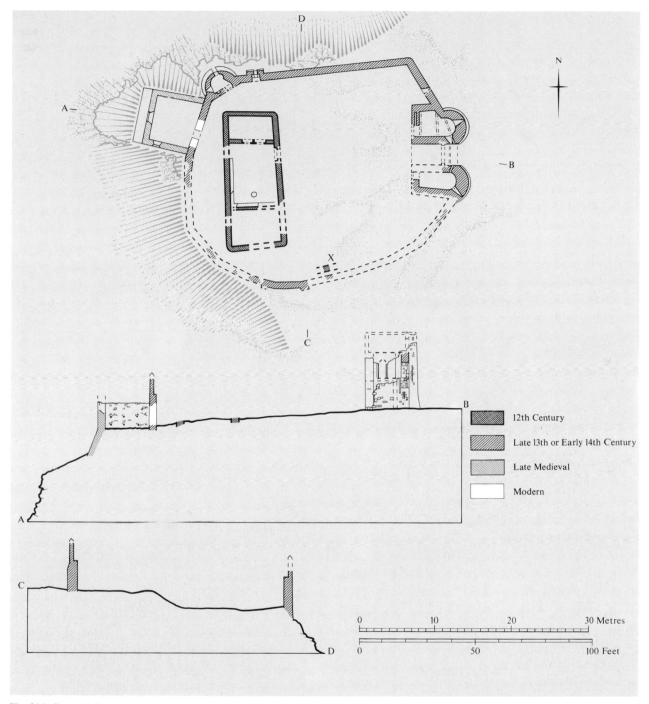

Fig. 216. Pennard Castle: plan and profiles.

S. side (X on plan, Fig. 216). This was bedded over 1.60m deep and beneath it a layer of charcoal covered the old turf-line. It is possible that this building, not further explored, was contemporary with the hall. The Buck brothers (1741) appear to depict a tall square tower in this area, but this is no more than the ill-shaded portrayal of the detached surviving section of the S. curtain which is still visible from their point of view.

The *masonry defences* are best-preserved on the N. and E., as they were when the Bucks chose these flanks for their depiction of the castle in the 18th century

(Fig. 214). Much of the N. curtain survives to its wall-walk, and the gatehouse dominating the E. front stands to the stumps of two merlons over its S. tower, though the unbroken crenellation of the Buck drawing is otherwise gone. The northern half of the W. front, overlooking Pennard Pill, also survives to its wall-walk, here saved from collapse by the square *Western Tower* added on a projecting spur of rock. Running S. from this tower, and following a bold curve to the gatehouse, the curtain is marked only by a few isolated traces of footings and one upstanding fragment near the S.E. corner of the hall. Excepting the added *Western Tower*, the masonry defences are of one build.

The curtain is 1.10m thick and its surviving wall-walk to the N. and behind the Western Tower averages 5.00m above the interior. The parapet rises intermittently and much reduced above the wall-walk, but old photographs, the Buck print and the very limited traces of the former crenellation have made it possible to attempt a reasoned reconstruction of the battlements (Figs. 218, 219). Alternate merlons were pierced by loops. The curtain displays tiers of putlog holes, all surmounted by a more regular line of identical holes serving to drain the wall-walk. One feature common to the N. curtain and the remaining tusk surviving on the S. is the clear indication of two phases of work marked by horizontal lines and a change of building stone. These changes must mark a seasonal break in construction, as a mere change of stone during activities would hardly effect such regular breaks

Fig. 217. Pennard Castle: external front of the Gatehouse.

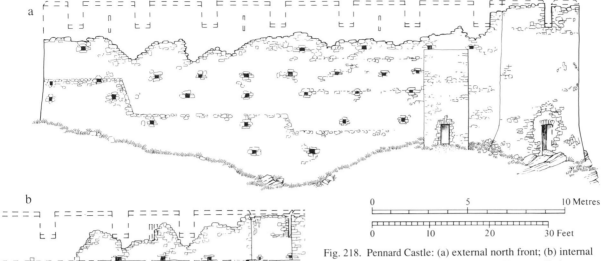

Fig. 218. Pennard Castle: (a) external north front; (b) internal elevation of the curtain on the west side. The crenellation restored in broken lines is based on early photographs, the Buck print, and slight surviving vestiges.

in the masonry. This break is most striking in the detached segment of curtain on the S. where the lower half surviving is of red sandstone conglomerate, while above this the white limestone of the site is used.[12] As late as the 1950s this section of walling retained its battlements.

The *Gatehouse* to the E. was probably the only entrance. With its flanking half-round towers and inward square projection this structure is clearly an 'Edwardian' gatehouse, but lacks the confident regularity of Caerphilly (LM 3). Its flanking guard-rooms are not symmetrical, that to the N. quite irregular

---

[12] This red stone outcrops on Cefn Bryn, but Mr Bernard Morris has indicated a more probable source in an outcrop only a hundred yards S. of the castle at SS 5435 8840. Professor Leslie Alcock has suggested that the red stone, also used for the earlier hall, may denote the re-use of material derived from the demolition of that building (*Morgannwg*, IV (1960), p. 701).

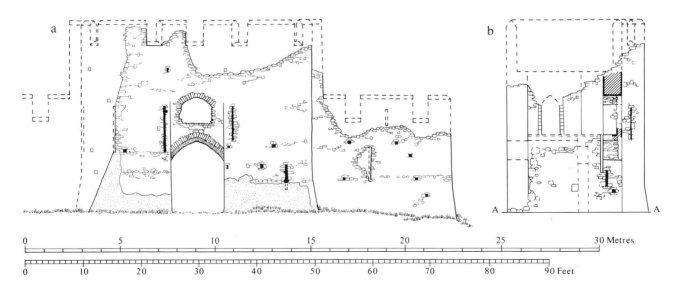

Fig. 219. Pennard Castle: (a) external east front; (b) cross-section of gatehouse, looking north.

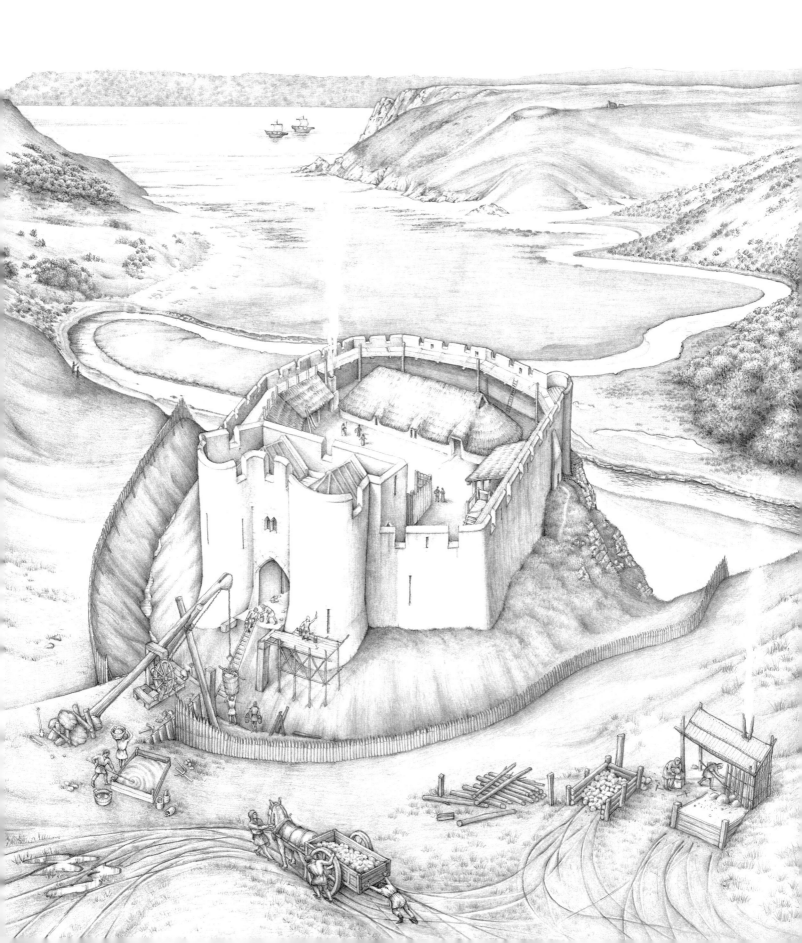

in plan. There are no side doors in the passage, and this could not be closed against the interior. The defences of the entrance are limited to a portcullis of simple form protecting double-doors and fronted by an oblique arrow-loop from the N. chamber – though without a loop on the S. side. The front of this gatehouse is comparatively intact, the inner half largely fallen. The guard-chambers were entered by doors at the rear, that to the N. provided with a draw-bar. As well as the loop covering the passage, the N. chamber also had a loop to the field. The S. chamber retains only one side of its door and, to the front, one particularly narrow splayed loop of no practical use and not flanking the approach to the passage. On the first floor, reached by vanished wooden steps, the provision of loops is again unequal. From each site, opposed loops fire across the immediate approach to the passage through deeply plunging cills. A third loop at this level is provided only on the S. side. The slot for the timber floor at this level is still visible in the rounded projection of the N. chamber.

Two particularly strange features of the gatehouse are the form of its portcullis and two oblique square holes running at ground level from the guard-rooms to the front of the passage on lines converging about 90cm in advance of the portcullis. They have been tentatively related to a form of drawbridge.[13] There was surely a ditch on this flank, and some form of footway that could be rolled back into the passage might be hesitantly conjectured; nothing could have been raised in the normal way by such low-seated pulley-holes, if such they were. Only excavation in the area might explain their purpose. The portcullis is peculiar in that its grooves are not carried to the floor but terminate 1.80m above, little below the springing of the arch. Quite clearly, we had here a particularly weak portcullis, shouldered and without the solidity of the usual continuous vertical hold of complete grooves.[14] There can be little doubt that this very weak and provincial copy of the Edwardian gatehouse was erected some time after the alarums of the Welsh wars, later rather than sooner, when familiarity with outward form did not go with practical experience of the serious purpose of such military constructions. Exceptionally strong lime-mortar is used throughout the castle, and this alone accounts for the survival of so much of its flimsy walling.

A small half-round mural turret at the N.W. angle

Fig. 220. *(Opposite)* Pennard Castle: conjectural reconstruction (*ca.* 1300).

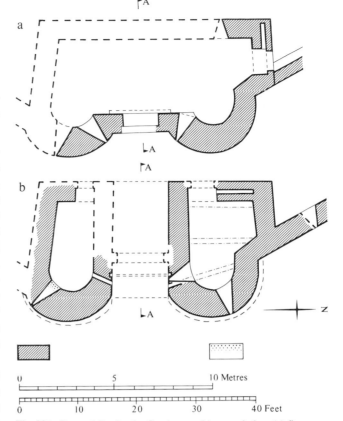

Fig. 221. Pennard Castle, the Gatehouse: (b) ground plan; (a) first floor plan.

with battered base is the only modest flanking provided but its position at the strongest point, where its only loop faces the W. precipice, does not suggest a military purpose, though its upper part was open to the court and its crenellations were followed by the continuation of the wall-walk. There was no stone stair, a characteristic shared with the gatehouse, and its lower chamber, entered by a door from the court, was ceiled in timber. The base of a latrine-chute pierces the outer wall. A further garderobe was provided a short distance E. along the N. curtain. This is housed in a squared projecting buttress, with central chute.

The Western Tower is clearly butted against the outer face of the W. curtain to utilize a boss of rock initially excluded. It is a large tower, clearly residential, with splayed windows in its walls to the W. and S. Its situation on the steep escarpment demanded a bold batter at its outer end. Its present entrance from the court is set in a crude modern patching which

[13] Morgan, *East Gower*, p. 206.
[14] G. T. Clark, *Arch. Camb.* (1893), pp. 306–7.

at least serves to maintain the original wall-walk above, much as similarly ugly modern buttressing protects the gatehouse. Again, there was no stone stair to the vanished upper floor of this tower.

King, p. 167.

Pennard

SS 58 N.W. (5442–8850)   6.viii.84   XXXI N.E.

MR 7   Rumney Castle (Cae-castell)

In 1801 Coxe described and illustrated a small 'encampment' with triangular 'outwork' at Rumney.[1] Only recently has this been identified as the Rumney Castle long known from the records. Mistakenly attributed to the Romans, most recently in 1953,[2] its tardy recognition is explained by its seclusion and subdivision in the back gardens of three adjacent late-Victorian villas flanking Newport Road on the E. outskirts of Cardiff (Fig. 222). In 1972, only an arc of ditch in the grounds of Oaklands was accessible; clearly medieval work, it was assumed to be the segment of a large motte and identified as Rumney Castle.[3] A far larger portion behind Tredelerch was masked by undergrowth and little remained of Coxe's 'outwork'. Prior to redevelopment, excavations were undertaken behind Oaklands in 1978 and behind Tredelerch in 1980–81. This work was directed by Mr K. W. B. Lightfoot for the Glamorgan-Gwent Archaeological Trust.[4] Almost the entire area of the main work was excavated (Fig. 224, a-f) and two sections were cut across its defences, confirming that it was Rumney Castle. A castle-ringwork of five periods, its bank was finally slighted and a short-lived manorial centre of minimal defensive strength raised in its place. Following the excavations the site was levelled, leaving only shortened re-entrants where its ditch and the northern dingle opened upon the sharp fall to the Afon Rhymni. Castle Drive was then carried across the S.E. side flanked by two new houses, No. 2 being raised over the final stone hall (Fig. 222). Oaklands is now The Oaklands Hotel.

Before excavation the segment in Oaklands accommodated a tennis court reached by a decayed footbridge across the deep ditch to the S.E. Clearance of undergrowth in the adjacent garden revealed the size and characteristics of the site and confirmed Coxe's account of 1801. Subdivided unequally by the party wall, a comparatively large horseshoe-shaped platform was set against the fall to the river on the N.W. Its level summit, rather above the 15m contour, measured 41m along the straight natural scarp, from which it extended for the same distance to the S.E. It was defined by a broad ditch opening upon the natural scarp to the S.W. and curving around to link with a natural re-entrant on the N.E. This ditch was impressive in Oaklands, with an average fall of 4m from the summit. Behind Tredelerch its continuation was less marked and largely infilled to facilitate the activities of a former market garden attested by the shallow foundations of greenhouses along the N.W. side. During its first five phases the platform was protected by a partial ring-bank with its open end set against the impregnable fall to the river. There was no superficial evidence for a counterscarp bank, nor for the successive entrances uncovered to the S. and S.E.

The small 'outwork' recorded by Coxe was surely a bailey. It largely fell within the bounds of Castlefield, now a Conservative Club, and measured about 32m to the N.E., against the ringwork ditch, and extended some 35m to an apex on the S.W. (Fig. 222). Only the N. angle survives, much disturbed and littered with rubbish. Most of it has been cut away to level a carpark.

The castle lies 3.9km N.E. of Cardiff on the further E. bank of the Afon Rhymni, 1.9km from its mouth.

Fig. 222. *(Opposite)* Rumney Castle: plan of the site during the excavations (1978-81) and indicating subsequent redevelopment which obliterated the remains. The position and approximate form of the bailey to the south-west is based on Coxe's plan of 1801.

[1] William Coxe, *An Historical Tour in Monmouthshire*, (London, 1801), Part I, p. 63 and plan facing p. 75.

[2] C. J. O. Evans, *Monmouthshire, its History and Topography*, 1953, p. 470. Large-scale O.S. maps had perpetuated the tradition of a 'Roman Camp', despite Walker's map of 1836, which labels the site 'Castle' (D. M. P. Michael, *The Mapping of Monmouthshire*, (Bristol, 1985), p. 111), and a brief anonymous note in *Arch. Camb.*, 1913, p. 69, equating it with Rumney Castle. These obscure references had been ignored, even in the standard history of Cardiff.

[3] C. J. Spurgeon and H. J. Thomas, *Arch. in Wales*, 1974, No. 14, pp. 37–8 and *Morgannwg*, XXII, (1978), p. 18.

[4] The Commission is much indebted to the Trust, and particularly to Mr Lightfoot. He has generously furnished copies of all his detailed drafts and illustrations in advance of his definitive publication and given valued advice in summarizing the complex results of his excavation. An illustrated final interim report has appeared in the Trust's *Annual Report* for 1981–82, pp. 1–7. The full report will appear in *Medieval Archaeology*.

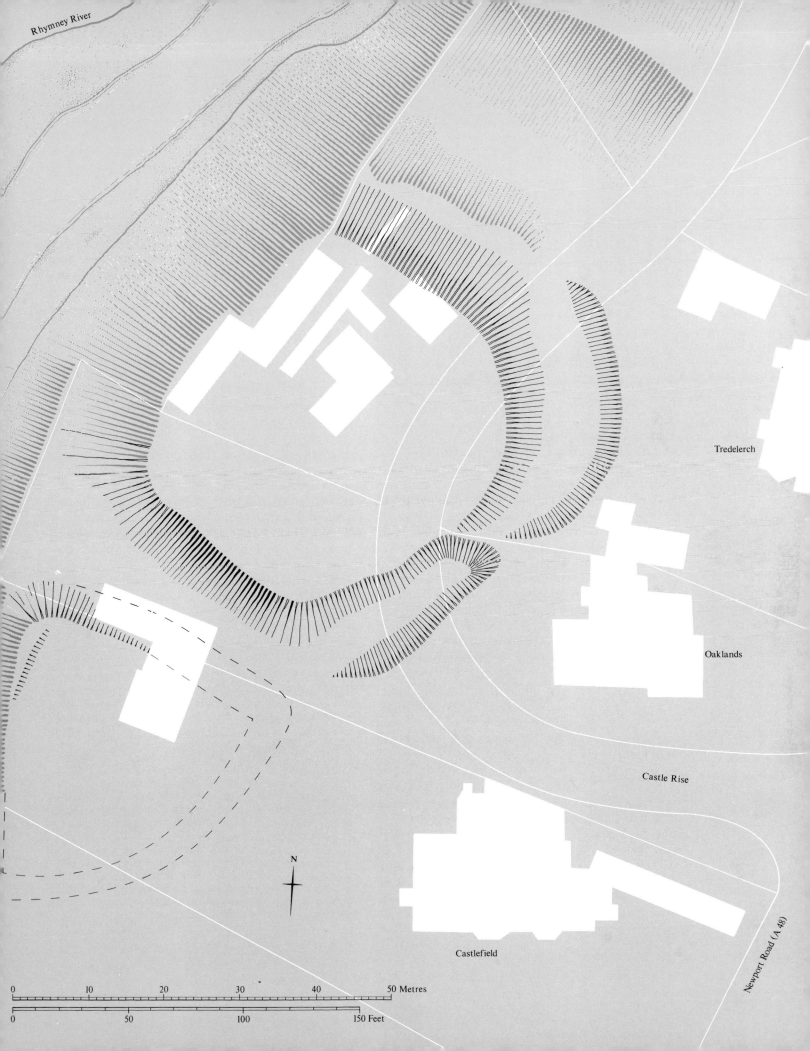

Rhymney River

Tredelerch

Oaklands

Castle Rise

Castlefield

Newport Road (A 48)

N

| 0 | | 10 | | 20 | | 30 | | 40 | | 50 Metres |

| 0 | | 50 | | 100 | | 150 Feet |

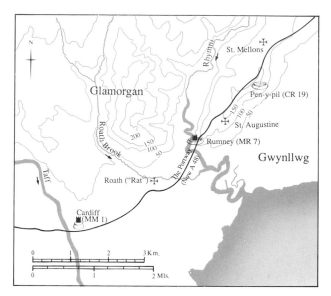

Fig. 223. Rumney Castle: location map.

This river separated the lordships of Glamorgan and Gwynllŵg and, until recently, the counties of Glamorgan and Monmouth. In 1938 Glamorgan absorbed the parish of Rumney (Tredelerch in Welsh) when it was incorporated in the City of Cardiff. Adjacent parts of the neighbouring parish of St Mellons were likewise absorbed in 1951. These changes brought Rumney Castle and Pen-y-pil, St Mellons (CR 19), into Glamorgan, though purists still regard them as Monmouthshire sites.[5] Though within Gwynllŵg, Rumney was a possession of the lords of Glamorgan, for both territories fell to Fitzhamon ca. 1093. Topographical considerations would suggest that the founding of Rumney Castle was not long delayed. At the S.W. end of a ridge, it dominates an ancient crossing of the Rhymni 300m to the S. (Map, Fig. 223). There is no other point of vantage; the ground opposite in Glamorgan is flat. Rumney Bridge is recorded in the late 12th century, but was of greater antiquity. The Roman road from Caerleon to Cardiff approaches this crossing along the ridge, its line approximating to the A48 which passes within 40m of the castle.[6] The location of the bridge was dictated by abrupt falls to the river upstream and the marshy tidal flats flanking its meandering lower reaches. The river was tidal and ships could discharge goods and men close to the castle, an asset shared with the lord's strongholds at Neath, Kenfig and Cardiff.[7] It is not improbable that Rumney Castle protected this natural gateway to Glamorgan from the outset, the chief lord's main castle at Cardiff being only a level 3.9km distant.

Even earlier it is the probable location of the battle in 1072 on the banks of the Rhymni, in which Norman help enabled Caradog ap Gruffydd, King of Gwynllŵg, to win mastery of Glamorgan.[8]

History and Descent

Although Rumney Castle is not recorded until the Welsh uprising of 1184, we have noted military considerations favouring a foundation soon after 1093. Evidence from the excavations is not incompatible with an early foundation: the Keep, presumably of late-12th-century date, was added as the first masonry in Period III, after two periods of development in earth and timber. Some evidence suggests that Fitzhamon granted lowland Gwynllŵg (Wentloog) to Robert de Haia, who might therefore, have founded the Castle.[9] De Haia, however, appears to have relinquished his lordship to Earl Robert of Gloucester (ca. 1114–47), who certainly held Rumney and granted 300 acres of its coastal levels to Morgan and Iorwerth of Machen, the upland Welshry of the lordship.[10] The charter recording this grant also mentions the church of St John of Rumney, 400m E.N.E. of the castle, which would soon gain its present dedication when Earl William (1147–83) granted it to the monks of St Augustine, Bristol. Earl William also granted the tithes of his mill of *Rumia* to St James's in the same city.[11]

When Earl William died, late in 1183, he left no male heir and Glamorgan and Gwynllŵg passed into royal custody. Henry II immediately faced a major

---

[5] E.g. King, *Cast. Ang.*, I, pp. 287–8.

[6] Ivan D. Margary, *Roman Roads in Britain*, revised ed., 1967, pp. 324–5. Pen-y-pil (CR 19) and a motte at Castleton also lie beside this route, respectively 2km and 6km to the N.E. of Rumney. The bridge is mentioned in the Pipe Roll of 1184–85 and rather later by Gerald of Wales: 'The River Rhymney . . . flows by Rumney Castle and through Rhymney bridge, and then enters the sea' (*Opera*, Rolls Series, 21, VI, p. 172).

[7] As late as 1771 ships unloaded at the bridge, *Cardiff Records*, Vol. II, p. 391.

[8] *Bruts: B.S.*, *Pen. 20*, and *R.B.*; *Glam. Co. Hist.*, III, pp. 6–7.

[9] Lloyd, *Hist. Wales*, II, p. 442, n.159; *Epis. Acts*, II, No. L13, p. 612; Patterson, *Glouc. Charters*, No. 156, p. 146 (n.); David Crouch, *Morgannwg*, XXIX, (1985), p. 29 and n.37, pp. 38–9; A. C. Reeves, *The Marcher Lords*, 1983, p. 139.

[10] Crouch, *ibid*, p. 39, n.54 and Appendix, p. 41 and *Journal of Medieval History*, II, (1985), p. 230, and n.6, pp. 241–2.

[11] Patterson, *Glouc. Charters*, No. 24, p. 45; No. 34, p. 53, and No. 36, p. 54. The dowager countess, Mabel, also granted lands in Rumney Marsh to St John's, Rumney: *ibid*, Nos. 31 and 167, pp. 49 and 152.

offensive by the Welsh under Morgan ap Caradog ap Iestyn. The insurgents concentrated their hostilities upon the western castles at Neath, Kenfig and Newcastle, but Cardiff and Newport were also attacked, and the Pipe Rolls for 1184 bear witness to the strategic importance of Rumney.[12] Robert Fitzwilliam was allowed £5. 4s. 8d. for serving eighteen months as Henry II's custodian of *Castellum de Remni*, and 31s. 6d. was charged for repairs to the bridge, including 4s. for a great rope (*magna corda*). To further facilitate communications with Cardiff the bridge over the Roath Brook was also repaired (map, Fig. 223).

The future King, John of Mortain, obtained Glamorgan and Gwynllŵg on his marriage to the heiress, Isobel, in 1189. The lordships passed to the Clares in 1217, under whom Rumney developed as a rich demesne manor.[13] When Gilbert de Clare, the Red, obtained seisin in 1263 he disputed the castles and manors assigned in dower to his mother, Countess Maud, bringing suit against her in 1266. As a result, a new dower settlement was agreed and Rumney was among the manors granted.[14] It is possible that Maud's tenure (1267–89) witnessed the drastic conversion of Rumney Castle into the lightly fortified manorial curtilage of its final phase, for with Gilbert's annexation of Senghennydd (1267) and the Gwynllŵg uplands of Machen (1270), the threatening hills flanking the Rhymni Valley were seemingly neutralized, and the approaches to Rumney protected by the new fortress at Caerphilly. Such confidence proved ill-advised, for in 1294–95 Morgan ap Maredudd, son of the disinherited Welsh lord of Machen, led a fresh revolt in Glamorgan.[15] Rumney Castle, now ill-protected and back in possession of Gilbert, was put to the flames – a fate not mentioned in the records but evidenced by the excavations, and reflected in the war damage suffered by its two water-mills which was recorded in 1296.[16] The dilapidated mills of 1296 were together valued at only 20s., but they were restored and worth £13. 6s. 8d. in 1307, increasing to £18 by 1314 when the manor was worth the high sum of £73. 19s. 10d.[17] While the manor recovered, however, the Castle was never restored. When in royal custody in 1316, following the death of the last Clare earl, the Rumney mills were again destroyed during the revolt of Llywelyn Bren.[18]

With the partition of the Clare lands in 1317 Gwynllŵg ended its long association with Glamorgan, passing to Hugh Audley, husband of Margaret de Clare. Through their daughter it passed to a succession of earls of Stafford before forfeiture to the Crown, in 1521, on the execution of the 8th earl. It was granted in 1547 to William Herbert, created earl of Pembroke in 1550. Throughout the 14th and 15th centuries no record is inconsistent with the archaeological evidence for the abandonment of the castle following the destruction in 1295, even though Rumney had become the most valuable demesne manor in Gwynllŵg by 1401, worth over £109. Surveys of 1401 and of 1447–48 merely note certain arable land next to the castle known as 'Castellond'.[19] Leland noticed no castle remains in the 1530s, though it was known to local residents in his time. A custumal of the manor dating to about 1532 notices '... *certein closez by rumpney bridge which be parcell of the demesne where sumtyme was buylded a Pile or Castel by the water*'. It was overgrown and occupied by Walter Herbert.[20] It does not seem to be noticed again until reported by Coxe in 1801.

The Excavations, 1978 and 1980–81

Excavations behind Oaklands (1978) were directed by Mr K. W. B. Lightfoot and Mr P. Stanley, and those behind Tredelerch (1980–81) by Mr. Lightfoot, who has generously furnished full details in advance of publication (see f/n. 4). When work concluded, almost the entire summit had been excavated over an area amounting to about 1,650 square metres. Only a 3m baulk centred on the party wall and two small peripheral areas extending from it at each end were not explored (Fig. 224, a–f). The tennis court in the Oaklands had inflicted some disturbance, but only superficial damage had been caused by the shallow greenhouse foundations and bean-trenches in the

---

[12] *Pipe Roll*, 31 Hen II, (1184–85), Vol. XXXIV, 1913, pp. 5 and 6; Clark, *Cartae*, I (clxxi), pp. 170–2 and n., p. 175. See also *Glam. Co. Hist.*, III, pp. 37–9; Pipe Roll, 30 Henry II, (1183–84), XXXIII, 1912, Introduction, p. xxvii and *Hist. Kings Works*, II, pp. 650–1.

[13] William Rees, *Journal of the British Arch. Assoc.*, New Series, XXXV, (1929), pp. 203–4 and 206.

[14] Altschul, *The Clares*, pp. 95–6, 99, 117 (n.85) and 244 (n.8).

[15] Altschul, *ibid*, pp. 154–5; *Glam. Co. Hist.*, III, pp. 59–60.

[16] *Cardiff Records*, I, p. 267 (*Inq. p.m.* Gilbert de Clare, 24 Edward I, 1295–96).

[17] *Cardiff Records*, I, p. 275 (*Inq. p.m.* of Gilbert and Joan de Clare) and p. 286–7 (*Inq. p.m.* of Gilbert de Clare, the Last).

[18] *Cardiff Records*, I, p. 146 (Ministers Accounts, 9 Edward II, 1316).

[19] T. B. Pugh, *The Marcher Lordships of South Wales 1415–1536*, U.W.P., 1963, pp. 150 and 187; *Cardiff Records*, I, p. 164.

[20] A. C. Reeves, 'The Custumal of Rumney Manor', *B.B.C.S.*, XXVII, part 2, pp. 298–302 (quotation pp. 301–2).

Trederlerch sector. In both cases the general levelling up of Period VI minimized disturbance.

Six periods of building were discerned, with a relatively secure terminal date for the final phase (1295). Throughout the first five periods the site was protected by a partial ring-bank. This has been conjecturally restored on the evidence of distinct traces of its truncated base around the perimeter (Fig. 224, a–e). Masonry was not introduced until the keep was inserted in the third period close to the gate. In Period V the timber gateway close to the keep was blocked and a new stone gatehouse inserted further W. The levelling of the ring-bank and the construction of a modestly fortified manorial complex followed in Period VI. The main features of each period may be summarized as follows:

Period I (Fig. 224a): A primary partial ring-bank, open towards the river, enclosed a metalled court with an average internal diameter of 35m. The bank survived to a maximum height of 1.50m on the S.E., where it was pierced by a gate-passage splaying wider towards the interior and marked by four large post-pits which may have carried a gate-tower. The doors seem to have been set back within the passage where this was crossed by four small pits. Three beam-slots flanking the entrance suggested a timber revetment on the external face of the bank. The entrance faced S.E. towards the most vulnerable approach from the higher ground of Rumney Hill. A small building of post construction, with a bowed N.E. end (A), was partially revealed beside the natural N.W. scarp. Two post-pits ranged along the scarp beyond its N. corner may indicate a palisade. A few abraded Romano-British sherds and an Early Christian glass bead from Ireland were not significant lying beside a Roman road; the earliest occupation, represented by a thin layer with unglazed sherds beneath the ring-bank to the N.E., did not greatly predate the castle and may relate to the initial building activities.

Period II (Fig. 224b): In this period a smaller timber gate structure was raised and Building A was replaced by a much larger single-aisled hall. The renewed entrance was defined by four post-pits set centrally within the passage and now of rectangular form. As before, the door appears to be marked by central transverse post-pits, two in this case, and now linked by two curved slots. The new hall (B) was of at least six bays defined by parallel rows of post-pits. The S.W. end was not located. The aisle was to the S.E., and five lesser pits towards the E. corner may indicate the door and a slightly projecting porch.

Period III (Fig. 224c): The hall (B) continued in use, but the defences were greatly improved. A square keep was raised over the rampart on the E. side near the entrance. Only fragmentary vestiges of two walls of this structure survived, together with remnants of a paved floor. The N.W. wall survived at foundation level, 2.5m wide and set in a trench cut into bedrock. It was constructed of limestone slabs pitched obliquely to hint at herring-bone construction, except at the W. angle which was coursed horizontally. Where fragments survived above the foundation course, there were traces of lime-mortar. An ill-defined projection at the N. corner was much disturbed. The S.W. wall was indicated by a robber trench 2.20m wide and filled with mixed sand, clay and lime-mortar. Internally, the W. angle was also defined by a right-angled shelf cut inwards from the respective foundation trenches and packed with clay and rubble after the raising of the walls. The S.W. wall was founded at a higher level than that to the N.W., rising over the remains of the bank. The outward facing walls and floor were raised over the ditch, but no trace was found of these walls; large trees impeded excavation in this direction and erosion, dumping and disturbance of the scarp may have removed all traces. During this period the timber gateway of Period II continued in use, but the ring-bank was strengthened by increasing its width inwards by about 2.0m. Around the reduced perimeter there were clear traces of an internal timber revetment retaining the thickened bank. Timber posts to support such a revetment were indicated by intermittent lines of pits along the tail of the bank, three towards the N. angle, five around the E. corner skirting the keep and four immediately W. of the entrance. Where these appeared to be in unbroken sequence they were spaced between 1.25m and 2.30m apart. A timber building (D) was suggested against the presumed revetment to the N., but its form could not be ascertained from a scatter of post-holes. A second lean-to (C) was better defined W. of the entrance. This small structure was between 2m and 2.5m wide and about 5.75m long. It had been destroyed by fire; coarse-ware sherds, animal bones and cereal grains recovered suggest that it may have been a kitchen.

Period IV (Fig. 224d): Of three features attributed to this phase, the most significant was the replacement of the hall of Period II (B) by a new hall (E). As with its predecessors on this site, its S.W. end was

Fig. 224. Rumney Castle: six periods of development discerned in excavations (1978, 1980-81), after plans by Mr. K.W.B. Lightfoot.

a

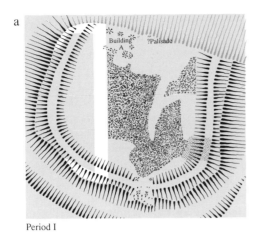

Building A   ?Palisade

Period I

b

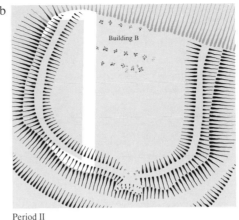

Building B

Period II

c

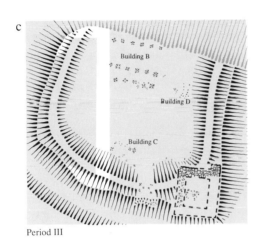

Building B

Building D

Building C

Period III

d

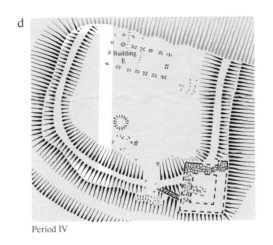

Building E

Period IV

e

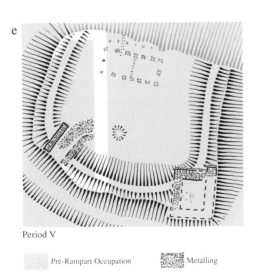

Period V

f

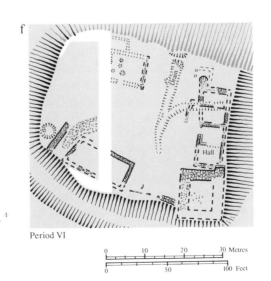

Drain

Hall

Period VI

Pre-Rampart Occupation   Metalling

0   10   20   30 Metres

0   50   100 Feet

301

not revealed beneath the baulk in this direction. It was a building of at least six bays defined by large rock-cut rectangular post-pits. A transverse beam slot marked the partition dividing the hall into two rooms, with a communicating door at its N. end indicated by the holes for its jambs and a slab threshold. The external door probably entered the N. room through its S.E. wall. Successive shallow drains linked with the N.W. scarp from the inner chamber. A line of seven pits along the scarp and roughly parallel with the adjacent hall may represent a renewal of the palisade suspected in Period I. Close to the presumed kitchen (C) a large pit was excavated to the limits of safety (1.80m) and interpreted as a well or cistern. The final addition of this phase was probably the clay-bonded stone revetment inserted between the gate and the keep.

Period V (Fig. 224e): The original gate-passage was now infilled and the ring-bank cut through for a new entrance about 26m further along the perimeter. This entrance was protected by a simple stone gate-tower with walls faced with rough limestone blocks set in lime mortar. The W. wall survived for several courses, but that to the E. was greatly disturbed and it was not possible to determine its relationship with the curving robber trench which continued the N. end of its foundation trench. The line of this feature was followed by the continuation of metalling laid in the gate-passage, but neither continued beyond the baulk.

Period VI (Fig. 224f): Only the keep appears to have survived a radical transformation in this final period. The entrance was rebuilt with a narrower W. wall set to narrow the external end of the passage which now widened towards the interior. The ring-bank was considerably reduced and its material used to bring the whole site to an enlarged level platform around which were ranged new buildings. A long irregular building ran E. from the rebuilt E. flank of the gateway, but scant vestiges of its sandstone foundations set in clay did not demonstrate the structural relationship between them. A more impressive range was raised to the N.E., consisting of a hall and service room in line. The hall measured 11m by 7m externally, with walls bonded with clay and lime-mortar and a roof of Pennant Sandstone with glazed ridge-tiles. Entered from the court by a door at the N. end, its S. end was raised as a dais. There were stone benches at the lower end. A conflagration destroyed the hall. Its charred roofing material sealed the remains of a wooden tub and carbonised grain at the lower end; more significantly it incorporated an important coin

hoard of the early 1290s which dated this destruction. The service-room was less completely preserved, but its N. gable retained traces of a round-ended projection – presumably an oven. The scant vestiges of this building were cut through by a short-lived drainage gully which was later infilled to level up the site of a new service-block at right-angles to the hall.

A timber building was built to the N.W., on the site of the successive earlier halls. As before, the S.W. end ran beneath the baulk and was not disclosed. The new hall was outlined by beam slots and had a door from the court to the S.E. Four clay-lined bowl-shaped pits with pierced bases were found within and interpreted as evidence of smelting. Immediately W. of the gate a large circular pit was dug 1.50m deep into the truncated base of the bank. Traces of lime and a stone rake-hole towards the scarp initially suggested a lime-kiln, but it is now thought to represent a signal beacon.[21] It may be assumed that the buildings which now flanked the court were linked by a curtilage wall along the scarp to the ditch which still provided a modicum of protection. Traces of such a wall only survived between the keep and long building on the S.E. side.

Chronology and Discussion

With the exception of the coin hoard dating the final destruction and abandonment of the site, the excavations failed to yield diagnostic artefacts to date the stratigraphically established sequence of building periods. This may only be tentatively attempted relative to historical probabilities and the characteristics of the site and its structures in each period.

The initial castle-ringwork of Periods I and II was probably founded soon after the arrival of Fitzhamon *ca.* 1093 for reasons of military necessity on the main route into Glamorgan. This case is argued above in considering the siting of the castle. It need only be added that the primary ringwork compares well with sites established *ca.* 1100. Its estimated diameter of 45m is close to that of Fitzhamon's Newcastle (EM 3; 42m) and the early ringworks at Ogmore (MR 5) and Coity (MR 1), which measured about 44m. The early-12th-century Llantrithyd ringwork (CR 13) had post-built structures, including an aisled hall. Castle

---

[21] For comparable pits thus interpreted at Merthyr Mawr (Glam.) and Niton Down (I.O.W.) see G. C. Dunning, *Arch. Camb.*, 1937, pp. 331–3. The Rumney example may post-date occupation and explain the carriage of 33 bundles of wood to the site in 1401 (*Cardiff Records*, I, p. 169).

Tower, Penmaen (CR 18), the castle of a knight's fee established before 1135, had a massive post-built gate-tower comparable to that of the early ringwork at Rumney; it also had a smaller post-built hall than Building A at Rumney and a presumed kitchen of similar construction.

The dating of the keep inserted into the defences in Period III is crucial in formulating a reasoned chronology. Its general form and suspected herring-bone masonry would favour a date in the latter half of the 12th century, particularly as allowance must be made for the two earlier periods of development, and for the two which followed before the drastic rebuilding of Period VI in the late 13th century. The size and shape of Rumney keep, as calculated by the excavator, are virtually identical to those of Turberville's Coity (MR 1) and much larger than the tower flanking the gate at Newcastle (EM 3), both of which were imposed on ringworks in the later 12th century, though those were integrated with contemporary stone curtains. The Rumney development is paralleled at Ogmore (MR 5) where an oblong keep of similar area, but earlier date, was similarly inserted beside the gate of a palisaded ringwork which was not converted to stone until the 13th century. The early-12th-century keep at Kenfig (EM 2) was also protected by a palisade as late as 1232. The most probable incentive for the building of Rumney keep and the strengthening of its ring-bank is the Welsh revolt of 1184, which also may have inspired the more thorough stonework at Newcastle and Coity.

The new hall (E) of Periods IV and V and the newly sited entrance and gate-tower may be reasonably ascribed to the first half of the 13th century. Only the final period of occupation (VI) may be dated with confidence to a specific and limited period terminating in 1295. The terminal date is based on an exceptional convergence of archaeological, numismatic and historical evidence: the virtually total excavation of the site yielded no evidence for continued occupation after a conflagration destroyed the final hall on the site; a hoard of 64 silver pennies of Edward I's reformed coinage, securely sealed by the collapse of the roof, has been authoritatively discussed in print and assigned to the early 1290s;[22] and finally, a Welsh revolt of 1294–95, led by the dispossessed lord of the adjacent Welshry of Machen, offers an irresistible context for the conflagration at Rumney.[23] A specific reference to an attack by Morgan ap Maredudd on the castle is lacking, but the record of damage to its mills, cited above, leaves no reasonable doubt that

the site must have suffered his attentions, particularly as it is absent from further cited extents in 1307 and 1314.

The inception of this ultimate period of occupation is less easily gauged, but may be estimated in the light of historical developments in the preceding decades and the nature of the site in its final years. During this period it was protected by little more than its ditch, a lightly defended enclosure offering only the obsolete keep as a last redoubt to its vulnerable occupants, a transformation comparable to even more drastic redevelopment in the early-13th century at Sully (EM 6), where the keep was also retained, but the ringwork was entirely erased and replaced by a much larger manorial enclosure disregarding earlier defences. With these changes Rumney and Sully were no more seriously fortified than the walled manorial centres at Landimôr, Marcross and Llandough (Vol. III, Part 1b, SH 1, 2 and TH 2).

One area furnished archaeological evidence relevant to the duration of Period VI: the hall and the adjacent service-block adjoining it on the N.E. side. Before the destruction of the hall this period had witnessed the abandonment of the initial service-block in line, its area being cut by a large drainage gully which was later filled to level the site of a final service-wing at right angles to the hall. Historical probability suggests that these phases of development fell within the period *ca.* 1270–95. It seems improbable that the slighting of the castle's defences would have been contemplated before the annexation by Gilbert de Clare of Senghennydd in 1267 and of Machen in 1270. These Welsh commotes flanked the Afon Rhymni a short distance N. of Rumney. After 1270, with the new fortress at Caerphilly policing the valley to the N., such a transformation would appear more explicable, especially as it had passed in dower to Maud de Clare in 1267. It is tempting to see the conversion as a work for her domestic convenience close to Cardiff – though no records indicate this. Soon after her death in 1289 the hoard of coins was secreted on a roof timber when the Welsh assault of 1295 was rightly feared.

King, p. 287 (under Monmouthshire).

Rumney (E); Cardiff (C).
ST 27 N.W. (2103–7893)   9.iii.87   XLIIIA N.W.

---

[22] George C. Boon, *Welsh Hoards*, Part III, pp. 83–90.

[23] John E. Morris, *The Welsh Wars of Edward I* (Oxford, 1901), pp. 251–2, 295; *Glam. Co. Hist.*, III, pp. 59–60.

Section EM: Early Masonry Castles

Monuments EM 1–6

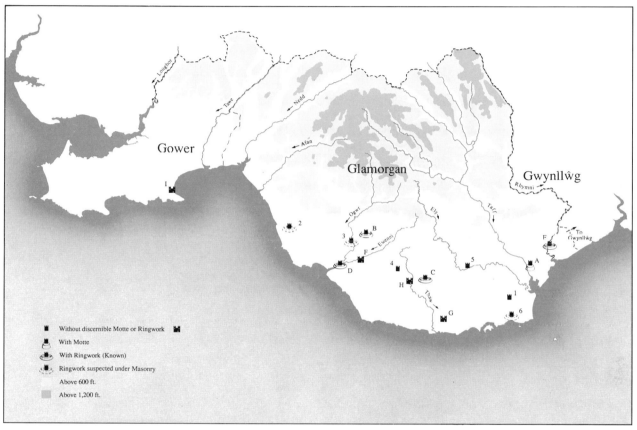

Fig. 226.

1 Dinas Powys Castle
2 Kenfig Castle
3 Newcastle, Bridgend
4 Penllyn Castle
5 Peterston Castle
6 Sully Castle

Early masonry Castles described in other sections
A   Cardiff   (MM 1)

B	Coity	(MR 1)
C	Llanquian	(MR 3)
D	Ogmore	(MR 5)
E	Rumney Castle	(MR 7)
F	Ewenny	(LM 5)
G	Fonmon	(LM 6)
H	Llanblethian	(LM 7)
I	Oystermouth	(LM 12)

Volume III
Part 1b

In this section 'early' implies a date in the 12th century. To qualify the title further, it should be understood that the six monuments included here are not the only stone castles which were built in Glamorgan in the Norman period. The two previous sections (MM and MR) deal with those Glamorgan castles which began as mottes and castle-ringworks, but whose timbers were later converted to stone. In some cases this conversion began in the 12th century. Other vestiges of 12th-century castle masonry are also known at some of the later castles described in Section LM, Part 1b, where the greater bulk and interest of their later masonry favours their inclusion there. In order to give this section the completeness that its title implies, these

Fig. 225. *(Opposite)* Newcastle, Bridgend (EM 3): Gateway.

305

other early stone castles are mapped and listed above (A–I).

It is very probable that most of the six castles described here began as castle-ringworks. They are not included in the appropriate section (MR, Masonry over Ringworks), though cross-referenced there, because they retain no certain visible trace of earlier earthworks, although such may be strongly argued form the near-circular plan of the walls of Kenfig and Newcastle, and from the segment of curving bank and ditch found in the excavations at Sully. In short, at the six sites to be described here the most significant remains consist of Norman masonry.

Their condition ranges from the substantial stonework of *Newcastle* to the vanished *Sully*, which is only known from the records and the excavations carried out there in the 1960s and earlier. The remains at *Kenfig* must also be substantial, but they are for the most part masked by encroaching sand-dunes. Considerable sections of 12th-century walling also survive at *Dinas Powys*, as well as the collapsed heap marking its keep. At *Penllyn* the keep fragment, which is all that survives, is of interest for its herring-bone walling. *Peterston* presents more scattered fragments than Penllyn, distributed about several gardens. Most of these are 13th-century or later in date, but one fragment is to be interpreted as the last remnant of a keep. This, rather than the widely scattered and largely indeterminate vestiges nearby, is the most interesting vestige, and the reason for placing the site in this section. Its later masonry is no great loss to Section LM and will be cross-referenced there.

All six sites have good documentary backing. Although specific references to the castles themselves may be few, their feudal context is clear. Two were castles of the chief lords of Glamorgan: *Newcastle*, first built by Robert Fitzhamon before 1106 and later converted to stone; and *Kenfig*, a castle, with adjacent borough, founded by Robert Consul, Earl of Gloucester and Henry I's son, probably in the 1120s. The remaining four castles were held by tenants-in-chief of the lords of Glamorgan. *Dinas Powys* was the castle of the Somery family, who figure in the *Liber Niger* list (1166) of those enfeoffed before 1135. The same list shows that Norris were at *Penllyn*, and le Sore at *Peterston*, by the same date. De Sully of *Sully* is not listed, but there is clear evidence of the family in Glamorgan at an early date.

Dinas Powys, *Kenfig* and *Newcastle* (EM 1–3) retain significant remains of Norman masonry, and the first two are relatively undisturbed, offering great potential for future clearance and excavation. The six monuments described in this section all incorporated square or rectangular keeps, though that formerly free-standing within Newcastle is long vanished. These keeps, and other characteristic features of the early stone castles described or listed here, are discussed in the Introduction (pp. 39–43).

Monuments retaining some Norman fabric, but more appropriately described in other sections, may be briefly noticed. In Section MM it is suggested that at *Cardiff* (MM 1) the late-11th-century motte was integrated with a walled enclosure largely incorporating the reconstructed stone wall of the late-Roman fort; the fine faceted shell-keep was raised upon the motte in the 12th century. Four of the masonry castles built upon ringworks, and described in Section MR, retain Norman fabric.* At *Coity* (MR 1) there are substantial remains of a Norman keep and an integrated and faceted curtain wall. *Llanquian* (MR 3) has traces of a crude ring-wall incorporating a small square tower or hall. At *Ogmore* (MR 5) the keep and 'cellar' are of the 12th century, while excavations at *Rumney* (MR 7) disclosed the vestiges of a Norman keep.

In Part 1b, Section LM will describe four monuments incorporating Norman fabric. The North and South Gatehouses in the precinct walls at *Ewenny Priory* (LM 5), enlarged *ca.* 1300, incorporate 12th-century gateways. At *Fonmon* (LM 6) a Norman keep is encased in later work. A great heap of collapsed masonry within the 14th-century walls of *Llanblethian* (LM 7) is best explained as a large square keep of the 12th century, while a similar date may be assigned to the rectangular first-floor hall on the highest ground at *Oystermouth* (LM 12) and encased in substantial later works.

Though excluded from the above list and map, the crudely-built ring-wall with imposed 13th-century gatehouse at *Llangynwyd* (MR 2) may be early. Also excluded are the purely domestic early masonry structures recorded within ringworks at Pennard (MR 6), Llantrithyd (CR 13) and Penmaen (CR 18).

---

* Loughor Castle (MR 4) may now be added; see postscript to the site account.

EM 1   Dinas Powys Castle

Dinas Powys Castle, *caput* of the large Somery lordship of Dinas Powys, valued at 3½ knights' fees, probably replaced the unfinished and briefly-occupied Dinas Powys Ringwork (CR 7), 670m distant to the N.W., which was dismantled and abandoned early in the 12th century. The later castle lies at 100ft above O.D. on the higher N.W. end of an isolated hill 5.7km S.W. of Cardiff. The only easy approach is from the S.E., where a gentle slope rises to the main entrance in the S.E. curtain. On the other flanks the falls are steep and wooded; Letton's Way occupies a dingle below the particularly abrupt S.W. flank, while a lesser fall to the N.E. side is skirted at its foot by a leat, tapping the adjacent Cadoxton River and formerly serving a mill of late-medieval foundation 90m to the S.E. The narrow defile of Cwm George, dominated at its N. end by the castle-ringwork, runs N.W. from a point some 200m to the N.W. The castle, like the ringwork, which lies in the neighbouring parish of Michaelston-le-Pit, is uncommonly far from its parish church of St. Andrew, which is 1.4km to the W. and retains a Norman font.

A late tradition claiming that Dinas Powys Castle was a seat of Iestyn ap Gwrgant may be dismissed (see CR 7). Equally unacceptable is the claim that it was ever a possession of the Reigny family, though they were tenants of Somery in the sub-manor of Michaelston-le-Pit.

Dinas Powys lordship comprised the parishes of St. Andrew's, Cadoxton-juxta-Barry, Merthyr Dyfan, Michaelston-le-Pit and Highlight. There is strong evidence that this large and fertile coastal tract, only rivalled by Penmark, St. Athan, and Ogmore, was acquired by Roger de Somery in the time of Fitzhamon. Roger, the probable builder of the nearby castle-ringwork, witnessed the gift of Basaleg Church to Glastonbury *ca.* 1102, in the company of known followers of Fitzhamon, who himself approved the deed.[1] Roger also granted two parts of the tithes of Dinas Powys to Fitzhamon's foundation at Tewkesbury, and may be numbered with the unnamed 'Barons of Robert Fitzhamon', whose gifts of tithes to the abbey were confirmed by Henry I in 1107.[2] The Somery family held Dinas Powys until their failure in the male line in 1321. Their descent is unclear.[3] Dinas Powys was peripheral to their widespread estates in England, especially after their acquisition of the barony of Dudley, Staffordshire, through marriage in 1194, in which context it may be significant that the latest fabric at the castle is little, if at all, later than that date.

The lordship was held by Adam de Somery, of the old enfeoffment (*i.e.* made by 1135), in the returns of 1166.[4] Possibly heir of Roger de Somery, it was no doubt this Adam who granted Margam Abbey 20 shillings of the rent of a mill and 12 acres of land.[5] He had a son John and a grandson Ralph.[6] Possibly Adam's son was the John de Somery who married Hawyse Pagenel and fathered a Ralph; Hawyse was the sister and heiress of Gervase Pagenel, Baron of Dudley. John predeceased Gervase, but his son Ralph succeeded to that barony in 1194.[7] In a deed made between 1193–1203 Ralph de Somery (*ob.* 1210) notified his confirmation of his grandfather Adam's grant of 20 shillings' rent to Margam. This deed furnishes the first mention of the castle; the sum was to be received at Michaelmas from his bailiffs at his castle of *Dinaspowis*.[8]

The castle is next mentioned in 1222, following the death of William de Somery of Dudley. The heir being a minor, Henry III dispatched Robert de Vallibus to receive custody of the castle (*castrum de Dinaunt Poys*) which was then in the hands of William Marshall the younger, Earl of Pembroke. Robert was to deliver the castle to Earl Gilbert de Clare, chief lord of Glamorgan, who was firmly ordered to abandon his preparations to seize the castle by force.[9] A note

[1] Clark, *Cartae*, I (xxxv), p. 38.

[2] Clark, *Cartae*, I (xxxvi–xxxvii), pp. 39–40; (cxxxvi), p. 134; and (cxciii), p. 200; *Epis. Acts*, II, L25, p. 614; L170, p. 659; and L229, p. 677.

[3] See Clark, *Limbus*, p. 431; Corbett, *Glamorgan Lordship*, pp. 95–8; Nichol, *Normans*, pp. 45–9.

[4] *Liber Niger*; *Liber Rubeus*; Corbett, *Glamorgan Lordship*, pp. 33, 118; Nichol, *Normans*, pp. 45.

[5] Clark, *Cartae*, I, p. 163 and (ccxviii) p. 224; II (cccxxv–cccxxvi), pp. 324, 327; (cccxlii) p. 342; and (cccxlix), p. 350; *Epis. Acts*, II, Nos. L279–81, pp. 689–90; Patterson, *Glouc. Charters*, Nos. 137, 139, 140, 144, 145, 148, 149.

[6] Corbett, *Glamorgan Lordship*, p. 95 – though wrongly stating that Roger held the lordship in 1166.

[7] H. Brakspear and A. A. Rollaston, *Official Guide to Dudley Castle*, Dudley, undated, p. 31.

[8] Clark, *Cartae*, I (ccxviii), p. 224; *Epis. Acts*, L298, pp. 694–5; Dating narrowed to 1203, at latest, by King, *Cast. Ang.*, I, p. 176, n.25.

[9] *Cal. P.R.* (1216–25), p. 346; Clark, *Land of Morgan*, p. 87. The Marshalls and Somerys were connected by marriage, see *Complete Peerage*, under Somery.

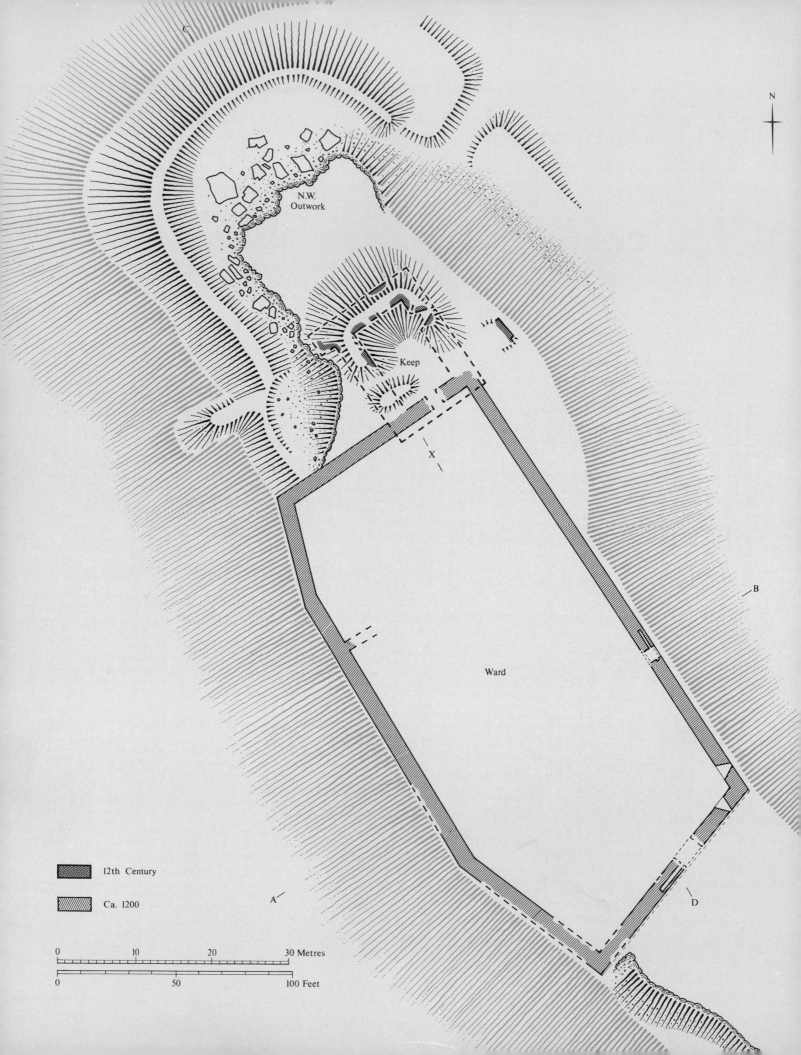

C

N

N.W.
Outwork

Keep

X

Ward

B

12th Century

Ca. 1200

A

D

0   10   20   30 Metres

0   50   100 Feet

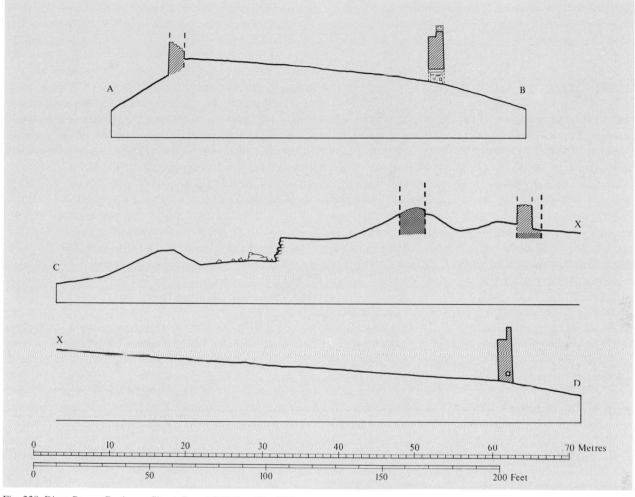

Fig. 228. Dinas Powys Castle; profiles A-B and C-X-D on Fig. 227.

subscribed to the royal mandate indicated that Earl Gilbert had actually besieged the castle.

In 1262, on the death of Earl Richard de Clare, Dinas Powys was held by Robert de Somery.[10] The castle is mentioned in 1275, when Aline, Countess of Norfolk, purchased the wardship of the manor until Roger de Somery was of age.[11] This Roger died in 1291, and his son John is recorded as lord of Dinas Powys in 1307, 1314 and 1317, though the castle is only mentioned in the first of these records.[12] John de Somery, the last of his name, died in 1321. Like Dudley, Dinas Powys was partitioned between his married sisters and coheiresses, Margaret Sutton and Joan de Botetourt. The castle fell within the Sutton moiety, and in an extent of 1330 it was said to be 'worth nil beyond reprises'.[13] The Botetourt moiety

Fig. 227. *(Opposite)* Dinas Powys Castle: general plan.

came to the chief lord, Edward le Despenser, before 1373, probably by purchase, escheating to the Crown in 1483; the Sutton moiety was purchased by Sir Matthew Cradock early in the 16th century, and through him came to the Herberts.[14]

The castle was 'al in ruine' by 1536, when noticed by Leland, though its walls survived to shelter a garden and were repaired by E. H. Lee who owned it

[10] Clark, *Cartae*, II (dcxv), p. 650; Corbett, *Glamorgan Lordship*, pp. 34, 97; *Glam. Co. Hist.*, III, p. 17.

[11] Clark, *Cartae*, III (dcciii), pp. 770–2; Corbett, *Glamorgan Lordship*, p. 98; Nichol, *Normans*, p. 48.

[12] *Cal. I.P.M.*, Vol. IV, No. 435, pp. 322–4; *Cardiff Records*, I, p. 271; Clark, *Cartae*, III (dccclii), p. 1000; Corbett, *Glamorgan Lordship*, p. 98.

[13] Clark, *Cartae* III (dccccxliii), p. 1163.

[14] Corbett, *Glamorgan Lordship*, pp. 98–101; Lewis, *Breviat*, p. 98, n.2; see also *Cal. Anc. Petitions*, p. 356, for the purchase of the advowson of the church of Dinas Powys by Despenser.

in the early 19th century.[15] More recently an orchard, a market garden and a piggery, the site had become completely overgrown by 1979 when Dinas Powys Civic Trust cleared the tangled undergrowth.

Architectural Description

The surviving remains (Fig. 227) comprise three components representing at least two periods of work that extend for 117m along the ridge. From the N.W. these are: (i) *The N.W. Outwork* on the tip of the ridge; (ii) *The Keep* on the highest point of the ridge; and (iii) *The Ward*, walled but unflanked. Formerly a further embanked outwork to the S.E. may have fronted the main entrance into the ward; now vanished, such an outwork was recorded in an unpublished note and sketch by G. T. Clark *ca.* 1860.[16] The relationship between the N.W. outwork and the keep is uncertain, but both predate the ward.

(i) *The N.W. Outwork* occupies the final 32m of gently sloping ground on the tip of the ridge. It is outlined by a well-marked penannular bank up to 2m high internally but without an outer ditch. This bank follows the crest of the steep natural slope, terminating on the N. close to the foot of the slope beneath a bold outcrop of Triassic rock. At its southern termination, below the W. angle of the keep, it has been truncated by a quarry-pit. By far the greater part of the original surface within this bank has been quarried away, the outcrop having been worked inwards from the rear of the bank to leave a vertical quarry-face and a floor littered with unhewn slabs and debris. Of regular form and earthen content, the bank is not easily explained as quarry dumping. A short hollow-way curves up behind its northern termination from an old track passing along the adjacent hillside. Crucial evidence is to be seen in the area of the southern termination of the bank. There it is clear that the quarry-face associated with the pit which truncates the bank continues on under the N.W. curtain of the ward; the curtain is stepped down over the quarry-face, 7m from the W. angle, and displays evidence of constructional difficulties detailed below. In this area, at least, the quarrying post-dates the outwork and is earlier than the curtain of *ca.* 1200. A small dump lies adjacent at the head of the natural scarp.

The purpose of the N.W. Outwork and its relationship to the keep is uncertain. Excavation might clarify matters, but meanwhile three interpretations might be postulated: (a) The outwork predates the keep and is the remnant of an earth-and-timber castle, the immediate successor of Dinas Powys Ringwork (CR 7); (b) it was contemporary with the keep and is the remnant of a palisaded bailey; or (c) it was contemporary with the keep, but served only as a defensive hornwork, perhaps augmented by the obstacles of the internal quarry-face and debris.

The purpose of the quarrying must also be considered. Except for scant imported dressings, the walls of the keep and ward are constructed of the Triassic Limestone quarried on the site. It seems probable that the earliest quarrying, predating the ward, furnished stone for the keep. This undoubtedly early quarrying may well have extended along the entire S.W. flank of the ward, and beyond, as will be suggested below, although that does not rule out the possibility that at a later date some of the quarrying within the outwork provided material for the ward. Undoubtedly, however, the final stage reached in quarrying rendered the outwork useless as a bailey, but effective as a hornwork.

(ii) *The Keep* is now represented by a crescentic bank up to 2.2m high, its ends embracing a hollow beyond the N.W. wall of the later ward. Clearance of thick undergrowth and debris revealed slight but consistent traces of the mortared masonry of the N.W. half of a large rectangular keep. Its walls are 3m thick, measured well above the level of any batter which may be buried. Two features were noted: the vestiges of the splays of a loop in the N.E. wall, and a projection at the E. angle, perhaps for a latrine. No visible trace of the S.E. half of the keep survives, but its lines are indicated by two ragged scars on the outer face of the adjacent curtain of the later ward, one at its N. angle, the other the requisite 3m wide and exactly in line with the known section of the S.W. keep wall. At the N. angle of the ward the scar corresponds with the known inner face of the N.E. keep wall, but continues around the ward angle, where the external keep face seemingly projected a little beyond that of the ward. These aligned scars on the thinner and better preserved curtain-wall suggest that the S.E. wall of the keep had collapsed, or been destroyed before its surviving walls were incorporated as an adjunct of the new ward adjacent, from which a narrow central door entered its basement. This door, now a ragged gap, retained a rebated jamb when seen by Clark, *ca.* 1860.[17]

[15] Leland, *Itin. Wales*, p. 23; Lewis, *Top. Dict.* (1833); Thomas David, *N.L.W.*, MS 253.

[16] Clark Papers, *N.L.W.*, MS 5215E.

Present vestiges indicate a massively walled keep measuring some 18.3m by 13.4m externally, and close in area to the largest keep in the county at Kenfig (EM 2). Besides Clark's unpublished notes, cited above, two earlier accounts confirm the existence of a keep at Dinas Powys and indicate that it had a vaulted basement. Iolo Morgannwg (Edward Williams) described the site in unpublished notes of *ca.* 1780:

'Without the walls to the northeast are apparent ruins of a much ancienter castle, probably Roman, and the mouth of a vault going under it still open. Close by ye north east corner huge mass of very ancient ruins at ye north end.'[18]

By 1833 the vault was no longer visible, but Samuel Lewis confirms local knowledge of its former existence, already quite misunderstood:

'On the outside of the great walls' (of the ward) 'at the north-western corner, there is a smaller heap of ruins, probably those of an ARX, or tower, appendant to the castle, with which it appears to have communicated by means of a narrow door; and, within the memory of persons now living, there was a subterraneous passage, commencing in the side of the rocky hill, forming the side of the castle, and proceeding in a direction towards this tower, but which has been filled up.'[19]

Clark's sketch outlines the keep and he also notes:

'The Keep seems to have been a small square tower placed outside the W. end (sic) but whether touching its wall is uncertain.'[20]

The vault observed by Iolo, and misunderstood by local inhabitants, presumably spanned the width of the keep and was entered by the door communicating with the ward. The keep at Kenfig (EM 2) also had one of its walls rebuilt less massively, though there the structure remained free-standing.

(iii) *The Ward* encloses a roughly quadrilateral area, slightly bowed out to the S.W., measuring 67m by 32m internally. There is a gentle slope along and across its interior (Fig. 228, profiles). Only the walls survive, but they retain slight traces of internal buildings and still rise above the level of the wall-walk on the N.E. and S.E. sides. The eroded battlements are best preserved to the N.E., with lesser traces surviving to the S.E. The walls are 2m thick, and built with Triassic Limestone rubble derived from the site, roughly coursed and laid in sandy mortar, and with imported Sutton and Tufa dressings. The less deeply bedded white Triassic Limestone generally predominates over the red variety, which is also used.

The *N.W. Curtain* survives to 3m or more in height. Its incorporation in the earlier keep, to form a renewed S.E. wall of that structure, has been noted, as also its awkwardly contrived construction over a pre-existing quarry face 7m from the W. angle. From the keep to this step in the ground surface the external face of the curtain is roughly coursed with predominantly red Triassic rubble, which facing terminates at a near vertical break directly above the quarry face. Beyond this break, where the curtain steps down, the facing is of smaller and generally white Triassic rubble coursed on a slope downwards to the W. angle. Internally this break is equally apparent, though the ground has been levelled up to mask the quarry face. Two phases of construction met at this difficult point, and it is possible that the quarry face extended along the entire S.W. flank of the ridge, for it reappears at a similar point beyond the S. angle of the ward and continues well beyond.

The *S.W. Curtain*, bowed outwards in three unequal straight lengths, survives internally to heights between 1 and 2m above the ground. Externally, however, it is carried down for some 4m as a revetment well below the internal level and founded, without a berm, on the top of a precipitous fall (Fig. 228, profile A–B). Its bowed line, greatly reduced height and deep outer revetment reflect its precarious position above the steepest fall from the site, adding to the suspicion of an inherent instability and a line imposed by a continuous quarry face. The only surviving feature on this curtain is the stub of a wall, 1.2m wide and bonded with the inner face 19m S. of the W. angle. In this area Lewis (1833) noted the foundations of walls forming two apartments, while Clark (*ca.* 1860) recorded similar traces of buildings and the finding of a 'water stoup ... of a chapel'.[21] Another record of internal buildings in this quarter, perhaps of Sutton Stone, is found in a manuscript by Thomas David (1837): '... inside of these North Westward parts there was another dwelling house where lately was found a Cross Wall of Spar stones.'[22]

The *N.E. Curtain* (Fig. 229b) is straight and sur-

[17] See f/n. 16.

[18] Iolo Morgannwg Papers, *N.L.W.*, MS 21413E.

[19] Lewis, *Top. Dict.* (1833).

[20] See f/n. 16.

[21] See f/ns. 16 and 19.

[22] Thomas David (Bard), 'The History of Dinaspowis Castle', 'finish December 1837', *N.L.W.*, MS 252. A second version of the same short manuscript (MS 253) gives similar information. The keep is the other 'house' – noted as 'a fine place of dwelling'.

311

vives to its full height. Although the external ground here falls away gently, before steepening, there is no external ditch. The wall-walk is almost 6m above internal level, with eroded battlements rising a further 1.8m. A postern gate (Fig. 230) 19m N. of the internal E. angle retains its segmental-vaulted rear arch, but internal and external dressings of Sutton Stone have been robbed, leaving only some roots of this stone in place. One dislodged moulded fragment of the outer arch was recovered from the foot of the outer N. jamb and matched five others described below. This dressing was deeply-incised with a triple roll-and-fillet moulding of Early English style. Draw-bar holes behind the outer arch survive on both sides, that to the N. being 2.44m deep. At 1.5m from the internal W. angle, a splayed loop pierces the curtain, its rear arch retaining two dressed Tufa voussoirs. Another similar loop is placed an equal distance along the adjacent S.E. curtain, both having probably served a vanished building at this point. In the absence of any scar or tusk on the curtain, a large square beam hole some 1.5m high and a little to the N. of the first-mentioned loop, may indicate a half-timbered structure. Internal lean-to buildings are certainly indicated by intermittent traces of horizontal flashing-creases both along the curtain N. of the postern and S. of the main entrance through the adjacent S.E. curtain.

Putlog holes penetrating the entire thickness of the

wall are a conspicuous feature of the N.E. and S.E. curtains. They are generally ranged in vertical or slightly staggered tiers of four holes, each tier about 3m apart.

The *S.E. Curtain* is now broken by a ragged gap E. of centre. Early accounts, already cited, indicate that a round-headed principal gateway survived *ca.* 1780 (Iolo Morgannwg),[23] but that it had fallen in to leave a wide breach by 1833 (Lewis).[24] A large draw-bar hole 40.2cm square still penetrates the truncated W. flank of the entrance to a depth of 3.8m. This most vulnerable flank would have been fronted by a ditch, now entirely vanished along with all traces of the embanked outwork noted and sketched by Clark.[25] The external S.E. facade (Fig. 229a) displays certain features reminiscent of the main entrance front of the late-12th-century Newcastle (EM 3). Large dressed alternating quoins of Sutton Stone survive above the reach of stone-robbers at the E. angle. At and near ground level they have been robbed, but more significantly this robbing has been continued unbroken along the curtain to the entrance in three horizontal steps, and beyond that for 11.5m in one continuous horizontal line, below which all original facing has gone. Above these horizontal robbing lines the roughly-coursed rubble face survives, suggesting most strongly that an ashlar plinth has been removed, as at Newcastle, where the ashlar also rose upwards to frame the dressings of the gate. It may also be significant that internal and external facing has entirely fallen away for a distance of 6m from the W. angle, a measurement exactly corresponding with the southward continuation of the quarry-face already noticed

---

[23] See f/n. 18.
[24] See f/n. 19.
[25] See f/n. 16.

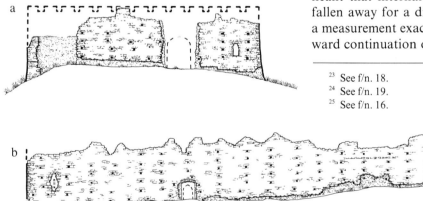

Fig. 229. Dinas Powys Castle: (a) external south-east elevation, gateway and crenellations restored as described by Iolo Morgannwg (*ca.* 1780); (b) external north-east elevation.

(plan, Fig. 227). The W. angle lacks Sutton quoins and has been rebuilt with a shallow plain buttress at its base, a further hint of settlement problems over the quarry.

Besides the few dressings still *in situ* (Sutton quoins at the E. angle and Tufa voussoirs over the adjacent loop), other loose dressings were found collected together in the garden of the cottage immediately beyond the main entrance (Old Mill Farmhouse). These included three Sutton voussoirs exactly matching that recovered from the postern gate and undoubtedly coming from the outer arch there, and two more identical voussoirs found during survey within the ward. All are now brought together in the garden, and the fact that all six voussoirs have lost their central roll must indicate mutilation when all formed part of the outer postern arch. An upper quernstone of conglomerate and part of a trefoiled window-head were also found and added to the same collection. Coins of 13th- to 15th-century date were found in the ward in 1965,[26] and during survey a rim-sherd of coarse ware of *ca.* 1200 was recovered from rubble near the loop in the keep.

Structural Development and Dating

Dismissing the late tradition that Dinas Powys was a seat of Iestyn ap Gwrgant, historical and archaeological evidence suggests that the castle was founded by the Somery lords to replace Dinas Powys ringwork (CR 7) in the early 12th century. Roger de Somery, lord under Fitzhamon, and Adam de Somery the elder, possibly Roger's son or grandson and still lord in 1166, are the only members of the family known to us who may have changed the site of their *caput*. The systematic way in which the ringwork was dismantled might well indicated that work on the new castle was already well advanced and ready to accommodate the administration of the lordship.

Without the evidence of excavation it is not possible to know whether the *Keep* and the *North-West Outwork* were both incorporated in the castle from the outset, or whether the keep was a later addition to an earthwork castle which would surely have been a promontory castle-ringwork like its predecessor. Substantial remains of the keep lie buried, but pending its excavation we may only deduce a 12th-century date from its massive construction and rectangular form, broad characteristics that do not exclude the possibility of erection early in that century. Fitzosbern's 'Great Tower' of the late 1060s at Chepstow is nar-

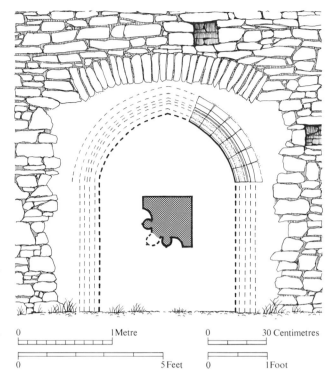

Fig. 230. Dinas Powys Castle: north-east postern, external elevation. Dressings restored from moulding (inset) recovered at its north jamb.

rower, if even longer. A further large rectangular 12th-century keep is known at Sully (EM 6), while smaller local examples are found at Ogmore (MR 5) and Penllyn (EM 4), the latter incorporating herring-bone masonry.

A date early rather than late in the 12th century for the building of the keep might also be surmised from the circumstances of its incorporation in the later ward. The S. wall of the keep required rebuilding, apparently from the ground up, though footings may await excavation. If structural weakness, rather than hostile action, necessitated this rebuilding, we might presume a lengthy period before instability became apparent. The only record of an attack on the castle, cited above,[27] is the siege mounted by Gilbert de Clare in 1222. This siege, however, could hardly explain the need to rebuild the keep, for by that date it is most probable that the ward had already been completed and integrated with the restored keep.

The dating of the *Ward* must at present rely on its form and surviving detail. Its form, a simple unflanked enclosure, outlined in a series of straight

---

[26] G. Dowdell, *Arch. in Wales.* 1965, p. 26.

[27] See f/n. 9.

lengths, evidently reflects the similar if more regular 12th-century faceted enclosures to be seen at Ogmore (MR 5), Coity (MR 1) and Newcastle (EM 3); the same technique is also seen at the 12th-century shell-keep on the motte at Cardiff (MM 1), and all four exemplify the use of alternating quoins of Sutton Stone at the angles, a feature surviving at the E. angle of Dinas Powys Castle. We have also noted the strong possibility that Dinas Powys Castle once had an ashlar plinth like that at Newcastle, which itself probably dates at the latest to the 1180s. The moulding of the postern arch, which was not an insertion, could certainly be dated well into the 13th century, but a late-12th-century date cannot be ruled out. On balance, a provisional date of *ca.* 1200 for the ward would best suit present information.

The lack of any certain 13th-century or later fabric might reflect the Somery acquisition of the barony of Dudley in 1194, to add to their already extensive English estates, which no doubt diminished their interest in Dinas Powys. Failure in the male line in 1321, and the resultant partition of the lordship, would have further reduced the likelihood of any major work at the castle. Perhaps abandoned before the close of the Middle Ages, it was in ruins by the early 16th century.

King, p. 163

St Andrews (E), St Andrews Major (C)
ST 17 S.E. (1527–7164)　　2.x.85　　XLVII S.W.

EM 2　Kenfig Castle

The scant and desolate vestiges of the castle of Kenfig, and its '... borough town sometime of good account' (Merrick), have been long abandoned to a forlorn wilderness of sand-dunes. Kenfig, established by Robert, Earl of Gloucester, Lord of Glamorgan *ca.* 1114–47, remained a demesne possession of successive chief lords throughout the medieval period. An enduring tradition that Kenfig was a castle of Iestyn ap Gwrgant, taken and strengthened by Robert Fitzhamon in the late 11th century,[1] must be rejected; its authority is the forged Gwentian *Brut*.[2] Its strategic and exposed position as a western outpost of the lords of Glamorgan explains its exceptionally full documentary record; no less than eight attacks on Kenfig are known to us, seven by the Welsh and one by an alliance of Welsh and English lords. But from the 14th century Kenfig progressively succumbed to the remorseless advance of the sands, its church of St James being replaced before 1485 by a new church of the same name at Pyle, on higher ground and 2.4km to the E.[3] In the 1530s Leland found only '... *a little village ... and a castel, both in ruine and almost shokid and devourid with the sands that the Severn Se there castith up.*'[4] Of the 142 burgages frequently recorded in the 13th and 14th centuries, only three survived by 1572, when most burgesses had resettled away from the old enclosed borough, including those established in 29 new burgages on Cefn Cribwr, near Pyle.[5] By 1665 only one cottage remained '... *on the scite of the ould castle*'.[6] Several villages and the castles of Penmaen (CR 18), Pennard (MR 6) and Candleston (TH 1) on the coasts of Gower and Glamorgan were similarly overwhelmed by sand in the same period (see Introductory Survey, Part 1b).

The Site and History of Kenfig

The lordship, castle and borough of Kenfig, like others in the county, derived its name from the river on which it stood, namely the Afon Cynffig, which rises on Margam Mountain 6km to the N.[7] The castle lies on its S. bank 2km from its present estuary, though this is a late-medieval deflection from a broad estuary which once extended inland almost to the site on its S.E.

[1] e.g.: Lewis, *Breviat*, p. 105; Clark, *Arch. Camb.* 1871, p. 173; Gray, *Kenfig*, pp. 36–45; Armitage, *Norman Castles*, p. 295; A. J. Richard, *Arch. Camb.* 1927, pp. 162–3; and I. Soulsby, *The Medieval Towns of Wales* (1983), p. 150.

[2] Exposed by J. E. Lloyd, *Proc. of the British Academy*, XIV (1928), pp. 376–7.

[3] L. S. Higgins, *Arch. Camb.*, LXXXVIII (1933), pp. 34–5, 64; F. J. North, *Sunken Cities*, Cardiff, 1957, pp. 115–18; Clark, *Cartae*, V (mccclxix), p. 1916; *Glam. Co. Hist.*, III, p. 354. The church of St. Mary Magdalen, at nearby Mawdlam, has a Norman font which may have come from the old St James (see *Arch. Camb.* 1898, pp. 132–3).

[4] Leland, *Itin. Wales*, p. 29; see also Merrick, *Morg. Arch.*, p. 105, and Lewis, *Breviat*, p. 101, for similar observations later in the same century.

[5] Clark, *Arch. Camb.* 1871, pp. 245, 253–4; Gray, *Kenfig*, pp. 168–9, 177–8.

[6] A. L. Evans, *The Story of Kenfig*, Port Talbot, 1960, pp. 39–40 (citing Bute MSS. *N.L.W.*); *Arch. Camb.*, CXXVI (1977), pp. 145–7.

[7] For the name, *Glam. Co. Hist.*, II, p. 457; Other Glamorgan castles and lordships named after rivers are Loughor, Ogmore, Rumney and Neath.

side and is now marked by the land-locked Kenfig Pool and lesser ponds to its N. (Map, Fig. 232).[8] The extensive dunes of Kenfig Burrows so mask the site that it may only be found in relation to modern features: it is immediately S. of railway sidings and 300m W. of the point at which an elevated section of the M4 crosses these sidings and the main railway line. The castle cannot lie far from the point at which the Roman road from Cardiff to Neath crossed the river (Vol. I, Part 2, No. 753). This ancient road, the medieval *Via Regalis*, *Via Maritima*, or Port Way, is not traced with certainty to the W. of Stormy Down, but a most convincing line follows Heol-y-sheet, *via* North Cornelly, to a crossing at Pont-felin-newydd, 560m E. of the castle, and beyond the river westwards to Margam as Water Street.[9] Roman brick and tile

are incorporated in the fabric of the keep at Kenfig, and two coin hoards and sherds of Roman date, as well as an Early Christian brooch, have been recovered from the immediate vicinity.[10]

Kenfig was pivotal to Earl Robert's westward advance from the line of the Ogmore Valley, the western limit of castle-building and appropriations under Fitzhamon.[11] Close to the Roman road and its import-

---

[8] In the lordship as a whole, the S. bank was effectively on the E. or Cardiff side; for the original estuary, see North, *op. cit.*, f/n. 3.

[9] Gray, *Kenfig*, pp. 30–2, map facing p. 318.

[10] *B.B.C.S.*, III, Part 1 (1926), p. 76 and XIV, Part 1 (1950), p. 87; *Arch. Camb.*, LXXXIII (1928), pp. 200–2; *Glam. Co. Hist.*, II, pp. 287, 331–4, 444b.

Fig. 231. Kenfig Castle: aerial view from the north-north-east. Castle beyond railway, centre; borough rampart visible top right, and rather lower top left.

ant river-crossing, Kenfig was respectively 10km N.W. and 10.5km W.N.W. of earlier castles at Ogmore (MR 5) and Newcastle (EM 3), the latter initially, by 1106, a solitary outpost on the W. bank of the Ogwr. Beyond the Afon Cynffig, from a point about 4km N. of Kenfig Castle, traffic westwards was constricted by a continuous line of steep hills to a narrow coastal strip for a further 8km, as far as the Afon Nedd. Before 1130 Earl Robert had advanced along this corridor to establish his furthermost demesne castle on the E. bank of the Nedd (LM 11), accompanied by his constable, Richard de Granville, who had raised a short-lived castle on the W. side of that river (VE 2). In 1130 Richard granted this castle and all his lands W. of the river to endow his new abbey at Neath, while Robert, clearly established by then on the E. bank, donated lands at Llansawel.[12] Robert and Richard probably advanced to the Afon Nedd in the early 1120s, and it is self-evident that this campaign would have been bolstered by first establishing a castle at Kenfig. Earl Robert was celebrated for his keep at Bristol. The smaller keep at Kenfig, as first built, was consistent with this reputation, to judge from its fine ashlar buttresses and the internal embellishment represented by the attached scalloped capital recovered within (below and Fig. 237).

Incontrovertible evidence for Earl Robert's presence at Kenfig is limited to a charter of 1140–47, in which he grants to Ewenny Priory '... *a burgage in the west street ... outside the gate of the vill of Kenefec* ...';[13] clearly a fortified vill had been established, and with it, we need not doubt, the castle. The lost Register of Neath, as cited by Merrick, also named Earl Robert as the founder of Kenfig, with the enigmatic marginal gloss '... *viz. Anno Domini* 1129 Kenfig rebuilt.'[14]

In 1147, the last year of his life, Robert founded Margam Abbey, granting it '... *all the land between the Cynffig and Afan rivers from the brow of the mountains to the sea ...*', a further proof of his presence in the lands between Afan and Ogwr. As to the land embraced by the Cynffig and Ogwr rivers, perhaps a former Welsh division, it was now divided into the two demesne lordships based respectively on Newcastle and Kenfig, while a third was soon established with its *caput* at Llangynwyd Castle (MR 2), which lordship became known as Tir Iarll (the Earl's Land) and was always associated with Kenfig. Among subtenants enfeoffed in the area in the 12th century were Scurlage and Sturmi, who built castles at Llangewydd (VE 3) and Stormy (MO 5).

In the time of Earl William (1147–83), though the castle is not mentioned, there are records of the borough and its church of St. James, founded 1151–54.[15] Of particular interest is Earl William's grant to Hugh of Hereford of 100 acres at Kenfig, for which Hugh owed 40 days castle-guard at one of the Earl's castles, an indication, perhaps, that castle-guard was computed at this rate by William.[16] Hugh's service was probably demanded at the Earl's western castles at Neath, Kenfig and Newcastle. The town of Kenfig (*Villa de Kenefeg*) was burned for the first time, according to the Margam Annals, in 1167.[17]

From 1183–89, following the death of Earl William, the lordship of Glamorgan was held by the Crown, until in the latter year it passed to John, Henry II's son, on his long-delayed marriage to the heiress Isabel of Gloucester. Though John and Isabel were already betrothed, the serious Welsh uprising which followed Earl William's death persuaded Henry II to retain the lordship and postpone the marriage. The revolt of 1183–84 centred especially in the western parts of the lordship, with determined assaults on Neath, Kenfig and Newcastle, probably led by Morgan ap Caradog of Afan. The attack on Kenfig furnishes our first known references to the castle, where the royal custodian was Reginald Fitzsimon. The attack was expected, for palisades (*palis*) were prepared in the woods near Chepstow and brought by boat at a cost of £22. 3s. 4d. These were used to enclose the town and castle, while three brattices (*bretescarum*) and 200 picks were despatched from Bristol. Despite these urgent preparations the town and its mill were burned by the insurgents and the castle damaged before the

Fig. 232. *(Opposite)* Kenfig Castle: location map. Kenfig pool, bottom left, marks the former estuary.

---

[11] *Glam. Co. Hist.*, III, p. 14, citing as one index of Fitzhamon's advance the limited distribution of the grants of land and churches to Tewkesbury. Though appropriated to that abbey and beyond the Ogwr, Kenfig church was not founded until 1151–57 (Patterson, *Glouc. Charters*, No. 271, p. 175; Clark, *Cartae*, I (CX), p. 111).

[12] Clark, *Cartae*, I (lxvii), p. 74 and II (cccxviii), p. 315.

[13] Patterson, *Glouc. Charters*, No. 68, p. 74; Clark, *Cartae*, I (ci), p. 103; *Epis. Acts*, II, L105, pp. 637–8; *Hist. et Cart. Gloucester*, Vol. II (dcxlvii), p. 135.

[14] Merrick, *Morg. Arch.* pp. 42, 101. For the reliability of Merrick's use of this lost source, see *ibid.*, pp. XXI and XXVIII and *Arch. Camb.* 1887, pp. 88–94.

[15] Patterson, *Glouc. Charters*, No. 182, p. 163 and No. 271, p. 175; Clark, *Cartae*, I (cv), p. 107 and (cx), p. 111; *Glam. Co. Hist.*, III, pp. 98, 338.

[16] Patterson, *Glouc. Charters*, No. 97, p. 98; Clark, *Cartae*, VI (mdli), p. 2272.

[17] *Ann. Margam*, p. 16.

N

Motorway

Water Street

Afon Cynffig

Former course
of river

Kenfig Castle

Heol-y-Sheet
"Roman Road

✝ Site of St. James's Church

Kenfig Burrows

St. Mary Magdalen's Church

Town Hall

Mawdlam

Kenfig Pool

(former estuary)

| 0 | 100 | 200 | 300 Metres |

| 0 | 500 | 1,000 Feet |

revolt was quelled in July 1184. In 1185 timber was brought in 24 ships to the castle, where £16. 11s. 6½d. was expended on repairs to gates, palisades and other unspecified works. The palisade defending the town was also repaired, at a cost of £16, and the mill was restored, while the burgesses were excused their rents on account of damages suffered.[18] Though it was damaged, the castle was not taken, which suggests that the stone keep was already built. There is no hint of any work in stone in the recorded repairs. The keep had probably been built by Earl Robert at the foundation of Kenfig, for he was celebrated for the especially strong keep he raised at Bristol.[19]

No record is known of Kenfig Castle during the long period of John's possession of the Lordship of Glamorgan 1189–1214, as king from 1199. Soon after he obtained siesin in 1189, John granted Newcastle to Morgan ap Caradog, the presumed leader of the revolt of 1183–84. Newcastle remained with Morgan's heir Leisan until at least 1213, but his brother and heir Morgan Gam was not enfeoffed by the first of the Clare lords, Earl Gilbert (1217–30). Not surprisingly, Morgan Gam was soon in arms against Gilbert, attacking Newcastle in 1226. In 1228, following Morgan Gam's capture and imprisonment by Gilbert, the struggle was taken up by Morgan's kinsman, Hywel ap Maredudd of Meisgyn, who burned the town of Kenfig.[20] Morgan, freed from the earl's prison in 1229, resumed his hostility during the minority of Gilbert's heir, Richard, when Hubert de Burgh held Glamorgan for the King. In 1231, along with Llywelyn ap Iorwerth of Gwynedd, Morgan destroyed Neath Castle (LM 11) and in the following year, on Llywelyn's orders, he moved against Kenfig; the town, excepting the church, was destroyed, but the keep (turris) withstood the assault, though its outer defences comprised only a ditch and palisade (fossa et sepe).[21]

After Morgan Gam's death, ca. 1241, Hywl ap Maredudd assumed leadership of the Welsh commotes, and in 1243, soon after Richard de Clare had obtained siesin of Glamorgan, he attacked Kenfig again, without recorded mention of the castle.[22]

Surprisingly, there is no mention of Kenfig in 1257 and 1258, when the castles of Llangynwyd (MR 2) and Neath (LM 11) were in turn destroyed by the Welsh, the first by Llywelyn ap Gruffydd of Gwynedd. The next recorded attack on Kenfig did not come until 1295, shortly before the death of Gilbert de Clare, the 'Red Earl'. This attack was carried out by the Welsh of the Blaenau led by Morgan ap Maredudd, and the damage inflicted is made clear in the earl's

inquisition post mortem; the castle had been 'recently burned' and although 142 burgages had been accounted for as recently as 1281, the burgage rents now returned only 13s.[23]

The town had recovered by 1314, when 142 burgages were again registered in the inquisition on the death of the last Clare, Earl Gilbert, at Banockburn.[24] With his passing Glamorgan once more reverted to the Crown, pending a settlement of the Clare inheritance on the late earl's three sisters. As in 1183, unrest soon broke out in the lordship, and though Kenfig was initially spared, it was attacked by the insurgent Welsh in 1316, during the more serious revolt of Llywelyn Bren of Senghennydd. Much of the town was devastated and its trade disrupted. The castle, though damaged, was again successfully held for the Crown by Leisan de Avene of Afan, much to the outrage of his rebellious compatriots.[25] An echo of the havoc wrought in this attack is to be found in the 1316 account of John Giffard, royal keeper of the lordship: 'The greater part of the town was burnt in the war', 42 burgages were in ashes and their owners fled. The castle required 2,000 roof shingles (scendulis) and nails to repair houses within it at a cost of 16s. 8d.[26]

The eighth and final recorded attack on Kenfig in 1321 was more destructive and quite different from those that had been suffered earlier. All previous attacks had been mounted by Welsh insurgents. On this occasion a coalition of Marcher lords and Welsh leaders, including Leisan de Avene who had defended Kenfig for the Crown in 1314–16, brought devastation

---

[18] Pipe Rolls (1183–84), 30 Henry II and (1184–85), 31 Henry II; Ann. Margam, pp. 17–18 (misdated to 1185); Glam. Co. Hist., III, pp. 37–8; Lloyd, Hist Wales, II, pp. 571–2; Hist. Kings Works, II, pp. 650–1.

[19] For the vanished Bristol keep, Hist. Kings Works, II, p. 578.

[20] Ann. Margam, pp. 35–6; Glam. Co. Hist., III, pp. 46–7.

[21] Ann. Margam, p. 39; Breviate Ann. (Arch. Camb. 1862, p. 278).

[22] Clark, Cartae, III (dcclviii), p. 859; Breviate Ann. (Arch. Camb. 1862, p. 279); Glam. Co. Hist., III, pp. 50, 338; A. L. Evans, Margam Abbey, 1958, p. 72.

[23] Cal. I.P.M. Vol. III, 24 Edward I, p. 244; Corbett, Glamorgan Lordship, pp. 141–2; Beresford, New Towns, pp. 256, 555; A. L. Evans, Margam Abbey, 1958, p. 76. The insurgents were pardoned in October 1295 (Cal. P.R., 1292–1301, p. 154).

[24] Cal. I.P.M., 8 Edward II, 43/38; Beresford, New Towns, p. 555.

[25] Cal. C.R., 1313–18, pp. 162, 406; Clark, Cartae, III (dccclxvii), p. 1024; Glam. Co. Hist., III, pp. 73, 79, 344; A. L. Evans, Margam Abbey, p. 77.

[26] Clark, Cartae, III (dccxlvii), pp. 835–6 (one of a series of Giffard's accounts transcribed by Clark, but all erroneously dated to 1281 on p. 812); Gray, Kenfig, pp. 60, 65.

to the lands of the recently enfeoffed Despenser lord, Hugh the Younger. Hugh, enfeoffed in 1317 as husband of Eleanor de Clare, had provoked this coalition by his unscrupulous and acquisitive aims and his malevolent influence over the king. In a swift and savage campaign, notwithstanding Hugh's foreknowledge and defensive preparations, a force of 800 men-at-arms, 500 light horse and 10,000 footmen spread desolation in his lands. Led by Humphrey de Bohun and Roger Mortimer, and with the support of the earl of Lancaster, Despenser's seven demesne castles in Glamorgan, including Kenfig, were destroyed. This was a punitive campaign of looting and destruction, not one of conquest. Goods and chattels, arms, engines and victuals to the value of £2,000 were carried away. The gates and houses of all Hugh's castles were destroyed and all their iron fittings and lead were taken, to the value of a further £2,000. A like value was put on the lord's muniments and charters which were taken or destroyed as well, not to mention the havoc wrought on mills, crops, animals and houses throughout the earl's demesnes.[27]

Kenfig Castle next figures in an inquisition of 1359.[28] In 1377 it was repaired by William Walsh, crown receiver during the minority of Thomas Despenser. Its central role in affairs of the borough was still evident in Lord Thomas Despenser's charter of 1379, the town's oldest extant charter. The constable of the castle, or the sheriff of Glamorgan, were to select the reeve annually from three burgesses elected by their peers; this reeve, and lesser officers, were to be sworn in at the castle before the constable or sheriff; the constable of the castle would act as coroner; no burgess would be imprisoned in the castle, except for flagrant felony or offences touching the lord himself.[29]

Thomas Despenser, author of the 1397 charter, was executed in 1400 and his lands were forfeited. Kenfig Castle and borough, however, were among lands granted in dower to his widow Constance, but in 1405 these dower lands were granted to Joan, Queen of England, during the minority of the heir, Richard Despenser.[30]

There is no evidence to support the claim that Kenfig was destroyed by Owain Glyndŵr or his followers.[31] This rests largely on a misinterpretation of an order to provision the castle of *Kenflyc* from Worcester in 1403; from the context that castle was Cefnllys, Radnorshire, and not Kenfig.[32]

At Kenfig, as elsewhere along the coasts of Gower and Glamorgan, the sands encroached steadily throughout the 15th century, and gradually the borough became so untenable that the burgesses moved to higher ground at Pyle and Mawdlam, so that only a little village and sand-choked castle met Leland in 1536. Municipal functions and organization persisted until 1883, when the Corporation was abolished.[33]

By 1924, when excavations were commenced, all but two insignificant fragments of the keep had been completely covered by the sands. The excavations uncovered large areas of the castle, and despite subsequent sand encroachment most of the structures explored are still visible. To facilitate the following descriptions and discussion of the structural development of the castle, Fig. 233 tabulates the eight known attacks on Kenfig.

Description and Structural Development

Visible remains of the castle (Fig. 234) comprise the base of a square keep and the vestiges of a gatehouse, a curtain-wall and other buildings exposed in the excavations of 1924–32. The castle occupies the N. angle of a quadrangular enclosure of about 8.25 acres (3.34ha) set against the river and defined at its W. and E. angles by visible traces of its rampart (Figs. 231–32). This enclosure is too extensive for a castle bailey and must represent Kenfig Borough although the church of St James is known to have stood outside, some 60m S. of the inferred S. angle.

Before excavation only two tusks of the core of the keep stood out above a high dune that had accumulated over the castle. The excavations, directed by the late Mr A. J. Richard, on behalf of the Aberafan and Kenfig Historical Society, uncovered the remains of the keep, the gatehouse and other parts of the castle, and these exposed vestiges remain largely visible, despite subsequent drifting and the erosion of exposed

[27] *Cal. C.R.*, 1318–23, pp. 541–2; *Cal. F.R.*, 1319–27, pp. 100, 189; J. Conway Davies, 'The Despenser War in Glamorgan', *Trans. Royal Hist. Soc.*, 3rd Series, IX (1915), pp. 21–64, and especially pp. 49, 53–7; *Glam. Co. Hist.*, III, pp. 170–1; A. J. Richard, *Arch. Camb.* 1927, p. 174; Corbett, *Glamorgan Lordship*, p. 148.

[28] *Cal. I.P.M.*, X, No. 523, p. 416; *Exchequer Accounts Various*, E/101/487/12.

[29] Clark, *Arch. Camb.* 1871, pp. 176–85; Gray, *Kenfig*, pp. 99–115.

[30] *Cal. P.R.* Henry IV, Vol. III (1405–08), p. 4; *Cal. Anc. Petitions*, p. 382; Gray, *Kenfig*, p. 66; *Arch. Camb.* 1927, pp. 180–1.

[31] e.g. Gray, *Kenfig*, pp. 65–6.

[32] *Cal. P.R.*, Henry IV, Vol II (1401–05), p. 296.

[33] Llewellyn, *Arch. Camb.* 1898, pp. 136–8; A. L. Evans, *The Story of Margam*, pp. 43–4.

	Date	Attackers	Borough	Castle	Source
1	1167	Welsh for 'first time'	Burned	No mention	*Ann. Margam*
2	1183–84	Welsh, probably led by Morgan ap Caradog of Afan	Burned, palisade and mill destroyed	Held, but gate and palisade damaged	*Pipe Rolls; Ann. Margam*
3	1228	Welsh, led by Hywel ap Maredudd of Meisgyn	Burned	No mention	*Ann. Margam*
4	1232	Welsh, led by Morgan Gam of Afan, on orders of Llewelyn ab Iorwerth	Destroyed, except for the church	Held. Tower (*turrem*), palisade and ditch mentioned	*Ann. Margam*
5	1243	Welsh, led by Hywel ap Maredudd of Meisgyn	Burned	No mention	*'Exchequer Domesday'*
6	1295	Welsh of the Blaenau, including Tir Iarll and Afan	Destroyed	Burned	*Patent Rolls; Inq. P.M.*
7	1316	Welsh of the Blaenau	'Greater part of town destroyed.' 42 burgages in ashes	Held, but damaged	*Close Rolls; Ministers' Accounts*
8	1321	Coalition of Barons and Welsh, led by de Bohuns and Mortimer, with support of Lancaster	Town devastated	Destroyed and pillaged	*Close Rolls; Fine Rolls*

Fig. 233. Table: Recorded assaults on the Castle and Borough of Kenfig.

masonry. There is no full excavation report in print, nor any account of the finds. Only the early stages of the excavation of the keep, up to April 1927, were published in any detail and with illustrations (Richard, iii).[34] Later work on the keep and all work on other parts of the castle and borough enclosure were only published in brief interim notes and a final but partial revision of earlier interpretations (Richard, i–ii and iv–xi, see f/n. 34). Despite such serious shortcomings, the following description and interpretation must rely largely on those scattered published details, which for convenience will be cited in parentheses, with page references only given to the one full-length account (Richard, iii).[34]

The castle consists of a square keep set within the north-eastern part of a roughly-circular ward which is 37m in diameter and bounded by a curtain constructed in short straight facets. The ward was entered through a gateway on the S.W., communicating with the borough enclosure. A late rectangular building abuts the S. curtain beside the gate, and the angle of another such building is visible immediately N.W.

of the keep. The castle was built on a very low glacial elevation. The river now runs sluggishly in a swampy hollow 30m to the W., but the excavations showed that it has changed course, having been choked and deflected by the sands accumulated over the castle (Richard, ix). Formerly the river followed a course around the N. and W. flanks of the castle, acting as its moat and continuing southwards to outline and protect the W. flank of the borough. The castle is

[34] Citations in parentheses refer to the following chronological list of Mr A. J. Richard's published report (iii) and his other short notes and comments on the excavations:
  i *B.B.C.S.*, II (1924), p. 264.
  ii *B.B.C.S.*, III (1926), pp. 241–2.
  iii *Arch. Camb.* 1927, pp. 161–82.
  iv *B.B.C.S.*, IV (1927), pp. 98–9.
  v *Arch. Camb.*, LXXXIII (1928), pp. 377–8.
  vi *B.B.C.S.*, IV (1928), p. 282.
  vii *B.B.C.S.*, V (1929), p. 91.
  viii *B.B.C.S.*, V (1930), p. 282.
  ix *B.B.C.S.*, VI (1931), p. 98.
  x *B.B.C.S.*, VI (1932), pp. 294–5.
  xi *Glamorgan Historian*, I (1963), p. 39.

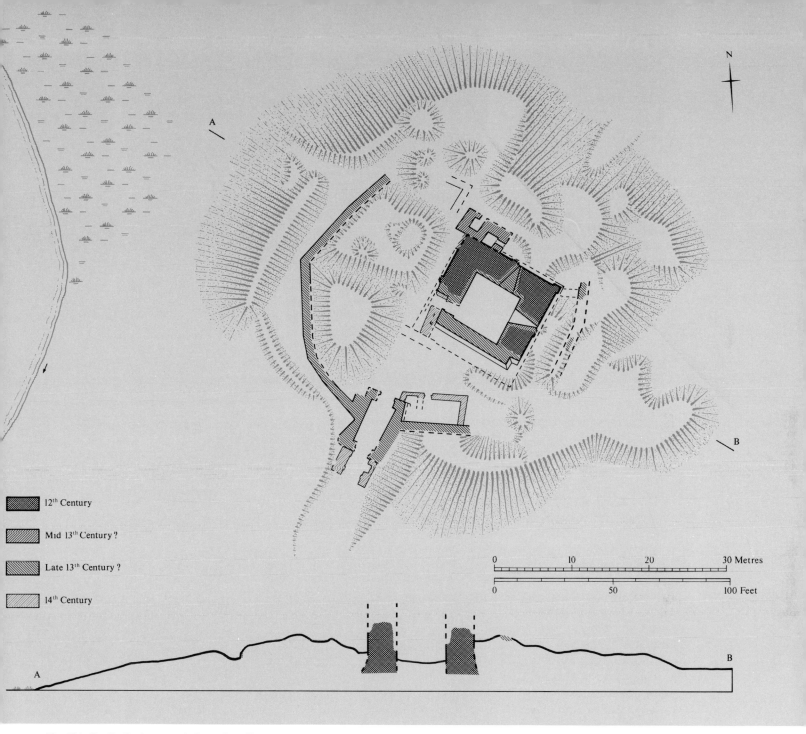

Fig. 234. Kenfig Castle: general plan and profile.

Legend:

12th Century

Mid 13th Century ?

Late 13th Century ?

14th Century

still much obscured by sand and pock-marked by the trenches and spoil-heaps of the excavation.

The Primary Castle

The records of 1183–84 and 1232 indicate a castle comprising a tower protected by a timber palisade and ditch. It has been claimed that that castle was a motte, upon which the keep had been raised.[35] The excavator suggested this in his last published com-ments on Kenfig (Richard, xi) though it contradicted his acceptable and reiterated earlier belief that the keep was founded on natural ground: 'Excavation has proved that there was no mound on the site of the stone structure (*i.e.* the keep) when the latter was first erected but that one was thrown up later' (Richard, iii, p. 165; a view he repeated in ii, v, and iii, pp.

---

[35] e.g. Armitage, *Norman Castles*, p. 296; Renn, *Norman Castles*, p. 211; King, *Cast. Ang.*, I p. 164.

167, 182). Richard's mound, 'thrown up later', cannot be interpreted as a motte, still less as a feature of the primary castle; it was due to a general levelling up which buried the lower part of the keep, and it was not undertaken until *ca.* 1300 (Richard, ii and iii, pp. 169–70). That there was no motte to begin with, as Richard first believed, is confirmed by levels recorded across the site (Fig. 234, profile A–B).

Although no earthworks of the primary castle are now visible, it surely began as a palisaded castle-ringwork enclosing a detached stone keep sited opposite the entrance. This ring-work, on the reasonable assumption that its palisade broadly followed the angular trace of the later stone curtain, would have been 37m in diameter, close to the mean size of Glamorgan castle-ringworks, slightly smaller than others converted to stone at Coity (44m), Ogmore (44m) and Rumney (46m), but larger than another similarly converted at Loughor (22m).

The narrow trench and irregular outer bank following the outer face of the W. curtain were created by the excavations, but the course of the moat around the castle was determined at four points. At the gate it was shown to be over 18m wide.

The closest parallel to the suggested primary castle at Kenfig is Ogmore (MR 5), where a primary ringwork was levelled up with material from its bank on conversion to stone, a process which partially buried a large square structure, the 'cellar', which was also placed opposite the entrance like Kenfig keep. A similarly positioned and detached keep existed formerly at Newcastle (EM 3), where a primary ringwork is also a probability. Other Glamorgan ringworks that were levelled up on conversion to stone are Loughor (MR 4), Rumney (MR 7) and Coity (MR 1).

The record of Morgan Gam's attack in 1232 shows that palisaded earth-and-timber defences still protected the stone keep at that date. Conversion to stone came at the end of the 13th century.

The Keep

The vestiges of the lower part of the keep (Figs. 235–38) display four main phases of development which were identified and illustrated by Richard. These four phases may also be applied to the castle in general. The keep is the largest in the county, and displays most fully the classic form.

Phase I (Richard, iii, pp. 167–9): When first built, the keep measured 14m square above its battered plinth, with walls 3.7m thick, and it had shallow clasp-

Fig. 235. Kenfig Castle: the north-east angle of the keep as exposed in excavations (repr. from *Arch. Camb,* 1927).

ing buttresses at the angles and a pilaster buttress at the centre of each side. These buttresses projected 17cm and were formed with fine ashlar (Fig. 235); only the buttress at the N.E. angle survives, but others, robbed for their ashlar, are indicated by scars in the masonry. The S. wall is a narrowed rebuilding of *Phase III* on the old foundations. The other three walls are substantially of Phase I, rising above the level of the basement as core, and built of random rubble uti-

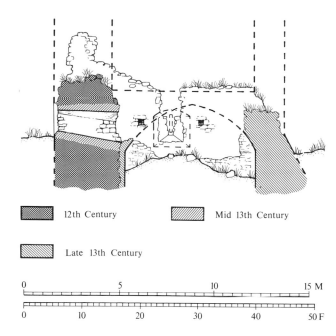

12th Century   Mid 13th Century

Late 13th Century

```
0            5            10           15 M
|||||||||||||||||||||||||||||||||||||||||||
0       10       20       30       40     50 F
```

Fig. 236. Kenfig Castle: section of Keep, looking south-east.

lizing Carboniferous Limestone, local Pennant Stone (from Pyle) and rounded glacial pobble stones, all laid in orange sandy mortar. Fragments of re-used Roman brick and tile are present in the face and core, particularly in the W. wall, and pieces of *opus signinum* occur occasionally in the mortar. The keep was originally unvaulted, its unlit basement accessible only by trap from the first floor. A first-floor entry was thought by Richard to have been towards the S. end of the W. wall, its position possibly marked by the straight joint rising up from a point just N. of the shoulder of the Phase IV door into the basement (Fig. 238, and Richard, iii, pp. 177–9, Fig. 10).

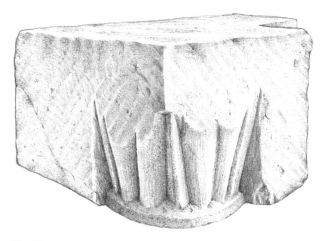

Fig. 237. Kenfig Castle: capital recovered from the Keep.

An early date for the keep, and an indication of the quality of its vanished first-floor hall, may be deduced from a Norman ornamental carving recovered from the keep during the excavations and now in the National Museum of Wales (Fig. 237; Richard v and vi; *N.M.W.*, Acc. No. 28/486). A scalloped and attached capital of Sutton Stone, it is quarter-round and fashioned at the angle of a dressed block to surmount a slender shaft, probably to flank the inner jamb of a window. A modest rebate to one side shows that shaft and capital projected a little from the face of the wall. Only Ogmore keep (MR 5) conserves comparable early Norman dressings in Glamorgan, *in situ* there but flanking its fireplace.

The *Phase I* keep presumably served at least until 1232, when it withstood Morgan Gam's attack upon the surrounding ditch and palisade.

Phase II (Richard, iii, pp. 168–9): towards the mid-13th century, perhaps responding to the attacks of 1232 and 1243, two splayed loops were inserted in the basement, one to the N. and one to the E. Only the N. loop still retains its segmental-headed rear arch. Two abutting garderobe pits were also added at this time at the W. end of the N. wall. The outlet from the E. pit retains a small pointed arch.

Phase III (Richard, iii, pp. 169–70): the third and most extensive alterations are assigned to very late in the 13th century, as they may well have been works following the destruction of both castle and town by the Welsh in 1295. Major work was not confined to the keep, for this phase also saw the construction of the gatehouse, and probably the curtain; it was at this time that the base of the keep was buried almost to first-floor level in the general raising of the ward, presumably with the material derived from the now obsolete ring-bank. The S. wall of the keep required complete rebuilding. The renewed wall was built over the old foundations. Being of lesser width, its inner face corresponded with the old wall, but its outer face was well within the original external line, and it tapered from W. to E., and formed re-entrants at the S. corners. In raising this new S. wall a barrel-vault was carried across the basement. This vault has now collapsed, except for its haunches along the N. and S. walls. On the N. wall this inserted vault caused the blocking of the *Phase II* loop, its cavity first having been filled with the glacial gravel and pebbles used to level up the surrounding ward. The line of the upper part of the vault would also have clipped the head of the E. loop (see Section C–D, Fig. 236). The interior of the basement was plastered, and for the first time a ground-floor entry was provided, set in the recessed re-entrant at the S.W. angle, its opening set back to half the width of the original W. wall. This new door into the basement was presumably reached by steps down from the newly-raised level of the ward, as at the 'cellar' at Ogmore (MR 5), though no trace of such steps were recorded by the excavators.

Phase IV (Richard, iii, pp. 169, 174–80): In the early 14th century the final phase of building involved the renewal of the basement door, additions to the gate-house and the addition of a building against the S. curtain. With the major reconstruction of the keep in Phase III assigned to the very late 13th century and probably following the Welsh destruction of 1295, only a further damaging attack within a short period thereafter could reasonably explain the need for the renewal of the basement door so soon. Kenfig Castle, if not the town, successfully withstood the Welsh attack of 1316, though it was damaged, but in 1321 the wholesale destruction wrought by the baronial coalition furnishes a very probable context for the work of Phase IV, particularly as it is known that their attacks on Despenser's castles involved the dismantling of doors and windows.[36]

The renewed basement door was set forward from that of Phase III, its dressed Sutton Stone frame and now vanished rear arch being carried on inserted blockings of the re-entrant within which the earlier door had been recessed, and built obliquely over the battered base of the original keep wall. The lower jambs survive, broad-chambered and with a broach-and-bar stop on the N.; when first exposed during the excavations of 1926, this door retained part of its head (Fig. 238), but this has since collapsed.

The blocking of the re-entrant on the S. side of the door was extended beyond the outer face of the narrowed S. wall to abut with the footings of a transverse wall fragment parallel to, and slightly in advance of, the line of the original outer face of the keep. The purpose of this extension and transverse wall is unclear.

The Curtain-Wall

The curtain-wall (Richard, ii; iii, pp. 168, 170; iv; vi) was built in *Phase III*, at the end of the 13th century, when the keep was rebuilt and altered, and the level of the ward was raised. It revetted the raised interior and took the form of a regular polygon of near-circular shape, being defined by short straight facets of differing lengths. This polygonal perimeter is

Fig. 238. Kenfig Castle: basement door of the Keep as revealed in excavations (repr. from *Arch. Camb*, 1927).

known for over half its course from surviving traces or from the details recorded during the excavations (Fig. 234). Nine facets are identified, and a further six or seven are now masked by sand. The wall was 1.22m thick above an external batter, and it bonded with the contemporary gatehouse sited to the S.W. From the W. side of the gatehouse a few courses of the outer face are visible, unbroken for six facets which define the W. side of the castle; sand and grass, at a higher level, cover all but the first 2.2m of the corresponding inner face. A further facet runs E. from the gatehouse; only 1.5m of its outer face is visible, but it can be traced for 9.0m internally, within a later

---

[36] *Cal. C.R.*, 1318–23, pp. 541–2 and n.27 above.

building set against it. Beyond this, the gap to the S.E. is probably closed by two buried facets linking with another two recorded close to the E. wall of the keep, but now under sand once more, though its core may still be made out on the surface, and a short stretch of inner face is visible 2.0m from the N.E. angle of the keep and clearly set directly upon gravelly soil well above the floor of the adjacent basement. Beyond this point a further four or five facets would have closed the large gap to the N., now covered by high dunes.

The Gatehouse

The surviving lower walls of the gatehouse (Richard, iv, vi–ix) are sufficient to define two periods of construction, the first of Phase III (late 13th century) and contemporary with the curtain, the second a cruder extension broadly dating from *Phase IV* (14th century). The gatehouse of *Phase III* straddles the curtain and has doors set at each end of a long passage which narrows outwards from 3.4 to 3.0m. Its internal walls were rendered in plaster. There is an external batter corresponding to that of the curtain. In plan the gatehouse is most irregular. Two halves of its inward projecting end are quite different in form; its very thick W. side may well have been the base of a stair to the upper floor of the gatehouse or to the curtain. At the outer end only the W. half is fully exposed, displaying a remarkable curved outer face forming a re-entrant with the curtain. The partly buried E. half presumably mirrors this form. A larger but earlier gatehouse of similar form was built at Grosmont (Mon.) by Hubert de Burgh (1219–32).

The *Phase IV* extension of the 14th century added a further 4.6m to the 8.5m-long passage of the earlier gate, as well as a third door at the outer end. The masonry of this extension is very crude, and no trace survives of a drawbridge pit and revetted causeway that was revealed beyond the extension.

Buildings Within the Ward

In addition to the keep and the unexplained wall-fragment close to its S.W. angle, the excavations revealed two other buildings within the ward. At the N. end a rectangular building was explored but there is no information as to its size or possible date. Its N.E. internal angle is still visible in a hollow in the sand, and a recent writer claims that it was 7.6m long.[37] The internal E. wall of this building is parallel to and

3.0m from the W. wall of the keep, and was mistaken by Richard for another section of the curtain (Richard, iii, p. 169, Fig. 6).

The lower walls of another rectangular building are still entirely exposed to the S. This building abuts the curtain and the E. side of the gatehouse, and must therefore be assigned to Phase IV (14th century). It was 7.4m long internally, with walls 1.2m thick. The stub of a cross-wall is visible towards its W. end, and just E. of this a splayed doorway faces into the ward, its dressings robbed.

The Borough Enclosure

The borough enclosure is defined by its rampart at the S.W. and N.E. angles, and by projecting these visible sections a roughly quadrangular enclosure of about 8.25 acres (3.34ha) may be surmised (Figs. 231–32). This fortified borough is fully treated in another section (Part 1b, TD 3); only its main characteristics need to be noted here, in so far as they relate to the castle.

The borough defences were linked to those of the castle, both being fed by the Afon Cynffig which formerly skirted the western flank. The castle occupied the N.W. angle of these joint defences and its gate opened into the town. In 1950 traces of a paved road were noted leading across the enclosure from this gate.[38] The N.E. salient is defined by a gently curving line of rampart which can be followed for 140m, though there is no trace of its ditch. To the S. this rampart disappears under the large dunes over the S.W. quarter of the town. To the N. it ends against the S. end of a building set at right-angles across the infilled ditch. This building, of four units, was explored by Richard (ix, x), and was thought to be of the 15th century.

The nature of the town defences is best seen to the S.W., where the rampart re-emerges from the dunes and runs straight for 76m to the S.W. angle, fronted by a wide ditch. A trench was cut across this stretch of the defences (Richard, i; iii, pp. 165, 168, Fig. 4). The rampart was found to be composed of gravel and glacial or river pebbles, and had been fronted by a ditch that was 14.7m wide and 4.3m deep. Close to the S.W. angle a causeway crosses the ditch.

---

[37] A. L. Evans, *The Story of Kenfig*, 1960, p. 20. Richard gives no information on this building.

[38] R. E. Kay, MSS. notes and plan in National Monuments Record for Wales, Aberystwyth. But note that a track is said to have been built by the army here in 1940, *ex inf.* Mr. C. N. Johns.

Beyond this, the angle is now defined by no more than a scarp, but was formerly embanked, the rampart running northwards along the W. front towards the castle for over 60m (Richard, iii, p. 166, Fig. 2).

The church of St James, which stood outside the town walls to the S., was not isolated. It is known that a hospital (*maladaria*) stood near, and traces of the buildings of an extra-mural settlement have been noticed in the dunes. The Margam Annals, in their account of Morgan Gam's attack of 1232, mention both 'the town within the gates' and 'the town without the walls'.[39] This extra-mural settlement was no doubt to the S. in the area of the church.

The Finds

Only two significant finds were mentioned in the scat-tered reports of the excavations: a 14th-century jug and the Norman capital described above. The jug was recovered from the garderobe pit of the keep and was almost complete, green-glazed with sagging thumb-pressed base and peletted chevron strips (Richard, viii). Together with the capital, this jug is now in the National Museum of Wales, along with potsherds, metalwork and other finds from the excavation.[40]

King, p. 164.

Pyle and Kenfig (E), Kenfig (C)
SS 88 S.W. (8009–8269)   16.xi.84   XXXIII S.E.

[39] *Ann. Margam*, p. 39.
[40] *N.M.W.*, Acc. Nos. 28.486b; 49.163, 1–29; and Z103, 1–13. For the Kenfig pottery, see *Medieval and Later Pottery in Wales*, No. 7, 1984, pp. 1–8.

EM 3   Newcastle, Bridgend

Newcastle is noteworthy for its 12th-century enceinte of one build, with its fine Norman doorway and two mural towers. It is likely that it was built by Earl William (*ob.* 1183), or by King Henry II who held it between 1183 and 1189. A dependable unpublished account of *ca.* 1835 (cited f/n. 28) indicates the former existence of a detached central keep. Later additions are negligible.

The primary castle established on this site before 1106 by Robert Fitzhamon was probably a castle-ringwork. It was strongly sited on the edge of a precipitous scarp on the W. flank of the Afon Ogwr. From a little over 100ft above O.D. it overlooked the flood plain and a ford at which the market town of Bridgend was to develop, on the opposite bank, at a much later period. St Leonard's, the parish church of Newcastle, lies adjacent to the castle on the less steeply sloping ground to the S., where the linear village of Newcastle developed on the trackway to the ford. There is level ground to the W. of the castle, but a slight re-entrant dingle gives added protection on the N.

Named Newcastle when first mentioned in 1106, it is most unlikely that this name implies a change of site, as has been argued in relation to Oldcastle (VE 4), 610m to the S.S.E. on the opposite bank of the Ogwr, particularly as the latter site was within the neighbouring lordship of Coity.

The history and descent of Newcastle, like its fabric, is exceptional and falls into four distinct tenurial phases: (*i*) *ca.* 1100–83 – the chief lords of Glamorgan;

(*ii*) 1183–89 – King Henry II; (*iii*) 1189–1214 – the Welsh lords of Afan; (*iv*) 1217 onwards – the Turbervilles and their successors, lords of Coity. The brief hiatus, 1214–17, saw a short reversion to the chief lords (Countess Isabel and Geoffrey de Mandeville), an inconsequential episode treated under (*iii*).

(*i*) *ca.* 1100–83: The Chief Lords of Glamorgan

In this phase Newcastle was a demesne possession of the first three lords of Glamorgan, Robert Fitzhamon (until 1107), Robert, Earl of Gloucester (*ca.* 1114–47) and Earl William (1147–83). Under Fitzhamon it was the only castle established to the W. of the Afon Ogwr, which otherwise marked the western limit of his appropriations and those of his followers.[1] One index of this limited advance under Fitzhamon is the distribution of the churches, tithes and lands granted by him and his 'barons', as they are termed, to his foundation at Tewkesbury. These included the church and two parts of the tithes of Newcastle (*Novo Castello*), as listed in Henry I's confirmation of 1106.[2]

From Newcastle it is doubtful whether Fitzhamon

[1] *Glam. Co. Hist.*, III, p. 14.
[2] Clark, *Cartae*, I (xxxvi–xxxvii), pp. 39–40; *Epis Acts*, II, L25, p. 614; Fitzhamon's grant of the church is also confirmed by Earl William (1148): Patterson, *Glouc. Charters*, No. 179, p. 161 and No. 288, p. 181; *Epis. Acts*, II, L182, p. 662.

could have exercised effective authority over the large lowland tract between the Afan and Ogmore rivers. The traditions of his conquest of this territory are now discredited, being derived from the forged Gwentian *Brut*. These western lowlands were not overrun until the time of Earl Robert, with his foundation of the demesne castles at Kenfig (EM 2) and Neath (LM 11). Fitzhamon's Newcastle, to judge from the line of its walls, was a castle-ringwork.

There is no record of the castle during the reversion to Henry I (1107–*ca.* 1114), or in the time of Earl Robert (*ca.* 1114–47), the King's natural son, who obtained seisin on marriage to Fitzhamon's heiress. Robert's new castles at Neath and Kenfig, both accessible from the sea, no doubt lessened the significance of land-locked Newcastle. The lands between the Cynffig and Ogwr were now sub-divided between the demesne lordships of Kenfig and Newcastle, within which lordships sub-tenants were enfeoffed after 1136, including the Scurlages of Llangewydd (VE 3) and

Fig. 239. Newcastle, Bridgend: elevated view from the church tower on the south side. The curtain-wall in the foreground masks a precipitous fall to the flood plain of the Afon Ogwr to the right.

the Sturmis of Stormy (MO 5). Two sub-tenants of Earl William (1147–83) were to be of significance in the later history of Newcastle, namely Walter Luvel and Payn Turberville. Luvel held lands near Newcastle, at Pen-y-fai in Llangewydd, and at Cornelly in Kenfig.[3] Payn Turberville, the lord of neighbouring Coity, was granted lands at 'Coitkard' in Newcastle.[4] Later, from 1217, the Turbervilles would possess the whole lordship.

Earl William's tenure of Glamorgan (1147–83) spans the earlier and greater part of the period to which the Norman fabric at Newcastle might be ascribed on architectural and historical grounds.

(ii) 1183–89:
King Henry II

Earl William died on 23rd November 1183 and before the end of the year the Welsh had risen in revolt, most probably led by Morgan ap Caradog ab Iestyn, lord of Afan.[5] It was so serious an uprising that Henry II retained the lordship of Glamorgan until he died in 1189, despite the prior betrothal of his son, Count John of Mortain, to Isabel, the heiress of Earl William.

The uprising lasted until the summer of 1184, and was pressed with particular vigour to the W., where Morgan ap Caradog sought to recover the lands of Neath, Kenfig and Newcastle. The castles were attacked and the towns at Neath and Kenfig burned. The *Pipe Rolls* for 1183–85 show substantial expenditure on their defence.[6] The custody of Newcastle was entrusted to Walter Luvel, the Newcastle sub-tenant, who was paid 40 shillings for a half-year, as well as other sums for the payment of 300 footmen and for the custody of Welsh prisoners, and 60 shillings for his loss of two war-horses.[7] Although the *Pipe Rolls* record expenditure on specific works at Neath, Kenfig and other castles in Glamorgan, none is recorded for Newcastle. Despite this, these years in royal custody seem a most likely and final occasion for the exceptionally good Norman masonry there, before Welsh tenure made such work improbable.

(iii) 1189–1214:
The Welsh Lords of Afan

On the 29th August 1189, seven weeks after Henry II's death, John finally married Isabel and in her right obtained Glamorgan, which he was to retain, despite divorce, until 1214, as king from 1199. In an extraordinary gesture of conciliation, for there is no other known explanation, the new lord of Glamorgan granted the lordship and castle of Newcastle (*Novum castellum de Ogmoer*) to Morgan ap Caradog, the presumed instigator of the savage revolt of 1183–84. Morgan held the lordship by the service of a fourth part of a knight's fee. He retained Newcastle until his death *ca.* 1208, and his son Leison still held it in 1213. John's enfeoffment of Morgan is only known from the records of a 16th-century lawsuit between Mansel and Gamage,[8] but his possession of the lordship is amply attested by contemporary deeds, as is that of Leison. Most specific are King John's charter to Margam (1205), confirming the monks in the lands given to them by Morgan and his men '... *in territorio Novi Castelli ...*', and Morgan's undated grant of land '... *de dominio meo in feudo Novi Castri ...*' to Roger Cole.[9] In many other charters Morgan gives his consent to the grants of land in Newcastle made to Margam by his men.[10] He is last mentioned in 1208, when he granted land at Laleston to the abbey.[11] Soon after this he was succeeded by Leisan, who had commanded 200 Welshmen in Normandy on the King's service in 1204, and who last appears as lord of Newcastle in 1213.[12] Leison died soon after, but his brother and heir, Morgan Gam, did not inherit Newcastle.

There now occurred the brief and inconsequential phase, 1214–17, during which the Welsh loss of Newcastle was incidental to the termination of the Crown's tenure of Glamorgan. John had divorced Isabel in 1199, but retained Glamorgan. In 1214 he gave her in marriage to Geoffrey de Mandeville, Earl of Essex, and granted the late Earl William's lands to them.[13] From various charters it is apparent that Newcastle

---

[3] Clark, *Cartae*, II (cclxviii), p. 265.

[4] Clark, *Cartae*, II (cccxci–cccxciii), pp. 384–7; *Epis. Acts*, II, L222, p. 674–5.

[5] *Ann. Margam*, pp. 17–18, but incorrectly under 1185; Lloyd, *Hist. Wales*, II, p. 571; *Glam. Co. Hist.*, III, pp. 37–9; J Beverley Smith, *Morgannwg*, II (1958), pp. 24–7; *Hist. Kings Works*, pp. 650–1.

[6] *Pipe Rolls*, 30 Henry II (1183–84) and 31 Henry II (1184–85).

[7] *Pipe Rolls*, 31 Henry II (1184–85), pp. 5–8; Clark, *Cartae*, I (clxxi), pp. 170–6.

[8] Clark, *Cartae*, V (mccxcvi), pp. 1791–2; *Glam. Co. Hist.*, III, pp. 38–9.

[9] Clark, *Cartae*, II (cclxxxvii), p. 291 and (cccxcxiii), p. 392.

[10] Clark, *Cartae*, II (cccxcix–cccci), pp. 393–5; (ccccliv–cccclvi), pp., 447–8; and (cccclviii), p. 450.

[11] Clark, *Cartae*, II (cccxxvii), p. 328.

[12] *Cal. Liberate Rolls*, 5 John, p. 88; *Glam. Co. Hist.*, III, p. 39; A. L. Evans, *Trans. Port Talbot Hist. Soc.*, No. 3, Vol. II (1974), p. 23.

[13] Clark, *Cartae*, II (cccxxxviii–cccxxxix), pp. 338–9.

reverted to Countess Isabel.[14] The circumstances of this reversion are not known, but it is clear that Morgan Gam was deeply affronted and harboured a strong desire to repossess the fee, to which end he often took up arms.

In 1217 Isabel's death left her sister Amice as the last of Earl William's daughters. She was married to Earl Richard de Clare, but as he died soon afterwards, it was their son Gilbert de Clare who assumed lordship.

It is not likely that the lords of Afan could have built the surviving 12th-century fabric of such high quality and advanced design. Its fine defensive enceinte was presumably completed when John granted it to them soon after he obtained Glamorgan in 1189, for the simple walled enclosure and tower at Plas Baglan (UW 5) is the only stone castle that may be claimed as their work.

(iv) 1217 onwards:
The Turbervilles and their Successors, Lords of Coity.

In 1217 the new lord, Earl Gilbert de Clare, granted Newcastle to Gilbert Turberville of Coity, descendant of the Payn who had been given lands in that lordship by Earl William. It is said that Gilbert Turberville was married to a lady of the house of Afan,[15] though the evidence is questionable. Turberville was admirably placed to hold Newcastle, directly facing Coity across the Afon Ogwr, and a lordship where he already held some land. Whether or not he was related by marriage to Morgan Gam, this Welsh claimant was rejected. Thus early appears the firmness of the Clares towards the Welsh, which under Earls Richard and Gilbert II would see the final annexation of the *Blaenau*.

Coity Castle (MR 1) is only 2.5km to the N.E. of Newcastle, and as it remained the chief residence of the Turbervilles it is not surprising that it displays a complex and continuous building history. At Newcastle, subordinated to such a nearby castle, it is apparent that little building was carried out by the lords of Coity, and what remains is almost entirely Norman.

Morgan Gam persisted in his claims to Newcastle and no doubt instigated the burning of the vills of Newcastle, Laleston and St. Nicholas in 1226, probably fulfilling the bold reservation he had made to his confirmation of Newcastle lands to Margam Abbey, namely that he might make war there with others.[16]

After a period in the earl's prison, Morgan next allied himself with Llywelyn ap Iorwerth in a successful and destructive attack on Neath Castle (LM 11) and Kenfig (EM 2) in 1231 and 1232 respectively. In 1233, with Llywelyn, he joined the baronial rising under Richard, Earl of Pembroke, no doubt hoping to recover Newcastle.[17] His hopes were to no avail and remained unfulfilled at his death *ca.* 1241.

In the Extent of 1262 Gilbert Turberville held Newcastle as one tenth of a knight's fee, valued at £10. This value had fallen to 40 shillings by the time of the Despenser survey of 1321, which recorded nine ploughlands there.[18] In the same year an anonymous and accurate warning of preparations being made by the barons was sent to King Edward II from Newcastle (*Noef Chastel*), which did not figure in the swift and destructive baronial campaign that duly followed.[19]

Successive failures in the male line brought Newcastle to the Berkerolles (1360), the Gamages (1411) and the Sidneys (1584). Of the minor additions made at Newcastle under these lords, only the traces of Elizabethan refurbishment of the S. tower by John, the last Gamage lord, can be closely dated by two 16th-century references to the work.[20] Robert Sidney, later Earl of Leicester, acquired Newcastle on his marriage to the Gamage heiress, Barbara, in 1584. By 1833 the castle was a garden, and by 1912 a market garden. It was taken into State guardianship in 1932, cleared and consolidated.[21]

Structural Development

Excepting slight Tudor insertions in the *South Tower*, the surviving defensive enceinte is a unitary 12th-century rebuilding in stone of Fitzhamon's castle of

---

[14] Patterson, *Glouc. Charters*, Nos. 142–145, pp. 132–6 and No. 147, pp. 138–9; Clark, *Cartae*, II (cccvlix), p. 350; VI (mdciii and mdcv), pp. 2323, 2326.

[15] Clark, *Arch. Camb.* 1867, p. 19; A. L. Evans, *Margam Abbey*, 1958, p. 68; Nicholl, *Normans*, pp. 153, 163.

[16] *Ann. Margam*, pp. 34–5; A. L. Evans, *Margam Abbey*, 1958, p. 68; Corbett, *Glamorgan Lordship*, pp. 65, 132; Clark, *Cartae*, VI (mdcxxii), pp. 2350–1.

[17] *Glam. Co. Hist.*, III, p. 48; A. L. Evans, *Trans. Port Talbot Hist. Soc.*, No. 3, Vol. II (1974), p. 27.

[18] Clark, *Cartae*, II (dcxv), p. 651; Merrick, *Morg. Arch.*, pp. 72, 74.

[19] *Cal. Anc. Corr.*, pp. 180–1.

[20] Merrick, *Morg. Arch.*, p. 105; Lewis, *Breviat*, p. 125.

[21] Lewis, *Top. Dict.* (1833); Armitage, *Norman Castles*, p. 295; B. H. St.J. O'Neil and H. J. Randall, *Newcastle, Bridgend* (Official Guide-book, 1949).

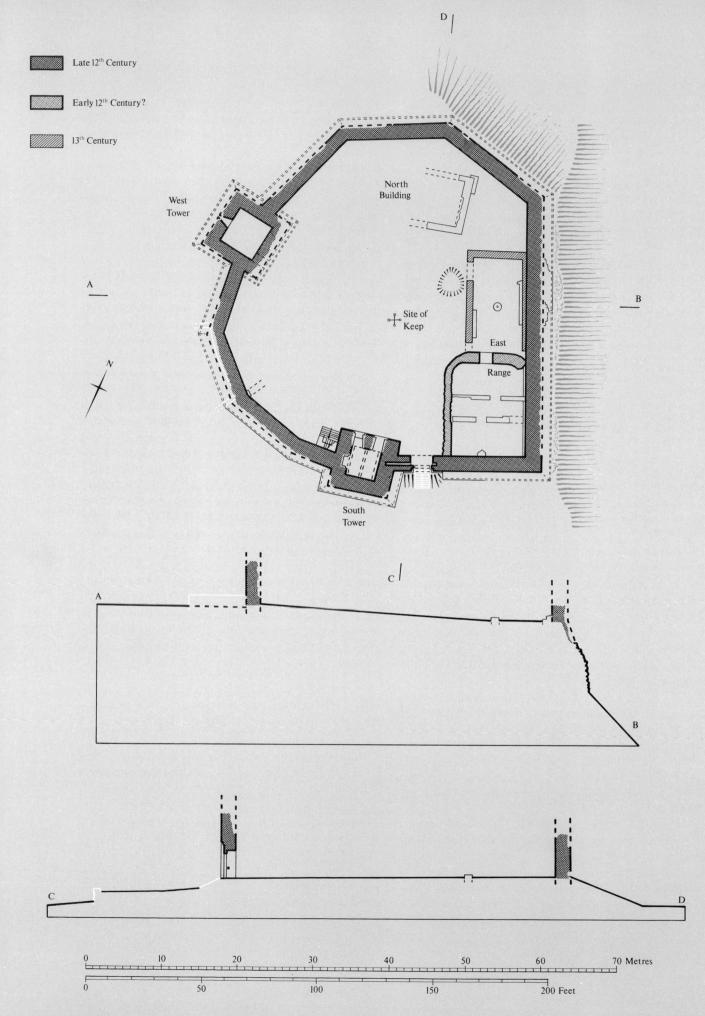

Late 12th Century

Early 12th Century?

13th Century

West Tower

North Building

Site of Keep

East Range

South Tower

A

B

C

D

A

B

C

D

| 0 | 10 | 20 | 30 | 40 | 50 | 60 | 70 Metres |

| 0 | 50 | 100 | 150 | 200 Feet |

ca. 1100 (Fig. 240). The round-cornered S. building of the *East Range* may be the only surviving structure of the primary castle-ringwork suggested by the trace of the curtain-walls. Stylistic and historical considerations imply that these walls replaced the palisade in one building campaign at some time between about 1150 and a certain terminal date of 1189, and during the tenure of either Earl William (1147–83) or King Henry II (1183–89). This definitive rebuilding probably included the central *Vanished Keep* (though on analogy with Kenfig (EM 2) this could have been raised within the palisade by Earl Robert before 1147). There is no evidence of subsequent building of a defensive nature, but merely internal additions and minor alterations of a domestic nature.

The *East Range* was completed with the addition of the narrower extension at its N. end. Its reduced width was perhaps dictated by the proximity of the now vanished keep, and its central hearth suggests that it was a 13th-century hall. The inserted cross-walls sub-dividing the older S. building may also be of this period.

The surviving E. end of the *North Building*, with its added clasping buttress, may be part of another later medieval addition. Alternatively, it could well be part of the 'pretty pile ... re-edified' by John Gamage before his death in 1584;[20] the windows inserted in the *South Tower* may certainly be ascribed to him, but this small tower hardly befits Rice Lewis' quoted complimentary description. If the *North Building* was a work of Gamage it is probable that it would have been incorporated with a 're-edified' adjacent keep, just like that refurbished and augmented early in the 16th century at his main castle of Coity (MR 1).

The minimal and purely domestic internal works in evidence at Newcastle subsequent to the building of the 12th-century stone castle reflect its tenurial history. As acquired by the Welsh lords of Afan in 1189 it had been recently rebuilt in stone, to an advanced design more than adequate to their needs, and greatly superior to work that might be attributed to them. From 1217 on the successive lords of Coity held Newcastle, but retained Coity Castle (MR 1) as their principal residence. There, in turn, the Turbervilles, Berkerolles and Gamages undertook extensive works on the defences, domestic quarters and services; their apparent neglect of Newcastle, only 2.5km away, is not surprising. The last Gamage lord's refurbishment of the domestic quarters at Newcastle seems to have been the only work of note by any Coity lord, and of that little remains. In 1584 the marriage of his heiress took both castles to the Sidneys, earls of Leicester. Absentee lords until the 18th century, they maintained Coity, but appear to have neglected Newcastle.

The 12th-Century Stone Castle

Despite the loss of its central keep, no Norman stone castle in Wales is comparably intact and so devoid of later modifications. Its walls, towers and gateway are clearly contemporary, but regrettably there is no record of its construction. Its attribution either to Earl William (1147–83) or King Henry II (1183–89) is based on the current ascription of the gateway to the period 1150–80, not unduly extended to include the King's tenure, which began with a violent Welsh revolt and witnessed works for him at other Glamorgan castles. Its construction after the King's death in 1189 is not conceivable during the ensuing tenure of the Welsh lords of Afan, given the simplicity of Plas Baglan (UW 5), the only certain Welsh stone castle in Glamorgan.

Some features of the design and detail of Newcastle are certainly appropriate to a castle of both Earl William and Henry II. The *vanished keep*, free-standing within and apparently square, would have been the dominant structure. The enceinte was characterised by its square *straddling mural towers* and its continuous external *battered plinth*. The lavish use of *freestone ashlar* of Sutton stone is exceptional; this sheathed the plinth and was used at all doors and angles, including changes in the alignment of the curtain where it furnished internal and external alternating quoins. The fine *Norman doorway* is accentuated by a particularly comprehensive ashlar facing of the surrounding wall-faces; this ashlar survives intact, though elsewhere it has been extensively stripped away to expose a rough core.

Earl William, unlike his father, Earl Robert, is not known for his castle-building, but the current ascription of *the gateway* to 1150–80 would favour construction during his tenure. He also possessed the extraordinary Sherborne Old Castle in Dorset, built before 1135 by Roger, Bishop of Salisbury, but foreshadowing features at Newcastle. Similarly polygonal, it had four square *straddling mural towers*, two being gatehouses, a *central square keep* (with exceptional integrated domestic block), and *battered plinths* and

Fig. 240. *(Opposite)* Newcastle, Bridgend: general plan and profiles. The trace of the curtain-wall suggests that the primary castle here was a Castle-ringwork.

freestone ashlar dressings.[22] The straddling mural towers at Sherborne appear to be the earliest of their type, providing an acceptable model for those he may have raised at Newcastle. The keeps at the castles of William's tenants-in-chief at Ogmore and Coity might also be cited as further models for the Newcastle mural towers, though only the former was certainly pre-existing. Both of these undoubted keeps straddled the curtain beside the gateway, just like the South Tower at Newcastle.

The violence of the Welsh uprising of 1183–84 compelled King Henry II to retain Glamorgan and Gwynllŵg until his death in 1189, despite his son's prior betrothal to the heiress. This period, given his renown as a builder of castles, and recorded work during his tenure at other castles in these lordships, would appear to be a most likely time for the construction of the excellent Norman fabric at Newcastle, and only marginally after the date span of 1150–80 attributed to the style of its gateway. The *Pipe Rolls*, however, only record expenditure on the royal garrison at the castle under Walter Luvel, but none on building works. Normally such a major building enterprise could not have escaped notice in these accounts of royal officers in escheated lordships. Here, this omission impels two possible conclusions: either Earl William had so recently rebuilt Newcastle in stone that it required no immediate improvement, or circumstances were sufficiently abnormal in Glamorgan for the expenditure to escape the cognizance or prerogative of royal officers, perhaps as direct royal expenditure in a lordship destined to pass to the king's son when conditions permitted his intended marriage. Though small, the castle certainly displays a quality and precocious design not unworthy of Henry II, particularly with the rediscovered evidence for the former central square keep, a feature particularly appropriate to a work of that king. Of Henry's many castles, Orford in Suffolk is of particular relevance.[23] Although its curtain-walls are vanished, John Norden's view of 1600–02 clearly portrays large square *straddling mural towers* on its line, that to the foreground clearly founded on a *boldly-battered plinth*, which was no doubt rendered in *freestone ashlar* like the plinth of the exceptional *central keep* still surviving within, and very like the Newcastle towers.

Architectural Description

The remains consist of a single ward of D-shaped but almost circular plan (Figs. 239, 240), about 40m in average internal diameter and enclosed by a curtain-wall still standing up to 6.30m high and 1.9m thick above a strikingly bold battered plinth 1.0m wide. No ditch was necessary on the precipitous E. flank; elsewhere it has been totally filled up. The single entrance is to the S., facing the church, with a large square salient tower straddling the curtain on its W. side. A second and similar tower faces the level ground to the W. The footings of two internal buildings abut the E. curtain, while those of the E. end of a free-standing building lie to the N. No visible trace remains of the central detached keep recorded early in the 19th century, to be mentioned below.

The Primary Castle of Fitzhamon was presumably a castle-ringwork which dictated the circuit of the later stone curtain. Its approximate internal diameter, on this assumption, would have been at least 40m, a size close to the Glamorgan mean and to that of Coity (44m), Ogmore (44m) and another demesne castle at Rumney (46m).

The Curtain-Wall is set out in a series of short straight facets, except to the E. where a longer line was imposed along the head of the steep natural scarp. Here a bold and continuous external battered plinth is particularly strong to support the wall above the steep slope, increasing to a width of 1.5m and carried well down the scarp to rest on a rock outcrop, where its base survives towards the centre for a distance of 5.0m. Elsewhere 1.0m wide, this plinth is clearly seen on the main S. front and around the South Tower, although robbed of its ashlar facing, and may be traced along the first two facets to the W. of this tower. Beyond this point the plinth is buried by a raised ground level, buts scars at the West Tower confirm its continuation.

The curtain stands up to 5.23m on the N. and up to 6.30m at its junction with the E. side of the South Tower, both heights measured from the level of the interior. Originally the wall rose much higher, for these highest surviving points retain no trace of the wall-walk and crenellations. The masonry of the curtain, as of the towers, is constructed of random limestone rubble brought irregularly to intermittent

---

[22] *Dorset Inventory*, RCHM, I (1952), pp. 64–6; *Hist. Kings Works*, II, pp. 832–3; Renn, *Norman Castles*, pp. 308–10. Its acquisition by Earl Robert and continued possession by Earl William was only noticed after Mr Derek Renn kindly drew attention to its straddling towers as a parallel to Newcastle.

[23] R. Allan; Brown, *Orford Castle* (Official Guide-book, 1964), Plate II; *Hist. Kings Works*, II, pp. 769–71, Plate 47A. A further possible parallel also kindly suggested by Mr Derek Renn.

Fig. 241. Newcastle, Bridgend: the Norman gateway.

The Gateway (Figs. 225, 241, 242a) is a simple opening constructed entirely of Sutton Stone and clearly coeval with the curtain and towers with which it shares the same ashlar dressings. The opening consists of a recessed segmental-headed arch with roll mouldings flanked by alternating sunken rectangular panels and strips of pellets. Within the angles of the recess attached columns with eroded Romanesque capitals support a round-headed and roll-moulded arch, the whole outlined on the external face with plain unchamfered blocks. The capitals differ, that to the W. being ornamented with strap-work and volutes, the other with leaves. The bases are of plain cushion form. Internally the rear arch is segmental, with plain Sutton voussoirs and jambs. A deep draw-bar hole extends 3.45m into the W. jamb, almost penetrating the full thickness of the adjacent tower wall and proving the two were contemporary. The present steps rising to the entrance are modern.

The recessed segmental inner arch set within its rounded outer arch is uncommon. There are several examples, much more ornately decorated, at Lilleshall Abbey, Shropshire, probably later than 1148, and another in the Norman gate-tower at Egremont, Cumberland. The panel-and-pellet ornament at Newcastle has only been paralleled by the ornate door of Quenington church, near Cirencester, Gloucestershire, where a recessed decorated tympanum forms a lintel replacing the segmental inner arch.[24] One authority has dated the Newcastle doorway to 1175–80; another has ascribed it to the third quarter of the 12th century and considers it to be in a style alien to the county.[25] These ascriptions would suggest construction by Earl William (1147–83), but the alien style and lavish use of ashlar could imply special circumstances, and with a date only marginally later, the royal custody of 1183–89 might furnish such circumstances.

The South Tower (Fig. 242) straddles the curtain to the W. side of the gateway. Its strong battered external plinth is robbed of its former sheathing except for a few fragments at its inner angles. Within the ward there is no plinth. The tower was of three storeys, all much altered in the 16th century. There are no loop-holes on the ground floor which is reached through a door in the N. wall. This door, and an

levelled courses, and pierced by rows of putlog holes. Dressed blocks of Sutton Stone are used to sheathe the plinth and for all doors and quoining, a characteristic use being the alternating internal and external quoins of this stone at every change of alignment of the curtain. This form of quoining in Sutton Stone it shares with the 12th-century faceted curtains at Coity (MR 1), and with that of the contemporary shell-keep at Cardiff (MM 1). The 12th-century castle at Dinas Powys (EM 1) retains identical quoining at one angle, as well as strong indications of an ashlar-dressed plinth. The use of ashlar at Newcastle, however, was particularly lavish, especially on part of the south front, where it rose above the plinth, now almost entirely robbed of its facing, to clad the wall around the gateway, where it survives (Elevation, Fig. 242a).

---

[24] S. E. Rigold, *Lilleshall Abbey*, (Official Guide-book, 1969); Egremont Castle and Quenington Church, *ex inf.* Mr Derek Renn (*in lit.*, 10.11.87), conveying Professor George Zarnecki's view that the door of the latter dated to *ca.* 1150–60 or later.

[25] O'Neil and Randall., *op. cit.*, n.21, p. 5; L. A. S. Butler, *Glam. Co. Hist.*, III, p. 385.

adjacent window are both refaced, but may be original features of the tower. Traces of a paved floor survive at the door and a short way into the room. A fireplace has been inserted in the W. wall. The ceiling was supported by three beams.

The first floor was reached by an external stair, now renewed, set in the angle made with the curtain on the W. This floor retains typical Elizabethan windows in the N. and S. walls. Though only fragments of their dressings survive, it is clear that each was of three transomed lights of local sandstone, sunk-chamfered and with labels. Again there are no defensive loop-holes, though one may have been opened out for the outward-facing Elizabethan window. This floor had a fireplace in the E. wall, and access to the second floor by a small newel stair in the N.W. corner, which retains traces of its lower steps.

Little remains at second-floor level, but sufficient to identify two Elizabethan windows in the N. and S. walls, repeating those on the floor below. There was a fireplace in the E. wall flanked by a recessed window overlooking the entrance.

The mortar lining all the openings in this tower is of chalky post-medieval character. These late alterations indicate that the tower, though cramped in space, had been converted for domestic use in the late-16th century, and they agree well with the recorded works carried out by John Gamage before his death in 1584, which created '... *a pretie pile newly begun to be re-edified by John Gamage esquiour that last was*' (Rice Lewis, *ca.* 1596).[26]

The West Tower (Fig. 242g). This was another square tower straddling the curtain. Only eroded vestiges of its ground floor remain. The entrance seems to have been at the S.E. corner. The only loop was in the W. wall towards the field. Lacking any fireplace or other domestic feature, this chamber must have served as a storeroom. The tower is slightly larger than that to the S., and scars on the internal face of the curtain at its angles made with the tower show that here the bold external batter continued around the internal part of the structure.

The North Building. Only the foundations of this building survive, representing the E. gable end of a rectangular detached structure set in the N. part of the ward. A secondary clasping buttress has been added at the N.W. corner.

The East Range consists of the foundations of two buildings set in line along the E. curtain, that to the S. lying within the angle made with the S. curtain. The much narrower northern building has been inter-

preted as the 12th-century hall, that to the S. being ascribed to the 16th century.[27] This sequence and dating for the two parts of the East Range is no longer tenable on any consideration of the existing remains. The larger south building is constructed with mortared walls, of which only the W. side and N. end walls survive. As existing, the N. angles are most clearly rounded, both internally and externally, which in itself is a most emphatic indication of a 12th-century and not a 16th-century date. It would also appear from the rough termination of the inward curving wall at its N.E. angle, that a former E. lateral wall has been demolished for the insertion of the curtain-wall in its place. A similar sequence seems probable to the S., where the curtain appears to overly the surviving footings of the W. side wall without any evident straight joint. After the insertion of the S. and E. curtain, the rebuilding of what remained of the south building is indicated by the two internal cross-walls. These are both clearly insertions post-dating both the building and the curtain. The general plan of the original south building is reminiscent of the 12th-century sub-rectangular halls at the castle-ringworks at Llantrithyd (CR 13), Penmaen (CR 18) and Pennard (MR 6), and at such domestic sites as Highlight (Vol. III, Part 2, MS 10). Its great internal width of 9.75m suggests that its roof may have been supported, as at Rumney (MR 7) and Llantrithyd, by an aisled arrangement of posts. This building is probably the earliest structure surviving on the site, and perhaps the hall of the primary ringwork.

The north building added to complete the East Range is undoubtedly later than the curtain, against which its E. lateral wall abuts. Within this building there are the remains of an inserted stone bench along the E. wall, while a central hearth, now marked by the fragments of a conglomerate millstone, suggests that it was a hall of the 13th century. There is a door towards the N. end of the W. wall. A distinct circular hollow now obstructs access to this door. The narrower width of this component of the East Range may have been dictated by the proximity of the now vanished keep.

Fig. 242. *(Opposite)* Newcastle, Bridgend: (a) section of South Tower, looking north, with elevation of adjacent curtain; (b) section of South Tower, looking east; (f) South Tower, ground floor; (e) South Tower, first floor; (c) South Tower, second floor; (d) windows in South Tower, first floor. (g) West Tower, ground floor.

---

[26] See note 20.
[27] O'Neil and Randall, *op. cit.*, n.21, p. 6 and plan.

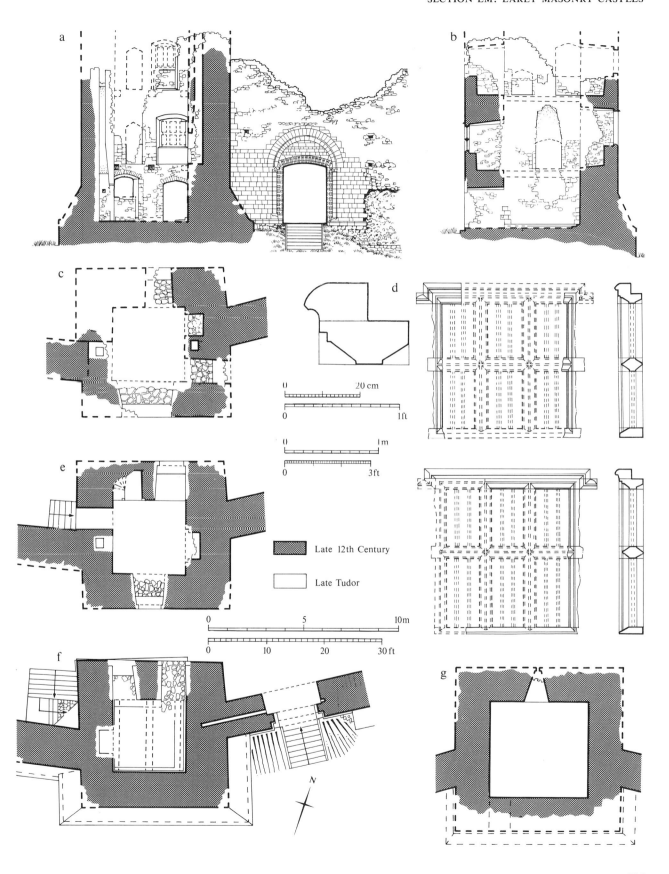

Late 12th Century

Late Tudor

The Vanished Keep. That most thorough of castle recorders, G. T. Clark, in a rough unpublished sketch plan of *ca.* 1835, noted a mound of debris, 'once a keep', in the centre of the ward, with an accompanying perspective sketch showing the foundations of a square structure in this position.[28] Clark does not mention this building in any of his published works, nor were any foundations in this position recorded during clearance. Mrs Armitage (1912) mentioned a motte in one corner, with the ruins of a tower upon it, but this could only have been the collapsed remains of the West Tower.[29]

Most Glamorgan keeps are placed on the line of the curtain, flanking the entrance, as at Coity (MR 1) and Ogmore (MR 5). There is, however, a detached internal keep at Kenfig (EM 2), and one should also note the strange free-standing 12th-century 'cellar' at Ogmore. Clark's observations cannot be ignored; recent excavations have confirmed the footings of a keep at Sully (EM 6), long vanished but also noted by Clark when briefly exposed in the 1830s.

Outworks. There are no traces of the castle ditch. The church to the S. no doubt began as the castle chapel, and the strong natural scarps defining the E. and S. sides of the churchyard suggest the possibility that it lay within a bailey. At the N.E. angle of the churchyard the vestiges of a mortared foundation project out from under the base of the modern yard wall and run for at least 4.0m in an oblique line down the steep natural scarp. This might have formed the revetment of a trackway leading up to the castle or church from the ford.

King, p. 161 (Bridgend).

Newcastle (E), Newcastle Higher (C)
SS 98 S.W. (9022–8007)   5.x.84   XL N.E.

---

[28] *N.L.W.*, G. T. Clark MSS. (Welsh Castles), Vol. I, MS. 5197C.

[29] Armitage, *Norman Castles*, p. 295.

EM 4   Penllyn Castle

Penllyn Castle is 2km N.W. of Cowbridge and only 700m N. of the Roman road and later Port Way, the main medieval E.–W. route across Glamorgan. It lies at over 300ft above O.D., on the edge of a rocky Carboniferous Limestone cliff which forms the W. side of the Thaw Valley. Except for this cliff to the E., the position has no natural defence, though a gradual fall to the S. gives extensive views towards the Port Way. The church 500m to the W. is modern; the Pen-llin parish church of Llanfrynach is 1.3km to the S. and beyond the Port Way. The castle was the *caput* of a manor held for the service of two knights by the Norris family from the early 12th century. Vestiges of the keep are all that survive, but these incorporate herringbone masonry and round-headed arches.

The lordship of Penllyn included the parishes of both Pen-llin and Llanmihangel which contained a total of about 2,370 acres. It was within the Shire-fee, but its N., E. and S. limits abutted the member lordships of Rhuthin, Talyfan and Llanblethian.

The earliest known lord of Penllyn was Robert Norris, who was enfeoffed before 1135, as may be deduced from the un-named fees listed in *Liber Niger* and *Liber Rubeus*.[1] Robert Norris was the sheriff of Glamorgan in the last years of Robert Consul, Earl of Gloucester (*ob.* 1147), who thus addressed him in

charters to Ewenny and St. Peter's, Gloucester (1140–47), and also to Margam Abbey (1147).[2] He continued to serve as sheriff under Earl William, but died before 1166.[3] Although Rice Merrick notices Robert Norris's service as sheriff under the two earls, he is mistaken in saying that Penllyn was granted to him by Earl William, as on the evidence of *Liber Niger* he was enfeoffed already by 1135.[4] Richard Norris appears in charters of 1186–91 and 1207–18.[5] In the extent of 1262, following the death of Earl Richard de Clare, the two fees of Penllyn were held by John le Norris.[6] Another John le Norris was lord in 1322 and was among those whose lands were taken into the king's

---

[1] *Liber Niger* and *Liber Rubeus*: . . . *feudo quod fuit Roberti Norensis, II milites.*; Corbett, *Glamorgan Lordship*, pp. 33, 118; Nicholl, *Normans*, pp. 72–3; *Glam. Co. Hist.*, III, p. 17.

[2] Patterson, *Glouc. Charters*, No. 68, p. 73 (=Clark, *Cartae*, I, ci, P. 103 and *Epis. Acts*, II, L105, pp. 637–8); Patterson, *Glouc. Charters*, No. 84, p. 87 (=Clark, *Cartae*, I, xcvii, p. 99 and *Epis. Acts*, II, L90, pp. 634–5); and Patterson, *Glouc. Charters*, No. 119, p. 114 (=Clark, *Cartae*, IV, dcccclxviii).

[3] Patterson, *Glouc. Charters*, Nos. 96, 122, 170 and 182, pp. 97, 116, 154 and 163; Clark, *Cartae*, I (cxviii).

[4] Merrick, *Morg. Arch.*, pp. 42, 63, 66.

[5] Clark, *Cartae*, II (cccxci), pp. 384–5 (=*Epis Acts*, II, No. L222, p. 675); Clark, *Cartae*, II (ccccxliv), pp. 432–3 (=*Epis. Acts*, II, L320, p. 701); Patterson, *Glouc. Charters*, No. 93, pp. 92–3.

Fig. 243. Penllyn Castle in 1786, viewed from the north-east. Engravings by: (a) Paul Sandby; (b) S. Sparrow for Grose's *Antiquities*. Engraving (a) clearly portrays the Tudor house beyond; both notice the herringbone work and the scarp-edge siting *(National Library of Wales)*.

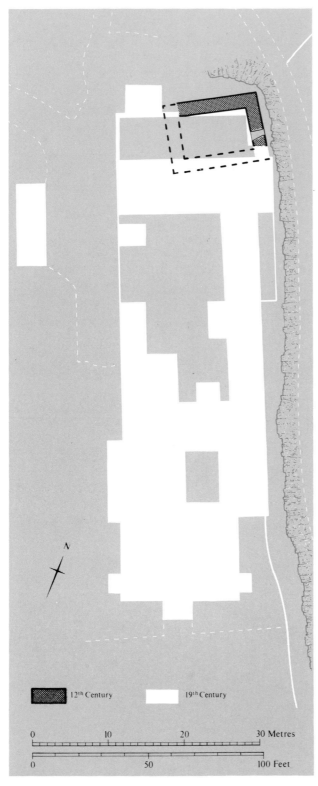

Fig. 244. Penllyn Castle: the Norman vestiges in relation to the nineteenth century mansion.

■ 12th Century   □ 19th Century

0   10   20   30 Metres

0   50   100 Feet

hands in 1322 for their part in the baronial uprising of the previous year.[7]

The Norris family retained Penllyn until the male line failed in *ca.* 1400, when four daughters divided the inheritance. One daughter, Wenllian Norris, held one portion of Penllyn according to Beauchamp's Survey of 1429, but her sister Lucy had taken that part containing the castle to her husband, Tomkin Turberville of Tythegston.[8] Even after this division of the inheritance, the Turbervilles, as holders of the castle, continued to render the full payment of 13*s.* 4*d.* as wardsilver appropriate to two fees, as in 1546 when Christopher Turberville paid this sum in respect of '... *ye Castle and 3rd parte of ye lordships of Penlline ... held of ye King as of his Castle of Cardiffe, by castle guard and knight service* ...'; and in 1597 when his son Jenkin Turberville paid the same amount.[9]

John Leland (1526–39) noted that the castle '... *yet stondith* ...' and alluded to the great strife between its owner Christopher Turberville and Watkin Lougher in 1535, when the latter's son-in-law beset the 'manor' of Penllyn with 100 armed men and set it on fire; Turberville survived within, though suffering '... *a greate pellet of lede through the hoses.*'[10] The Turbervilles of Penllyn long adhered to the Roman faith, and although Richard Turberville tardily conformed in 1592, his successors reverted to it, and it was at Penllyn castle that the missionary priest John Lloyd was apprehended in 1678, before his trial and execution in Cardiff in the following year.[11]

In the 16th century the Turbervilles built a large manor-house on the site of the castle. The keep survived beside the new house, but most of the remaining parts of the castle seem to have been destroyed, to judge from the vagueness of a description of Penllyn

[6] Clark, *Cartae*, II (dcxv), p. 650; Corbett, *Glamorgan Lordship*, p. 34; John also figures in a charter of *ca.* 1270: Clark, *Cartae*, II (dcxliv), pp. 698–700.

[7] *The 'Spenser' Survey* (1320), transcribed by Merrick, *Morg. Arch.*, pp. 72, 74; *Cal, F.R.*, III, Edw. II (1319–27), p. 100.

[8] Clark, *Limbus*, p. 424; Clark, *Cartae*, II, p. 700, n.; Lewis, *Breviat*, p. 118, n.4 and p. 130, n.4; Nicholl, *Normans*, pp. 73–4; Cardiff Library, MS. 3.464 (17th-century copy of Beauchamp's Survey (1429), fols. 126–7).

[9] Cardiff Library, MS. 3.464, fols. 135–7: 'A Survey of all ye Knights fees in Glamorgan. 1546'; Inquisition *post mortem* of Jenkin Turberville (1597): Clark, *Cartae*, VI (mccclxxvi), p. 2123.

[10] Leland, *Itin. Wales*, p. 32; *Morgannwg*, VII (1963), p. 31 (citing Star Chamber Proceedings); J. B. Davies, *Saints and Sailing Ships* (Vale of Glamorgan Series, Vol. IV), 1962, pp. 91–2.

[11] *Glam. Co. Hist.*, IV, pp. 235–6, 475; J. B. Davies, *op. cit.* (n.10), pp. 92–3.

in 1652 as a ruined castle with 'adjoining to it, or in the place of it, a fair house'.[12]

The Turberville connection with Penllyn ended in 1703 with its sale by the brothers John and Thomas Turberville to Richard Seys of Boverton. Then it changed hands in quick succession, which no doubt explains the early abandonment and dereliction of the Turberville house. Richard Seys' son Jevan sold it in 1717 to Sir Edward Stradling, on whose demise it passed to Bussy, the last Lord Mansel. Lord Mansel's daughter and heiress, Lady Vernon, then bequeathed it to her friend Miss Emilia Gwinnett.[13]

The house was derelict by 1786, when a print depicts the N. face of the keep, beyond which is visible a roofless ruin with tall chimneys and a labelled three-light window of typical early-Tudor form (Fig. 243a). Two antiquarian descriptions by Iolo Morgannwg and the anonymous 'C.C.', both also of the 1780s,

describe the site as comprising a tower, identified as Norman by virtue of its semicircular arches and herringbone masonry. This stood on the N. side. Access to its upper floor is described as through a narrow (? mural) stair, the arch of the doorway being semicircular. The ruined buildings occupying the southern portion of the site were noted as having the aspect of a private house of 'considerably later date' in the 'Gothic' style of architecture. It contained a hall and various apartments, all 'small and low' but possessing good quality freestone chimney-pieces, doors and window cases.[14] By 1789 Miss Gwinnett had inherited the

---

[12] J. Taylor, *A Short Relation of a Long Journey Through Wales Made in the Year 1652*, Ed. J. O. Halliwell, London, 1859.

[13] Davies, *op. cit.* (n.10), pp. 93, 96–7; Lewis, *Top. Dict.*; 'C.C.'s Tour in Glamorgan, 1789', *Glamorgan Historian*, II (1965), p. 128.

[14] Descriptions by Iolo Morgannwg, *ca.* 1782, *N.L.W.* MS 13115B, fol. 291; 'C.C.'s tour, 1789', *op. cit.*, n.13.

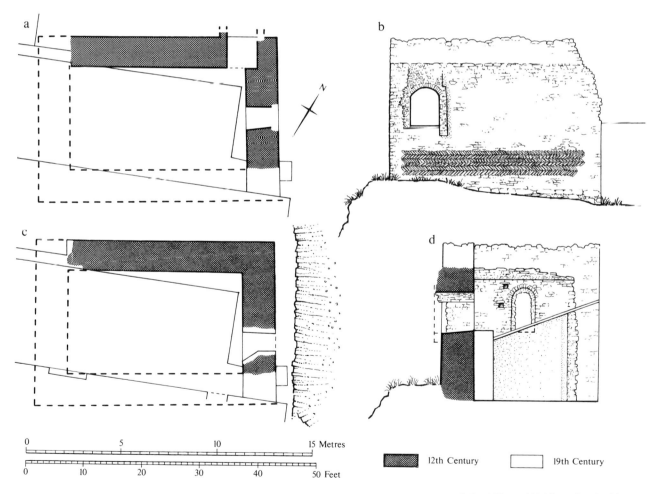

Fig. 245. Penllyn Castle, the Keep: (c) ground floor; (a) first floor; (b) north-west external elevation (*cf.* Fig. 243 a and b) (d) section, looking north-east and passing through first-floor door on left.

ruin and began to build what Lewis (1833) was to describe as an '... *elegant modern mansion, in which some remains of the ancient edifice were incorporated.*' Miss Gwinnett's house was soon replaced by the present castellated mansion to the S., erected by John Homfray soon after his purchase of Penllyn in 1846.[15]

Architectural Description

The only part of the castle to survive consists of the N. and E. walls of the keep, incorporated in a disused stable on the N. side of the mid 19th-century house (Fig. 244). These walls stand to a height of 8.5m and indicate a keep which was very probably about 12.5m by 8.5m overall, and had walls 1.7m thick (Fig. 245, a–d). It was sited to benefit from the protection afforded by a re-entrant angle of the cliff, which gave strength to both surviving walls and is well portrayed, if exaggerated, in 18th-century prints (Fig. 243, a–b). The masonry is of random Carboniferous Limestone rubble for the most part, but the N. wall is especially noteworthy for a bank of six courses of thin slabs laid in herringbone fashion towards its base. Dressed quoins seem to have been robbed and replaced with rough stone. The upper part of the keep has been raised by about 1.3m at some indeterminate period. The ground floor probably served as a basement, as the two surviving walls retain no original openings at this level. On the first floor are the remains of an entrance at the N.E. angle with a round-headed arch. Traces of a projecting toothing, both on the wall near the jambs and above the arch, indicate the former existence of a fore-building which would have enclosed the top of a vanished external stone stair occupying the full width of the narrow berm formed by the re-entrant cliff. The only other surviving feature is a round-headed and recessed window in the E. wall, now robbed of its dressings.

The rectangular keeps of Glamorgan are usually associated with castle-ringworks. At Coity (MR 1) and Ogmore (MR 5) the keep is placed on the line of the ring-bank and later curtain-wall but it was internal and detached at Kenfig (EM 2) and at Newcastle (EM 3). At Penllyn, standing above the cliff as it does, the keep must have stood on the perimeter of any former ringwork that may well have occupied the area to the S., where the Turbervilles erected the house portrayed by Sandby in 1786.

G. T. Clark ascribed an early-12th-century date to the Penllyn keep; at first he favoured Earl Robert but later Robert Norris as its builder, the latter being rather more probable. For the herringbone masonry he deduced an early date, which would agree with the accepted view that this form of walling is characteristic of early Norman work.[16]

King, p. 167 (Penlline)

Pen-llin
SS 97 N.E. (9789–7609)   13.xi.85   XLI S.W.

[15] Lewis, *Top. Dict.*; J. B. Davies, *op. cit.* (n.10), p. 97.
[16] Clark, *The Land of Morgan*, pp. 35–6 and *Cartae*, II (dcxliv), p. 700, n.; M. Wood, *Norman Domestic Architecture*, Royal Archaeological Institute, 1974, p. 76.

EM 5   Peterston Castle

A singular manorial status provides some interest to the scant surviving vestiges of Peterston Castle. Although this castle and lordship was within the shire-fee of Glamorgan, it was not held directly of the chief lord but was a demesne lordship of his le Sore tenant of the adjoining fee of St. Fagans, for which the usual knight-service was rendered. The slight remains of the castle lie 9.5km W. of Cardiff Castle within the village of Peterston-super-Ely, and dispersed within the grounds of four houses which now occupy the site. The parish church is 900m to the W., on the fringe of the village. The castle is not strongly sited, at rather less than 100ft above O.D.; its S. flank falls away gradually to the flood-plain of the Ely River, but in other directions the ground is level. The river flows eastwards for some 7km and successively defines the southern boundaries of Peterston and St Fagans, before turning S.E. towards the sea. St Fagans Castle (LM 17) is only 3.5km to the E., on a similar but more elevated site on the N. side of the river.

Peterston, along with St Fagans, was appropriated early in the 12th century by le Sore. It was not the only early sub-manor of St Fagans: le Sore also sub-enfeoffed the Hawey family in the detached manor of Gelli-garn (CR 8), 12km to the W. of Peterston, but permitted them to exchange it with Neath Abbey between 1154 and 1183.[1] The contiguous estates of

[1] Clark., *Cartae*, II (cccxviii), p. 315, 318, n.; Corbett, *Glamorgan Lordship*, p. 237; Merrick, *Morg. Arch*, pp. 57–8.

le Sore at Peterston and St Fagans were on the northern fringe of the shire-fee and represent its only extension into the heavy soils to the N. of the Ely River.[2] Neither lordship is coterminous with its respective parish, which in each case extends northwards beyond the Shire-fee into the Welsh territory of Meisgyn that remained autonomous until the mid 13th century; the small lordships occupying the southern parts of these parishes have the appearance of lands annexed from Meisgyn, which must surely have extended anciently to the natural line of the Ely.

Robert le Sore is first recorded in the company of Robert Fitzhamon in South Wales *ca.* 1102, as witness to a deed concerning Basaleg church.[3] Odo le Sore next appears, witnessing Earl Robert of Gloucester's concord with Bishop Urban of Llandaff in 1126, and that with the Abbot of Fécamp in 1128.[4] When Earl Robert was the leading supporter of the empress against Stephen, Odo was one of eight hostages given by the earl to Miles, Earl of Hereford, in 1141–43.[5] He appears also during the early part of Earl William's tenure of the lordship of Glamorgan, granting houses at Bristol to Margam Abbey.[6] This Odo, if not the Robert le Sore of *ca.* 1102, was certainly enfeoffed in St Fagans, valued at one knight's fee, before 1135, since his fee is listed in 1166 as of the 'old enfeoffment', and its early possession may be deduced from Tewkesbury's enjoyment of half of its tithes.[7] Therefore it may be assumed that the manor of Peterston had been acquired equally early and its first castle raised beside the river to buttress the W. flank of St Fagans.

Ca. 1150, Odo's son John confirmed his father's grant in Bristol to Margam, and a little later he allowed the exchange of his sub-manor of Gelli-garn with Neath Abbey.[8] Jordan le Sore had succeeded by the date of *Liber Niger* (1166); William le Sore assisted in the defence of Neath Castle during the uprising of 1183–84, and he or another William was witness to many charters between 1186–91 and 1216.[9]

William le Sore was in possession at the extent of 1262, but by the end of the 13th century an heiress had taken St Fagans to the le Veles, though strangely the sub-manor of Peterston remained with le Sores, presumably of a cadet branch. About the middle of the 14th century one of this line appears to have sold a moiety of Peterston to Lord Edward Despenser (*ob.* 1375), while the remaining moiety came to John Butler by 1382.[10] Before 1459 the Butler moiety, which included the village and castle, was further partitioned, half going to Mathew of Radyr. Thus it remained *ca.* 1536, when Leland said of Peterston,

'*B(utler) and George Mathew be lordes of the village'*, and the castle was '... almost al in ruine'.[11] By this date the Despenser moiety was with the Crown, having come to Henry VII; it was granted to John Basset in 1545, from whom it passed to Mansel and Aubrey.

There is no specific record of Peterston castle, and since the manor was not held directly of the chief lord it escaped notice in general medieval surveys and inquisitions. Nevertheless, there is no doubt that it was held by le Sores of St Fagans from the early-12th century until the mid-14th century. The 16th century historians are not credible in two of their assertions regarding Peterston:[12] the place-name appears to have persuaded them that a Peter le Sore was numbered with Fitzhamon's knights, and enfeoffed by him at Peterston, but no record substantiates this claim. Merrick also relates a further unacceptable tradition claiming that Owain Glyndŵr captured Peterston Castle and beheaded its lord, Sir Mathew le Sore, whose skull was displayed in Peterston Church in his time. As we have seen, the castle had passed to the Butlers over twenty years before the Glyndŵr uprising.

Description of the Remains

The ruins were sketched for Jeston Homfray in 1828, when the site was already occupied by two houses,

[2] *Glam. Co. Hist.*, III, p. 21.

[3] Clark, *Cartae*, I (xxxv), p. 38; *Glam. Co. Hist.*, III, p. 286; R. A. Griffiths, *Glamorgan Historian*, III (1966), p. 164.

[4] Clark, *Cartae*, I (1), p. 56 (= *Epis. Acts*, II, L45, pp. 620–1 and Patterson, *Glouc. Charters*, No. 109, p. 106). That Odo was Robert's son appears from the witness list to the foundation charter of Neath Abbey (1130): Clark, *Cartae*, I (lxvii), p. 75.

[5] Patterson, *Glouc. Charters*, No. 95, p. 5; *Glam. Co. Hist.*, III, p. 27.

[6] Clark, *Cartae*, I (cviii), p. 110 (= *Epis. Acts*, II, L167, p. 658 and Patterson, *Glouc. Charters*, No. 126, p. 118); Clark *Cartae* I (clxvii), p. 166 (= Patterson, *Glouc. Charters*, No. 121, p. 116).

[7] *Liber Niger*; *Liber Rubeus*; Corbett, *Glamorgan Lordship*, pp. 33, 118; Nicholl, *Normans*, pp. 6–7; *Epis. Acts*, II, L170, p. 659; W. Rees, *South Wales and Monmouth Record Soc.*, Publication No. 2, 1950, p. 143.

[8] Clark, *Cartae*, I (cxxix), p. 126; Merrick, *Morg. Arch.*, citing the lost Register of Neath Abbey: pp. 58, 64. See also n.1.

[9] *Pipe Rolls* (1184–85), 31 Henry II; *Glam. Co. Hist*, III, p. 38. For the charters, too numerous to cite, see Clark, *Cartae*; *Epis. Acts*, II; and Patterson, *Glouc. Charters*.

[10] *Cal. Anc. Petitions*, p. 356; Corbett, *Glamorgan Lordship*, pp. 235, 241.

[11] Leland, *Itin. Wales*, p. 26.

[12] Merrick, *Morg. Arch.*, pp. 27, 57 (Appendix 2, pp. 153, 160 for Sir Edward Stradling's similar version); Lewis, *Breviat*, p. 130.

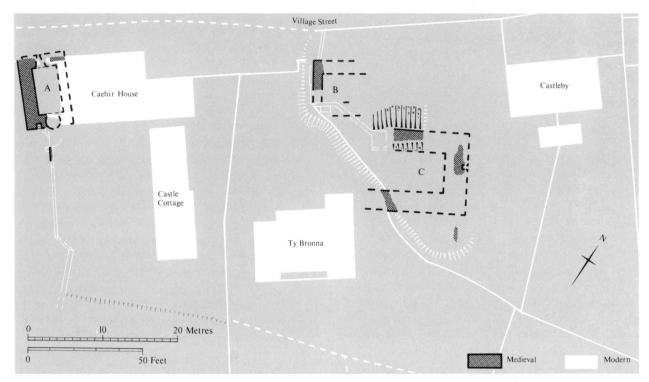

Fig. 246. Peterston Castle: general plan to locate its scattered vestiges. A. The north-west angle-tower; B. Suspected gate-tower; C. Suspected keep.

one of which was thatched and apparently of 16th- or 17th-century appearance. The thatched house is no longer standing, and the castle site is now occupied by four houses of recent date, *viz*, from W. to E., Caehir House, Castle Cottage, Ty Bronna and Castleby (plan, Fig. 246).

The remains of masonry belonging to the castle, A, B, and C, lie within the grounds of Caehir House to the W. and Castleby to the centre. **A**, is the most substantial, and represents a rectangular angle-tower. B represents another and smaller rectangular tower, possibly connected with a gate, since like the N.W. tower it lies beside the main village street running E.–W. along the N. side. No trace remains of a curtain-wall to link these two towers, or of one running E. to a vanished N.E. angle-tower in the area of the modern Castleby. The third and final remnant of masonry, C, seems to be the oldest fabric on the site, retaining slight hints of 12th-century detail and distinguished from the other two by its orange sandy mortar, theirs being sandy but very white.

This, the earliest fragment, seems to represent a detached keep. It occupies the highest ground, though this may be no more than the build-up created by its collapsed masonry. Only its N. wall stands above

ground, to a height of about 4m, and this only for a short section. What stands, however, retains in its severed E. end the voussoirs of a clearly round-headed opening into the first floor, though whether of a door or a window it is impossible to say. The masonry of this building C is of irregularly squared blocks of Lias Limestone, set in random fashion, but here and there brought to roughly levelled courses. The E. wall is represented by a mass of its well-mortared rubble core, retaining the inner part of a latrine chute, and roughly defined, as to its line and width, by the stony bank above which it protrudes a little. The third known side, that to the S., may be discerned at present only at the top of the recent 'quarry-face' made to level the grounds of the new bungalow called Ty Bronna, and defining its boundary. Here both sides of the S. wall can be located in section, and it is clear that the S.W. angle has been lost, though the footings of that to the N.W. may survive. The remains thus defined would indicate a rectangular building measuring 11.5m by at least 17m externally, with strong well-mortared walls 3m thick. Such a structure could hardly have been anything but a 12th-century keep. Larger than that of Ogmore (MR 5; 14.5m by 10m), the Peterston keep is closer in size to those at Sully

(EM 6; approximately 18m by 12m) and Dinas Powys (EM1; 18.3m by 13.4m).

The N.W. angle-tower A, a roofless shell incorporated in the W. end of Caehir House, is the most substantial fragment to survive. Its projecting W. wall stands to a surviving height of rather over 6m. This wall retains the returns of the western ends of the adjoining N. and S. walls, while a straight joint near the N.W. corner of Caehir House, facing the street, defines the width of the tower and shows that its E. wall, at least in part, is incorporated in the house. The tower was about 10m by 7m externally, with walls 1.6m thick. The W. wall retains remains of a first-floor splayed window with segmental-headed rear arch. At the level of its inner arch a line of joist-holes marks the line of the second floor. A garderobe chute is incorporated in the wall at the S.W. angle, with an outfall contained within the angle made with the W. curtain-wall. A flat lintel carried on corbels spans the outfall below remains of a squinch. The severed end of the N. wall still has remains of the W. splays of windows at ground- and first-floor levels, beyond which further traces of the projecting N. wall, or rather its core, are incorporated in Caehir House abutting the straight joint already mentioned. The S. wall, at its junction with the curtain, retains part of the curved recess of a newel stair. To the S. of this, the garden wall running S. appears ancient at its base, and must lie over the curtain and define the W. side of the castle. A row of external corbels supporting the second floor was noted on the W. wall of the tower in 1963, but this has now mostly fallen.

Fragment B, at 35m E. of the N.W. Tower, uses the same white sandy mortar as in that tower. Only a part of its W. wall survives, and this stood to a height of 5.49m when initially surveyed in 1963, but it had been greatly reduced by 1985. No features now survive. The fragment defines the N.W. angle of a rectangular tower, its length set along the line of the vanished N. curtain and the adjacent parallel street. Perhaps it flanked or incorporated the gateway.

Heavy boulder footings noted along the S. flank in 1963, together with traces of a rubble wall noted but not defined to the E., give approximate indications of the extent of the castle. From these it would seem to have been a rectangular enclosure measuring 40m E.–W. by 35m N.–S. If it had a rectangular tower at each corner like that on the N.W., its enceinte may have been of the late 13th or 14th century. The more massive keep, which would have stood detached in the N.E. quarter of such a later enclosure, was surely of the 12th century, and was perhaps initially surrounded by a palisaded enclosure like that recorded at Kenfig (EM 2), where it accompanied a stone keep until at least 1232.

King, p. 168.

Peterston-super-Ely.
ST 07 N.E. (0839–7641)   1.x.85   XLII S.E.

EM 6   Sully Castle

Sully Castle is no more; its site is now occupied by houses built after excavations carried out for the Ancient Monuments Branch of the Ministry of Works by Mr. G Dowdell between 1963 and 1969. The site is 8.6km to the S.W. of Cardiff, and only 400m from the sea. With the village of Sully, it occupies a low ridge with no natural defence but a wide outlook over the Bristol Channel to the S. and Sully Moors to the N. The parish church lies beside the castle to the W. Before the recent excavations the site was wooded and densely overgrown; little was to be seen. Excavations were undertaken here in the mid 19th century, with the cognizance of, and possibly under the direction of, G. T. Clark, who then worked for the Guests of Dowlais. The Guests owned the adjacent Sully House, and Lady Charlotte is known to have excavated at Morlais Castle, near Merthyr (LM 10). The foundations of a keep uncovered at Sully are mentioned in Clark's scattered lists of such structures in his published works.[1] No details were published, but his plans and notes survive in the National Library.[2] The foundations were soon buried once more. When Fox visited the site in 1924 and 1934 only vestiges of the much later curtain-wall enclosing the keep were visible, and on his second visit the best-preserved fragment, that to the N., was being demolished for houses beside the Sully Inn.[3]

The excavations of 1963–69 uncovered substantial

---

[1] Clark, *Land of Morgan*, pp. 35–6, 48; Clark, *Med. Milit. Arch.* I, pp. 113, 148; *Handbook of the British Association*, Cardiff meeting 1891, Ed. D. I. James, p. 51.

[2] *N.L.W.*, Welsh Castles, MS. 5198E, Vol. II, p. 56; MS. 9198E, Vol. II, p. 54; MS. 5215E, Vol. VII.

[3] *N.M.W.*, Fox notebook, No. 2, p. 51.

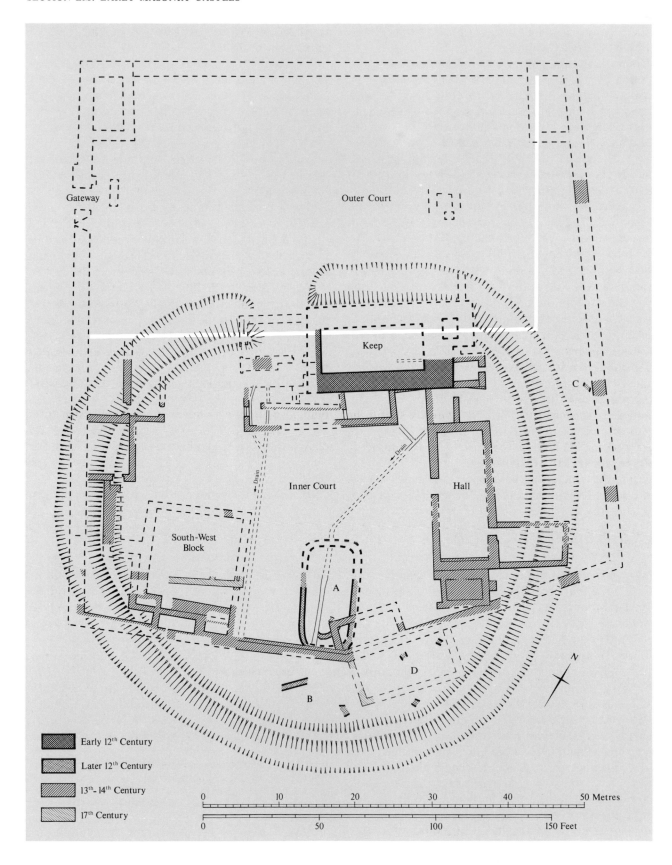

Gateway

Outer Court

Keep

C

Drain

Drain

Inner Court

Hall

South-West
Block

A

D

B

N

Early 12th Century

Later 12th Century

13th–14th Century

17th Century

| 0 | 10 | 20 | 30 | 40 | 50 Metres |

| 0 | | 50 | | 100 | | 150 Feet |

traces of the keep and confirmed Clark's plans and descriptions of it. A long and complex building history was worked out, which will be summarised here through the kindness of Mr. Dowdell in communicating a copy of his report prior to its publication.*

Sully Castle, from the 12th to the early 14th centuries, was the *caput* of a lordship held by the Sully family. They do not appear in the *Liber Niger* list of fees held of Earl William of Gloucester, only emerging in the Glamorgan records of the last quarter of the 12th century. Yet the evidence revealed by the excavations supports those historians who have long suspected that they were at Sully early in the 12th century, unnoticed perhaps because their adoption of the name Sully came later.[4] The first on record is Walter de Sully, who figures frequently as a witness to charters in the period 1190–1214.[5] They appear throughout the 13th century, and in the extent made following the death of Earl Richard de Clare in 1262, when another Walter de Sully held four fees by knight service, two at Sully valued at £20 and two at Wenvoe, valued at £10.[6] Briefly Glamorgan was retained by the Crown at this date, during the minority of the heir, Earl Gilbert de Clare, and Walter de Sully was appointed *custos* of the lordship. Already sheriff, he is described at this time as '*bonus homo et potens in provincia*'.[7] The four fees were held by Raymond de Sully in 1314, according to the inquisition on the late Earl Gilbert de Clare, but by 1317 he too was dead, the last of his line. Sully seems to have passed briefly to Breos by marriage to an heiress, but about the middle of the century it was purchased by one of the Despenser lords of Glamorgan.[8] The chief lords held the manor for the rest of the Middle Ages, but at some stage, it appears, the castle was given up for a new administrative centre at the moated site of Middleton, 520m to the N. on Sully Moors (Vol. III, Part 2, MS 11).

The Structural Development of Sully Castle

The excavations of 1963–69 on the site of the castle revealed six phases of occupation ranging from the Romano-British to the 17th or 18th century. Four were medieval (phases 2–5) from which were deduced two main periods of building: *I*, an earthwork of the

Fig. 247. *(Opposite)* Sully Castle: Plan after that of the excavator (Mr. Gareth Dowdell) and others by G.T. Clark. The hypothetical castle-ringwork is inferred from the segment of bank and ditch observed within the south-west angle of the later walled enclosure.

12th century to which a stone-built keep was added (phases 2–3), and *II*, a fortified manor-house of the 13th and early 14th centuries imposed upon the previous earthwork but regardless of its plan (phases 4–5).

Period I, The 12th-Century Castle

The primary castle was inferred from the segment of a curving bank and external ditch observed beneath the buildings contained within the S.W. angle of the later 13th-/14th-century enclosure (Plan, Fig. 247). Contemporary with this bank and ditch, and presumably enclosed by its undetermined circuit, were flimsy structures of timber underlying the hall of *Period II*, as well as a more massively timbered structure partly beneath the keep. Slight though this evidence is, it indicates the existence of a large castle-ringwork during the first period.

Later in the 12th century (phase 3) the defences were strengthened by the imposition of a dry-stone revetment on the bank, and by the erection of a stone keep to replace the timber structure to the N., while four sub-rectangular buildings (A, B, C and D) were built, also of stone, to replace flimsy timber structures. This rebuilding, judging from archaeological evidence, was undertaken before *ca.* 1150, which would therefore suggest that the keep was raised in the time of Earl Robert of Gloucester (*ca.* 1114–47).

The ringwork is conjecturally shown on the plan (Fig. 247), continuing the known segment so as to embrace four of the five round-cornered buildings and also the keep, assuming that it was just inside the northern front by analogy with Coity and Ogmore castles (MR 1, 5). Slight though they were, the remains of this ringwork matched those of better-preserved examples which cluster in the eastern part of the Vale of Glamorgan. Likewise the buildings with rounded

[4] Clark, *Land of Morgan*, pp. 31, 48; Corbett, *Glamorgan Lordship*, pp. 35, 118–19, 127.

[5] Clark, *Cartae*, II (cccxci), pp. 384–5 (=*Epis. Acts*, II, L222, pp. 674–5); *Cartae*, II (cccclii), p. 441 (=*Epis Acts*, II, L227, pp. 676–7); *Cartae*, II (ccxx), pp. 225–6 (=*Epis. Acts*, II, L242, p. 680); *Cartae*, II (cclxxii), pp. 269–70 (=*Epis. Acts*, II, L254, p. 683); *Cartae*, II (cccxxv), pp. 323–5 (=*Epis. Acts*, II, L279, p. 690); *Cartae*, II (cccxlii), p. 441.

[6] Clark, *Cartae*, II (dcxv), p. 650 and *Land of Morgan*, p. 33; Corbett, *Glamorgan Lordship*, pp. 34–5.

[7] Clark, *Land of Morgan*, pp. 123 (citing the Annals of Tewkesbury).

[8] *Cal. Anc. Petitions*, No. 10442, p. 356; Nicholl, *Normans*, p. 51.

corners matched those found in ruin in the early-12th-century ringworks at Llantrithyd (CR 13), Penmaen (CR 18) and Pennard (MR 6). At both Penmaen and Llantrithyd, as at Sully, the sub-rectangular buildings were preceded by timber structures. Likewise the dry-stone revetment of the bank at Sully is paralleled at the castle-ringworks of Dinas Powys (CR 7) and North Hill Tor (CR 15).

The hypothetical ringwork at Sully, defined by the contemporary features it would have contained, would have had a diameter of about 53m. This is the largest diameter of its class in Glamorgan, but not improbably so. That de Sully might have built the largest ringwork in the county need not surprise us. They ranked with the fortunate holders of the richest and most extensive estates ranged along the sea coast: those of de Londres at Ogmore, Nerber at St Athan, and Umfraville at Penmark. The Sully lands bounded with those of Umfraville and formed the final large coastal holding at the E. end of the Vale, extending close to Cardiff. Each of these large holdings was valued at four knights' fees. Sully, only recorded at this valuation in 1262, but evidently fortified from early in the 12th century, gives complete symmetry to the Norman feudal partition of the coastal lowlands, with two leading followers either side of the chief lord's demesne manor at Llantwit.

The keep (Fig. 247), when uncovered by Dowdell, was represented only by the footings and the lower courses of its S. half, rectangular and unbuttressed, corresponding to and confirming G. T. Clark's complete ground plan.[9] Clark recorded the masonry of the S. wall as standing to a height of 1.6m, but this had diminished to between 0.6m and 0.9m above the footings, with a maximum of three courses of original facing. The S. wall was 2.7m thick, the E. wall 3.6m without the former projection for a cess-pit seen by Clark. The W. wall, of which most of the inner face was found, had been 2.1m thick as seen by Clark, who recorded the N. wall as 2.7m thick like that to the S. Thus, excluding the N.E. projection, it formerly measured 19m by 11.5m externally, and was almost as large as the keeps at Dinas Powys and Kenfig (EM 1, 2), the former having a similar projection, the latter having had an added latrine-turret. Any stair was presumably in the very massive E. wall, but no trace of it was found.

Before considering the later castle, it should be noted that the adjacent church of the 13th century replaces a Norman foundation; footings of an apsidal chancel were observed during restoration in 1833.[10]

Period II,
The 13th- and Early-14th-Century Castle

The most striking aspect of the later castle is the disregard its layout shows for the earlier defences. To the W. the new curtain-wall runs over the in-filled earlier ditch, while buildings against it overlie the levelled bank. To the S. an arc of the former ringwork was left outside the new enclosure, while to the N. and E. this enclosure extended well beyond. There was not the usual simple replacement of the old defences here, as at Coity and Ogmore, but a new and much extended roughly quadrangular perimeter was set out without regard to the previous plan. The new castle was built, it seems likely, in the first half of the 13th century (*phase 4*), and modified late in the 13th or early 14th century (*phase 5*). The keep was retained, now occupying a central position within the new perimeter. It remained the lord's residence, to judge by the improved accommodation furnished by chambers now added against its W. and S. walls.

The *Curtain-Wall* was only 1.52m thick and without any flanking towers. It clearly represents a fortified manorial curtilage rather than a castle. Its approximation to a quadrangular plan furnished the form most convenient for the arrangement of the domestic quarters and services. Similarly, for domestic rather than military needs there were additions to the flanks of the keep. A gateway flanked by two small slightly projecting towers seems to have existed towards the N. end of the W. wall, facing the church. In 1934 Fox and O'Neil visited the site while the northern curtain was being demolished.[11] They noted the remains of small rectangular towers, both about 10m by 6m, set within the N. angles, neither of which projected beyond the curtain. Their simple sketch is fortunately augmented by more detailed unpublished plans by Clark.[12]

The *South-West Block* in the S.W. angle represented a building of some importance, though lacking any hint of defensibility. Its large northern component produced slight evidence of culinary activity.

In the final phase of medieval building (phase 5) a large new *Hall* to the E. replaced the keep as the main accommodation. This, with the further addition

---

[9] See f/n. 2.
[10] J. K. Knight, *Trans., Cardiff Nat. Soc.*, XCIX (1976–78), 1981, pp. 60–1; M. R. Spencer, *Annals of South Glamorgan*, (Carmarthen, 1913), pp. 184–5.
[11] See note 3.
[12] See note 2.

of a range of three well-appointed chambers along the W. curtain, apparently formed an inner residential court, presumably with a gate to the outer court on the W. side of more additions made in this phase to the keep.

The later castle at Sully was no more than a stronghouse, its castellation symbolic rather than functional. Such later medieval crenellated curtilages, not seriously fortified, are to be seen elsewhere in Glamorgan at Landimôr (SH 1), Marcross (SH 2), Llandough (TH 2) and, in its early medieval form, at Beaupre (Vol. IV, Part I, No. 1).

Occupation seems to have ceased very soon after the failure of the Sully line early in the 14th century. The later de Sullys must certainly have undertaken the final developments of substance on the site. In 1349, after the fief had been purchased by Despenser, the inquisition on Hugh le Despenser notes:

'Sully . . . In which manor there is a certain messuage enclosed by a stone wall, with a garden annexed, and valued by the year 10s. Also there is in the same place a certain stone dovecot which is valued by the year 6s. 8d.'[13]

It is not possible to say whether this relates to the castle or to Middleton Moat nearby, which replaced the castle as the manorial centre under the Despensers.

King, p. 172 (under vanished castles)

Sully
ST 16 N.E. (1516–6834) 25.viii.68 LI N.W.

---

[13] *N.L.W.,* MS 3748D, Floyd Transcripts: Inquisition *P.M.* of Hugh le Despenser, lord of Glamorgan, 1349.

* * * *

Abbreviated Titles of References

Alcock, *Dinas Powys* Leslie Alcock, *Dinas Powys: An Iron Age, Dark Age and Early Medieval Settlement in Glamorgan*, Board of Celtic Studies (Cardiff, 1963).

Altschul, *The Clares* Michael Altschul, *A Baronial Family in Medieval England: The Clares 1217–1314* (Baltimore, 1965).

Ann. Camb. *Annales Cambriae*, ed. J. Williams ab Ithel (Rolls Series, 1860).

Ann. Margam *Annales de Margam* (Printed in *Annales Monastici*, ed. H. R. Luard, Rolls Series, Vol. I, 1864).

Ann. Theokes. *Annales de Theokesberia* (Printed in *Annales Monastici*, ed. H. R. Luard, Rolls Series, Vol. I, 1864).

Antiq. Journ. *Antiquaries Journal*, The Society of Antiquaries, London.

Arch. Camb. *Archaeologia Cambrensis*, The Cambrian Archaeological Association, Cardiff.

Arch. in Wales *Archaeology in Wales*, Newsletter of the Council for British Archaeology, Group 2, Wales.

Armitage, *Norman Castles* Ella S. Armitage, *The Early Norman Castles of the British Isles* (London, 1912).

B.B.C.S. *Bulletin of the Board of Celtic Studies*, University of Wales, Cardiff.

Beresford, *New Towns* Maurice Beresford, *New Towns of the Middle Ages* (London, 1967).

Boon, *Welsh Hoards* George C. Boon, *Welsh Hoards 1979–1981*, N.M.W., 1986.

Breviate Ann. Annals from A.D. 600–1298 inserted in Breviate of Domesday (P.R.O., E. 164/1) and printed in *Arch. Camb.* 1862, pp. 272–83.

Brut, B.S. *Brenhinedd y Saesson or The Kings of the Saxons*, ed. and transl. T. Jones, Board of Celtic Studies, History and Law Series, No. 25 (Cardiff, 1971).

Brut, Pen 20 *Brut y Tywysogyon or The Chronicle of the Princes* (Peniarth MS 20 version), ed. and transl. T. Jones, Board of Celtic Studies, History and Law Series, No. 11 (Cardiff, 1952).

Brut, R.B.H. *Brut y Tywysogyon or The Chronicle of the Princes* (Red Book of Hergest version), ed. and transl. T. Jones, Board of Celtic Studies, History and Law Series, No. 16 (Cardiff, 1955).

Cal. Anc. Corr. *Calendar of Ancient Correspondence Concerning Wales*, ed. J. Goronwy Edwards, Board of Celtic Studies, History and Law Series, No. 2 (Cardiff, 1935).

Cal. Anc. Petitions *Calendar of Ancient Petitions Relating to Wales (13th–16th century)*, ed. William Rees, Board of Celtic Studies, History and Law Series, No. 28 (Cardiff, 1975).

Cal. C.R. *Calendar of the Close Rolls*, Edward I–Henry VII (London, 1892–1975) and, though not calendared, *Close Rolls of the Reign of Henry III*, 15 vols. (London, 1902–38, 1975).

Cal. I.P.M. *Calendar of Inquisitions Post Mortem and other analogous documents*, Henry III–Edward III (London, 1904–1974).

Cal. P.R. *Calendar of Patent Rolls*, Henry III–Elizabeth I (London, 1902–1982).

Cardiff Records J. H. Matthews (ed.), *Cardiff Records, Materials for a History of the County Borough*, 6 vols. (Cardiff, 1898–1911).

Carlisle, *Top. Dict.* N. Carlisle, *A Topographic Dictionary of Wales* (London, 1811).

Château Gaillard	*Château Gaillard, Études de Castellologie Médiévale*, Centre de Recherches Archéologiques Médiévales (Caen, 1964–).
Clark, *Cartae*	G. T. Clark, *Cartae et alia munimenta quae ad dominium de Glamorgancia pertinent*, 2nd. edn., 6 vols. (Cardiff, 1910).
Clark, *Land of Morgan*	G. T. Clark, *The Land of Morgan: Being a Contribution Towards the History of the Lordship of Glamorgan* (London, 1833).
Clark, *Limbus*	G. T. Clark, *Limbus Patrum Morganiae et Glamorganiae, being the genealogies of the older families of the lordships of Morgan and Glamorgan* (London, 1886).
Clark, *Med. Milit. Arch.*	G. T. Clark, *Mediaeval Military Architecture in England*, 2 vols. (London, 1884).
Corbett, *Glamorgan Lordship*	J. S. Corbett, *Glamorgan: Papers and Notes on the Lordship and its Members*, ed. D. R. Paterson (Cardiff, 1925).
Dict. Welsh Biog.	*The Dictionary of Welsh Biography down to 1940*, ed. Sir John Lloyd, *et al.* (London, 1959).
Epis. Acts	*Episcopal Acts and Cognate Documents relating to Welsh Dioceses, 1066–1272*, ed. J. Conway Davies, 2 vols., Historical Society of the Church in Wales (Cardiff, 1946, 1948).
Glam. Co. Hist.	*Glamorgan County History* (General Editor Glanmor Williams): Vol. III, *The Middle Ages*, ed. T. B. Pugh (Cardiff, 1971). Series now completed with Vols. I, II, IV, V, and VI (Cardiff, 1936, 1984, 1974, 1980, 1988).
Glamorgan Historian	*Stewart Williams' Glamorgan Historian*, ed. Stewart Williams *et al.*, 11 vols. (Cowbridge and Barry, 1963–79).
Gray, *Kenfig*	Thomas Gray, *The Buried City of Kenfig* (London, 1909).
Hist. King's Works	*The History of the King's Works*, ed. R. Allan Brown, H. M. Colvin and A. J. Taylor, Vols. I and II, *The Middle Ages* (London, 1963).
King, *Cast. Ang.*	David J. Cathcart King, *Castellarium Anglicanum, an Index and Bibliography of the Castles in England, Wales and the Islands*, 2 vols. (New York, 1983).
King	Relevant page references to King, *Cast. Ang.* (*supra*), Vol. I, pp. 159–78, 287–88 are cited thus at the end of inventory accounts.
Leland, *Itin. Wales*	*The Itinerary of John Leland in or about the years 1536–1539*, Vol. III, *Wales*, ed. L. Toulmin Smith (London, 1906, repr. 1964).
Lewis, *Breviat*	'A Breviat of Glamorgan, 1596–1600', by Rice Lewis, ed. William Rees (*S. Wales and Mon. Rec. Soc. Pubns.* No. 3, 1954).
Lewis, *Top. Dict.*	S. Lewis, *A Topographical Dictionary of Wales*, 2 vols. (London, 1833).
Lhuyd, *Parochialia*	*Parochialia, being a summary of answers to 'Parochial Queries' issued by Edward Lhwyd*, Pts. I–III, ed. R. H. Morris. (*Arch. Camb.* supplements, 1909–11.) [pp. 116–47 of Pt. III (Peniarth MS. 120E) form part of Merrick's *Morg. Arch.*]
Liber Land.	*The Text of the Book of Llan Dav*, ed. J. Gwenogvryn Evans and John Rhys (Oxford, 1893. Facsimile edn., N.L.W., 1979.)
Liber Niger	*Liber Niger Scaccarii*, ed. Thomas Hearne, 2 vols. (Oxford, 1728; 2nd. edn., London, 1771; repr. 1774).
Liber Rubeus	*Liber Rubeus de Scaccario, The Red Book of the Exchequer*, ed. Hubert Hall, Rolls Series, 3 vols. (London, 1896).
Lloyd, *Hist. Wales*	J. E. Lloyd, *A History of Wales from the Earliest Times to the Edwardian Conquest*, 2 vols. (London, 1911, repr. 1912, 1939, 1948).
Med. Arch.	*Medieval Archaeology*, Journal of the Society for Medieval Archaeology.

Merrick, *Morg. Arch.*	Rice Merrick, *Morganiae Archaiographia: A Book of the Antiquities of Glamorganshire*, ed. Brian Ll. James (S. Wales Record Society, Vol. I, 1983).
Morgan, *East Gower*	W. Ll. Morgan, *Antiquarian Survey of East Gower* (London, 1899).
Morgannwg	*Morgannwg, Transactions of the Glamorgan Local History Society* (from 1971 *The Journal of Glamorgan History*).
Nicholl, *Normans*	Lewis D. Nicholl, *The Normans in Glamorgan, Gower and Kidweli* (Cardiff, 1936).
N.L.W.	National Library of Wales, Aberystwyth.
N.L.W. Journal	*The National Library of Wales Journal.*
N.M.W.	National Museum of Wales, Cardiff.
O.D.	Ordnance Datum.
O.S.	Ordnance Survey.
Patterson, *Glouc. Charters*	*Earldom of Gloucester Charters. The Charters and Scribes of the Earls and Countesses of Gloucester to a.d. 1217*, ed. R. B. Patterson (Oxford, 1973).
Phillips, *Vale of Neath*	D. R. Phillips, *History of the Vale of Neath* (Swansea, 1925).
Pierce, *Dinas Powys*	G. O. Pierce, *The Place-names of Dinas Powys Hundred* (Cardiff, 1968).
P.R.O.	Public Record Office, London.
R.C.A.M.	Royal Commission on Ancient and Historical Monuments in Wales.
Rees, *Cardiff*	William Rees, *Cardiff, a History of the City*, 2nd. edn. (Cardiff, 1969).
Rees, *Map*	William Rees, *A Map of South Wales and the Border in the Fourteenth Century* (O.S., 1932).
Rees, *Order of St John*	William Rees, *A History of the Order of St John of Jerusalem in Wales and on the Welsh Border* (Cardiff, 1947).
Renn, *Norman Castles*	D. F. Renn, *Norman Castles in Britain*, 2nd. edn. (London, 1973).
Trans. Cardiff Nat. Soc.	*Transactions of the Cardiff Naturalists' Society.*
Trans. Port Talbot Hist. Soc.	*Transactions of the Port Talbot Historical Society.*

List of Ecclesiastical Parishes

With incidence of Monuments

This list corresponds with the map, Fig. 248, and indicates the ecclesiastical subdivision of Glamorgan into parishes as it stood *ca.* 1850, before any of the changes of names and boundaries which have taken place for administrative purposes (*cf.* Fig. 249 and list on p. 355).

Ecclesiastical parishes are noted at the end of Inventory entries, distinguished by the letter (E) when the monument concerned stands in a civil parish of a different name (C). Spellings used are as shown on the left; the forms found on the earlier editions of the O.S. maps are given in square brackets. The Welsh forms, which follow the recommendations of the Board of Celtic Studies, are given on the right only when they differ from those already adopted for use in this Inventory.

Nos. 5, 68 and 77 are parts of parishes which straddle the Monmouthshire border. Nos. 102 and 117 are included as a result of the expansion of Cardiff.

No.	Parish name used	Correct Welsh form	Monument Nos.
1	Aberavon	Aberafan	VE 1
2	Aberdâr [Aberdare]	—	UW 4
3	Baglan	—	UW 3, UW 5

No.	Parish name used	Correct Welsh form	Monument Nos.
4	Barry	Y Barri	—
5	Bedwas (Van hamlet)	—	CR 9
6	Betws [Bettws]	—	—
7	Bishopston	Llandeilo Ferwallt	CR 1
8	Bonvilston	Tresimwn	CR 2
9	Briton Ferry	Llansawel	—
10	Cadoxton-juxta-Barry	Tregatwg	—
11	Cadoxton-juxta-Neath	Llangatwg Nedd	UW 1, VE 2
12	Caerau	—	CR 4
13	Cardiff St. John	Caerdydd	MM 1
14	Cardiff St. Mary	Caerdydd	—
15	Cheriton	—	CR 15
16	Cilybebyll	—	—
17	Coety [Coity]	—	VE 4, MR 1
18	Colwinston	Tregolwyn	—
19	Coychurch	Llangrallo	—
20	Eglwys Brewys [Eglwysbrewis]	—	—
21	Eglwysilan	—	—
22	Ewenni [Ewenny]	—	—
23	Flemingston	Trefflemin	

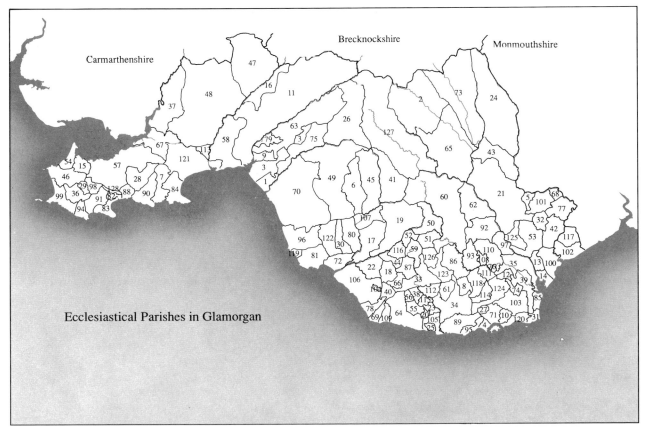

Fig. 248. Ecclesiastical Parishes. Numbers correspond to those in the list.

No.	Parish name used	Correct Welsh form	Monument Nos.
24	Gelli-gaer	—	MO 9
25	Gileston	Silstwn	—
26	Glyncorwg	—	—
27	Highlight	Uchelola	—
28	Ilston	Llanilltud Gŵyr	—
29	Knelston	Llan-y-tair-mair	—
30	Laleston	Trelales	VE 3
31	Lavernock	Larnog	—
32	Lisvane	Llys-faen	—
33	Llanblethian	Llanfleiddan	MR 3
34	Llancarfan	—	CR 17, CR 21
35	Llandaf [Llandaff]	—	—
36	Llanddewi	—	—
37	Llandeilo Tal-y-bont	—	MO 6
38	Llandough (near Cowbridge)	Llandochau	—
39	Llandough, Cogan a Leckwith	Llandochau, Cogan a Lecwydd	CR 3
40	Llandŵ [Llandow]	—	CR 11
41	Llandyfodwg	—	—
42	Llanedern [Llanedeyrn]	—	—
43	Llanfabon	—	—
44	Llan-gan	—	—
45	Llangeinwyr [Llangeinor]	—	—
46	Llangennith	Llangynydd	—
47	Llanguicke	Llan-giwg	
48	Llangyfelach	—	UW 2
49	Llangynwyd	—	MR 2
50	Llanharan	—	—
51	Llanhari [Llanharry]	—	—
52	Llanilid	—	CR 12
53	Llanisien [Llanishen]	—	—
54	Llanmadog [Llanmadoc]	—	—
55	Llanmaes	Llan-faes	—
56	Llanmihangel	Llanfihangel y Bont-faen	—
57	Llanrhidian	—	CR 5
58	Llansamlet	—	—
59	Llansanwyr [Llansannor]	—	—
60	Llantrisant	—	MO 2
61	Llantrithyd	Llantriddyd	CR 13
62	Llantwit Fardre	Llanilltud Faerdref	MO 7
63	Llantwit-juxta-Neath	Llanilltud Nedd	—
64	Llantwit Major	Llanilltud Fawr	—
65	Llanwynno [Llanwonno]	—	—
66	Llyswyrny [Llysworney]	—	—
67	Loughor	Casllwchwr	MR 4
68	Machen (Rhyd-y-gwern hamlet)	—	—
69	Marcros [Marcross]	—	—
70	Margam	—	—
71	Merthyr Dyfan	—	—
72	Merthyr Mawr	—	—

No.	Parish name used	Correct Welsh form	Monument Nos.
73	Merthyr Tudful [Merthyr Tydfil]	—	—
74	Michaelston-le-Pit	Llanfihangel-y-pwll	CR 7
75	Michaelston-super-Avon	Llanfihangel-ynys-Afan	—
76	Michaelston-super-Ely	Llanfihangel-ar-Elái	—
77	Michaelston-y-Vedw (Llanfedw hamlet)	Llanfihangel-y-fedw	MO 4
78	Monknash	Yr As Fawr	—
79	Neath	Castell-nedd	—
80	Newcastle	Y Castellnewydd	EM 3
81	Newton Nottage	Drenewydd yn Notais	—
82	Nicholaston	—	—
83	Oxwich	—	CR 16
84	Oystermouth	Ystumllwynarth	—
85	Penarth	—	—
86	Pendeulwyn [Pendoylan]	—	MO 10
87	Pen-llin [Penllyn]	—	EM 4
88	Pen-maen	—	CR 18
89	Pen-marc [Penmark]	—	—
90	Pennard	—	MR 6
91	Penrice	Pen-rhys	CR 14
92	Pen-tyrch	—	—
93	Peterston-super-Ely	Llanbedr-y-fro	EM 5
94	Port Einon [Porteynon]	—	—
95	Porthkerry	Porthceri	—
96	Pyle and Kenfig	Y Pîl a Chynffig	EM 2
97	Radur [Radyr]	—	MO 3
98	Reynoldston	—	—
99	Rhosili [Rhossili]	—	—
100	Roath	Y Rhath	—
101	Rudry	Rhydri	—
102	Rumney (formerly in Monmouthshire)	Tredelerch	MR 7
103	St. Andrews	Saint Andras	EM 1
104	St. Andrews Minor		—
105	St. Athan	Sain Tathan	—
106	St. Brides Major and Wick	Saint-y-brid ac Y Wig	MR 5
107	St. Brides Minor	Llansannffraid-ar-Ogwr	—
108	St. Brides-super-Ely	Llansannffraid-ar-Elái	—
109	St. Donats	Sain Dunwyd	—
110	St. Fagans with Llanilterne	Sain Ffagan gyda Llanilltern	—
111	St. George	Sain Siorys	—
112	St. Hilary	Saint Hilari	—
113	St. John-juxta-Swansea	—	—
114	St. Lythans	Llwyneliddon	—
115	St. Mary Church	Llan-fair	CR 10
116	St. Mary Hill	Eglwys Fair y Mynydd	CR 8
117	St. Mellons (part, formerly in Monmouthshire)	Llaneirwg	CR 19
118	St. Nicholas	Sain Nicolas	MO 1, CR 6, CR 20

No.	Parish name used	Correct Welsh form	Monument Nos.
119	Sker (extra-parochial)	Y Sgêr	—
120	Sully	Sili	EM 6
121	Swansea	Abertawe	—
122	Tythegston	Llandudwg	MO 5
123	Welsh St. Donats	Llanddunwyd	—
124	Wenvoe	Gwenfô	—
125	Whitchurch	Yr Eglwys Newydd	MO 8, MM2
126	Ystradowen	—	MO 12
127	Ystradyfodwg	—	MO 11
128	Land common to five parishes: Llanrhidian, Nicholaston, Pen-maen, Penrice, Reynoldston		

List of Civil Parishes

With incidence of Monuments

This list corresponds with the map, Fig. 249, and indicates the civil subdivision of Glamorgan into parishes as it stood at the end of 1970. The boundaries and the names have undergone many changes since the original adoption of the ecclesiastical pattern for secular administrative purposes (*cf.* Fig. 248 and list on p. 351), and modifications will continue to be made.

Civil parishes are noted at the end of Inventory entries, distinguished by the letter (C) when the monument concerned stands in an ecclesiastical parish of a different name (E). Spellings used are as shown on the left; the forms found on the earlier editions of the O.S. maps are given in square brackets. The Welsh forms, which follow the recommendations of the Board of Celtic Studies, are given on the right only when they differ from those already adopted for use in this Inventory.

No.	Parish name used	Correct Welsh form	Monument Nos.
1	Aberdâr [Aberdare]	—	UW 4
2	Baglan Higher	—	—
3	Barry	Y Barri	—
4	Betws [Bettws]	—	—
5	Bishopston	Llandeilo Ferwallt	CR 1
6	Blaen-gwrach	—	—
7	Blaenhonddan	—	—
8	Bonvilston	Tresimwn	CR 2
9	Bridgend	Pen-y-bont ar Ogwr	VE 4
10	Cardiff	Caerdydd	MO 8, CR 19, MM 1, MM 2, MR 7
11	Cheriton	—	CR 15
12	Cilybebyll	—	—
13	Clyne	Y Clun	—
14	Coed-ffranc	—	UW 1
15	Coety Higher [Coity H.]	Coety Uchaf	MR 1
16	Colwinston	Tregolwyn	—
17	Cowbridge	Y Bont-faen	—

No.	Parish name used	Correct Welsh form	Monument Nos.
18	Coychurch Higher	Llangrallo Uchaf	—
19	Coychurch Lower	Llangrallo Isaf	—
20	Cwm-du	—	—
21	Dulais Higher [Dylais H.]	Dulais Uchaf	—
22	Dulais Lower [Dylais L.]	Dulais Isaf	—
23	Dyffryn Clydach		—
24	Eglwys Brewys [Eglwysbrewis]	—	—
25	Eglwysilan	—	—
26	Ewenni [Ewenny]	—	—
27	Flemingston	Trefflemin	—
28	Gelli-gaer	—	MO 9
29	Gileston	Silstwn	—
30	Glyncorrwg	—	—
31	Gowerton	Tre-gŵyr	—
32	Ilston	Llanilltud Gŵyr	—
33	Kenfig	Cynffig	EM 2
34	Knelston	Llan-y-tair-mair	—
35	Laleston	Trelales	VE 3
36	Lavernock	Larnog	—
37	Leckwith	Lecwydd	CR 3
38	Lisvane	Llys-faen	

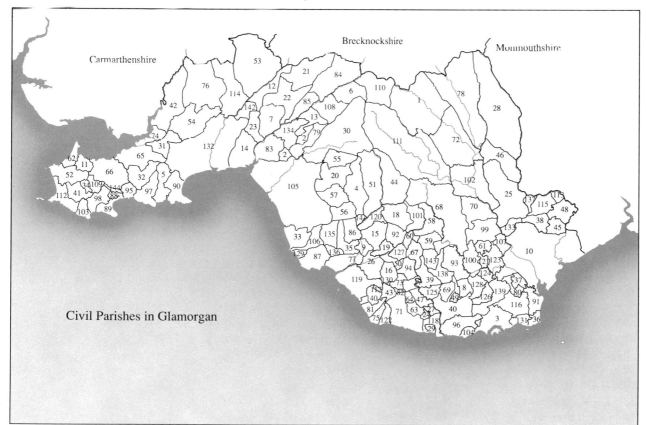

Fig. 249. Civil Parishes. Numbers correspond to those in the list.

No.	Parish name used	Correct Welsh form	Monument Nos.
39	Llanblethian	Llanfleiddan	MR 3
40	Llancarfan	—	CR 17, CR 21
41	Llanddewi	—	—
42	Llandeilo Tal-y-bont	—	MO 6
43	Llandŵ [Llandow]	—	CR 11
44	Llandyfodwg	—	—
45	Llanedern [Llanedeyrn]	—	—
46	Llanfabon	—	—
47	Llan-fair	—	CR 10
48	Llanfedw	—	MO 4
49	Llanfythin	Llanfeuthin	—
50	Llan-gan	—	—
51	Llangeinwyr [Llangeinor]	—	—
52	Llangennith	Llangynydd	—
53	Llanguicke	Llan-giwg	—
54	Langyfelach	—	—
55	Llangynwyd Higher	Llangynwyd Uchaf	—
56	Llangynwyd Lower	Llangynwyd Isaf	—
57	Llangynwyd Middle	Llangynwyd Ganol	MR 2
58	Llanharan	—	—
59	Llanhari [Llanharry]	—	—
60	Llanilid	—	CR 12
61	Llanilltern [Llanilterne]	—	—
62	Llanmadog [Llanmadoc]	—	—
63	Llanmaes	Llan-faes	—
64	Llanmihangel	Llanfihangel y Bont-faen	—
65	Llanrhidian Higher	Llanrhidian Uchaf	—
66	Llanrhidian Lower	Llanrhidian Isaf	CR 5
67	Llansanwyr [Llansannor]	—	—
68	Llantrisant	—	MO 2
69	Llantrithyd	Llantriddyd	CR 13
70	Llantwit Fardre	Llanilltud Faerdref	MO 7
71	Llantwit Major	Llanilltud Fawr	—
72	Llanwynno [Llanwonno]	—	—
73	Llyswyrny [Llysworney]	—	—
74	Loughor Borough	Casllwchwr	MR 4
75	Marcroes [Marcross]	—	—
76	Mawr	—	—
77	Merthyr Mawr	—	—
78	Merthyr Tudful [Merthyr Tydfil]	—	—
79	Michaelston Higher	Llanfihangel-ynys-Afan	—
80	Michaelston-le-Pit	Llanfihangel-y-pwll	CR 4, CR 7
81	Monknash	Yr As Fawr	—
82	Nash	Yr As Fach	—
83	Neath	Castell-nedd	VE 2
84	Neath Higher	Castell-nedd Uchaf	—
85	Neath Lower	Castell-nedd Isaf	—
86	Newcastle Higher	Castellnewydd Uchaf	EM 3
87	Newton Nottage	Drenewydd yn Notais	—

No.	Parish name used	Correct Welsh form	Monument Nos.
88	Nicholaston	—	—
89	Oxwich	—	CR 16
90	Oystermouth	Ystumllwynarth	—
91	Penarth	—	—
92	Pen-coed	—	—
93	Pendeulwyn [Pendoylan]	—	MO 10
94	Pen-llin [Penllyn]	—	EM 4
95	Pen-maen	—	CR 18
96	Pen-marc [Penmark]	—	—
97	Pennard	—	MR 6
98	Penrice	Pen-rhys	CR 14
99	Pen-tyrch	—	—
100	Peterston-super-Ely	Llanbedr-y-fro	EM 5
101	Peterston-super-Montem	Llanbedr-ar-fynydd	—
102	Pontypridd	—	—
103	Port Einon [Porteynon]	—	—
104	Porthkerry	Porthceri	—
105	Port Talbot	—	UW 3, UW 5, VE 1
106	Pyle	Y Pîl	—
107	Radur [Radyr]	—	MO 3
108	Resolfen [Resolven]	—	—
109	Reynoldston	—	—
110	Rhigos	Rugos	—
111	Rhondda	—	MO 11
112	Rhosili [Rhossili]	—	—
113	Rhyd-y-gwern	—	—
114	Rhyndwyglydach [Rhyndwyclydach]	—	UW 2
115	Rudry	Rhydri	—
116	St. Andrews Major	Saint Andras	EM 1
117	St. Andrews Minor		
118	St. Athan	Sain Tathan	—
119	St. Brides Major	Saint-y-brid	MR 5
120	St. Brides Minor	Llansanffraid-ar-Ogwr	—
121	St. Brides-super-Ely	Llansanffraid-ar-Elái	—
122	St. Donats	Sain Dunwyd	—
123	St. Fagans	Sain Ffagan	—
124	St. George	Sain Siorys	—
125	St. Hilary	Saint Hilari	—
126	St. Lythans	Llwyneliddon	—
127	St. Mary Hill	Eglwys Fair y Mynydd	CR 8
128	St. Nicholas	Sain Nicolas	MO 1, CR 6, CR 20
129	Sker	Y Sgêr	—
130	Stembridge	—	—
131	Sully	Sili	EM 6
132	Swansea	Abertawe	—
133	Tongwynlais	—	—
134	Tonna	—	—
135	Tythegston Higher	Llandudwg Uchaf	MO 5

357

No.	Parish name used	Correct Welsh form	Monument Nos.
136	Tythegston Lower	Llandudwg Isaf	—
137	Van	Y Fan	CR 9
138	Welsh St. Donats	Llanddunwyd	—
139	Wenvoe	Gwenfô	—
140	Wick	Y Wig	—
141	Ynysawdre	—	—
142	Ynysymwn [Ynysymond]	—	—
143	Ystradowen	—	MO 12
144	Land common to six parishes: Llanrhidian Higher & Lower, Nicholaston, Pen-maen, Penrice, Reynoldston		

Index of National Grid References

This index gives the eight-figure grid reference and corresponding monument number, name and ecclesiastical parish for every site described in Volume III, Part 1a of the Inventory. Its purpose is to furnish direct reference to the entry corresponding to a site located according to the National Grid, for which the proper name is unknown or uncertain. Rejected sites will be indexed in Volume III, Part 1b. With the monuments in each section arranged in alphabetical order it would be an arduous task to check such cases with the fortuitously ordered National Grid references at the end of entries.

Glamorgan falls within four 100 km squares of the National Grid, an 'upper' or more northerly pair, SN and SO, and a 'lower' pair, SS and ST. Only three monuments fall within SN and none within SO; the rest are almost equally divided between SS and ST. The references are arranged in a simple eastward progression within each 100 km square, beginning with SN and ending with ST, and without regard to the sections in which monuments are placed. Each reference leads to the classification and descriptive entry of a site and gives its name and ecclesiastical parish. Its civil parish, where it is of a different name, will be found at the end of the entry.

Note: Two vanished sites (VE 2, 3) are believed to have been near the grid references marked with asterisks.

G.R.	INV.	Name	Eccles. Parish
SN 5868 0267	MO 6	Talybont Castle (Castle Du; Castell Hu; Banc-y-rhyfel)	Llandeilo Tal-y-bont
SN 6941 0473	UW 2	Cae-castell, Rhyndwyglydach	Llangyfelach
SN 9651 0016	UW 4	Castell Nos, Aberdâr	Aberdâr (Aberdare)
SS 4530 9381	CR 15	North Hill Tor	Cheriton
SS 4915 8677	CR 16	Norton Camp	Oxwich
SS 4922 8786	CR 14	Mountyborough (Mounty Brough)	Penrice
SS 5069 9222	CR 5	Cil Ifor Ring	Llanrhidian
SS 5341 8804	CR 18	Penmaen, Castle Tower	Pen-maen
SS 5442 8850	MR 6	Pennard Castle	Pennard
SS 5642 9798	MR 4	Loughor Castle	Loughor
SS 5820 9001	CR 1	Bishopston Old Castle (Barland Castle)	Bishopston
SS 7315 9403	UW 1	Briton Ferry (Hen Gastell)	Cadoxton-juxta-Neath
SS 7480 9780*	VE 2	Granville's Castle, Neath	Cadoxton-juxta-Neath
SS 7562 9230	UW 5	Plas Baglan	Baglan
SS 7622 9012	VE 1	Aberafan Castle	Aberafan
SS 7679 9202	UW 3	Castell Bolan (Cwm Clais)	Baglan

G.R.	INV.	Name	Eccles. Parish
SS 8009 8269	EM 2	Kenfig Castle	Pyle and Kenfig
SS 8458 8153	MO 5	Stormy Castle	Tythegston
SS 8516 8866	MR 2	Llangynwyd Castle	Llangynwyd
SS 8755 8092*	VE 3	Llangewydd Castle	Laleston
SS 8819 7698	MR 5	Ogmore Castle	St Brides Major and Wick
SS 9022 8007	EM 3	Newcastle, Bridgend	Newcastle
SS 9053 7951	VE 4	Oldcastle, Nolton (Bridgend)	Coety (Coity)
SS 9232 8149	MR 1	Coity Castle	Coety (Coity)
SS 9418 7321	CR 11	Llandow	Llandŵ (Llandow)
SS 9603 7869	CR 8	Gelli-Garn Ringwork and Bailey	St Mary Hill
SS 9778 8132	CR 12	Llanilid	Llanilid
SS 9879 7606	EM 4	Penllyn Castle	Pen-llin (Penllyn)
SS 9948 9278	MO 11	Ynyscrug	Ystradyfodwg
ST 0050 7212	CR 10	Howe Mill Enclosure	St Mary Church
ST 0108 7765	MO 12	Ystradowen	Ystradowen
ST 0189 7444	MR 3	Llanquian Castle	Llanblethian
ST 0455 7273	CR 13	Llantrithyd Ringwork	Llantrithyd
ST 0461 7705	MO 10	Tŷ Du	Pendeulwyn (Pendoylan)
ST 0467 7001	CR 17	Pancross, Llancarfan	Llancarfan
ST 0606 7926	MO 2	Felin Isaf	Llantrisant
ST 0682 7123	CR 21	Walterston, Llancarfan	Llancarfan
ST 0706 7336	CR 2	Bonvilston	Bonvilston
ST 0809 7450	MO 1	Cottrell Castle Mound	St Nicholas
ST 0828 7366	CR 6	Coed-y-cwm	St Nicholas
ST 0839 7641	EM 5	Peterston Castle	Peterston-super-Ely
ST 0846 7476	CR 20	St Nicholas Gaer	St Nicholas
ST 0916 8647	MO 7	Tomen-y-clawdd	Llantwit Fardre
ST 1281 8189	MO 3	Morganstown Castle Mound	Radur (Radyr)
ST 1354 7509	CR 4	Caerau, Ely	Caerau
ST 1368 9694	MO 9	Twyn Castell, Gelli-gaer	Gelli-gaer
ST 1468 7439	CR 3	Brynwell, Leckwith	Llandough, Cogan and Leckwith
ST 1482 7224	CR 7	Dinas Powys Ringwork	Michaelston-le-Pit
ST 1516 6834	EM 6	Sully Castle	Sully
ST 1527 7164	EM 1	Dinas Powys Castle	St Andrews
ST 1538 8220	MO 8	Twmpath, Rhiwbina	Whitchurch
ST 1560 8040	MM 2	Treoda	Whitchurch
ST 1751 8789	CR 9	Gwern-y-domen	Bedwas (Van Hamlet)
ST 1808 7659	MM 1	Cardiff Castle	Cardiff, St John
ST 2103 7893	MR 7	Rumney Castle (Cae-castell)	Rumney (formerly in Mon.)
ST 2270 8035	CR 19	Pen-y-pil, St Mellons (Cae'r Castell)	St Mellons (formerly in Mon.)
ST 2233 8670	MO 4	Ruperra Motte (Castell Breiniol; Castell-y-ddraenen)	Michaelston-y-Vedw

Glossary: General

Most technical terms defined concern general and medieval military architecture. Terms special to medieval Historical studies, including some in French and Latin, are indicated by (Hist.), (Fr.), and (Lat.) respectively. Welsh terms are treated separately in the succeeding glossary.

Abutment – Solid masonry placed to counteract the lateral thrust of a bridge, arch or vault.

Advowson (Hist.) – The right to present a priest to a church benefice exercised by lay or clerical patrons.

Alternating Quoins – See **Quoin**.

Angle Buttress – See **Buttress**.

Angle-Spurs – Semi-pyramidal buttresses rising at the angles of a square-based tower in order to support a round or polygonal superstructure. Most commonly encountered in South Wales from ca. 1300.

Arcade – A range of arches carried on piers or columns, either open as in a nave arcade, or blind, i.e. attached to a wall.

Arch – The head of an opening (Excepting the **Relieving Arch**, q.v.). Forms encountered are classified as follows:

Flat or square-headed – Spanning at the level of the springing.

Four-centred or *depressed* – A pointed arch struck from four centres, two on the line of the springing with short radii giving a sharp curve rising from the springing, and two below the line of the springing with wider radii giving a gentler curve towards the pointed apex. A late medieval form similar to the Tudor arch below.

Lancet – A pointed arch struck from two centres on the line of the springing but outside the jambs.

Round or Semicircular – A single arc struck from a centre on the line of the springing. The characteristic Norman arch.

Segmental – pointed – A pointed arch, struck from two centres below the springing line.

Tudor – A pointed arch struck from two centres on the line of the springing with short radii close to the jambs, which are continued as gently ascending straight lines towards the apex. Similar to *four-centred* above.

Two-centred – A pointed arch struck from two centres on the springing line with radii equal to the span; less sharply pointed than the similar *lancet* above.

Arrow Slit or **Loop-Hole** (Fr. **Meutrière**) – A narrow vertical slit in a wall or **Merlon** (q.v.) which splayed internally to provide a wide arc of fire to defending archers or crossbowmen.

Ashlar – Blocks of masonry wrought to an even face with square edges.

Assommoir (Fr.) – See **Murder Hole**.

Bailey – A fortified enclosure, particularly the outer court of an earthwork castle; sometimes used of a walled enclosure which is more appropriately termed a **Ward** (q.v.)

Ball Stop – See **Stop**.

Barrel Vault – See **Vault**.

Batter – An outward sloping revetement reinforcing the foot of a wall or tower. Of modest proportions as a simple structural feature; greatly augmented in some later castles to deter sapping and mining and to deflect projectiles from above on to attackers.

Battlementing – See **Crenellation**.

Bay – A unit of a building or its external elevation delimited by recurring features (windows, columns, buttresses, roof-trusses).

Bay Window – A fenestrated angular or curved projection of a building. If curved, also called a **Bow Window**. If on an upper floor only, called an **Oriel** or **Oriel Window**.

Berm – A level space between the bank or wall of a fortification and its protecting ditch or scarp.

Boss – An ornamental knob or projection covering the intersection of the ribs in a vault or the timbers of a ceiling or roof.

Brattice – Usually a removable timber structure projecting from the parapets of castle walls and towers. Assembled and mounted in beam-holes provided when danger threatened. Openings in the floor facilitated the defence of the base by the wall (see **Machicolation**). Sometimes it constituted a temporary palisaded enclosure, e.g. to protect building works. Often prefabricated for a campaign.

Bressumer – A massive beam spanning an opening, particularly a fireplace; also the principal horizontal rail in timber framing.

Broach Stop – See **Stop**.

Bull-Nose Stop – See **Stop**.

Burgage – Plot or tenement in a medieval borough held by a **Burgess** (q.v.). Usually long and narrow and set end-on to a street.

Burgess – Member of a borough and possessor of one or more **Burgages**, or a fraction of a burgage. He enjoyed the privileges conferred by the borough charter and participated in its governance.

Buttery – A store room for provisions, especially drinks.

Buttress – A vertical projection from a wall-face giving it additional stability. Two buttresses at an angle of 90 degrees at the corner of a building are termed **Angle Buttresses; A Clasping Buttress** encases the angle. The **Pilaster Buttress**, of small projection and largely decorative, was a feature of Norman architecture.

Cantref – See Glossary of Welsh terms.

Capital – The head of a column, usually carved or moulded. The Romanesque **Cushion Capital** is cut from a cube, its lower parts rounded off to adapt to a circular shaft and presenting flat lunate faces to each side. The **Scalloped Capital** is an elaborated cushion capital in which the lunate faces are moulded into a series of truncated cones.

Capite, In (Hist.; Lat.) – Feudal term applied to a lordship or manor held directly (or 'in chief') from the King or chief-lord.

Caput (Hist.) – Feudal term for the administrative centre of a lordship; usually a castle.

Carucate, Hide, or **Ploughland** (Hist.) – Originally, in the Danelaw, the carucate or ploughland was the extent of land that could be tilled in one year with one ploughteam. It was similar to the West Saxon hide, the acreage necessary to support one peasant household. Both varied in different localities between 60 and 180 acres on account of variable soil characteristics and the diverse combinations of draught animals used. In Glamorgan it was 80 (statute) acres. These units were also frequently used for fiscal assessment.

Castle-Guard (Hist.) – A feudal service owed at the overlord's castle by the tenant of a **Knight's Fee** (q.v.) This later became commuted to a money payment, **Wardsilver**, which in Glamorgan was computed at 6s. 8d., a **Noble** or half a **Mark** (q.v.) for each fee.

Castle Mound or **Mount** – See **Mottes**.

Castle-Ringwork – An early form of earthwork castle contemporary with the **Motte** (q.v.). Usually defined by a circular or oval **Ring-Bank** and external ditch. The bank is often very strong for the limited area protected (averaging thirty-seven metres in diameter in Glamorgan). A **Partial-Ringwork** was occasionally but not invariably used where a strong natural scarp on one flank, surmounted by a palisade, would have provided adequate defence. Very rarely, the interior may have been artificially raised (See **Ring-Motte**).

Castlery or **Castelry** (Hist.) – The territory subject to a castle and organized for its protection and economic sustenance.

Chamfer – The plane formed when the sharp edge or angle of a squared stone block or timber beam is cut away, usually flat and at an angle of 45 degrees to the flanking surfaces. The plane might also be variously moulded, for which see **Moulding.**

Chimneypiece – The frame surrounding a fireplace, frequently including an overmantel or hood above it.

Clasping Buttress – See **Buttress.**

Comitatus (Hist.; Lat.) – According to context, an earldom, a county or a county court. In Glamorgan the county or shire court was also the court of the **Honour** (q.v.), and the term **Comitatus** also meant the territory of the **Honour**, i.e. **Shire-Fee.**

Commotal Lordship – A lordship, usually Welsh but sometimes Anglo-Norman, which corresponded with a pre-Norman Welsh **Commote** (q.v. in Glossary of Welsh terms).

Commote – See Glossary of Welsh terms.

Corbel – A stone or timber projection from the face of a wall which supported a floor or roof beam, the hood of a fireplace, or other superimposed feature of a building.

Corbel Table – A range of **Corbels** (q.v.) supporting a structure projecting from the general face of a wall (e.g. a latrine, a chimney, or a parapet). The most developed corbel tables supported **Machicolation** (q.v.).

Counterscarp – The outer slope of a defensive ditch. A subsidiary bank crowning this slope is termed a **Counterscarp Bank**.

Creasing – A groove in a wall-face ensuring a weatherproof junction with a roof or chimney which abuts it. To this end the groove might house **Flashing**, a projecting strip of metal, usually lead.

Crenel – See **Crenellation.**

Crenellation or **Battlementing** – The alternating sequence of **Crenels** and **Merlons** outlining the tops of the **Parapets** crowning the walls and towers of castles. The **Crenels** (or openings) and **Merlons** (or solids – sometimes pierced by arrowslits) provided cover and firing points for defenders. In origin defensive, crenellation became a purely decorative and prestigious feature of lordly residences.

Cross Oillet – See **Oillet.**

Cruck – One of a pair of large curved timbers rising from, or from near, ground level towards a common apex so as to carry a roof by a ridge-beam and through-purlins.

Curtain or **Curtain Wall** – The battlemented wall which joins towers, bastions and gateways to enclose a castle.

Cushion Capital – See **Capital.**

Cushion Stop – See **Stop.**

Cusps – The projecting points in a Gothic window or other opening which separate the **Foils.**

Custos (Lat.) – The temporary custodian or govenor of a castle or lordship.

Cyma or **Ogee** – See **Moulding.**

Demense (Hist.) – Land retained by the lord. A lord kept certain manors of his lordship for his own use and might establish **Demense Castles** on them. Similarly, tenants holding manors of the lord retained part of their estates 'in demesne', the remainder being held by free or unfree sub-tenants.

Depressed Arch - See **Arch.**

Diagonal-Cut Stop – See **Stop.**

Diagonal Tooling – See **Tooling.**

Drawbar – A sliding wooden bar to secure a door in the closed position. Normally lodged in a deep socket in one jamb, behind the door, it could be swiftly drawn out to engage in an opposed and lesser socket in the opposed jamb to secure the door.

Drawbridge – A hinged or pivoted bridge spanning the ditch fronting an entrance to a castle which could be raised to block the entry on the approach of an enemy force. A simple hinged drawbridge was raised by lifting-chains fixed at the outer end. A pivoted or **Turning Bridge** was balanced on a central axle and its weighted or counterpoised inner end could be lowered into a pit in the gate-passage to ease the effort required in raising the outer section.

Dressings; Dressed Stone – Stones worked to a smooth or moulded face and used to outline angles, windows, doors, or other features.

Drip-Stone – See **Hood-Mould.**

Drum Tower – A large circular or drum-shaped mural tower.

Dry-Stone – Masonry constructed without mortar, clay, or other bonding agent.

Dwarf Wall – Low modern wall marking early footings or foundations too insignificant to be restored for display.

Embrasure – A splayed opening in a wall or parapet. It might accommodate a window or an **Arrow Slit** (q.v.).

Enceite (Fr.) – The entire protective ring of defences enclosing a castle or walled town.

Enfeoff, Enfeoffment (Hist.) – The feudal term for granting legal possession of a holding to a tenant. **Knights' Fees** granted before the death of Henry I (1135) were described as of **'The Old Enfeoffment'**; after that date they were of **'The New Enfeoffment'**.

Englishry (Hist.) – In Medieval Wales, that part of the lordship (almost always the most fertile) where English customs (including inheritance practices and annual dues), law and administration prevailed. Many, though by no means necessarily the majority, of the tenants were English.

Escheat (Hist.) – The reversion of an estate to the king or a lord. Estates escheated if a tenant died without an heir or forfeited his estate by treason or felony. The term does not technically apply to **Wardship** (q.v.), which concerned the custody of an heir and his estates during a minority.

Extent (Hist.) – A detailed descriptive survey of the extent and valuation of a lordship and its tenancies.

Facet, Faceted – In castles a **Facet** is a straight line of defensive walling; in combination such **Facets** produce a simple **Faceted**, polygonal, or multangular plan characteristic of many 12th century castles lacking the later mural towers commonly raised at the angles.

Fan-Tooling – See **Tooling.**

Fealty (Hist.) – A tenant's formal acknowledgement of his acceptance of the personal authority of his lord. The tenant swore an oath of fealty, promising faithful service to his lord against all men; even unfree tenants might swear fealty.

Fee, Fief – See **Knight's Fee.**

Fenestration – The arrangement of windows in a building.

Fine Rolls (Hist.) – Rolls recording **Fines**, i.e. monies to be paid to the Exchequer by subjects in return for a wide variety of royal favours. **Fine**, meaning making an end of a matter by a money composition should be distinguished from an amercement, a money penalty imposed as a punishment for an offence.

Flanking – Defence augmented by **Mural** or **Flanking Towers** (or **Bastions**) projecting beyond the line of the walls to enable archers to enfilade the front of the defences by shooting along the line of the walls as well as outwards from them.

Flashing – See **Creasing.**

Flat Arch – See **Arch.**

Foil – A leaf shape formed between the curved sides of two adjacent **Cusps** (q.v.) on the head or sides of an opening or panel. The number of such foils is indicated by the terms trefoil, quatrefoil, cinquefoil, etc.

Forebuilding – A projecting building designed to protect an entrance; in a Norman **Keep** it houses a staircase to the first-floor entrance.

Four-Centred Arch – See **Arch.**

Freestone – Any stone which is easily cut and moulded, especially fine-grained limestone or sandstone. In Glamorgan Sutton Stone, a variety of **Lias Limestone** (q.v.), was such a freestone widely used for dressings in medieval times.

Garderobe – A medieval privy or lavatory. Usually set in the thickness of the wall at an upper level and above a shaft discharging at the foot of the external wall through an **Outfall.** Less commonly, it was carried out boldly on projecting corbels, avoiding the need for a shaft, or accommodated in a projecting **Garderobe Tower.**

Gatehouse – A strong storeyed building enclosing a fortified gate. It sheltered the guards and could house the machinery necessary to operate a **Portcullis** and **Drawbridge.** It further improved the defence of a weak point by rising higher than the flanking walls. From the simple square gatehouse towers enclosing the gateway, the form reached its climax with the great 13th-century **Keep-Gatehouse.** Also known as a **Great Gate**, its entrance was defended at each end and flanked by strong towers projecting to the field and united at the rear, forming a large independently defensible block.

Glazing Rebate – See **Rebate.**

Great Gate – See **Gatehouse.**

Gun Stones – Medieval term for spherical stones for cannons; cannon balls.

Hall – The principal room of a medieval house or castle, used especially on ceremonial or festive occasions. It may be on the ground or first floor.

Haunch – The part of an arch or vault between the crown and the springing.

Heriot (Hist.) – A form of death duty. The term derived from the Anglo-Saxon *heregeatu*, 'army apparel'. On a tenant's death his heir was obliged to surrender to the king or his lord the tenant's military equipment or a money equivalent before he could enter his inheritance. After the Norman Conquest **Heriot** was in effect replaced by **Relief** (q.v.) for tenants by military service. Lesser tenants however, still paid **Heriot** – typically the deceased's best beast or a money payment in lieu.

Herringbone Masonry – Stone, brick or tiles laid diagonally instead of horizontally. Alternate courses are inclined in opposite directions to produce a zig-zag pattern on the wall face. Frequently employed to line fire-places throughout the Middle Ages and later, but in general walling it is most usually encountered in Norman work.

Herse (Fr.) - **Portcullis** (q.v.).

Hide (Hist.) – See **Carucate.**

Hipped Roof – A pitched roof with sloping ends rather than vertical gables.

Hoard, Hoarding, Hourding – A timber gallery projecting from a castle wall-head to give increased fire-power over ground below through openings in its floor (cf. **Brattice, Machicolation**).

Hollow Moulding – See **Moulding.**

Hollow – See **Chamfer.**

Honour (Hist.) – A large and important feudal estate, often highly privileged, comprising many manors and knights' fees, administered as a unit from a centre, usually a castle, the *caput honoris*, where the honorial knights owed **Castle-Guard** and suit to the honour court. Unlike many English honours, Glamorgan was territorially compact.

Hood – The projecting and usually backward inclined canopy set on corbels and an advanced **Bressummer** or **Lintel** (q.v.) above a hearth. A functional and sometimes decorative feature to deflect smoke from a chamber.

Hood-Mould, Label, Drip-Stone – A moulding projecting from the face of a wall above and around an arch, doorway or window. It was functional, throwing off rainwater, but was also used decoratively and might be square in outline or shaped to follow the form of the opening.

Hornwork – An outer earthwork obstacle usually set before an entrance, or on the line of easiest approach, to impede attackers and hinder the advance of siege engines.

Inquisition Post Mortem (Hist.) – Inquest held on the death of any tenant-in-chief of the king to enable the latter to exercise his rights of relief, wardship and escheat. The jury declared what lands the deceased tenant held at his death, their value and by what services or rents they were held, and the identity and age of the heir.

Inspeximus (Hist., Lat.) – A charter or *letter patent* in which the grantor recites *verbatim* earlier charters which he has inspected and confirmed, possibly with additional grants.

Iure Uxoris (Lat.) – Tenure obtained by marrying an heiress; Lit. 'by right of his wife'.

Jamb – The vertical side of a doorway, window, archway or fireplace opening.

Keel Moulding – See **Moulding.**

Keel Stop – See **Stop.**

Keep – The principal tower of a castle, capable of sustaining resistance when the rest of the castle had fallen to the enemy. It generally contained the residential quarters of the lord.

Keystone – The central and usually wedge-shaped stone at the top of an arch. Often ornamented.

Knight's Fee (Hist.) – Land held of the king or a lord by the military service of one knight, both in the lord's army and in garrison of a lord's castle. Larger estates were assessed, commensurate with their value, at a number of knight's fees. Personal military service came to be replaced by the payment of **Scutage** and castle-guard by the payment of **Wardsilver** (q.v.).

Label – See **Hood-Mould.**

Lancet, Lancet Arch – See **Arch.**

Lias Limestone – The characteristic stone of the Vale of Glamorgan. Of variable quality but normally a brittle light blue-grey stone, making good mortar. Tougher littoral varieties can be worked as **Freestone** (q.v.), notably **Sutton Stone**, a conglomerate limestone quarried at Southerndown and Sutton on the coast near Ogmore.

Liber Niger, Liber Rubeus (Hist.) – The Black Book and the Red Book of the Exchequer. Miscellaneous compilations of the early-13th century. Both transcribe the important lists of **Knight's Fees**, classified as of 'the Old' or 'the New Enfeoffment' (i.e. established before or after 1135 – See **Enfeoff**).

Lintel – A horizontal beam or stone placed over the head of a door or window and supporting the wall above.

Loop-Hole – See **Arrow Slit.**

Machicolation – Openings in the floor of a projecting parapet or fighting gallery, through which missiles could be directed at attackers approaching the foot of the wall. Machicolation could be solidly built in masonry and supported on a row of large corbels; for less substantial timber fighting galleries serving the same purpose, see **Brattice** and **Hoard.**

Mark – A unit of account, though not a coin, valued at 13s. 4d.

Mason's Mark – A device cut on dressed stone by a mason to identify his work.

Member Lordship (Hist.) – A lordship held on generous terms and free of military service (see **Castle Guard**). In the honour of Glamorgan both Welsh and Normans held member lordships (see **Commotal Lordship**).

Merlon – The solid upstanding parts of a parapet. See **Crenellation.**

Mesne Lord (Hist.) – See **Subinfeudation.**

Messuage – A house with its outbuildings and yard. **A Capital Messuage** denoted a large house or mansion.

Mezzanine – A floor or landing between two main storeys. Also called an **Entresol.**

Military Tenure – See **Knight's Fee.**

Moated Site – A manor house, farm, parsonage or grange enclosed by a wide wet moat, usually square or rectangular. Such moats might also protect subsidiary areas such as gardens or orchards. Formerly termed 'homestead moats'.

Moiety (Hist.) – A share or portion of a subdivided estate, usually but not invariably a half share.

Motte, Castle-Mound or **Castle-Mount** – A flat-topped and steep-sided mound formerly supporting a palisaded timber tower. Either entirely artificial, or formed by scarping and re-shaping natural features or rock outcrops. With or without an accompanying **Bailey** (q.v.), it constituted the most common form of castle introduced by the Normans.

Moulding – A continuous ornamental contour formed on a surface or bevelled edge (**Chamfer**, q.v.). Common types are:

Cyma or *Ogee* – A double curve. In a *cyma recta* or *ogee*, the upper is concave and the lower is convex; these positions are reversed in the *cyma reversa* or *reverse ogee*.

Hollow or *Cavetto* – A hollow, usually a quadrant in section.

Keel – Pointed in section like the Keel of a ship.

Quarter-round or *Ovolo* – Convex, usually a quadrant in section.

Roll – Plain convex of semicircular or rounder section.

Sunk – With a flat surface recessed from its arrises or edges.

There are also various combinations of these mouldings, e.g. *roll and hollow*, *double ogee*, and *ogee and hollow*.

Mullion – A vertical post or upright of stone or wood separating the lights of a window.

Multivallate – Many-ramparted. Mainly applied to Iron Age hill-forts which may be uni-, bi-, or multivallate, depending on the number of earthen ramparts surrounding them. Medieval earthwork castles are rarely multivallate; the only example in Glamorgan is the castle-ringwork at Dinas Powys (CR 7).

Murage – Tolls or taxes levied by borough authorities, by licence of the king or their lord, to build or repair the town defences.

Mural Tower – See **Flanking.**

Murder Hole (Fr. – **Assommoir**) – An opening formed in the vault above a gate-passage to enable the defenders to harass attackers from above and extinguish fires lit against the gate. The French equivalent, **Assommoir** (derived from *assommer*, to batter or club to death) should not be confused with a **Meurtrière** which denotes an **Arrow Slit** (q.v.).

Newel Stair – A circular or winding stair. Its treads radiate from the **Newel**, a central post or column. The term **Newel** also denotes the principal posts at the end of a straight flight of stairs.

Noble – A third of a pound or half a **Mark**. This sum (6s. 8d.) was the commuted payment made in lieu of military service to the lord of Glamorgan by a knight in respect of each **Knight's Fee** he held (see **Castle-Guard**). Like the **Mark** it was only money of account until 1344, when Edward III issued a gold coin, the **Noble**, worth 6s. 8d.

Offset – A slope or ledge on a wall or a buttress where the upper face is set back. Internal **Offset** ledges were usually contrived to help support floors.

Ogee or **Cyma** – See **Mouldings.**

Oillet – The widening of the extremity of an **Arrow Slit** to improve the archer's view. An **Arrow Slit** with a cross-arm is termed a **Cross Oillet** when its four arms are widened at their ends.

Old Enfeoffment – See **Enfeoff.**

Opus Signinum (Lat.) – Roman lime concrete containing crushed brick and ceramic fragments which give a characteristic reddish colour.

Outfall – See **Garderobe.**

Outshut – A lateral projection of a building which is covered by the continuation downwards of the main roof.

Ovolo or **Quarter Round** – See **Moulding.**

Palisade – A defence formed by strong upright timbers set in the ground or in the complementary earthworks of a castle. More developed forms seem to have been wooden versions of the familiar **Battlemented** castle-walls.

Parados – A wall protecting the inner side of the **Wall Walk** of an enbattled **Curtain.**

Parapet – In military architecture, the battlemented or **Crenellated** wall protecting the outer side of a **Wall Walk**. It provided cover and firing points for defenders.

Partial Ringwork – See **Castle-Ringwork.**

Pellet – A small circular boss.

Pilaster Buttress – See **Buttress.**

Pillow Mound – A low ditched mound, usually oblong, which served as an artificial rabbit warren.

Pipe Rolls (Hist.) – Rolls of the Exchequer which recorded, county by county, the annual accounts of sheriffs for crown revenues derived from the farm of the county, feudal sources, profits of justice, taxation etc. Allowances were made for expenses incurred on behalf of the crown. Accounts of other officers and crown debtors came to be included. One roll from 1131 survives and from 1156 an unbroken series has been preserved. **Pipe Rolls** were so called from their resemblance when rolled to drainage or similar pipes.

Piscina – A stone basin near the altar for washing the communion vessels; provided with a drain and usually set in a niche.

Plinth – The projecting base of a wall or column. Its upper part was generally chamfered or moulded.

Ploughland – See **Carucate.**

Pobble Stones – Rounded glacial pebbles.

Portcullis – A heavy iron or iron-shod grille made to slide up and down in grooves set forward on either side of a gate-passage. Designed as an outer protection for the doors, it was controlled from a chamber above the passage into which it was raised when the gateway was opened. In a *Keep-gatehouse* a second Portcullis similarly protects doors at the inner end of the gate-passage (see **Gatehouse**).

Postern – A small subordinate entrance. Usually at the rear of a castle and permitting only pedestrian access.

Principia (Lat.) – The headquarters building of a Roman fort, centrally placed fronting the main cross-street.

Putlog Hole – One of a series of square holes which carried the horizontal timbers of scaffolding used during construction and subsequent repair or rendering. Usually in horizontal tiers; occasionally sloped to support oblique ramps.

Pyx – Ornamented casket holding the consecrated host. Placed upon or suspended above the altar.

Quarter Round or **Ovolo** – See **Moulding.**

Quern – Simple implements for grinding grain by hand. A *rotary quern* consisted of an upper stone disc rotated on a static lower stone.

Quoin – An external angle of a wall or building, from French *coin;* more commonly, the **Dressed Stones** often forming such angles. **Alternating Quoins** are set lengthwise in turn to each side of the angle.

Radyr Stone – A Triassic sandstone, reddish or brown in colour, suitable for dressing and formerly quarried at Radyr, north-west of Cardiff.

Rafter – A roof timber sloping up from the wall-plate to the ridge, either a subordinate **Common Rafter** or a more substantial **Principal Rafter** forming one half of a roof truss.

Rampart – A defensive bank of earth or rubble; sometimes applied to the defended **Wall Walk** (q.v.) crowning the walls of masonry castles.

Random Rubble - See **Rubble.**

Rear-Arch – The arch on the inside of a wall, spanning an opening.

Rear-Vault – The vaulted space between the **Rear-Arch** and the window frame on the outer wall-face.

Rebate – A continuous rectangular step or groove cut on an edge or face to receive a plank, door, or glazed window etc. In the latter case it is known as a **Glazing Rebate.**

Relief (Hist.) – A feudal incident. An heir to an estate was required to pay a sum of money to his lord before he could enter on his inheritance. In the 12th century £5 came to be regarded as a 'reasonable relief' for one **Knight's Fee.**

Relieving Arch – A false arch, usually of rough construction, which is built up into the walling over the head of a window or over the true open arch of a doorway. A structural device to help support the weight of the masonry of the wall above and relieve the pressure on the head of the opening below.

Retaining Wall – See **Revetment.**

Revetment – A retaining wall of masonry or timber to support a bank of earth or rubble and avoid erosion. In defensive works the **Revetment** confronted attackers with a steep or vertical face.

Ribbed Vault – See **Vault.**

Ring Bank – See **Castle-Ringwork.**

Ring-Motte – Formerly the term used for the **Castle-Ringwork** (q.v.). Obsolete since the recognition that few such sites are raised internally above the external level. The few thus elevated, and particularly such sites with ring-banks imposed on natural elevations, might still merit this term, effectively combining the characteristics of mottes and castle-ringworks [See Gwern-y-domen (CR 9) and Llanilid (CR 12)].

Ringwork – Any circular or oval fortification enclosed by an earthen rampart. This generic term applies to a wide range of such earthworks attributable to many periods. Many date to the prehistoric Iron Age or the Romano-British period. The **Rath** of Ireland and south-west Wales was a ringwork. To differentiate the special case of the medieval earthwork castle of this form it is termed a **Castle-Ringwork** (q.v.).

Roll Moulding – See **Moulding.**

Round or **Semicircular Arch** – See **Arch.**

Rubble – Walling of rough, undressed stones. It may be laid as rough courses or as **Random Rubble** without courses.

Scalloped Capital – See **Capital.**

Scarp, Scarping – A **Scarp** is the inner face or slope of a defensive ditch facing the opposed outer slope or **Counterscarp. Scarping** is the artificial cutting back of a natural slope to enhance its defensibility.

Screens Passage – A cross-passage at the service end of a medieval **Hall** from which it was separated by a timber or stone partition. This passage facilitated movement between the **Hall** and the service areas (kitchen, buttery, and pantry).

Segmental-Pointed Arch – See **Arch.**

Seisin (Hist.) – A term in common law meaning possession, not legal ownership, particularly of landed estate. To gain possession an heir to, or a grantee of an estate had to receive 'livery of seisin' from his lord, usually by the handing over of an object symbolizing the property, frequently a stick or a turf. A written deed of conveyance was not essential in the Middle Ages. Once in possession, a tenant was 'seised' of his estate; if dispos-

sessed he was 'disseised'.

Semicircular or **Round Arch** – See **Arch.**

Serjeanty – A feudal tenure granted for the performance of a wide variety of specialised personal services to the overlord. In Glamorgan the Turbervilles held Coity by 'serjeanty of hunting', presumably maintaining a chase for their lord.

Shell-Keep – A ring of walling replacing the original **Palisade** round the summit of a motte. Not a true keep, which was properly a true tower, but it similarly constituted the inner stronghold of a castle.

Shingles – Wooden tiles for covering roofs. (Lat. – *scendulis*).

Shire-Fee (Hist.) – See **Comitatus.**

Siegework – An earthwork raised for the protection of a force besieging a castle. It might shield offensive artillery engines or merely ensure against a sudden sally by the besieged garrison.

Sill, Sill Beam – The lowest horizontal member of a window-frame, timber-framed wall, or partition.

Solar – A private chamber (Lat. *solarium*). Generally a first-floor room near the dais end of the **Hall**. Reserved for the private use of the lord and his family.

Splay – The oblique face of the jamb of an opening, and particularly of a window, where that opening is wider internally than on the outer face of the wall.

Springal – A military engine worked by tension like a catapult. Mounted on wheels and used as a mobile artillery piece to throw heavy missiles.

Springer, Springing – The lowest tilted stones of an arch or vault; the point at which the arch or vault meets its supporting vertical member.

Spur - See **Angle-Spur.**

Square-Headed Arch – See **Arch.**

Squinch – An arch or corbelling, single or multiple, built diagonally across an internal angle to support a superstructure crossing that angle (e.g. a wall-walk, a latrine, or a means of access between two upper chambers).

Stop – A carved device terminating a continuous moulding or chamfer. The principal stops encountered are:

Broach – With two sloping facets, like a half-pyramid.

Bull-nose or *Ball* – Of bulbous, rounded form.

Cushion – Similar to *bull-nose* but with central crease.

Diagonal-cut – With a single facet at right-angles to the chamfer but tilted upwards from a horizontal arris on the external wall-face; the commonest stop in Glamorgan.

Straight-cut – A single sloping facet below or beyond the straight junction with the chamfer.

Straight-Cut Stop – See **Stop.**

String Course – A horizontal projecting moulding or band on the face of a wall.

Strong House – A modestly fortified seigneurial dwelling in which the residential element predominates over the defensive; a fortified manor house. Some elements of defensibility, but not deserving of the term castle.

Sub-Fee - See **Sub-Infeudation.**

Sub-Infeudation (Hist.) – A feudal practice often resulting in tenurial fragmentation. The granting by a **Tenant-In-Chief** of **Sub-Fees** or **Sub-Manors** to **Mesne Lords** who rendered specified military or other services to the grantor's overlord appropriate to the value of their **Sub-Fees.** The grantor's personal burden of services to the overlord was thus eased with no diminution of the total due to his overlord. This process was subject to no limit; five or six **Mesne Lords** might be interposed between the King and the tenant in actual possession.

Sunk Chamfer – See **Chamfer, Moulding.**

Sutton Stone – See **Lias Limestone.**

Tenant-In-Chief – See **Capite, In.**

Tithe – A due or payment of one tenth of all agrarian produce payable for the support of the clergy.

Tooling – The striations scored on the surface of ashlar in the process of **Dressing** it to an even face. **Fan Tooling** was produced when a narrow single-toothed chisel was employed, creating irregular fanned-out score-marks. **Diagonal Tooling** was produced using a wide multi-toothed chisel which produced parallel score-marks across the face of the stone, generally set diagonally. **Fan-Tooling** is an early feature, found in **Norman** work.

Toothing – See **Tusks, Tusking Stones.**

Tower House – Fortified residential tower, usually square, which may or may not be associated with a lightly defended yard or **Barmkin.** Numerous in Ireland, Scotland and the North of England, rare to the south and in Wales.

Tracery – The ornamental work in the head of a window, screen, panel etc. formed by curving bars of stone or wood.

Transom – A horizontal bar of stone or wood dividing the lights of a **Mullioned** window.

Trefoil – See **Foil.**

Truss – A framework of timber members supporting a roof.

Tudor Arch – See **Arch.**

Tufa – A durable building stone formed by successive layers of volcanic dust. Extensively used by the Romans.

Turning Bridge – See **Drawbridge.**

Turret – A small tower, sometimes placed on top of a larger tower to cover the stair-head.

Tusks, Tusking Stones, Toothing – Short stubs of walling protruding from a building with the intention of forming a bond with another building.

Two-Centred Arch – See **Arch.**

Tympanum – An enclosed space between the **Lintel** of a doorway and the arch above it. In classical architecture, the triangle of a pediment.

Undercroft – A vaulted basement.

Vault – An arched roof or ceiling of stone or brick. **A Barrel Vault** is an uninterrupted vault of semicircular section. Many other variants include the **Groined Vault** (formed by the intersection of two **Barrel Vaults** producing groins where they meet) and the many forms of **Ribbed Vault** (where arched ribs replace the groins).

Vill – A township, sometimes equivalent to a hamlet, village, manor or parish, sometimes a sub-division of them.

Volute – A spiral scroll distinctive of an Ionic capital. Smaller modified versions also figure in Corinthian and Composite capitals. The **Volute**, a Classical form, is retained on some Norman capitals.

Voussoirs – The stones or bricks, usually wedge-shaped, used in the construction of an **Arch.**

Ward – A fortified enclosure, particularly a walled area rather than an earthwork, which is usually called a **Bailey** (q.v.).

Wardship – Guardianship of minor heirs or heiresses and their lands until they attained a majority. See **Escheat.**

Wardsilver – The commuted payment made to a lord in lieu of military service. See **Castle-Guard.**

Wall-Plate – A beam laid along the lateral wall tops to receive the feet of the **Rafters.**

Wall-Walk – The footway along the top of a defensive wall, protected on the outer side by a battlemented **Parapet.** Sometimes a lesser plain wall, a **Parados**, was provided on the inner side.

Welshry – In medieval Wales, that part of a lordship (usually the least fertile) where Welsh customs, dues, laws and administration normally prevailed. See also **Englishry.**

Wing Wall – A wall crossing a ditch or descending a **Scarp** to join two **Wards**, or a **Keep** to its **Ward.**

Glossary:

Welsh terms and place-name elements

Frequently encountered mutated forms are given in parenthesis and cross-referenced. Only the singular form is given.

Ap (Ab) – Son of (before name, like Scots 'Mac' and Norman 'Fitz', e.g. Hywel ap Maredudd, Gruffydd ab Ifor), 'ap' before consonant; 'ab' before vowels.
Aber – Mouth of river; confluence.
Afon – River.
Allt (gallt) – Hill; hillside; slope; cliff.
Bach (fach); bychan *(masc.)* ; **bechan (fechan)** *(fem.)* – Little; minor; small.
Blaenau – A hilly area, especially the north part of Glamorgan ('Blaenau Morgannwg').
Bont – See Pont.
Bro (Fro) – A lowland area, especially the south part of Glamorgan ('Bro Morgannwg').
Bryn – Hill.
Cae – Field.
Caer (Gaer) – Fort; fortress, especially of Iron Age or Roman origin.
Cantref – An early Welsh administrative district (lit. a 'hundred hamlets', cf. the English Hundred), usually containing two or more *commotes* (q.v.).
Carn (Garn) – Cairn.
Castell – Castle, especially medieval works, but sometimes applied to earlier fortifications.
Cefn – Back; ridge.
Celli (Gelli) – Grove.
Clawdd – Dyke; embankment; hedge.
Coch (Goch) – Red.
Coed – Wood; timber; trees.
Commote, Cwmwd – An early Welsh administrative district, being a sub-division of a *Cantref* (q.v.).
Craig (Graig) – Rock.
Crug (Grug) – Hillock; heap; cairn.
Cwm – A narrow, steep-sided valley. cf. English 'coomb'.
Cwmwd – See Commote.
Cwrt - Court.
Dinas (Ddinas) – City; settlement; fort, especially of the Iron Age.
Domen – See Tomen.
Du (Ddu) – Black.
Eglwys - Church.

Fach – See Bach.
Fawr - See Mawr.
Fechan – See Bach, bychan.
Felin – See Melin.
Ffordd – Road; way.
Fro – See Bro.
Garth – Enclosure; garden; hill.
Gaer – See Caer.
Gallt – See Allt.
Garn – See Carn.
Gelli – See Celli.
Glyn – Glen; valley.
Goch – See Coch.
Graig – See Craig.
Grug – See Crug.
Gwern – Alder-grove; meadow; swamp.
Hen – Ancient; of old; old.
Heol – Road; track.
Iarll – Earl (e.g. 'Tir Iarll' = The Earl's Land).
Is (isaf) – Below; inferior; lower; under (strictly speaking **isaf** = lowest).
Llan – Sacred enclosure; church-yard; church. The most frequent place-name and parish prefix in Wales, often followed by a saint's name, e.g. Llanilltud ('The church of St. Illtud') Llandeilo ('The church of St. Teilo'), Llantrisant ('The church of three saints').
Llys – Court; hall; mansion.
Maen – Stone.
Maes – Field.
Mawr (fawr) – Big; great; large.
Melin (felin) – Mill.
Mynydd – Mountain.
Nant – Brook; stream; ravine.
Newydd – New; novel.
Nos – Night.
Pen – Chief; head; headland; summit; top.
Plas – Hall; mansion; palace.
Pont – Bridge.
Porth – Gate; gateway; porch.
Pwll – Pit; pool; pond.

Tomen (domen) – Dunghill; heap; mound. Commonly applied to *Mottes* (q.v. – in General Glossary).
Tref (tre) – Town; township; hamlet (see *Cantref*).
Twmpath – Tump, hillock.
Tŵr – Tower.
Twyn – Hill; hillock; knoll.

Tŷ – House.
Uchaf – Highest; uppermost.
Uwch – Above; higher; over.
Ynys – Island; river meadow.
Ystrad – Dale; vale; flat.

Sêl Morgan Gam, arglwydd Afan (*fl.* 1217 - 41)
Seal of Morgan Gam, lord of Afan (*fl.* 1217 - 41)

List of Figures, including Maps and Photographs

ACKNOWLEDGEMENTS.

Acknowledgement for permission to reproduce copyright material is made to the following: British Library, Figs. 120 (b) and 122; Cardiff Castle Archives, Figs. 117 (b) and 124; Cardiff City Library, Fig. 136; Committee for Aerial Photography, Cambridge University, Fig. 43; National Library of Wales, Figs. 117 (a), 118, 119, 120 (a), 134 (a) and (b), 135, 152, 214 and 243 (a) and (b); National Museum of Wales, Fig. 123 (a); Mark Sorrell, Esq., Fig. 85; Institute of Geological Sciences, Fig. 11. The copyright of these belongs to the parties named. Figs. 13 (part), 47, 107, 123 (b), 235 and 238 are redrawn or reproduced from sources cited in the captions. The remaining Figures are the work of the Commission staff, based on the Ordnance Survey in the case of most maps, and are Crown Copyright.

Front end-paper: Map: Monuments treated in Part 1a.
Back end-paper: Map: Monuments treated in Part 1b.

Fig.	Title	Page

Fig.   Title   Page

Fig.   Title   Page

General Index

Bold type readily identifies the section letters and serial numbers of monuments treated, given in brackets, and the page numbers of the main descriptive and historical accounts. The letters 'a' or 'b' indicate the left-hand or right-hand column respectively. For such families as de Clare, de Braose, and le Sore, *see under* Clare, Braose, and Sore. If possible, members of families are listed chronologically.

Village enclosures, at Walterston, 132ab; suspected at Penmark, 132b–133a.

Villers, family, of Loughor, 269a; Henry de, 25b, 29a, 33a, 64b, 66a, 265a, 268ab.

'Villa Sturmi' ('Sturmieston'), see Stormy Castle.

Walsh, family, of Llandough near Cowbridge, 13b, 105a.

Walsh, William, king's receiver in Glamorgan, 1377, 169a, 319a.

Walter of Llanblethian, early lord of that fee, before 1107, 13a, 14a.

Walters, R. A., geologist, cited, 34b.

Walterston chapel, Gower, granted to Knights Hospitallers before 1165, 30a, 90b, 119b.

Walterston, Llancarfan, castle-ringwork, 34a, 44a, 46a, 48b, 80b, 81a, 123a, **(CR 21) 132a–133b,** 154b, 290b; observed disturbances at, during survey, 132a.

Ward, John, excavations at Cardiff Castle (1889–1923), 163b (f/n 7), 187a, 190ab.

Ward silver, 13b, 31a, 63b, 158b, 338b.

Warren Hill, Iron Age hill-fort, 139a.

Warwick Castle, Guy's Tower at, 177a; William I's motte at, 164a.

Webster, Peter, archaeologist, excavations at Cardiff Castle, 163ab, 210b–211b.

Welsh castles, 31b; listed and discussed, 135a–139b; Welsh masonry castles, 138ab; attributions rejected, 139ab.

Welsh raids, on Gower lordship, listed, 28b, 66b; on Kenfig listed, 316a–318b, 320ab. Specific raids on the lowlands in: GLAMORGAN LORDSHIP, on Aberafan, in 1153 (15b, 17b, 20a, 137a, 138b, 141b, 155b); on Cardiff, in 1158 (17b, 70b, 165b); on Kenfig, in 1167, 1228, 1232, 1243, 1295, and 1316 (40a, 259a, 316b, 318a, 320ab); on Laleston vill, in 1226 (329a); on Llangynwyd Castle, in 1257 (318a, 259ab–postscript); on Neath, in 1231 and 1257 (318a); on Newcastle, in 1226 (318a, 329a); on St. Nicholas, in 1226 and 1229 (130b, 329a); and the lowlands, unspecified, in 1257 (19a) GOWER LORDSHIP, on Loughor and Talybont, in 1116, 1151, and 1215 (28b, 66ab, 268a, 269ab); on Oystermouth, and 'all the castles of Gower', in 1215 (27a, 66b, 269b); on Swansea, in 1192 and 1212 (27a, 28b, 66b, 269b); general incursions from Deheubarth, listed, 28b.

Welsh uprisings, in GLAMORGAN LORDSHIP: in 1135–36, of limited extent, 16b, 156b, 165b, 176b; in 1183–84, serious and widespread, 18ab, 139a, 166a, 220a, 259a, 298b–299a, 303a, 316b–318a, 328a, 332a; in 1294–95, on death of Gilbert II de Clare, 214a, 259a, 299a, 303a, 318ab, 323b, 324a; in 1314, on death of Gilbert III de Clare, 168a, 214a; in 1316, the revolt of Llywelyn Bren, 168ab, 214ab, 299a, 318b, 324a; in 1402–05, the early years of Glyndŵr's rebellion (1400–15), 165a, 169b–170a, 220b–222b, 223a, 276a, 319a. In GOWER LORDSHIP: in 1135–36, 16b, 26a, 156b, 268b–269a; in 1215, 27ab, 66b, 269b. See also under Baronial revolt (1233), and Despenser War (1321), for uprisings by disaffected anglo-Norman lords.

Wentloog, the coastal lowlands of Gwynllŵg, 10b–11a, 16b, 18a, 21ab, 24a, 32b, 298b.

Wenvoe Castle (Part 1b, PC 11), possible castle, vanished, 154b.

Wenvoe, fee of, held by de Sully family and adjoining Sully fee, 13a, 83ab, 85a, 129b.

Weobley, Gower, 'ancient fee' of, 30b, 90b, 92a.

Weobley Castle (Part 1b, LM 20), 43b, 44b, 92a, 117b.

West Plas, late medieval house, now vanished, at Coity, 218a.

Wheeler, J., architect, traced plan of apartments at Cardiff Castle before 1776, 178a–179b.

Whitchurch (Album Monasterium, Blancminster), demesne manor of, 68a, 70b, 163a, 211a, 212a, 214ab; mottes at, see Treoda, and Twmpath (Rhiwbina); chapel of ('Stuntaf'), 70b, 212b.

White Castle (Mon.), keep at, 43a.

William I, king of England (1066–87), his primary settlement at Cardiff, 8b–10b, 11a, 21a, 32a, 38b, 52b, 139a, 164ab, 190a, 211b; his mottes, 10a, 164a.

William II, king of England (1087–1100), his obscurely recorded punitive campaign of 1075, 9a; rewards loyalty of Henry de Beaumont and Robert Fitzhamon, 25b.

William, earl of Gloucester, lord of Glamorgan (1147–83), 8b, 17a–18a, 40b, 41b, 63a, 86b, 102b, 137ab, 141a, 155b, 165b, 176ab, 220a, 226b, 227a, 298b, 316ab, 326ab, 327a, 329a, 331ab, 332a, 333b, 336b; abducted by Welsh from Cardiff Castle (1158), 17b, 70b, 165b.

William Marshal, see Marshal, earls of Pembroke.

Wiltshire, estates held in by lords enfeoffed in Glamorgan, 20b–21b.

Windsor, family, lords of Glamorgan, 1704–76, 172a.

'Winning of Glamorgan', the, Merrick's mythical account of the Norman Conquest, 10a, 11b, 98b–100a, 136a, 137a, 155ab, 157a, 219a, 306a, 313a, 314a.

Winton, family, of Llandow, reputedly of Llanquian, 13b, 81b, 107b, 264a
ROGER, recorded 1148–1202, 107b
WILLIAM (1262), 107b.

Wiston Castle (Pembs.), shell keep at, 39a.

Woodstock, Agreement of (1126), 14b, 70b, 77a, 165ab, 212b, 219a.

Worleton, episcopal manor and moated site of, St. Nicholas, 94a, 129b.

Wotherton (Salop), diminutive motte at, 72a.

Wyatt, Sir Matthew Digby, his abortive neo-gothic scheme for Penllyn Castle, 185a.

Wyndham, family, of Dunraven, lords of Coity in 19th century, 223a.

Ynyscrug, fragment of motte, 44a, 46a, 53a, **(MO 11) 73a–74b,** 138b, 139b, 154b; observed disturbances during survey, 74b.

York, William I's motte at, 10a, 164a.

Ystrad Meurig (Cards.), early masonry at, 38a, 43a.

Ystradowen, unfinished motte, 34a, 70a, 74b, **(MO 12) 75a–77b,** 100a, 145a.

Ystum Enlli (Carms.), motte at, 64a; slighted castle-ringwork nearby, 64a, 98a.

Caerphilly Castle (LM3), Volume III, Part 1b.

390

Alphabetical list: sites treated in Part 1b

The fifty-one sites to be considered in Part 1b of Volume III have all been inspected and only unforeseen new discoveries might marginally alter the following arrangement of that Part:

Section LM, Later Masonry Castles (LM 1–20)
Section TH, Tower Houses (TH 1–5)
Section SH, Strong Houses (SH 1–3)
Section TD, Town Defences (TD 1–5)
Section PC, Possible Castles or Strong Houses (PC 1–12)
Section FO, Forts and other Post-Medieval Fortifications (FO 1–6)

The sites considered in Sections TD and PC are largely vanished. The fifty-one accepted sites are listed below, together with cross-referenced alternative names applied to some of them; they are also plotted on the map given on the back end-paper. The list and the map both exclude rejected sites which will be given in an annotated list in Part 1b (Section RS, at present containing fifty-nine entries).

Barry Castle (LM 1).
Bishops Castle, Llandaf (LM 2).
Bovehill Castle, *see* Landimôr.
Cadoxton Court (PC 1).
Caerphilly Castle (LM 3).
Caerphilly Civil War Redoubt (FO 1).
Candleston Castle (TH 1).
Cardiff Town Defences (TD 1).
Castell Coch (LM 4).
Castleton, St. Athan (PC 2).
Castle-upon-Alun, *see* Old Castle-upon-Alun.
Cogan, Old Cogan (PC 3).
Cosmeston (PC 4).
Cowbridge Town Defences (TD 2).
Culver Hole, Port Eynon (PC 5).
Dunraven Castle (PC 6).
Ewenny Priory (LM 5).
Flat Holm Batteries (FO 2).
Fonmon Castle (LM 6).
Kenfig Town Defences (TD 3).
Landimôr, or Bovehill Castle (SH 1).
Lavernock Batteries (FO 3).
Llanblethian Castle, or St. Quintins Castle (LM 7).
Llandaf Castle, *see* Bishops Castle.
Llandough, near Penarth (PC 7).
Llandough Castle, near Cowbridge (TH 2).
Llanmaes Castle, or Malifant Castle (TH 3).
Llantrisant Castle (LM 8).
Malifant Castle, *see* Llanmaes Castle.
Marcross (SH 2).

Marsh House Fortified Warehouse (FO 4).
Morgraig Castle (LM 9).
Morlais Castle (LM 10).
Mumbles Battery (FO 5).
Neath Castle (LM 11).
Neath Town Defences (TD 4).
North Cornelly (TH 4).
Old Castle-upon-Alun (PC 8).
Old Cogan, *see* Cogan.
Oxwich Tower (PC 9).
Oystermouth Castle (LM 12).
Penlle'r Castell (LM 13).
Penmark Castle (LM 14).
Penrice Castle (LM 15).
Port Eynon Castle, *see* Culver Hole.
St. Athan, *see* Castleton.
St. Donats Castle (LM 16).
St. Fagans Castle (LM 17).
St. Georges Castle (PC 10).
St. Quintins Castle, *see* Llanblethian Castle.
Salt House, Port Eynon (FO 6).
Swansea Castle (LM 18).
Swansea Town Defences (TD 5).
Talyfan Castle (LM 19).
Trecastell (SH 3).
Tythegston (TH 5).
Wenvoe Castle (PC 11).
Weobley Castle (LM 20).
Wrinston (PC 12).

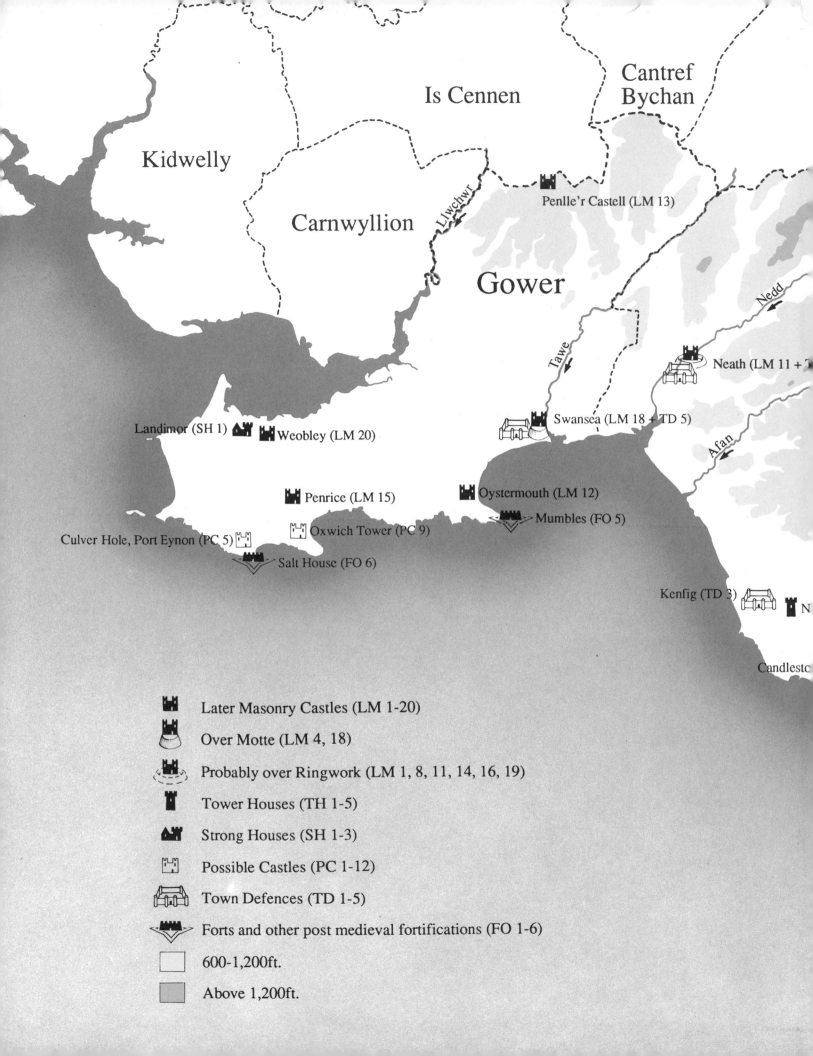

Is Cennen

Cantref Bychan

Kidwelly

Carnwyllion

Llwchwr

Gower

Penlle'r Castell (LM 13)

Nedd

Tawe

Neath (LM 11 + 7

Landimor (SH 1) Weobley (LM 20)

Swansea (LM 18 + TD 5)

Afan

Penrice (LM 15)

Oystermouth (LM 12)

Mumbles (FO 5)

Culver Hole, Port Eynon (PC 5) Oxwich Tower (PC 9)

Salt House (FO 6)

Kenfig (TD 3)

N

Candlesto

Later Masonry Castles (LM 1-20)

Over Motte (LM 4, 18)

Probably over Ringwork (LM 1, 8, 11, 14, 16, 19)

Tower Houses (TH 1-5)

Strong Houses (SH 1-3)

Possible Castles (PC 1-12)

Town Defences (TD 1-5)

Forts and other post medieval fortifications (FO 1-6)

600-1,200ft.

Above 1,200ft.